100 BULLETS: A FOREGONE TOMORROW

100 BULLETS: A FOREGONE TOMORROW

Brian Azzarello Writer **Eduardo Risso** Artist **Patricia Mulvihill** Colorist
Clem Robins Letterer **Dave Johnson** Original Series Covers

**Lee Bermejo   Jordi Bernet   Tim Bradstreet   Mark Chiarello   Dave Gibbons
J.G. Jones   Joe Jusko   Jim Lee   Frank Miller   Paul Pope** Guest Artists

100 BULLETS created by Brian Azzarello and Eduardo Risso

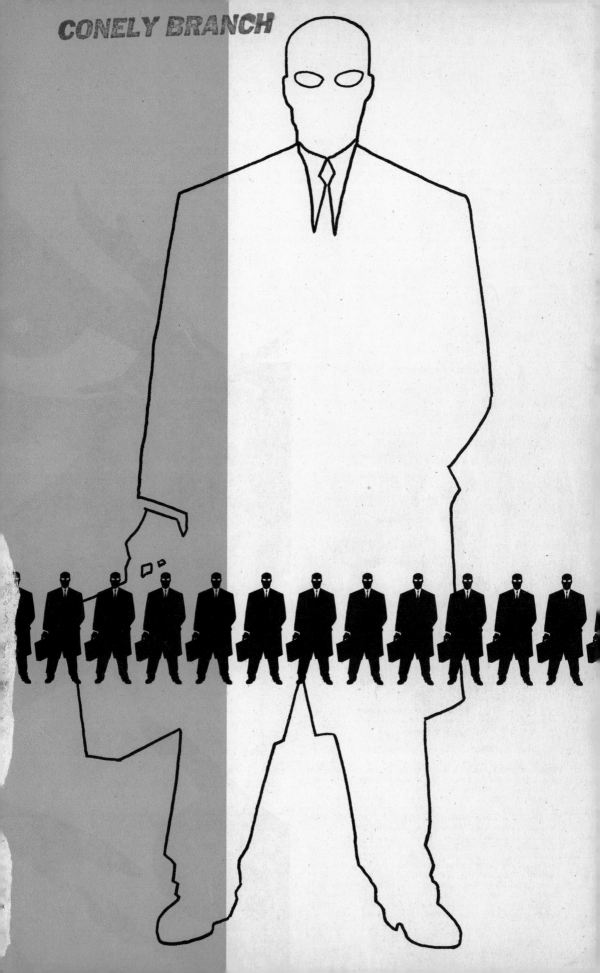

100 BULLETS: A FOREGONE TOMORROW

*Published by DC Comics. Cover, introduction and compilation
copyright © 2002 DC Comics. All Rights Reserved. Originally
published in single magazine form as 100 BULLETS 20-30.
Copyright © 2001, 2002 Brian Azzarello, Eduardo Risso and
DC Comics. All Rights Reserved. All characters, their distinc-
tive likenesses and related indicia featured in this publication
are trademarks of DC Comics. The stories, characters, and
incidents featured in this publication are entirely fictional.
DC Comics does not read or accept unsolicited submissions of
ideas, stories or artwork. DC Comics, 1700 Broadway,
New York, NY 10019. A division of Warner Bros. - An AOL Time
Warner Company. Printed in Canada. Second Printing. ISBN:1-
56389-827-6. Cover illustration by Dave Johnson and Eduardo
Risso. Publication design by Louis Prandi. Special thanks to
Nicolas Choisnel, Jean-Christophe Lips and Eduardo A.
Santillan Marcus for their translating assistance.*

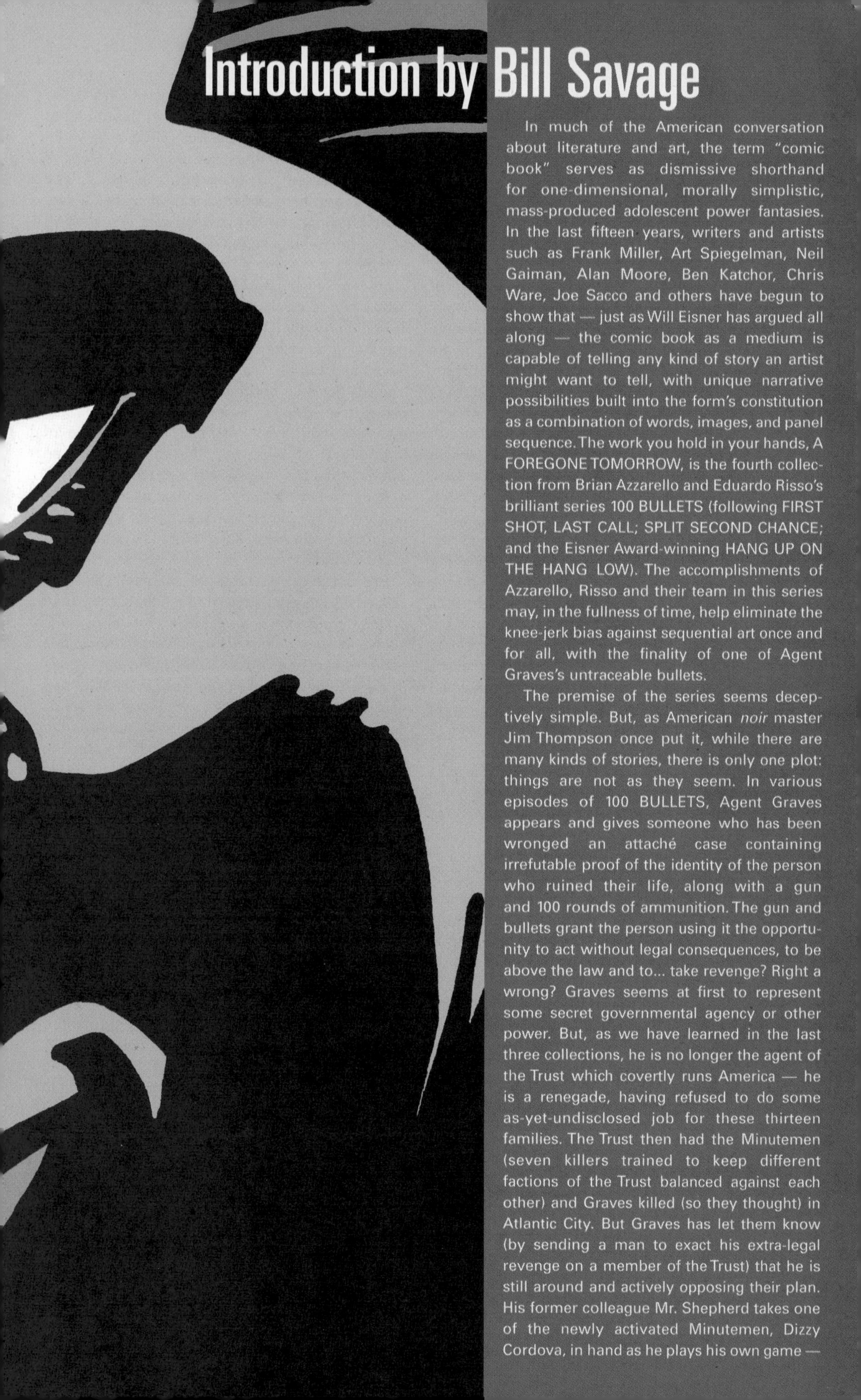

Introduction by Bill Savage

In much of the American conversation about literature and art, the term "comic book" serves as dismissive shorthand for one-dimensional, morally simplistic, mass-produced adolescent power fantasies. In the last fifteen years, writers and artists such as Frank Miller, Art Spiegelman, Neil Gaiman, Alan Moore, Ben Katchor, Chris Ware, Joe Sacco and others have begun to show that — just as Will Eisner has argued all along — the comic book as a medium is capable of telling any kind of story an artist might want to tell, with unique narrative possibilities built into the form's constitution as a combination of words, images, and panel sequence. The work you hold in your hands, A FOREGONE TOMORROW, is the fourth collection from Brian Azzarello and Eduardo Risso's brilliant series 100 BULLETS (following FIRST SHOT, LAST CALL; SPLIT SECOND CHANCE; and the Eisner Award-winning HANG UP ON THE HANG LOW). The accomplishments of Azzarello, Risso and their team in this series may, in the fullness of time, help eliminate the knee-jerk bias against sequential art once and for all, with the finality of one of Agent Graves's untraceable bullets.

The premise of the series seems deceptively simple. But, as American *noir* master Jim Thompson once put it, while there are many kinds of stories, there is only one plot: things are not as they seem. In various episodes of 100 BULLETS, Agent Graves appears and gives someone who has been wronged an attaché case containing irrefutable proof of the identity of the person who ruined their life, along with a gun and 100 rounds of ammunition. The gun and bullets grant the person using it the opportunity to act without legal consequences, to be above the law and to... take revenge? Right a wrong? Graves seems at first to represent some secret governmental agency or other power. But, as we have learned in the last three collections, he is no longer the agent of the Trust which covertly runs America — he is a renegade, having refused to do some as-yet-undisclosed job for these thirteen families. The Trust then had the Minutemen (seven killers trained to keep different factions of the Trust balanced against each other) and Graves killed (so they thought) in Atlantic City. But Graves has let them know (by sending a man to exact his extra-legal revenge on a member of the Trust) that he is still around and actively opposing their plan. His former colleague Mr. Shepherd takes one of the newly activated Minutemen, Dizzy Cordova, in hand as he plays his own game —

both ends against the middle, perhaps. Or perhaps not. Things are not as they seem.

Eduardo Risso's artwork is as good a place as any to begin. While other commentators have called Risso's art minimalist, I would argue that it's really impressionistic — especially regarding the physicality of the characters, who he depicts in slightly exaggerated forms which represent both their inner reality and their social position. Again in contrast to what most Americans think of when they think of comic books, 100 BULLETS is no world of cleft-jawed, noble-browed heroes and curvaceous beauty-pageant heroines in tights. Every character, from the major figures to the bit players in the background, is individually imagined and realized, and Risso's expressive range astounds. He doesn't just depict muscular heroes, he creates different sorts of muscularity: the lean controlled menace of Cole Burns, and the broad rampant madness of Lono. He has young people and old: every mile of travel and every moral choice offered is etched in Agent Graves's face, while Benito Medici's youth and privilege sits easy on him. Risso draws short skinny psycho punks and fat people — and the fat people are different sorts of fat, from the gangbanger Eight Ball's massive bulk to the Trust's Daniel Peres's lifetime of indulgence and Mr. Branch's despairing indolence. Yet even with its impressionistic aspects, Risso draws a realistic physical world, one with consequences: when people get beat up in 100 BULLETS, they sport bruises, broken teeth, blood, and scars.

Risso sometimes takes a minimalist approach, usually in his settings, but his minimalism deserves none of the negative overtones that evaluation can imply. Risso draws panels of heightened or lessened detail to stress particular aspects of the narrative; he often evokes a street scene or a bar or a building with a few strokes, paring the visual elements of what he depicts down to its essential shapes and relations. But these depictions aren't corner-cutting or random: they always occur at moments where the reader should attend to something other than the background: to the fully depicted action, the thing most essential for telling the story at hand. Risso's minimalism works hand in glove with Azzarello's prose as an aesthetic strategy to highlight the narrative. When something in the background matters — as in the scene on the boardwalk at the end of "Red Prince Blues," where the fact that Peres is meeting Agent Graves in a crowd is part of the point — Risso draws that entire background in rich and full detail.

As for the depiction of female characters, sure, dangerous curves abound, but Risso's art enhances the way each of Azzarello's women is far more than the run-of-the-mill *noir femme fatale*. The two main female characters so far — former gangbanger Dizzy Cordova and the Trust's Megan Dietrich — are both sexy as hell, but their sexual appeal operates in visually opposite ways to deepen their character-ization. In "Red Prince Blues," Azzarello and Risso explore Megan's cold, cutthroat power. While she uses her sexuality, her power is not based on her looks — as a member of the Trust, she'd be powerful if she looked like twenty miles of bad road. Megan's power is based on education, experience, and ruthlessness (a cold-heartedness which has a very human failing: she has a weak spot and a warm feeling for Benito, and things might have gone very differently at the end of "Red Prince Blues" had she not been thinking with something other than her head when accompanying Daniel Peres out from the Trust Summit). In "¡Contrabandolero!," we see the continuing education of Dizzy as Mr. Shepherd leads her further... astray, perhaps, or further towards her own position of confident power as a player in a world far larger and more complicated than she had ever imagined in the *barrio* of Chicago's West Side. And the contrast between Dizzy's Latina beauty — whether you think it marred or enhanced by the gang-tattoo tear on her cheek — and Megan's Aryan arrogance suggests a great deal about the world Azzarello and Risso have imagined and depicted.

Beyond his depiction of character and his aesthetic strategy of stress through the combination of detail and minimalism, Risso is a master of imaginative panel sequence, perspective, and mood. See page seven of part two of "Sell Fish and Out to Sea," or the lengthy smuggling sequence in the third part of "¡Contrabandolero!" — two instances where panel sequence tells the story in a way prose or film could not. His compositions roam so far beyond the standard filmic perspectives routinely used in comics that it demonstrates yet again the ways in which the medium has its own unique storytelling capabilities, echoing nothing so much as Will Eisner's SPIRIT. Risso gives us points of view from under water looking up, inside pinball machines, within canvases being painted — angles which place the reader in the action and which suggest far more than words can directly communicate and so invite readers to contemplate their meaning. And his use of silhouette and close-ups at key moments further enhances the book's narrative punch and the depth of its characterization.

The contributions of colorist Patricia Mulvihill, letterer Clem Robins and cover artist Dave Johnson should not be overlooked either. The stark cold light of the television set pervades the dingy home of compulsive gambler Hank and his dying wife, suggesting the stakes for which Hank is really playing. The alternating bright and dark in the final part of "Red Prince Blues" as Graves and Daniel meet on the Boardwalk while Benito and Megan handle Hank's demands at gunpoint in the hotel adds tremendous emotional weight to the story. Throughout the series, the coloring suggests different qualities of light, different moods, communicating emotion in a way only comics can. Similarly, the lettering suggests different sorts of noise — a visual and orthographic representation of how bouncers shouting over the music in a night club sound, for instance, in "Sell Fish and Out to Sea." Cover artist Dave Johnson also makes a tremendous impact. His covers consistently depict the meat of the story at hand without relying on plot elements or details. On the cover of "Idol Chatter" or the first part of "Sell Fish..." for instance, Johnson epitomizes the stories perfectly, without relying on the action scenes so often overused in comics cover art. His dramatically juxtaposed montages of character and setting consistently capture the mood of the series.

The overall visual style of the book is pure *noir*: a world of dingy bars and glittering casinos, both lit with omnipresent neon refracted by smoke; streetcorner drug deals and cross-border smuggling; lowlifes and high rollers both living on the edge and hence living life all the way. A world where the smallest misstep can lead to disaster, where one wrong word can lead to death. A world where what you don't know *can* hurt you — and what you do know can get you killed.

But Azzarello's writing provides more than just *noir* style; it delivers American substance in two ways. First, one of the traditional formal knocks on the comics medium has been its serial nature. Every month, the superhero foils the evil plans of one archenemy, the criminal is punished for his misdeeds, and tranquility returns to the City — for four weeks, until it's time to repeat with some variation, a different villain, another dastardly crime. But the problem with this scenario is not the serial *per se*: it's mediocrity, repetition, and lack of a coherent and fully thought-out fictive world sustained and elaborated from issue to issue. In the world of 100 BULLETS, Azzarello makes full use of the many rich narrative possibilities offered by the serial form: his literally and figuratively killer plots never fail to provide cliffhanger endings to draw the reader back for more, both within and between story arcs. But more important, Azzarello gives you something most serials (admittedly, produced over years or decades by different writers, editors and artists) never aspire to, much less achieve: an ever-growing complexity not just of plot, but of intellectual content. His plot twists aren't a journeyman writer's tricks of the trade, like the obligatory car chase or red digital readout of the generic Hollywood action movie. Azzarello's elaborate plots provide him the space to create a deepening moral complexity and narrative sophistication as story arc builds on story arc. (And, I write in my best professorial voice, as in any serious work of art, you'd better pay attention to every detail: seemingly minor actions or images in the background of a single panel can mean life or death later in the story, or in another story altogether. Something as minor as the name on a stolen credit card in "¡Contrabandolero!" for instance.)

His substantive plots show how Azzarello's work is related to the best American *noir* crime and detective writers: Raymond Chandler, Dashiell Hammett, Jim Thompson, Chester Himes, and David Goodis, writers whose work exposed the bleak dehumanizing violence at the heart of the American experience. The world of 100 BULLETS, like all great *noir*, is our world, twisted just a bit, turned up in intensity a notch. A mirror held up to the face of America, a mirror slightly darkened, slightly warped, 100 BULLETS engages with fundamental questions about individual identity; race, gender and, especially, class; the corruption of power — and the principled resistance to power; alienation and belonging; loyalty and treachery; violence and criminality; guilt and innocence; illusion and reality; freedom and servitude. For anyone who finds Azzarello's basic premise a bit unbelievable, let me just point out one thing: We live right now in a nation whose President is the son of a President and grandson of a Senator, who defeated a former Vice President, himself the son and grandson of Senators, in an election in part decided by a Supreme Court Justice appointed by the winner's father. Such a world of self-perpetuating political power is not that far off, really, from Azzarello's vision of the thirteen families of the Trust running America from behind a screen of absolute secrecy and murderous violence.

Second, Azzarello's brilliant use of American speech places 100 BULLETS firmly in the tradition not just of American *noir*, but of American literature in general: Poe, Melville and the darker Twain; Ernest Hemingway, William Faulkner, F. Scott Fitzgerald, Richard Wright and Nelson Algren; Jack Kerouac and William S. Burroughs; Toni Morrison and Don DeLillo. Since Twain's *Adventures of Huckleberry Finn*, one of the challenges to the American writer is to make great art with the language Americans actually speak — and Azzarello's command of the vernacular is unparalleled in comics and has few rivals in prose fiction or film. From their places scanning for the police and rival gangbangers on ghetto streetcorners or looking down over a city from the luxurious heights power affords them, Azzarello's people speak not like alter egos of the writer or derivative characters from other works, but like real people from real places. The *noir* genre provides a range of stock characters, yet Azzarello avoided central casting to create characters compelling in their originality and humanity — the psycho punk with his own monogrammed Ping-Pong paddle, the junkie bouncer whose former girlfriend is an artist, the compulsive gambler who would do anything for his sick wife.

If you haven't read the previous three collections and don't want to wait before diving in here, reading "Mr. Branch's Family Tree" might not be the worst way to enter the fictive world of 100 BULLETS (provided, of course, your French is better than mine. Yet another mark of the seriousness of this work is its resolute realism with language: Mexican hijackers speak Spanish, Parisians speak French —

no subtitles, no translations). This collection contains several brief story arcs (as well as, in the background of "Idol Chatter," the seeds of the next arc). In "The Mimic" and "Red Prince Blues," we see the tragic difference between the stakes for small fry and the big fish, and we learn more of Mr. Shepherd and the Trust's simmering conflict with Agent Graves and the renegade Minutemen. More hints come our way about the causes of Agent Graves's... rebellion? Defection? Heroism? In "¡Contrabandolero!," we discover more of the role of Mr. Shepherd and Dizzy in relation to Graves and the rival factions within the Trust. Stories also appear which might seem stand-alones unrelated to the larger narrative — like "Sell Fish and Out to Sea" — but given what we've seen earlier in this series, these apparent asides may very well come back to haunt someone — Agent Graves, Mr. Shepherd, the Trust, or the reader. Azzarello's plot construction is so imaginative, so full of unexpected twists and abrupt turns, that I've learned to put nothing past him, as "Idol Chatter" will show, with its utterly audacious take on the interrelated fates of three American icons. Throughout all of the stories in this collection, Azzarello and Risso's 100 BULLETS delivers its usual combination of breakneck narrative pacing, spectacular violence, dark humor, and genuine moral reflection.

Regardless of its medium — prose, film, drama, comics — a great work of narrative art is one which makes full use of the aesthetic resources offered by its medium to tell a compelling story. 100 BULLETS does that, in the written words, the images, the composition of panel and page sequences, coloring, and lettering. Every weapon in the arsenal of the comics medium is deployed to its best effect to tell a tale which doesn't just exist in its own world, but which illuminates the America we live in as well. There is nothing better being done in comics today. The cultural bias against the comic book form in American culture is so deeply embedded that it may take the entire projected run of 100 issues of this series to finally finish it off. But given the sustained artistic brilliance, the deepening moral complexity, the growing narrative sophistication and the sheer virtuoso exuberance of Azzarello and Risso's work so far, eventually 100 BULLETS may indeed deliver that long-awaited *coup de grâce*.

—Bill Savage

Bill Savage earned his Ph.D. in American literature at Northwestern University, where he currently teaches. Since its publication in 2000, he has included the collection 100 BULLETS: FIRST SHOT, LAST CALL in his courses, "Crime and Punishment in American Literature," "Crime Novels, Criminal Novels, and the Canon" and "Chicago Writers: Building the City of Words." There, Azzarello and Risso's work has been studied in the company of texts such as Twain's Pudd'nhead Wilson, *Hawthorne's* The Scarlet Letter, *Chandler's* The Big Sleep, *Thompson's* The Killer Inside Me, *Wright's* Native Son, *Algren's* The Man with the Golden Arm, *Burroughs's* Naked Lunch, *De Palma and Mamet's* The Untouchables, *and Tarantino's* Pulp Fiction. *Up against this competition, Azzarello and Risso have more than held their own.*

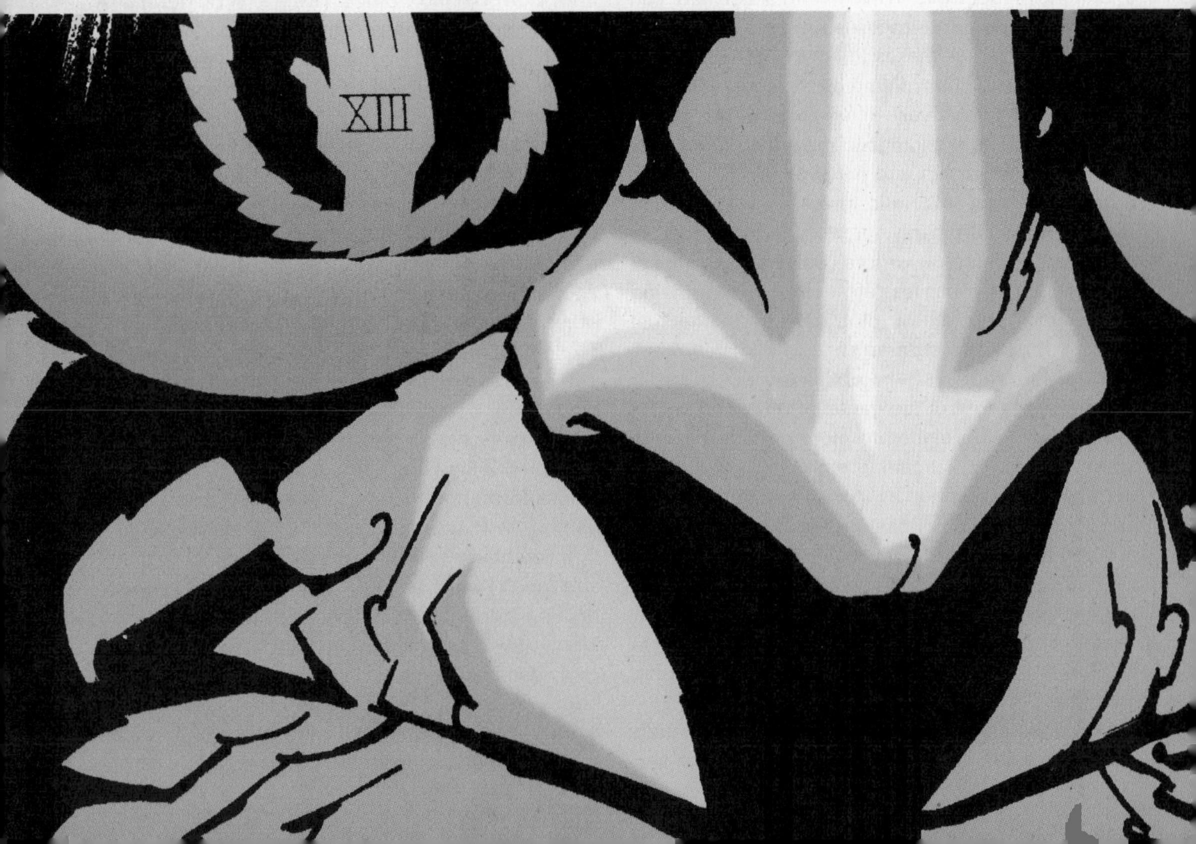
XIII

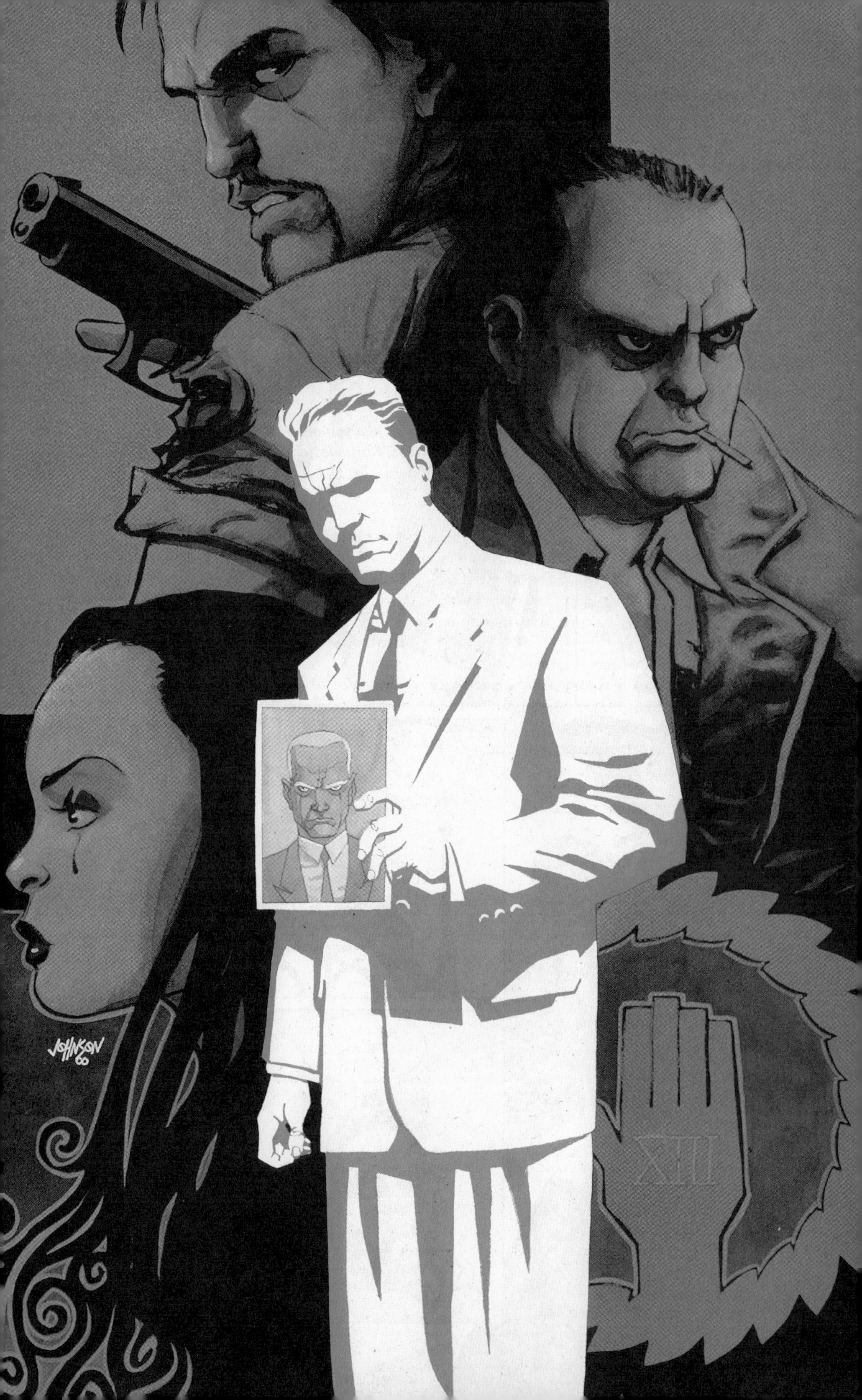
JOHNSON 00
XIII

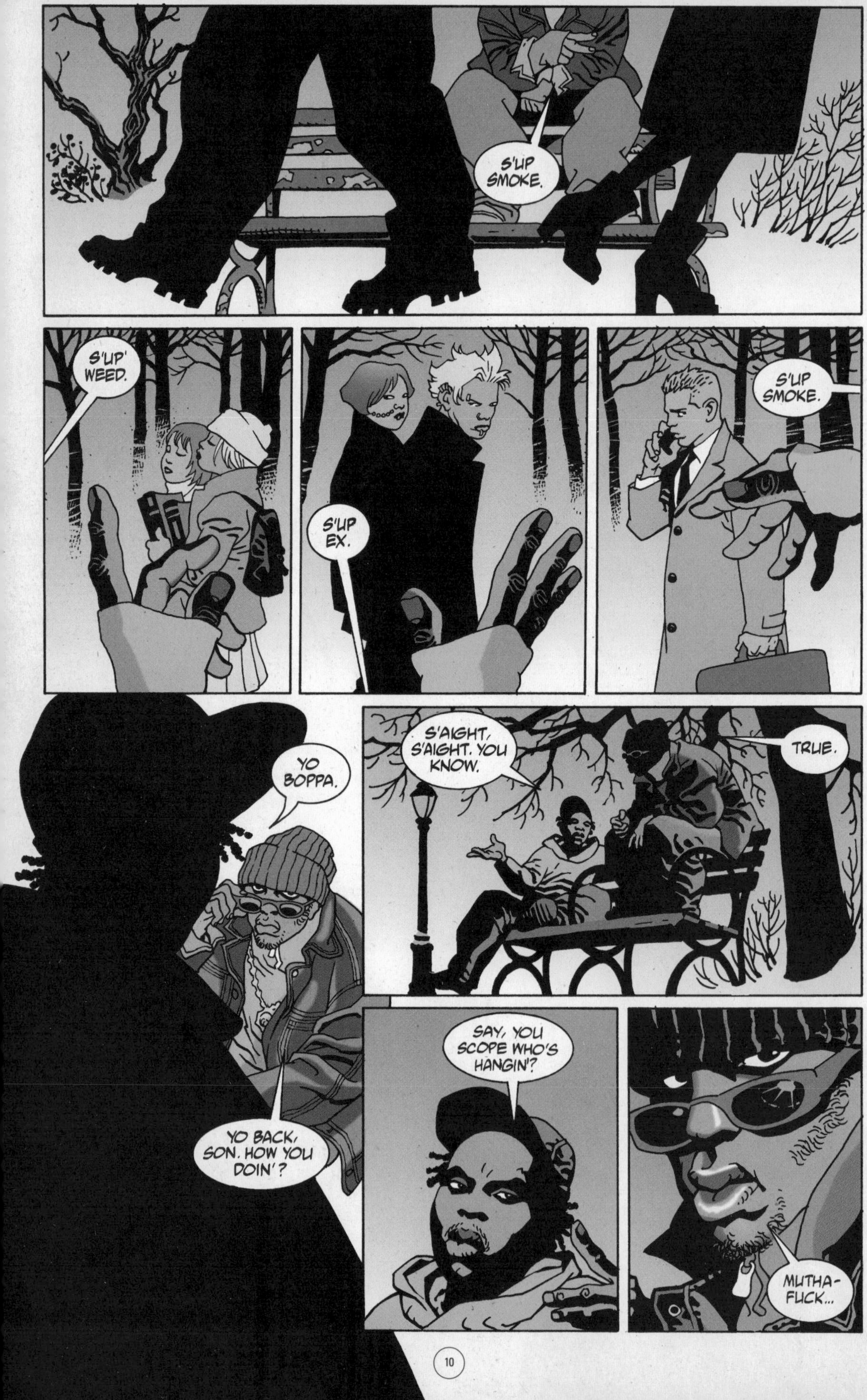
S'UP SMOKE.
S'UP' WEED.
S'UP EX.
S'UP SMOKE.
YO BOPPA.
YO BACK, SON. HOW YOU DOIN'?
S'AIGHT, S'AIGHT. YOU KNOW.
TRUE.
SAY, YOU SCOPE WHO'S HANGIN'?
MUTHA-FUCK...

...THAT BITCH GOT HIM SOME BALLS.
the MIMIC
BRIAN AZZARELLO
WRITER
EDUARDO RISSO
ARTIST
PATRICIA MULVIHILL, COLORS
DIGITAL CHAMELEON, SEPS
CLEM ROBINS, LETTERS
DAVE JOHNSON, COVER
WILL DENNIS, EDITOR

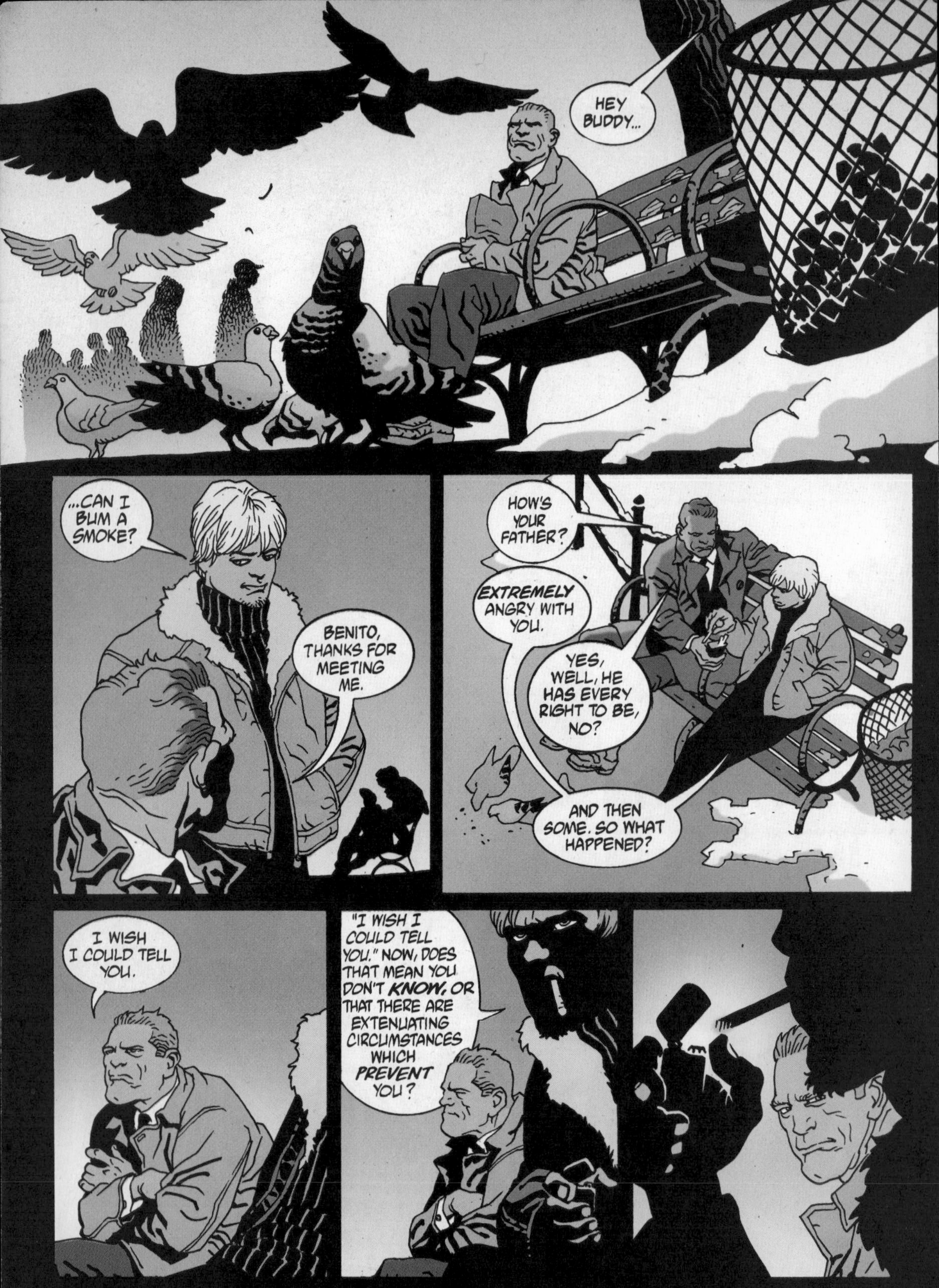
HEY BUDDY...
...CAN I BUM A SMOKE?
BENITO, THANKS FOR MEETING ME.
HOW'S YOUR FATHER?
EXTREMELY ANGRY WITH YOU.
YES, WELL, HE HAS EVERY RIGHT TO BE, NO?
AND THEN SOME. SO WHAT HAPPENED?
I WISH I COULD TELL YOU.
"I WISH I COULD TELL YOU." NOW, DOES THAT MEAN YOU DON'T KNOW, OR THAT THERE ARE EXTENUATING CIRCUMSTANCES WHICH PREVENT YOU?

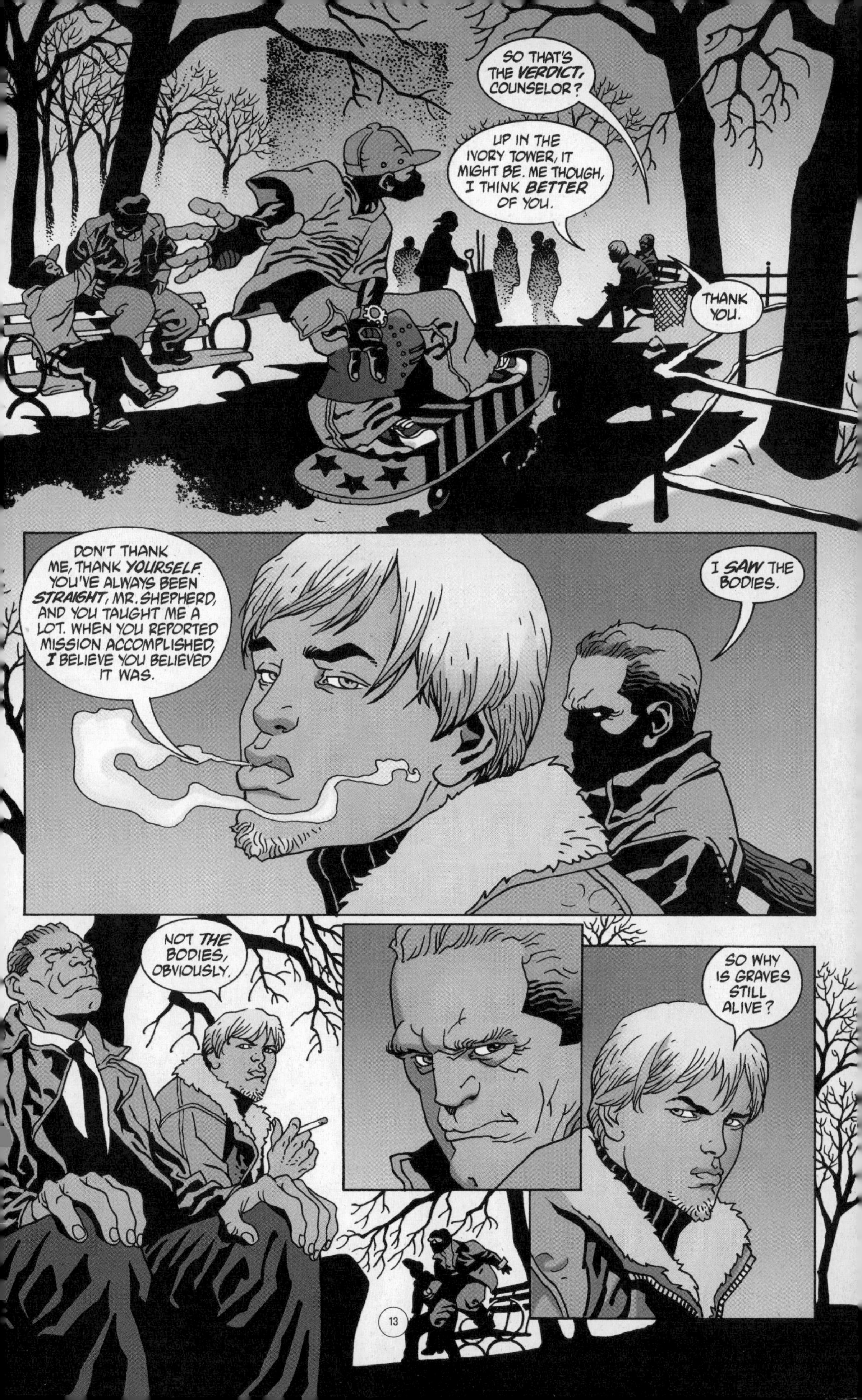
SO THAT'S THE VERDICT, COUNSELOR?
UP IN THE IVORY TOWER, IT MIGHT BE. ME THOUGH, I THINK BETTER OF YOU.
THANK YOU.
DON'T THANK ME, THANK YOURSELF. YOU'VE ALWAYS BEEN STRAIGHT, MR. SHEPHERD, AND YOU TAUGHT ME A LOT. WHEN YOU REPORTED MISSION ACCOMPLISHED, I BELIEVE YOU BELIEVED IT WAS.
I SAW THE BODIES.
NOT THE BODIES, OBVIOUSLY.
SO WHY IS GRAVES STILL ALIVE?

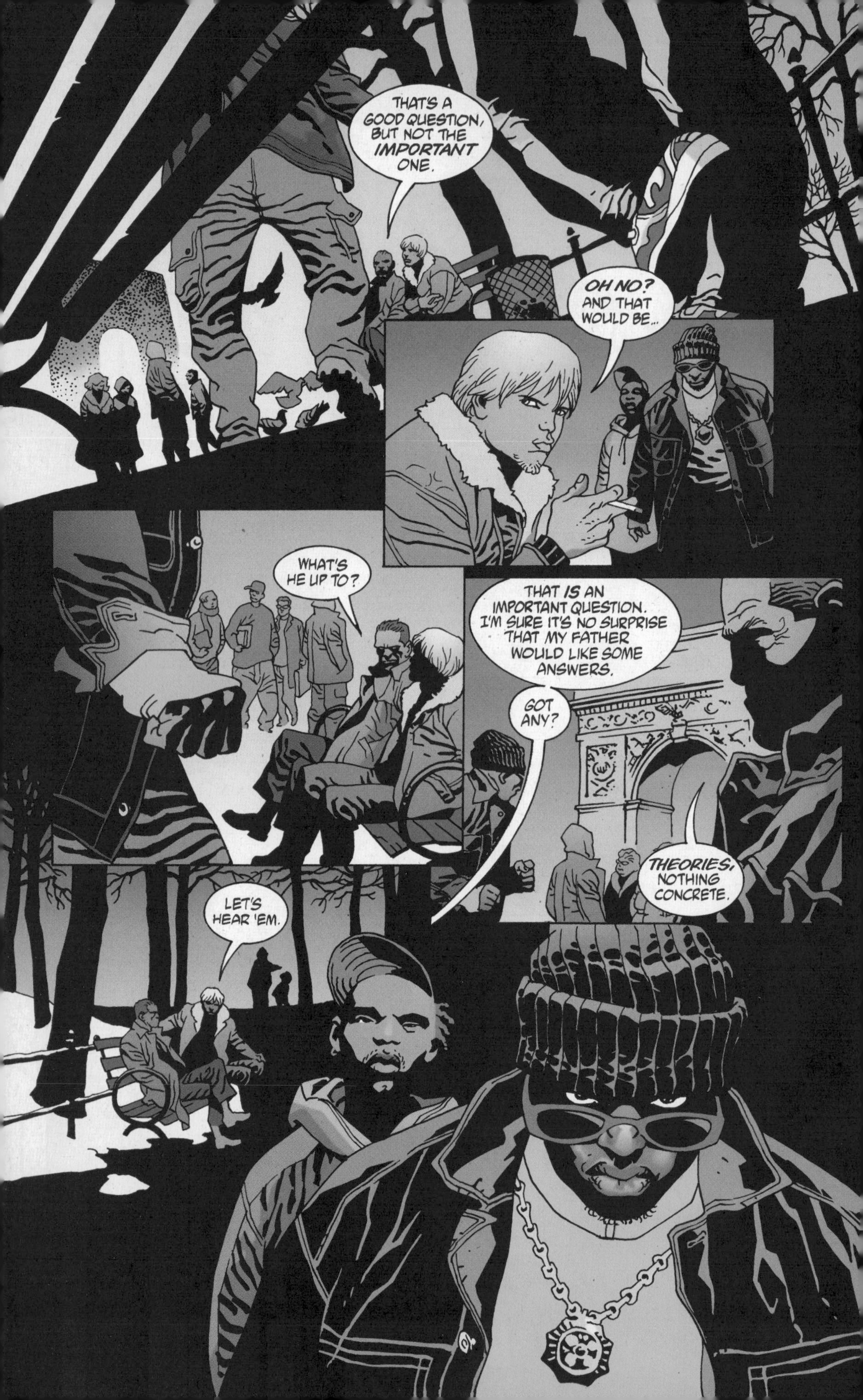
THAT'S A GOOD QUESTION, BUT NOT THE IMPORTANT ONE.
OH NO? AND THAT WOULD BE...
WHAT'S HE UP TO?
THAT IS AN IMPORTANT QUESTION. I'M SURE IT'S NO SURPRISE THAT MY FATHER WOULD LIKE SOME ANSWERS.
GOT ANY?
THEORIES. NOTHING CONCRETE.
LET'S HEAR 'EM.

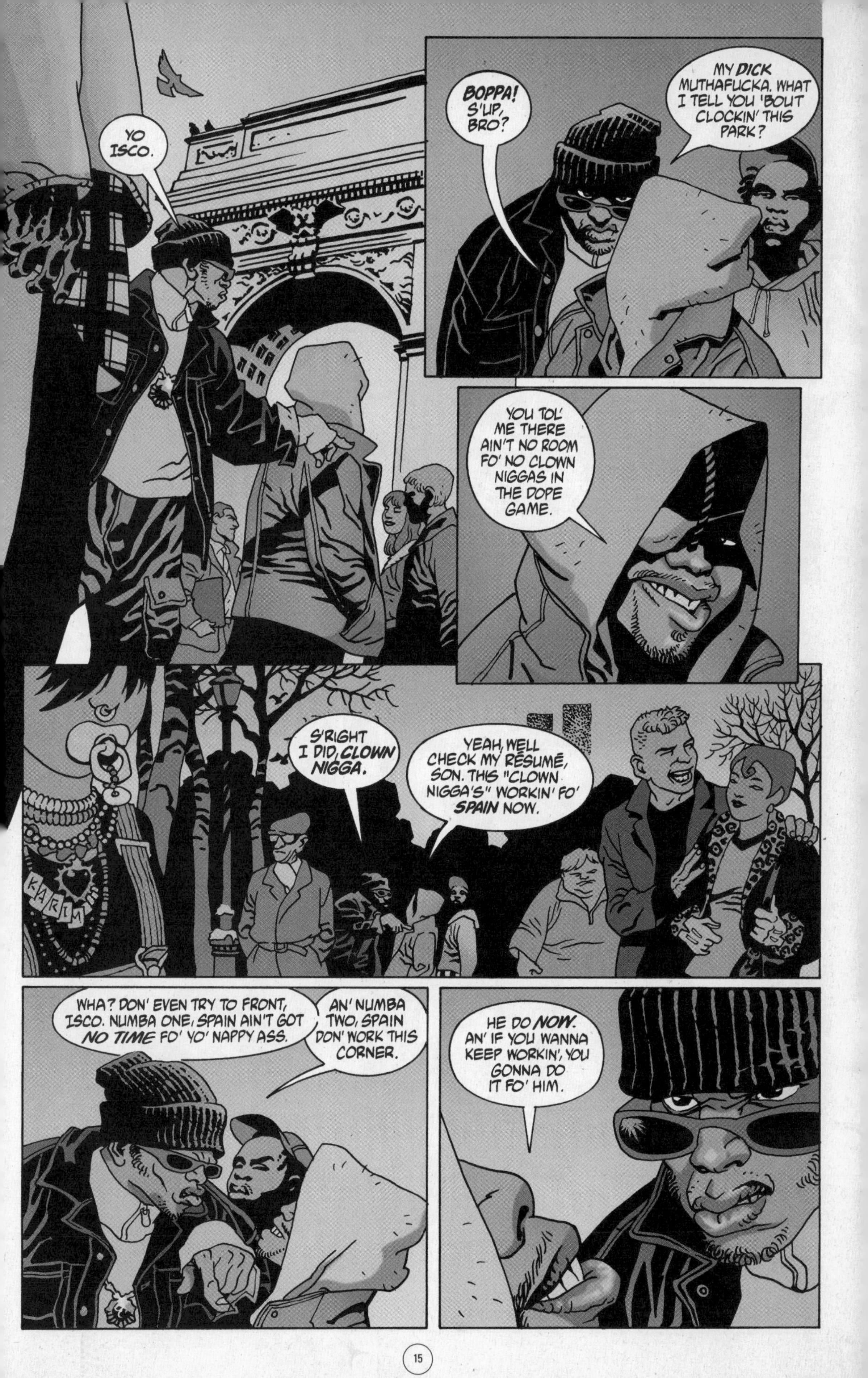
YO ISCO.
BOPPA! S'UP, BRO?
MY DICK MUTHAFUCKA. WHAT I TELL YOU 'BOUT CLOCKIN' THIS PARK?
YOU TOL' ME THERE AIN'T NO ROOM FO' NO CLOWN NIGGAS IN THE DOPE GAME.
S'RIGHT I DID, CLOWN NIGGA.
YEAH, WELL CHECK MY RÉSUMÉ, SON. THIS "CLOWN NIGGA'S" WORKIN' FO' SPAIN NOW.
KARIM
WHA? DON' EVEN TRY TO FRONT, ISCO. NUMBA ONE, SPAIN AIN'T GOT NO TIME FO' YO' NAPPY ASS.
AN' NUMBA TWO, SPAIN DON' WORK THIS CORNER.
HE DO NOW. AN' IF YOU WANNA KEEP WORKIN', YOU GONNA DO IT FO' HIM.

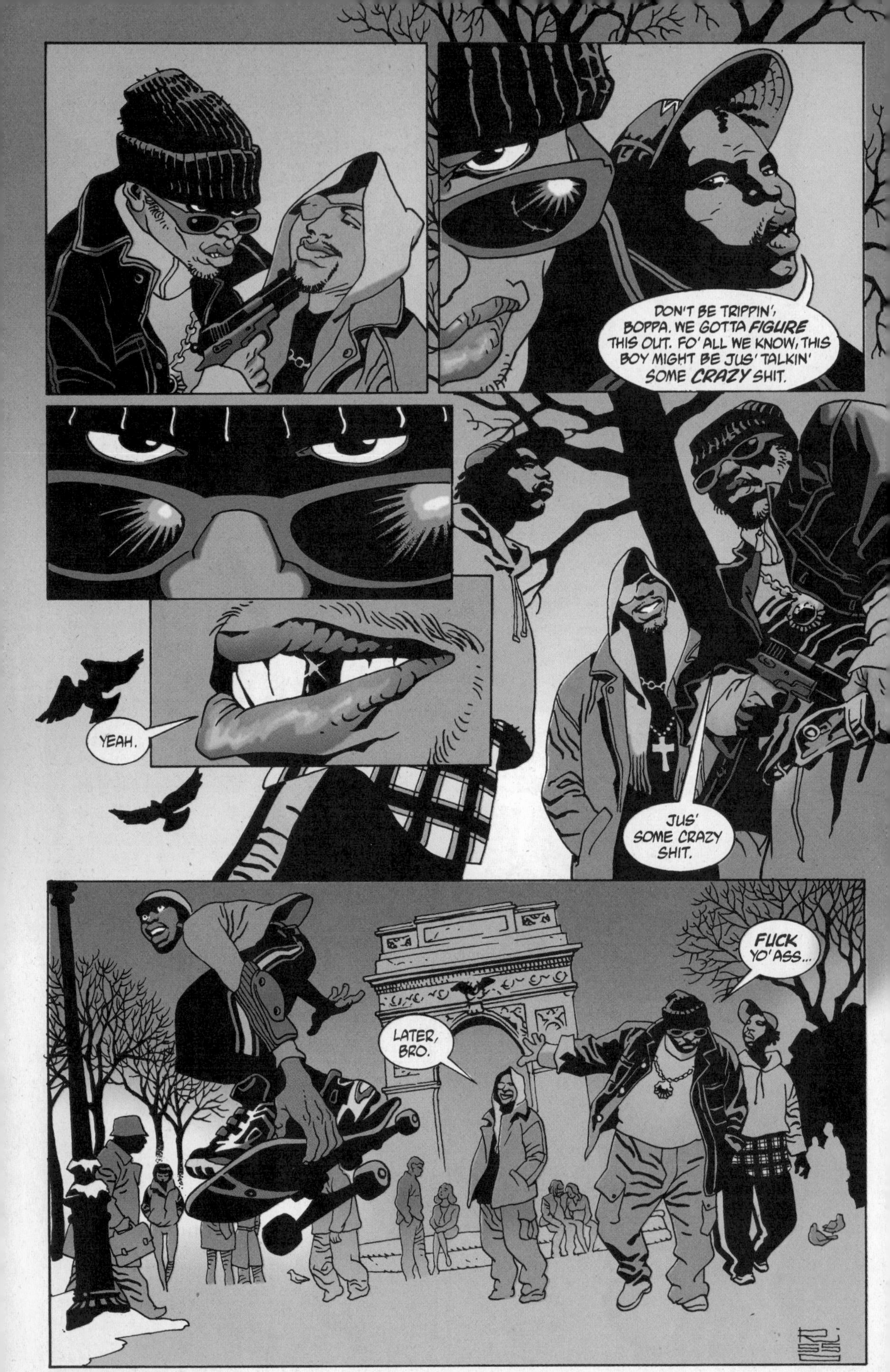

DON'T BE TRIPPIN', BOPPA. WE GOTTA FIGURE THIS OUT. FO' ALL WE KNOW, THIS BOY MIGHT BE JUS' TALKIN' SOME CRAZY SHIT.
YEAH.
JUS' SOME CRAZY SHIT.
FUCK YO' ASS...
LATER, BRO.

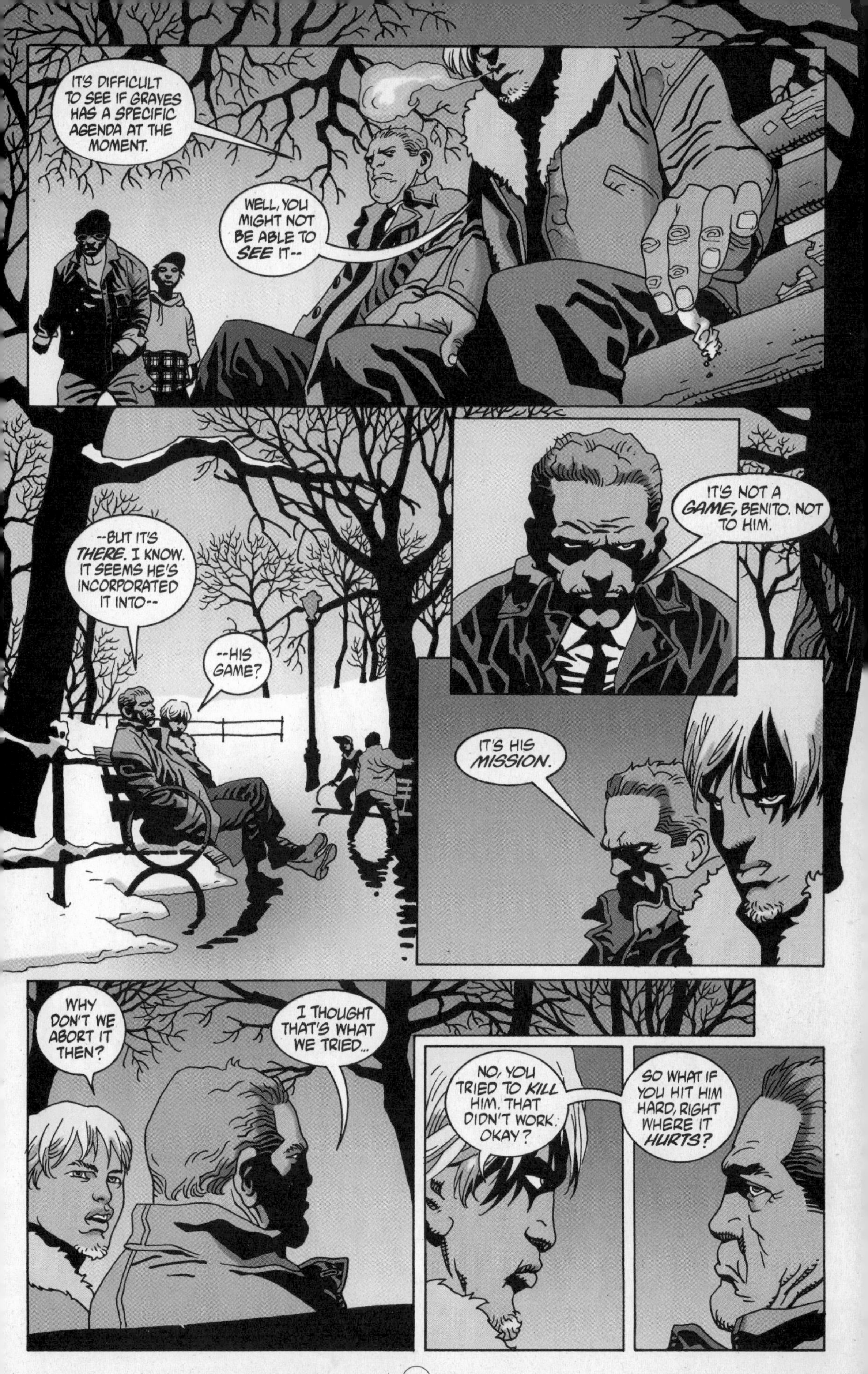
IT'S DIFFICULT TO SEE IF GRAVES HAS A SPECIFIC AGENDA AT THE MOMENT.
WELL, YOU MIGHT NOT BE ABLE TO *SEE* IT--
--BUT IT'S *THERE*. I KNOW. IT SEEMS HE'S INCORPORATED IT INTO--
--HIS GAME?
IT'S NOT A *GAME*, BENITO. NOT TO HIM.
IT'S HIS *MISSION*.
WHY DON'T WE ABORT IT THEN?
I THOUGHT THAT'S WHAT WE TRIED...
NO, YOU TRIED TO *KILL* HIM. THAT DIDN'T WORK. OKAY?
SO WHAT IF YOU HIT HIM HARD, RIGHT WHERE IT *HURTS*?

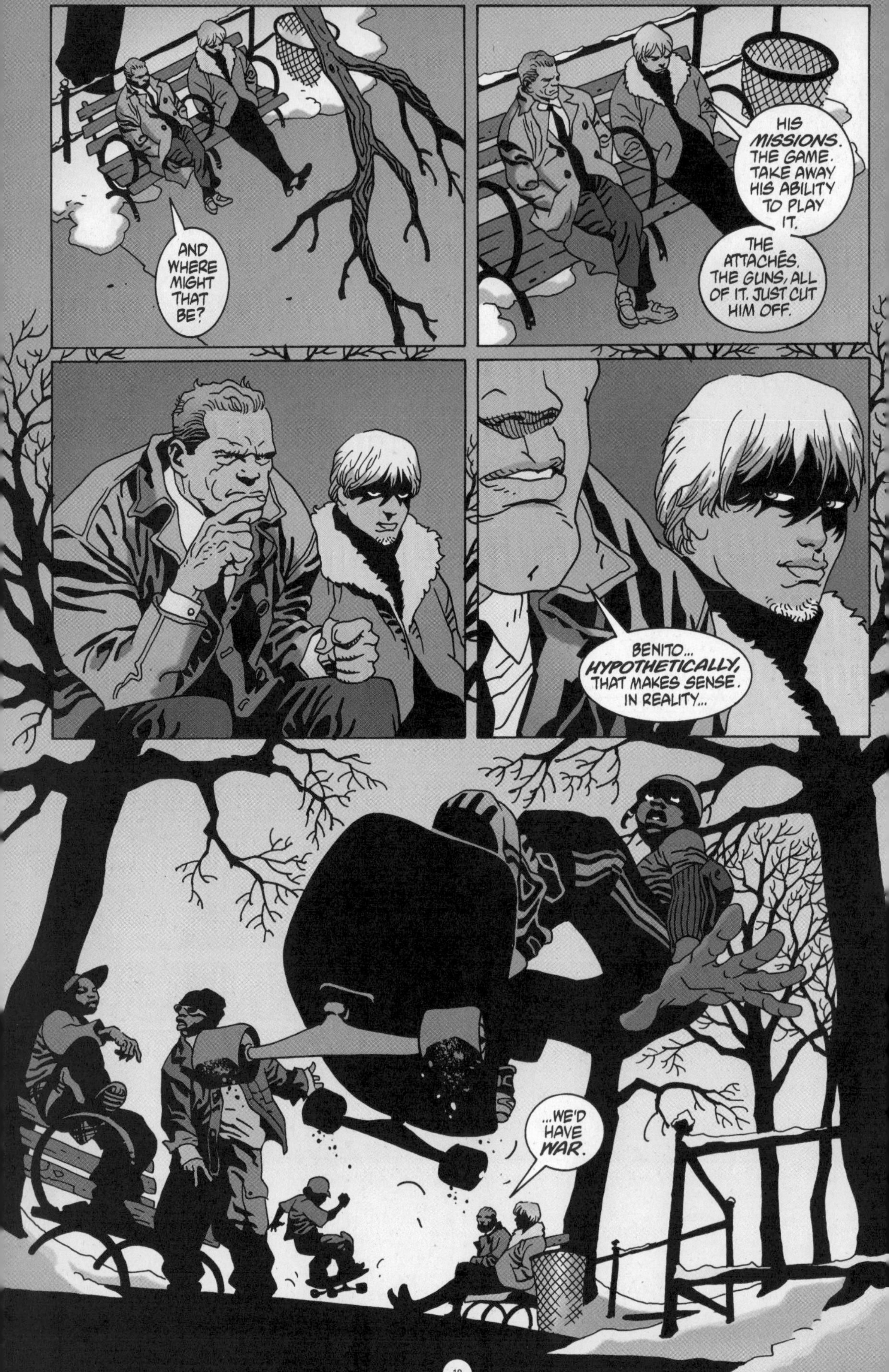
AND WHERE MIGHT THAT BE?
HIS MISSIONS. THE GAME. TAKE AWAY HIS ABILITY TO PLAY IT.
THE ATTACHÉS. THE GUNS, ALL OF IT. JUST CUT HIM OFF.
BENITO... HYPOTHETICALLY, THAT MAKES SENSE. IN REALITY...
...WE'D HAVE WAR.

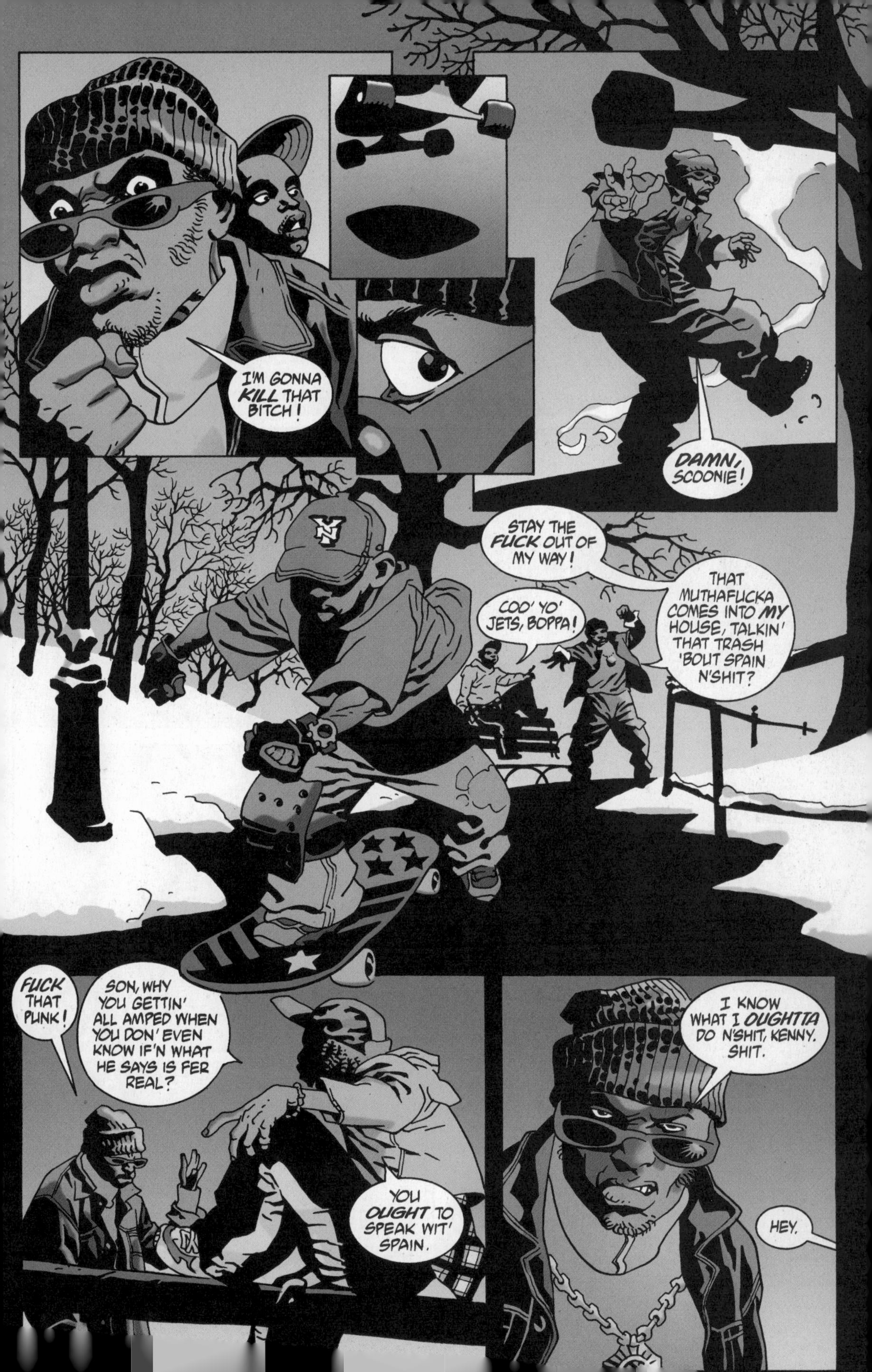

I'M GONNA KILL THAT BITCH!
DAMN, SCOONIE!
STAY THE FUCK OUT OF MY WAY!
COO' YO' JETS, BOPPA!
THAT MUTHAFUCKA COMES INTO MY HOUSE, TALKIN' THAT TRASH 'BOUT SPAIN N'SHIT?
FUCK THAT PUNK!
SON, WHY YOU GETTIN' ALL AMPED WHEN YOU DON' EVEN KNOW IF'N WHAT HE SAYS IS FER REAL?
YOU OUGHT TO SPEAK WIT' SPAIN.
I KNOW WHAT I OUGHTTA DO N'SHIT, KENNY. SHIT.
HEY.

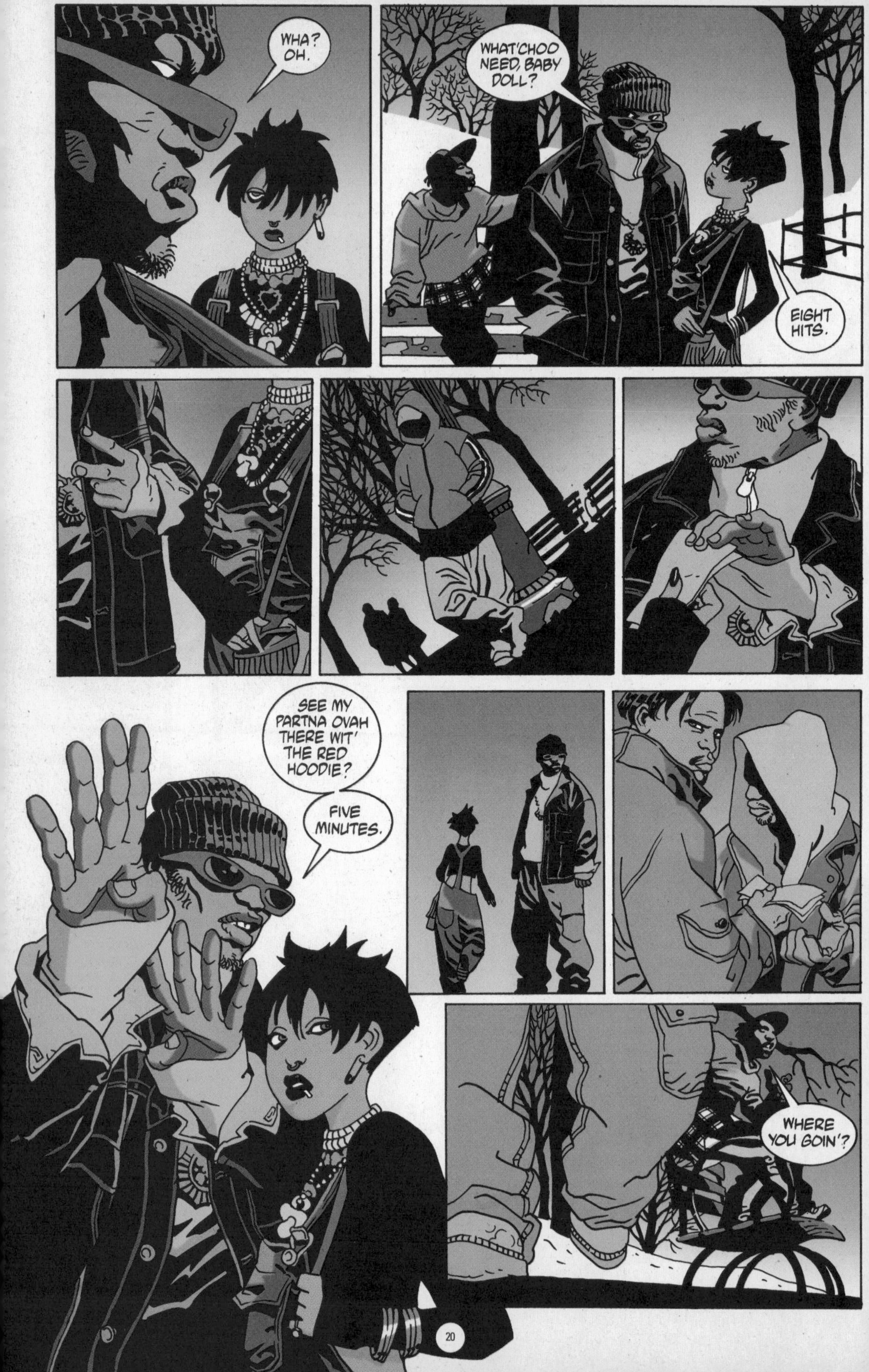
WHA? OH.
WHAT'CHOO NEED, BABY DOLL?
EIGHT HITS.
SEE MY PARTNA OVAH THERE WIT' THE RED HOODIE?
FIVE MINUTES.
WHERE YOU GOIN'?

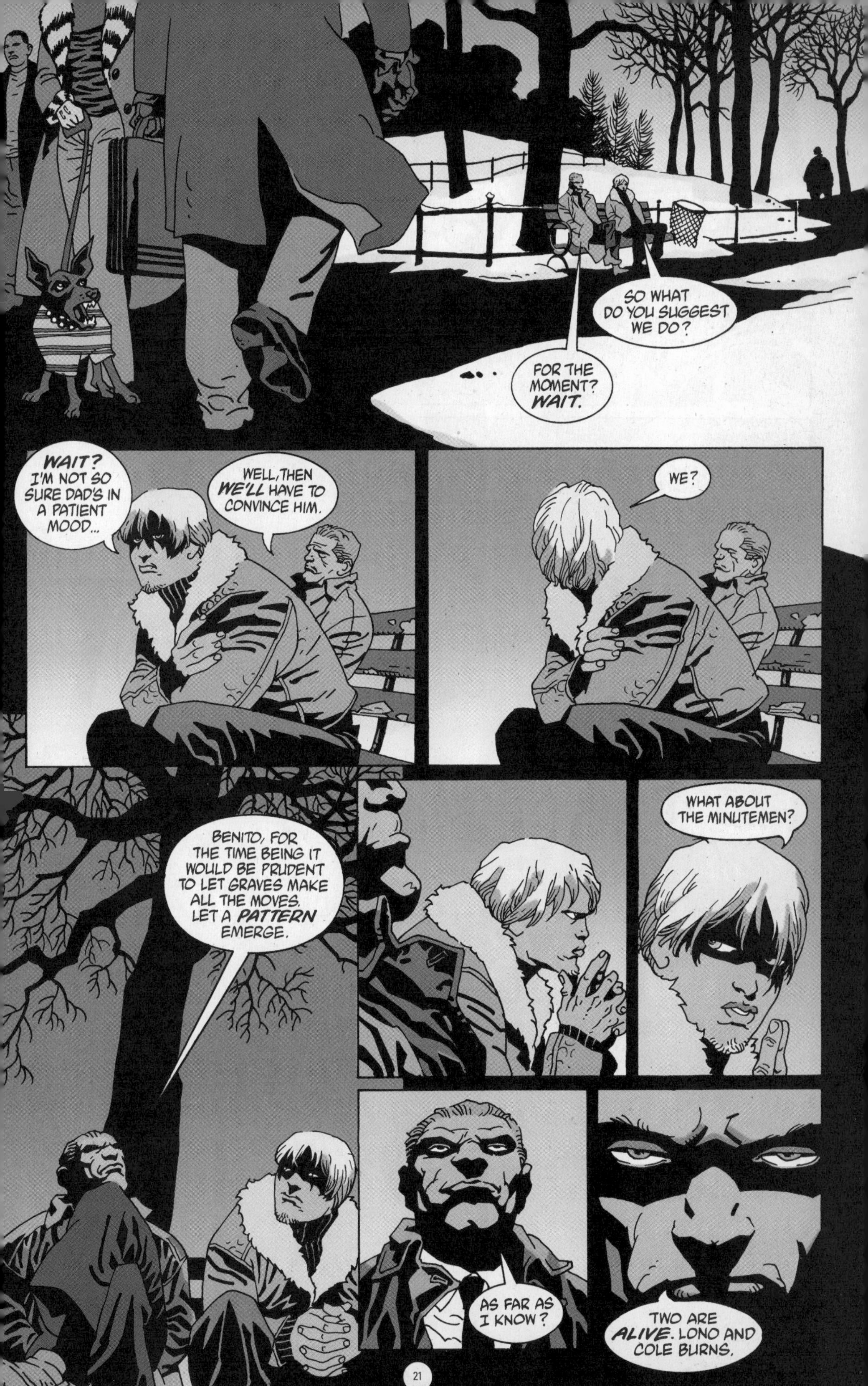
SO WHAT DO YOU SUGGEST WE DO?
FOR THE MOMENT? WAIT.
WAIT? I'M NOT SO SURE DAD'S IN A PATIENT MOOD...
WELL, THEN WE'LL HAVE TO CONVINCE HIM.
WE?
BENITO, FOR THE TIME BEING IT WOULD BE PRUDENT TO LET GRAVES MAKE ALL THE MOVES. LET A PATTERN EMERGE.
WHAT ABOUT THE MINUTEMEN?
AS FAR AS I KNOW?
TWO ARE ALIVE. LONO AND COLE BURNS.

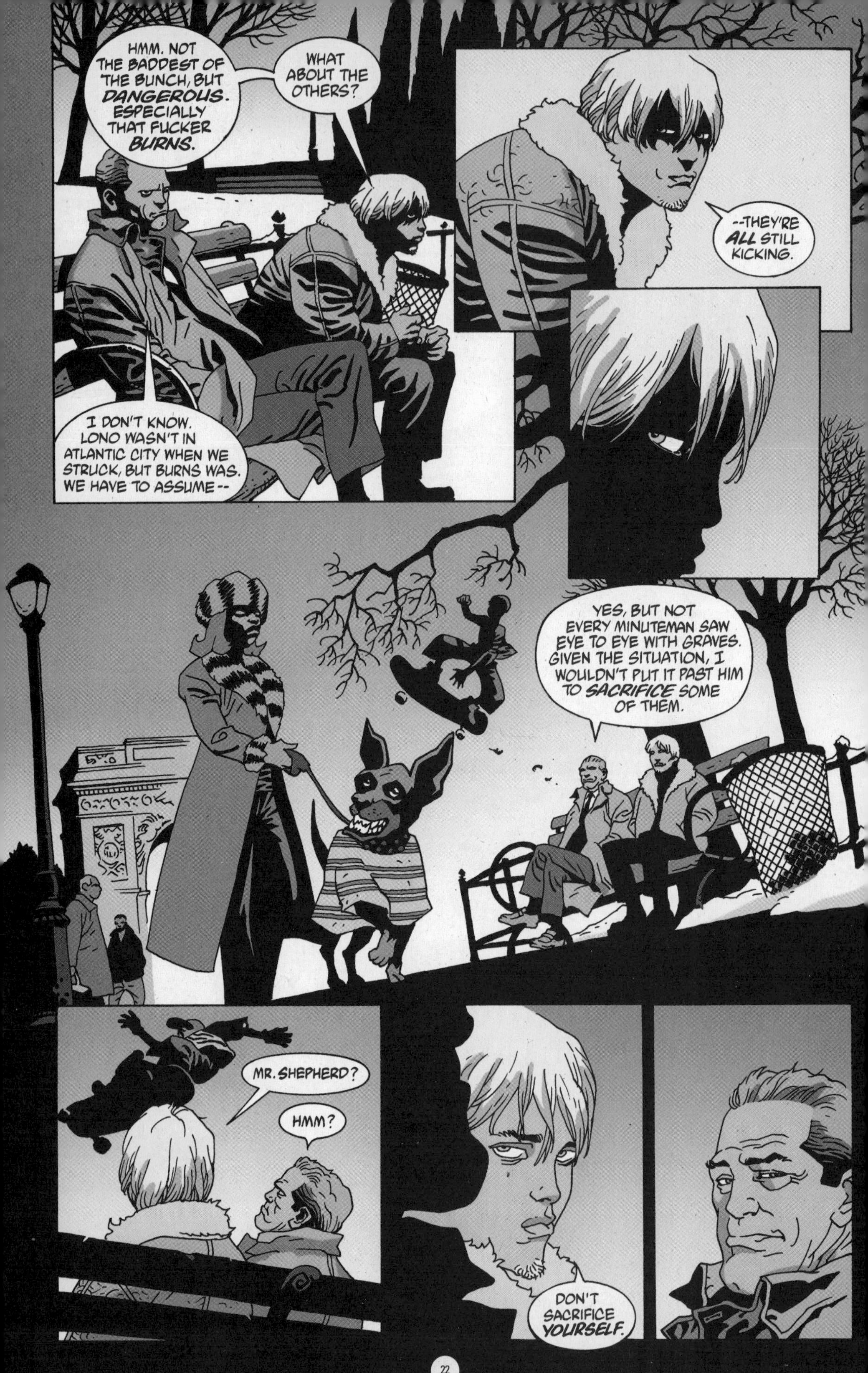
HMM. NOT THE BADDEST OF THE BUNCH, BUT DANGEROUS. ESPECIALLY THAT FUCKER BURNS.
WHAT ABOUT THE OTHERS?
I DON'T KNOW. LONO WASN'T IN ATLANTIC CITY WHEN WE STRUCK, BUT BURNS WAS. WE HAVE TO ASSUME--
--THEY'RE ALL STILL KICKING.
YES, BUT NOT EVERY MINUTEMAN SAW EYE TO EYE WITH GRAVES. GIVEN THE SITUATION, I WOULDN'T PUT IT PAST HIM TO SACRIFICE SOME OF THEM.
MR. SHEPHERD?
HMM?
DON'T SACRIFICE YOURSELF.

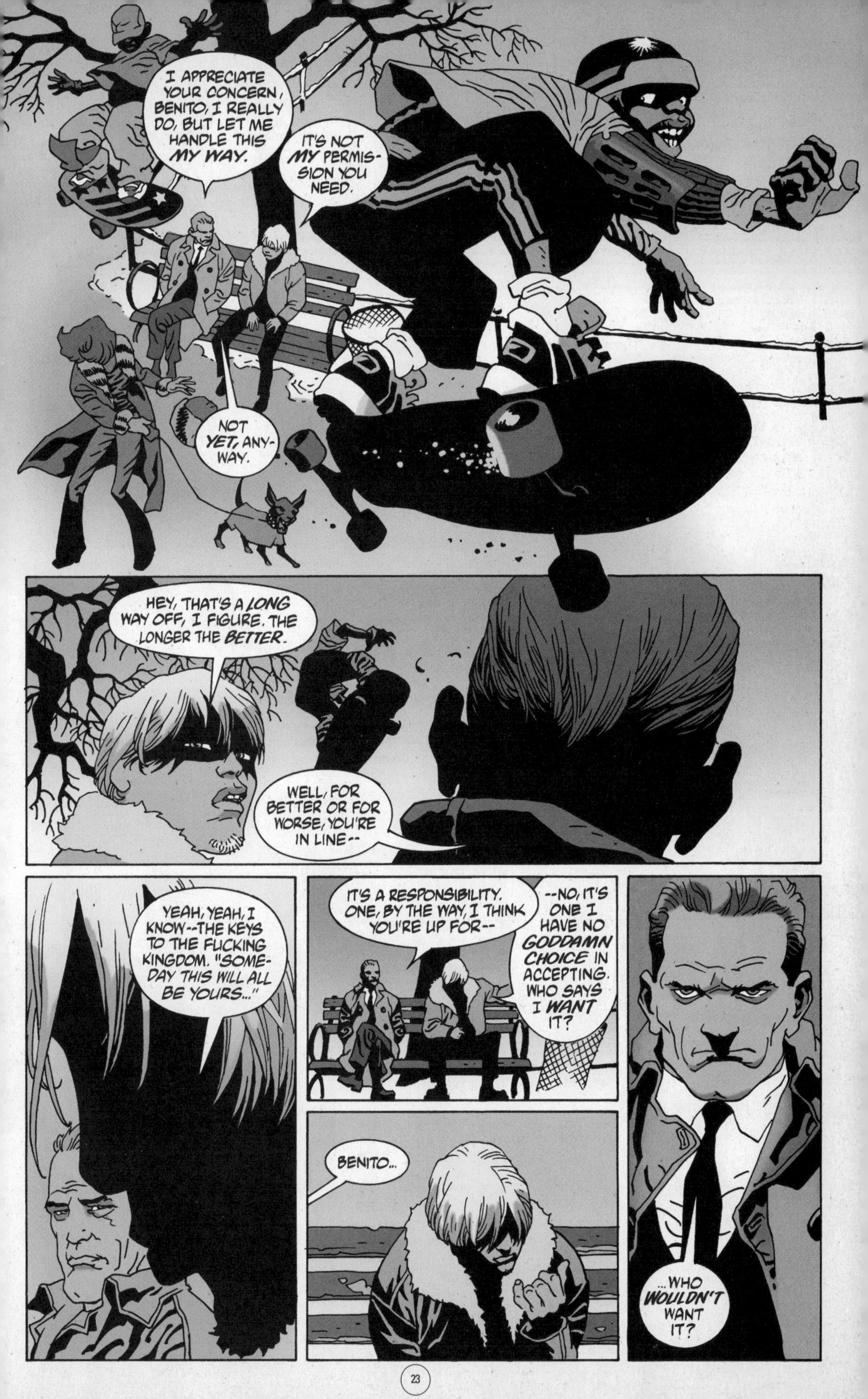
I APPRECIATE YOUR CONCERN, BENITO, I REALLY DO, BUT LET ME HANDLE THIS MY WAY.
IT'S NOT MY PERMISSION YOU NEED.
NOT YET, ANYWAY.
HEY, THAT'S A LONG WAY OFF, I FIGURE. THE LONGER THE BETTER.
WELL, FOR BETTER OR FOR WORSE, YOU'RE IN LINE--
YEAH, YEAH, I KNOW--THE KEYS TO THE FUCKING KINGDOM. "SOMEDAY THIS WILL ALL BE YOURS..."
IT'S A RESPONSIBILITY. ONE, BY THE WAY, I THINK YOU'RE UP FOR--
--NO, IT'S ONE I HAVE NO GODDAMN CHOICE IN ACCEPTING. WHO SAYS I WANT IT?
BENITO...
...WHO WOULDN'T WANT IT?

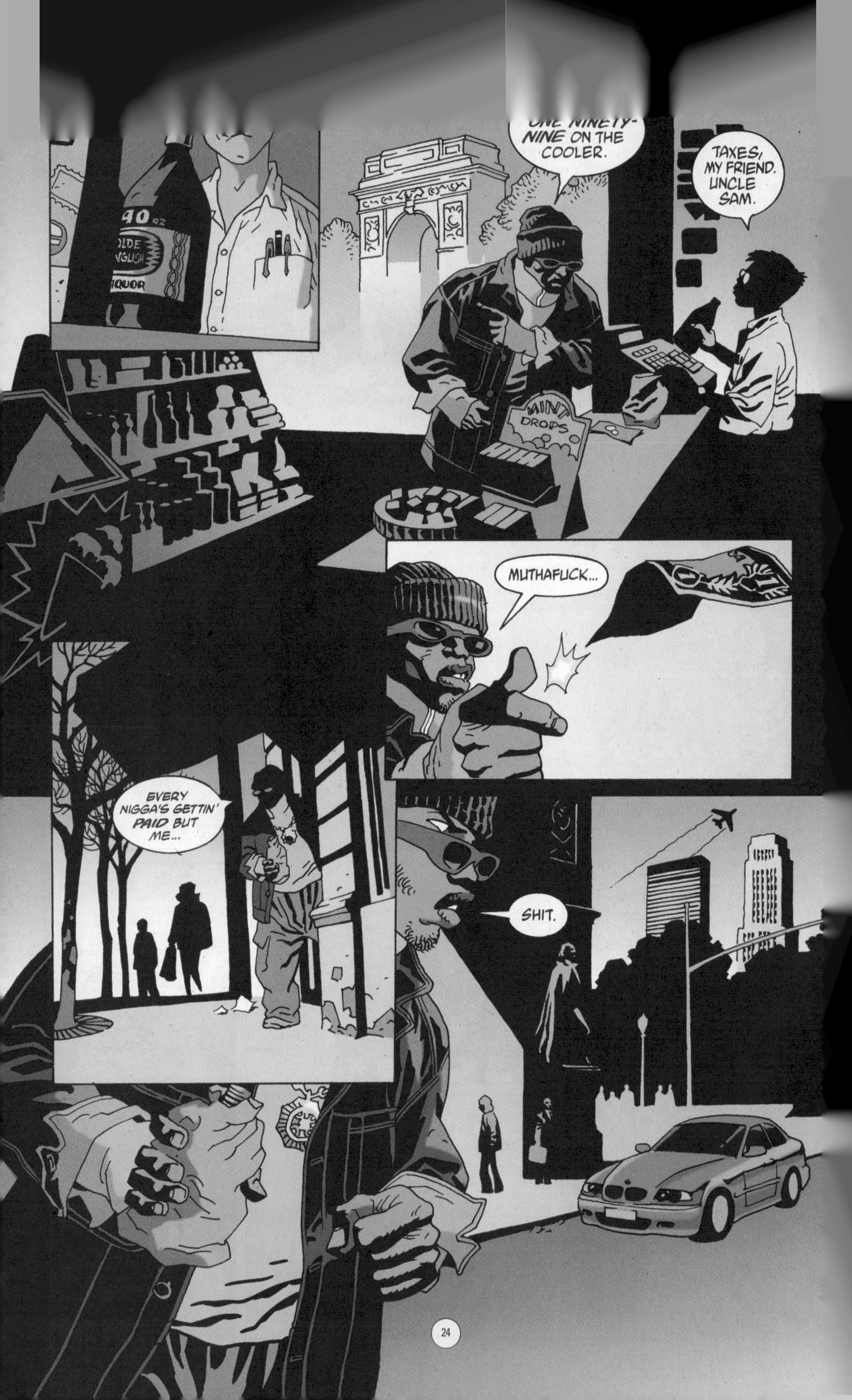
40 oz
OLDE ENGLISH
LIQUOR
ONE NINETY-NINE ON THE COOLER.
TAXES, MY FRIEND. UNCLE SAM.
MINT DROPS
MUTHAFUCK...
EVERY NIGGA'S GETTIN' PAID BUT ME...
SHIT.

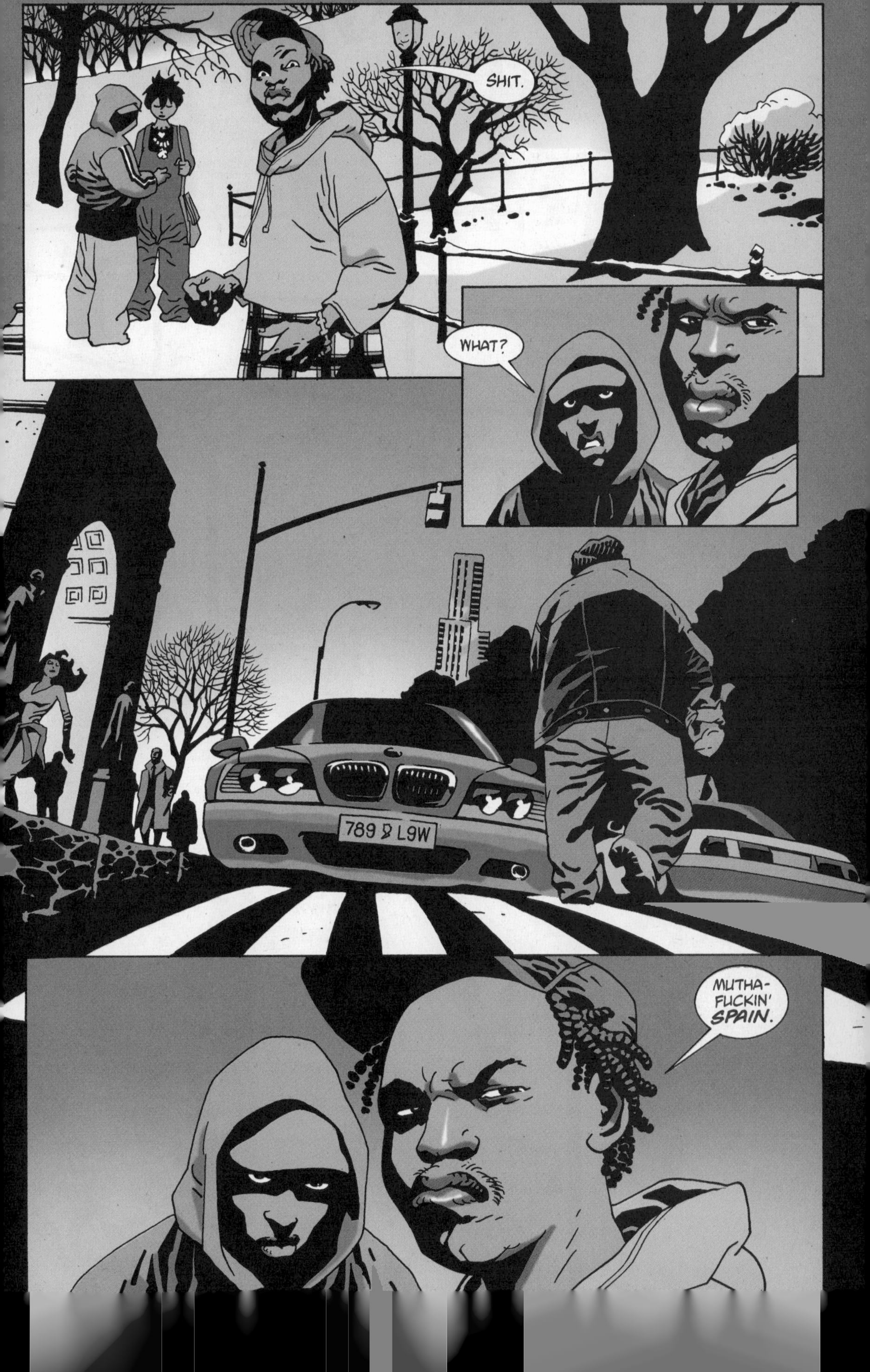
SHIT.
WHAT?
789 B L9W
MUTHA-FUCKIN' SPAIN.

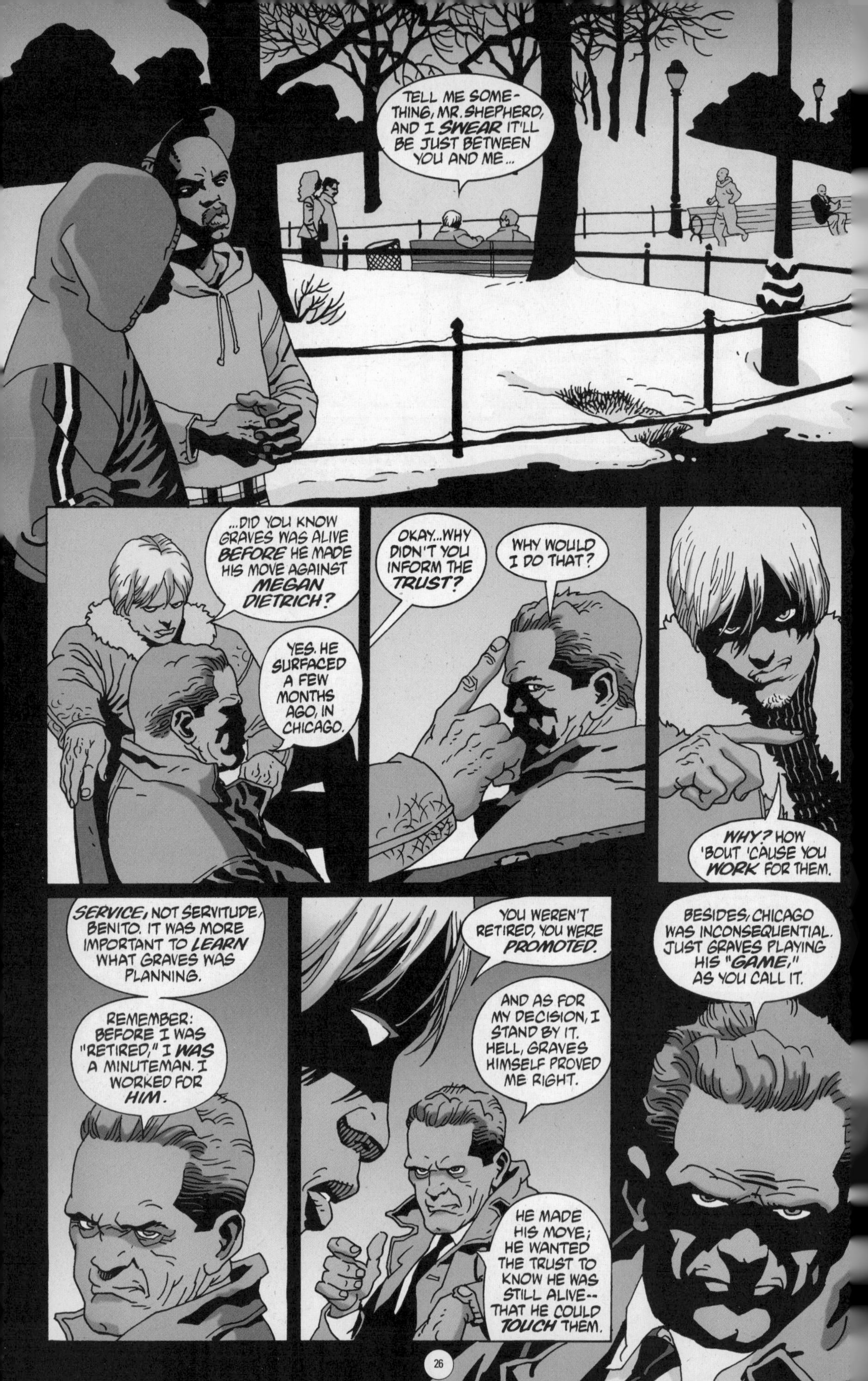
TELL ME SOMETHING, MR. SHEPHERD, AND I SWEAR IT'LL BE JUST BETWEEN YOU AND ME...
...DID YOU KNOW GRAVES WAS ALIVE BEFORE HE MADE HIS MOVE AGAINST MEGAN DIETRICH?
YES. HE SURFACED A FEW MONTHS AGO, IN CHICAGO.
OKAY...WHY DIDN'T YOU INFORM THE TRUST?
WHY WOULD I DO THAT?
WHY? HOW 'BOUT 'CAUSE YOU WORK FOR THEM.
SERVICE, NOT SERVITUDE, BENITO. IT WAS MORE IMPORTANT TO LEARN WHAT GRAVES WAS PLANNING.
REMEMBER: BEFORE I WAS "RETIRED," I WAS A MINUTEMAN. I WORKED FOR HIM.
YOU WEREN'T RETIRED, YOU WERE PROMOTED.
AND AS FOR MY DECISION, I STAND BY IT. HELL, GRAVES HIMSELF PROVED ME RIGHT.
HE MADE HIS MOVE; HE WANTED THE TRUST TO KNOW HE WAS STILL ALIVE-- THAT HE COULD TOUCH THEM.
BESIDES, CHICAGO WAS INCONSEQUENTIAL. JUST GRAVES PLAYING HIS "GAME," AS YOU CALL IT.

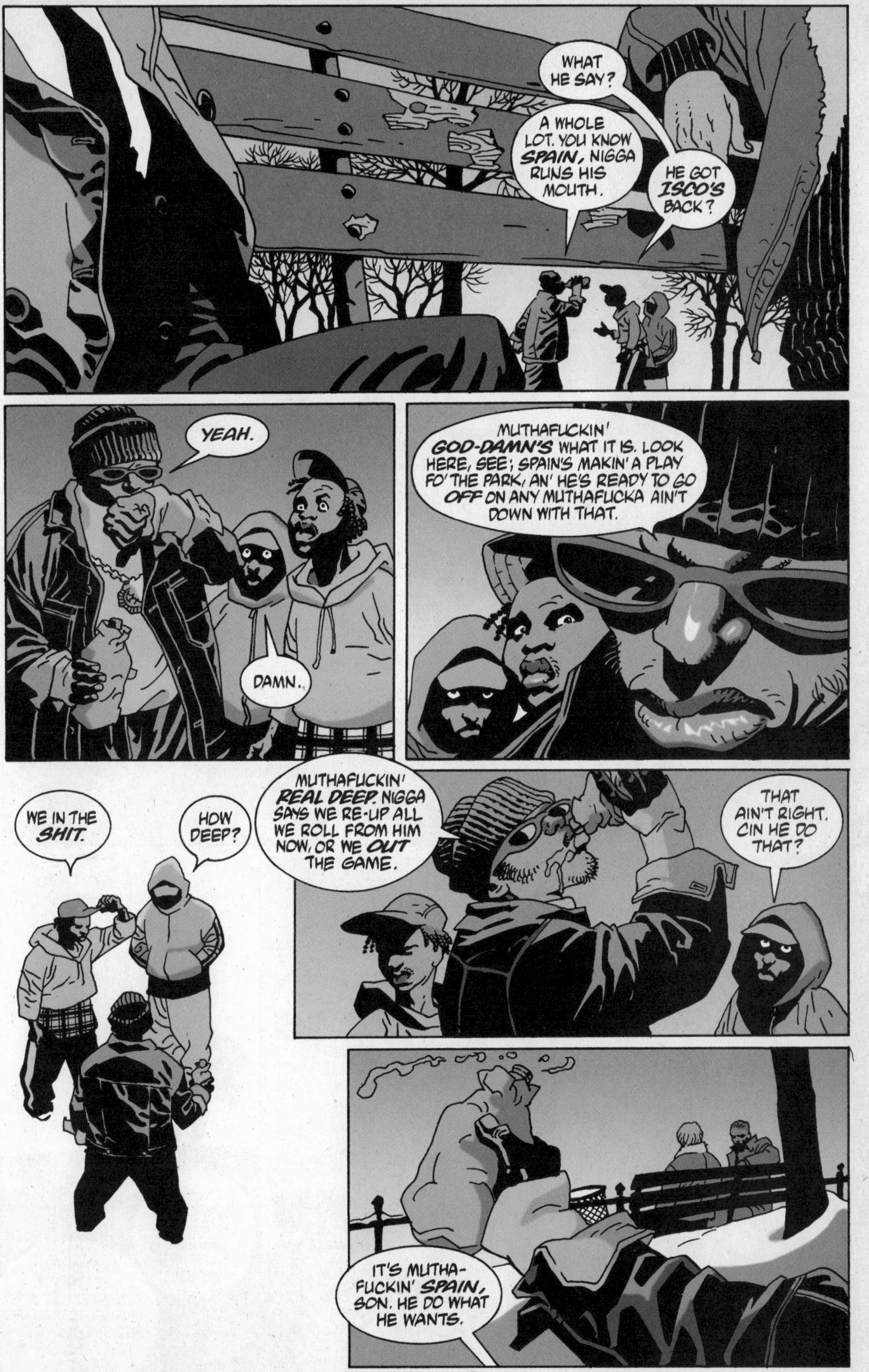
WHAT HE SAY?
A WHOLE LOT. YOU KNOW SPAIN, NIGGA RUNS HIS MOUTH.
HE GOT ISCO'S BACK?
YEAH.
DAMN.
MUTHAFUCKIN' GOD-DAMN'S WHAT IT IS. LOOK HERE, SEE; SPAIN'S MAKIN' A PLAY FO' THE PARK, AN' HE'S READY TO GO OFF ON ANY MUTHAFUCKA AIN'T DOWN WITH THAT.
WE IN THE SHIT.
HOW DEEP?
MUTHAFUCKIN' REAL DEEP. NIGGA SAYS WE RE-UP ALL WE ROLL FROM HIM NOW, OR WE OUT THE GAME.
THAT AIN'T RIGHT. CIN HE DO THAT?
IT'S MUTHA-FUCKIN' SPAIN, SON. HE DO WHAT HE WANTS.

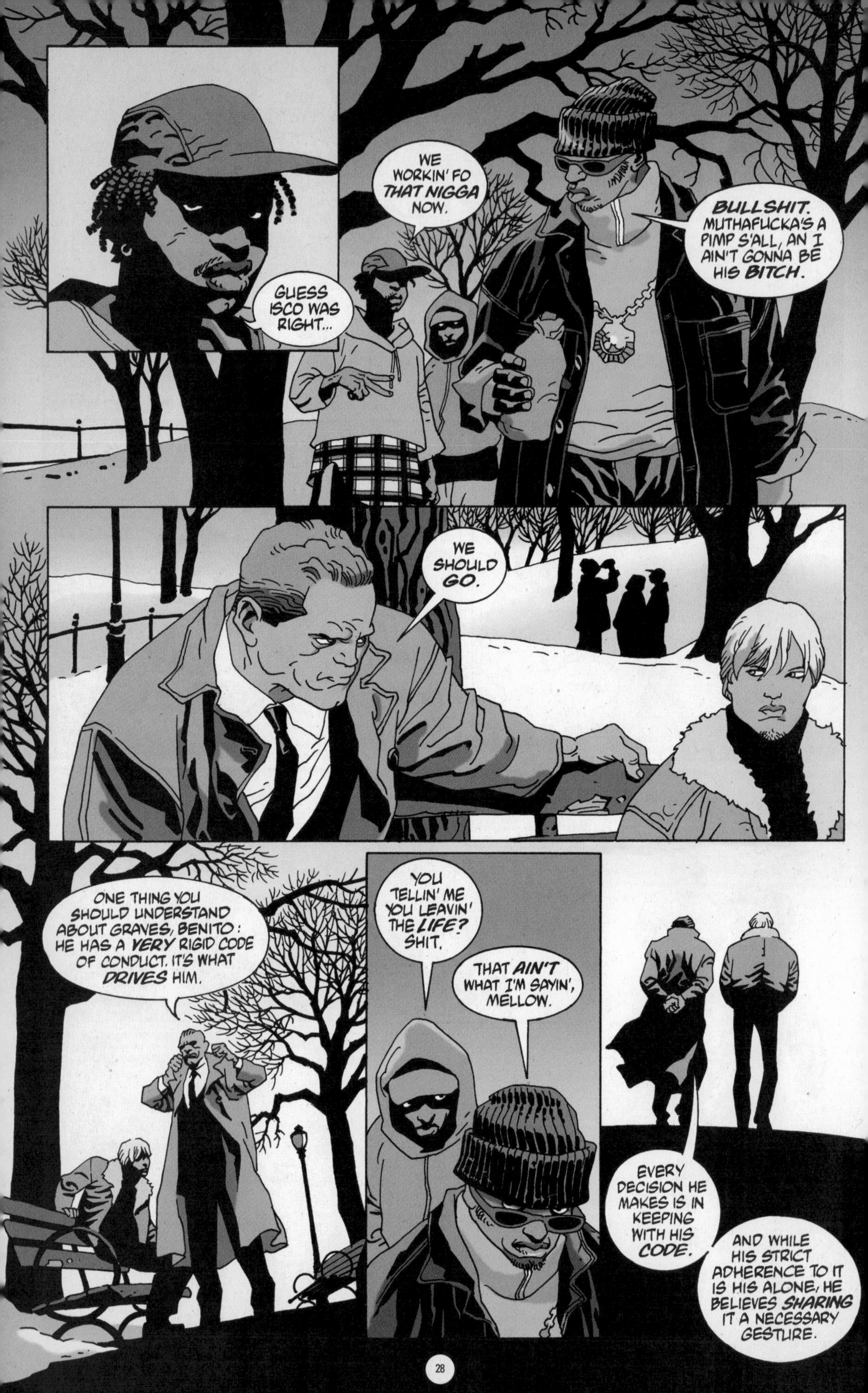
WE WORKIN' FO THAT NIGGA NOW.
GUESS ISCO WAS RIGHT...
BULLSHIT. MUTHAFUCKA'S A PIMP S'ALL, AN I AIN'T GONNA BE HIS BITCH.
WE SHOULD GO.
ONE THING YOU SHOULD UNDERSTAND ABOUT GRAVES, BENITO: HE HAS A VERY RIGID CODE OF CONDUCT. IT'S WHAT DRIVES HIM.
YOU TELLIN' ME YOU LEAVIN' THE LIFE? SHIT.
THAT AIN'T WHAT I'M SAYIN', MELLOW.
EVERY DECISION HE MAKES IS IN KEEPING WITH HIS CODE.
AND WHILE HIS STRICT ADHERENCE TO IT IS HIS ALONE, HE BELIEVES SHARING IT A NECESSARY GESTURE.

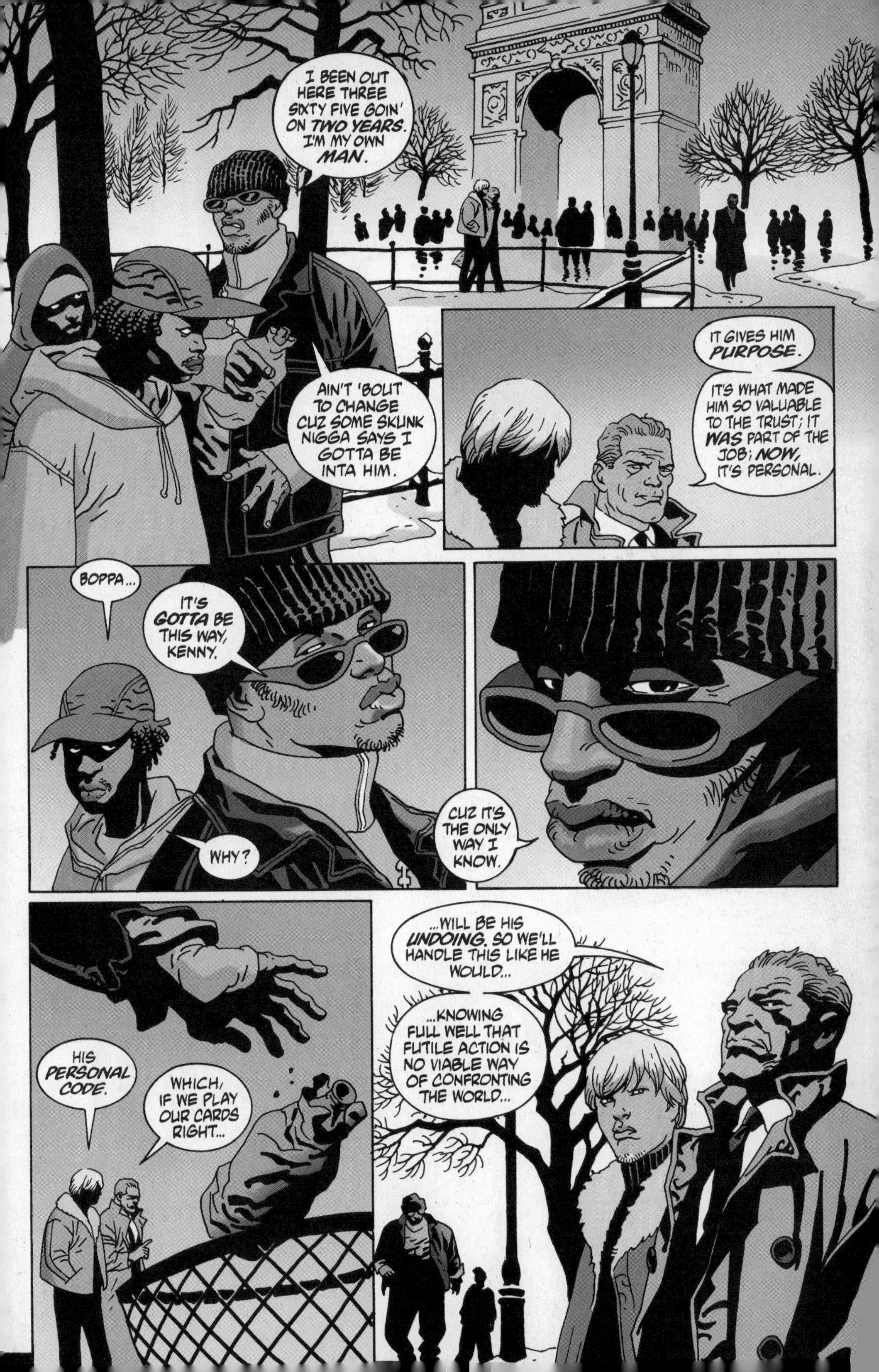
I BEEN OUT HERE THREE SIXTY FIVE GOIN' ON TWO YEARS. I'M MY OWN MAN.
AIN'T 'BOUT TO CHANGE CUZ SOME SKUNK NIGGA SAYS I GOTTA BE INTA HIM.
IT GIVES HIM PURPOSE.
IT'S WHAT MADE HIM SO VALUABLE TO THE TRUST; IT WAS PART OF THE JOB; NOW, IT'S PERSONAL.
BOPPA...
IT'S GOTTA BE THIS WAY, KENNY.
WHY?
CUZ IT'S THE ONLY WAY I KNOW.
HIS PERSONAL CODE.
WHICH, IF WE PLAY OUR CARDS RIGHT...
...WILL BE HIS UNDOING. SO WE'LL HANDLE THIS LIKE HE WOULD...
...KNOWING FULL WELL THAT FUTILE ACTION IS NO VIABLE WAY OF CONFRONTING THE WORLD...

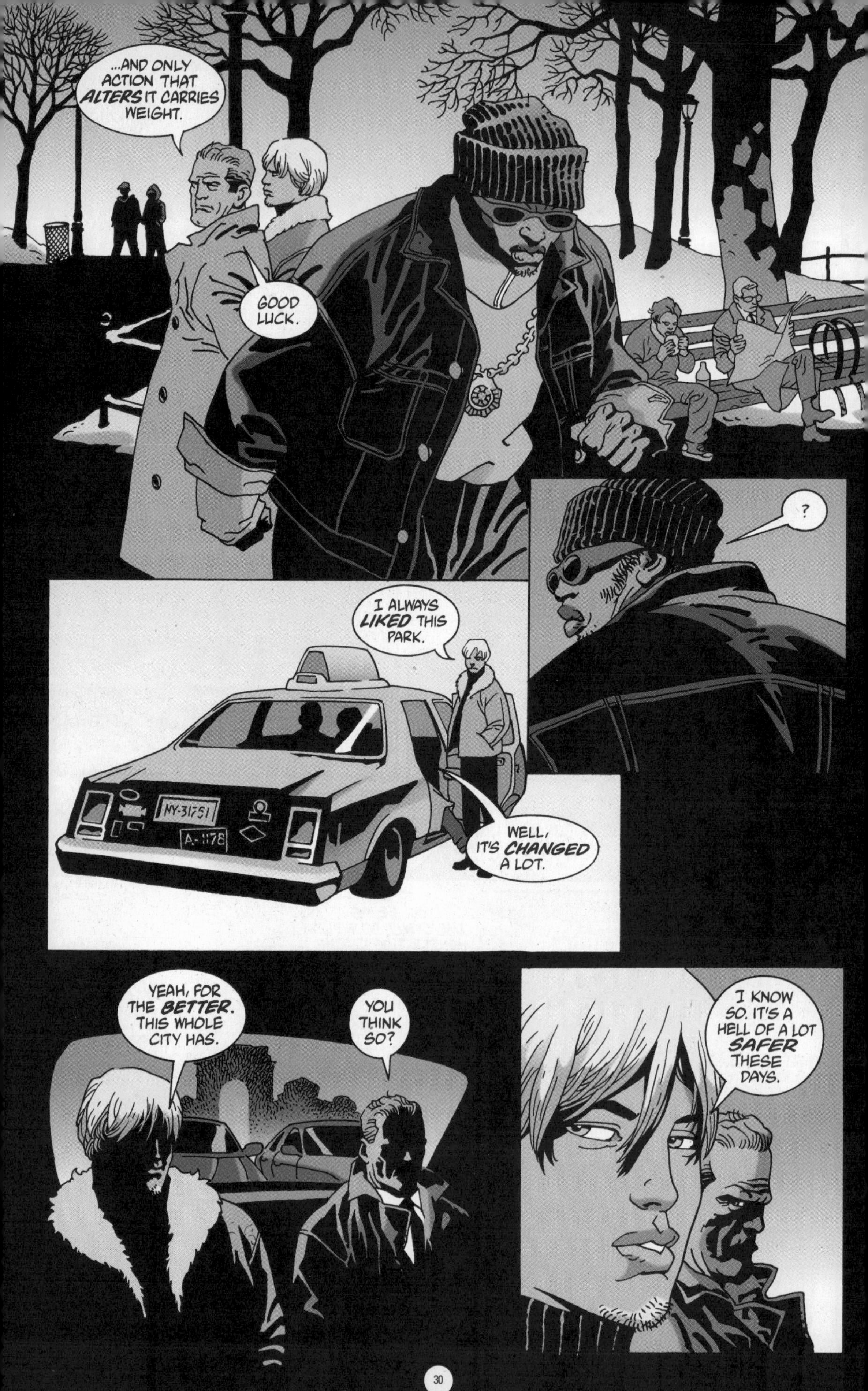
...AND ONLY ACTION THAT ALTERS IT CARRIES WEIGHT.
GOOD LUCK.
?
I ALWAYS LIKED THIS PARK.
NY-31751
A-1178
WELL, IT'S CHANGED A LOT.
YEAH, FOR THE BETTER. THIS WHOLE CITY HAS.
YOU THINK SO?
I KNOW SO. IT'S A HELL OF A LOT SAFER THESE DAYS.

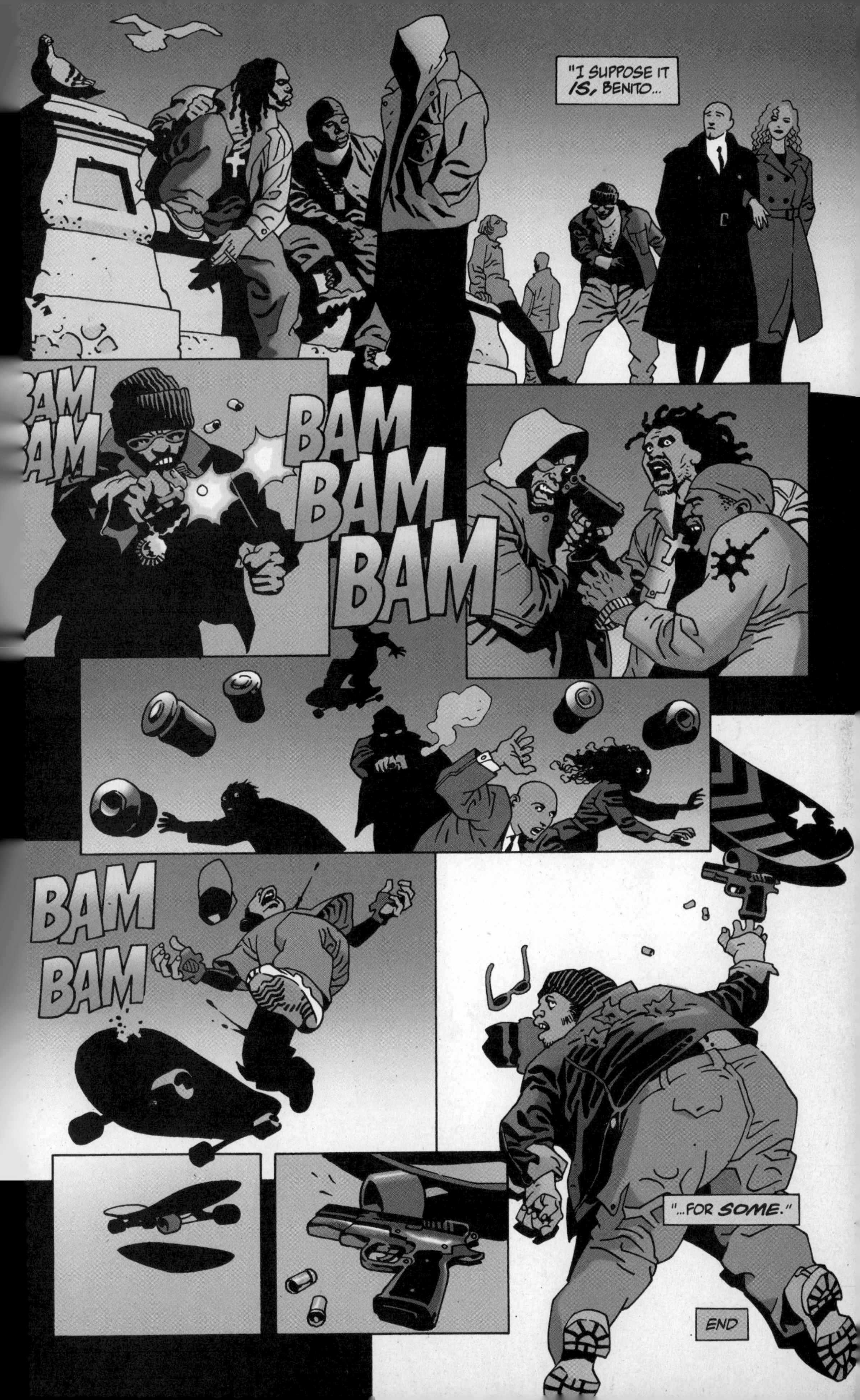
"I SUPPOSE IT IS, BENITO...
BAM BAM
BAM BAM BAM BAM
BAM BAM
"...FOR SOME."
END

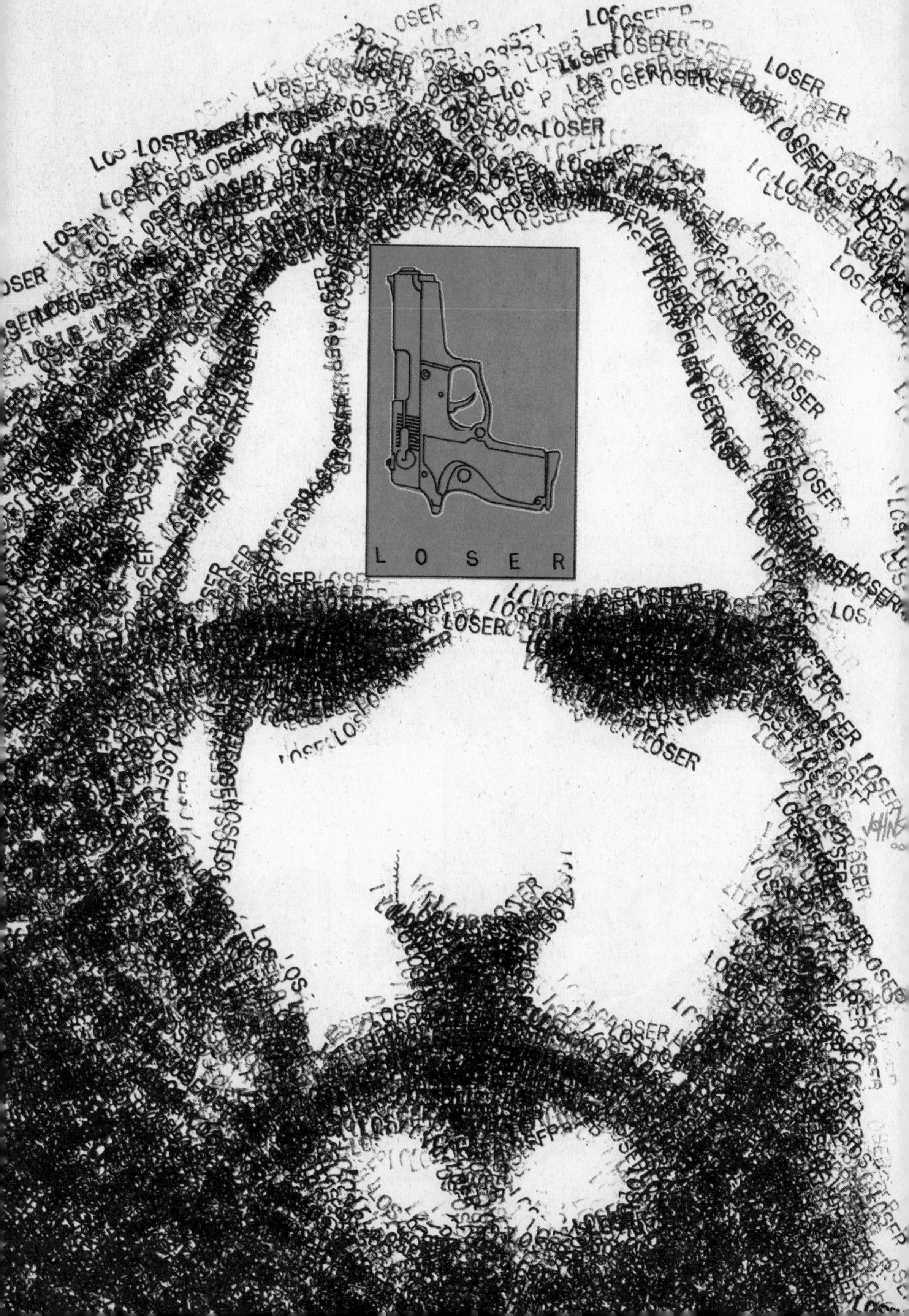
L O S E R

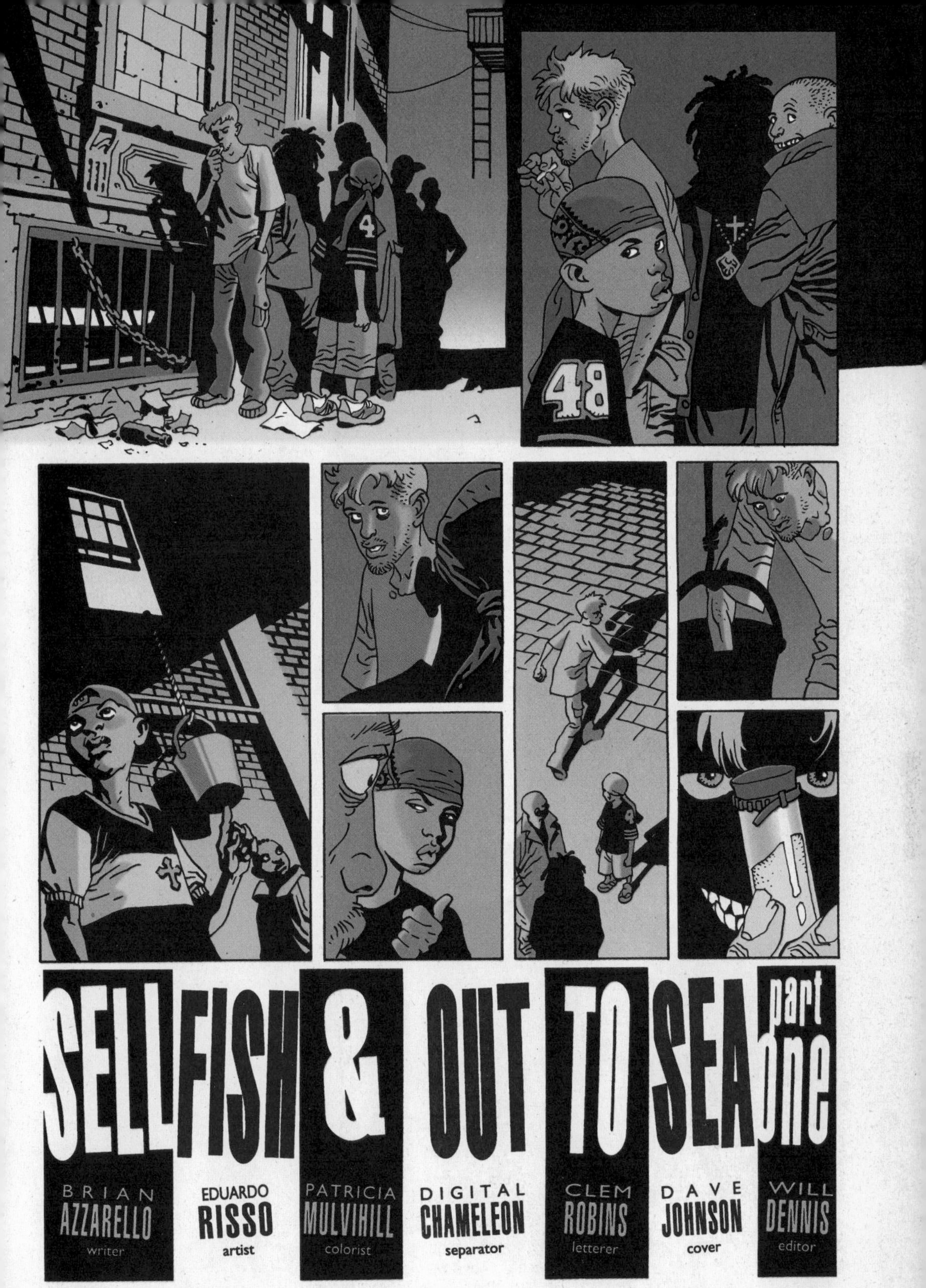
48

SELLFISH & OUT TO SEA part one

BRIAN AZZARELLO writer

EDUARDO RISSO artist

PATRICIA MULVIHILL colorist

DIGITAL CHAMELEON separator

CLEM ROBINS letterer

DAVE JOHNSON cover

WILL DENNIS editor

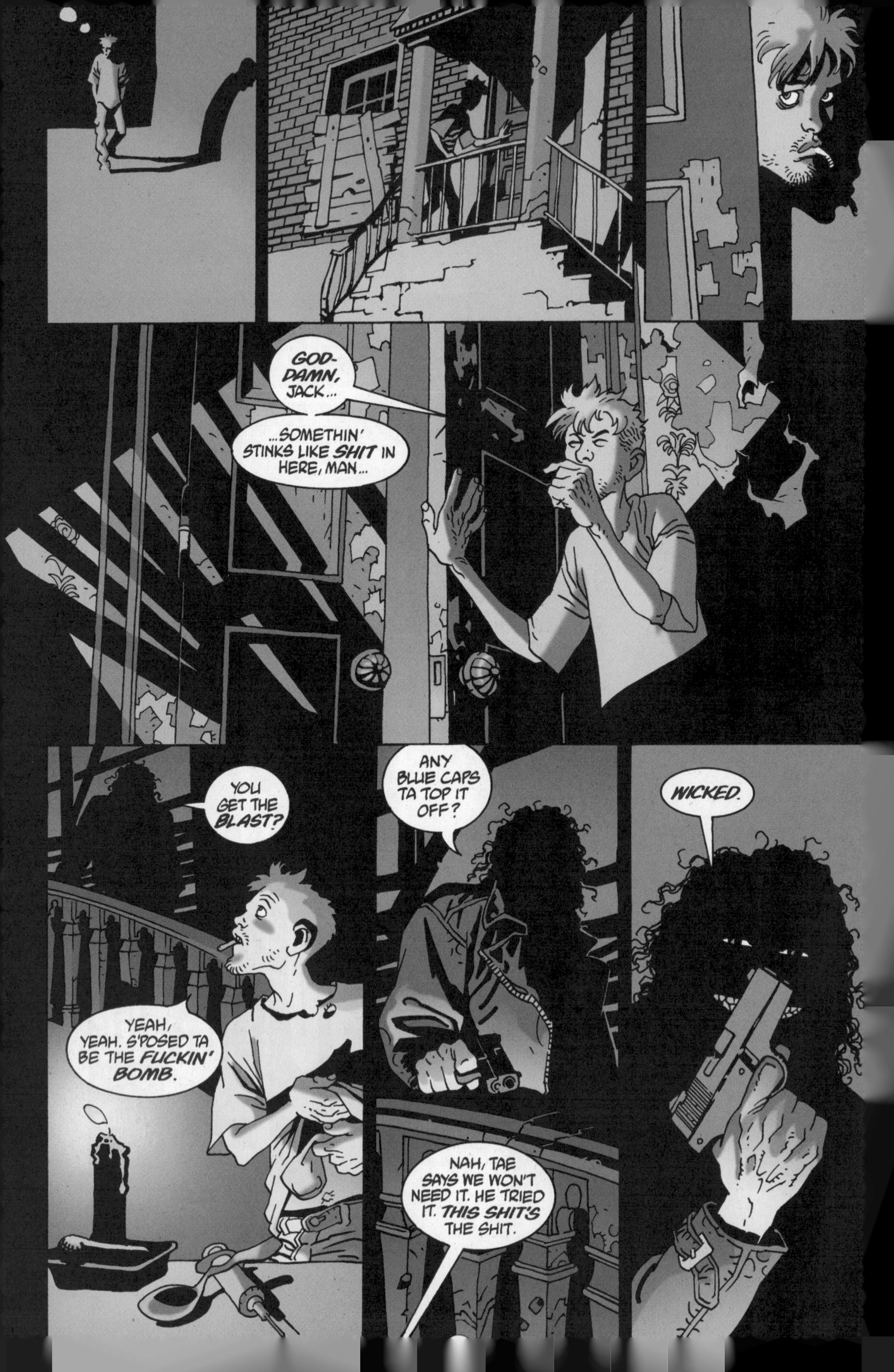
GOD-DAMN, JACK...
...SOMETHIN' STINKS LIKE SHIT IN HERE, MAN...
YOU GET THE BLAST?
YEAH, YEAH. S'POSED TA BE THE FUCKIN' BOMB.
ANY BLUE CAPS TA TOP IT OFF?
NAH, TAE SAYS WE WON'T NEED IT. HE TRIED IT. THIS SHIT'S THE SHIT.
WICKED.

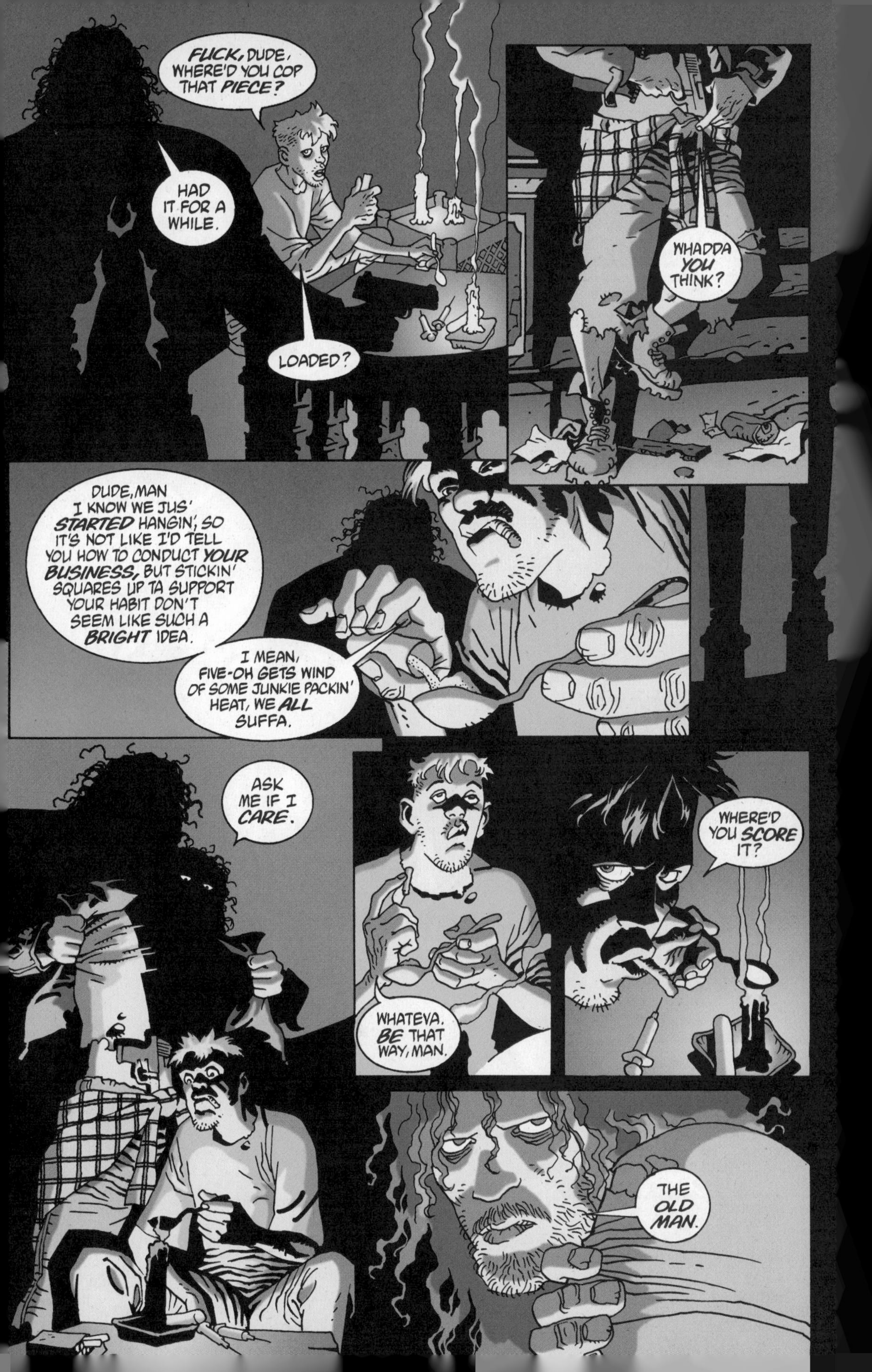

FUCK, DUDE, WHERE'D YOU COP THAT PIECE?
HAD IT FOR A WHILE.
LOADED?
WHADDA YOU THINK?
DUDE, MAN I KNOW WE JUS' STARTED HANGIN', SO IT'S NOT LIKE I'D TELL YOU HOW TO CONDUCT YOUR BUSINESS, BUT STICKIN' SQUARES UP TA SUPPORT YOUR HABIT DON'T SEEM LIKE SUCH A BRIGHT IDEA.
I MEAN, FIVE-OH GETS WIND OF SOME JUNKIE PACKIN' HEAT, WE ALL SUFFA.
ASK ME IF I CARE.
WHATEVA. BE THAT WAY, MAN.
WHERE'D YOU SCORE IT?
THE OLD MAN.

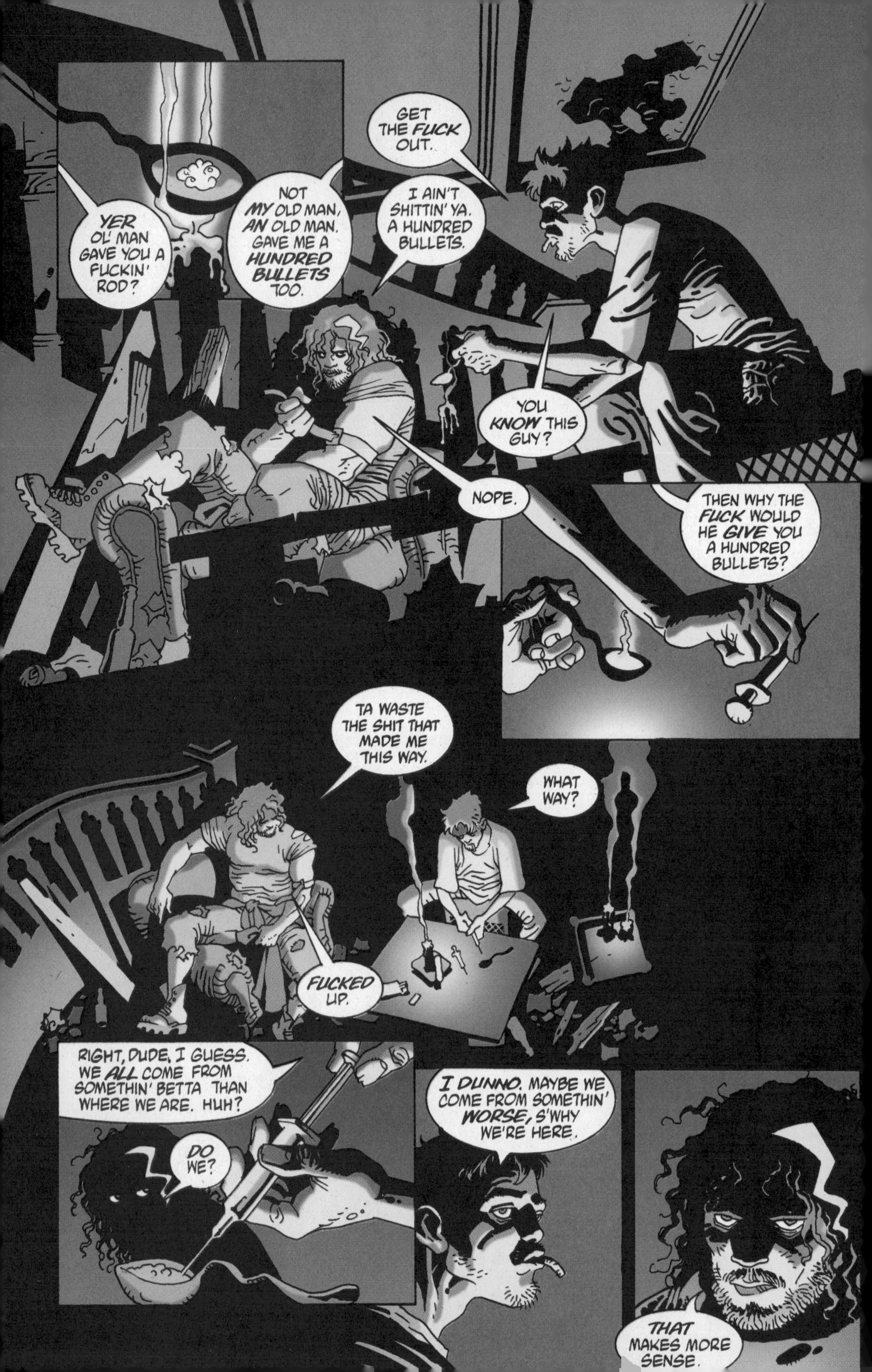

YER OL' MAN GAVE YOU A FUCKIN' ROD?
NOT MY OLD MAN, AN OLD MAN. GAVE ME A HUNDRED BULLETS TOO.
GET THE FUCK OUT.
I AIN'T SHITTIN' YA. A HUNDRED BULLETS.
YOU KNOW THIS GUY?
NOPE.
THEN WHY THE FUCK WOULD HE GIVE YOU A HUNDRED BULLETS?
TA WASTE THE SHIT THAT MADE ME THIS WAY.
WHAT WAY?
FUCKED UP.
RIGHT, DUDE, I GUESS. WE ALL COME FROM SOMETHIN' BETTA THAN WHERE WE ARE. HUH?
DO WE?
I DUNNO. MAYBE WE COME FROM SOMETHIN' WORSE, S'WHY WE'RE HERE.
THAT MAKES MORE SENSE.

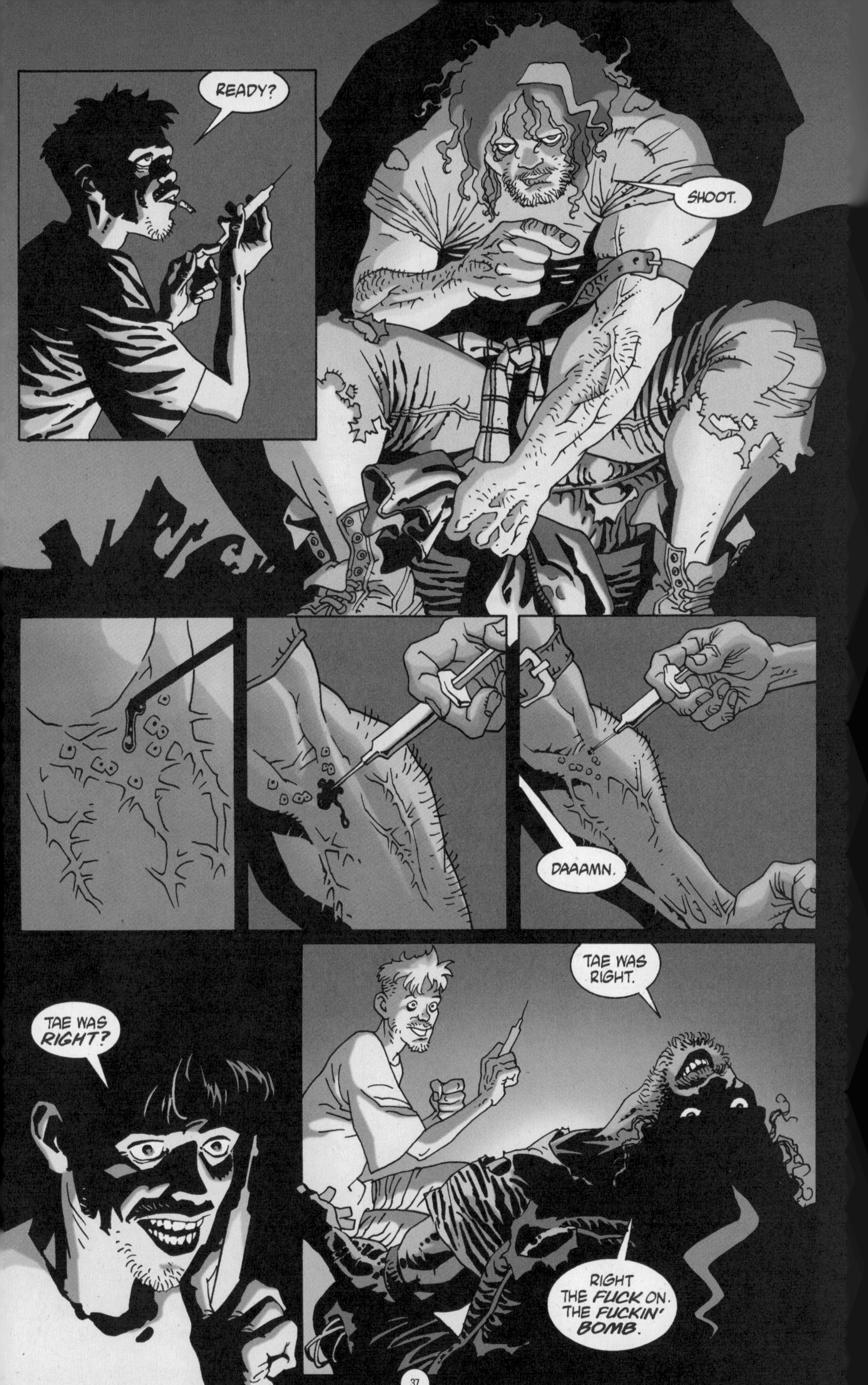
READY?
SHOOT.
DAAAMN.
TAE WAS RIGHT?
TAE WAS RIGHT.
RIGHT THE FUCK ON. THE FUCKIN' BOMB.

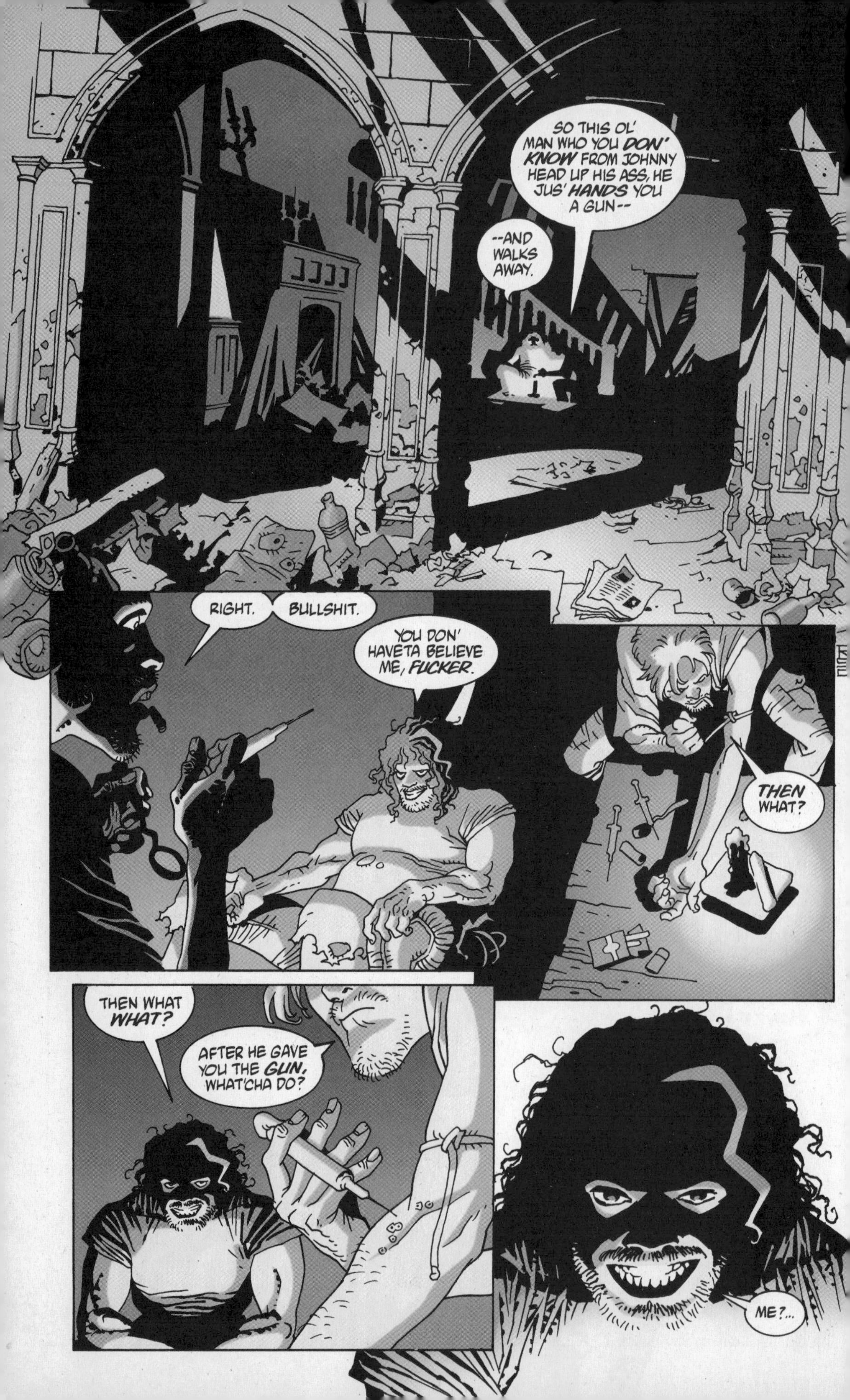
SO THIS OL' MAN WHO YOU DON' KNOW FROM JOHNNY HEAD UP HIS ASS, HE JUS' HANDS YOU A GUN--
--AND WALKS AWAY.
RIGHT.
BULLSHIT.
YOU DON' HAVETA BELIEVE ME, FUCKER.
THEN WHAT?
THEN WHAT WHAT?
AFTER HE GAVE YOU THE GUN, WHAT'CHA DO?
ME?...

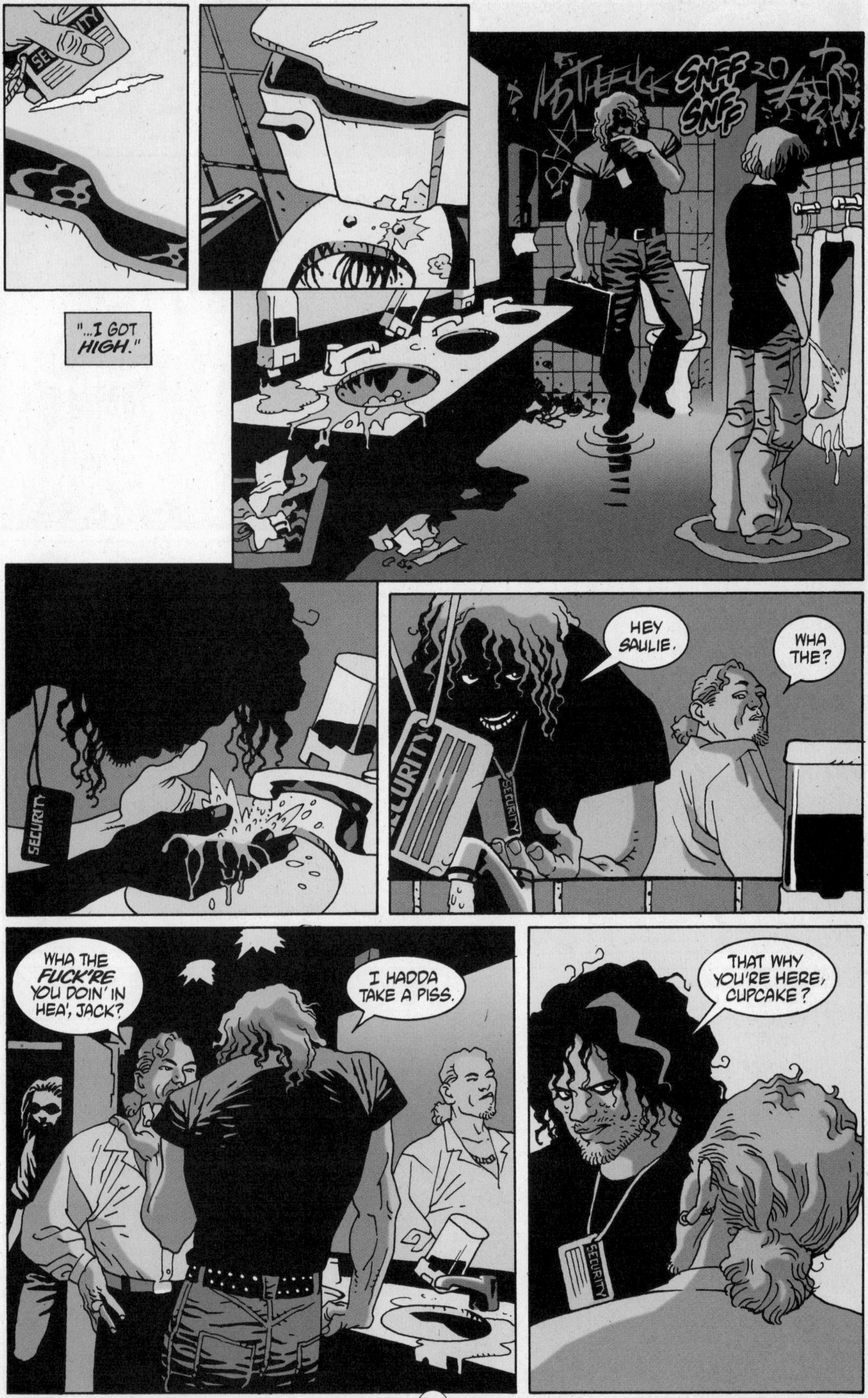
SECURITY
"...I GOT HIGH."
SNFF
SNFF
HEY SAULIE.
WHA THE?
WHA THE FUCK'RE YOU DOIN' IN HEA', JACK?
I HADDA TAKE A PISS.
THAT WHY YOU'RE HERE, CUPCAKE?

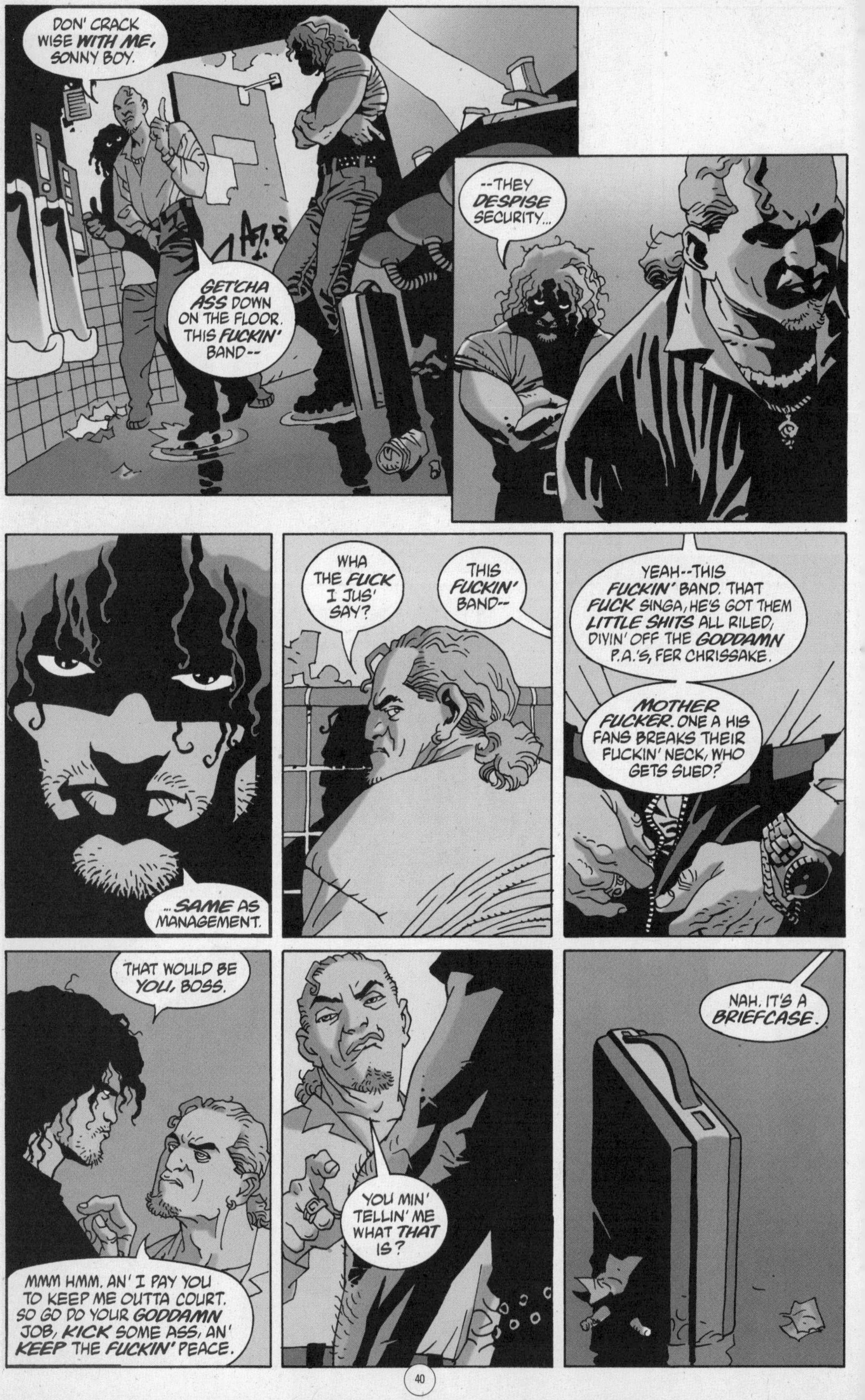
DON' CRACK WISE WITH ME, SONNY BOY.
GET'CHA ASS DOWN ON THE FLOOR. THIS FUCKIN' BAND--
--THEY DESPISE SECURITY...
...SAME AS MANAGEMENT.
WHA THE FUCK I JUS' SAY?
THIS FUCKIN' BAND--
YEAH--THIS FUCKIN' BAND. THAT FUCK SINGA, HE'S GOT THEM LITTLE SHITS ALL RILED, DIVIN' OFF THE GODDAMN P.A.'S, FER CHRISSAKE.
MOTHER FUCKER. ONE A HIS FANS BREAKS THEIR FUCKIN' NECK, WHO GETS SUED?
THAT WOULD BE YOU, BOSS.
MMM HMM. AN' I PAY YOU TO KEEP ME OUTTA COURT. SO GO DO YOUR GODDAMN JOB, KICK SOME ASS, AN' KEEP THE FUCKIN' PEACE.
YOU MIN' TELLIN' ME WHAT THAT IS?
NAH. IT'S A BRIEFCASE.

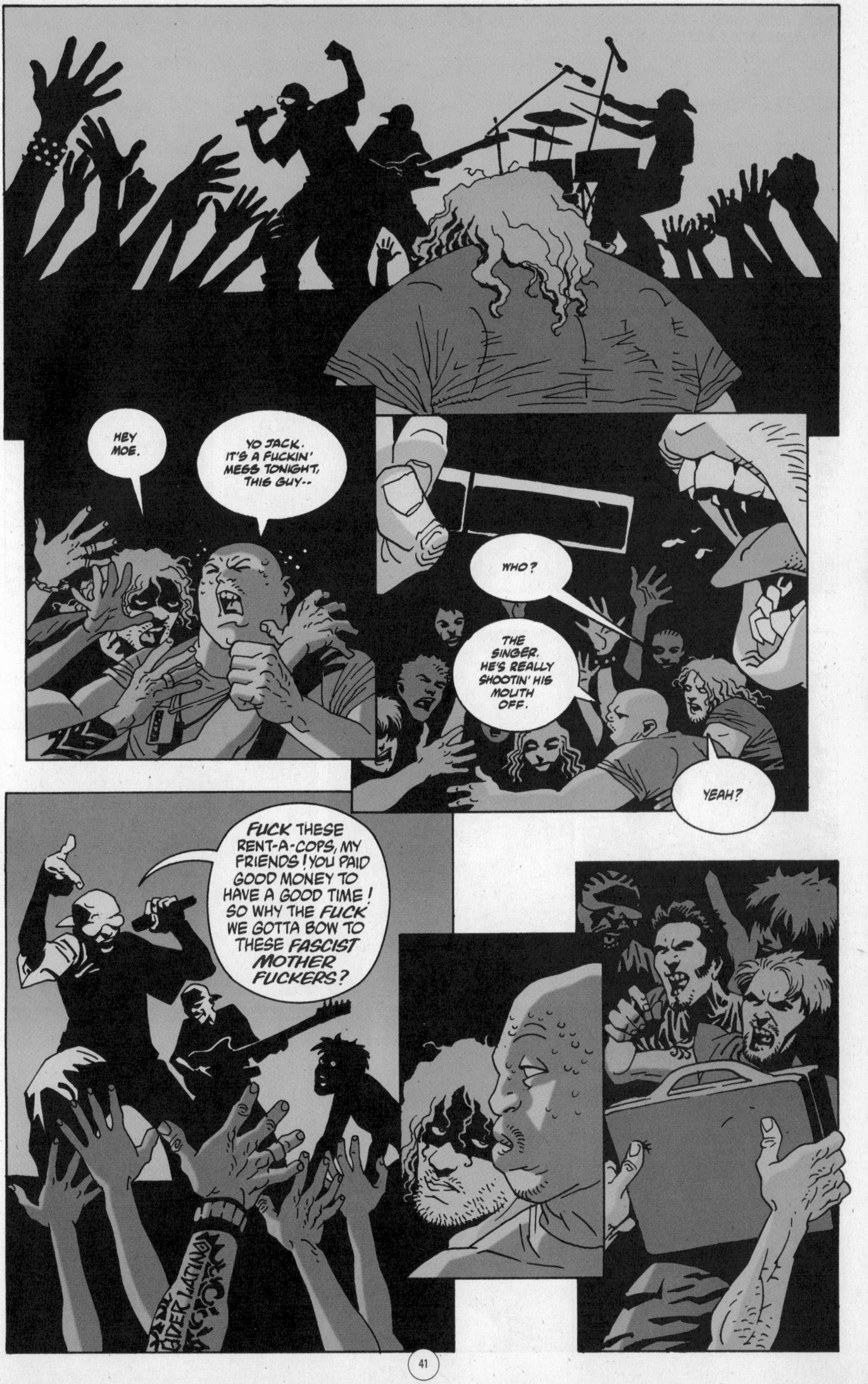
HEY MOE.
YO JACK. IT'S A FUCKIN' MESS TONIGHT, THIS GUY--
WHO?
THE SINGER. HE'S REALLY SHOOTIN' HIS MOUTH OFF.
YEAH?
FUCK THESE RENT-A-COPS, MY FRIENDS! YOU PAID GOOD MONEY TO HAVE A GOOD TIME! SO WHY THE FUCK WE GOTTA BOW TO THESE FASCIST MOTHER FUCKERS?

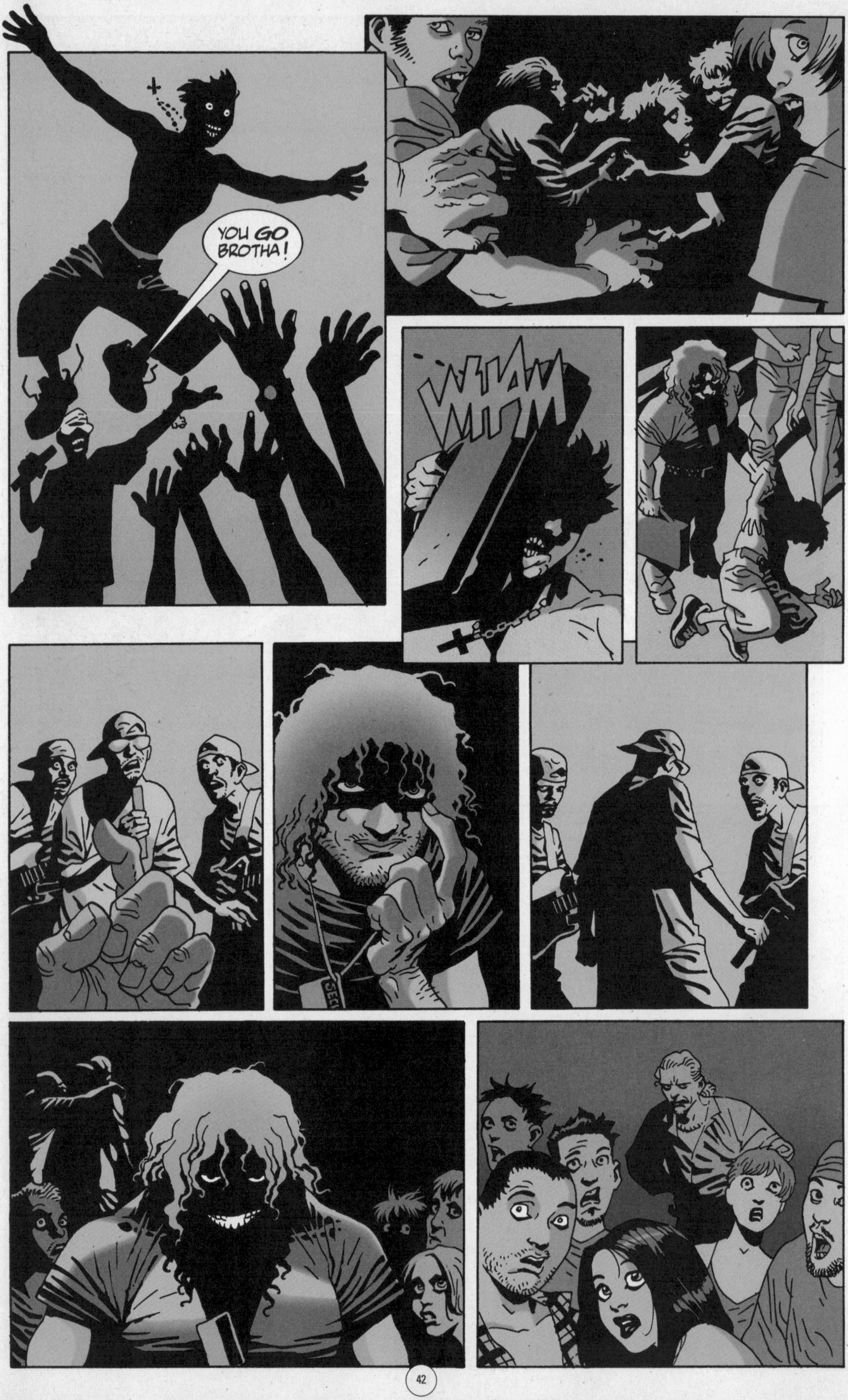
YOU GO BROTHA!
WHAM

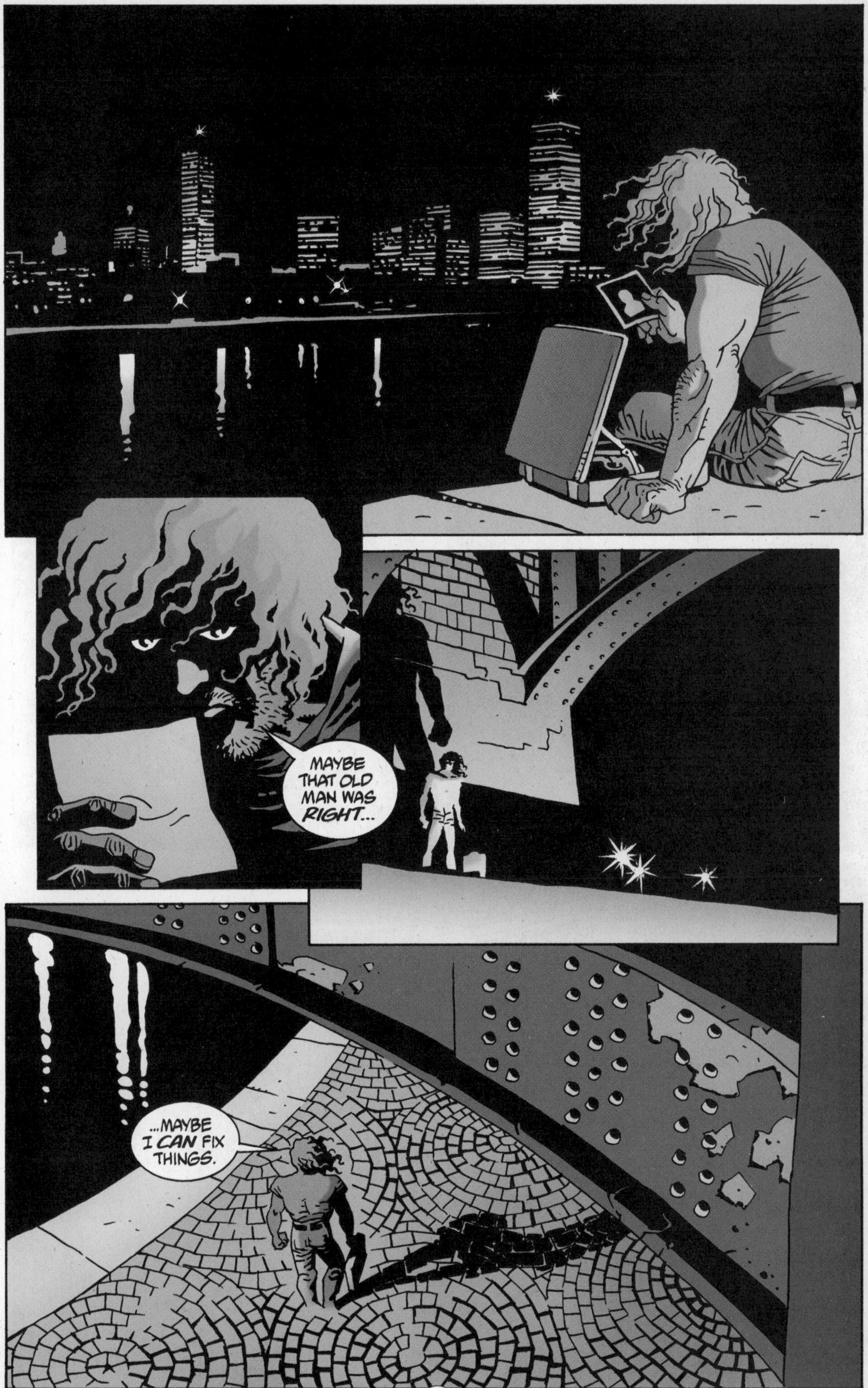
MAYBE THAT OLD MAN WAS RIGHT...
...MAYBE I CAN FIX THINGS.

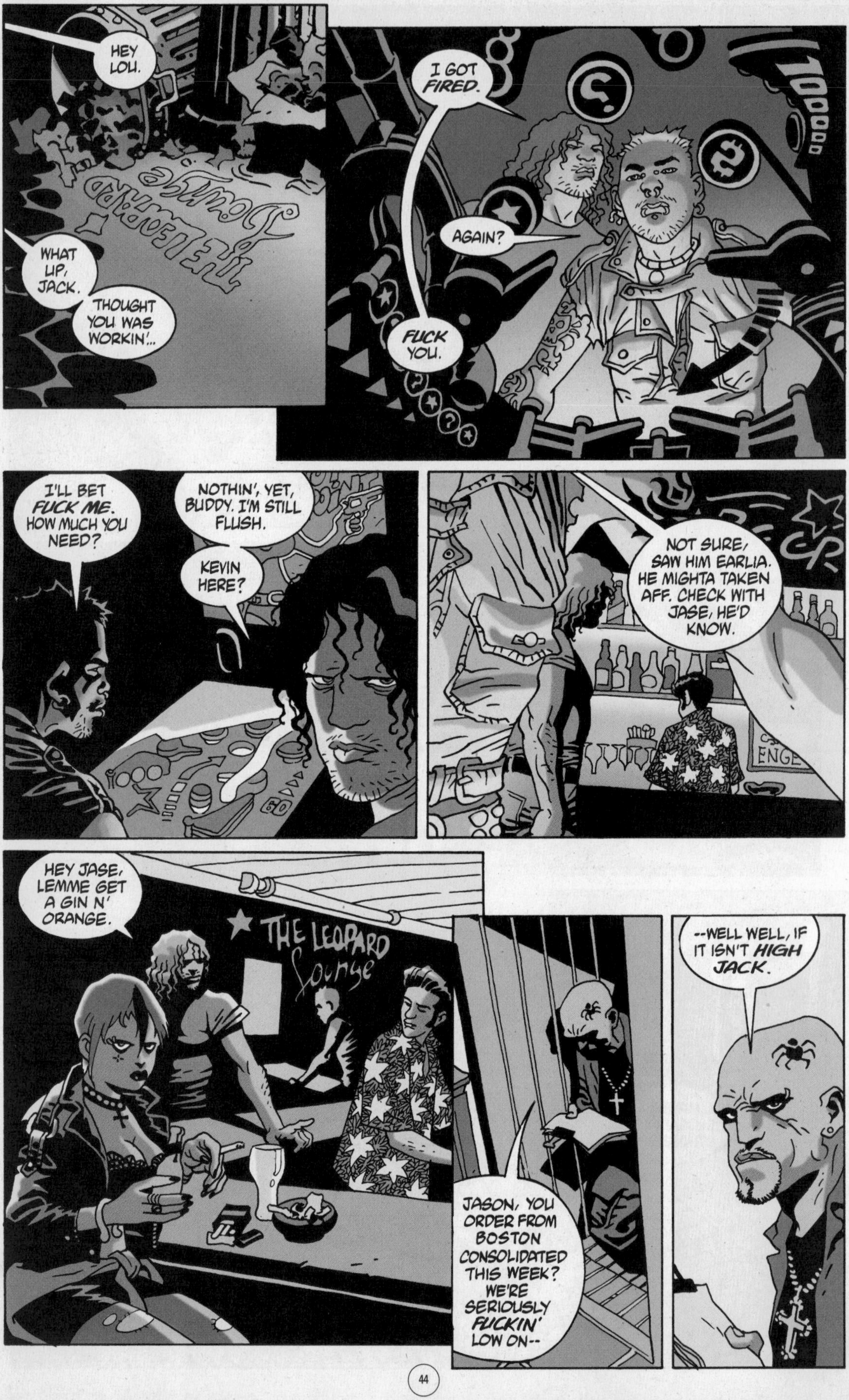
HEY LOU.
WHAT UP, JACK.
THOUGHT YOU WAS WORKIN'...
I GOT FIRED.
AGAIN?
FUCK YOU.
I'LL BET FUCK ME. HOW MUCH YOU NEED?
NOTHIN', YET, BUDDY. I'M STILL FLUSH.
KEVIN HERE?
NOT SURE, SAW HIM EARLIA. HE MIGHTA TAKEN AFF. CHECK WITH JASE, HE'D KNOW.
HEY JASE, LEMME GET A GIN N' ORANGE.
THE LEOPARD Lounge
JASON, YOU ORDER FROM BOSTON CONSOLIDATED THIS WEEK? WE'RE SERIOUSLY FUCKIN' LOW ON--
--WELL WELL, IF IT ISN'T HIGH JACK.

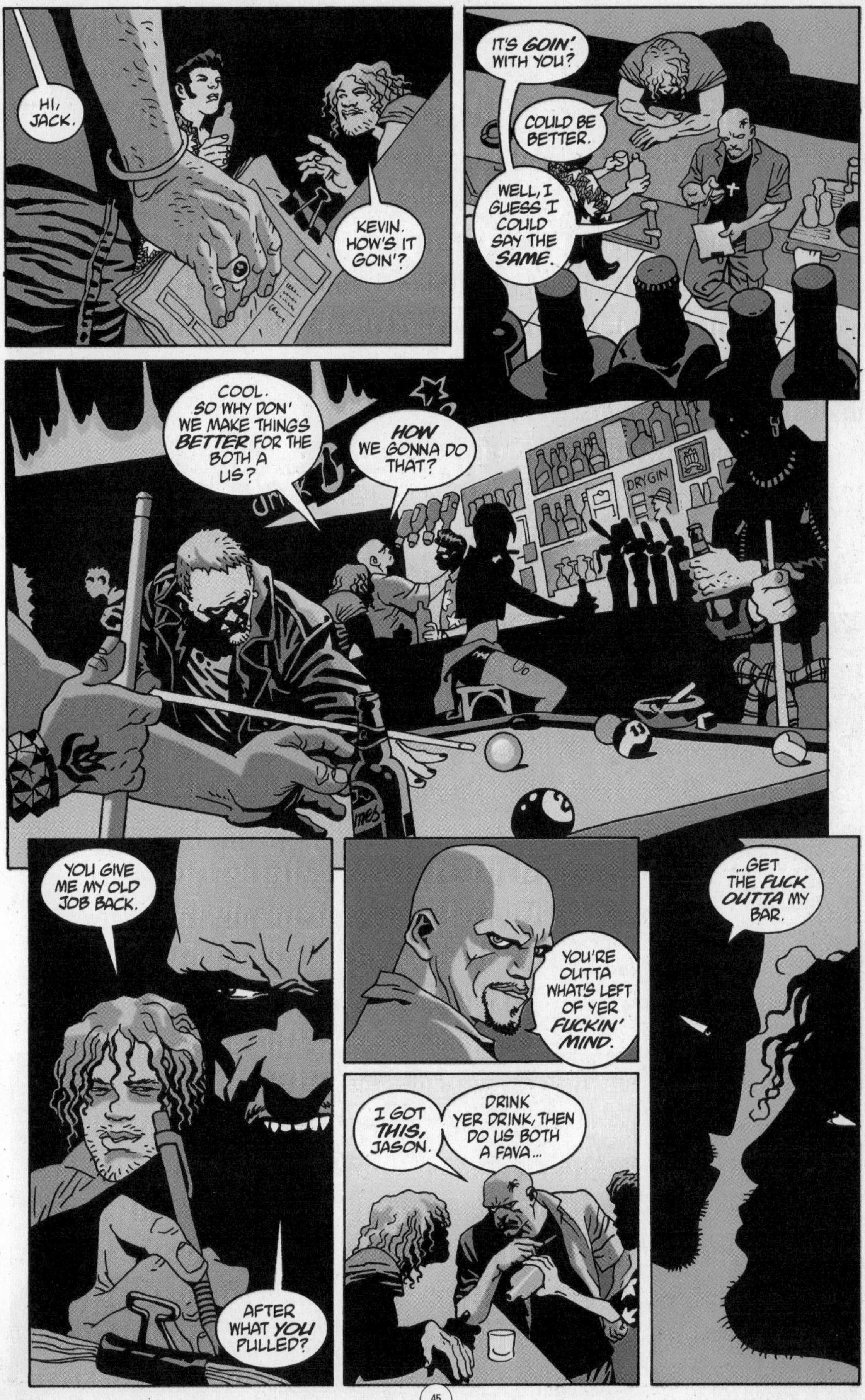
HI, JACK.
KEVIN. HOW'S IT GOIN'?
IT'S GOIN'. WITH YOU?
COULD BE BETTER.
WELL, I GUESS I COULD SAY THE SAME.
COOL. SO WHY DON' WE MAKE THINGS BETTER FOR THE BOTH A US?
HOW WE GONNA DO THAT?
DRY GIN
YOU GIVE ME MY OLD JOB BACK.
AFTER WHAT YOU PULLED?
YOU'RE OUTTA WHAT'S LEFT OF YER FUCKIN' MIND.
I GOT THIS, JASON.
DRINK YER DRINK, THEN DO US BOTH A FAVA...
...GET THE FUCK OUTTA MY BAR.

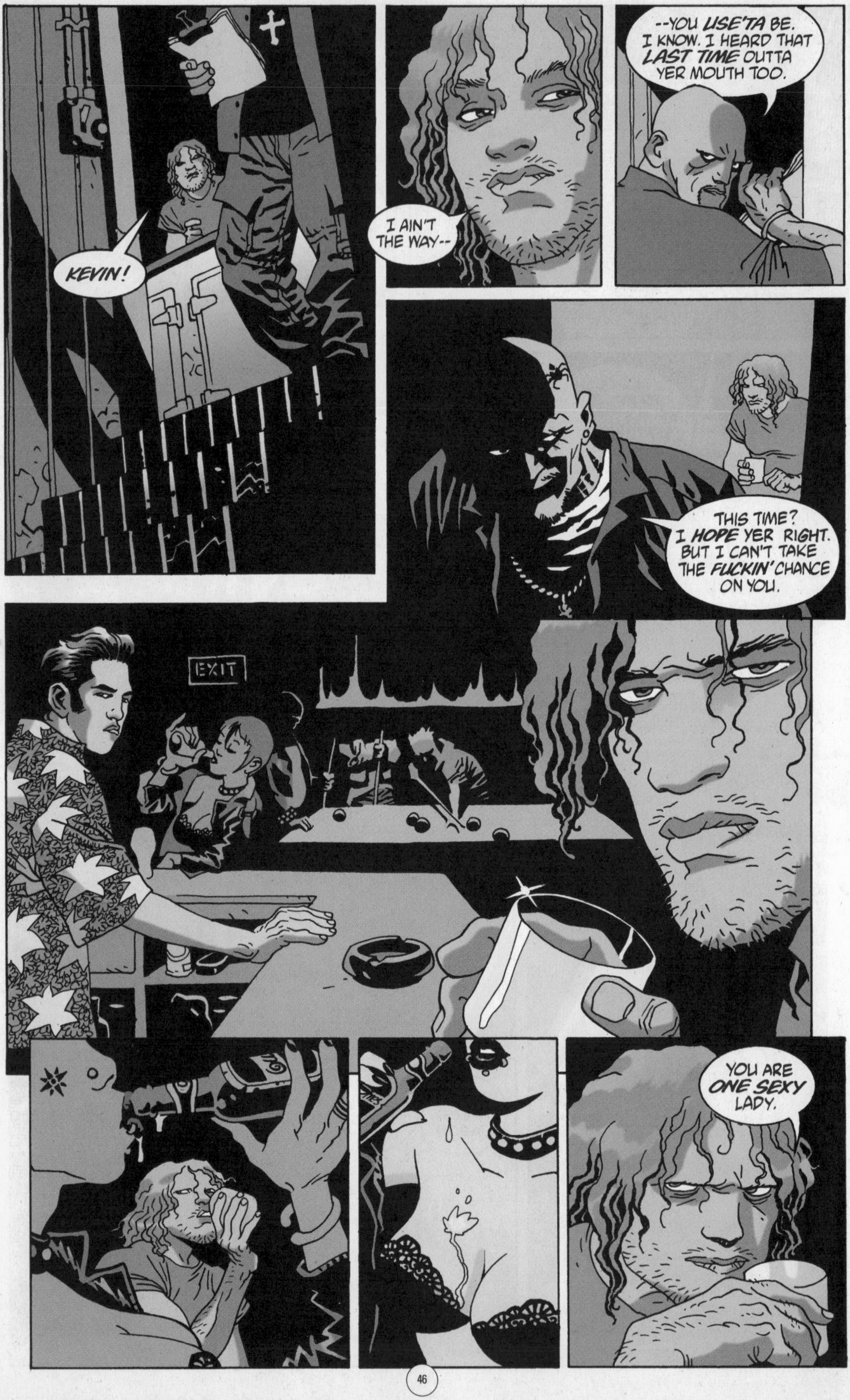
KEVIN!
I AIN'T THE WAY--
--YOU USE'TA BE. I KNOW. I HEARD THAT LAST TIME OUTTA YER MOUTH TOO.
THIS TIME? I HOPE YER RIGHT. BUT I CAN'T TAKE THE FUCKIN' CHANCE ON YOU.
EXIT
YOU ARE ONE SEXY LADY.

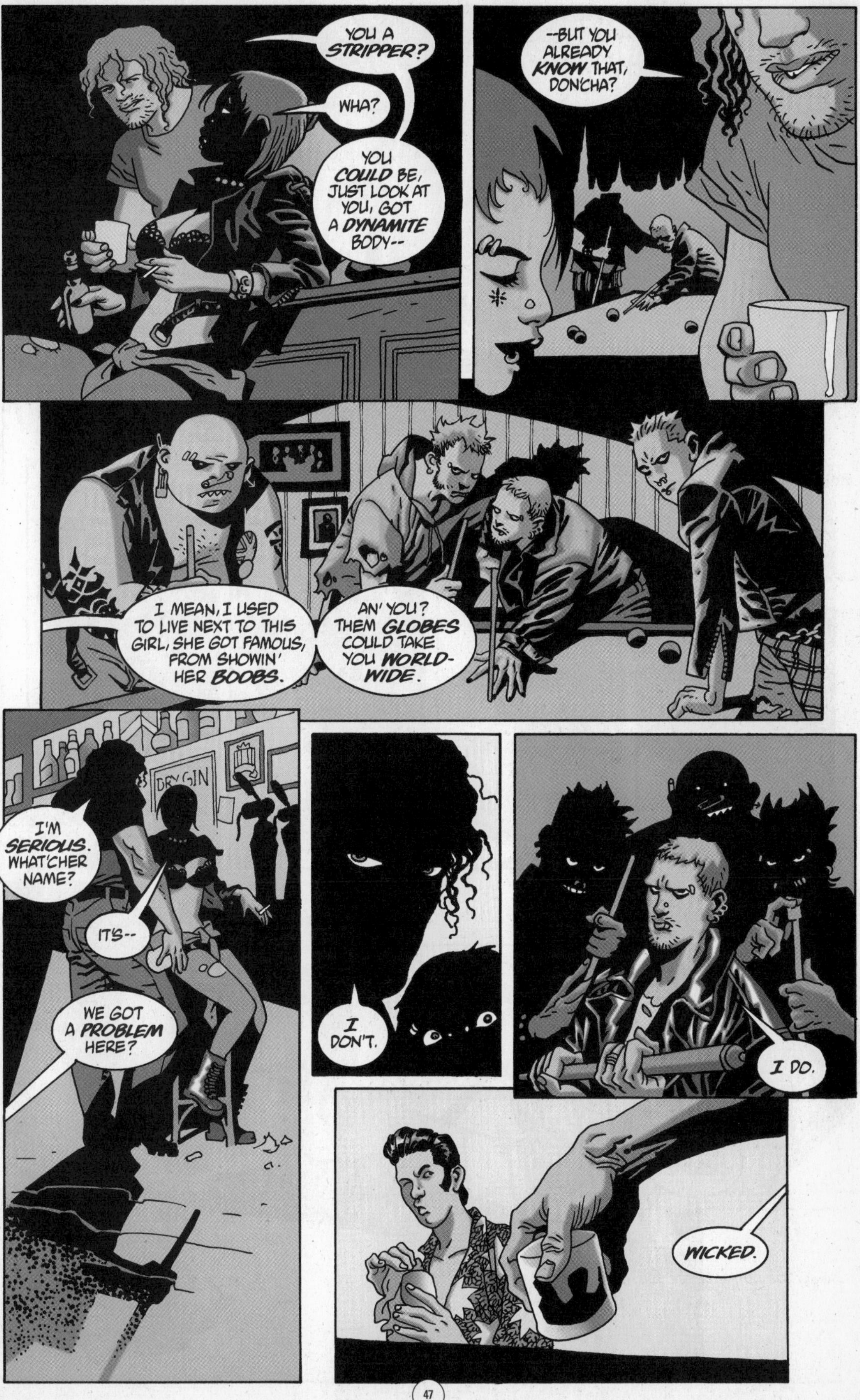
YOU A STRIPPER?
WHA?
YOU COULD BE, JUST LOOK AT YOU, GOT A DYNAMITE BODY--
--BUT YOU ALREADY KNOW THAT, DON'CHA?
I MEAN, I USED TO LIVE NEXT TO THIS GIRL, SHE GOT FAMOUS, FROM SHOWIN' HER BOOBS.
AN' YOU? THEM GLOBES COULD TAKE YOU WORLD-WIDE.
DRY GIN
I'M SERIOUS. WHAT'CHER NAME?
IT'S--
WE GOT A PROBLEM HERE?
I DON'T.
I DO.
WICKED.

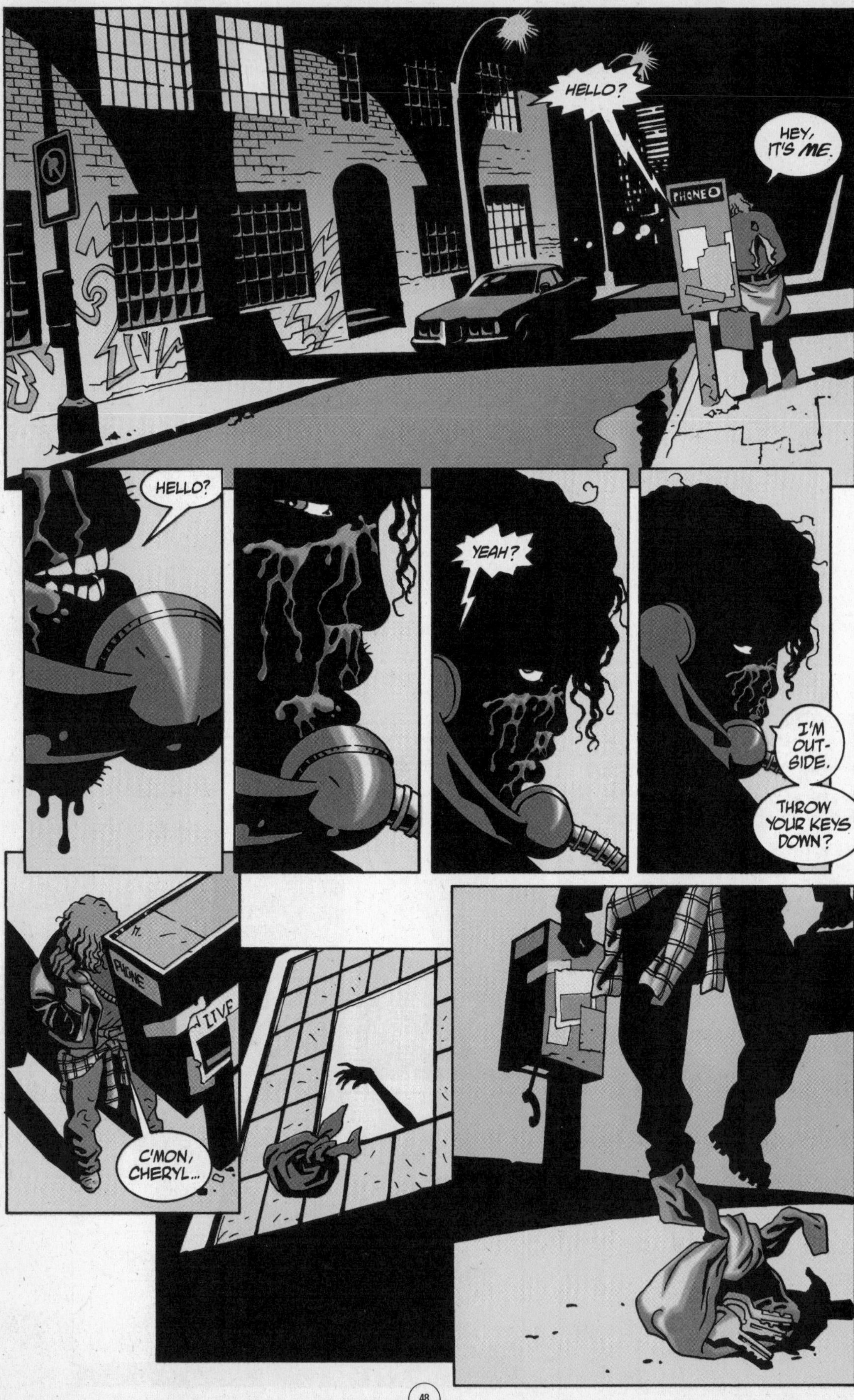
HELLO?
HEY, IT'S ME.
HELLO?
YEAH?
I'M OUT-SIDE.
THROW YOUR KEYS DOWN?
C'MON, CHERYL...
PHONE
LIVE

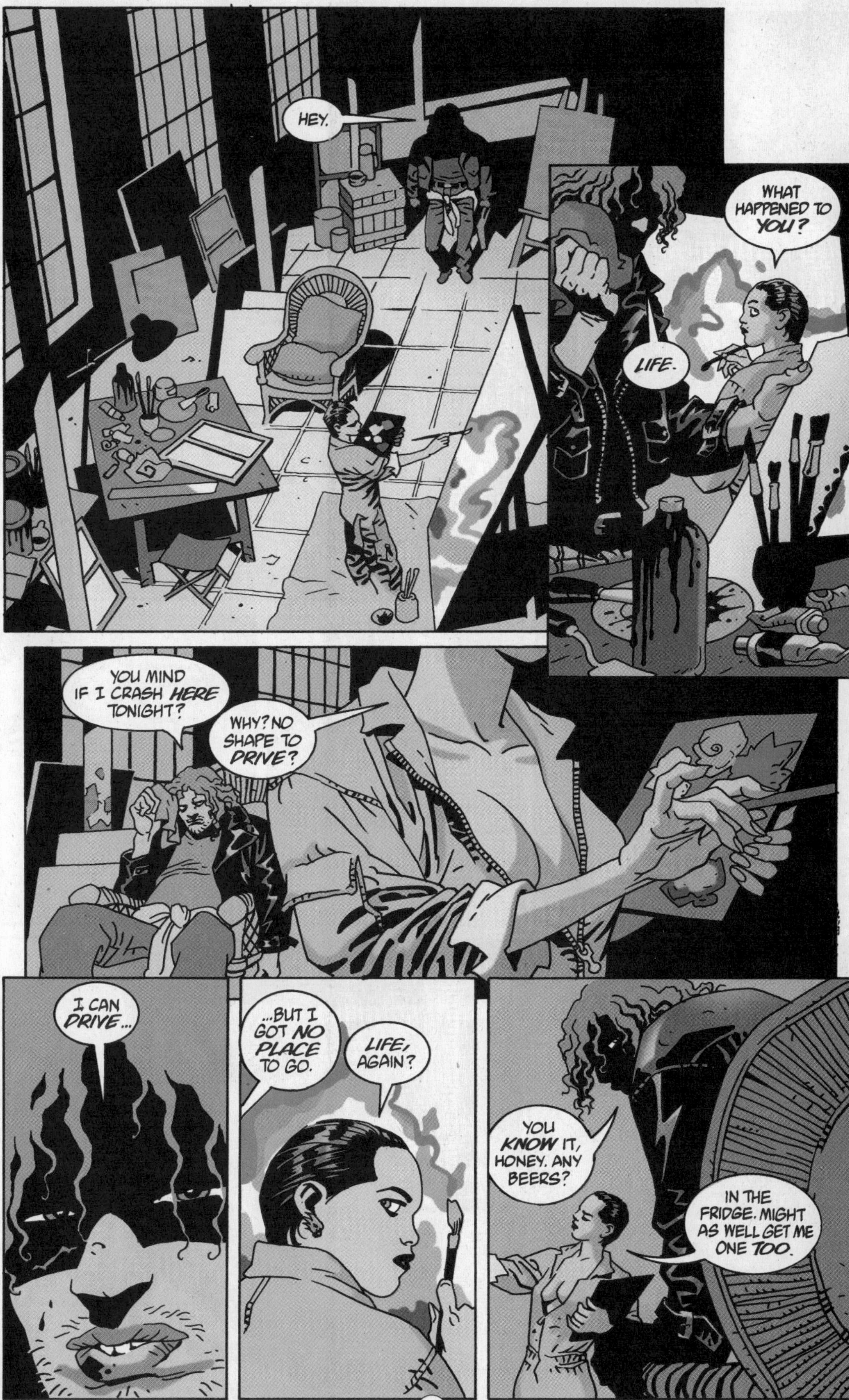
HEY.
WHAT HAPPENED TO YOU?
LIFE.
YOU MIND IF I CRASH HERE TONIGHT?
WHY? NO SHAPE TO DRIVE?
I CAN DRIVE...
...BUT I GOT NO PLACE TO GO.
LIFE, AGAIN?
YOU KNOW IT, HONEY. ANY BEERS?
IN THE FRIDGE. MIGHT AS WELL GET ME ONE TOO.

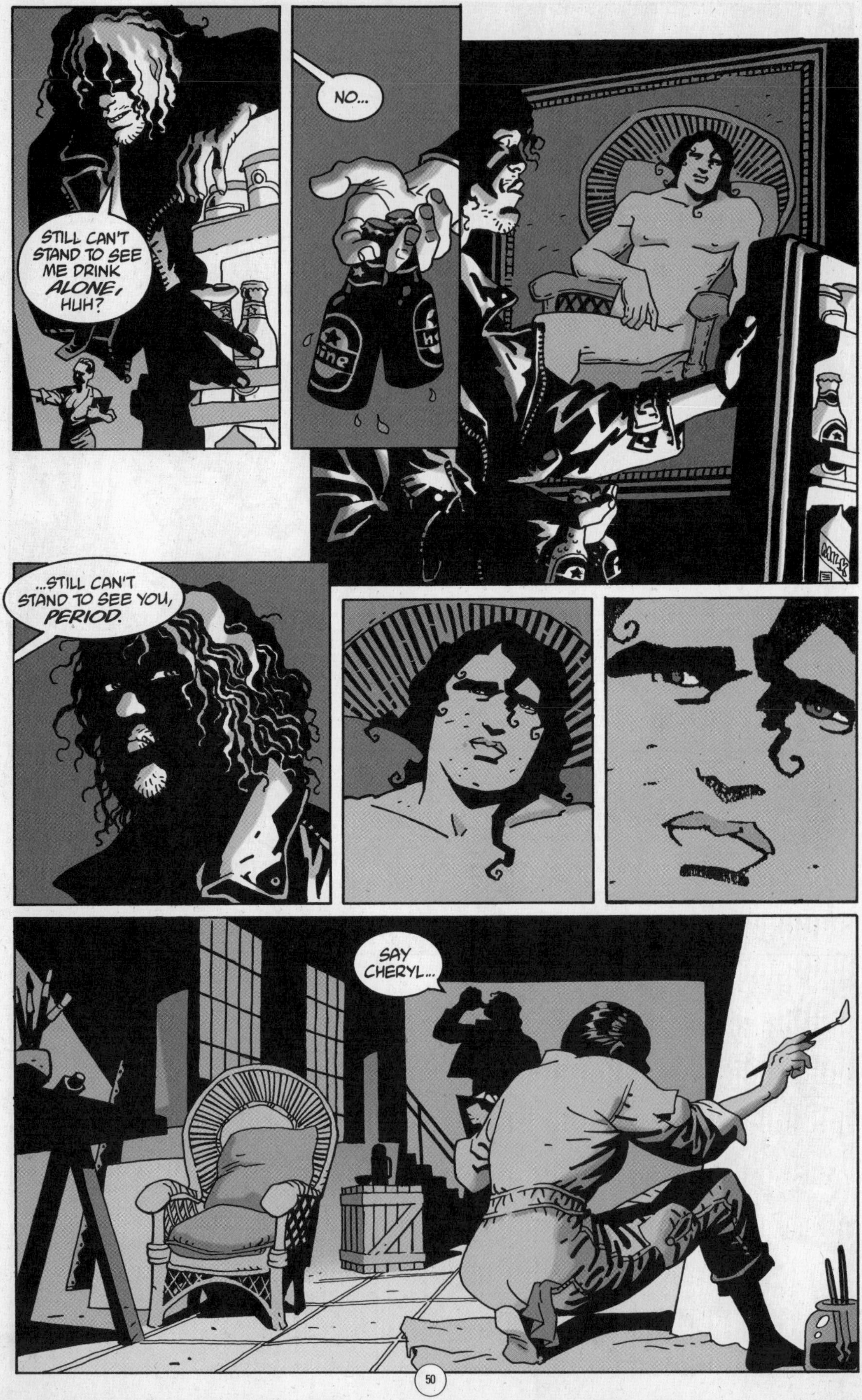

STILL CAN'T STAND TO SEE ME DRINK *ALONE*, HUH?
NO...
...STILL CAN'T STAND TO SEE YOU, *PERIOD*.
SAY CHERYL...

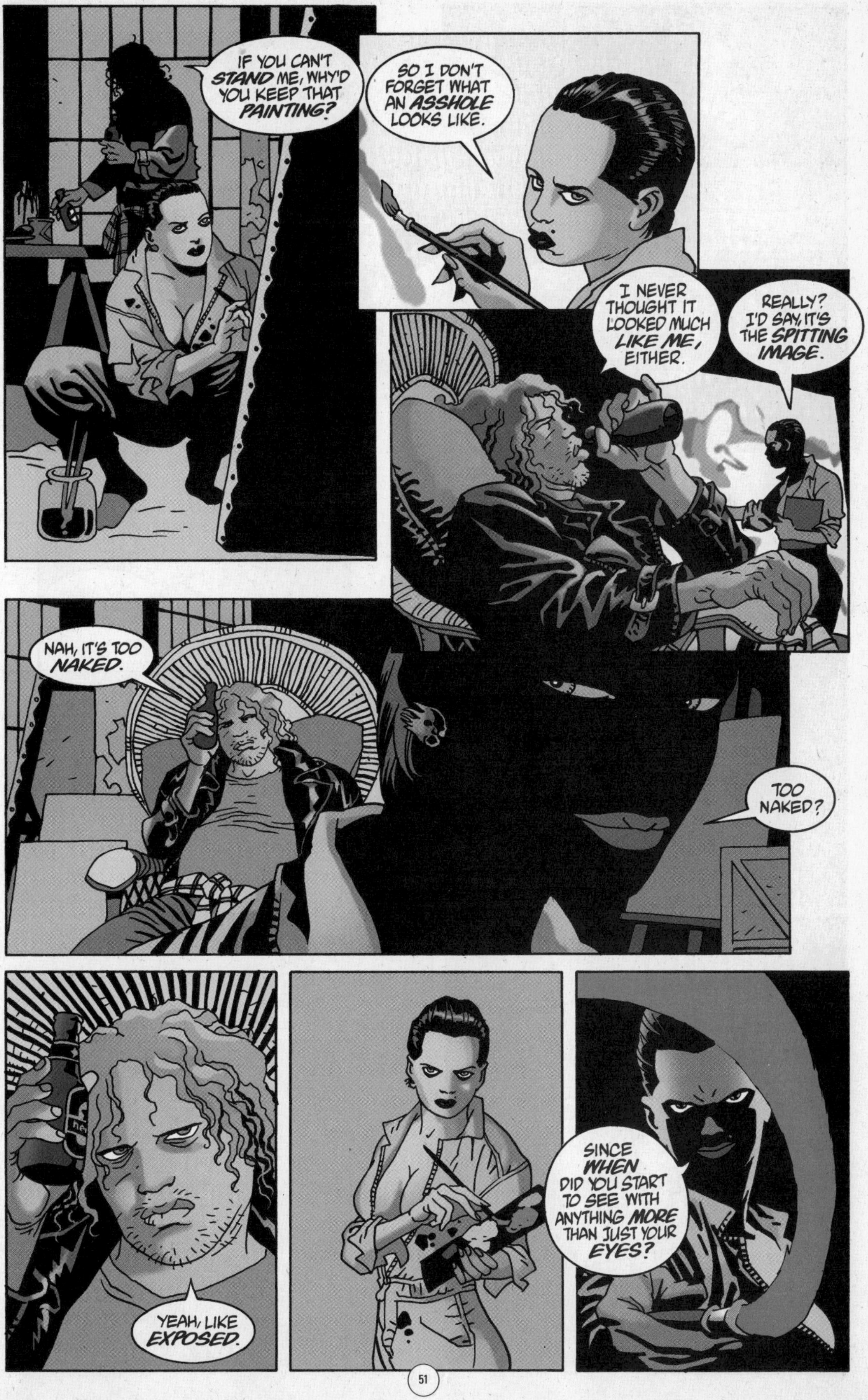

IF YOU CAN'T STAND ME, WHY'D YOU KEEP THAT PAINTING?
SO I DON'T FORGET WHAT AN ASSHOLE LOOKS LIKE.
I NEVER THOUGHT IT LOOKED MUCH LIKE ME, EITHER.
REALLY? I'D SAY, IT'S THE SPITTING IMAGE.
NAH, IT'S TOO NAKED.
TOO NAKED?
YEAH, LIKE EXPOSED.
SINCE WHEN DID YOU START TO SEE WITH ANYTHING MORE THAN JUST YOUR EYES?

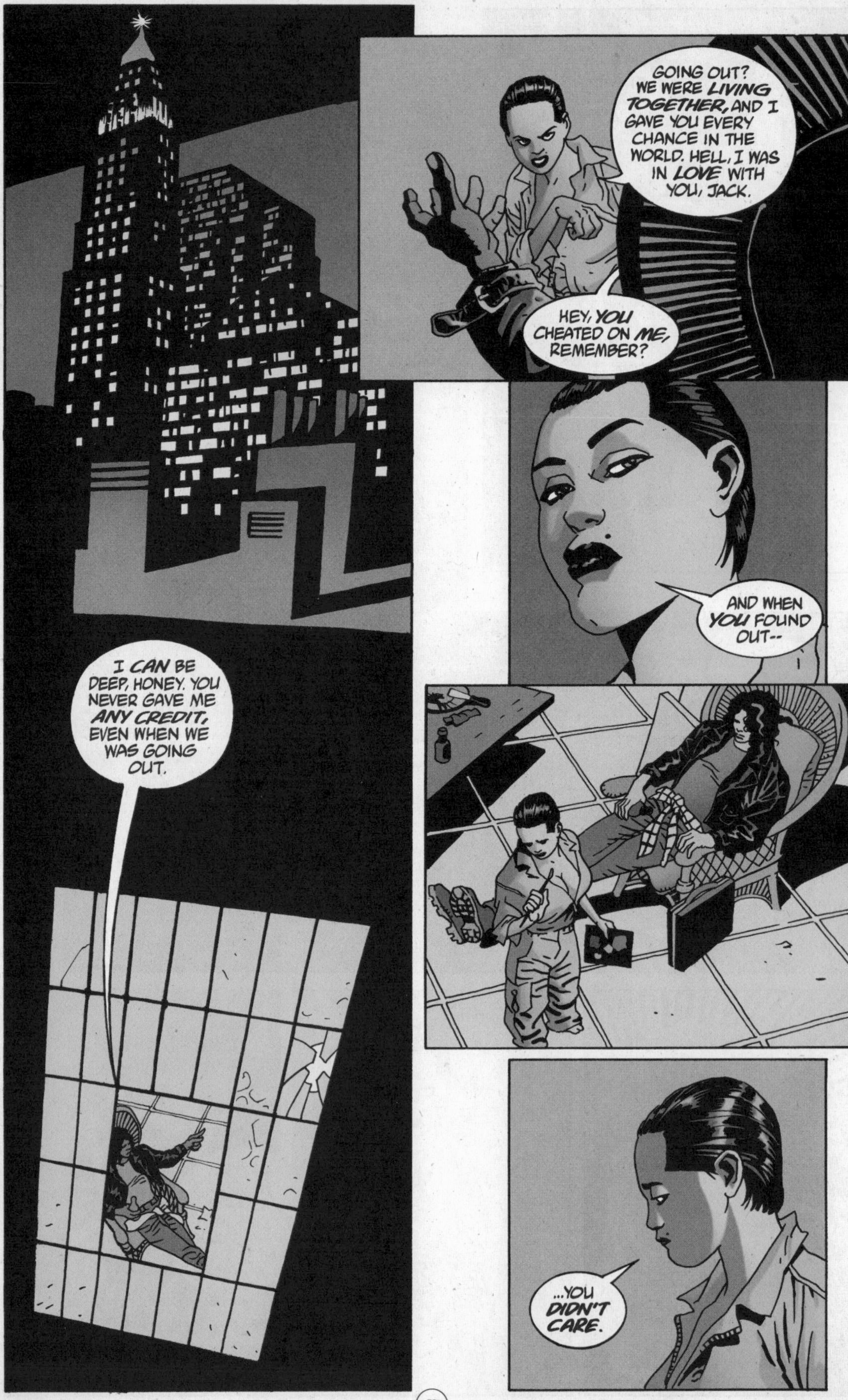
GOING OUT? WE WERE LIVING TOGETHER, AND I GAVE YOU EVERY CHANCE IN THE WORLD. HELL, I WAS IN LOVE WITH YOU, JACK.
HEY, YOU CHEATED ON ME, REMEMBER?
AND WHEN YOU FOUND OUT--
I CAN BE DEEP, HONEY. YOU NEVER GAVE ME ANY CREDIT, EVEN WHEN WE WAS GOING OUT.
...YOU DIDN'T CARE.

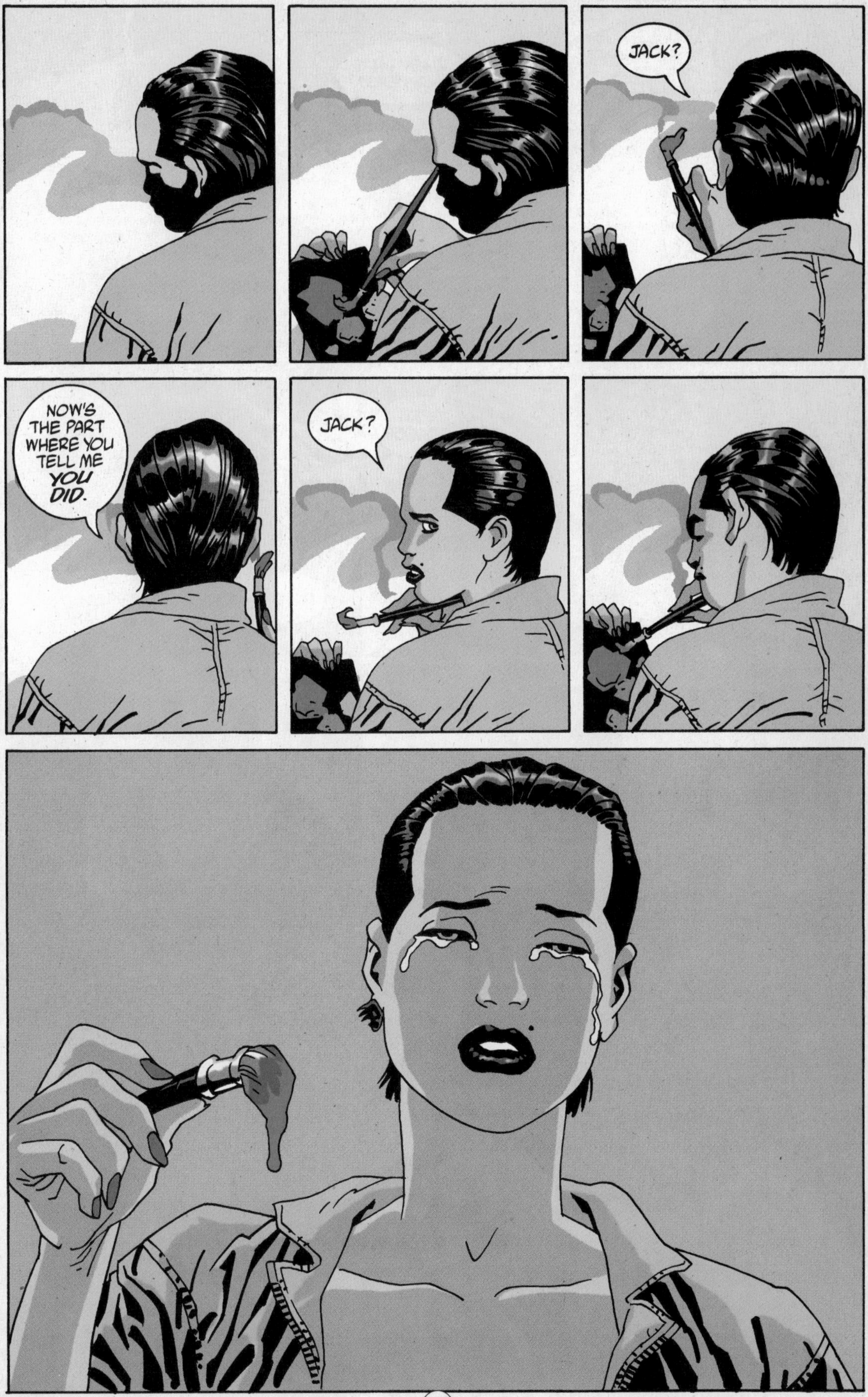
JACK?
NOW'S THE PART WHERE YOU TELL ME *YOU DID*.
JACK?

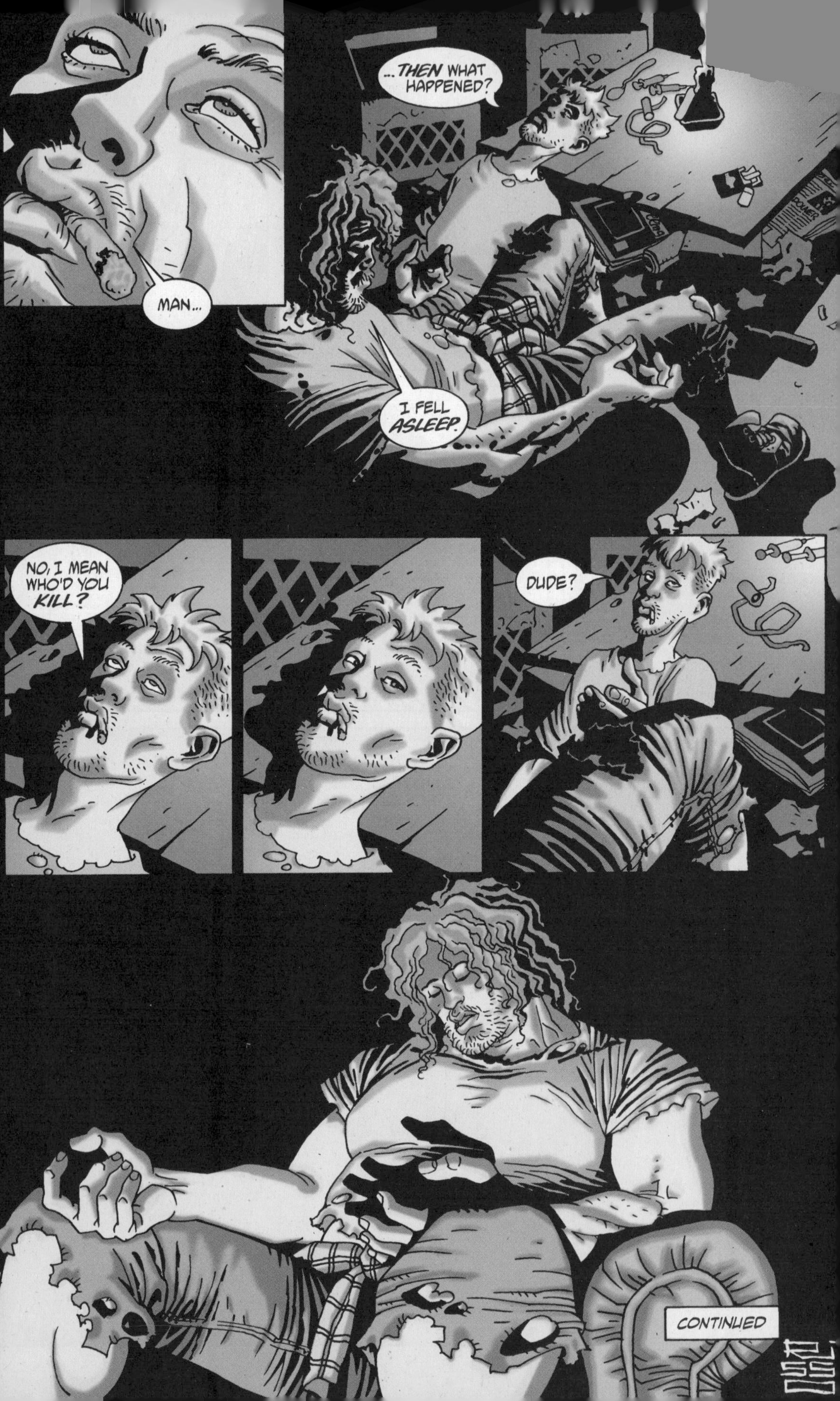
MAN...
...THEN WHAT HAPPENED?
I FELL ASLEEP.
NO, I MEAN WHO'D YOU KILL?
DUDE?
CONTINUED

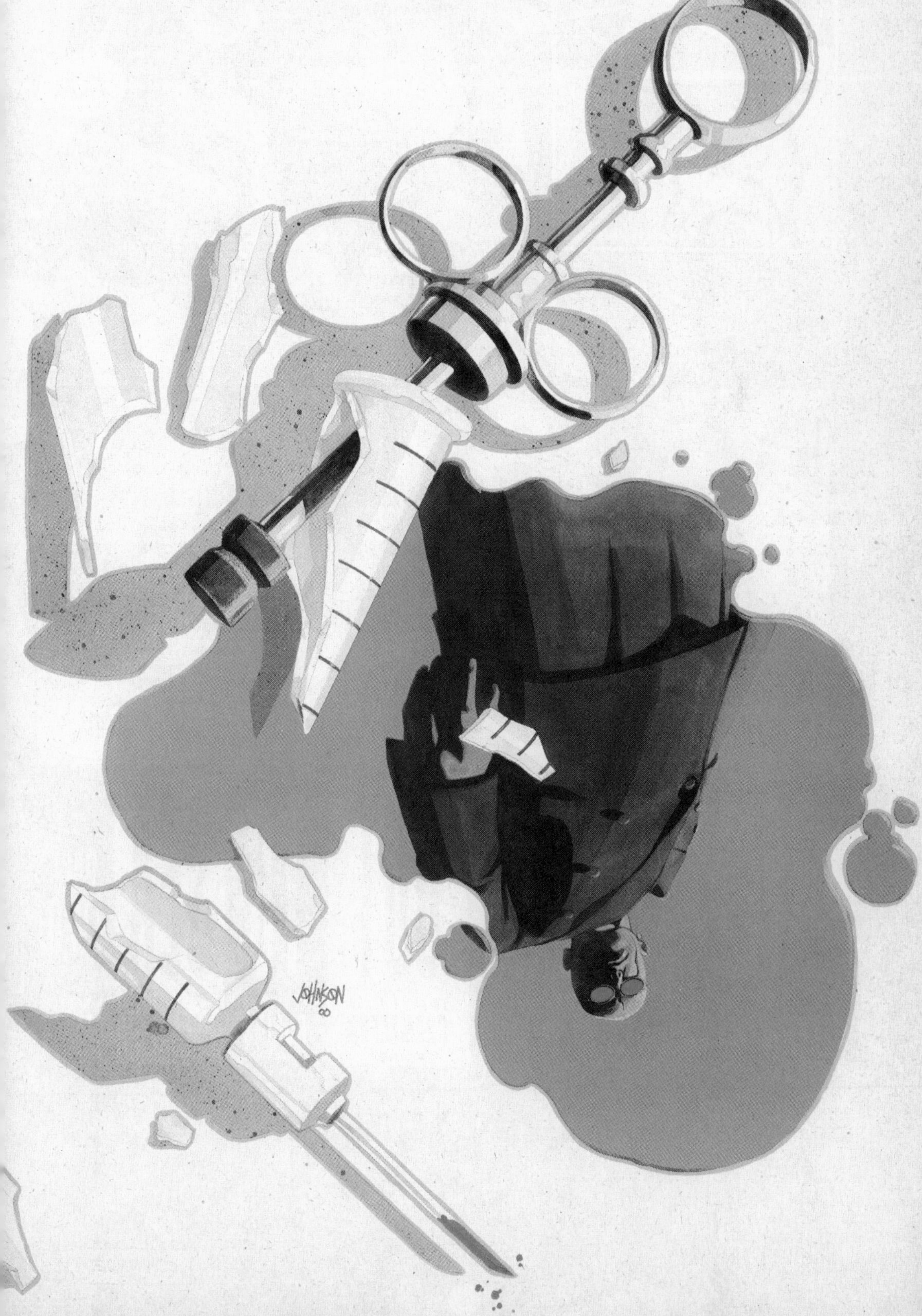
JOHNSON
00

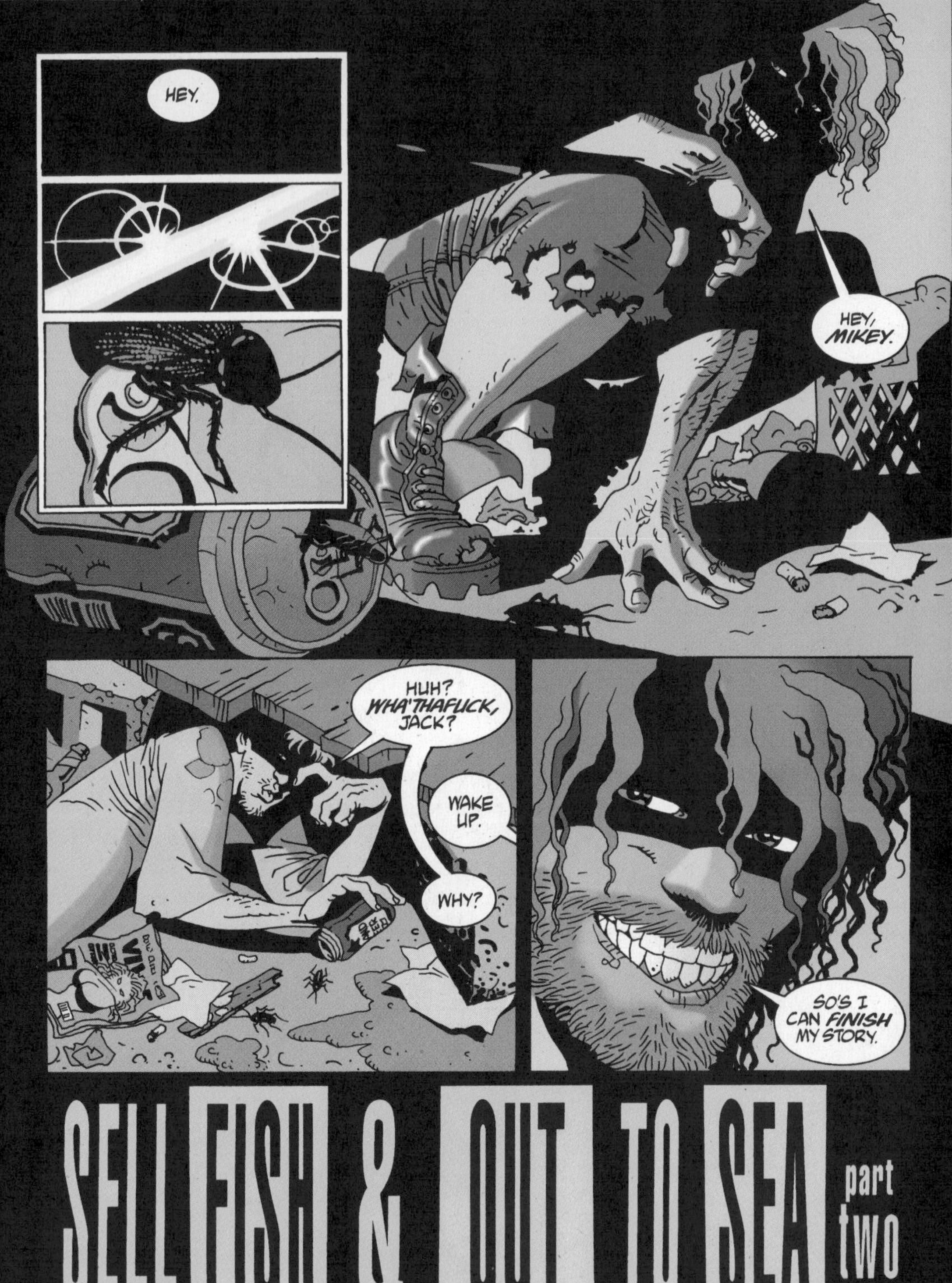
HEY.
HEY, MIKEY.
HUH? WHA'THAFUCK, JACK?
WAKE UP.
WHY?
SO'S I CAN FINISH MY STORY.

SELL FISH & OUT TO SEA part two

BRIAN **AZZARELLO** writer
EDUARDO **RISSO** artist
PATRICIA **MULVIHILL** colorist
DIGITAL **CHAMELEON** separator
CLEM **ROBINS** letterer
DAVE **JOHNSON** cover
WILL **DENNIS** editor

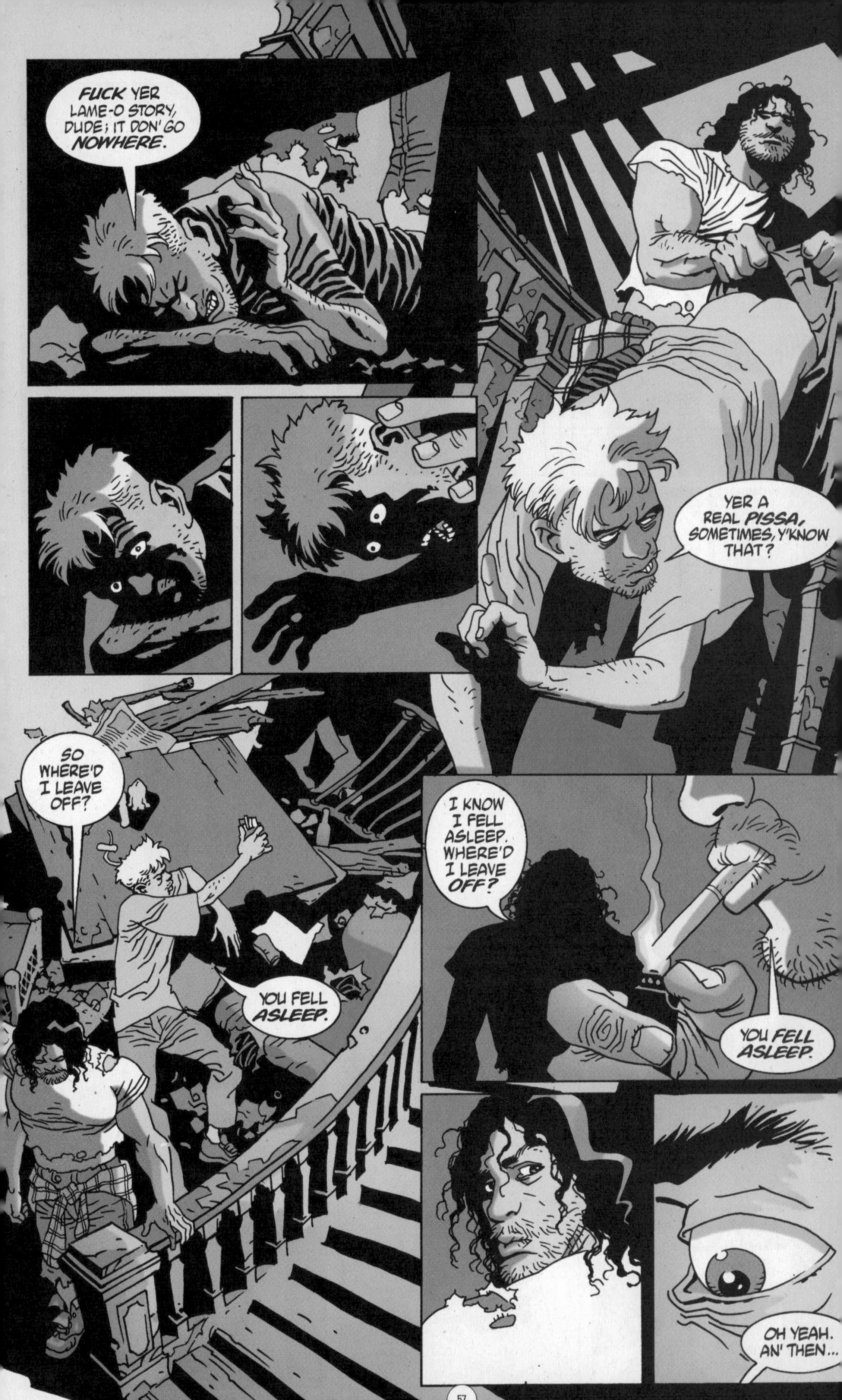
FUCK YER LAME-O STORY, DUDE; IT DON' GO NOWHERE.
YER A REAL PISSA, SOMETIMES, Y'KNOW THAT?
SO WHERE'D I LEAVE OFF?
YOU FELL ASLEEP.
I KNOW I FELL ASLEEP. WHERE'D I LEAVE OFF?
YOU FELL ASLEEP.
OH YEAH. AN' THEN...

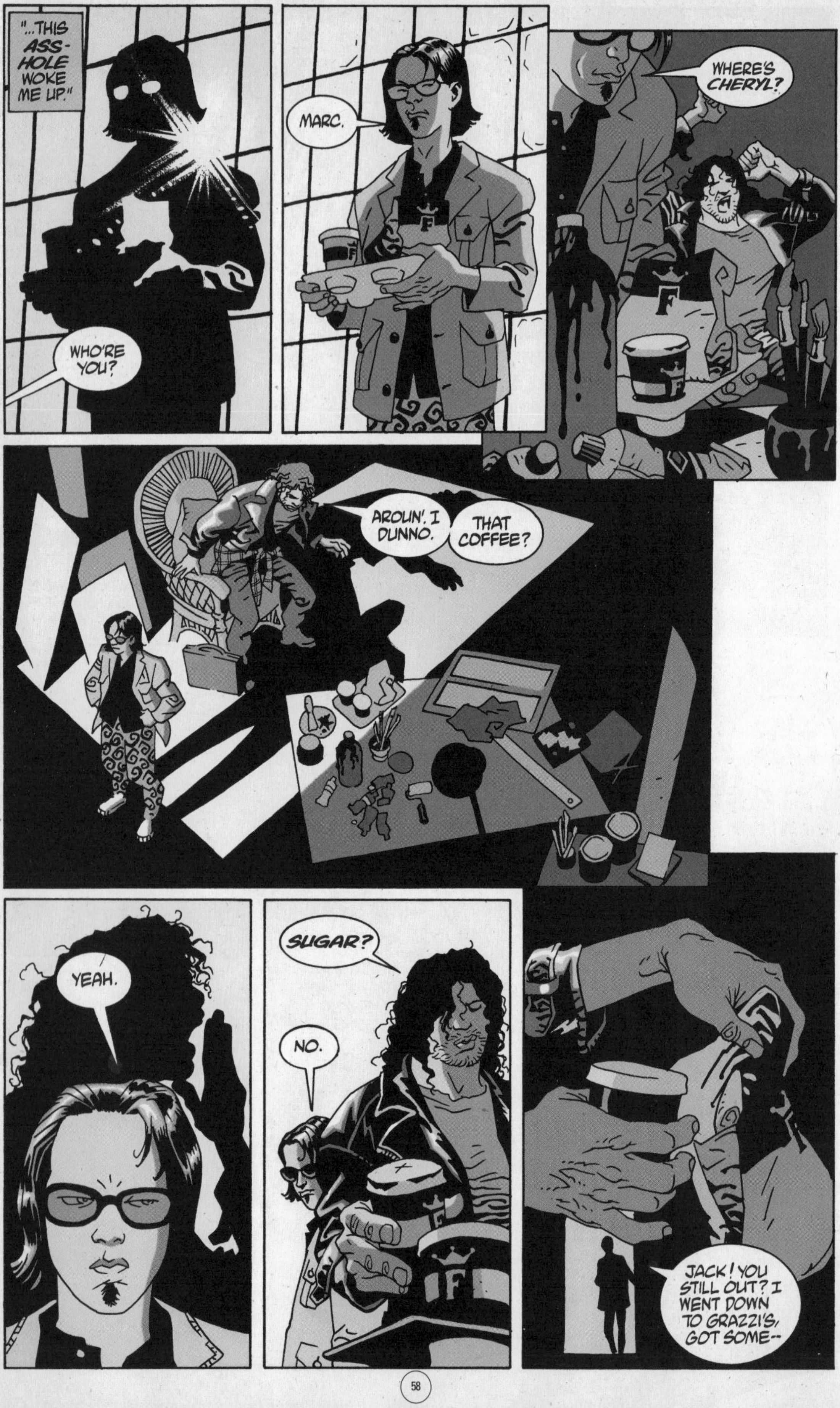
"...THIS ASS-HOLE WOKE ME UP."
WHO'RE YOU?
MARC.
WHERE'S CHERYL?
AROUN'. I DUNNO.
THAT COFFEE?
YEAH.
SUGAR?
NO.
JACK! YOU STILL OUT? I WENT DOWN TO GRAZZI'S, GOT SOME--

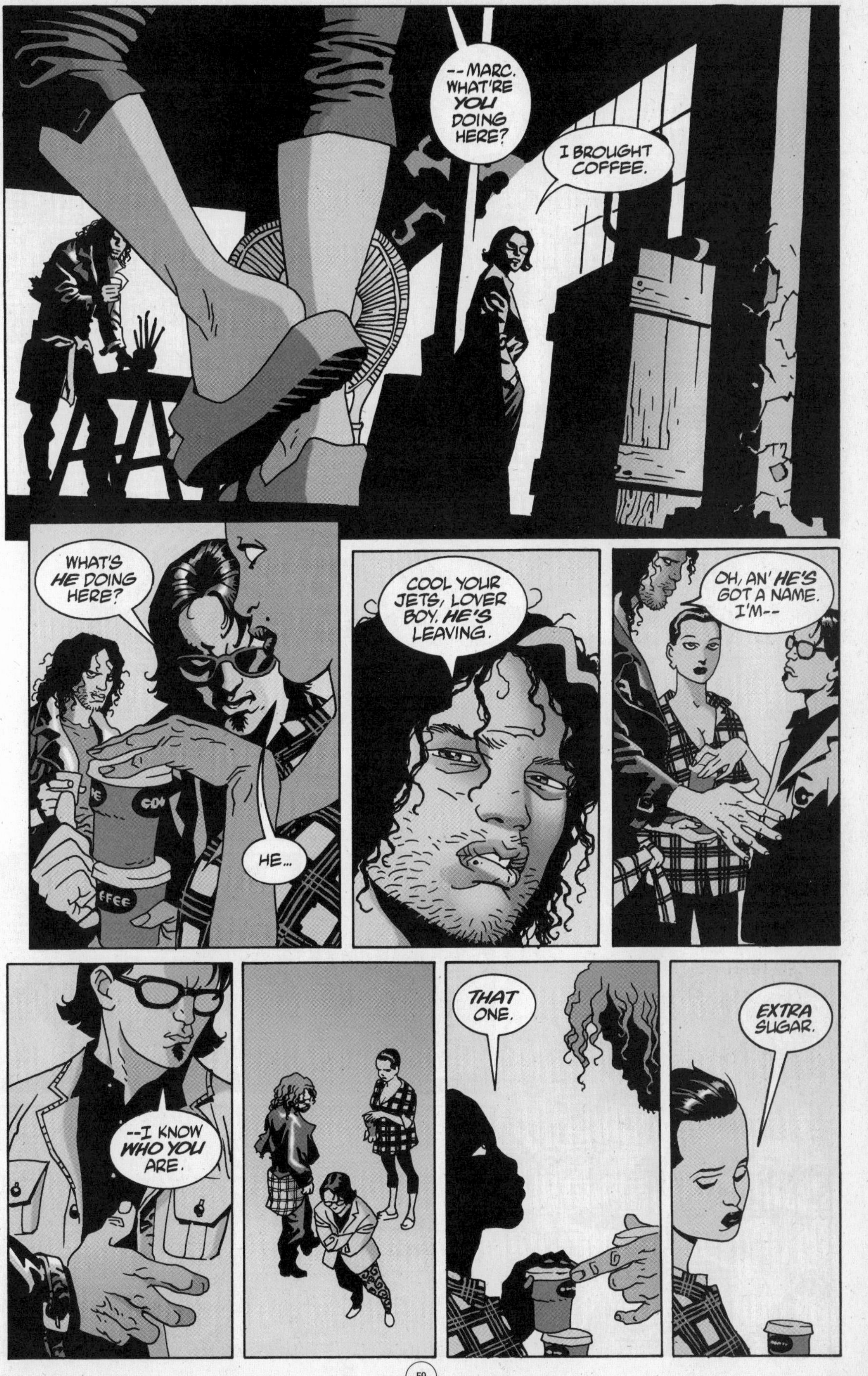

--MARC. WHAT'RE *YOU* DOING HERE?
I BROUGHT COFFEE.
WHAT'S *HE* DOING HERE?
HE...
COOL YOUR JETS, LOVER BOY. *HE'S* LEAVING.
OH, AN' *HE'S* GOT A NAME. I'M--
--I KNOW *WHO YOU* ARE.
THAT ONE.
EXTRA SUGAR.

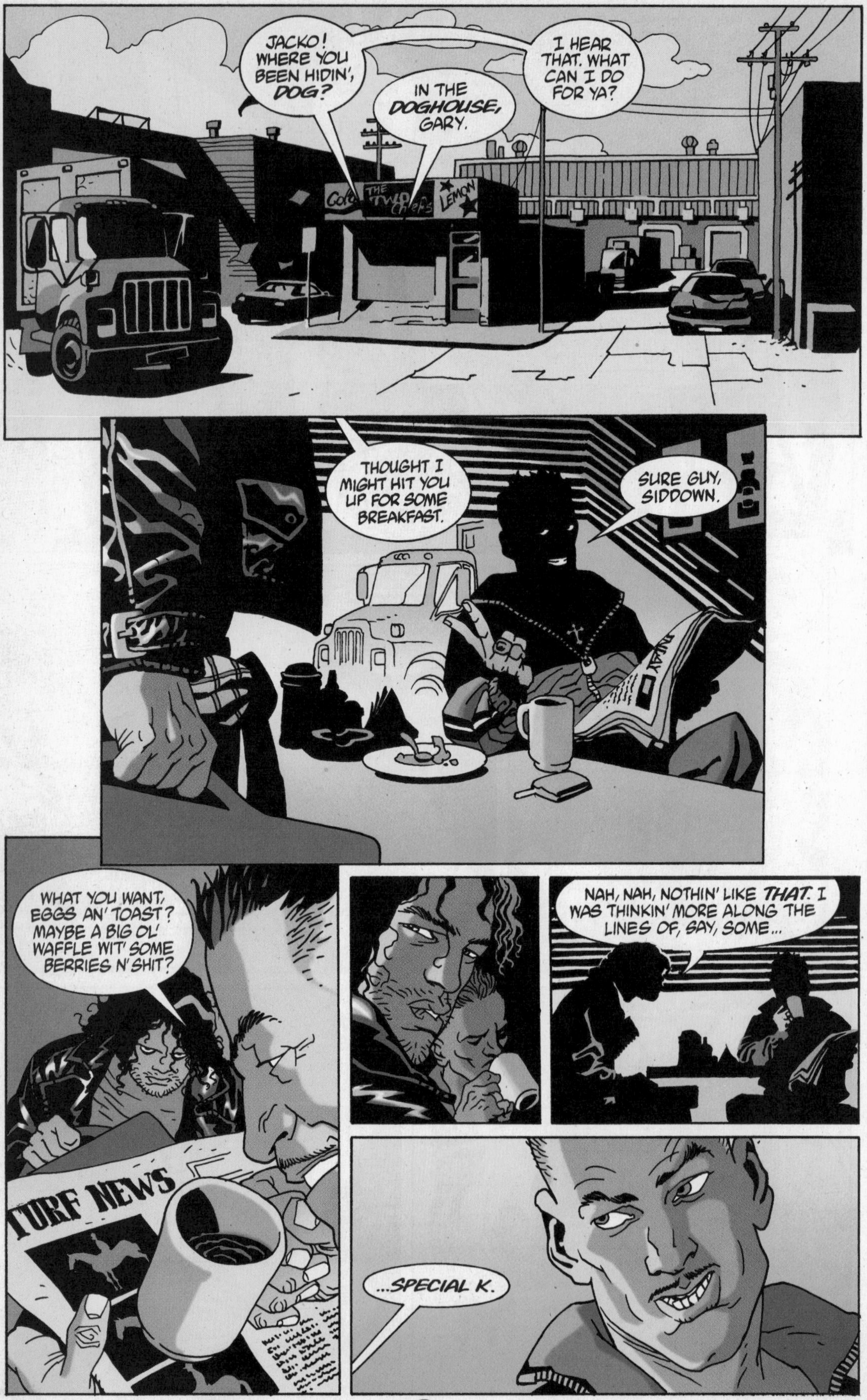
JACKO! WHERE YOU BEEN HIDIN', DOG?
IN THE DOGHOUSE, GARY.
I HEAR THAT. WHAT CAN I DO FOR YA?
THE TWO CHEFS
LEMON
THOUGHT I MIGHT HIT YOU UP FOR SOME BREAKFAST.
SURE GUY, SIDDOWN.
WHAT YOU WANT, EGGS AN' TOAST? MAYBE A BIG OL' WAFFLE WIT' SOME BERRIES N' SHIT?
TURF NEWS
NAH, NAH, NOTHIN' LIKE THAT. I WAS THINKIN' MORE ALONG THE LINES OF, SAY, SOME...
...SPECIAL K.

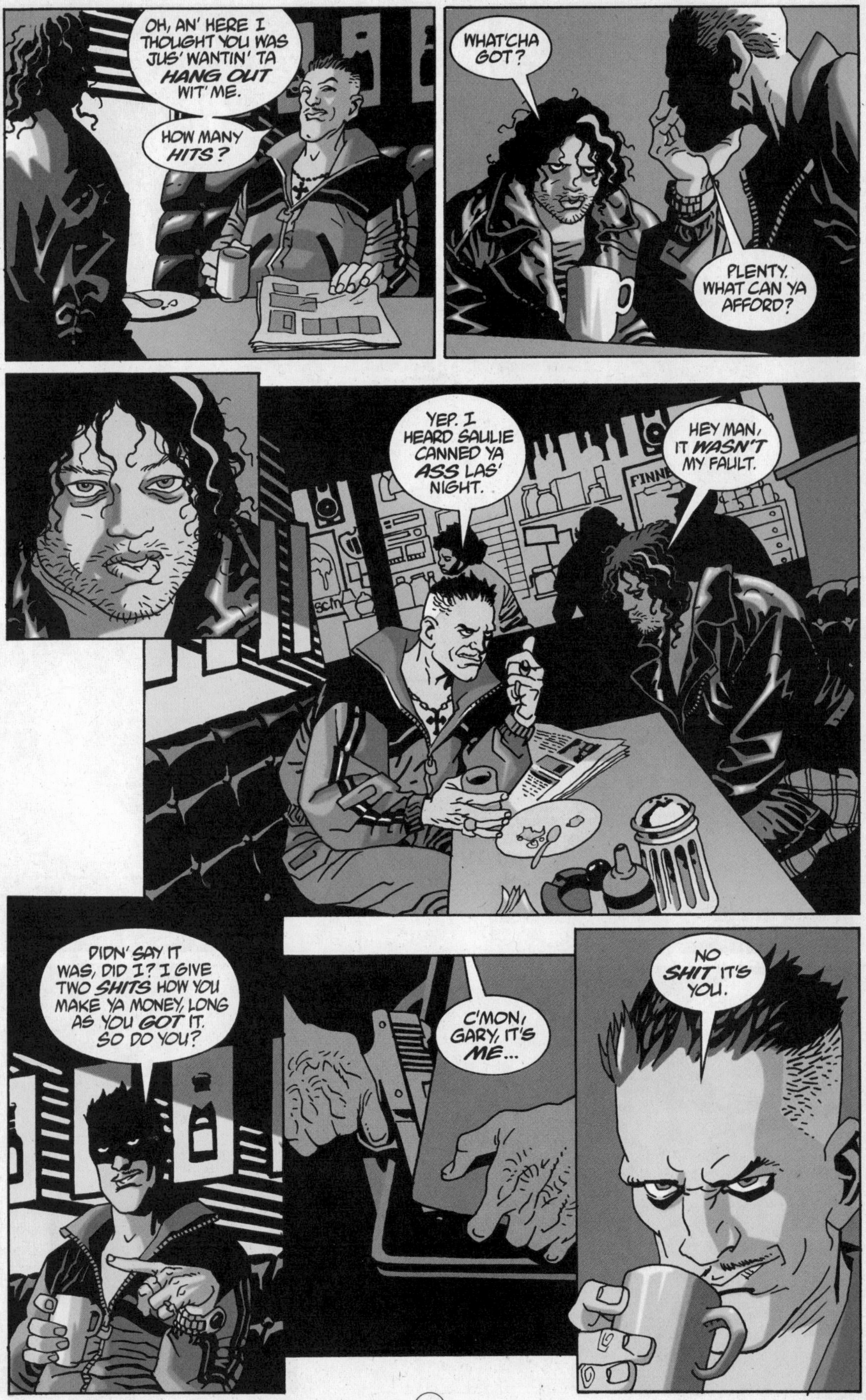
OH, AN' HERE I THOUGHT YOU WAS JUS' WANTIN' TA HANG OUT WIT' ME.
HOW MANY HITS?
WHAT'CHA GOT?
PLENTY. WHAT CAN YA AFFORD?
YEP. I HEARD SAULIE CANNED YA ASS LAS' NIGHT.
HEY MAN, IT WASN'T MY FAULT.
FINNE
DIDN' SAY IT WAS, DID I? I GIVE TWO SHITS HOW YOU MAKE YA MONEY, LONG AS YOU GOT IT. SO DO YOU?
C'MON, GARY, IT'S ME...
NO SHIT IT'S YOU.

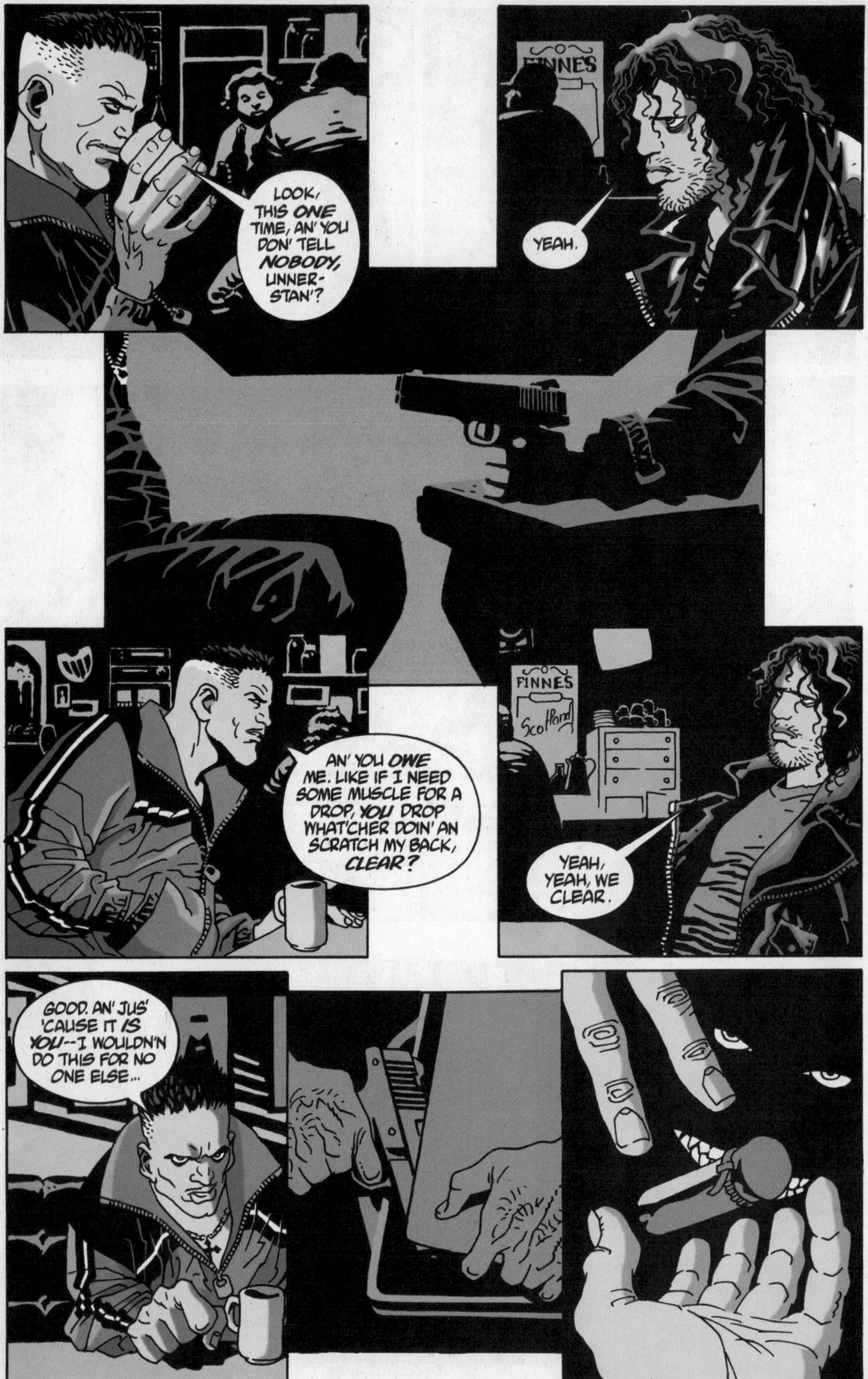
LOOK, THIS ONE TIME, AN' YOU DON' TELL NOBODY, UNNER-STAN'?
FINNES
YEAH.
AN' YOU OWE ME. LIKE IF I NEED SOME MUSCLE FOR A DROP, YOU DROP WHAT'CHER DOIN' AN SCRATCH MY BACK, CLEAR?
FINNES
YEAH, YEAH, WE CLEAR.
GOOD. AN' JUS' 'CAUSE IT IS YOU--I WOULDN'N DO THIS FOR NO ONE ELSE...

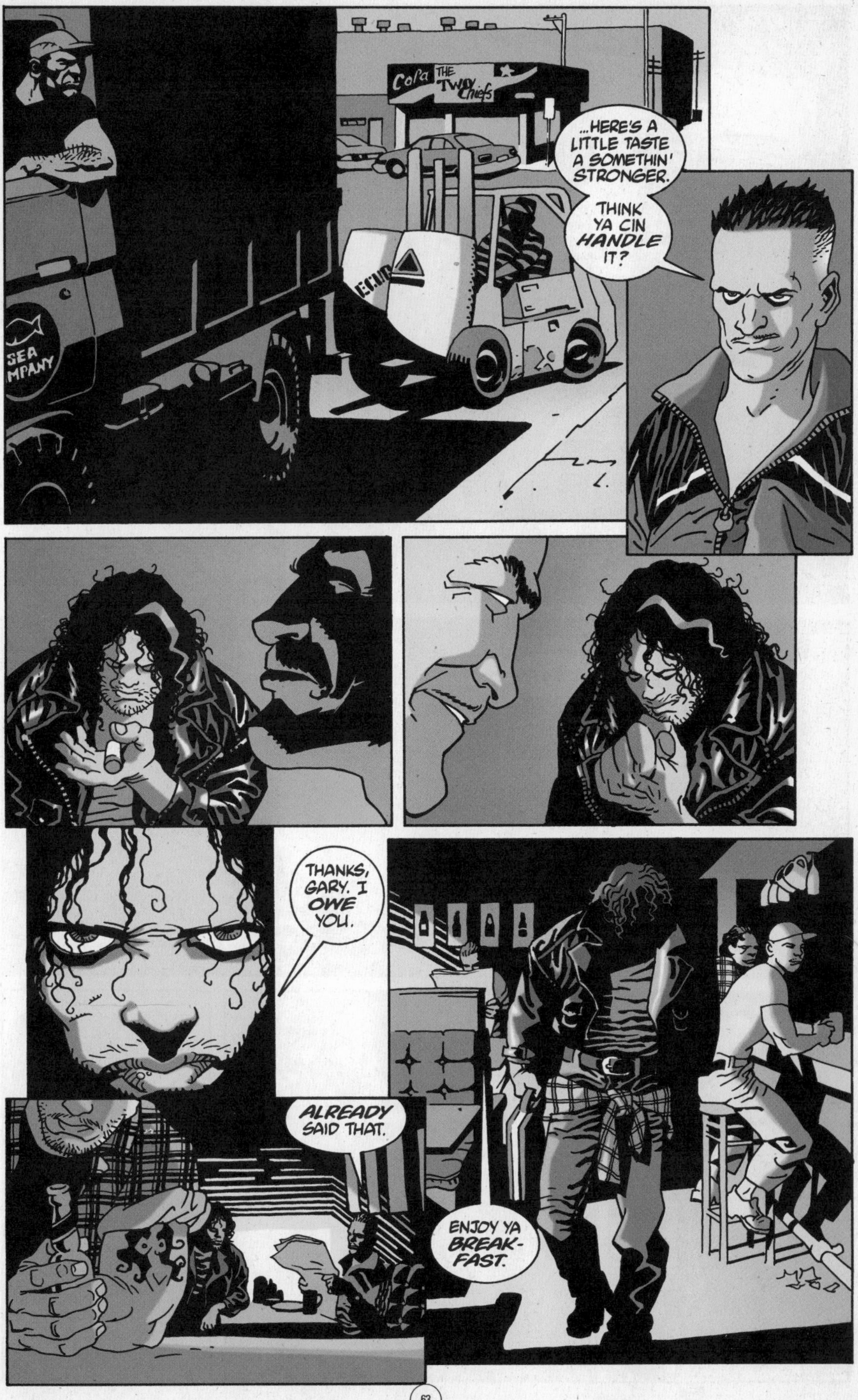
Cola THE TWO Chiefs
...HERE'S A LITTLE TASTE A SOMETHIN' STRONGER.
THINK YA CIN HANDLE IT?
SEA MPANY
THANKS, GARY. I OWE YOU.
ALREADY SAID THAT.
ENJOY YA BREAK-FAST.

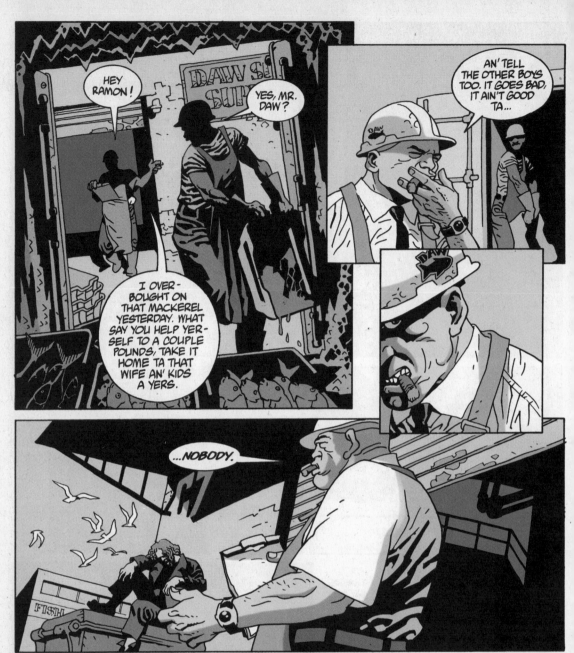

HEY RAMON!

YES, MR. DAW?

AN' TELL THE OTHER BOYS TOO. IT GOES BAD, IT AIN'T GOOD TA...

I OVER-BOUGHT ON THAT MACKEREL YESTERDAY. WHAT SAY YOU HELP YER-SELF TO A COUPLE POUNDS, TAKE IT HOME TA THAT WIFE AN' KIDS A YERS.

...NOBODY.

GARBAGE LIKE YOU...

...S'POSED TO BE IN THE DUMPSTA, NOT ON IT.

CAN IT, DAVID.

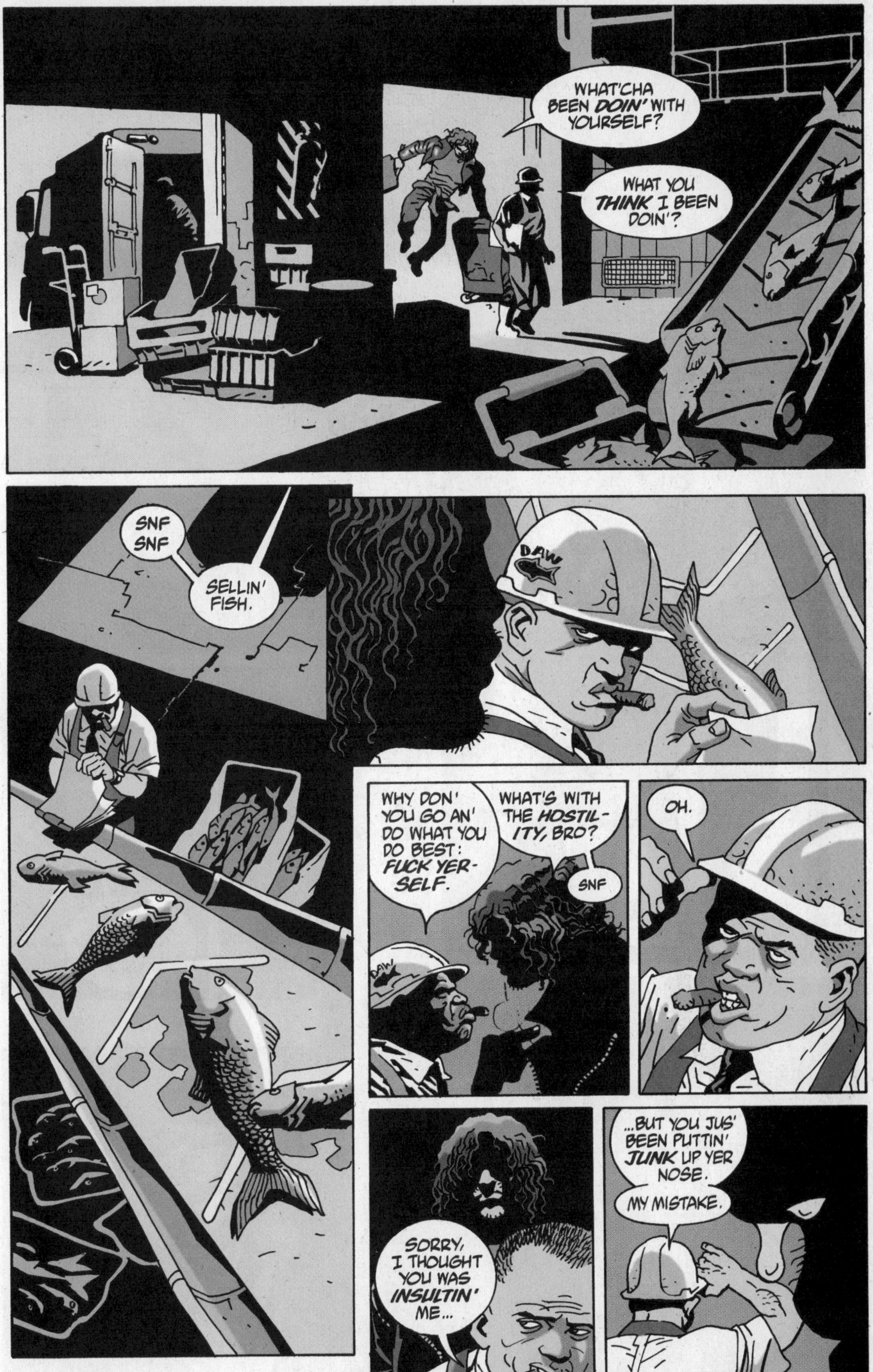
WHAT'CHA BEEN DOIN' WITH YOURSELF?
WHAT YOU THINK I BEEN DOIN'?
SNF SNF
SELLIN' FISH.
WHY DON' YOU GO AN' DO WHAT YOU DO BEST: FUCK YERSELF.
WHAT'S WITH THE HOSTILITY, BRO?
SNF
OH.
SORRY, I THOUGHT YOU WAS INSULTIN' ME...
...BUT YOU JUS' BEEN PUTTIN' JUNK UP YER NOSE.
MY MISTAKE.

YEAH. I WOULDN'N INSULT YOU.

COULD'N'N BE BOTHERED?

SURE I COULD. WHY YOU SAY THAT?

WHY? MMM, MAYBE 'CAUSE YOU CRAPPED OUT ON THE FAMILY FOR ALL THEM YEARS AFTER DAD...

...LOOK, WHY YOU HERE, JACK?

I CAME TO SEE THE OL' LADY. SHE ROUN'?

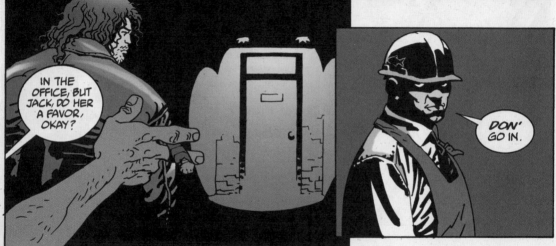

IN THE OFFICE, BUT JACK, DO HER A FAVOR, OKAY?

DON' GO IN.

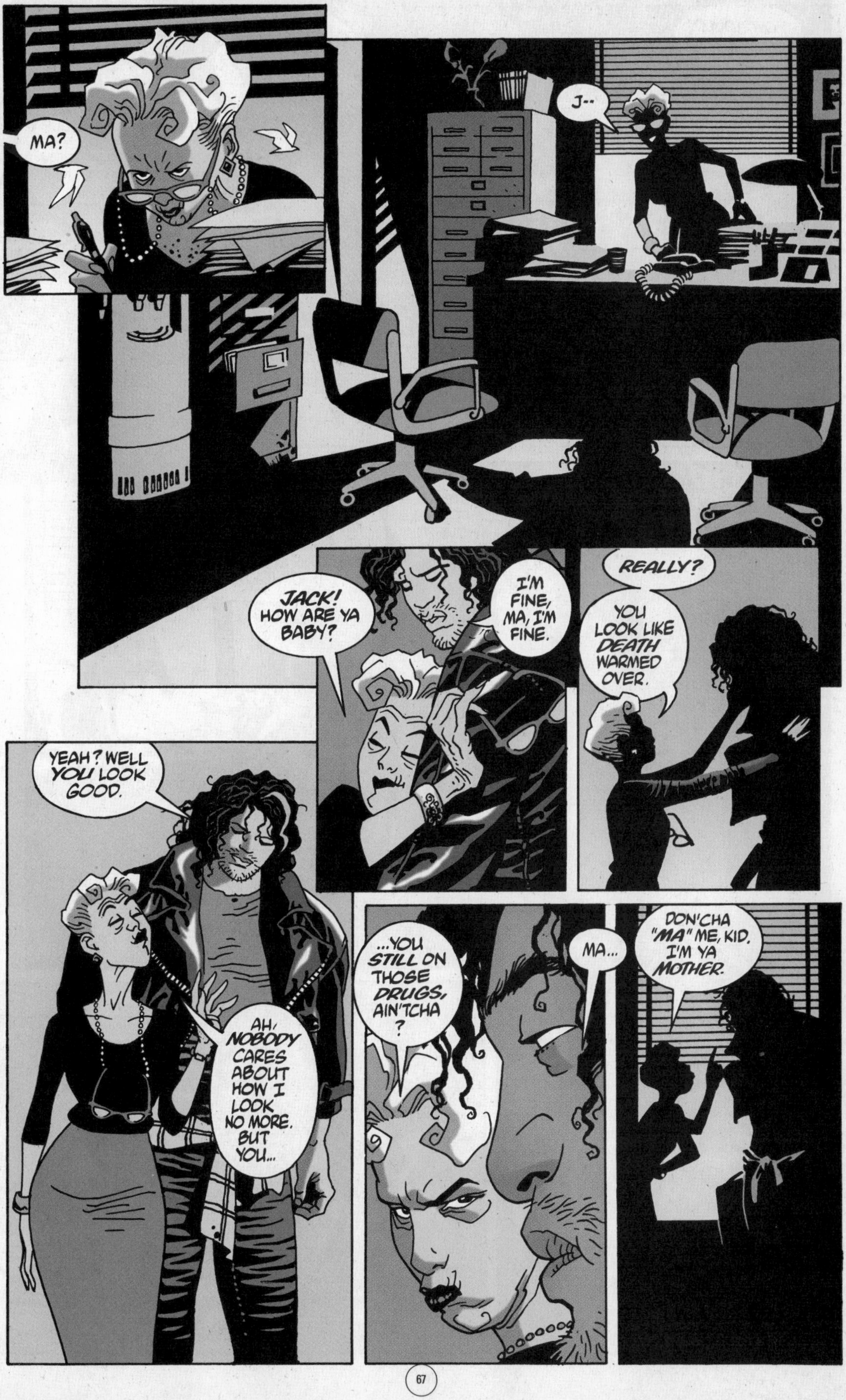

MA?
J--
JACK! HOW ARE YA BABY?
I'M FINE, MA, I'M FINE.
REALLY?
YOU LOOK LIKE DEATH WARMED OVER.
YEAH? WELL YOU LOOK GOOD.
AH, NOBODY CARES ABOUT HOW I LOOK NO MORE. BUT YOU...
...YOU STILL ON THOSE DRUGS, AIN'TCHA ?
MA...
DON'CHA "MA" ME, KID. I'M YA MOTHER.

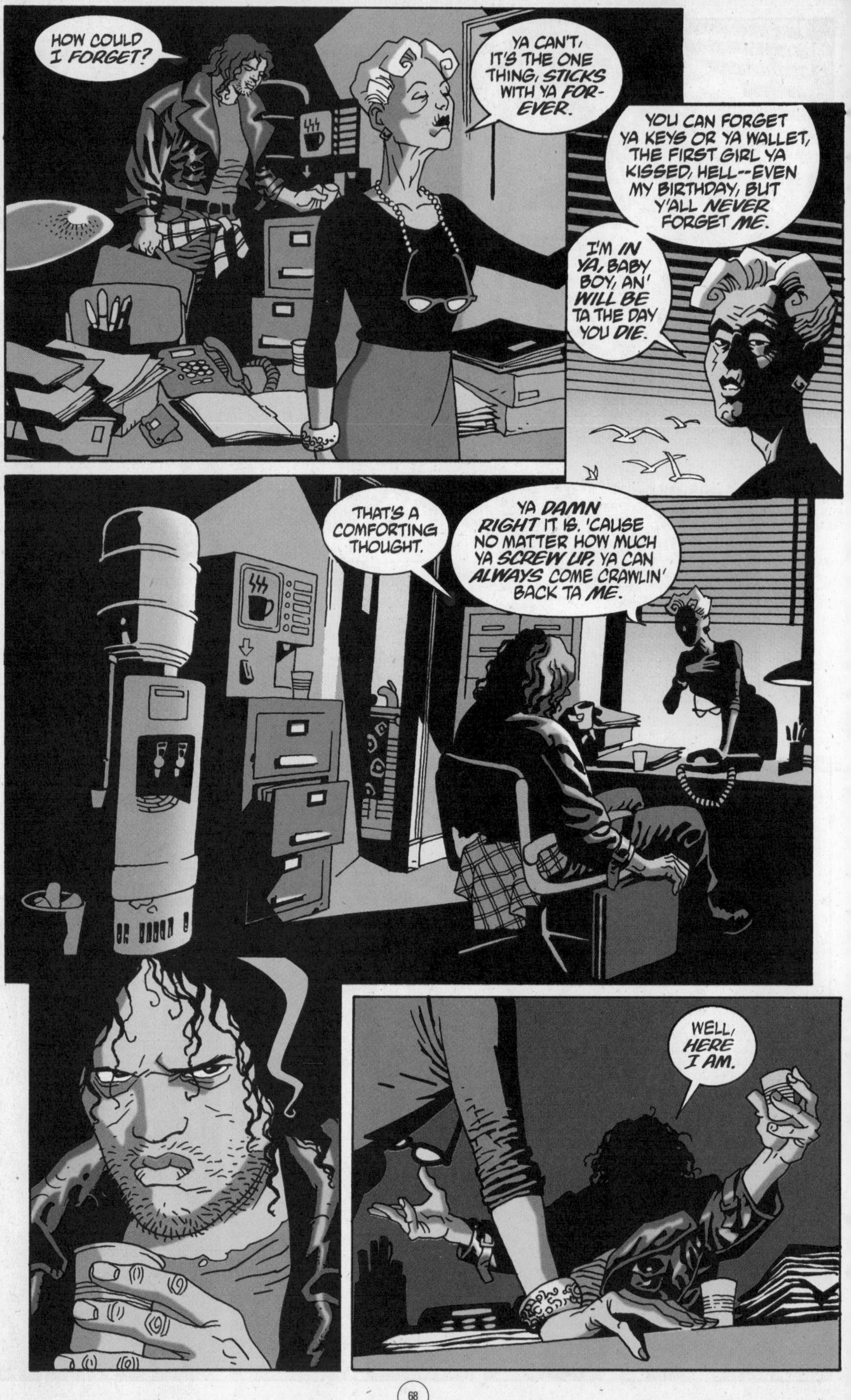
HOW COULD I FORGET?
YA CAN'T, IT'S THE ONE THING, STICKS WITH YA FOREVER.
YOU CAN FORGET YA KEYS OR YA WALLET, THE FIRST GIRL YA KISSED, HELL--EVEN MY BIRTHDAY, BUT Y'ALL NEVER FORGET ME.
I'M IN YA, BABY BOY, AN' WILL BE TA THE DAY YOU DIE.
THAT'S A COMFORTING THOUGHT.
YA DAMN RIGHT IT IS. 'CAUSE NO MATTER HOW MUCH YA SCREW UP, YA CAN ALWAYS COME CRAWLIN' BACK TA ME.
WELL, HERE I AM.

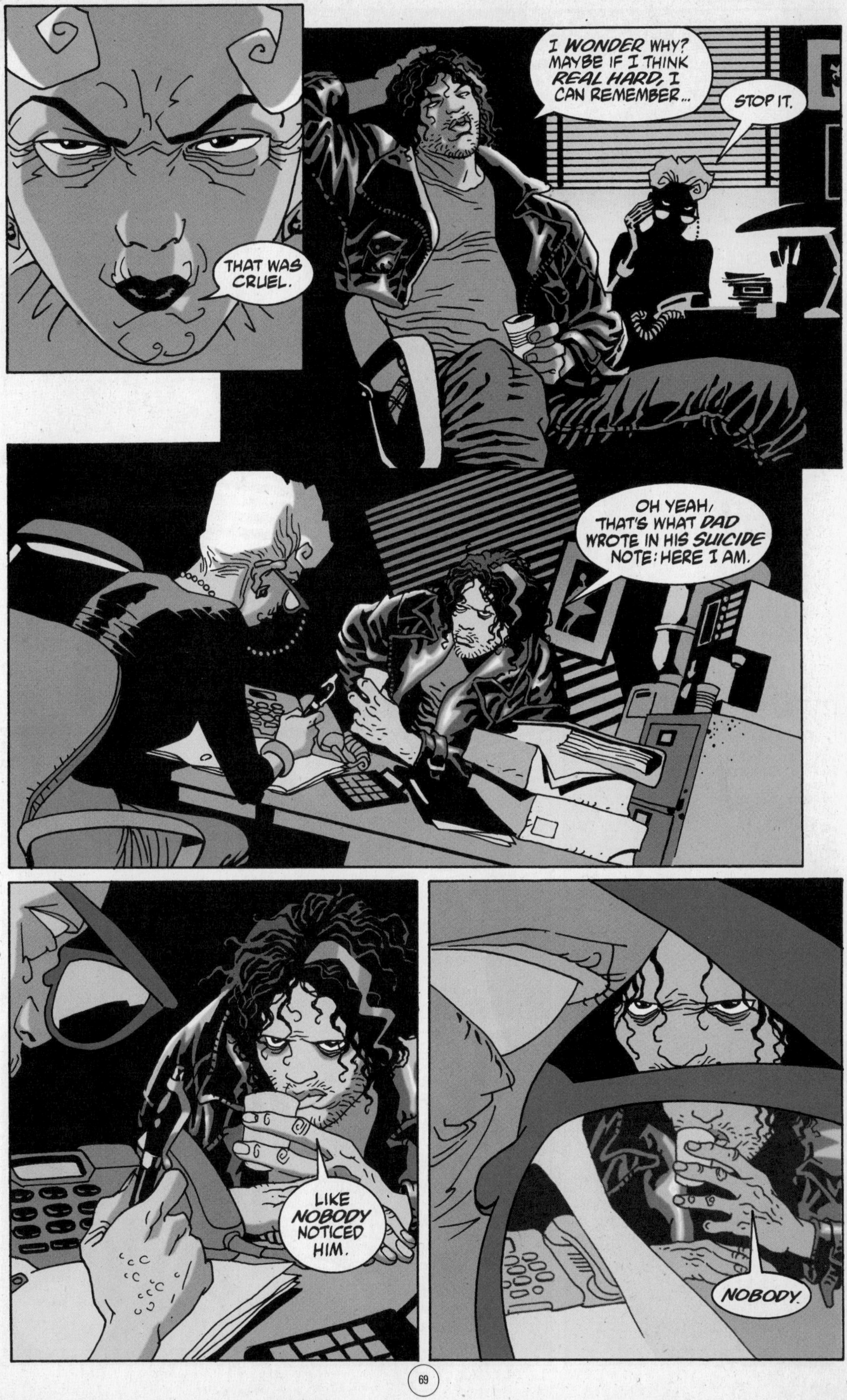
THAT WAS CRUEL.
I WONDER WHY? MAYBE IF I THINK REAL HARD, I CAN REMEMBER...
STOP IT.
OH YEAH, THAT'S WHAT DAD WROTE IN HIS SUICIDE NOTE: HERE I AM.
LIKE NOBODY NOTICED HIM.
NOBODY.

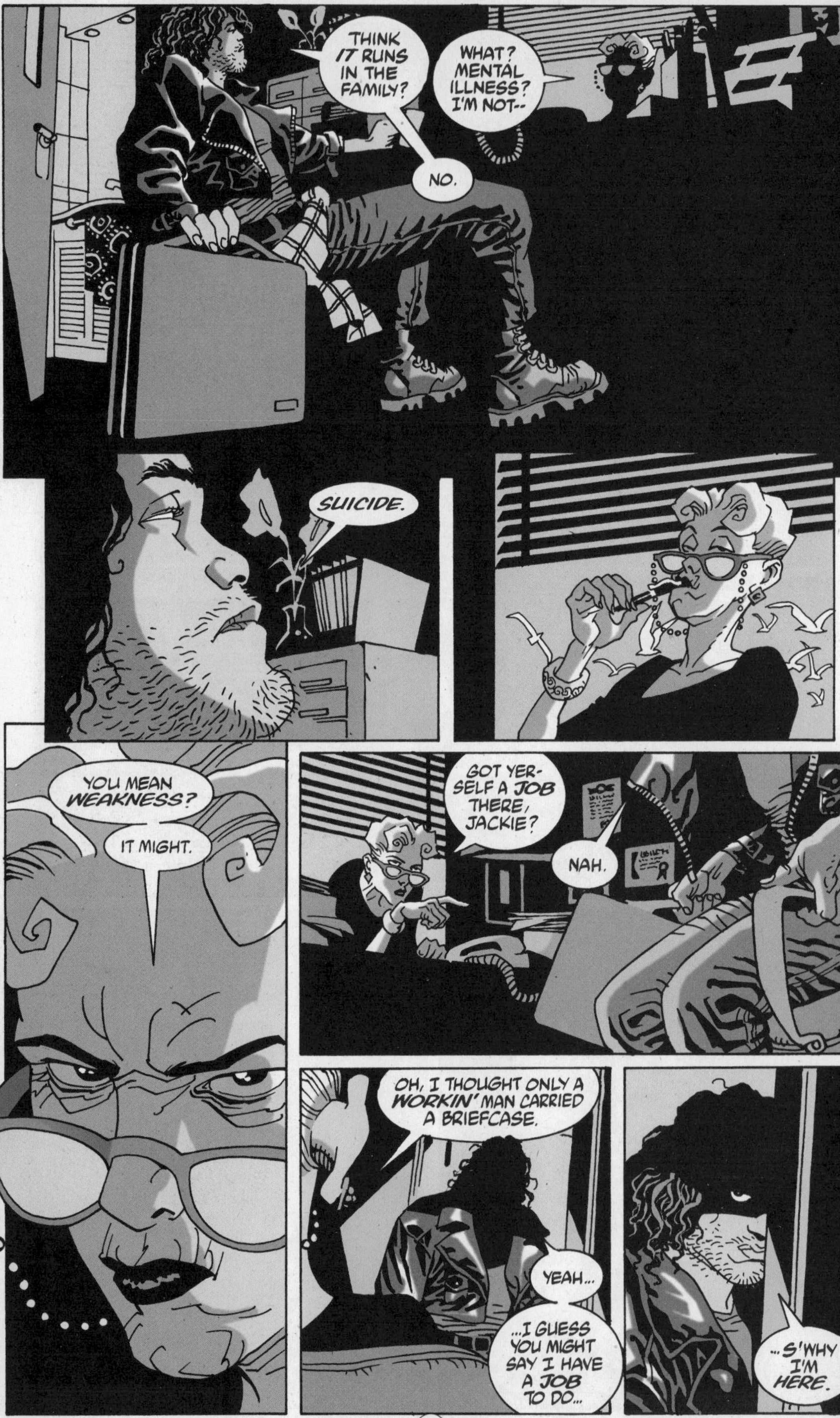

THINK IT RUNS IN THE FAMILY?
WHAT? MENTAL ILLNESS? I'M NOT--
NO.
SUICIDE.
YOU MEAN WEAKNESS?
IT MIGHT.
GOT YER-SELF A JOB THERE, JACKIE?
NAH.
OH, I THOUGHT ONLY A WORKIN' MAN CARRIED A BRIEFCASE.
YEAH...
...I GUESS YOU MIGHT SAY I HAVE A JOB TO DO...
...S'WHY I'M HERE.

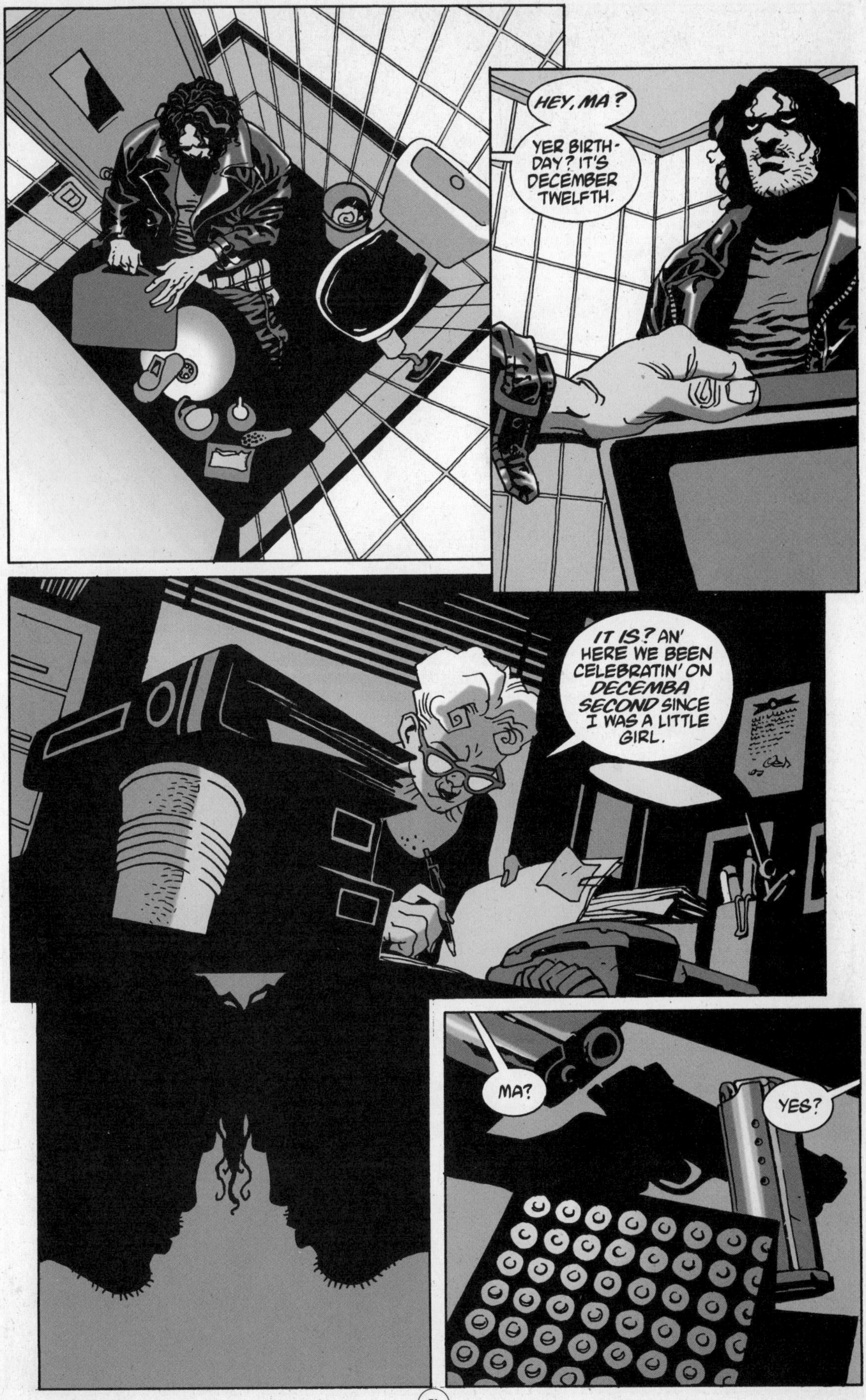
HEY, MA?
YER BIRTHDAY? IT'S DECEMBER TWELFTH.
IT IS? AN' HERE WE BEEN CELEBRATIN' ON DECEMBA SECOND SINCE I WAS A LITTLE GIRL.
MA?
YES?

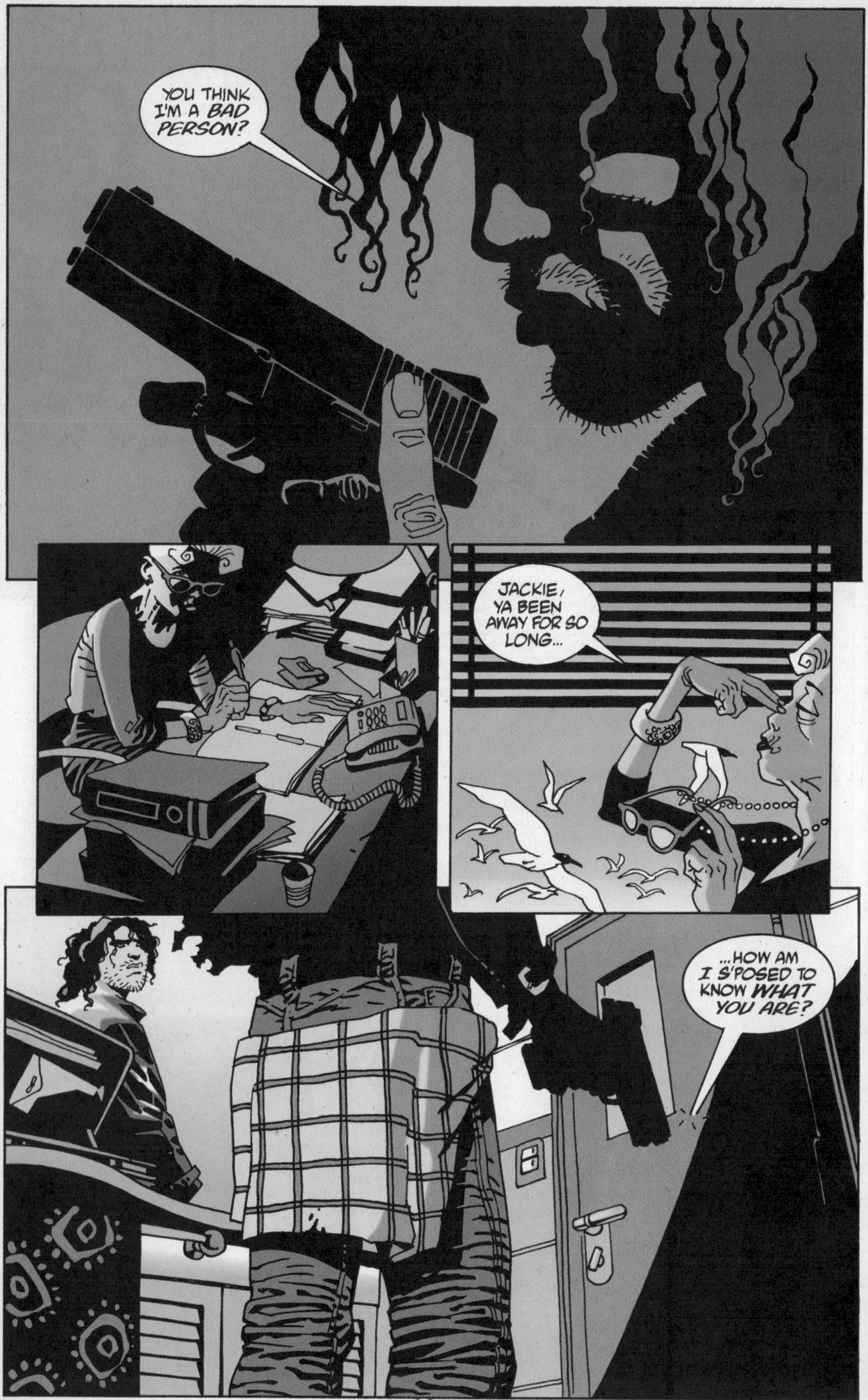
YOU THINK I'M A *BAD PERSON?*
JACKIE, YA BEEN AWAY FOR SO LONG...
...HOW AM I S'POSED TO KNOW *WHAT* YOU ARE?

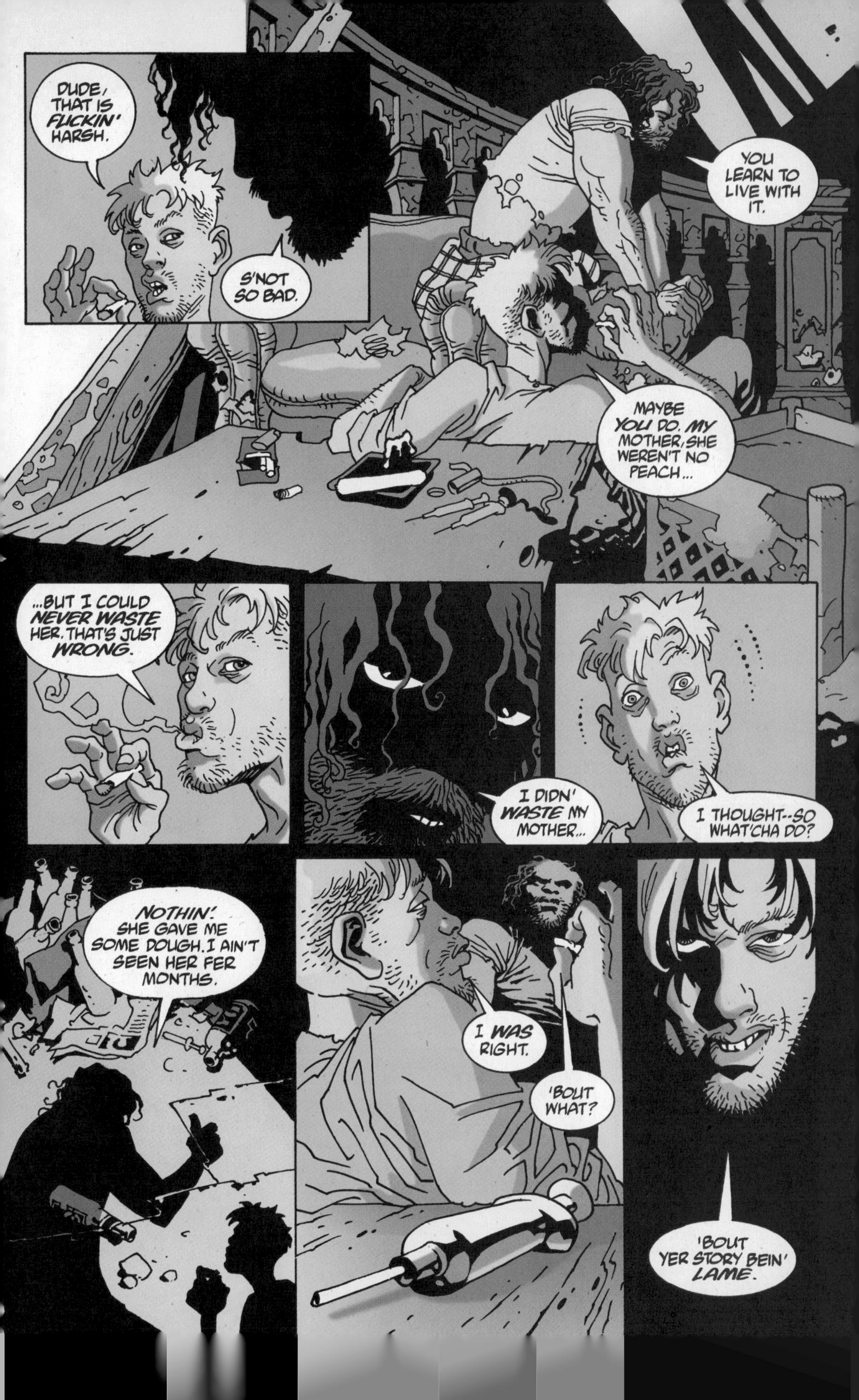
DUDE, THAT IS FUCKIN' HARSH.
S'NOT SO BAD.
YOU LEARN TO LIVE WITH IT.
MAYBE YOU DO. MY MOTHER, SHE WEREN'T NO PEACH...
...BUT I COULD NEVER WASTE HER. THAT'S JUST WRONG.
I DIDN' WASTE MY MOTHER...
I THOUGHT--SO WHAT'CHA DO?
NOTHIN'. SHE GAVE ME SOME DOUGH. I AIN'T SEEN HER FER MONTHS.
I WAS RIGHT.
'BOUT WHAT?
'BOUT YER STORY BEIN' LAME.

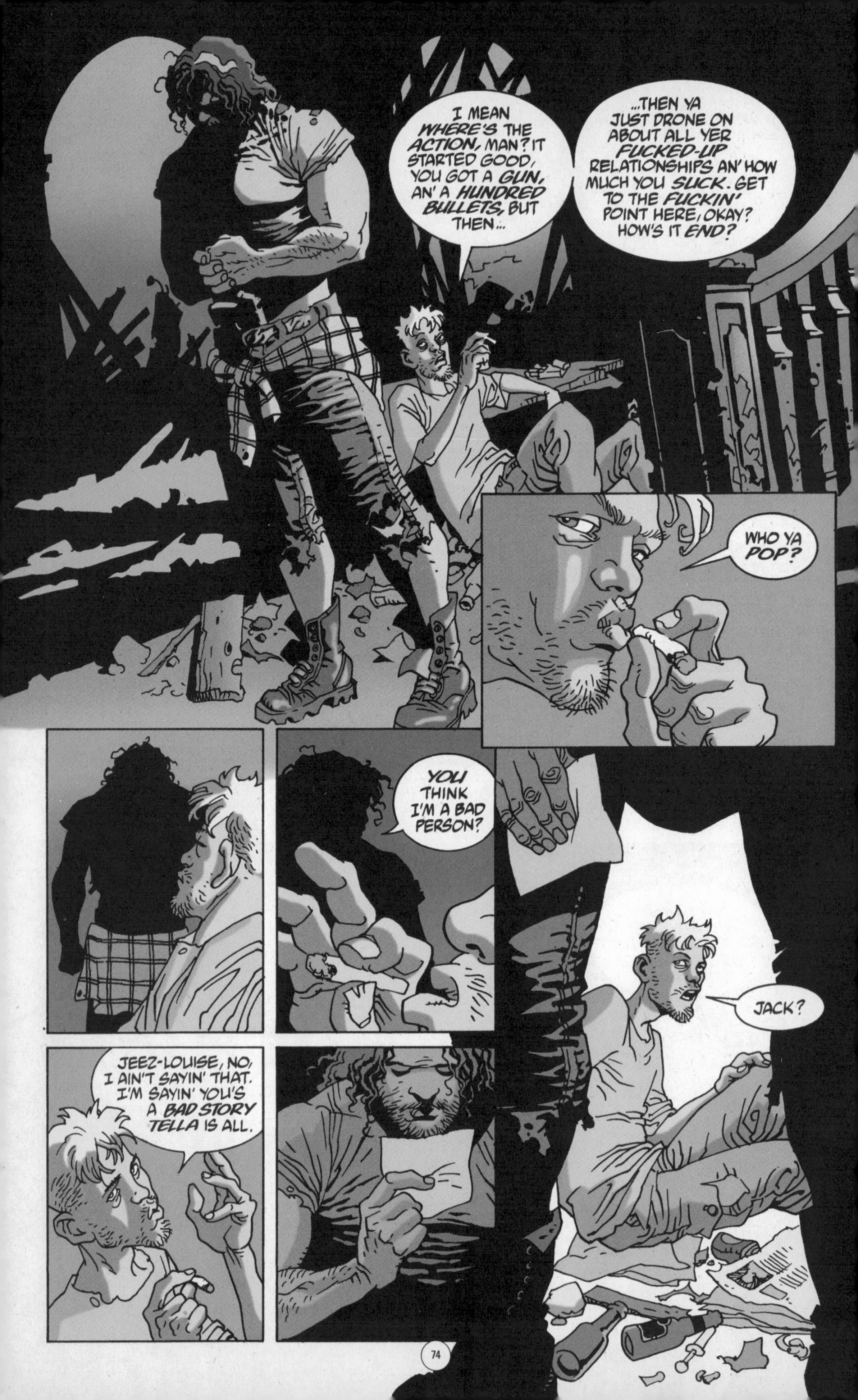
I MEAN WHERE'S THE ACTION, MAN? IT STARTED GOOD, YOU GOT A GUN, AN' A HUNDRED BULLETS, BUT THEN...
...THEN YA JUST DRONE ON ABOUT ALL YER FUCKED-UP RELATIONSHIPS AN' HOW MUCH YOU SUCK. GET TO THE FUCKIN' POINT HERE, OKAY? HOW'S IT END?
WHO YA POP?
YOU THINK I'M A BAD PERSON?
JACK?
JEEZ-LOUISE, NO, I AIN'T SAYIN' THAT. I'M SAYIN' YOU'S A BAD STORY TELLA IS ALL.

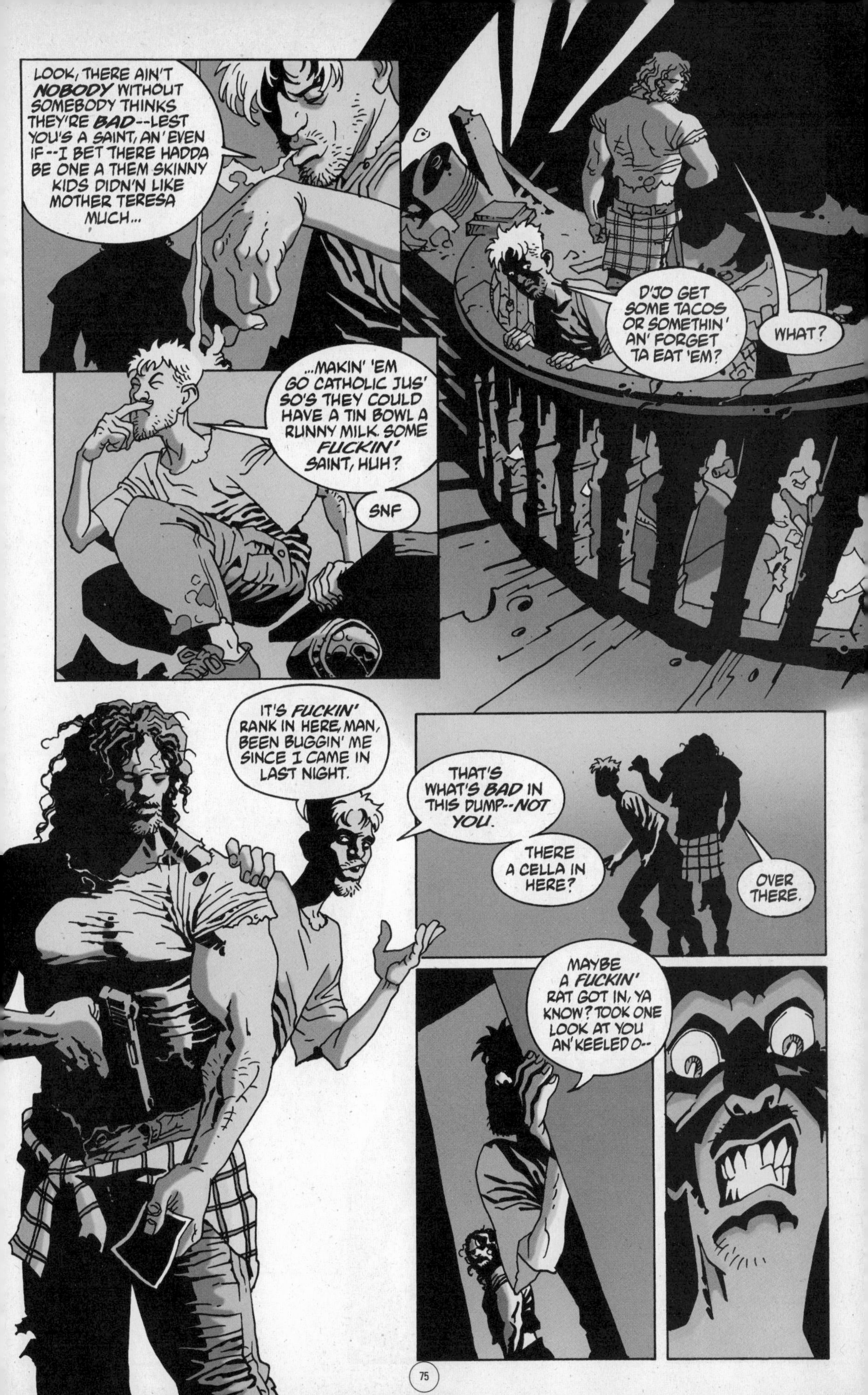
LOOK, THERE AIN'T NOBODY WITHOUT SOMEBODY THINKS THEY'RE BAD--LEST YOU'S A SAINT, AN' EVEN IF--I BET THERE HADDA BE ONE A THEM SKINNY KIDS DIDN'N LIKE MOTHER TERESA MUCH...
...MAKIN' 'EM GO CATHOLIC JUS' SO'S THEY COULD HAVE A TIN BOWL A RUNNY MILK. SOME FUCKIN' SAINT, HUH?
SNF
D'JO GET SOME TACOS OR SOMETHIN' AN' FORGET TA EAT 'EM?
WHAT?
IT'S FUCKIN' RANK IN HERE, MAN, BEEN BUGGIN' ME SINCE I CAME IN LAST NIGHT.
THAT'S WHAT'S BAD IN THIS DUMP--NOT YOU.
THERE A CELLA IN HERE?
OVER THERE.
MAYBE A FUCKIN' RAT GOT IN, YA KNOW? TOOK ONE LOOK AT YOU AN' KEELED O--

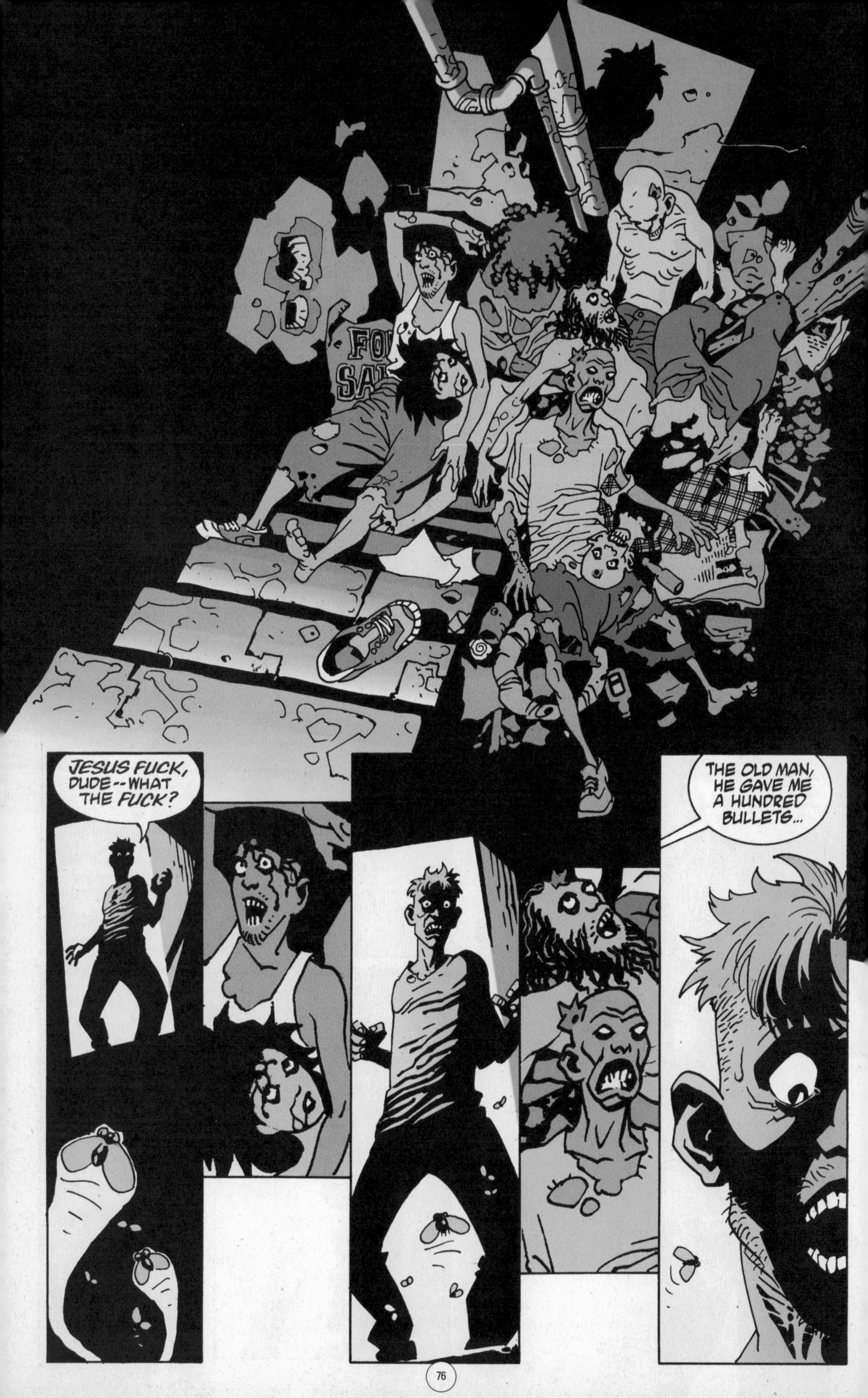

JESUS FUCK, DUDE--WHAT THE FUCK?
THE OLD MAN, HE GAVE ME A HUNDRED BULLETS...

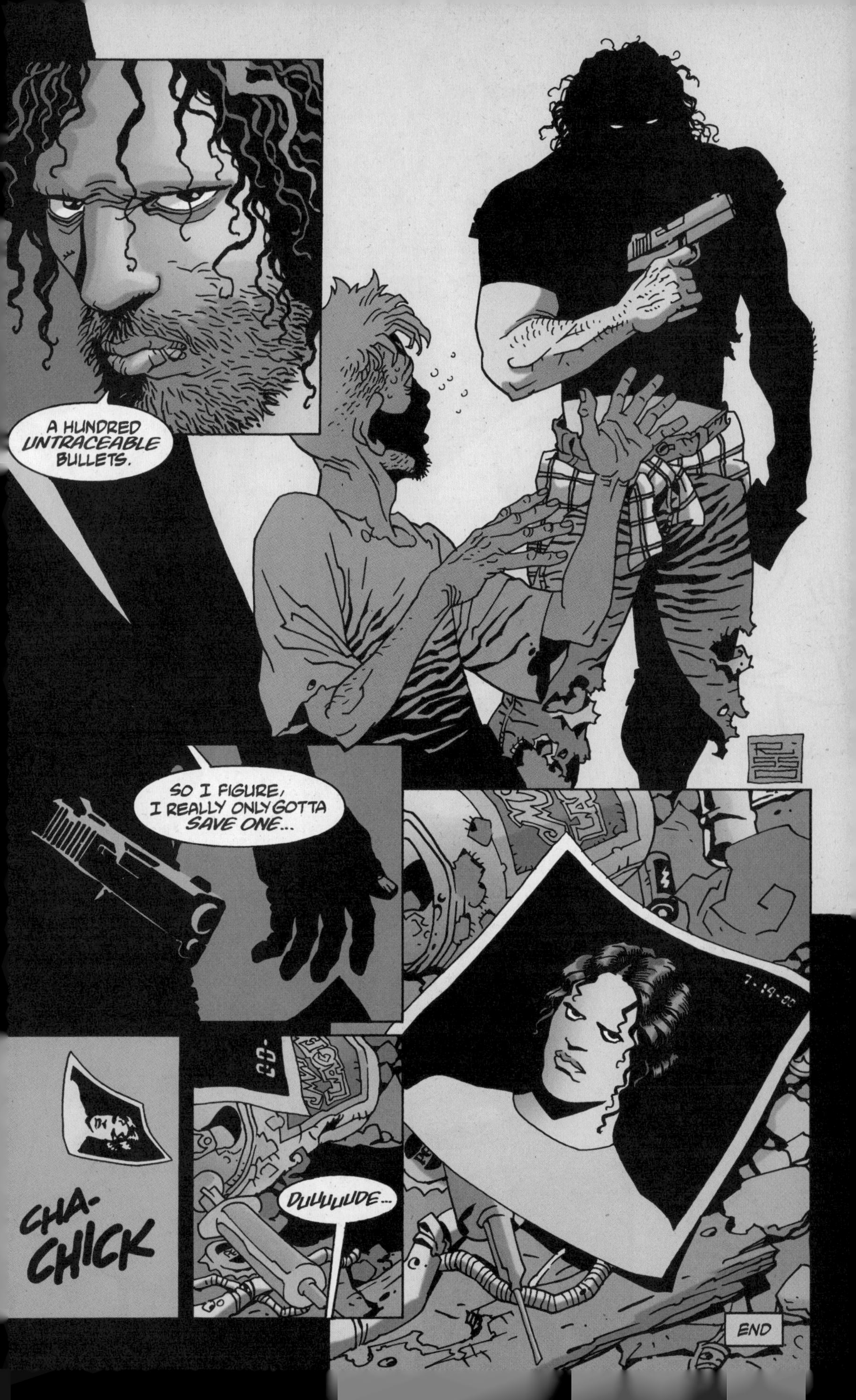
A HUNDRED UNTRACEABLE BULLETS.
SO I FIGURE, I REALLY ONLY GOTTA SAVE ONE...
CHA-CHICK
DUUUUUDE...
7-19-00
END

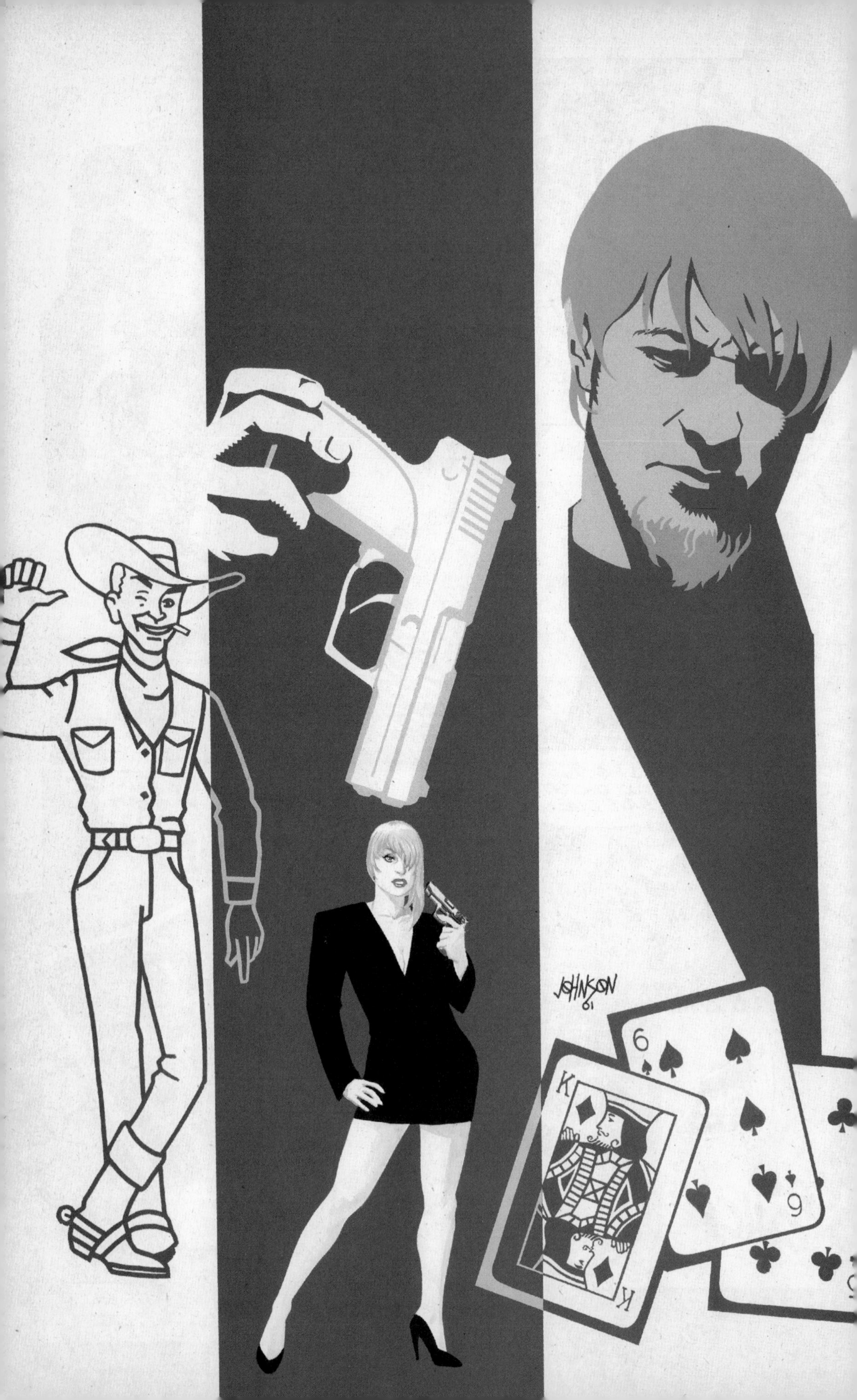
JOHNSON

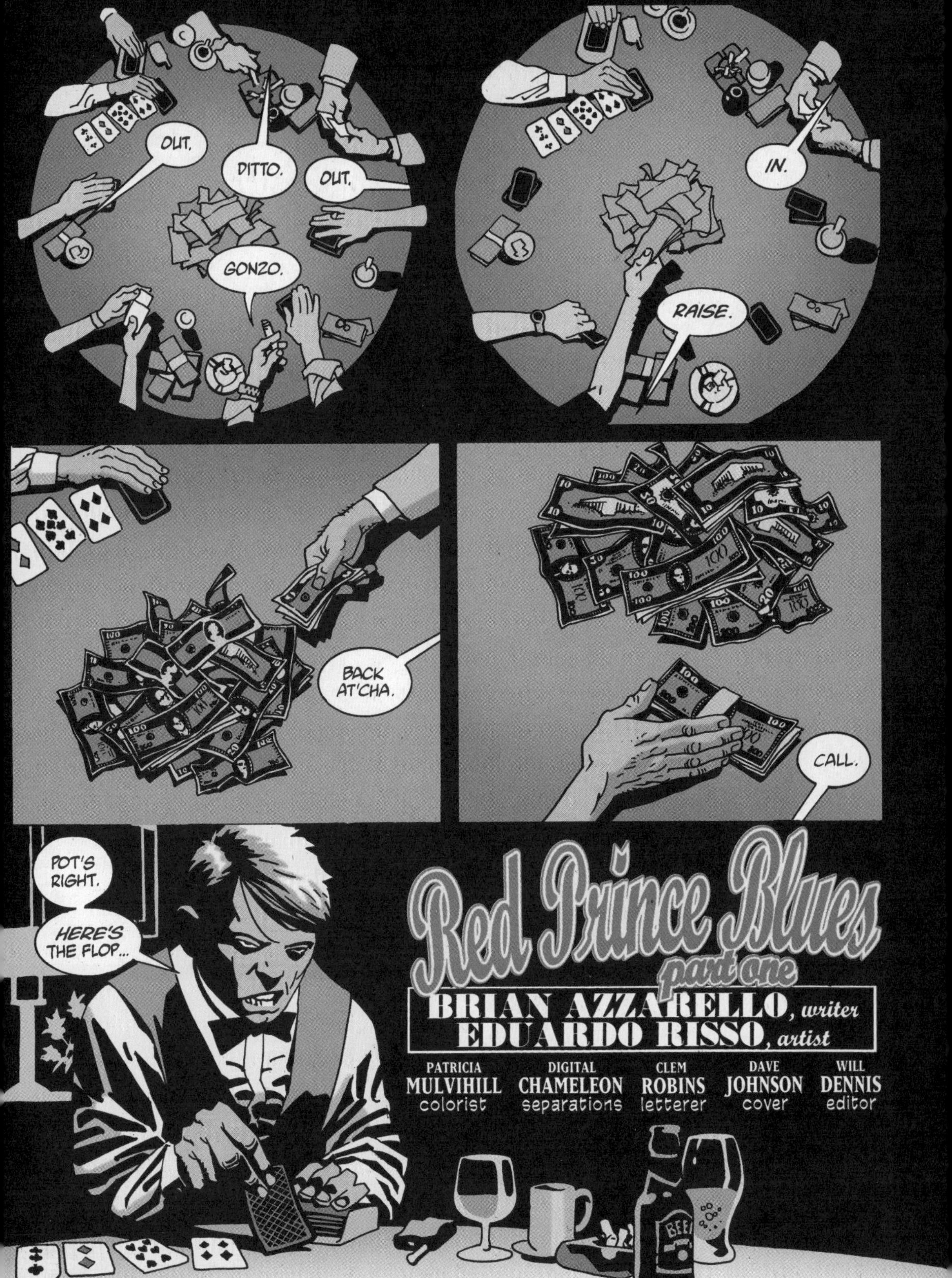
OUT.
DITTO.
OUT.
GONZO.
IN.
RAISE.
BACK AT'CHA.
CALL.
POT'S RIGHT.
HERE'S THE FLOP...
Red Prince Blues
part one
BRIAN AZZARELLO, writer
EDUARDO RISSO, artist
PATRICIA MULVIHILL colorist
DIGITAL CHAMELEON separations
CLEM ROBINS letterer
DAVE JOHNSON cover
WILL DENNIS editor
BEER

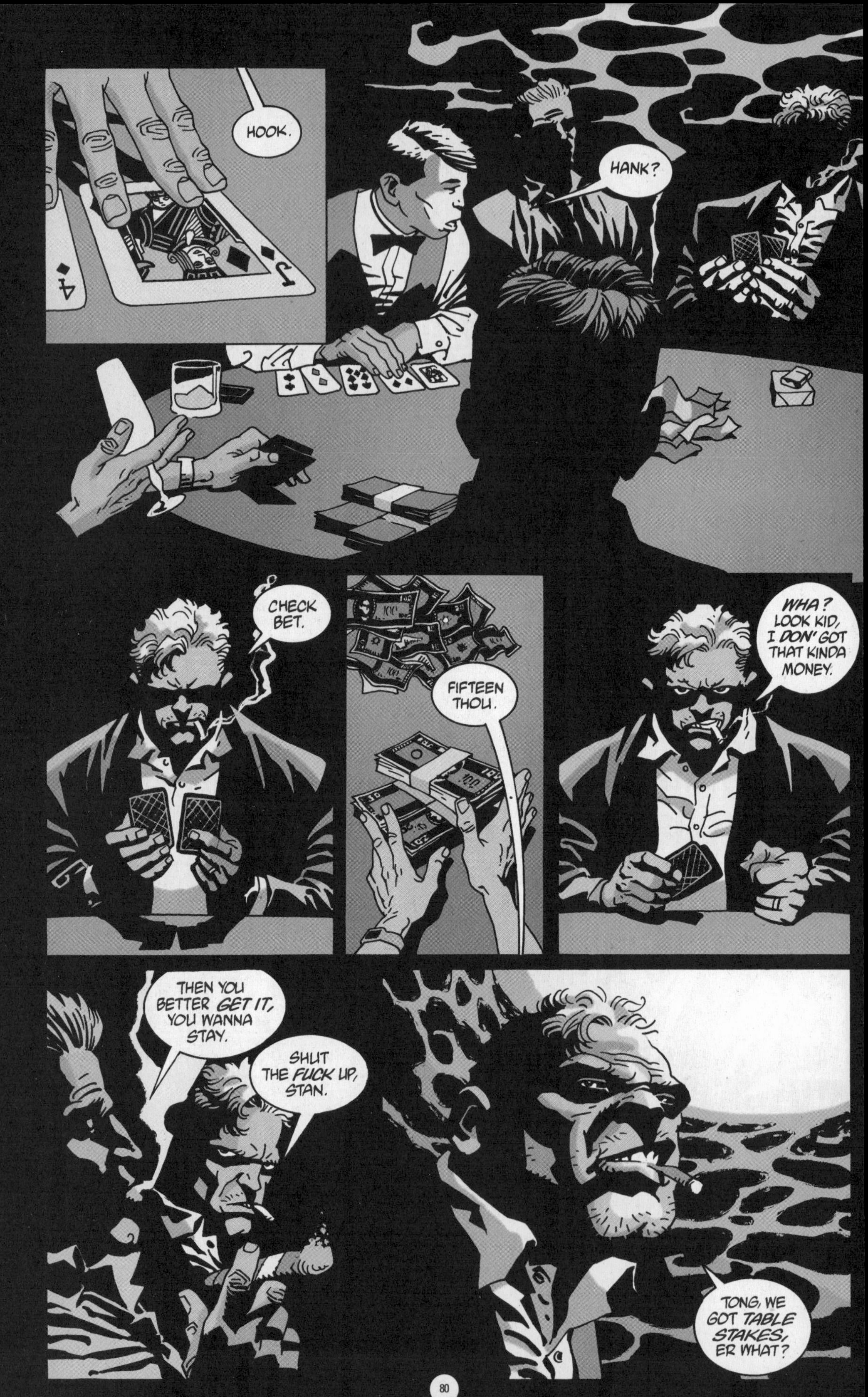
HOOK.
HANK?
CHECK BET.
FIFTEEN THOU.
WHA? LOOK KID, I DON' GOT THAT KINDA MONEY.
THEN YOU BETTER GET IT, YOU WANNA STAY.
SHUT THE FUCK UP, STAN.
TONG, WE GOT TABLE STAKES, ER WHAT?

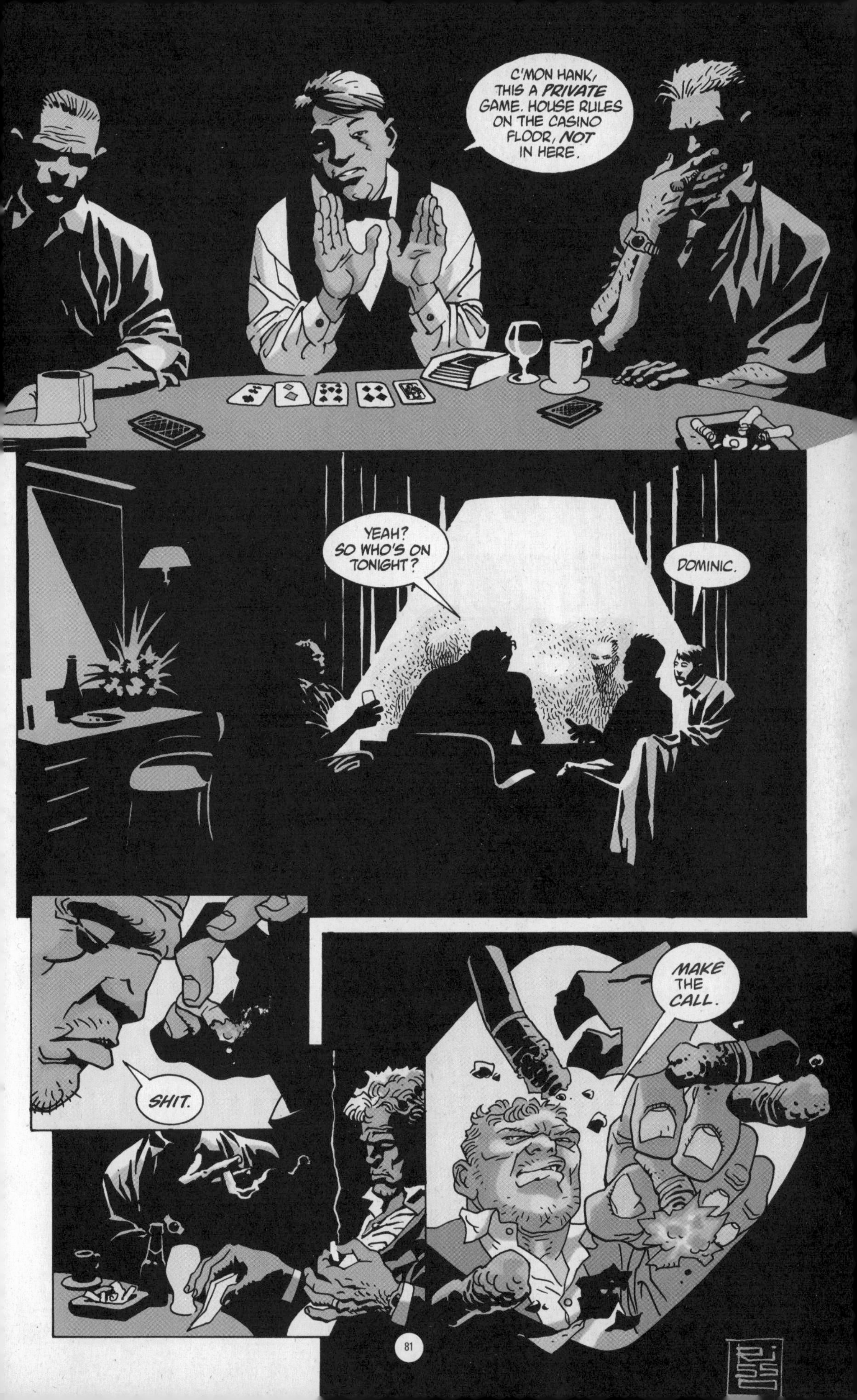
C'MON HANK, THIS A PRIVATE GAME. HOUSE RULES ON THE CASINO FLOOR, NOT IN HERE.
YEAH? SO WHO'S ON TONIGHT?
DOMINIC.
SHIT.
MAKE THE CALL.

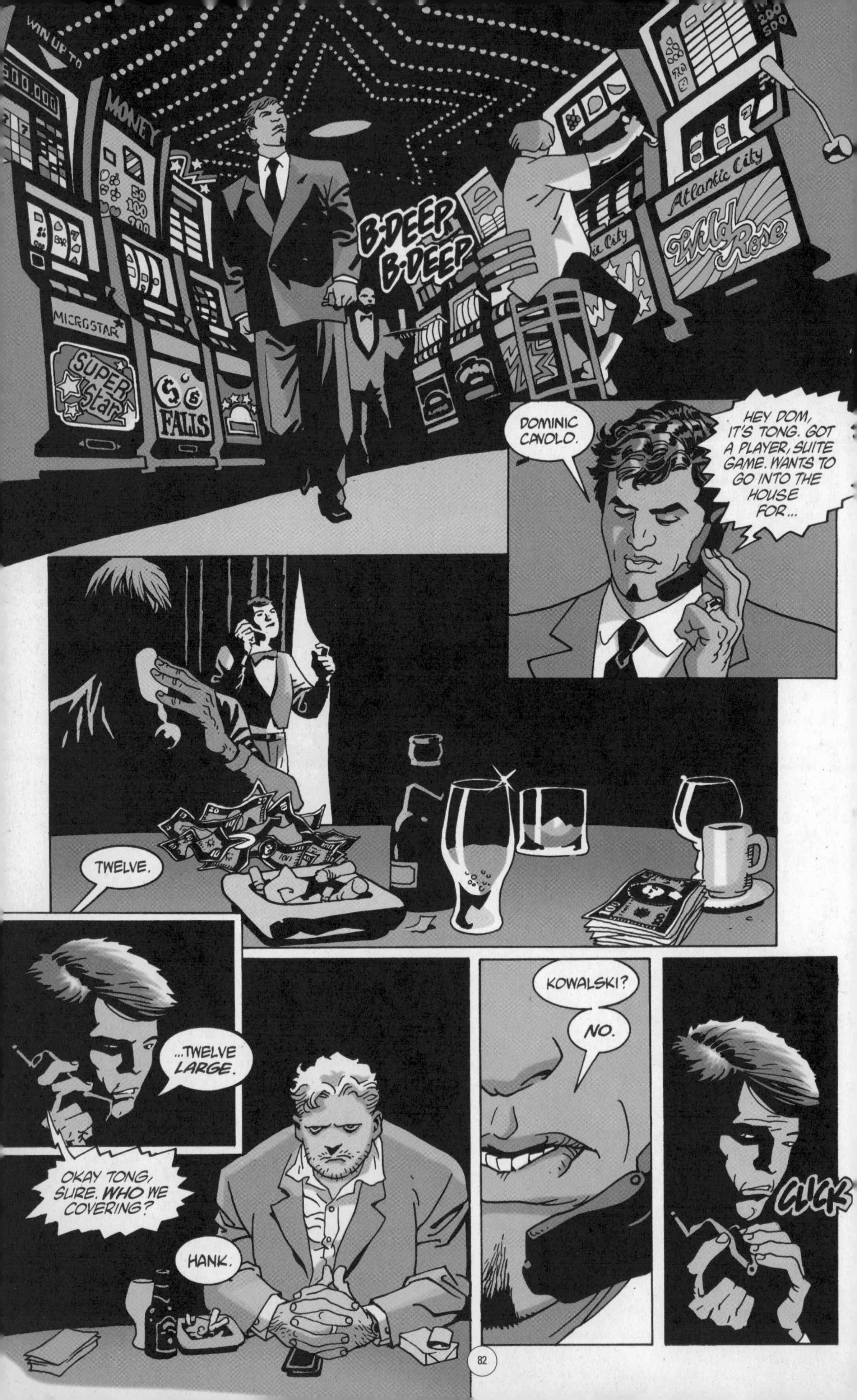
WIN UP TO
MONEY
MICROSTAR
SUPER Star
FALLS
Atlantic City
Wild Rose
B-DEEP B-DEEP
DOMINIC CAVOLO.
HEY DOM, IT'S TONG. GOT A PLAYER, SUITE GAME. WANTS TO GO INTO THE HOUSE FOR...
TWELVE.
...TWELVE LARGE.
OKAY TONG, SURE. WHO WE COVERING?
HANK.
KOWALSKI?
NO.
CLICK

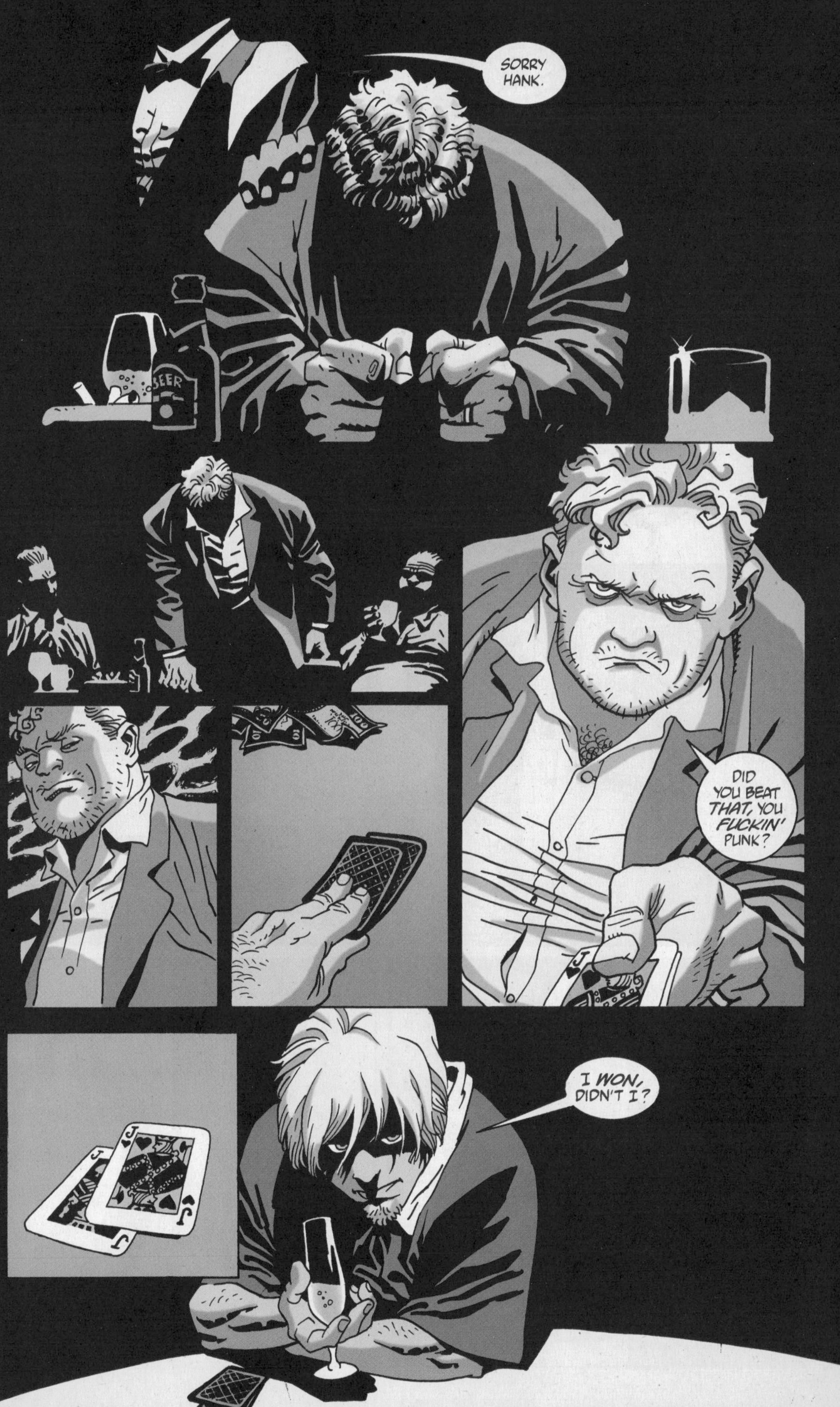
SORRY HANK.
BEER
DID YOU BEAT THAT, YOU FUCKIN' PUNK?
I WON, DIDN'T I?

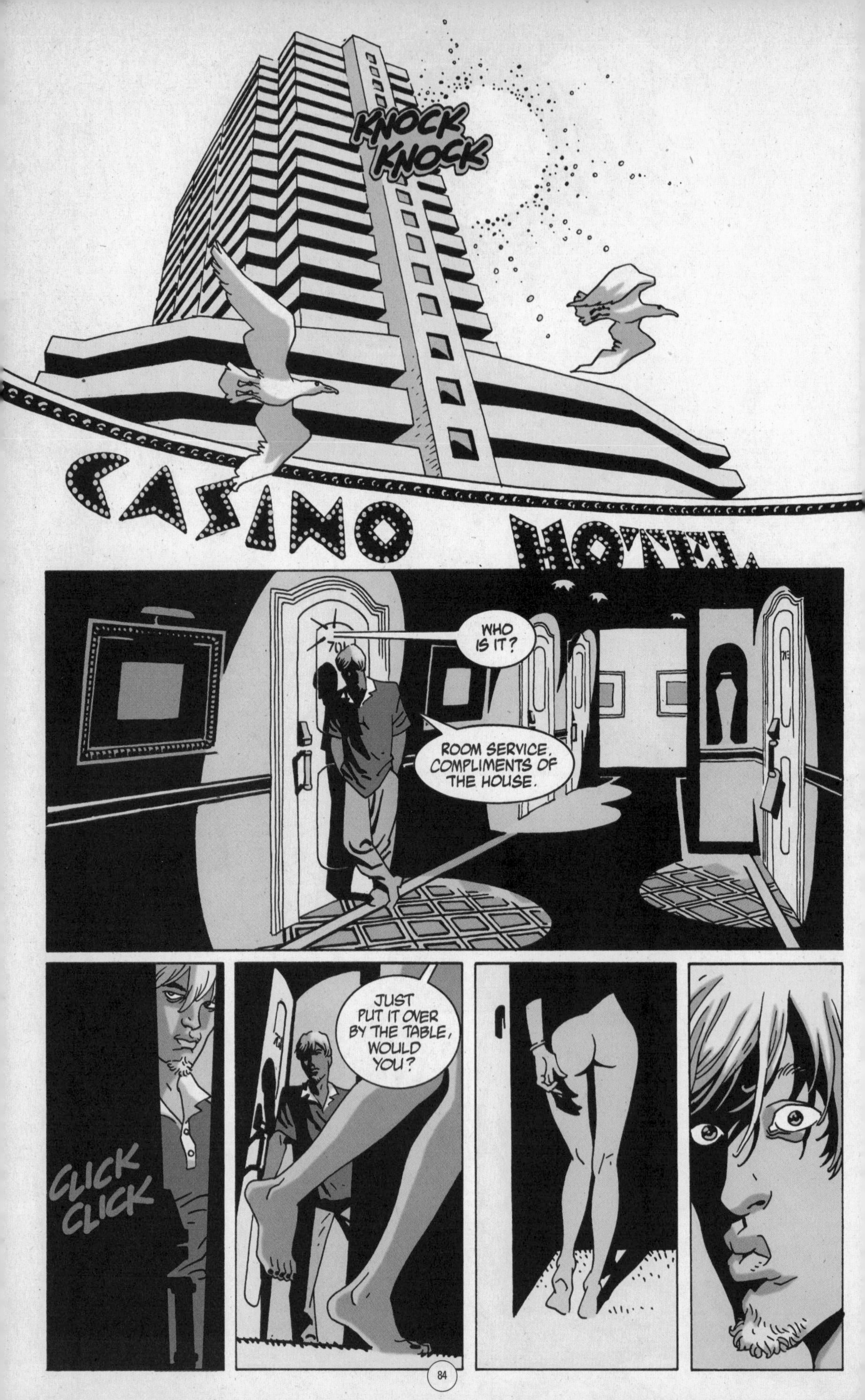
KNOCK KNOCK
CASINO HOTEL
WHO IS IT?
ROOM SERVICE, COMPLIMENTS OF THE HOUSE.
CLICK CLICK
JUST PUT IT OVER BY THE TABLE, WOULD YOU?

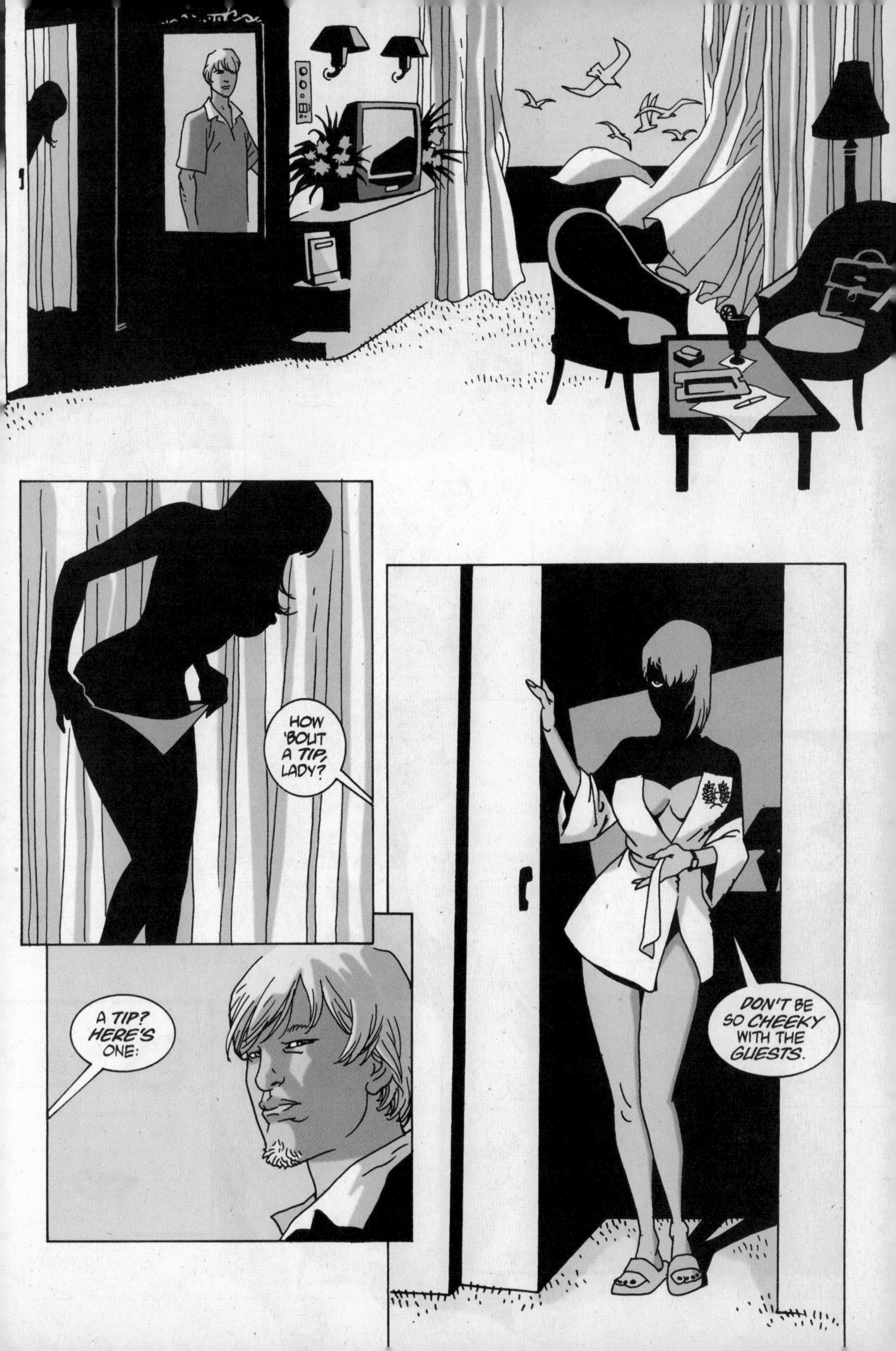
HOW 'BOUT A TIP, LADY?
DON'T BE SO CHEEKY WITH THE GUESTS.
A TIP? HERE'S ONE:

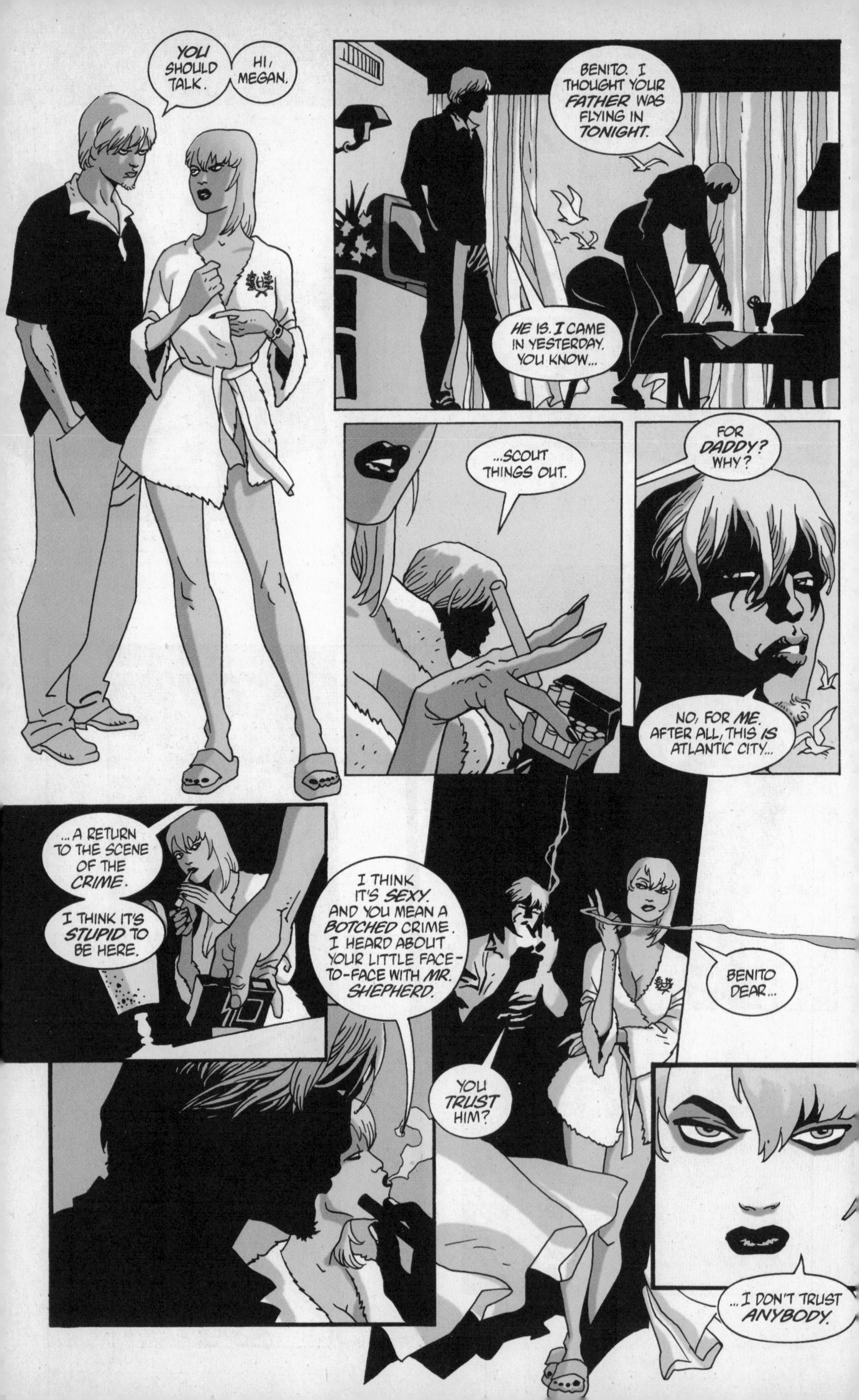

HI, MEGAN.
YOU SHOULD TALK.
BENITO. I THOUGHT YOUR FATHER WAS FLYING IN TONIGHT.
HE IS. I CAME IN YESTERDAY. YOU KNOW...
...SCOUT THINGS OUT.
FOR DADDY? WHY?
NO, FOR ME. AFTER ALL, THIS IS ATLANTIC CITY...
...A RETURN TO THE SCENE OF THE CRIME.
I THINK IT'S STUPID TO BE HERE.
I THINK IT'S SEXY. AND YOU MEAN A BOTCHED CRIME. I HEARD ABOUT YOUR LITTLE FACE-TO-FACE WITH MR. SHEPHERD.
BENITO DEAR...
YOU TRUST HIM?
...I DON'T TRUST ANYBODY.

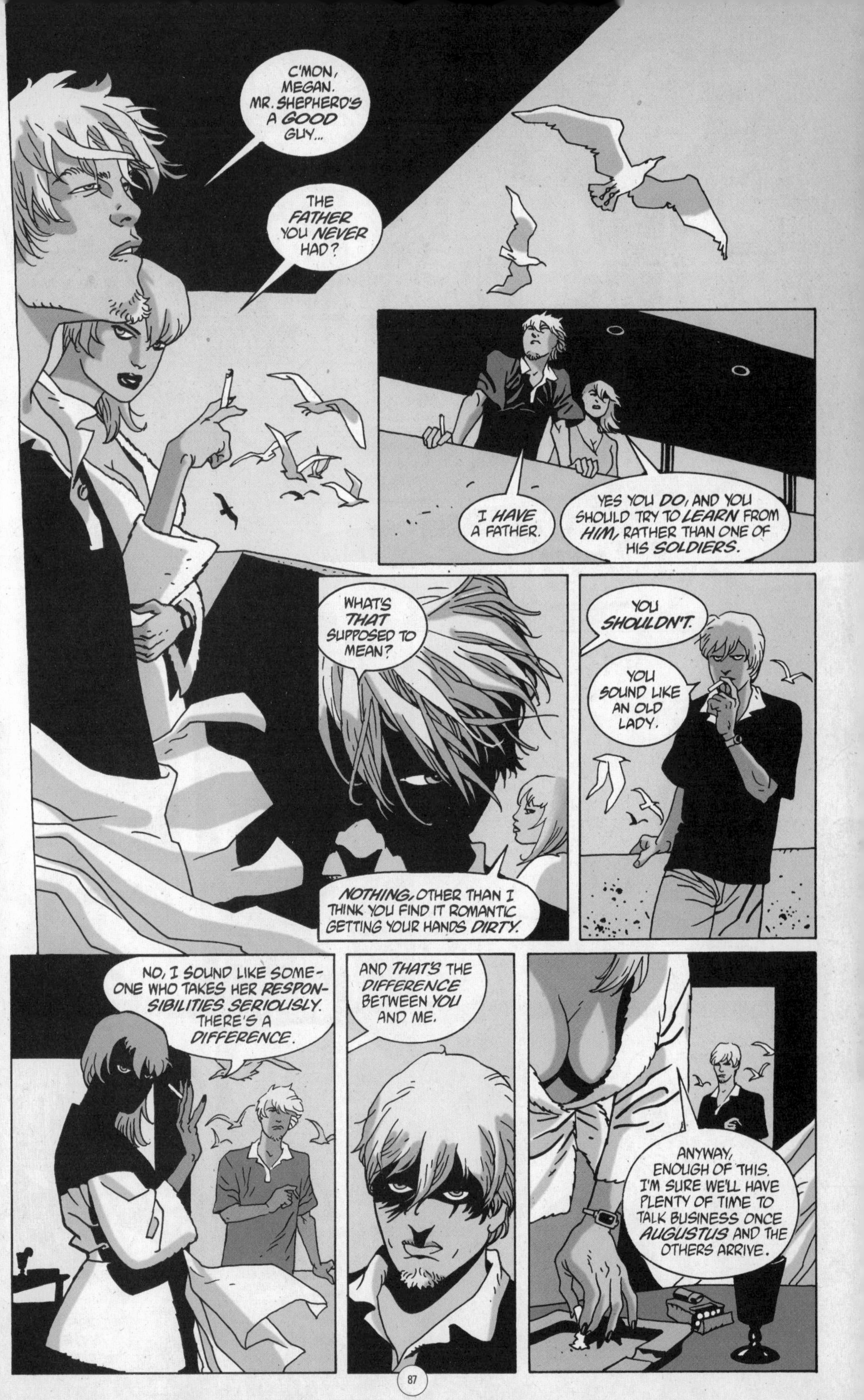
C'MON, MEGAN. MR. SHEPHERD'S A GOOD GUY...
THE FATHER YOU NEVER HAD?
I HAVE A FATHER.
YES YOU DO, AND YOU SHOULD TRY TO LEARN FROM HIM, RATHER THAN ONE OF HIS SOLDIERS.
WHAT'S THAT SUPPOSED TO MEAN?
NOTHING, OTHER THAN I THINK YOU FIND IT ROMANTIC GETTING YOUR HANDS DIRTY.
YOU SHOULDN'T.
YOU SOUND LIKE AN OLD LADY.
NO, I SOUND LIKE SOME-ONE WHO TAKES HER RESPON-SIBILITIES SERIOUSLY. THERE'S A DIFFERENCE.
AND THAT'S THE DIFFERENCE BETWEEN YOU AND ME.
ANYWAY, ENOUGH OF THIS. I'M SURE WE'LL HAVE PLENTY OF TIME TO TALK BUSINESS ONCE AUGUSTUS AND THE OTHERS ARRIVE.

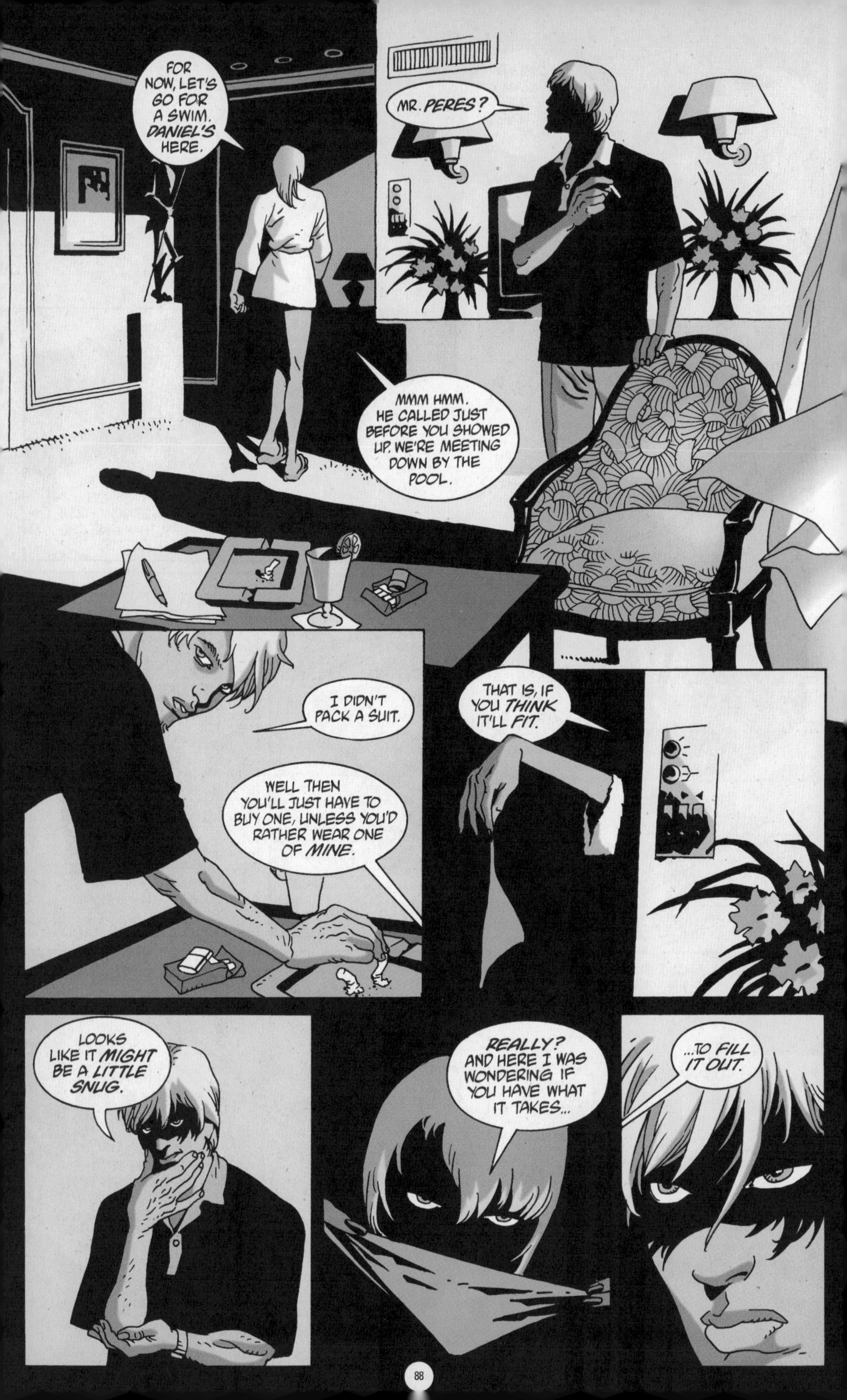
FOR NOW, LET'S GO FOR A SWIM. DANIEL'S HERE.
MR. PERES?
MMM HMM. HE CALLED JUST BEFORE YOU SHOWED UP. WE'RE MEETING DOWN BY THE POOL.
I DIDN'T PACK A SUIT.
WELL THEN YOU'LL JUST HAVE TO BUY ONE, UNLESS YOU'D RATHER WEAR ONE OF MINE.
THAT IS, IF YOU THINK IT'LL FIT.
LOOKS LIKE IT MIGHT BE A LITTLE SNUG.
REALLY? AND HERE I WAS WONDERING IF YOU HAVE WHAT IT TAKES...
...TO FILL IT OUT.

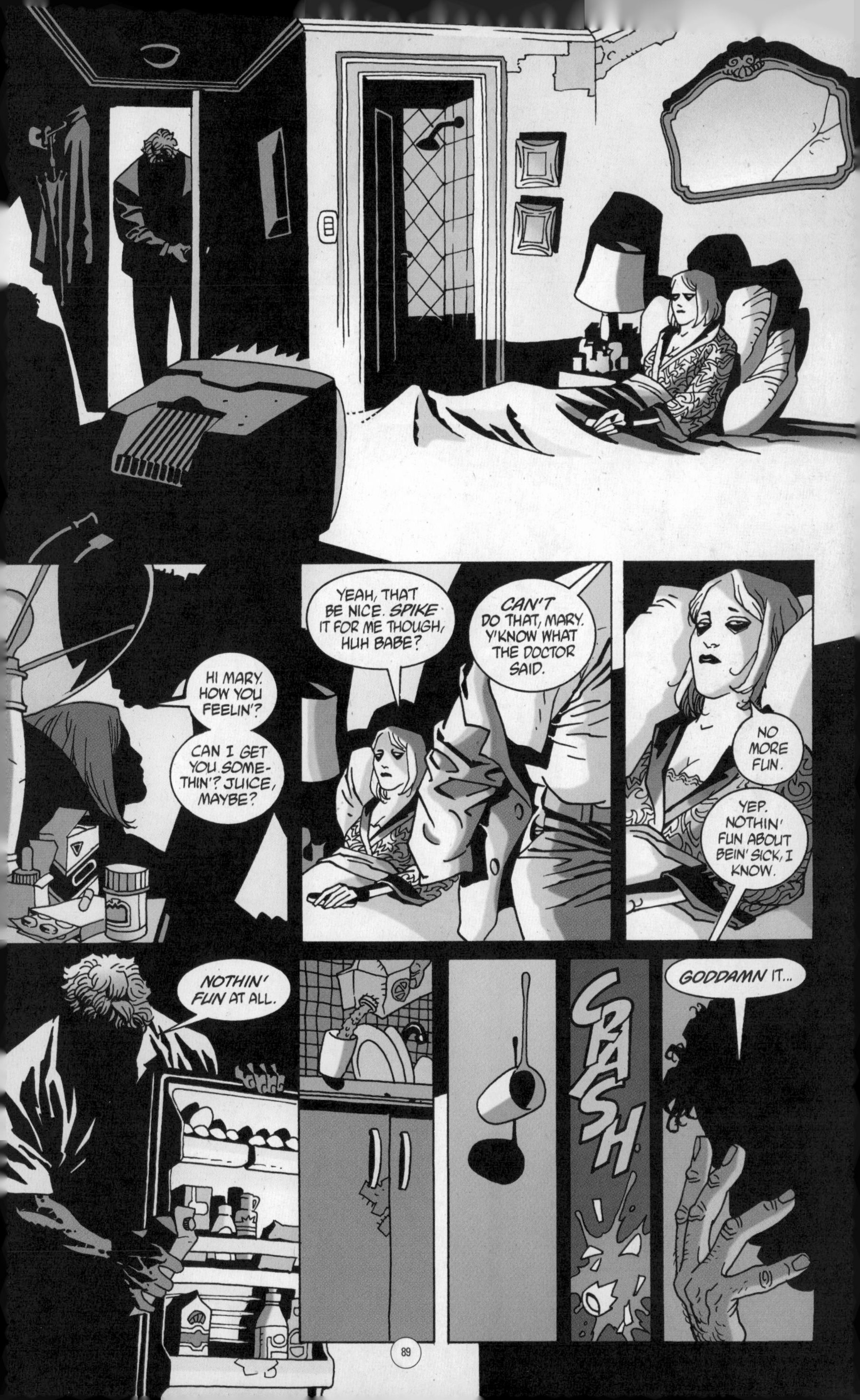
HI MARY. HOW YOU FEELIN'?
CAN I GET YOU SOME-THIN'? JUICE, MAYBE?
YEAH, THAT BE NICE. SPIKE IT FOR ME THOUGH, HUH BABE?
CAN'T DO THAT, MARY. Y'KNOW WHAT THE DOCTOR SAID.
NO MORE FUN.
YEP. NOTHIN' FUN ABOUT BEIN' SICK, I KNOW.
NOTHIN' FUN AT ALL.
CRASH
GODDAMN IT...

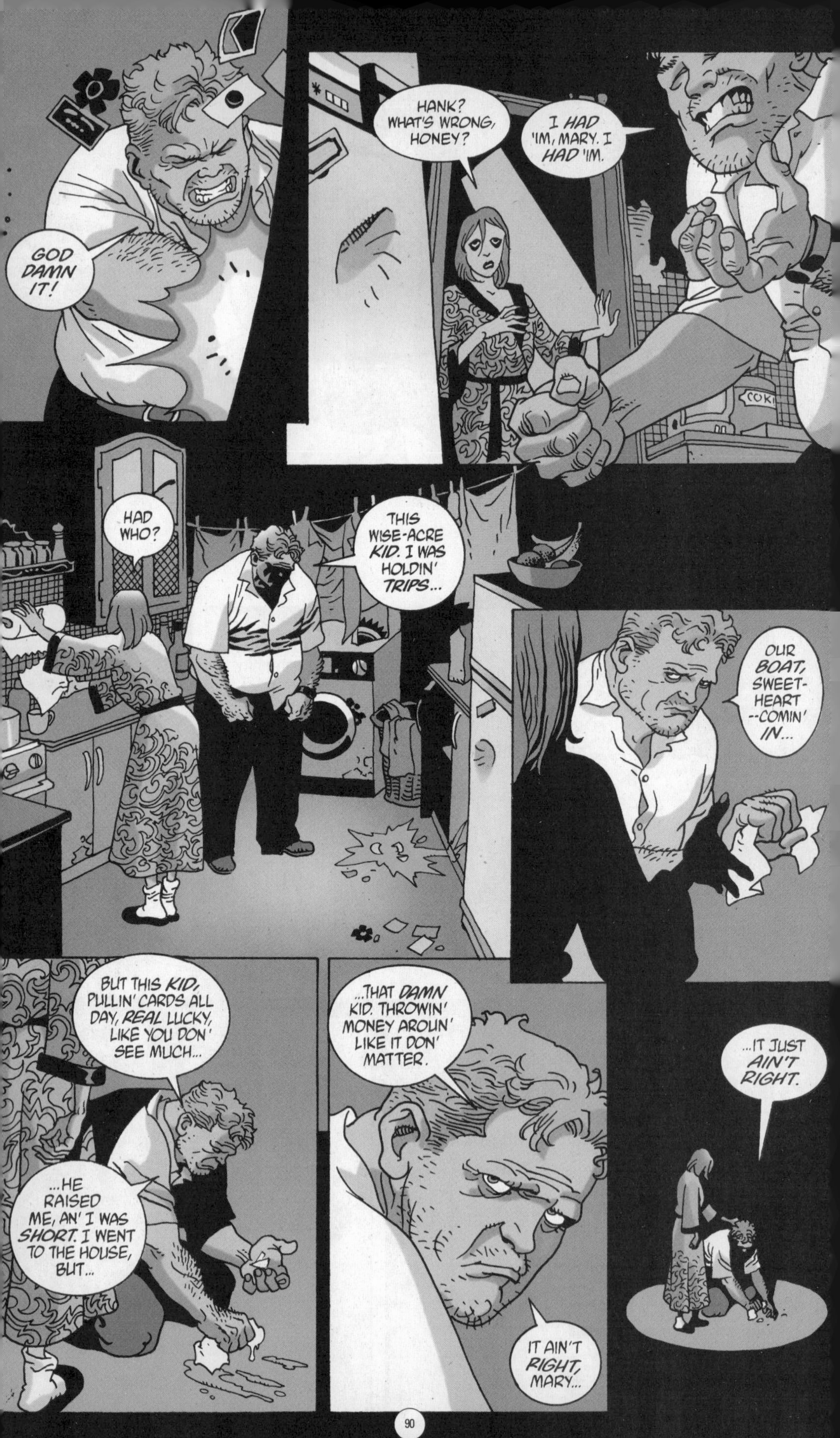
GOD DAMN IT!
HANK? WHAT'S WRONG, HONEY?
I HAD 'IM, MARY. I HAD 'IM.
COKE
HAD WHO?
THIS WISE-ACRE KID. I WAS HOLDIN' TRIPS...
OUR BOAT, SWEET-HEART --COMIN' IN...
BUT THIS KID, PULLIN' CARDS ALL DAY, REAL LUCKY, LIKE YOU DON' SEE MUCH...
...HE RAISED ME, AN' I WAS SHORT. I WENT TO THE HOUSE, BUT...
...THAT DAMN KID. THROWIN' MONEY AROUN' LIKE IT DON' MATTER.
IT AIN'T RIGHT, MARY...
...IT JUST AIN'T RIGHT.

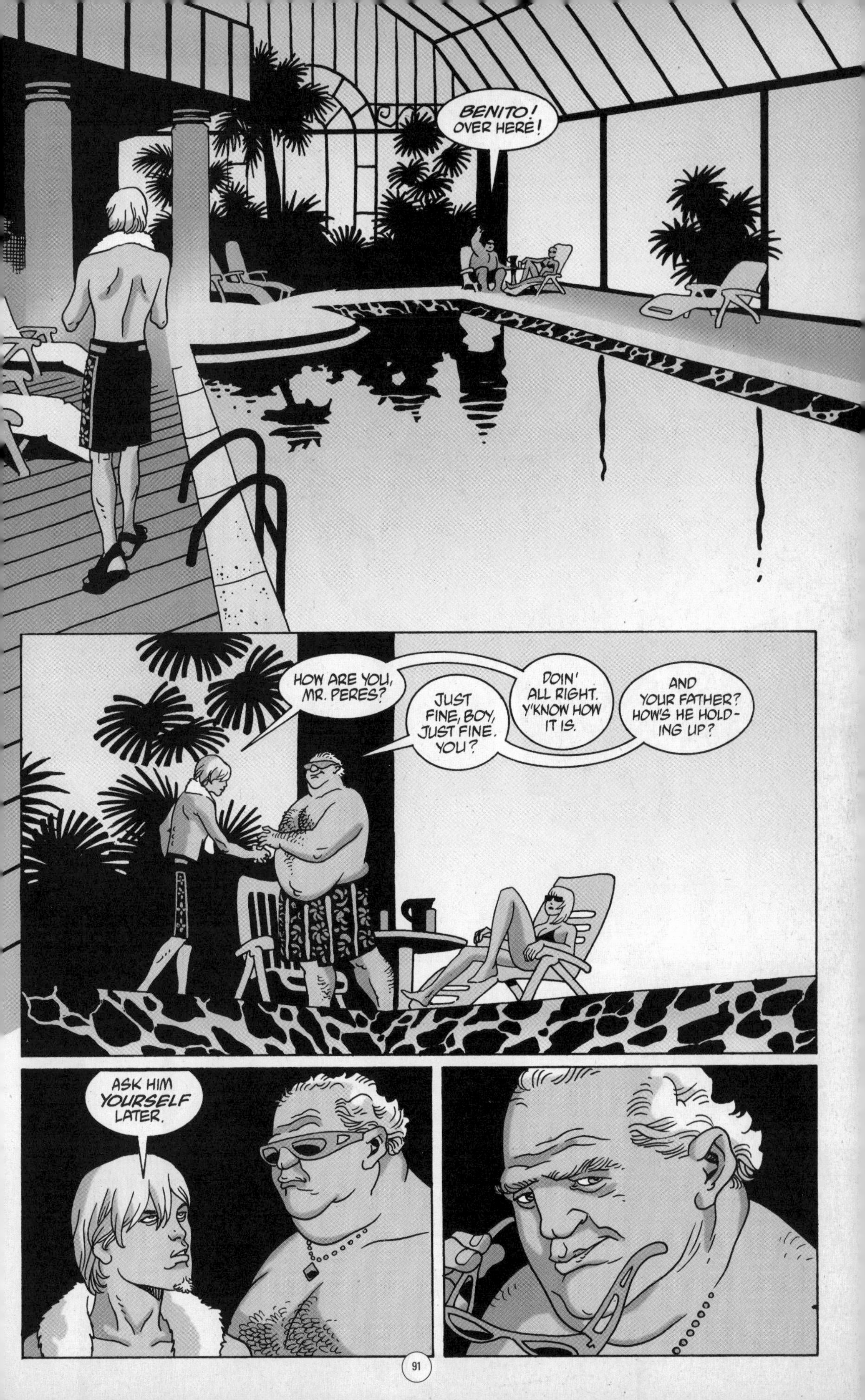
BENITO! OVER HERE!
HOW ARE YOU, MR. PERES?
JUST FINE, BOY, JUST FINE. YOU?
DOIN' ALL RIGHT. Y'KNOW HOW IT IS.
AND YOUR FATHER? HOW'S HE HOLDING UP?
ASK HIM YOURSELF LATER.

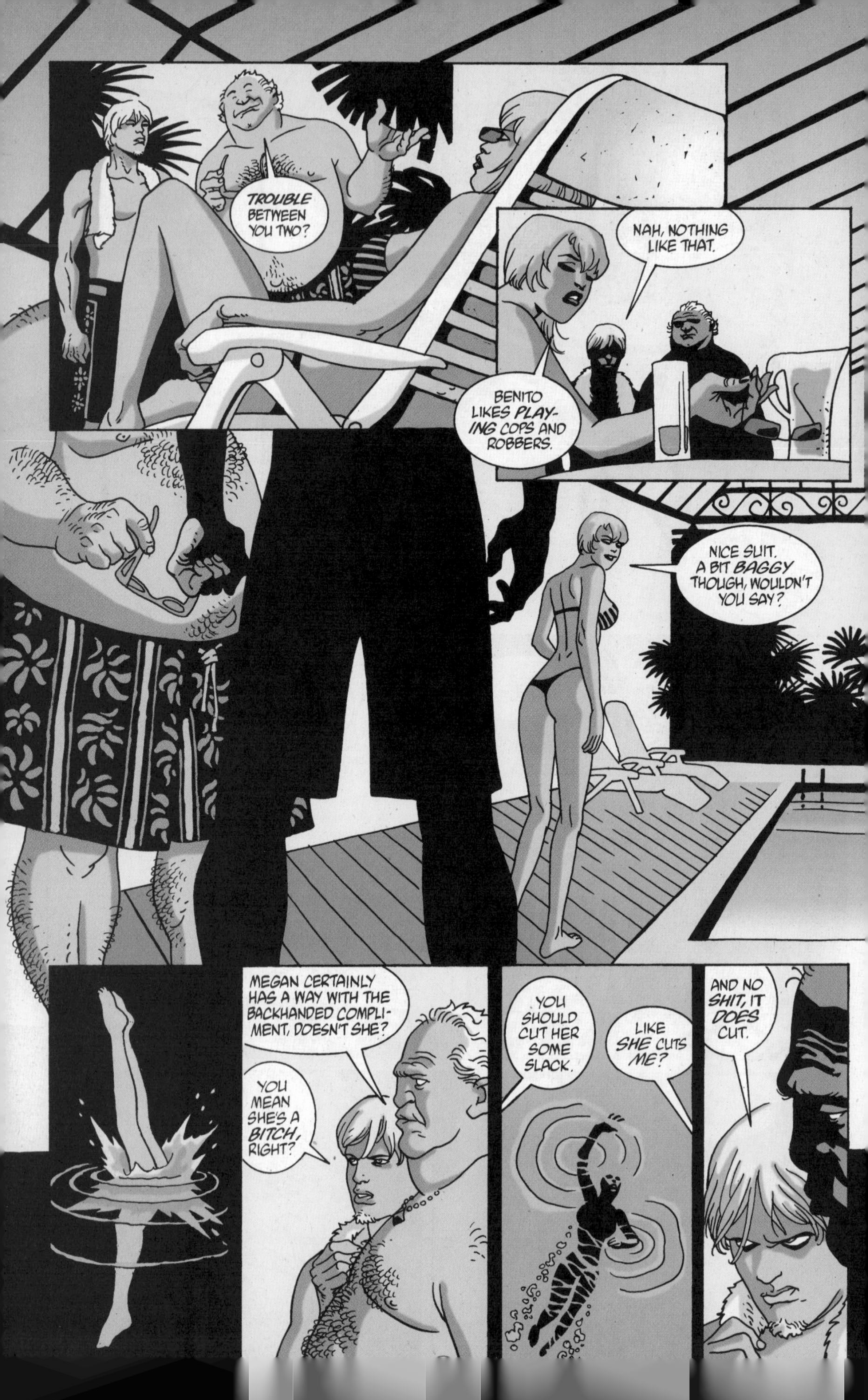
TROUBLE BETWEEN YOU TWO?
NAH, NOTHING LIKE THAT.
BENITO LIKES PLAYING COPS AND ROBBERS.
NICE SUIT. A BIT BAGGY THOUGH, WOULDN'T YOU SAY?
MEGAN CERTAINLY HAS A WAY WITH THE BACKHANDED COMPLIMENT, DOESN'T SHE?
YOU MEAN SHE'S A BITCH, RIGHT?
YOU SHOULD CUT HER SOME SLACK.
LIKE SHE CUTS ME?
AND NO SHIT, IT DOES CUT.

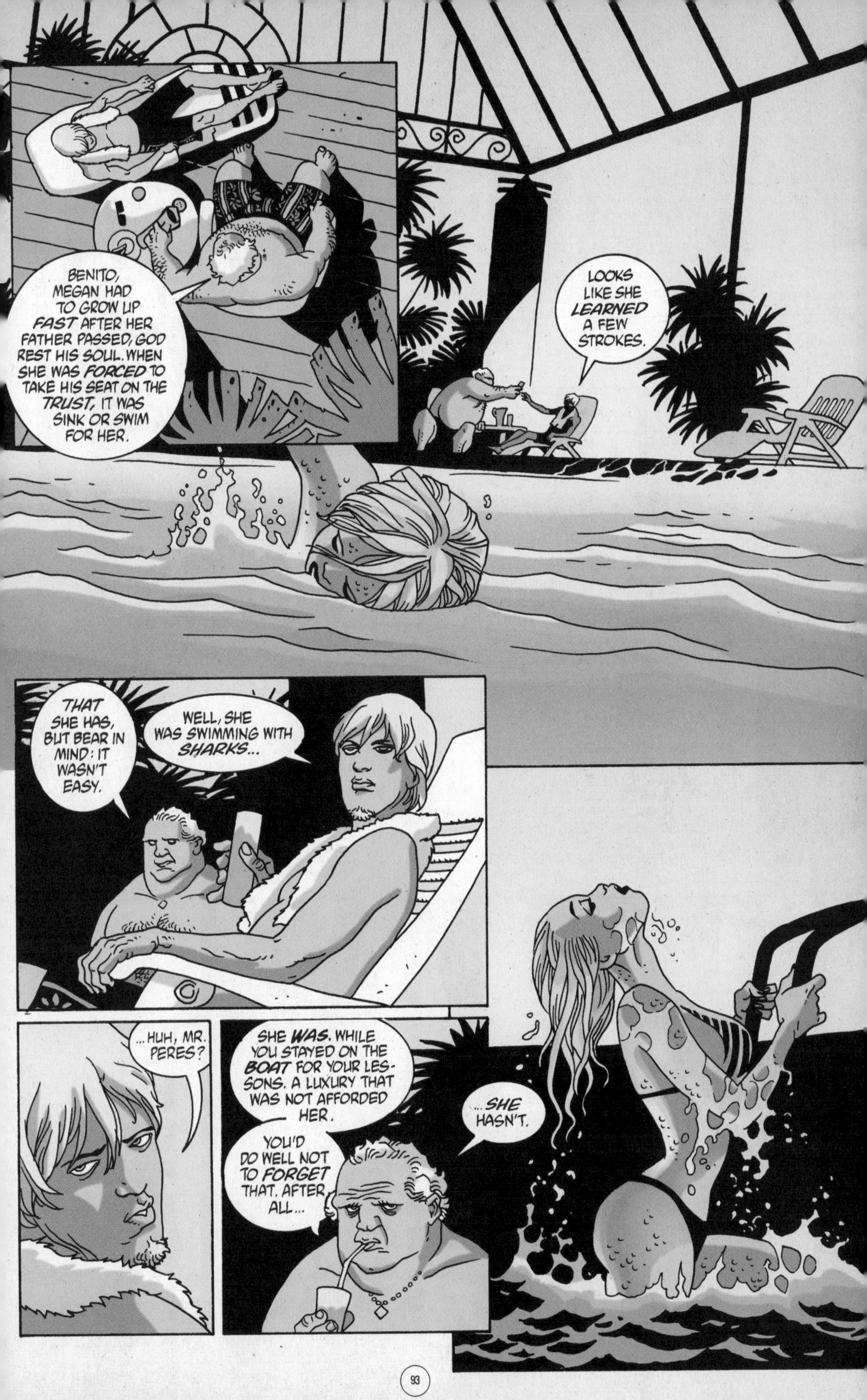
BENITO, MEGAN HAD TO GROW UP FAST AFTER HER FATHER PASSED, GOD REST HIS SOUL. WHEN SHE WAS FORCED TO TAKE HIS SEAT ON THE TRUST, IT WAS SINK OR SWIM FOR HER.
LOOKS LIKE SHE LEARNED A FEW STROKES.
WELL, SHE WAS SWIMMING WITH SHARKS...
THAT SHE HAS, BUT BEAR IN MIND: IT WASN'T EASY.
...HUH, MR. PERES?
SHE WAS. WHILE YOU STAYED ON THE BOAT FOR YOUR LESSONS. A LUXURY THAT WAS NOT AFFORDED HER.
YOU'D DO WELL NOT TO FORGET THAT. AFTER ALL...
...SHE HASN'T.

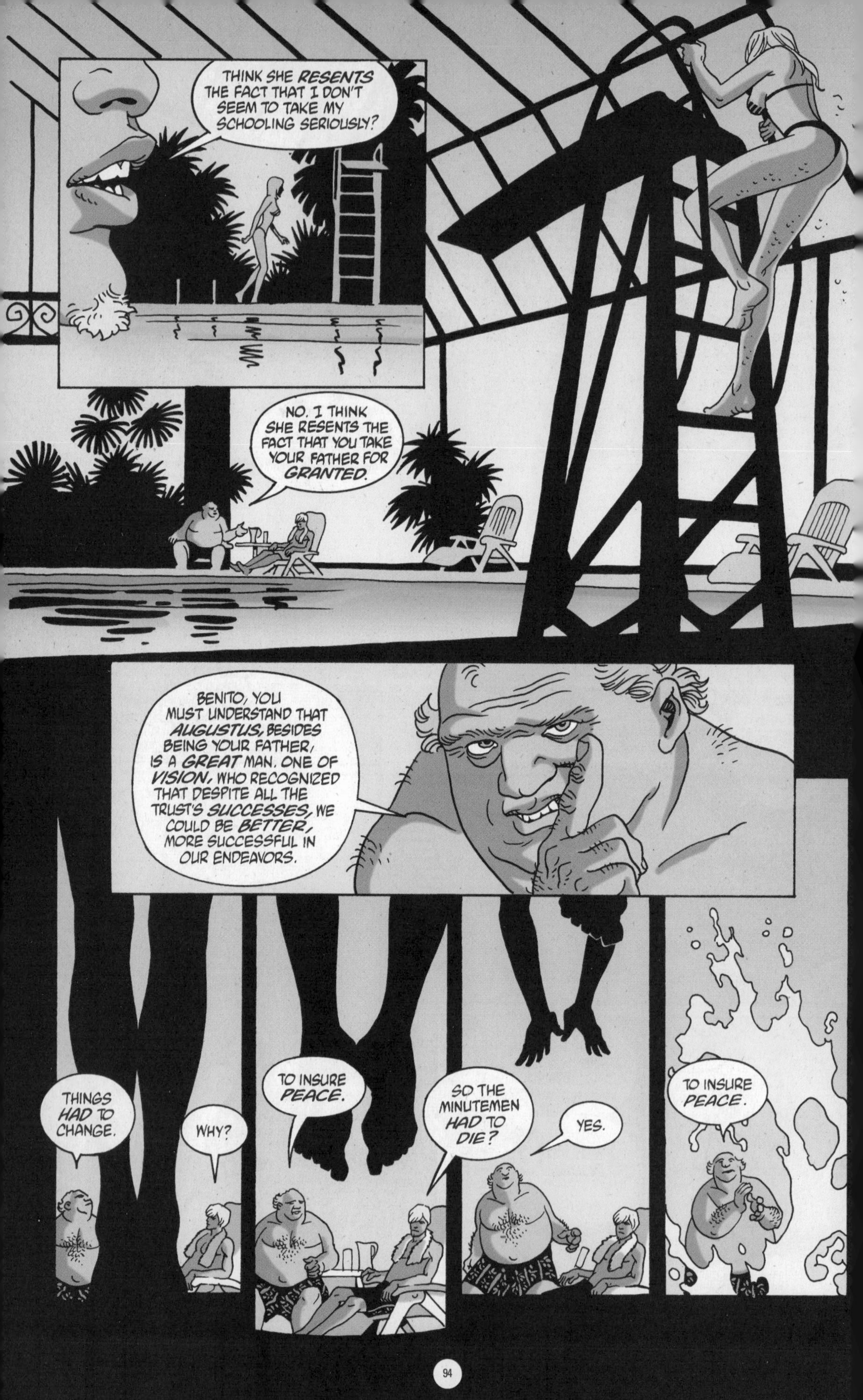
THINK SHE RESENTS THE FACT THAT I DON'T SEEM TO TAKE MY SCHOOLING SERIOUSLY?
NO. I THINK SHE RESENTS THE FACT THAT YOU TAKE YOUR FATHER FOR GRANTED.
BENITO, YOU MUST UNDERSTAND THAT AUGUSTUS, BESIDES BEING YOUR FATHER, IS A GREAT MAN. ONE OF VISION, WHO RECOGNIZED THAT DESPITE ALL THE TRUST'S SUCCESSES, WE COULD BE BETTER, MORE SUCCESSFUL IN OUR ENDEAVORS.
THINGS HAD TO CHANGE.
WHY?
TO INSURE PEACE.
SO THE MINUTEMEN HAD TO DIE?
YES.
TO INSURE PEACE.

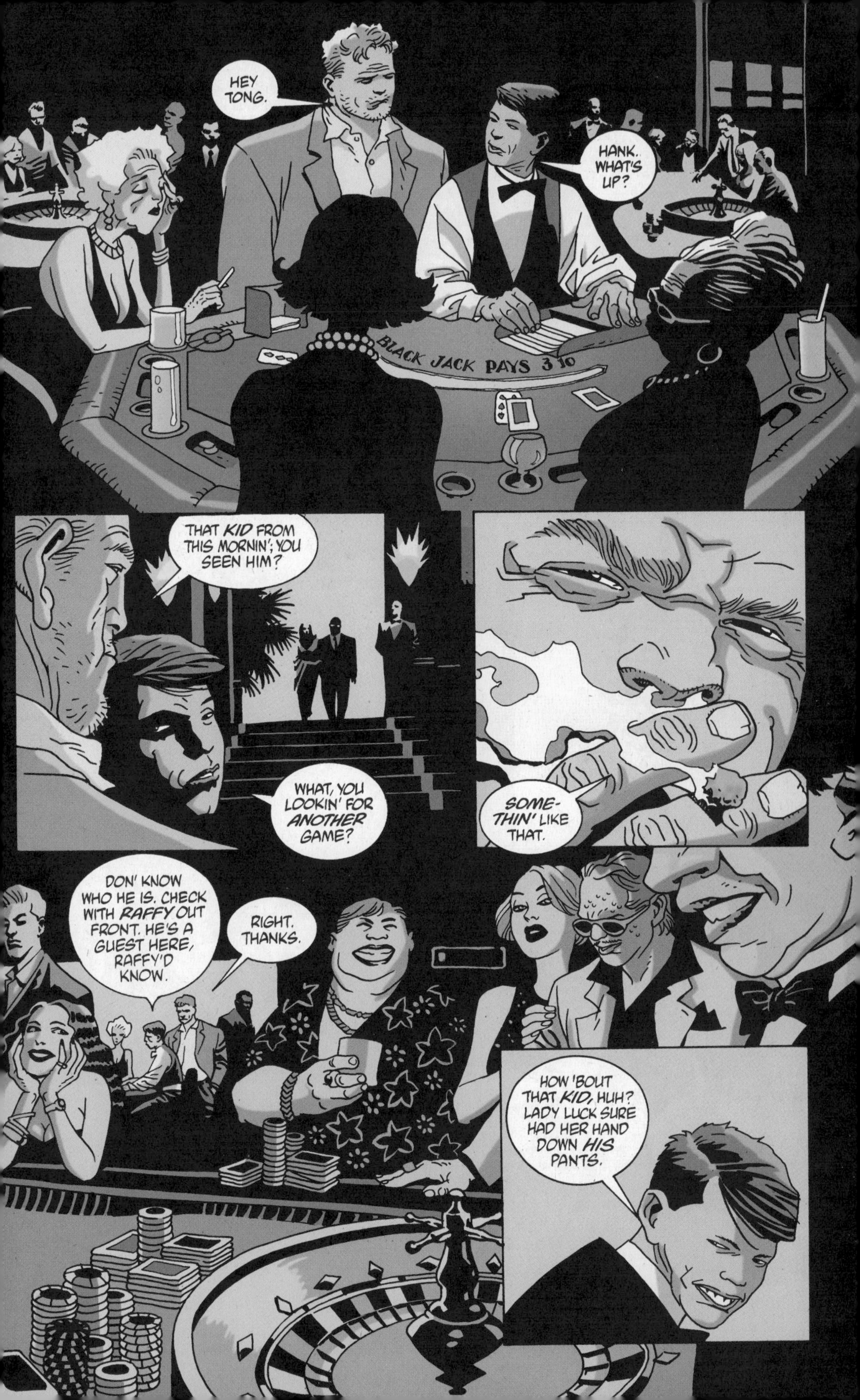
HEY TONG.
HANK.. WHAT'S UP?
THAT KID FROM THIS MORNIN'; YOU SEEN HIM?
WHAT, YOU LOOKIN' FOR ANOTHER GAME?
SOME-THIN' LIKE THAT.
DON' KNOW WHO HE IS. CHECK WITH RAFFY OUT FRONT. HE'S A GUEST HERE, RAFFY'D KNOW.
RIGHT. THANKS.
HOW 'BOUT THAT KID, HUH? LADY LUCK SURE HAD HER HAND DOWN HIS PANTS.
BLACK JACK PAYS 3 to

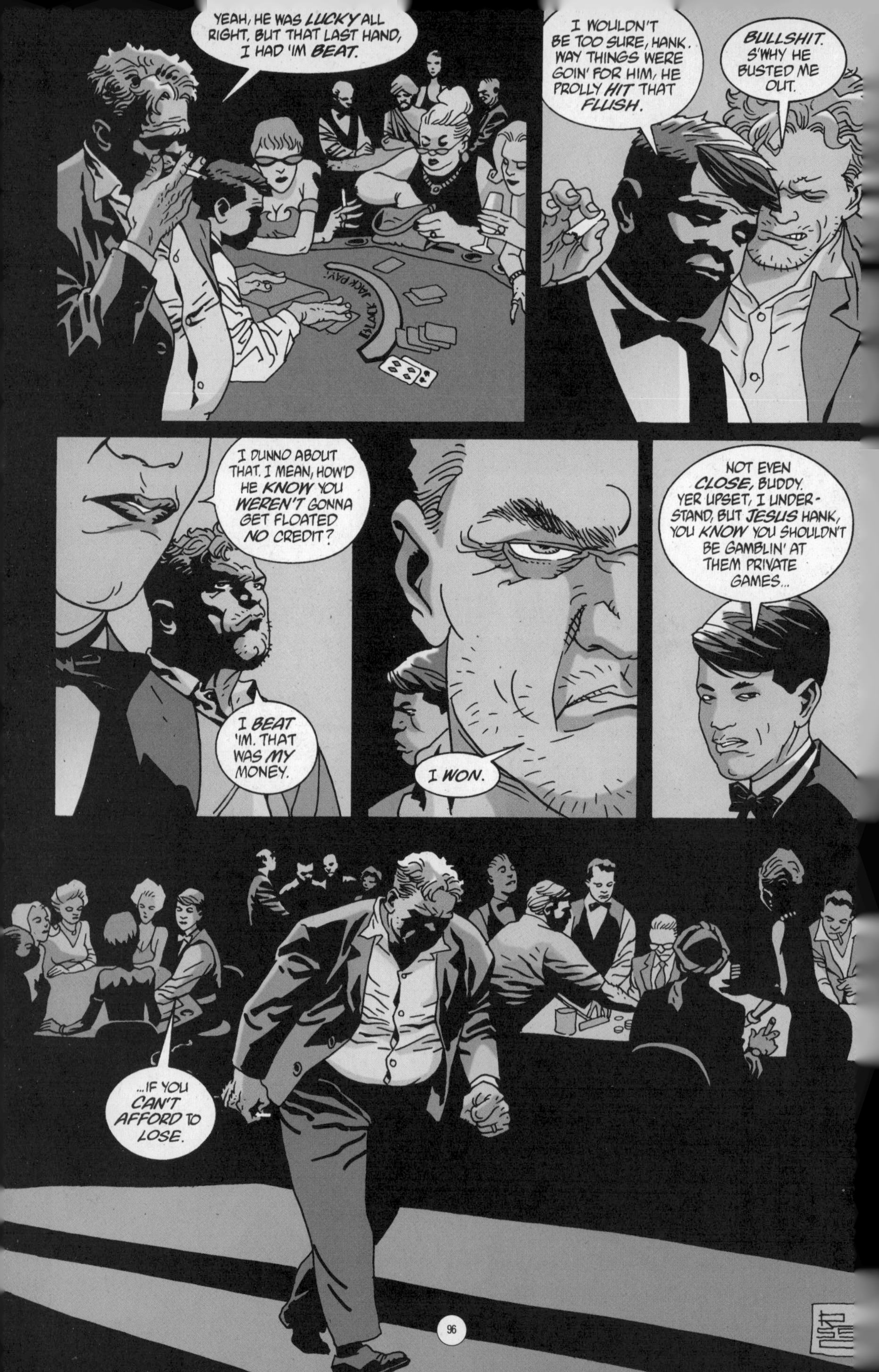
YEAH, HE WAS LUCKY ALL RIGHT, BUT THAT LAST HAND, I HAD 'IM BEAT.
BLACK JACK PAYS
I WOULDN'T BE TOO SURE, HANK. WAY THINGS WERE GOIN' FOR HIM, HE PROLLY HIT THAT FLUSH.
BULLSHIT. S'WHY HE BUSTED ME OUT.
I DUNNO ABOUT THAT. I MEAN, HOW'D HE KNOW YOU WEREN'T GONNA GET FLOATED NO CREDIT?
I BEAT 'IM. THAT WAS MY MONEY.
I WON.
NOT EVEN CLOSE, BUDDY. YER UPSET, I UNDER-STAND, BUT JESUS HANK, YOU KNOW YOU SHOULDN'T BE GAMBLIN' AT THEM PRIVATE GAMES...
...IF YOU CAN'T AFFORD TO LOSE.

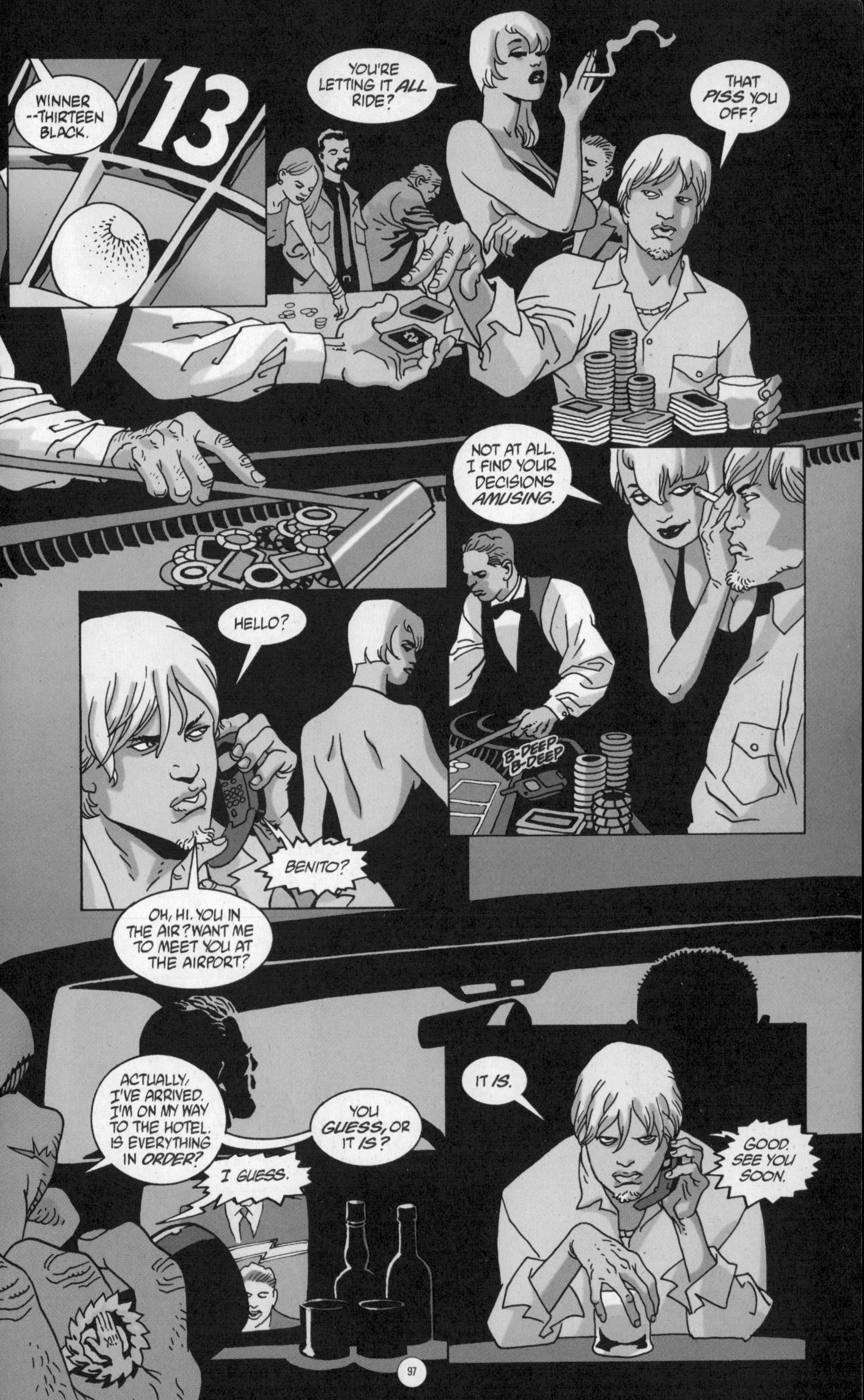

WINNER --THIRTEEN BLACK.
13
YOU'RE LETTING IT ALL RIDE?
THAT PISS YOU OFF?
NOT AT ALL. I FIND YOUR DECISIONS AMUSING.
B-DEEP B-DEEP
HELLO?
BENITO?
OH, HI. YOU IN THE AIR? WANT ME TO MEET YOU AT THE AIRPORT?
ACTUALLY, I'VE ARRIVED. I'M ON MY WAY TO THE HOTEL. IS EVERYTHING IN ORDER?
I GUESS.
YOU GUESS, OR IT IS?
IT IS.
GOOD. SEE YOU SOON.

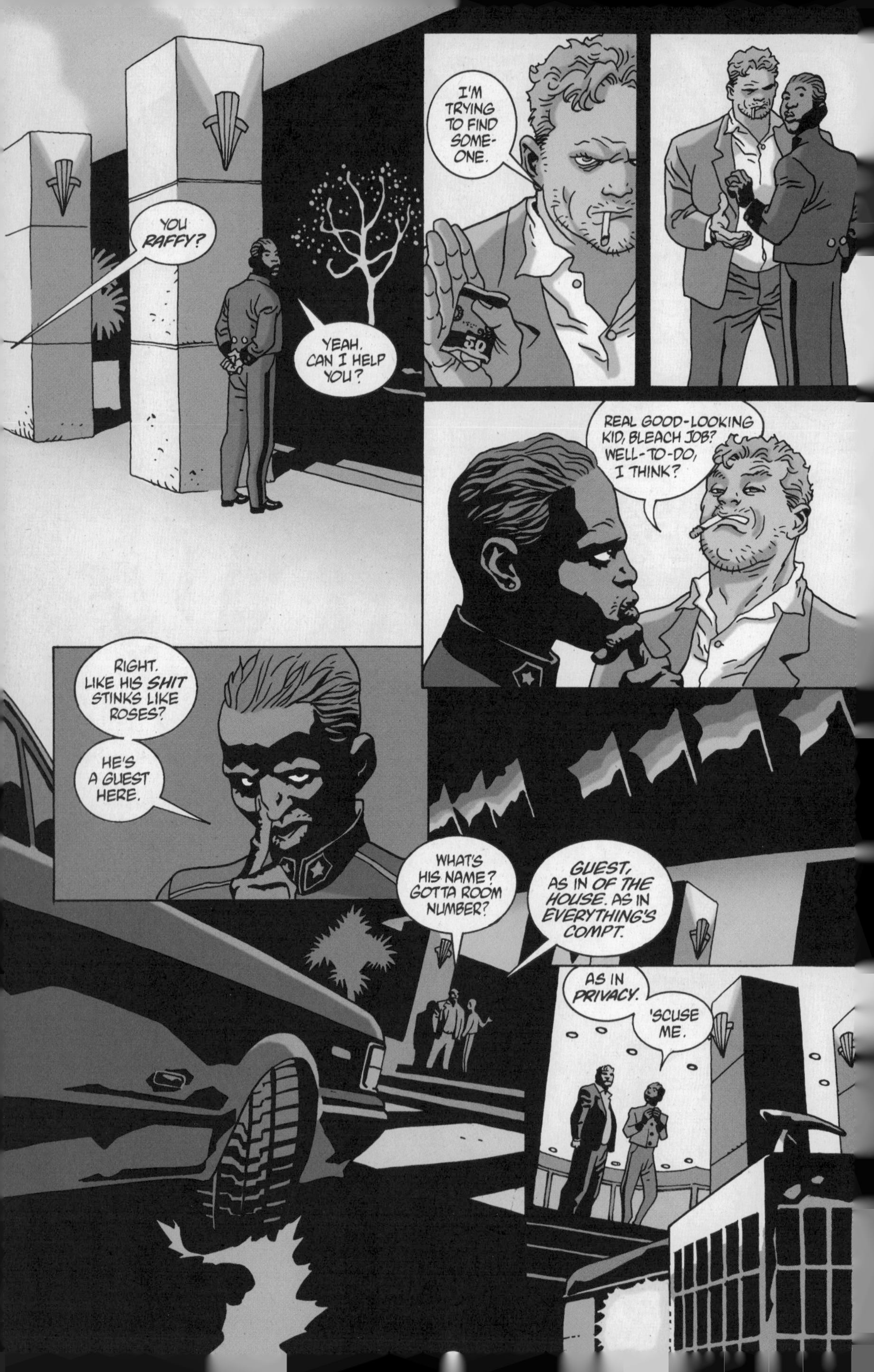
YOU RAFFY?
YEAH. CAN I HELP YOU?
I'M TRYING TO FIND SOME-ONE.
REAL GOOD-LOOKING KID, BLEACH JOB? WELL-TO-DO, I THINK?
RIGHT. LIKE HIS SHIT STINKS LIKE ROSES?
HE'S A GUEST HERE.
WHAT'S HIS NAME? GOTTA ROOM NUMBER?
GUEST, AS IN OF THE HOUSE. AS IN EVERYTHING'S COMPT.
AS IN PRIVACY.
'SCUSE ME.

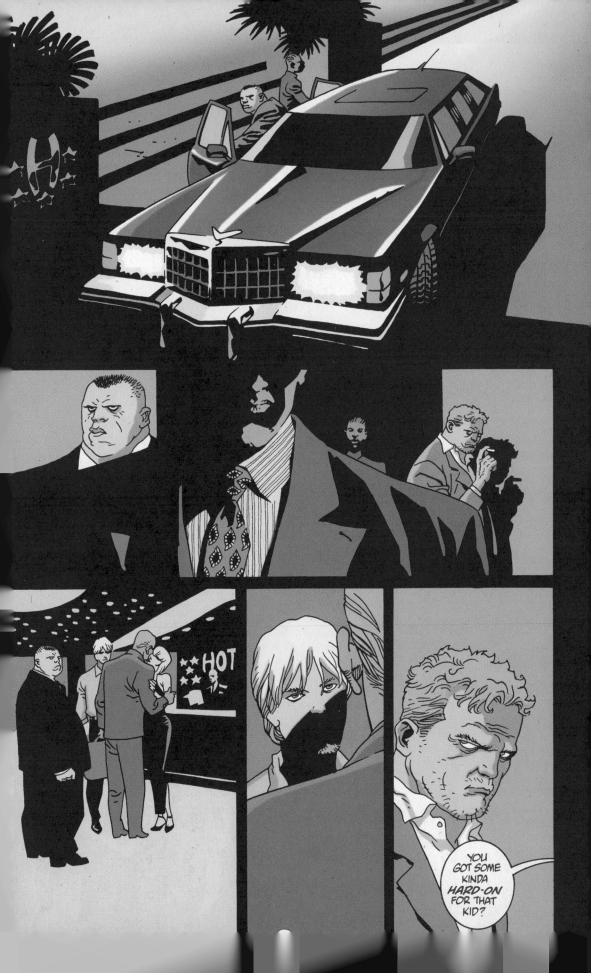

YOU GOT SOME KINDA *HARD-ON* FOR THAT KID?

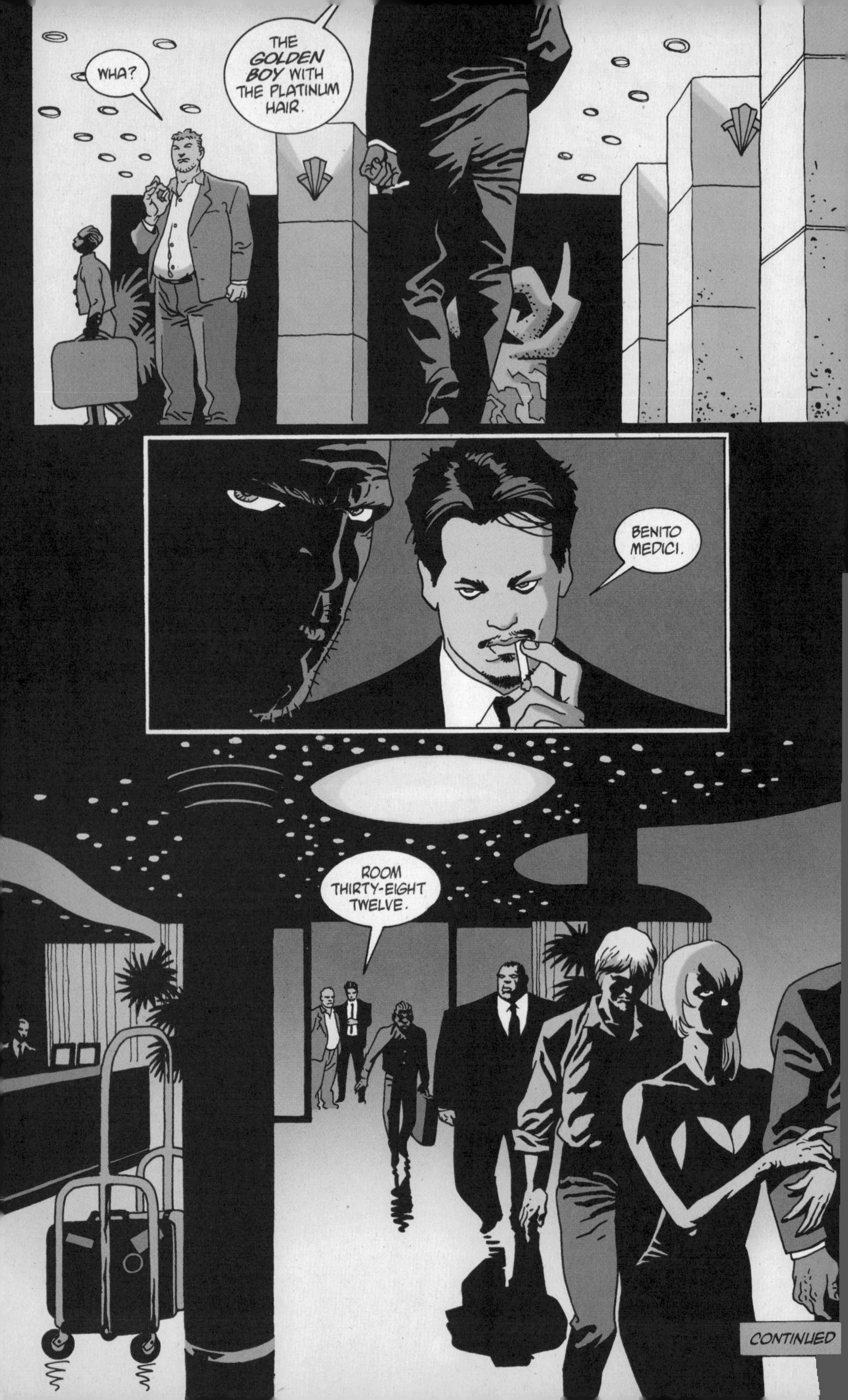
WHA?
THE GOLDEN BOY WITH THE PLATINUM HAIR.
BENITO MEDICI.
ROOM THIRTY-EIGHT TWELVE.
CONTINUED

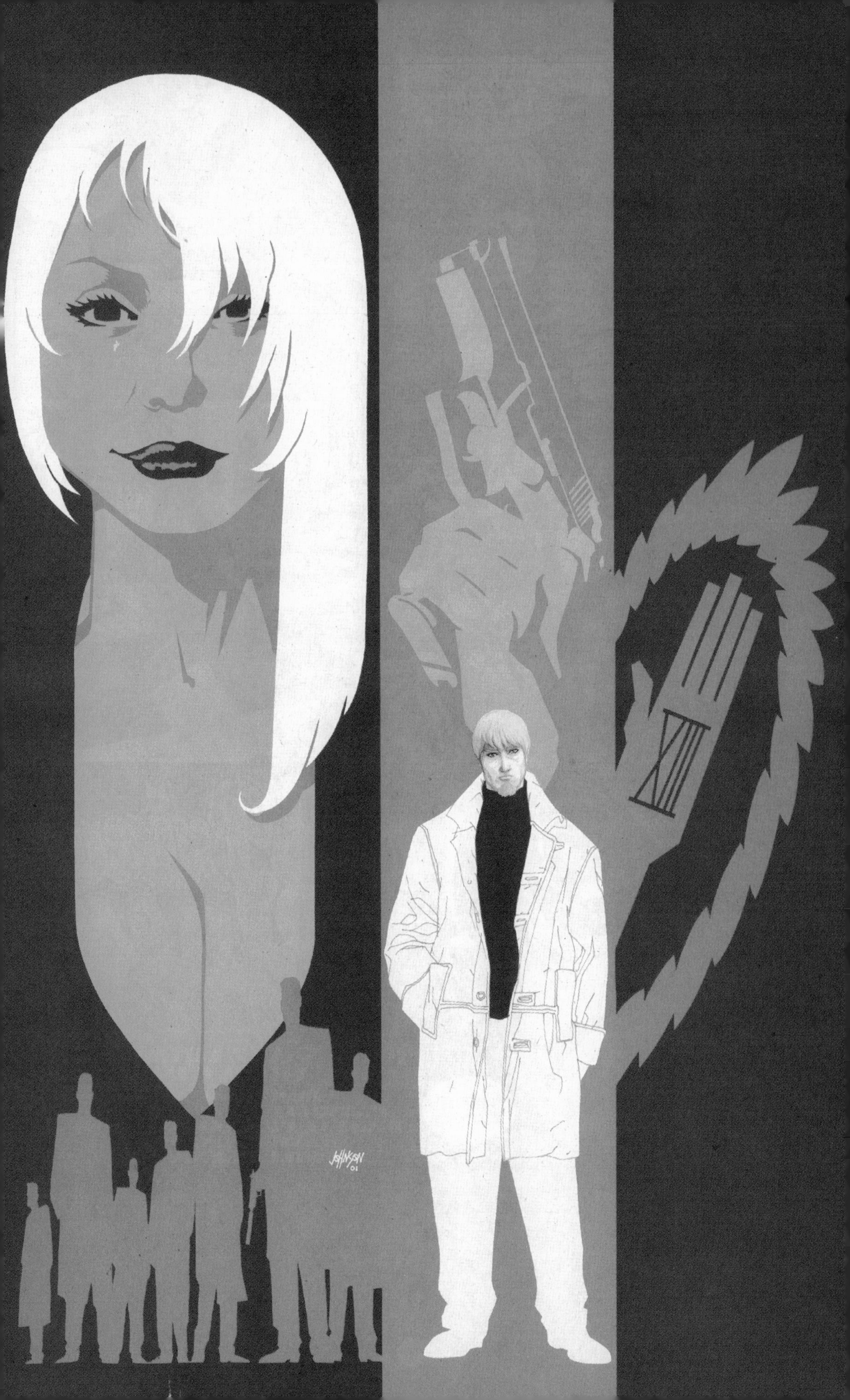
XIII
JOHNSON '01

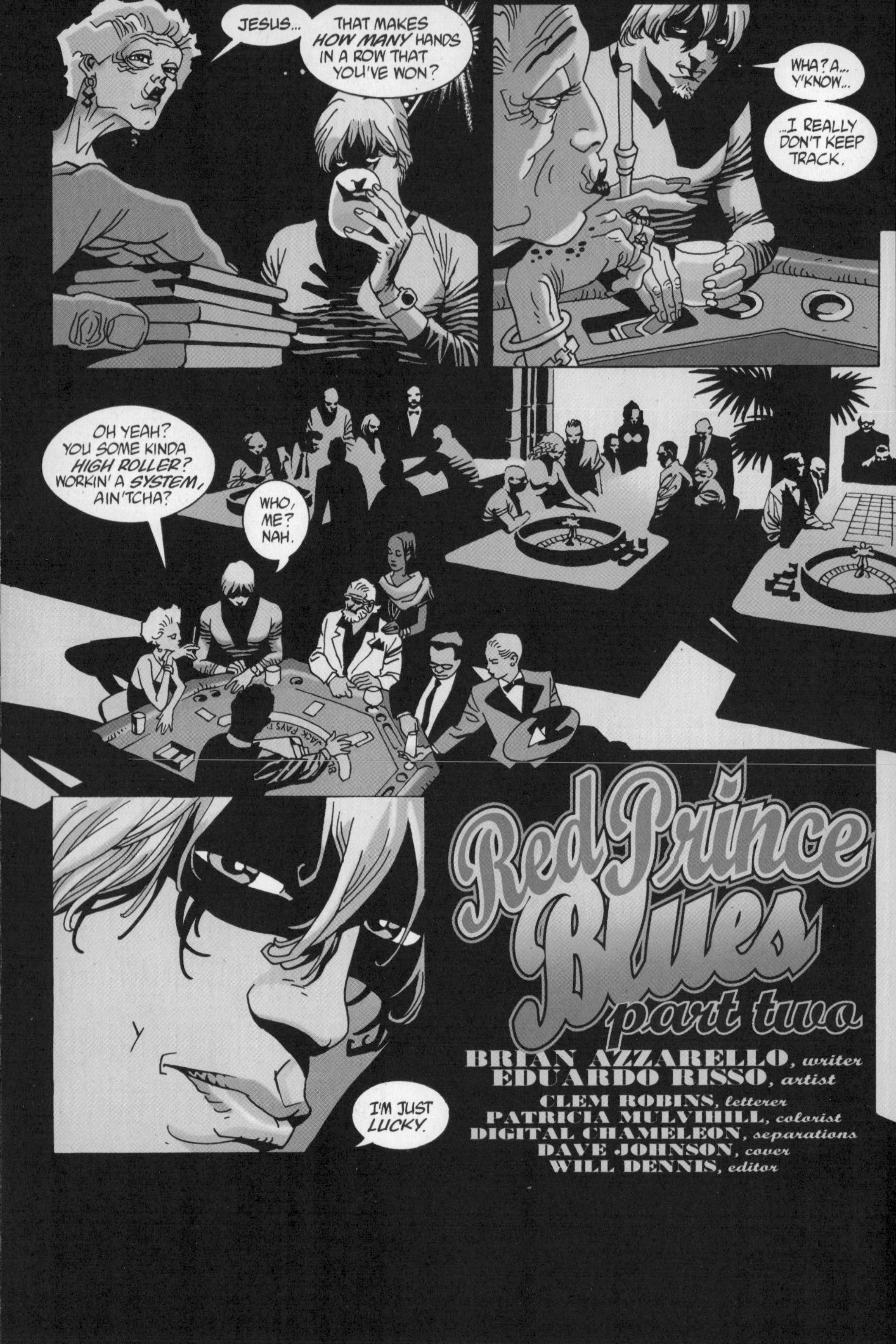
JESUS...
THAT MAKES HOW MANY HANDS IN A ROW THAT YOU'VE WON?
WHA? A... Y'KNOW...
...I REALLY DON'T KEEP TRACK.
OH YEAH? YOU SOME KINDA HIGH ROLLER? WORKIN' A SYSTEM, AIN'TCHA?
WHO, ME? NAH.
I'M JUST LUCKY.
Red Prince Blues
part two
BRIAN AZZARELLO, writer
EDUARDO RISSO, artist
CLEM ROBINS, letterer
PATRICIA MULVIHILL, colorist
DIGITAL CHAMELEON, separations
DAVE JOHNSON, cover
WILL DENNIS, editor

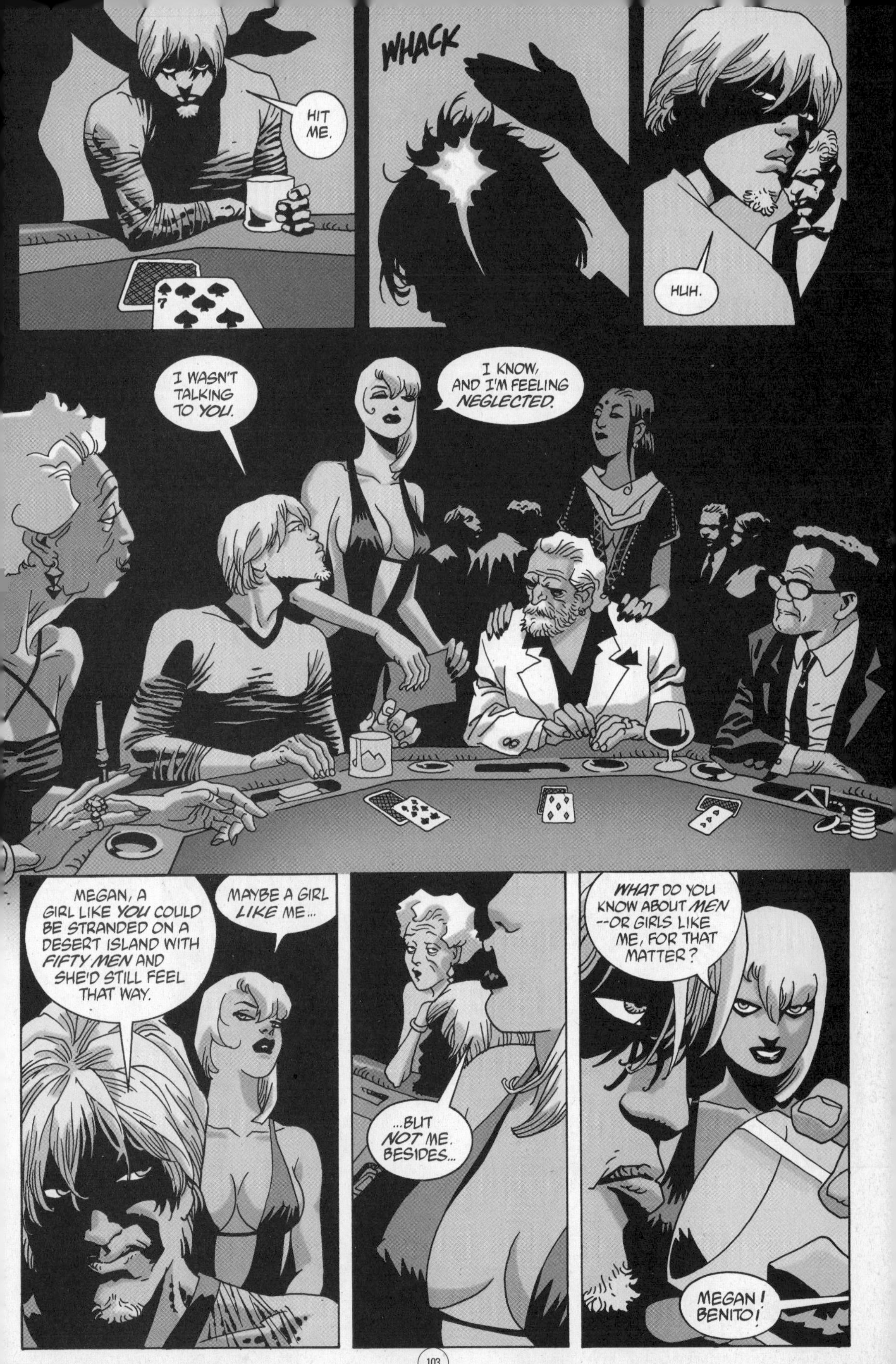

HIT ME.
WHACK
HUH.
I WASN'T TALKING TO YOU.
I KNOW, AND I'M FEELING NEGLECTED.
MEGAN, A GIRL LIKE YOU COULD BE STRANDED ON A DESERT ISLAND WITH FIFTY MEN AND SHE'D STILL FEEL THAT WAY.
MAYBE A GIRL LIKE ME...
...BUT NOT ME. BESIDES...
WHAT DO YOU KNOW ABOUT MEN --OR GIRLS LIKE ME, FOR THAT MATTER?
MEGAN! BENITO!

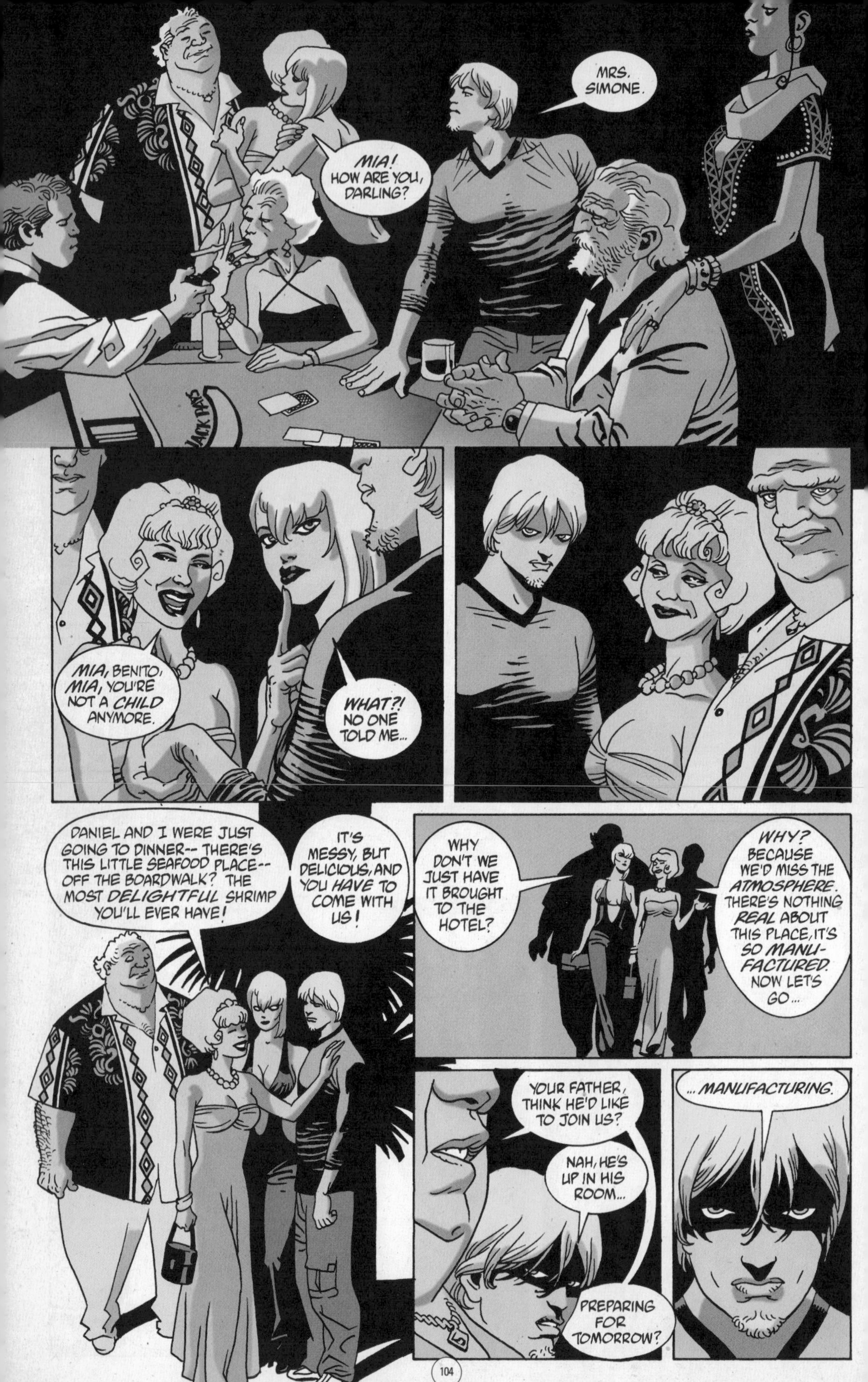
MRS. SIMONE.
MIA! HOW ARE YOU, DARLING?
MIA, BENITO. MIA, YOU'RE NOT A CHILD ANYMORE.
WHAT?! NO ONE TOLD ME...
DANIEL AND I WERE JUST GOING TO DINNER-- THERE'S THIS LITTLE SEAFOOD PLACE-- OFF THE BOARDWALK? THE MOST DELIGHTFUL SHRIMP YOU'LL EVER HAVE!
IT'S MESSY, BUT DELICIOUS, AND YOU HAVE TO COME WITH US!
WHY DON'T WE JUST HAVE IT BROUGHT TO THE HOTEL?
WHY? BECAUSE WE'D MISS THE ATMOSPHERE. THERE'S NOTHING REAL ABOUT THIS PLACE, IT'S SO MANUFACTURED. NOW LET'S GO...
YOUR FATHER, THINK HE'D LIKE TO JOIN US?
NAH, HE'S UP IN HIS ROOM...
PREPARING FOR TOMORROW?
...MANUFACTURING.

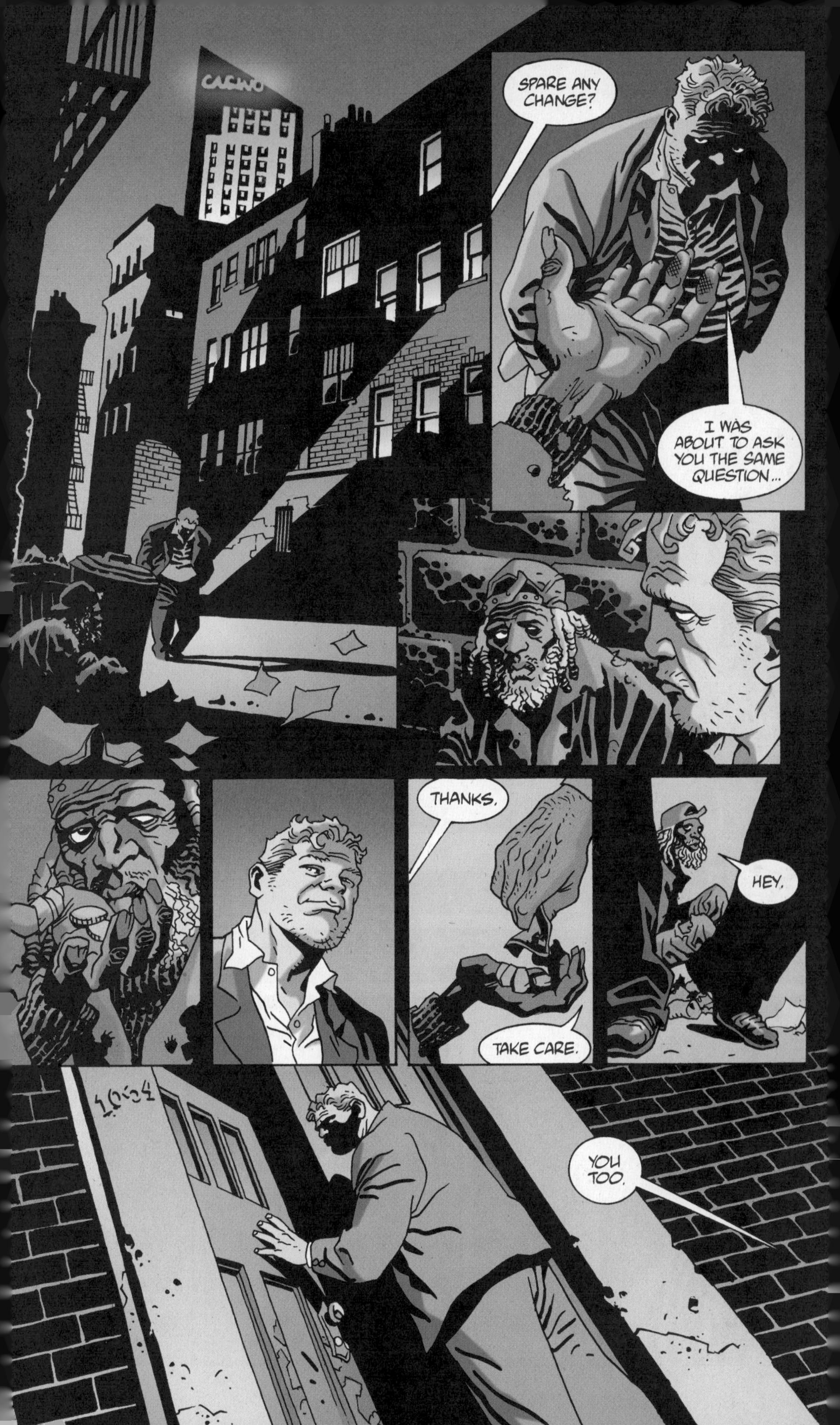
CASINO
SPARE ANY CHANGE?
I WAS ABOUT TO ASK YOU THE SAME QUESTION...
THANKS.
TAKE CARE.
HEY.
YOU TOO.

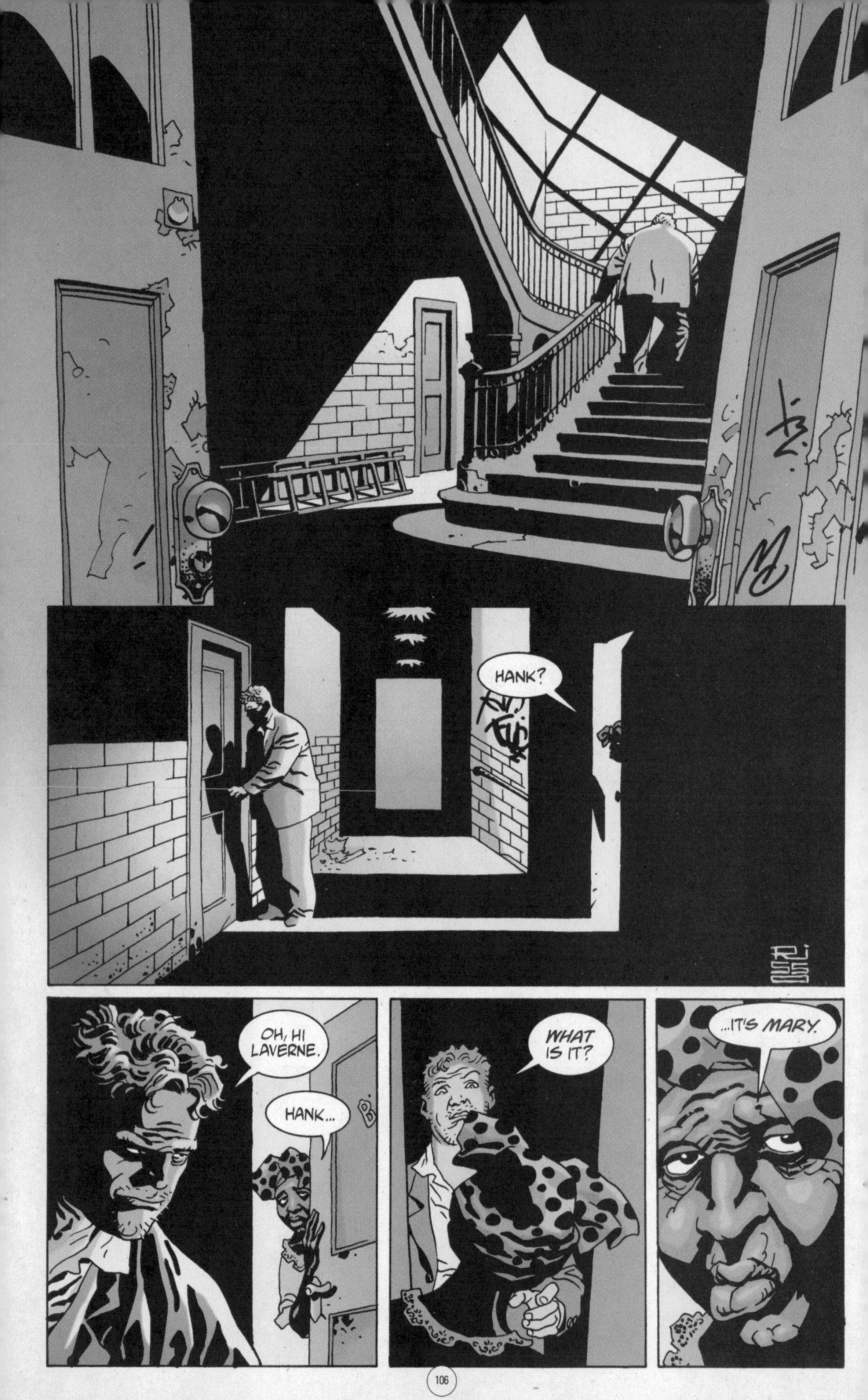
HANK?
OH, HI LAVERNE.
HANK...
WHAT IS IT?
...IT'S MARY.

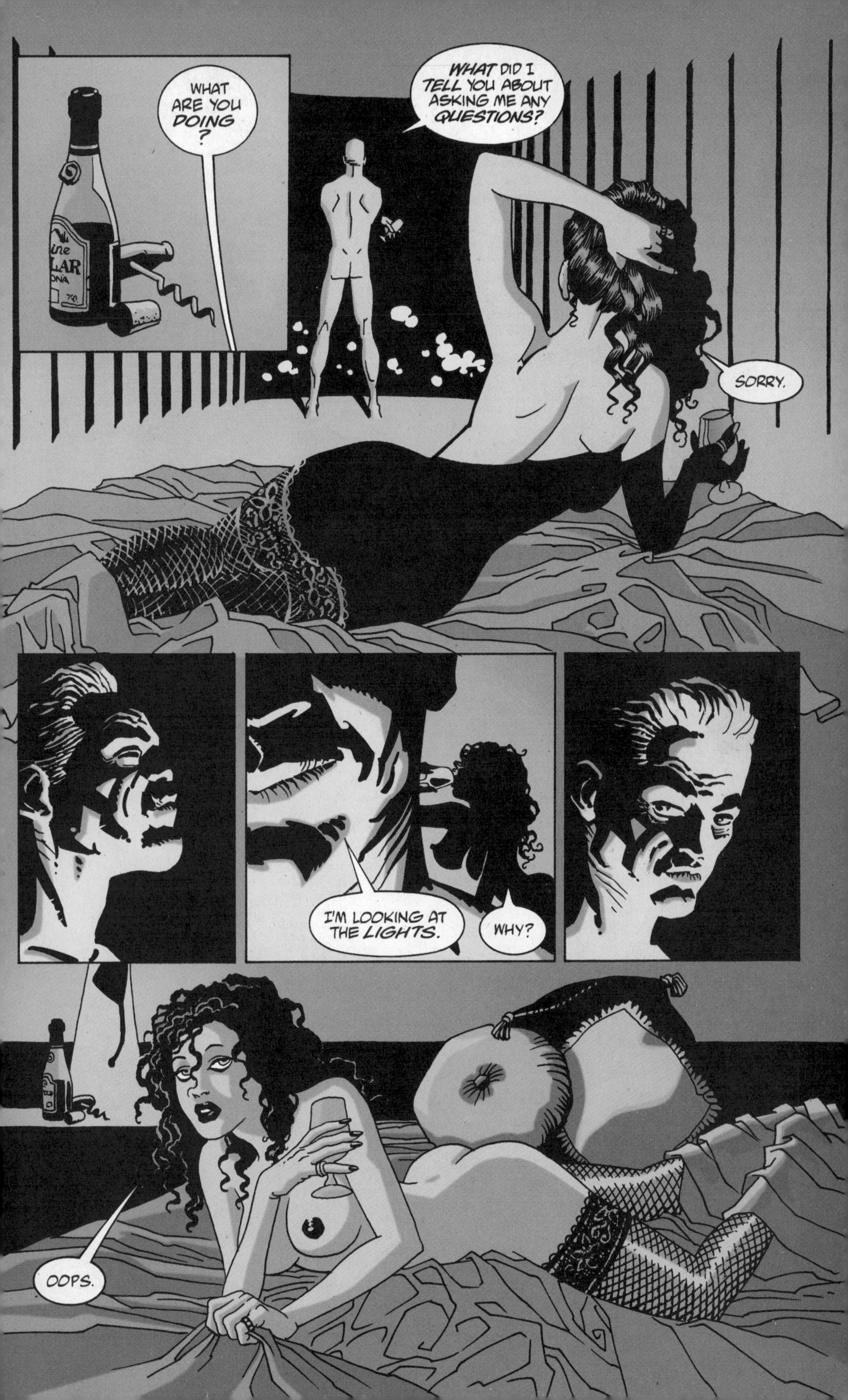
WHAT ARE YOU DOING ?
WHAT DID I TELL YOU ABOUT ASKING ME ANY QUESTIONS?
SORRY.
I'M LOOKING AT THE LIGHTS.
WHY?
OOPS.

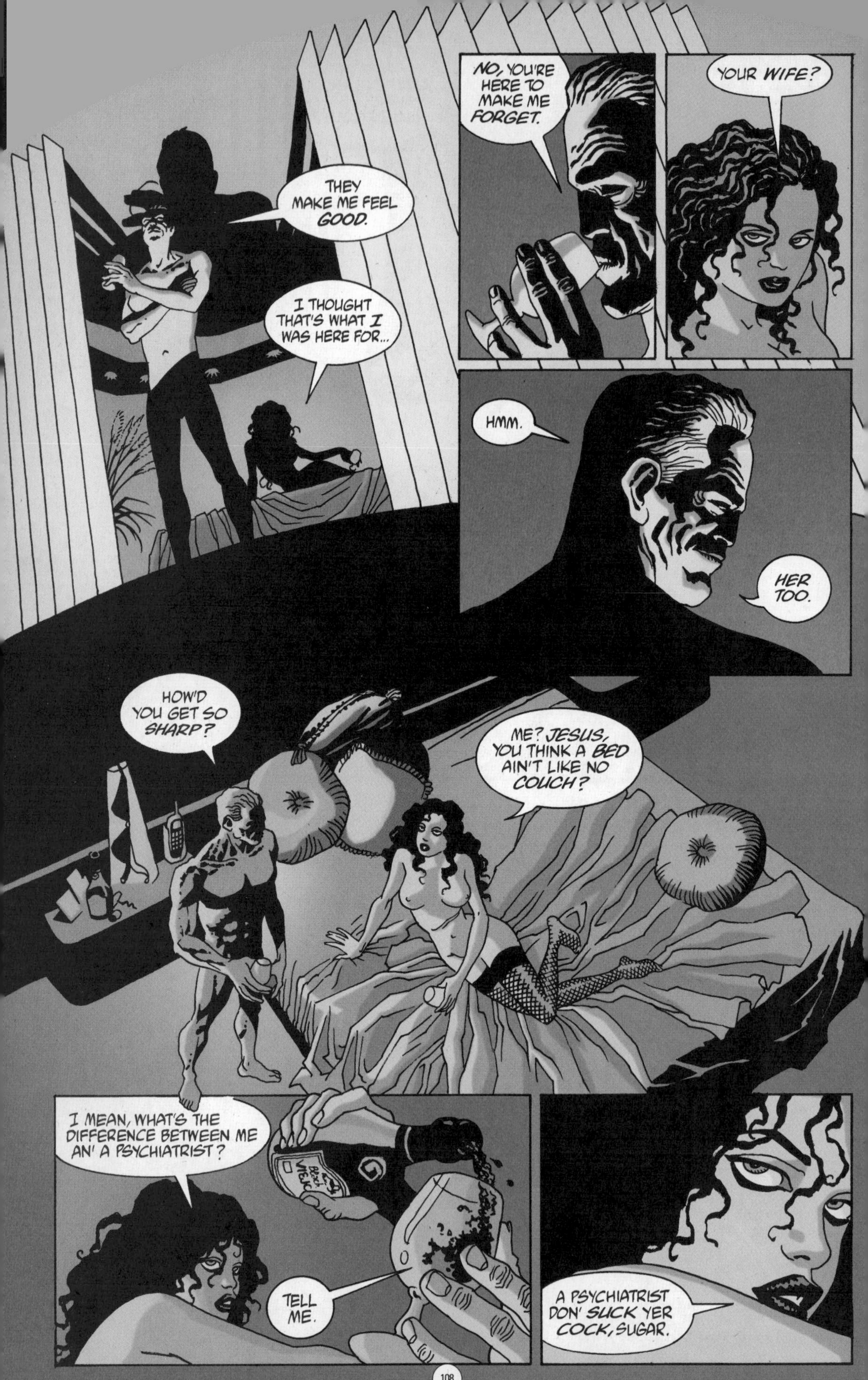
THEY MAKE ME FEEL GOOD.
I THOUGHT THAT'S WHAT I WAS HERE FOR...
NO, YOU'RE HERE TO MAKE ME FORGET.
YOUR WIFE?
HMM.
HER TOO.
HOW'D YOU GET SO SHARP?
ME? JESUS, YOU THINK A BED AIN'T LIKE NO COUCH?
I MEAN, WHAT'S THE DIFFERENCE BETWEEN ME AN' A PSYCHIATRIST?
TELL ME.
A PSYCHIATRIST DON' SUCK YER COCK, SUGAR.

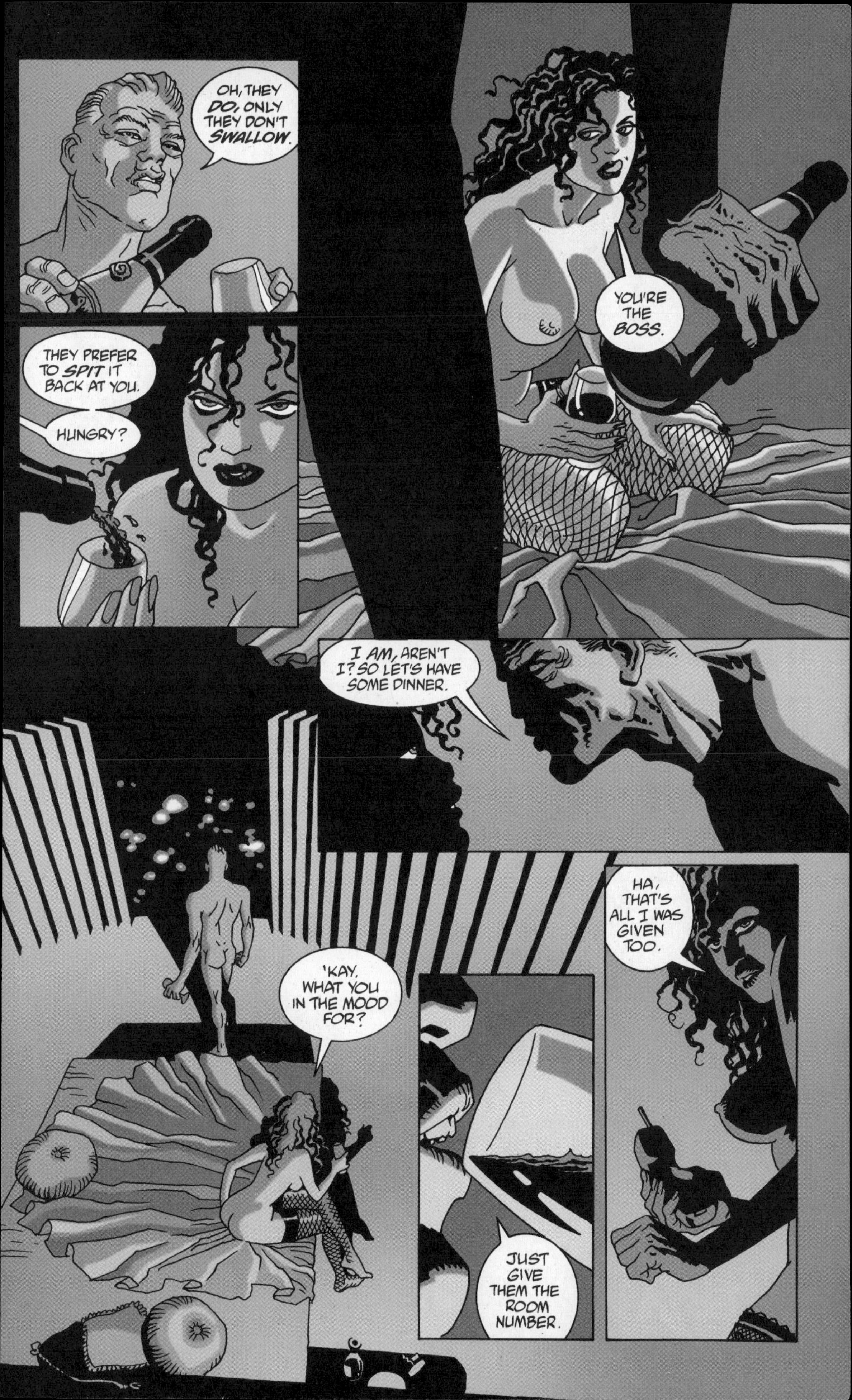
OH, THEY DO, ONLY THEY DON'T SWALLOW.
YOU'RE THE BOSS.
THEY PREFER TO SPIT IT BACK AT YOU.
HUNGRY?
I AM, AREN'T I? SO LET'S HAVE SOME DINNER.
'KAY. WHAT YOU IN THE MOOD FOR?
JUST GIVE THEM THE ROOM NUMBER.
HA, THAT'S ALL I WAS GIVEN TOO.

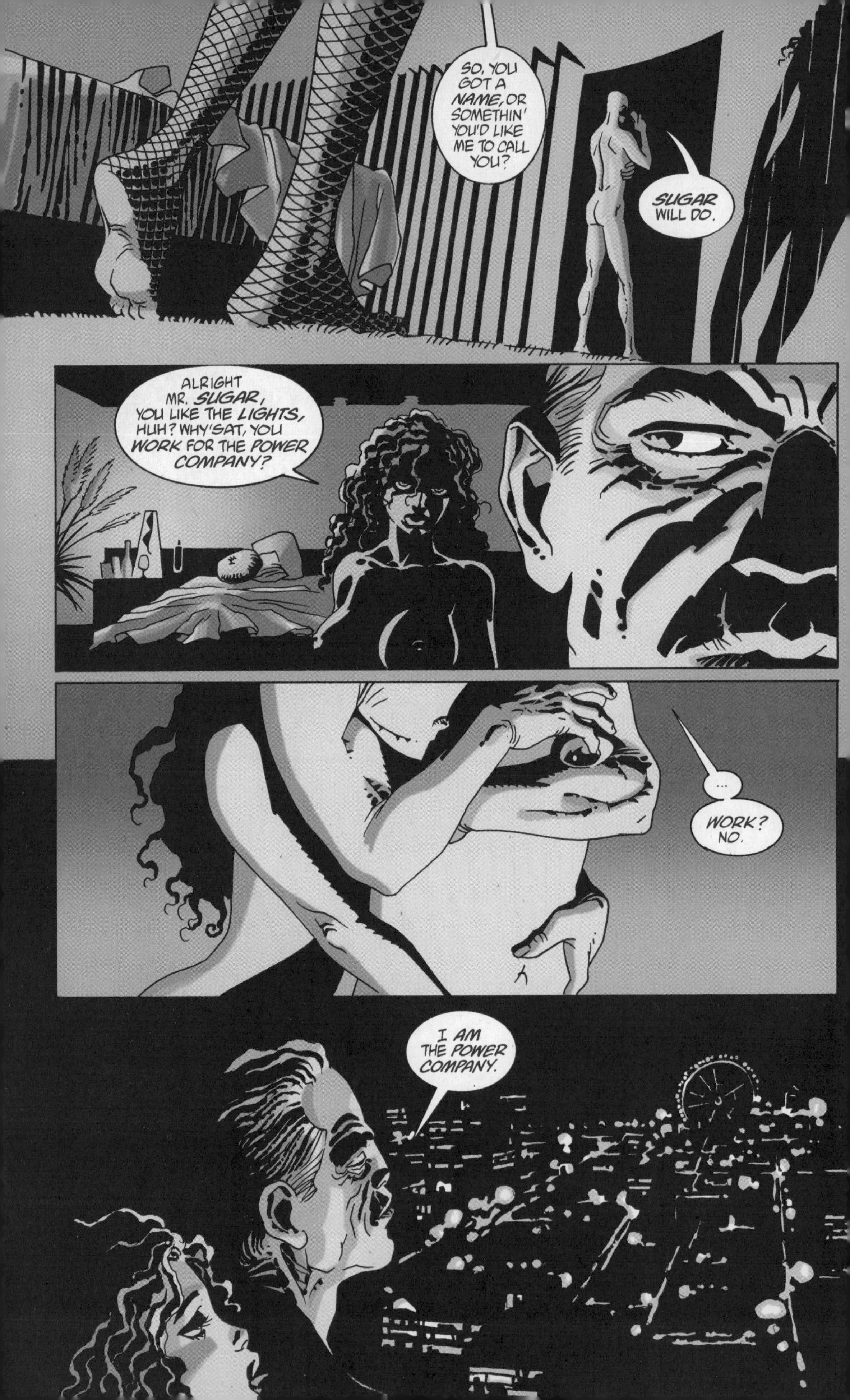
SO, YOU GOT A NAME, OR SOMETHIN' YOU'D LIKE ME TO CALL YOU?
SUGAR WILL DO.
ALRIGHT MR. SUGAR, YOU LIKE THE LIGHTS, HUH? WHY'SAT, YOU WORK FOR THE POWER COMPANY?
...
WORK? NO.
I AM THE POWER COMPANY.

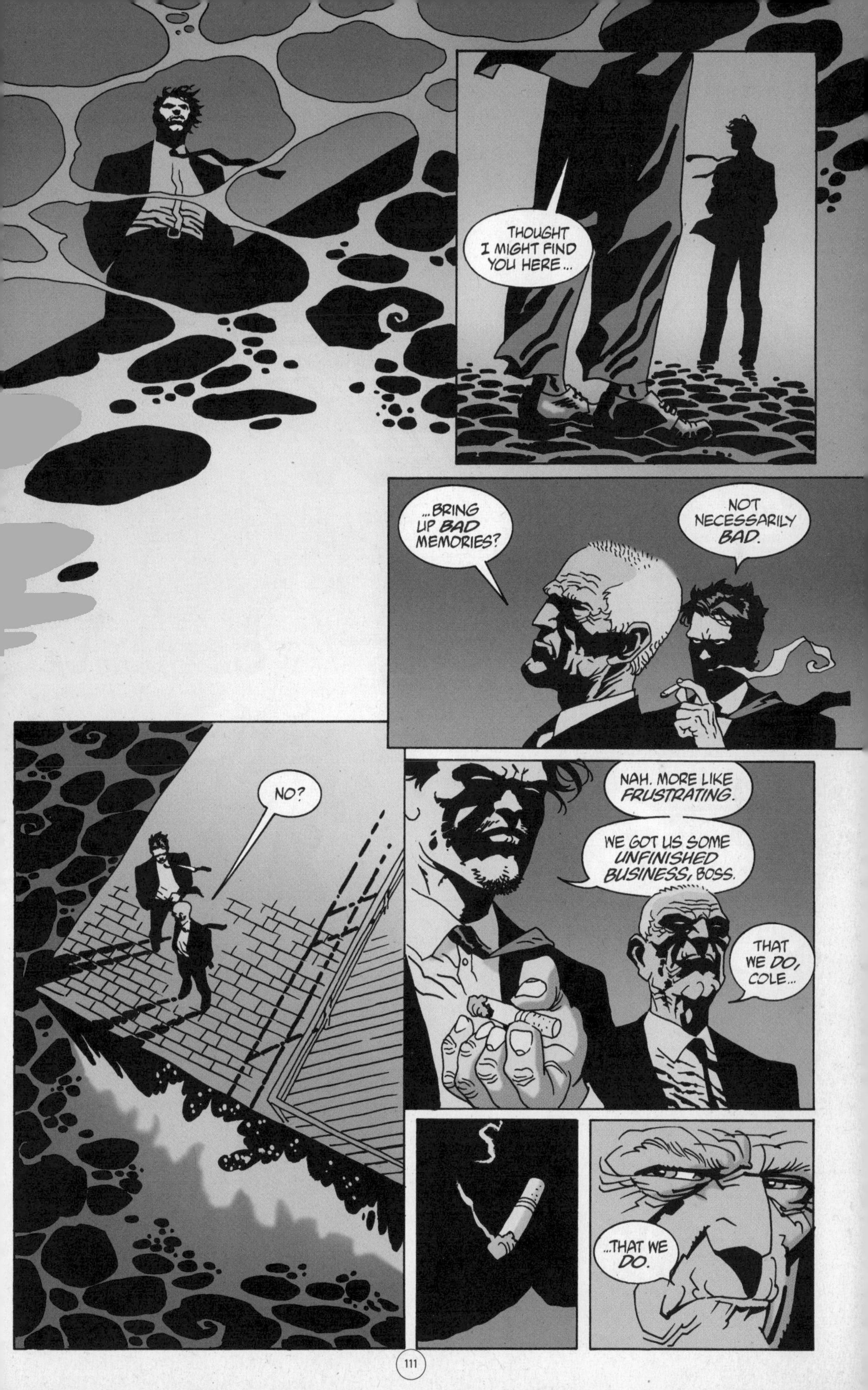
THOUGHT I MIGHT FIND YOU HERE...
...BRING UP BAD MEMORIES?
NOT NECESSARILY BAD.
NO?
NAH. MORE LIKE FRUSTRATING.
WE GOT US SOME UNFINISHED BUSINESS, BOSS.
THAT WE DO, COLE...
...THAT WE DO.

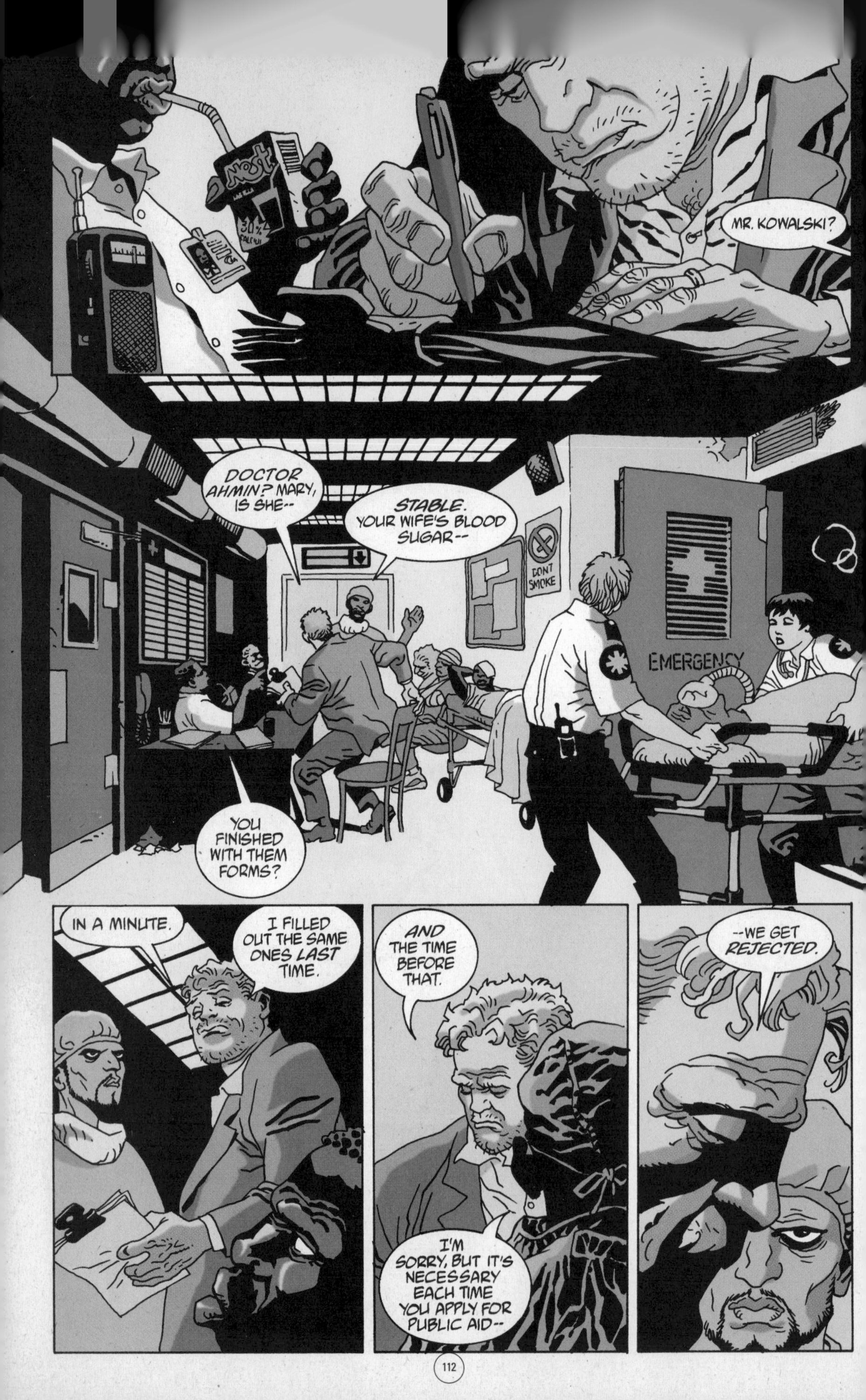

MR. KOWALSKI?
DOCTOR AHMIN? MARY, IS SHE--
STABLE. YOUR WIFE'S BLOOD SUGAR--
DON'T SMOKE
EMERGENCY
YOU FINISHED WITH THEM FORMS?
IN A MINUTE.
I FILLED OUT THE SAME ONES LAST TIME.
AND THE TIME BEFORE THAT.
I'M SORRY, BUT IT'S NECESSARY EACH TIME YOU APPLY FOR PUBLIC AID--
--WE GET REJECTED.

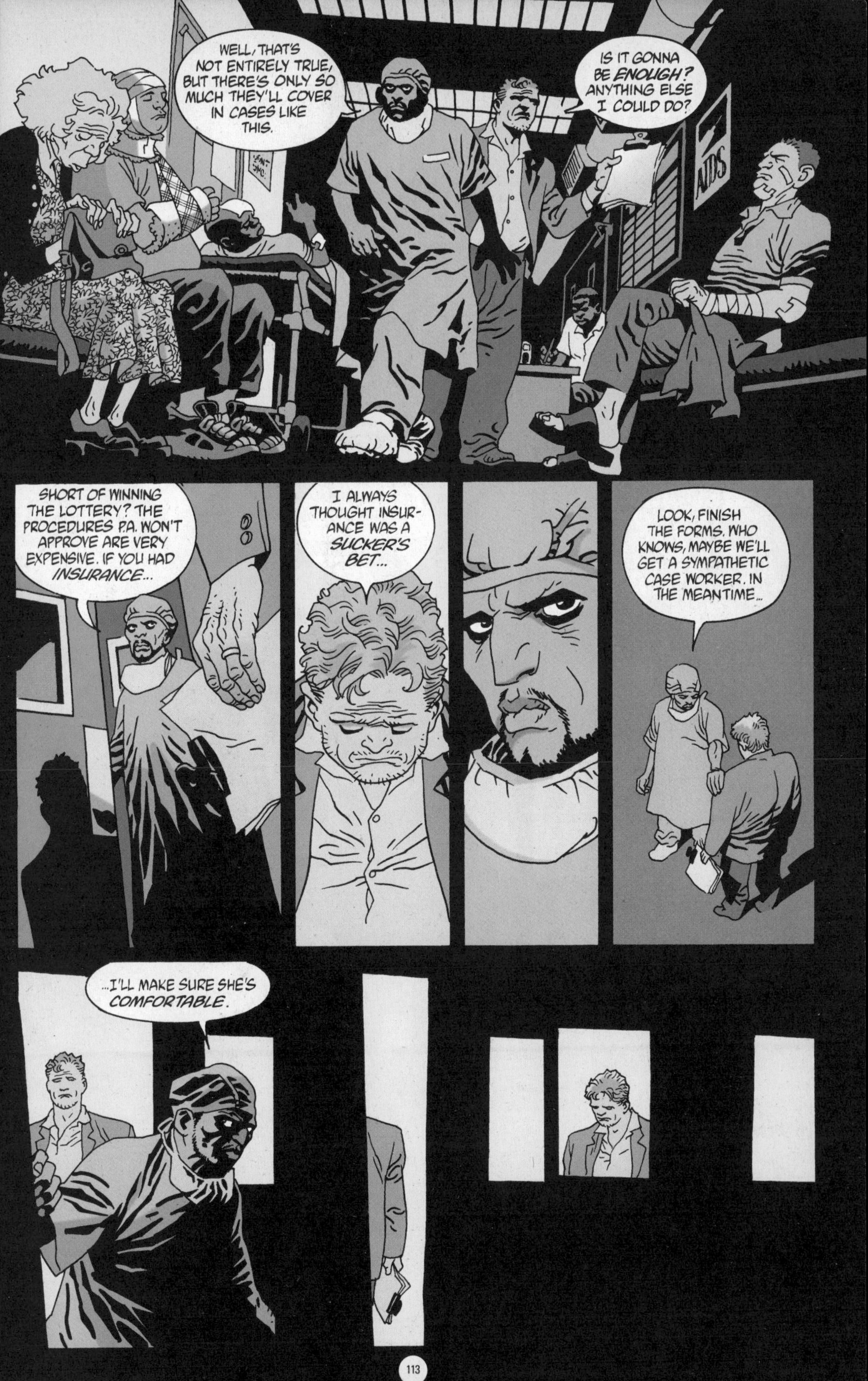
WELL, THAT'S NOT ENTIRELY TRUE, BUT THERE'S ONLY SO MUCH THEY'LL COVER IN CASES LIKE THIS.
IS IT GONNA BE ENOUGH? ANYTHING ELSE I COULD DO?
AIDS
SHORT OF WINNING THE LOTTERY? THE PROCEDURES P.A. WON'T APPROVE ARE VERY EXPENSIVE. IF YOU HAD INSURANCE...
I ALWAYS THOUGHT INSURANCE WAS A SUCKER'S BET...
LOOK, FINISH THE FORMS. WHO KNOWS, MAYBE WE'LL GET A SYMPATHETIC CASE WORKER. IN THE MEANTIME...
...I'LL MAKE SURE SHE'S COMFORTABLE.

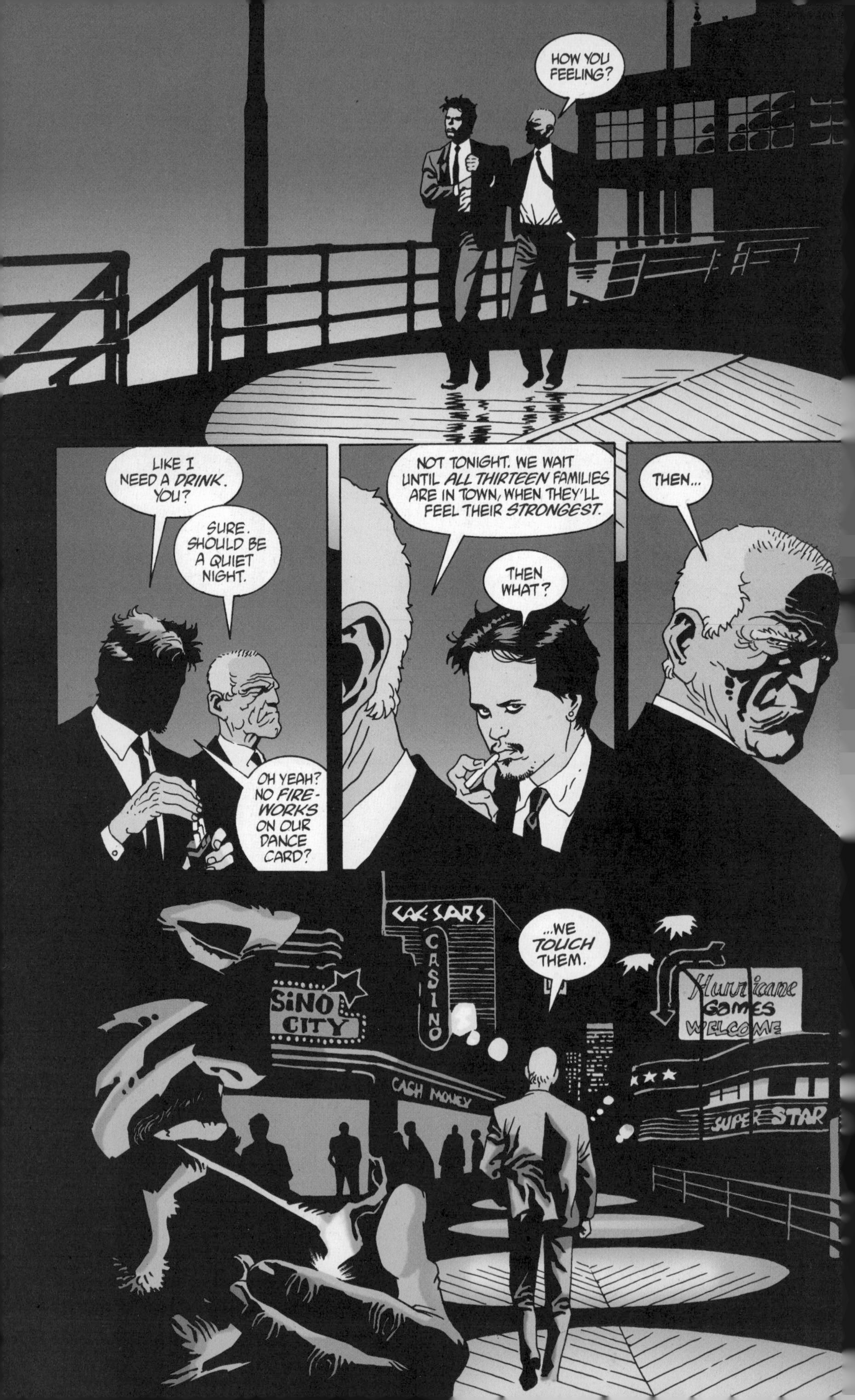

HOW YOU FEELING?
LIKE I NEED A DRINK. YOU?
SURE. SHOULD BE A QUIET NIGHT.
OH YEAH? NO FIRE-WORKS ON OUR DANCE CARD?
NOT TONIGHT. WE WAIT UNTIL ALL THIRTEEN FAMILIES ARE IN TOWN, WHEN THEY'LL FEEL THEIR STRONGEST.
THEN WHAT?
THEN...
...WE TOUCH THEM.
CAESARS
CASINO
SINO CITY
CASH MONEY
Hurricane Games WELCOME
SUPER STAR

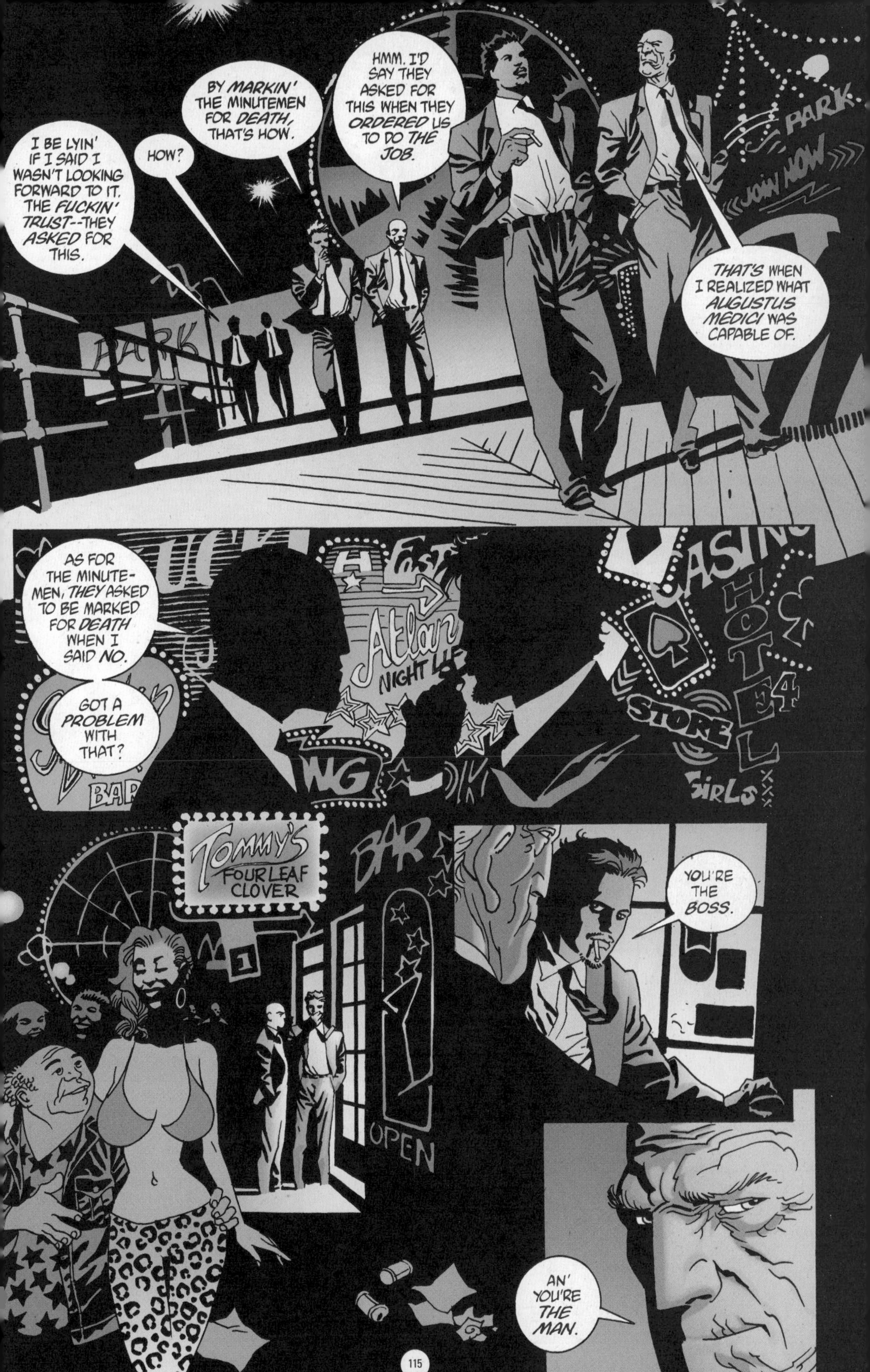
I BE LYIN' IF I SAID I WASN'T LOOKING FORWARD TO IT. THE FUCKIN' TRUST--THEY ASKED FOR THIS.
HOW?
BY MARKIN' THE MINUTEMEN FOR DEATH, THAT'S HOW.
HMM. I'D SAY THEY ASKED FOR THIS WHEN THEY ORDERED US TO DO THE JOB.
PARK
JOIN NOW
THAT'S WHEN I REALIZED WHAT AUGUSTUS MEDICI WAS CAPABLE OF.
AS FOR THE MINUTE-MEN, THEY ASKED TO BE MARKED FOR DEATH WHEN I SAID NO.
GOT A PROBLEM WITH THAT?
CASINO
HOTEL
STORE
GIRLS
BAR
TOMMY'S FOUR LEAF CLOVER
BAR
OPEN
YOU'RE THE BOSS.
AN' YOU'RE THE MAN.

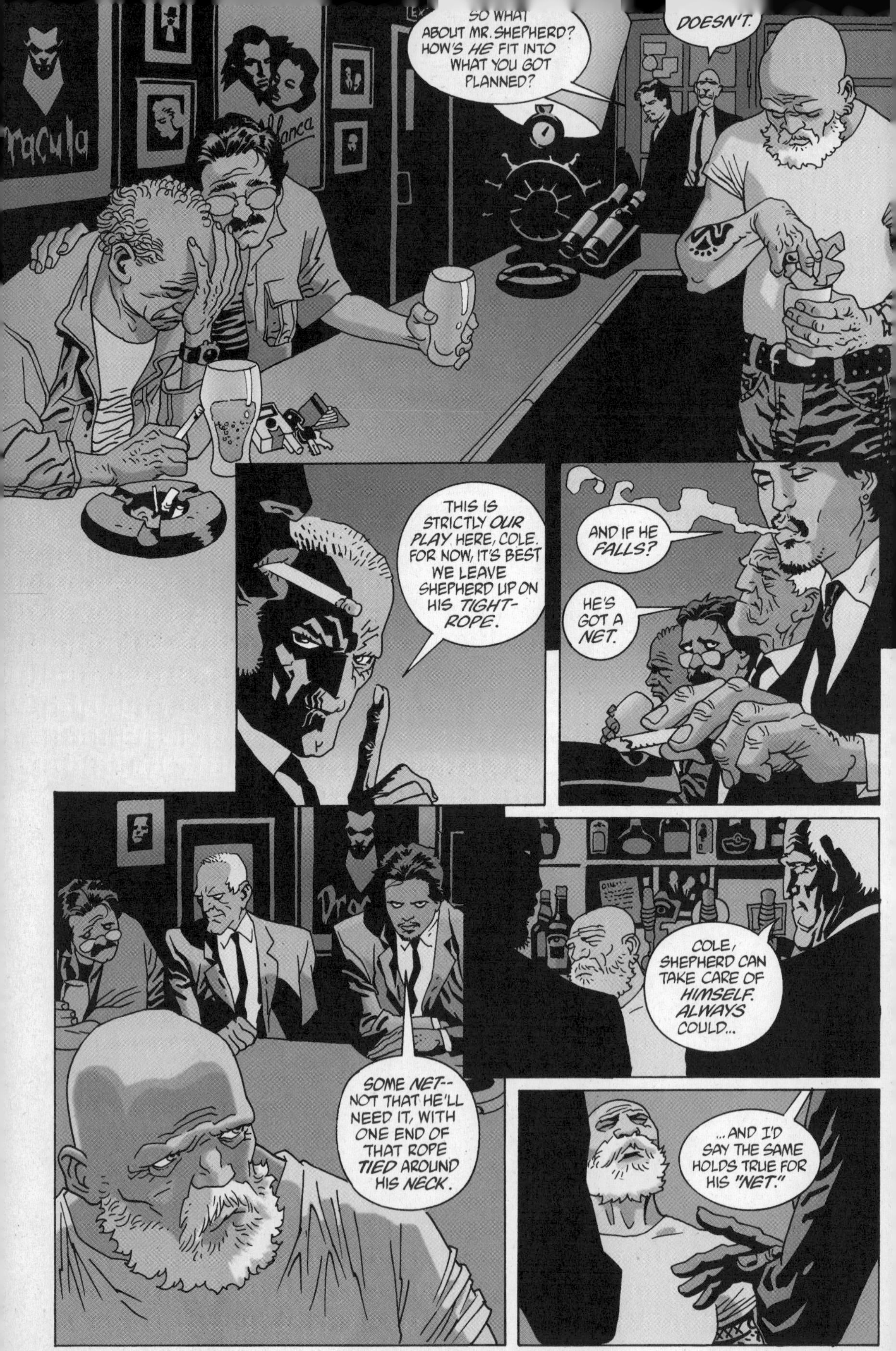
SO WHAT ABOUT MR. SHEPHERD? HOW'S HE FIT INTO WHAT YOU GOT PLANNED?
DOESN'T.
THIS IS STRICTLY OUR PLAY HERE, COLE. FOR NOW, IT'S BEST WE LEAVE SHEPHERD UP ON HIS TIGHT-ROPE.
AND IF HE FALLS?
HE'S GOT A NET.
SOME NET-- NOT THAT HE'LL NEED IT, WITH ONE END OF THAT ROPE TIED AROUND HIS NECK.
COLE, SHEPHERD CAN TAKE CARE OF HIMSELF. ALWAYS COULD...
...AND I'D SAY THE SAME HOLDS TRUE FOR HIS "NET."

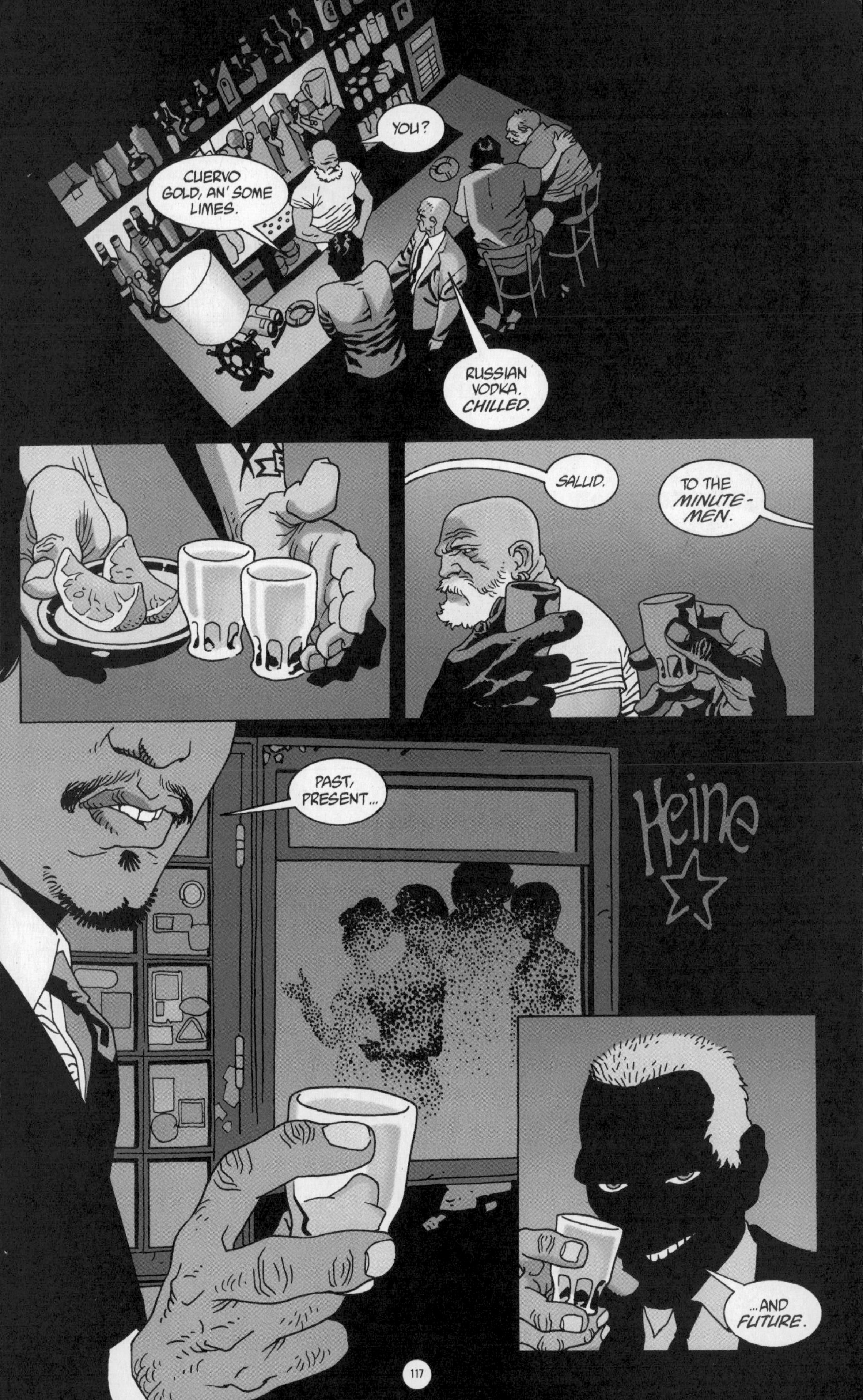
YOU?
CUERVO GOLD, AN' SOME LIMES.
RUSSIAN VODKA, CHILLED.
SALUD.
TO THE MINUTE-MEN.
PAST, PRESENT...
Heine
...AND FUTURE.

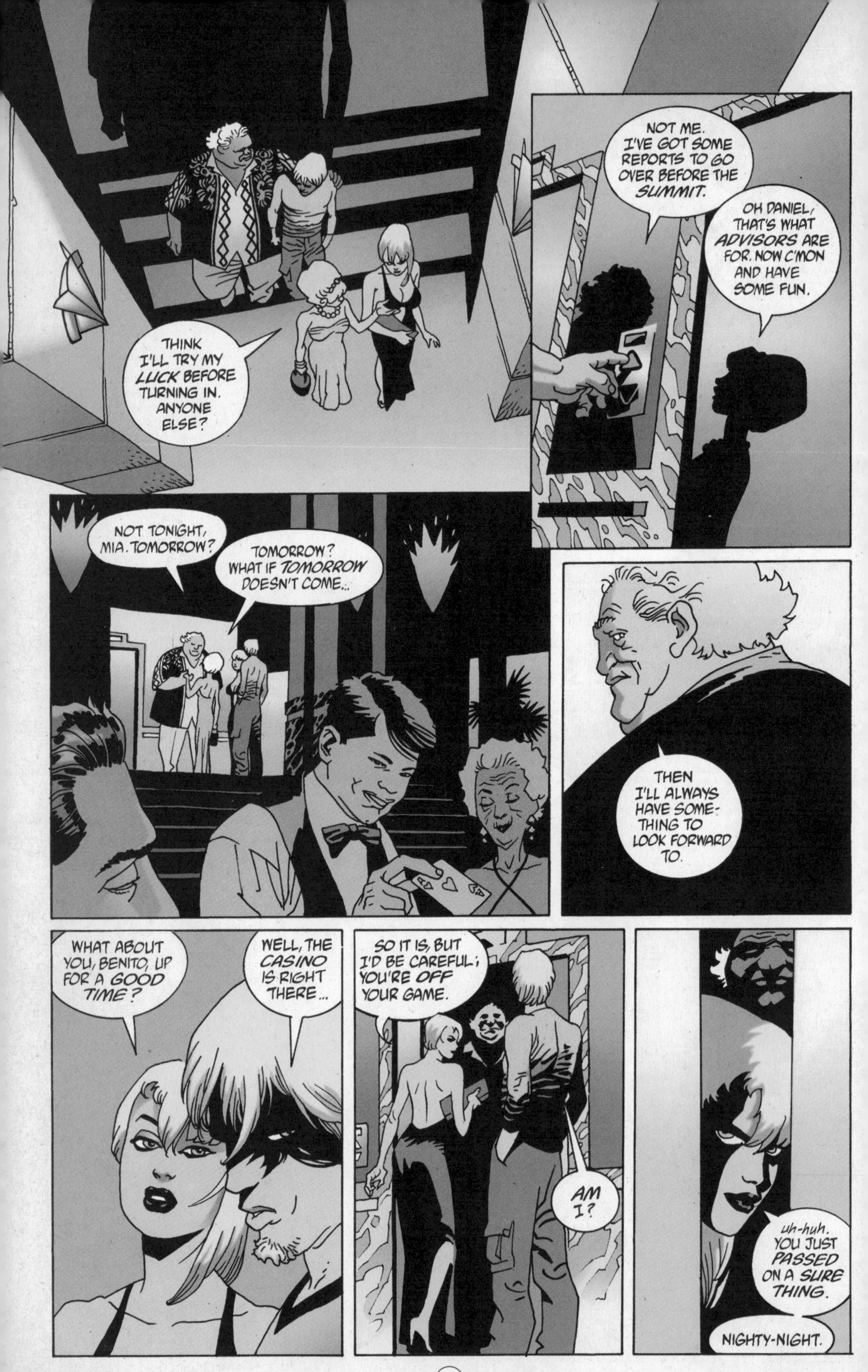
THINK I'LL TRY MY LUCK BEFORE TURNING IN. ANYONE ELSE?
NOT ME. I'VE GOT SOME REPORTS TO GO OVER BEFORE THE SUMMIT.
OH DANIEL, THAT'S WHAT ADVISORS ARE FOR. NOW C'MON AND HAVE SOME FUN.
NOT TONIGHT, MIA. TOMORROW?
TOMORROW? WHAT IF TOMORROW DOESN'T COME...
THEN I'LL ALWAYS HAVE SOME-THING TO LOOK FORWARD TO.
WHAT ABOUT YOU, BENITO, UP FOR A GOOD TIME?
WELL, THE CASINO IS RIGHT THERE...
SO IT IS, BUT I'D BE CAREFUL; YOU'RE OFF YOUR GAME.
AM I?
uh-huh. YOU JUST PASSED ON A SURE THING.
NIGHTY-NIGHT.

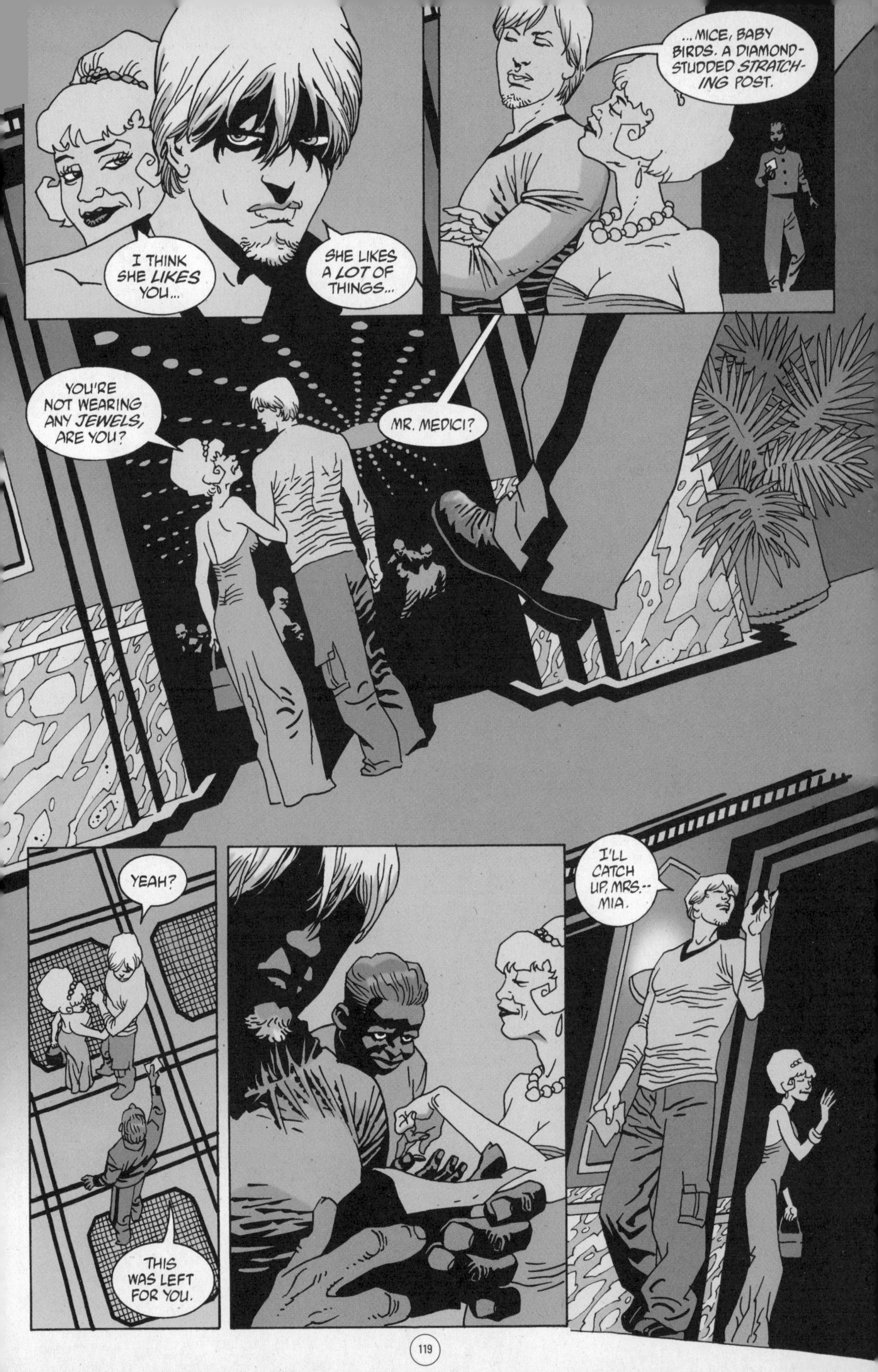
I THINK SHE LIKES YOU...
SHE LIKES A LOT OF THINGS...
...MICE, BABY BIRDS. A DIAMOND-STUDDED STRATCHING POST.
YOU'RE NOT WEARING ANY JEWELS, ARE YOU?
MR. MEDICI?
YEAH?
THIS WAS LEFT FOR YOU.
I'LL CATCH UP, MRS.-- MIA.

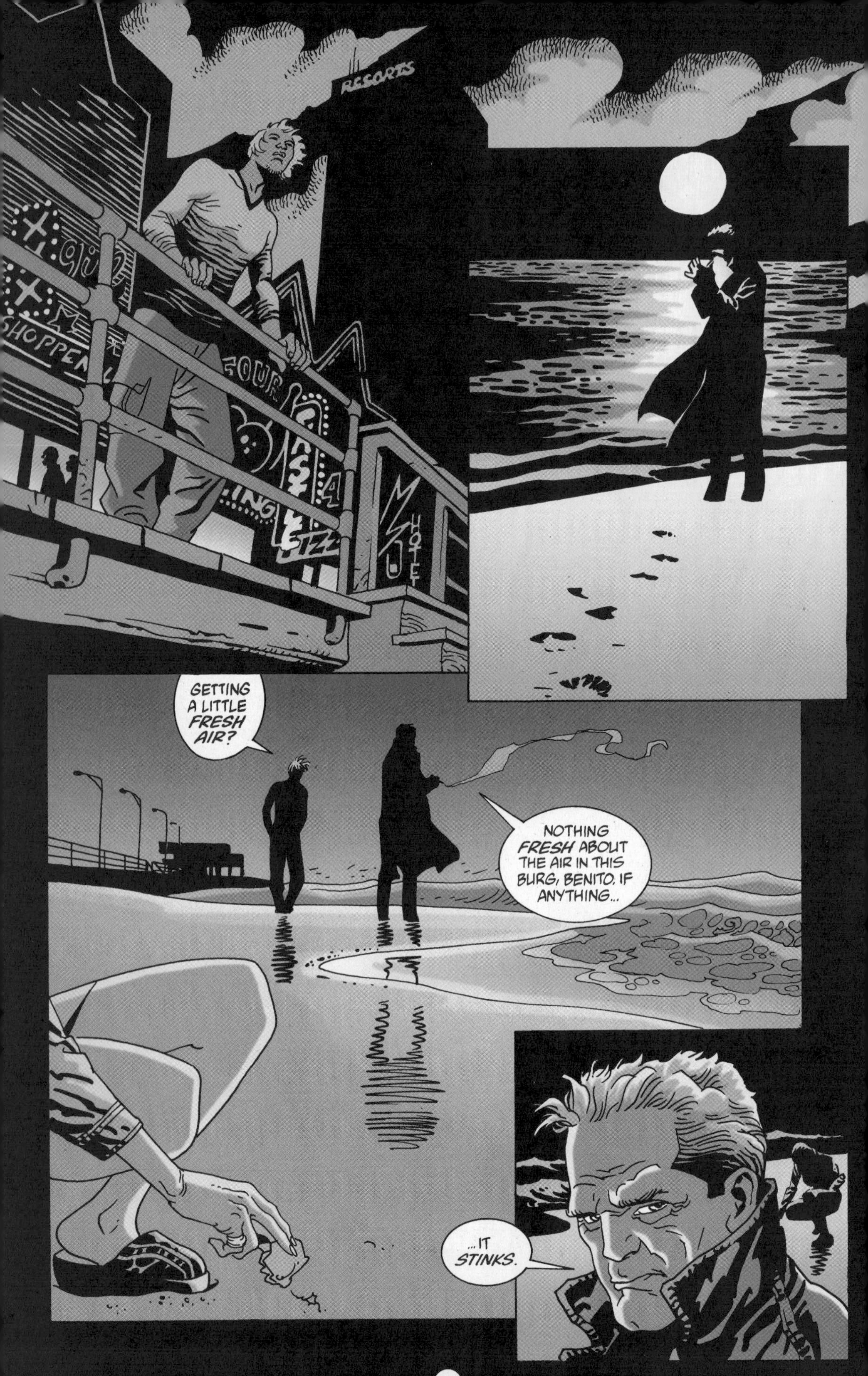
RESORTS
SHOPPEN
FOUR
HOTEL
GETTING A LITTLE FRESH AIR?
NOTHING FRESH ABOUT THE AIR IN THIS BURG, BENITO. IF ANYTHING...
...IT STINKS.

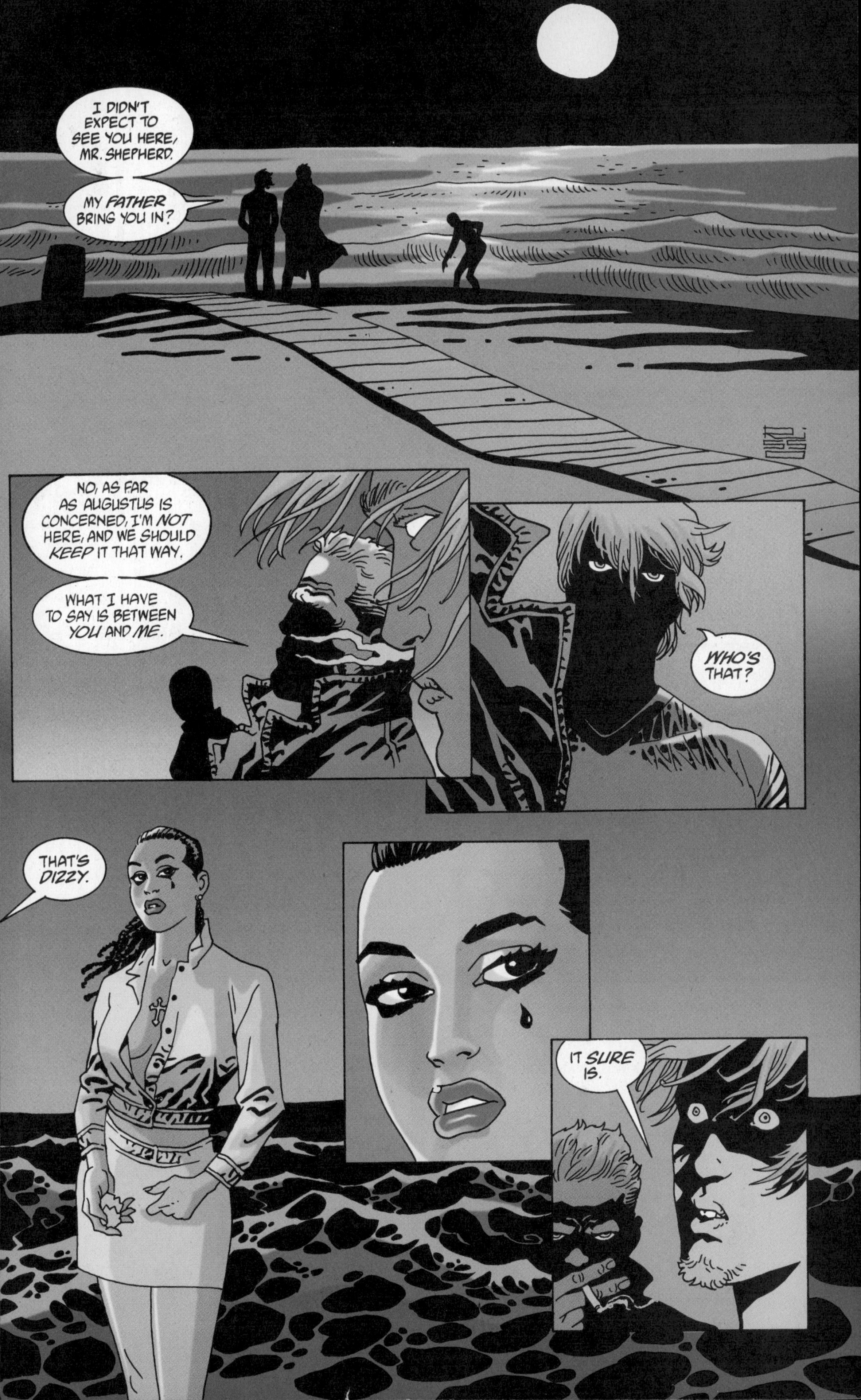
I DIDN'T EXPECT TO SEE YOU HERE, MR. SHEPHERD.
MY FATHER BRING YOU IN?
NO, AS FAR AS AUGUSTUS IS CONCERNED, I'M NOT HERE, AND WE SHOULD KEEP IT THAT WAY.
WHAT I HAVE TO SAY IS BETWEEN YOU AND ME.
WHO'S THAT?
THAT'S DIZZY.
IT SURE IS.

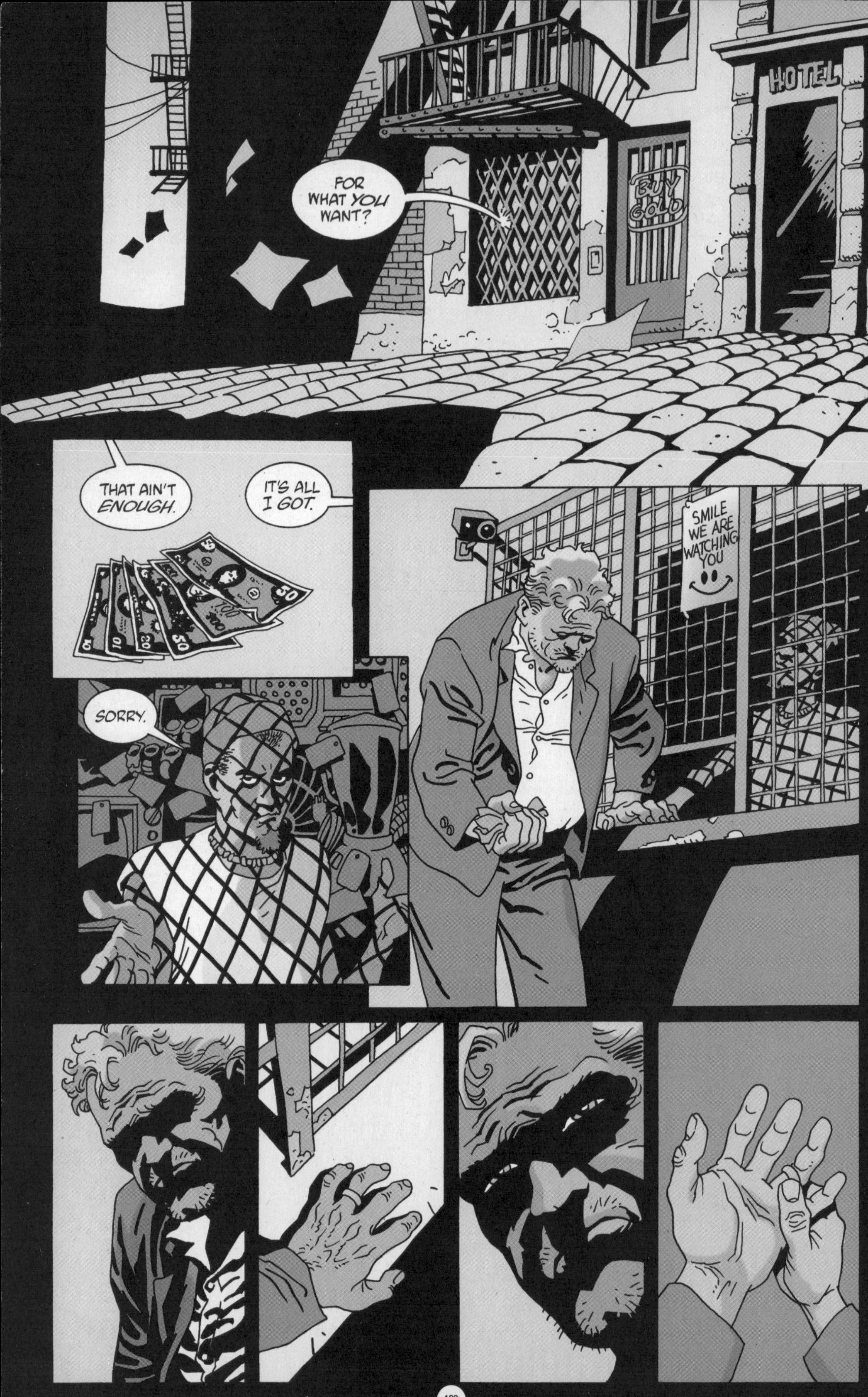

HOTEL
BUY GOLD
FOR WHAT YOU WANT?
THAT AIN'T ENOUGH.
IT'S ALL I GOT.
SMILE WE ARE WATCHING YOU
SORRY.

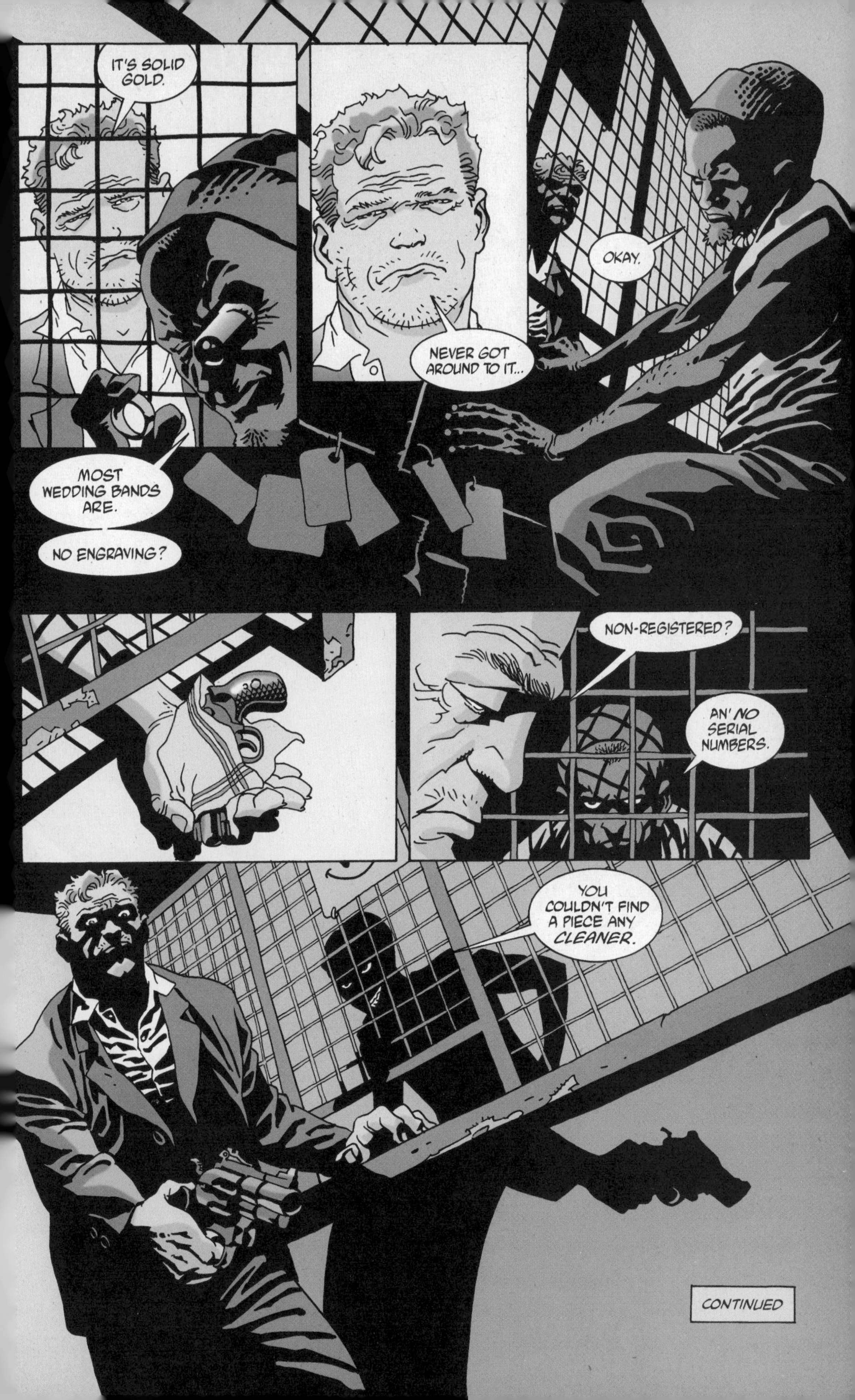
IT'S SOLID GOLD.
NEVER GOT AROUND TO IT...
OKAY.
MOST WEDDING BANDS ARE.
NO ENGRAVING?
NON-REGISTERED?
AN' NO SERIAL NUMBERS.
YOU COULDN'T FIND A PIECE ANY CLEANER.
CONTINUED

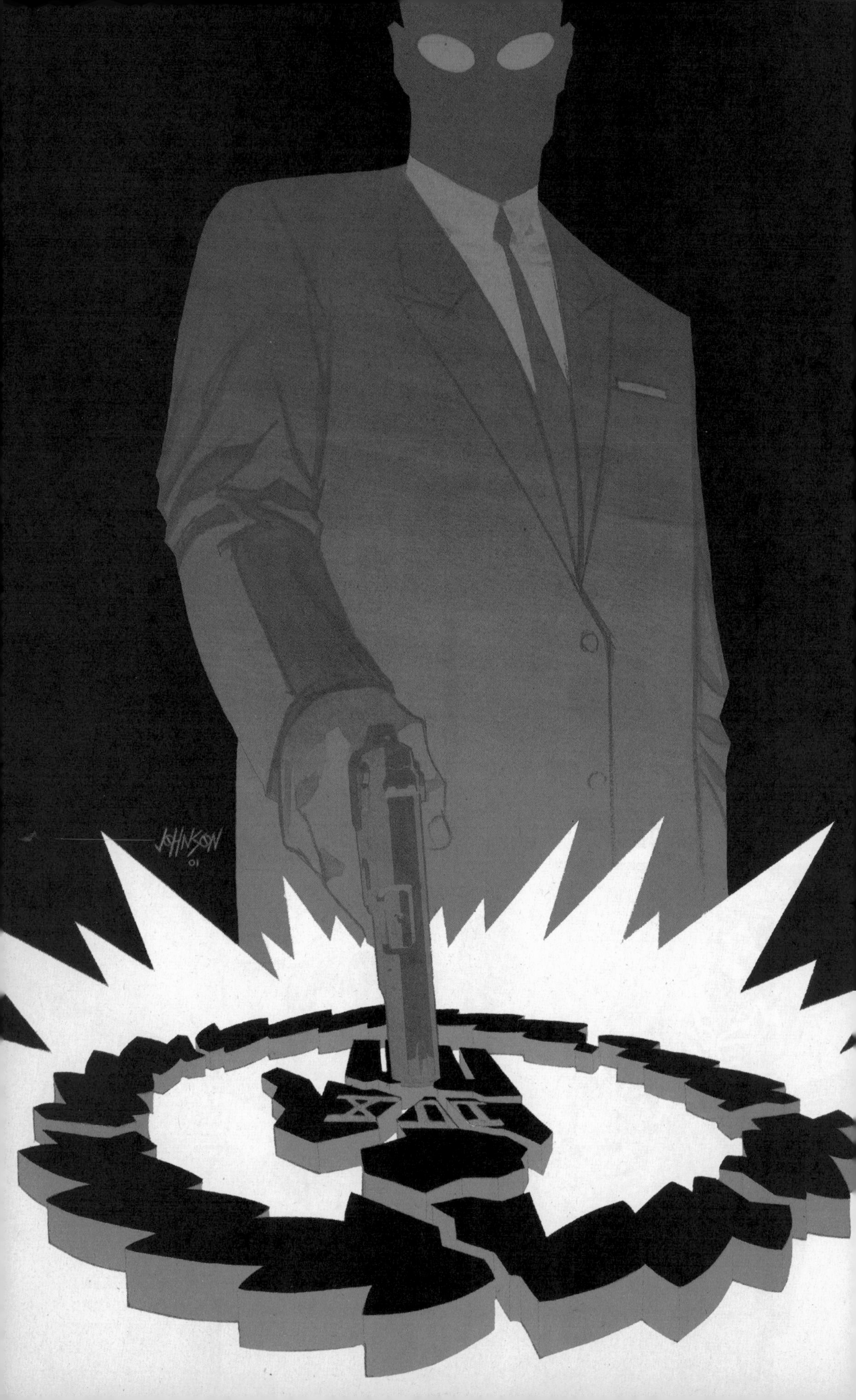
JOHNSON
01

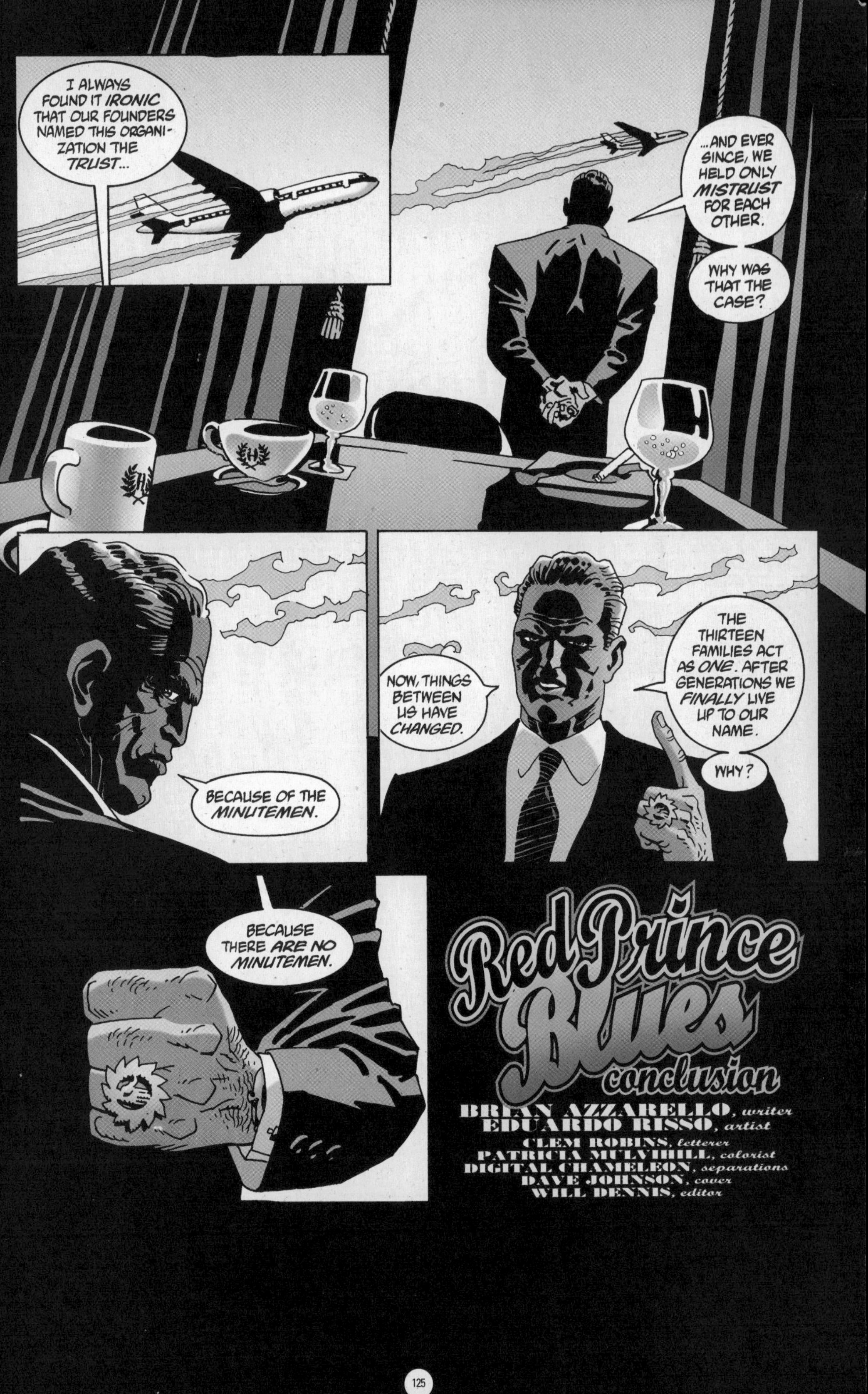

I ALWAYS FOUND IT IRONIC THAT OUR FOUNDERS NAMED THIS ORGANIZATION THE TRUST...
...AND EVER SINCE, WE HELD ONLY MISTRUST FOR EACH OTHER.
WHY WAS THAT THE CASE?
BECAUSE OF THE MINUTEMEN.
NOW, THINGS BETWEEN US HAVE CHANGED.
THE THIRTEEN FAMILIES ACT AS ONE. AFTER GENERATIONS WE FINALLY LIVE UP TO OUR NAME.
WHY?
BECAUSE THERE ARE NO MINUTEMEN.
Red Prince Blues conclusion
BRIAN AZZARELLO, writer
EDUARDO RISSO, artist
CLEM ROBINS, letterer
PATRICIA MULVIHILL, colorist
DIGITAL CHAMELEON, separations
DAVE JOHNSON, cover
WILL DENNIS, editor

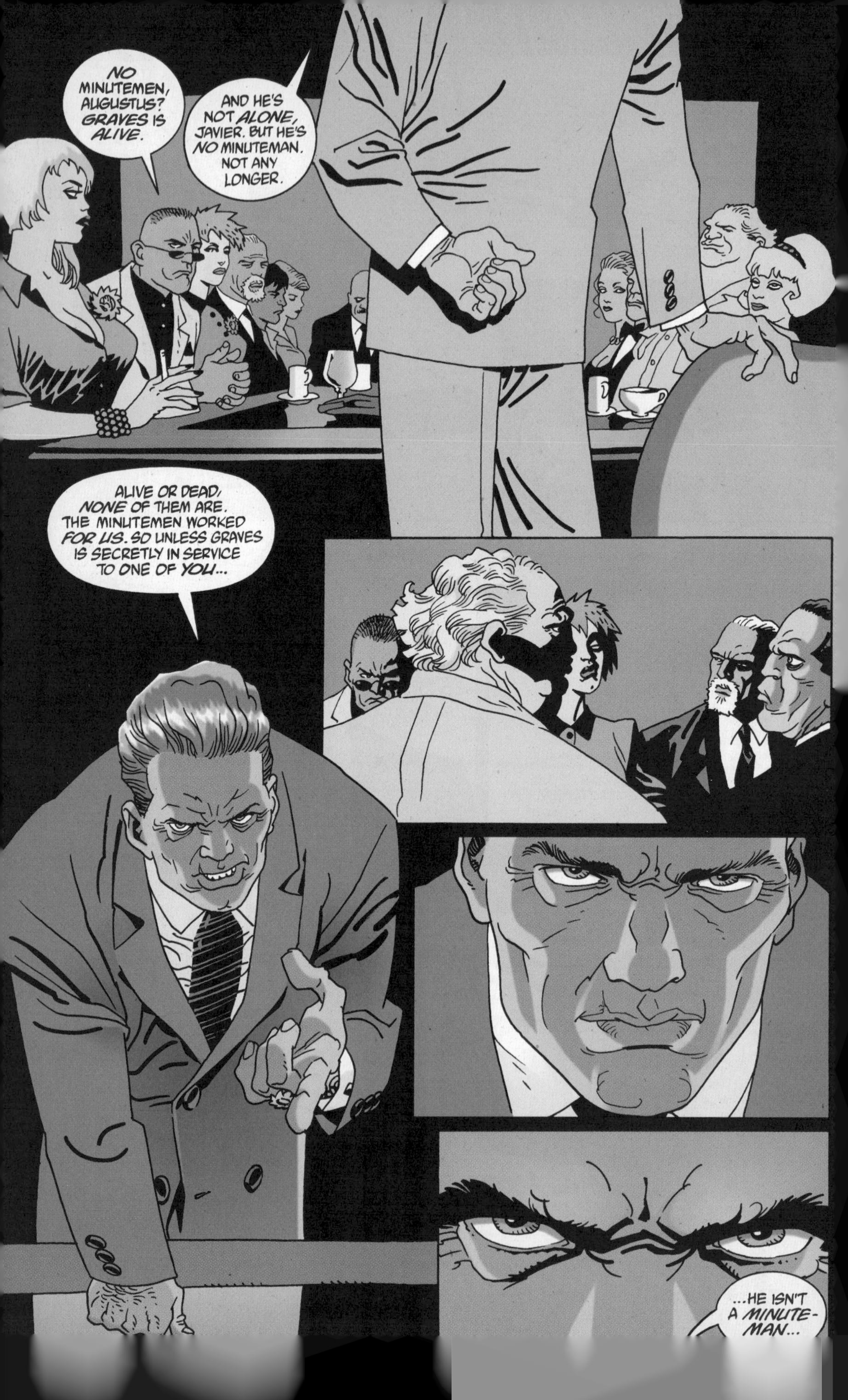
NO MINUTEMEN, AUGUSTUS? GRAVES IS ALIVE.
AND HE'S NOT ALONE, JAVIER. BUT HE'S NO MINUTEMAN. NOT ANY LONGER.
ALIVE OR DEAD, NONE OF THEM ARE. THE MINUTEMEN WORKED FOR US. SO UNLESS GRAVES IS SECRETLY IN SERVICE TO ONE OF YOU...
...HE ISN'T A MINUTE-MAN...

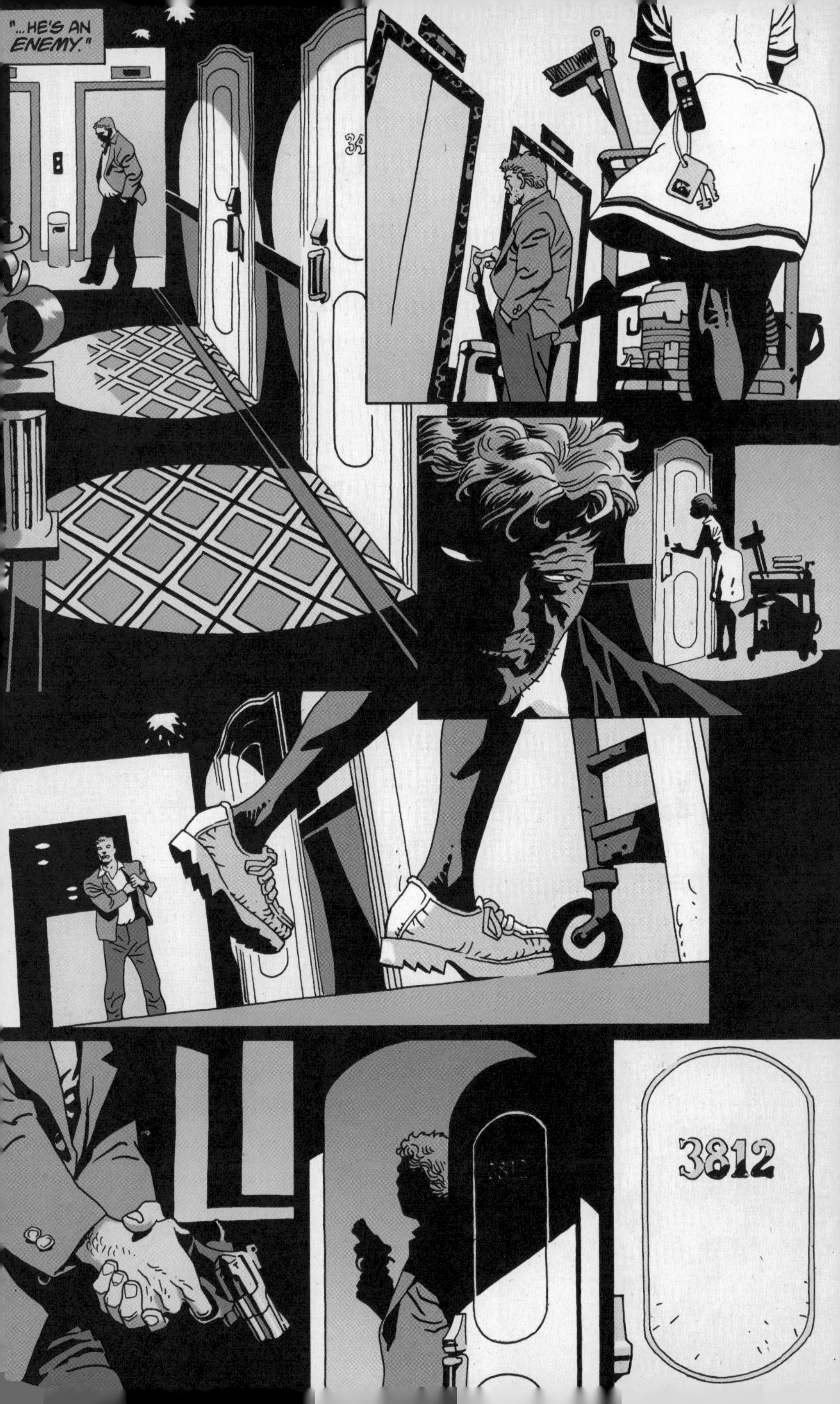
"...HE'S AN ENEMY."
3812

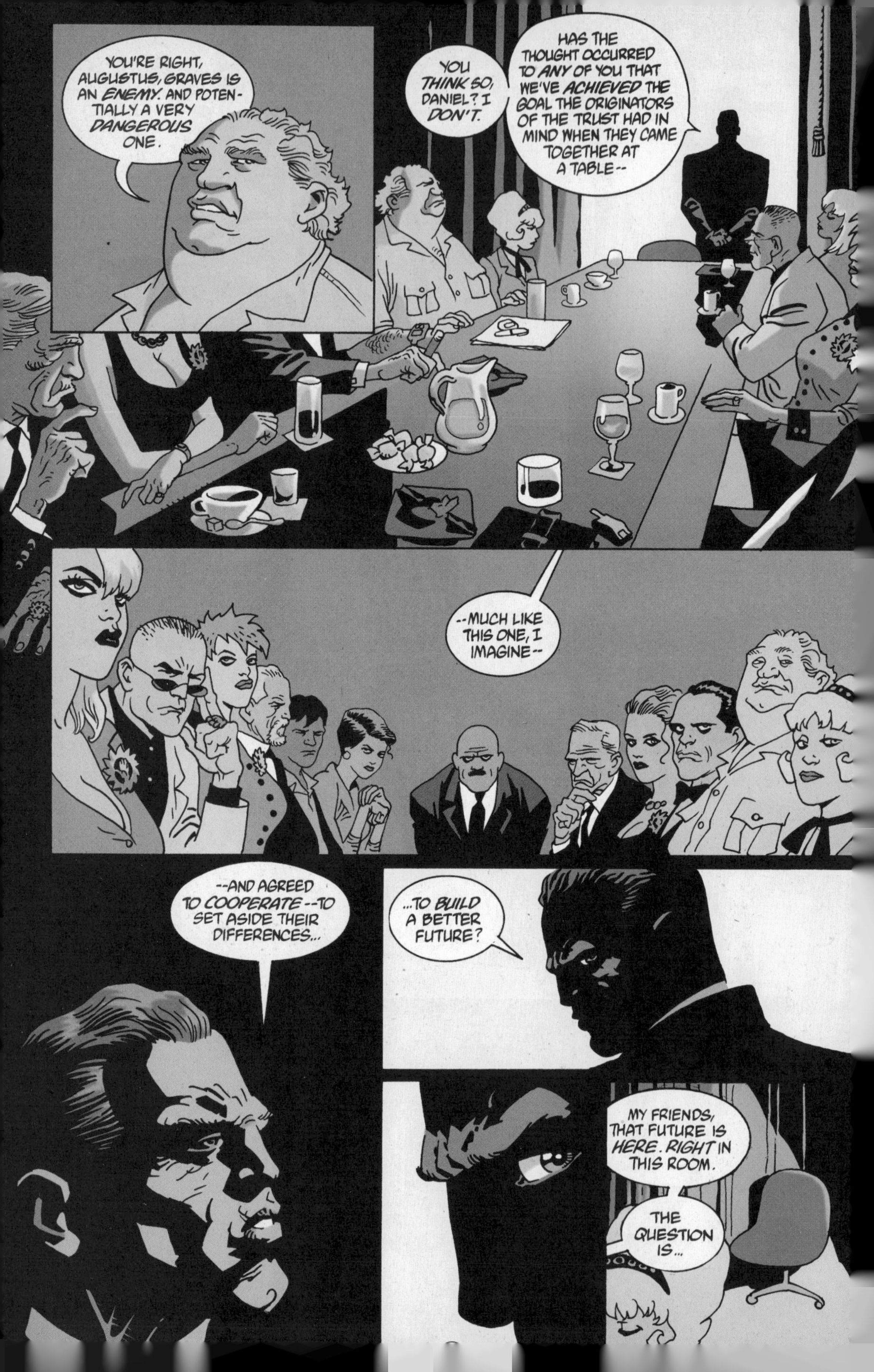
YOU'RE RIGHT, AUGUSTUS, GRAVES IS AN ENEMY. AND POTENTIALLY A VERY DANGEROUS ONE.
YOU THINK SO, DANIEL? I DON'T.
HAS THE THOUGHT OCCURRED TO ANY OF YOU THAT WE'VE ACHIEVED THE GOAL THE ORIGINATORS OF THE TRUST HAD IN MIND WHEN THEY CAME TOGETHER AT A TABLE--
--MUCH LIKE THIS ONE, I IMAGINE--
--AND AGREED TO COOPERATE--TO SET ASIDE THEIR DIFFERENCES...
...TO BUILD A BETTER FUTURE?
MY FRIENDS, THAT FUTURE IS HERE. RIGHT IN THIS ROOM.
THE QUESTION IS...

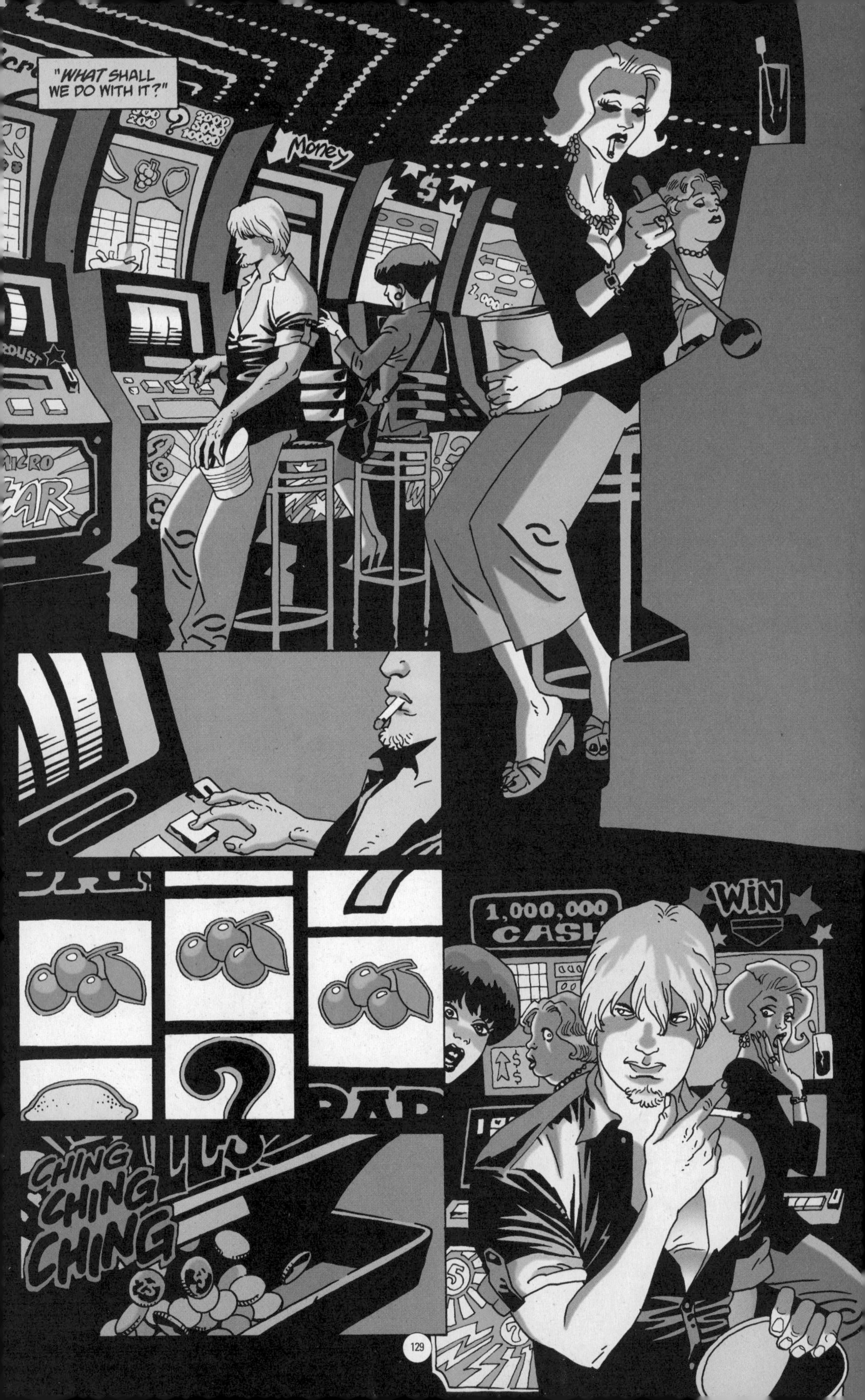
"WHAT SHALL WE DO WITH IT?"
Money
1,000,000
WIN
CHING
CHING
CHING

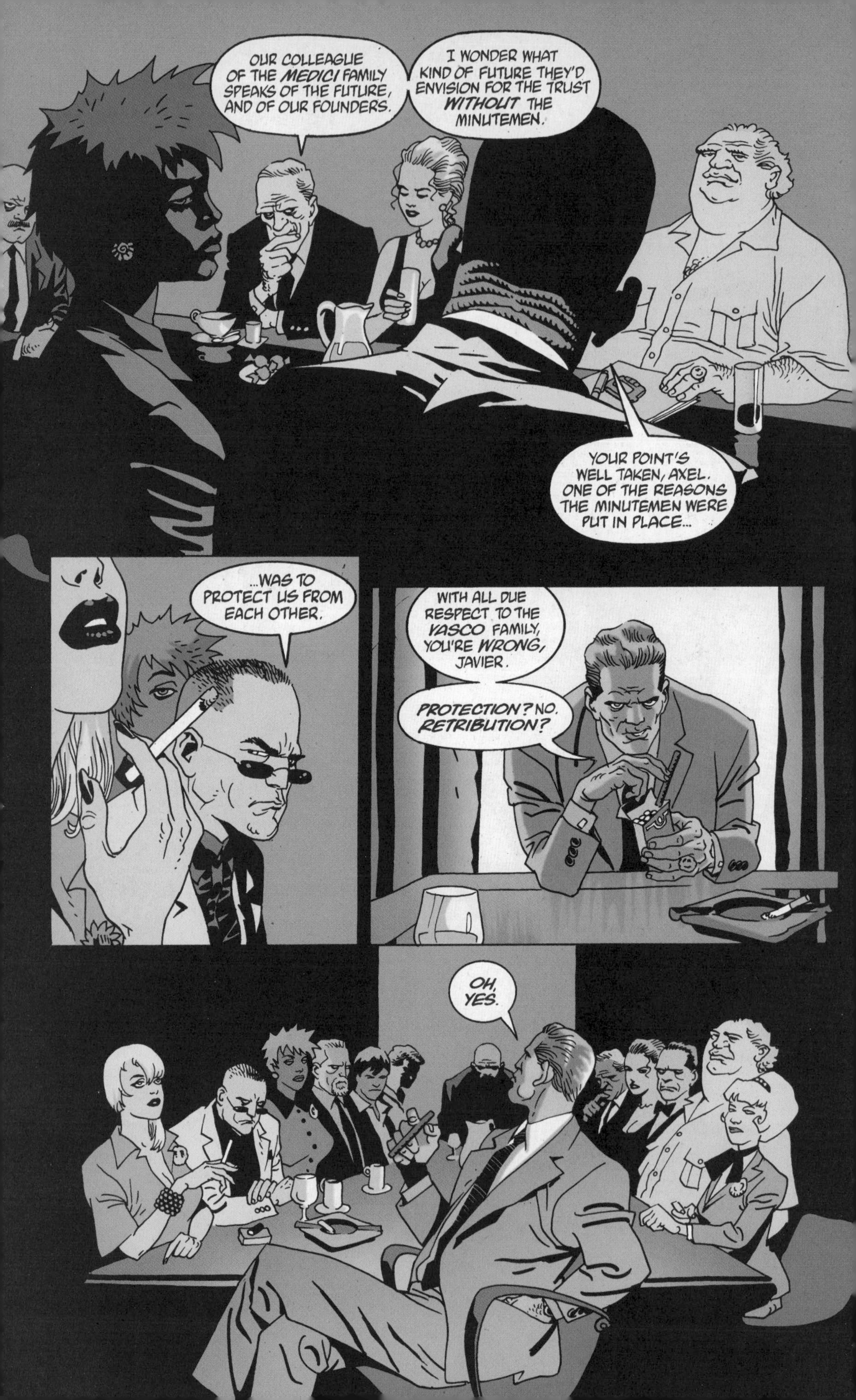
OUR COLLEAGUE OF THE *MEDICI* FAMILY SPEAKS OF THE FUTURE, AND OF OUR FOUNDERS.
I WONDER WHAT KIND OF FUTURE THEY'D ENVISION FOR THE TRUST *WITHOUT* THE MINUTEMEN.
YOUR POINT'S WELL TAKEN, AXEL. ONE OF THE REASONS THE MINUTEMEN WERE PUT IN PLACE...
...WAS TO PROTECT US FROM EACH OTHER.
WITH ALL DUE RESPECT TO THE *VASCO* FAMILY, YOU'RE *WRONG*, JAVIER.
PROTECTION? NO. *RETRIBUTION?*
OH, YES.

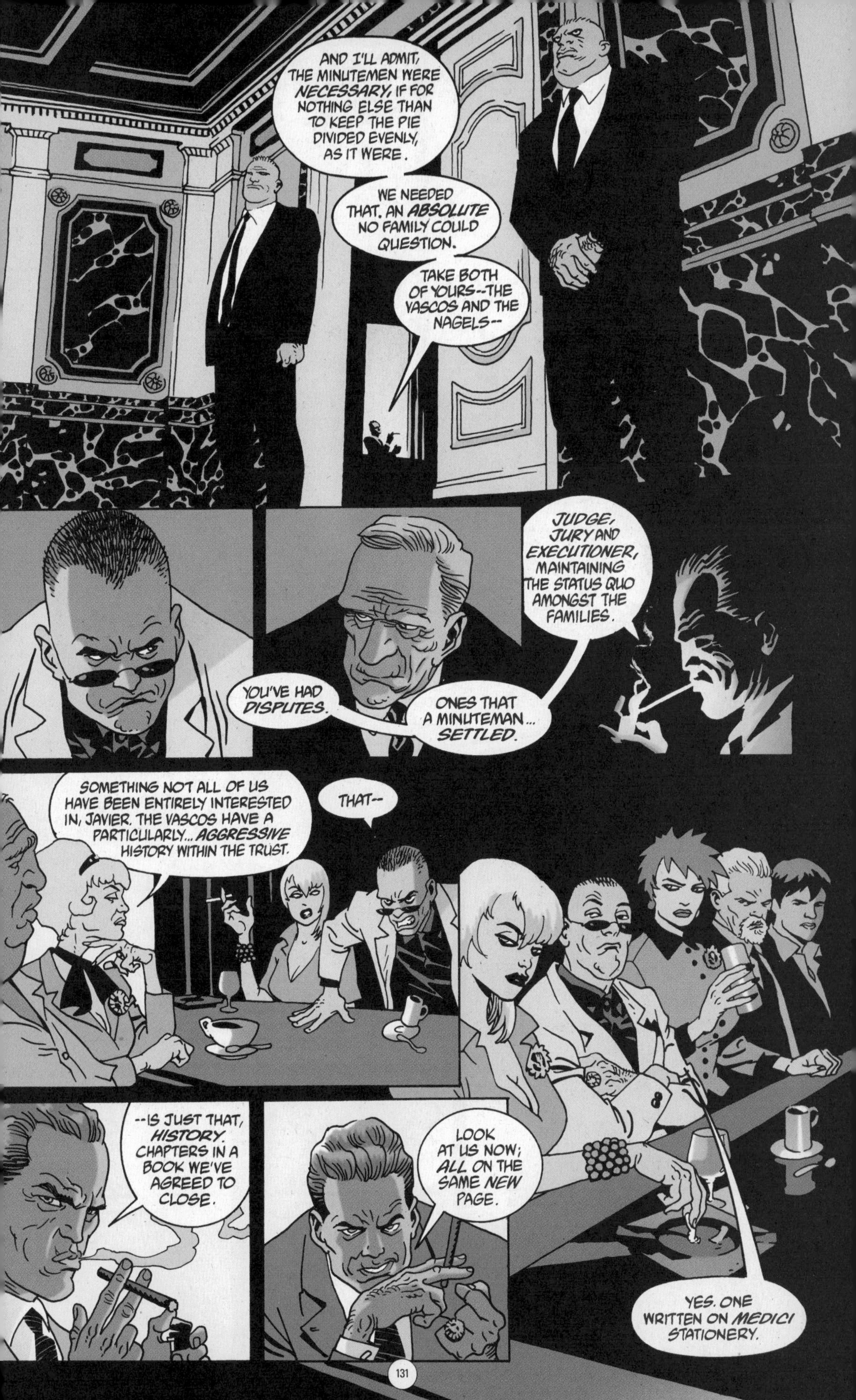
AND I'LL ADMIT, THE MINUTEMEN WERE NECESSARY, IF FOR NOTHING ELSE THAN TO KEEP THE PIE DIVIDED EVENLY, AS IT WERE.
WE NEEDED THAT. AN ABSOLUTE NO FAMILY COULD QUESTION.
TAKE BOTH OF YOURS--THE VASCOS AND THE NAGELS--
JUDGE, JURY AND EXECUTIONER, MAINTAINING THE STATUS QUO AMONGST THE FAMILIES.
YOU'VE HAD DISPUTES.
ONES THAT A MINUTEMAN... SETTLED.
SOMETHING NOT ALL OF US HAVE BEEN ENTIRELY INTERESTED IN, JAVIER. THE VASCOS HAVE A PARTICULARLY... AGGRESSIVE HISTORY WITHIN THE TRUST.
THAT--
--IS JUST THAT, HISTORY. CHAPTERS IN A BOOK WE'VE AGREED TO CLOSE.
LOOK AT US NOW; ALL ON THE SAME NEW PAGE.
YES. ONE WRITTEN ON MEDICI STATIONERY.

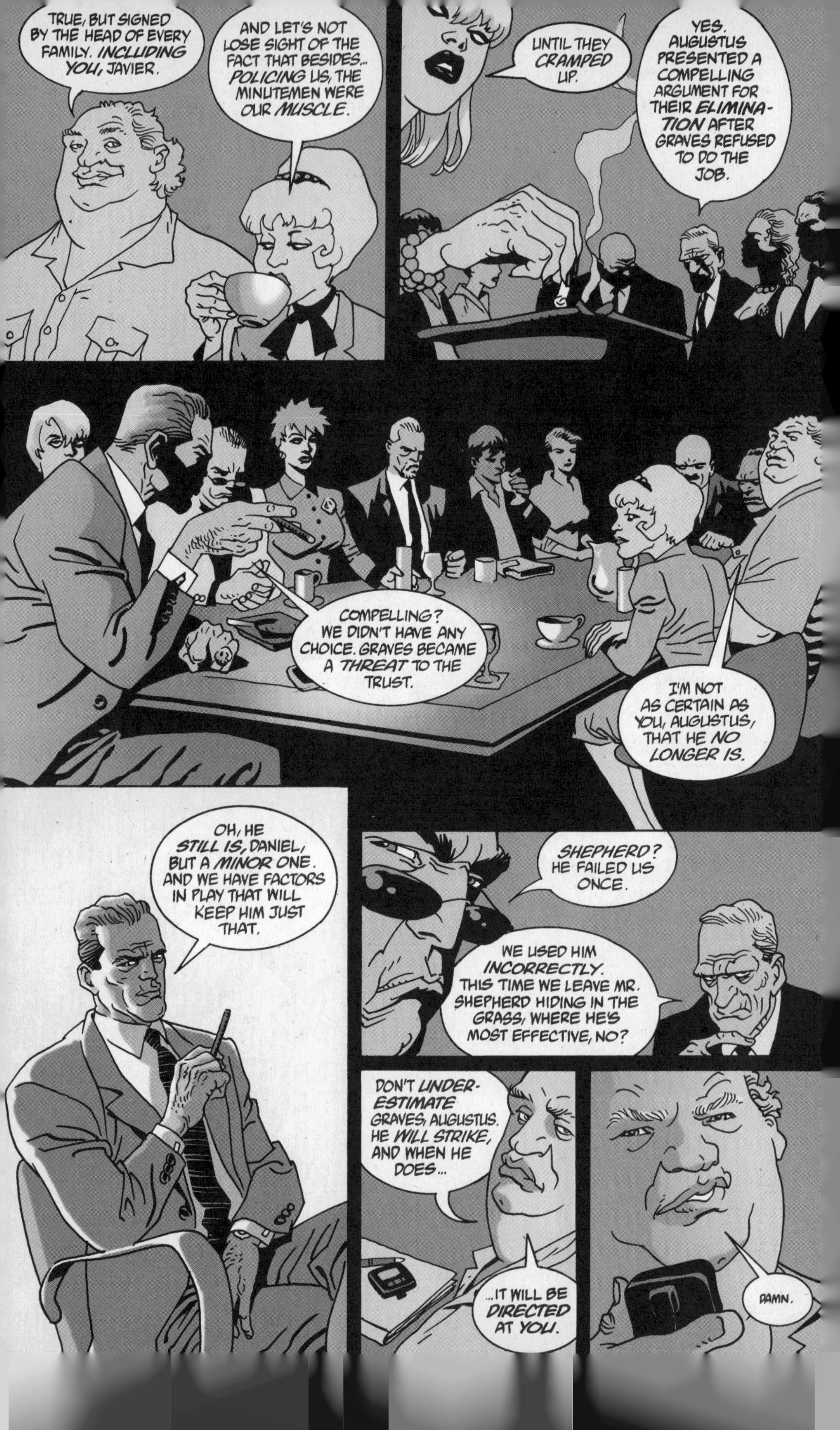
TRUE, BUT SIGNED BY THE HEAD OF EVERY FAMILY. INCLUDING YOU, JAVIER.
AND LET'S NOT LOSE SIGHT OF THE FACT THAT BESIDES... POLICING US, THE MINUTEMEN WERE OUR MUSCLE.
UNTIL THEY CRAMPED UP.
YES. AUGUSTUS PRESENTED A COMPELLING ARGUMENT FOR THEIR ELIMINATION AFTER GRAVES REFUSED TO DO THE JOB.
COMPELLING? WE DIDN'T HAVE ANY CHOICE. GRAVES BECAME A THREAT TO THE TRUST.
I'M NOT AS CERTAIN AS YOU, AUGUSTUS, THAT HE NO LONGER IS.
OH, HE STILL IS, DANIEL, BUT A MINOR ONE. AND WE HAVE FACTORS IN PLAY THAT WILL KEEP HIM JUST THAT.
SHEPHERD? HE FAILED US ONCE.
WE USED HIM INCORRECTLY. THIS TIME WE LEAVE MR. SHEPHERD HIDING IN THE GRASS, WHERE HE'S MOST EFFECTIVE, NO?
DON'T UNDERESTIMATE GRAVES, AUGUSTUS. HE WILL STRIKE, AND WHEN HE DOES...
...IT WILL BE DIRECTED AT YOU.
DAMN.

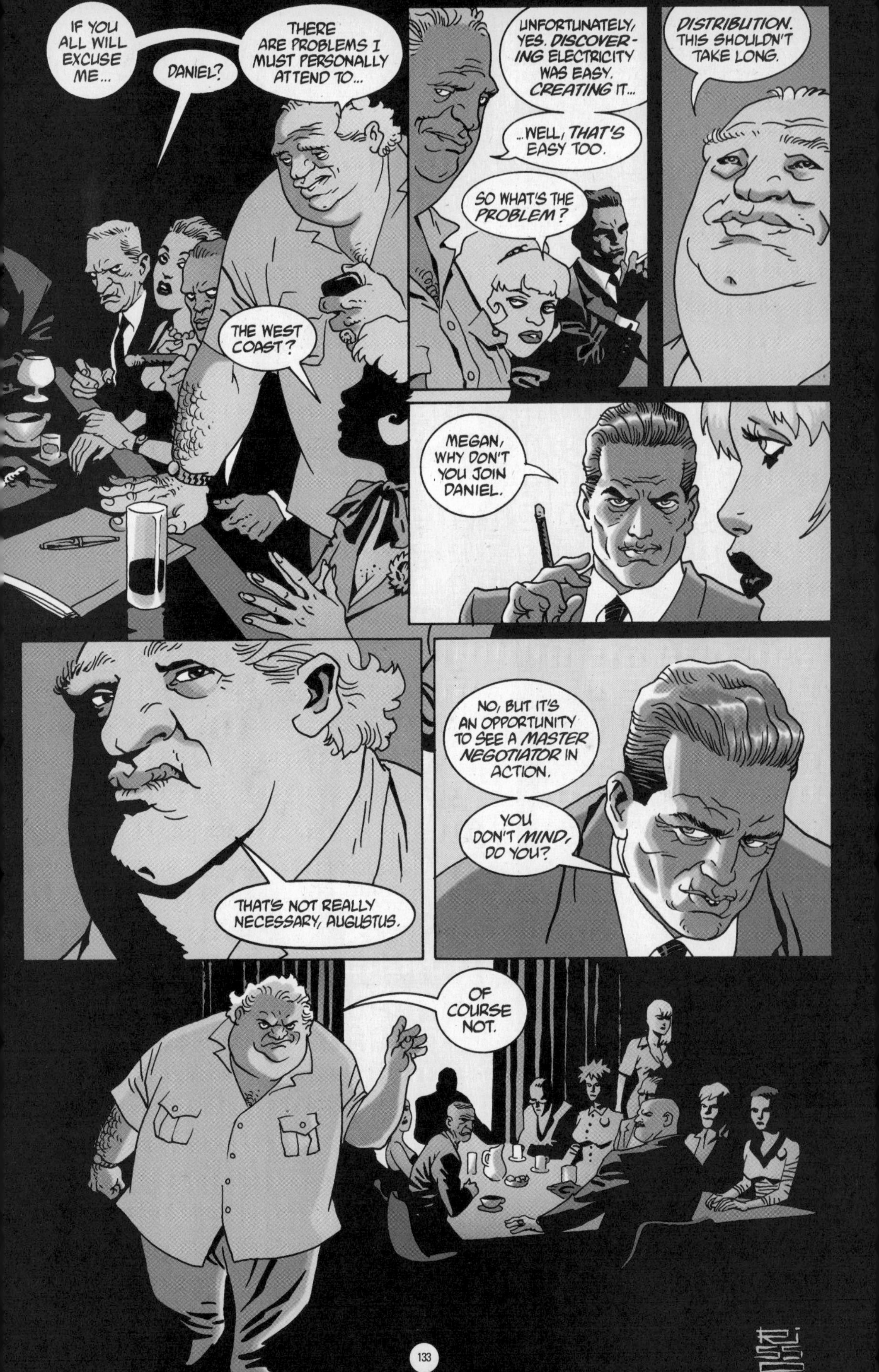
IF YOU ALL WILL EXCUSE ME...
DANIEL?
THERE ARE PROBLEMS I MUST PERSONALLY ATTEND TO...
THE WEST COAST?
UNFORTUNATELY, YES. DISCOVERING ELECTRICITY WAS EASY. CREATING IT...
...WELL, THAT'S EASY TOO.
SO WHAT'S THE PROBLEM?
DISTRIBUTION. THIS SHOULDN'T TAKE LONG.
MEGAN, WHY DON'T YOU JOIN DANIEL.
THAT'S NOT REALLY NECESSARY, AUGUSTUS.
NO, BUT IT'S AN OPPORTUNITY TO SEE A MASTER NEGOTIATOR IN ACTION.
YOU DON'T MIND, DO YOU?
OF COURSE NOT.

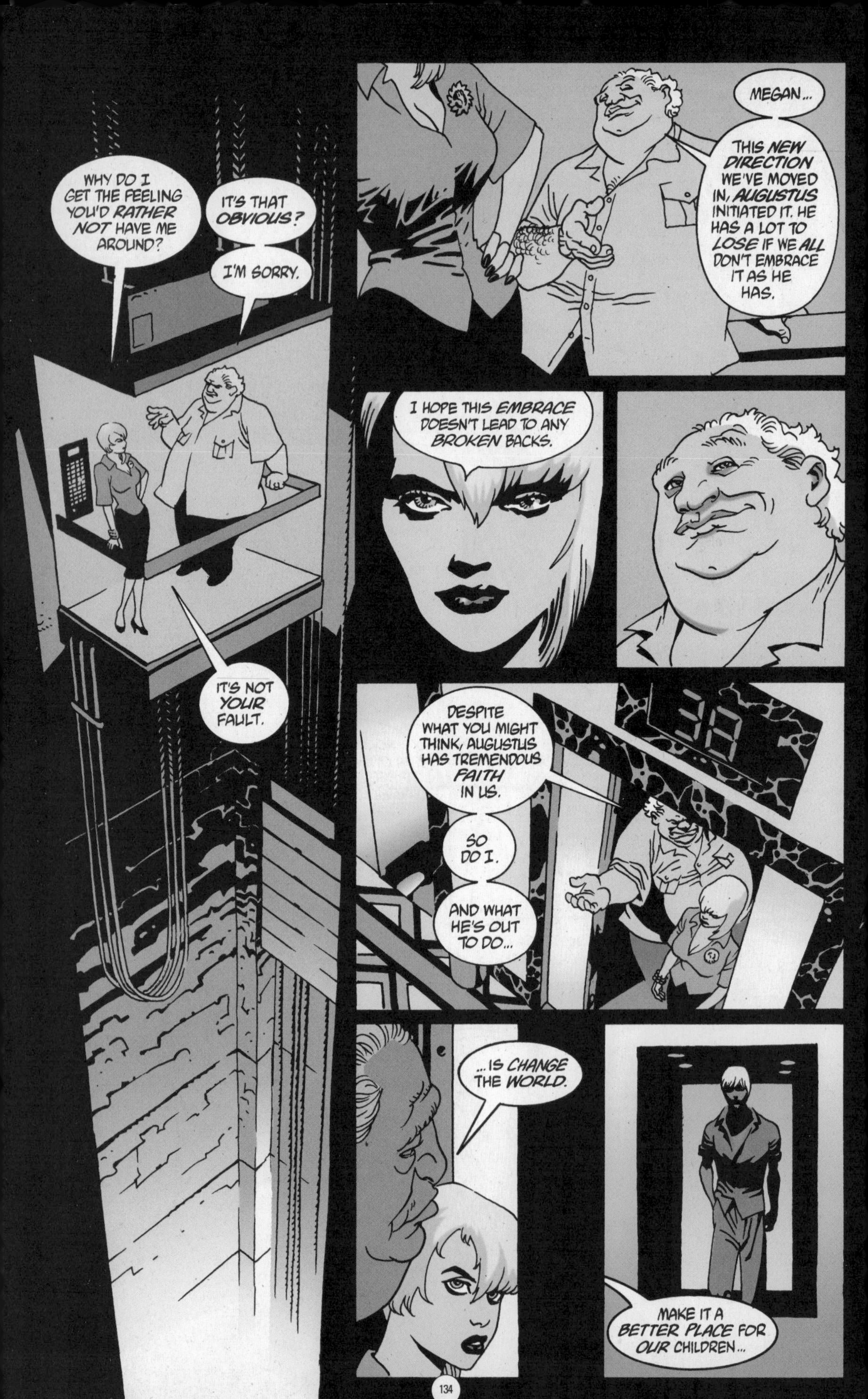
WHY DO I GET THE FEELING YOU'D RATHER NOT HAVE ME AROUND?
IT'S THAT OBVIOUS?
I'M SORRY.
IT'S NOT YOUR FAULT.
MEGAN...
THIS NEW DIRECTION WE'VE MOVED IN, AUGUSTUS INITIATED IT. HE HAS A LOT TO LOSE IF WE ALL DON'T EMBRACE IT AS HE HAS.
I HOPE THIS EMBRACE DOESN'T LEAD TO ANY BROKEN BACKS.
DESPITE WHAT YOU MIGHT THINK, AUGUSTUS HAS TREMENDOUS FAITH IN US.
SO DO I.
AND WHAT HE'S OUT TO DO...
...IS CHANGE THE WORLD.
MAKE IT A BETTER PLACE FOR OUR CHILDREN...

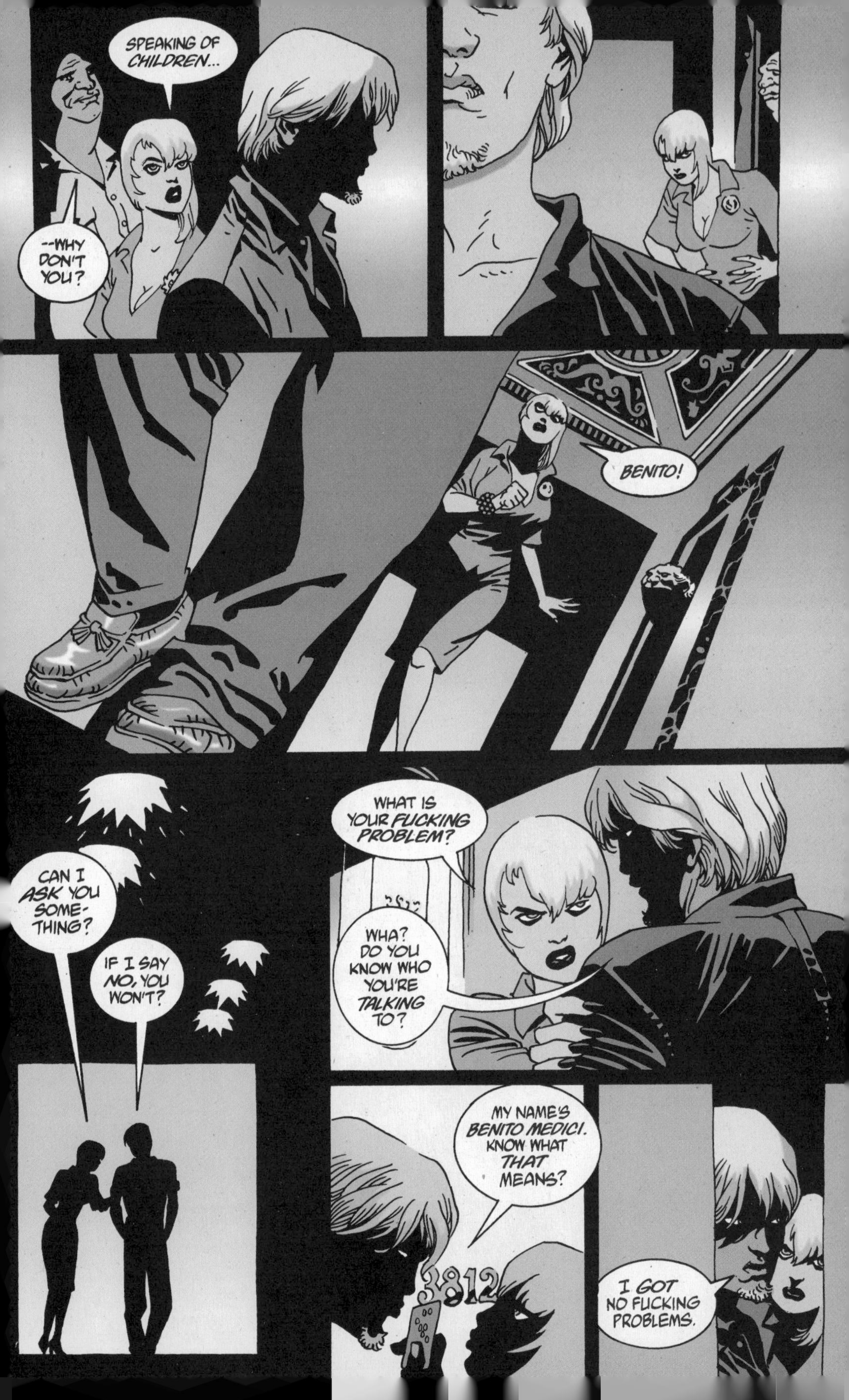
SPEAKING OF CHILDREN...
--WHY DON'T YOU?
BENITO!
CAN I ASK YOU SOME-THING?
IF I SAY NO, YOU WON'T?
WHAT IS YOUR FUCKING PROBLEM?
WHA? DO YOU KNOW WHO YOU'RE TALKING TO?
MY NAME'S BENITO MEDICI. KNOW WHAT THAT MEANS?
I GOT NO FUCKING PROBLEMS.

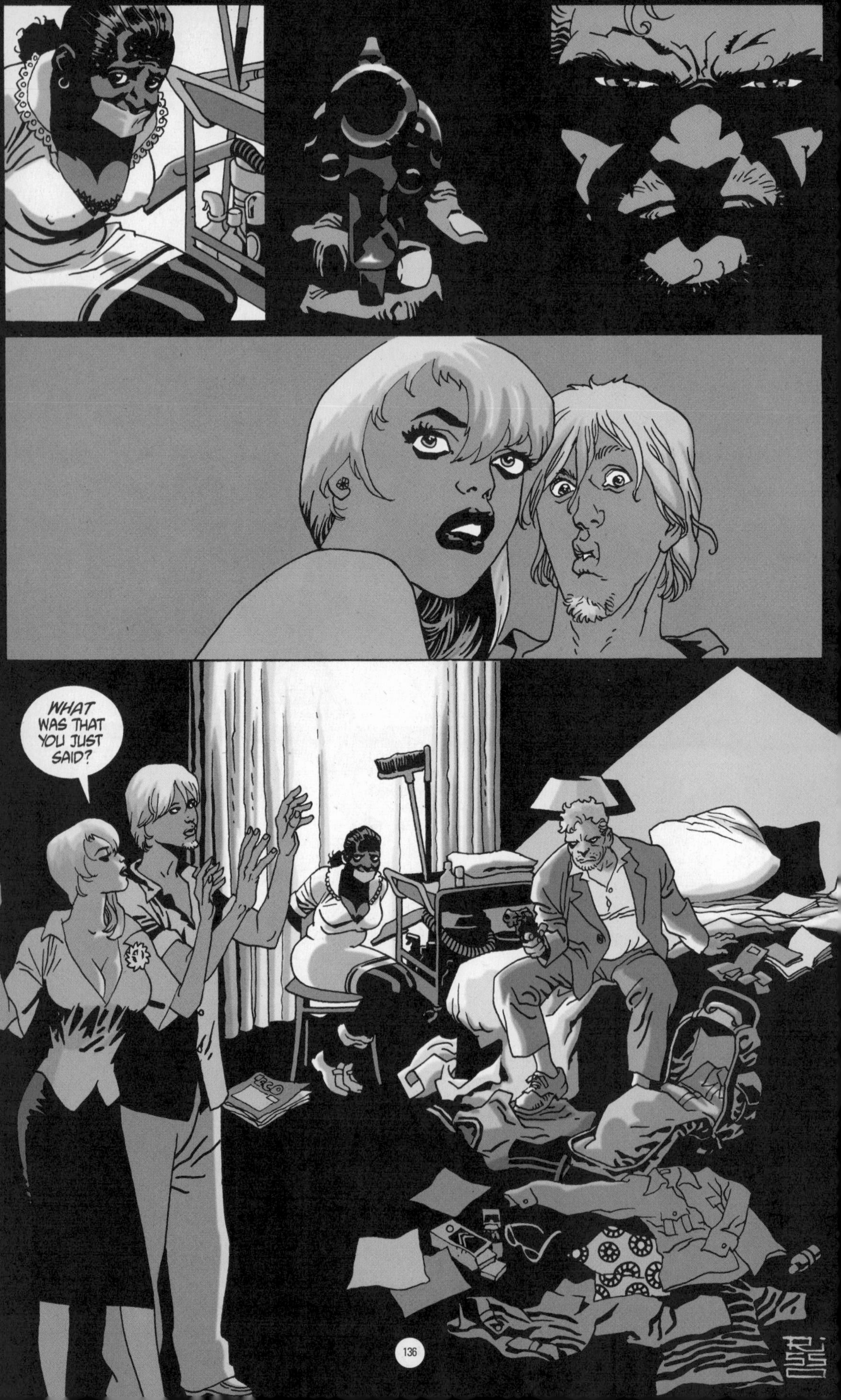
WHAT WAS THAT YOU JUST SAID?

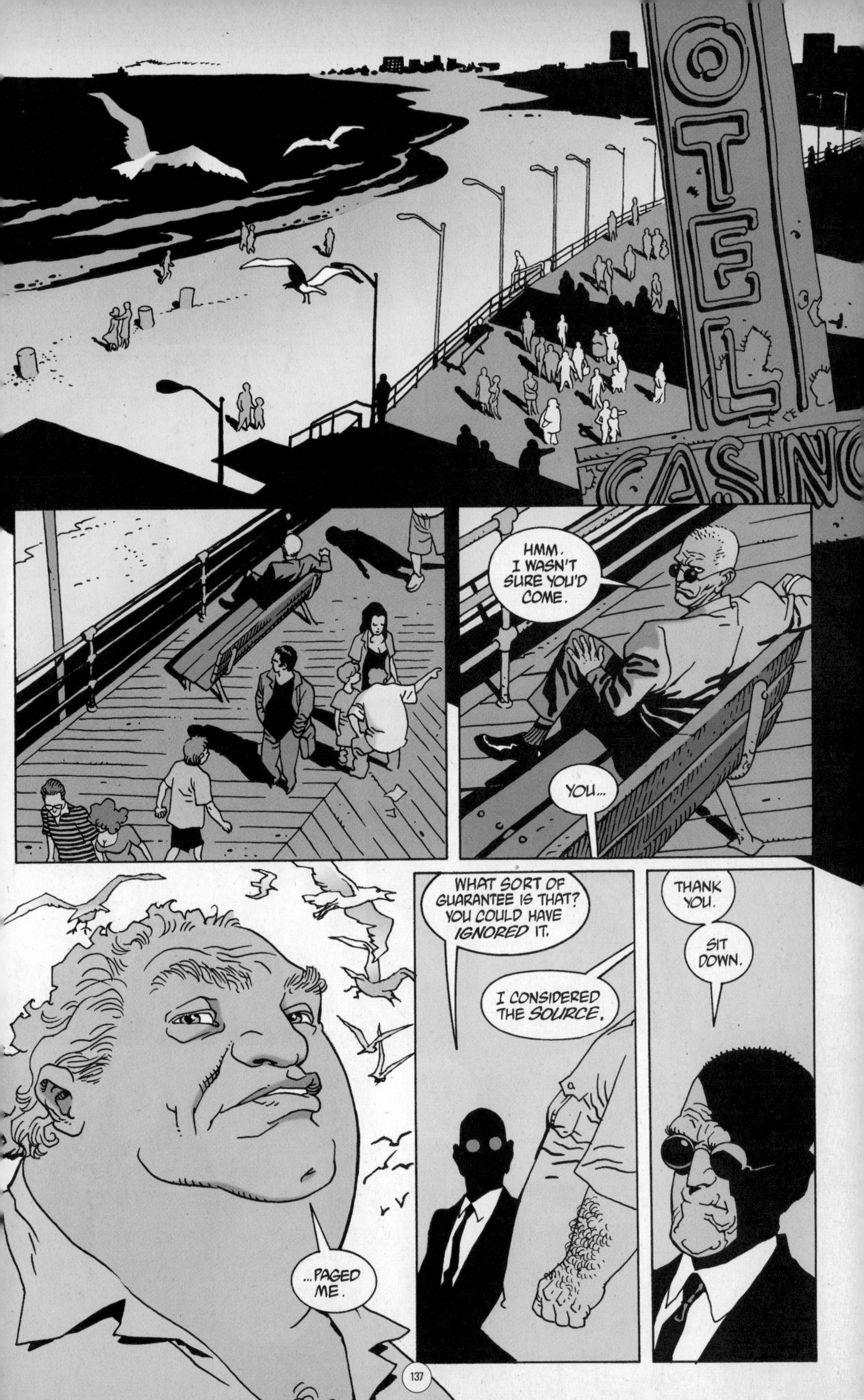
OTEL
CASINO
HMM. I WASN'T SURE YOU'D COME.
YOU...
...PAGED ME.
WHAT SORT OF GUARANTEE IS THAT? YOU COULD HAVE *IGNORED* IT.
I CONSIDERED THE *SOURCE*.
THANK YOU.
SIT DOWN.

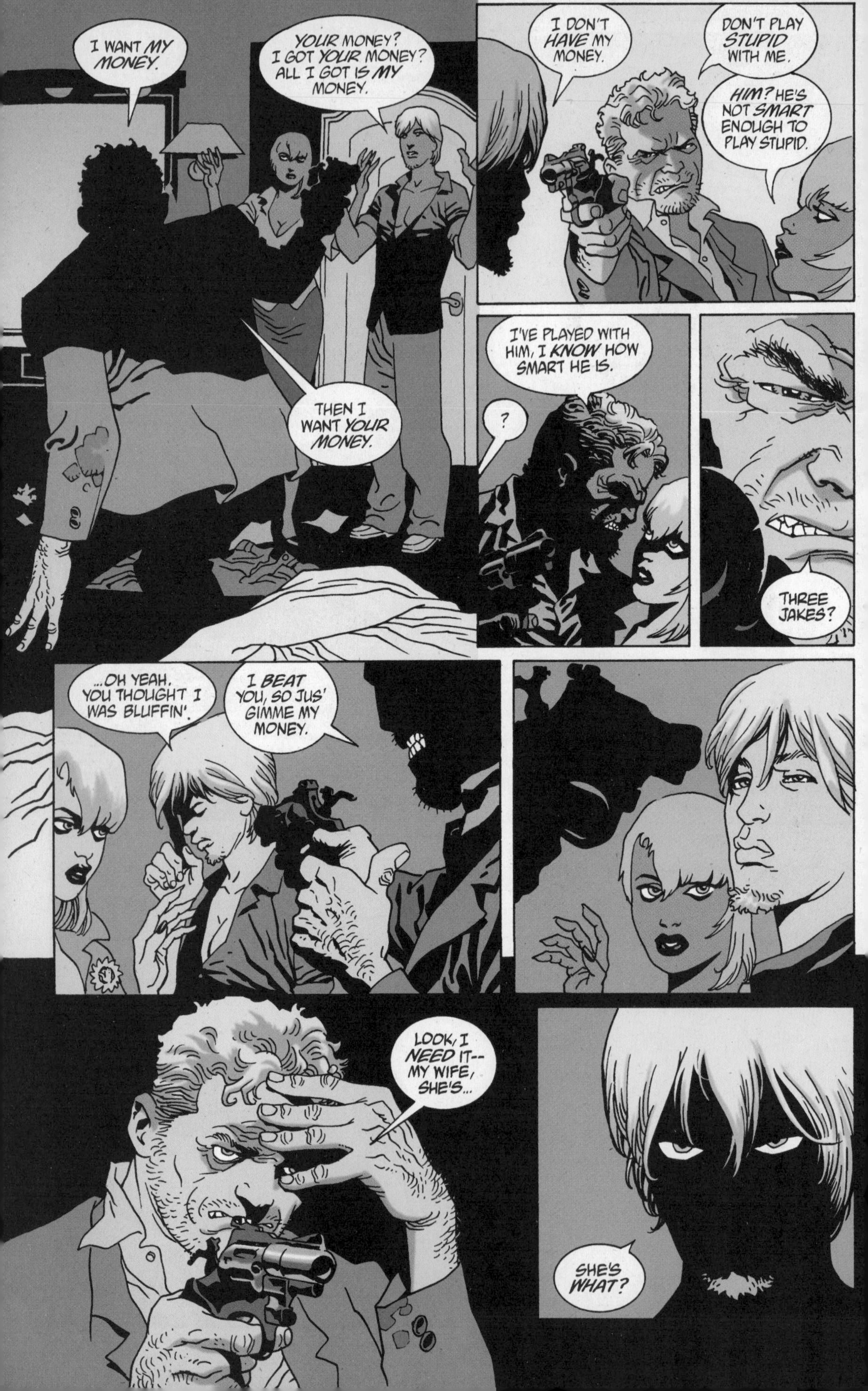
I WANT MY MONEY.
YOUR MONEY? I GOT YOUR MONEY? ALL I GOT IS MY MONEY.
THEN I WANT YOUR MONEY.
I DON'T HAVE MY MONEY.
DON'T PLAY STUPID WITH ME.
HIM? HE'S NOT SMART ENOUGH TO PLAY STUPID.
I'VE PLAYED WITH HIM, I KNOW HOW SMART HE IS.
?
THREE JAKES?
...OH YEAH. YOU THOUGHT I WAS BLUFFIN'.
I BEAT YOU, SO JUS' GIMME MY MONEY.
LOOK, I NEED IT-- MY WIFE, SHE'S...
SHE'S WHAT?

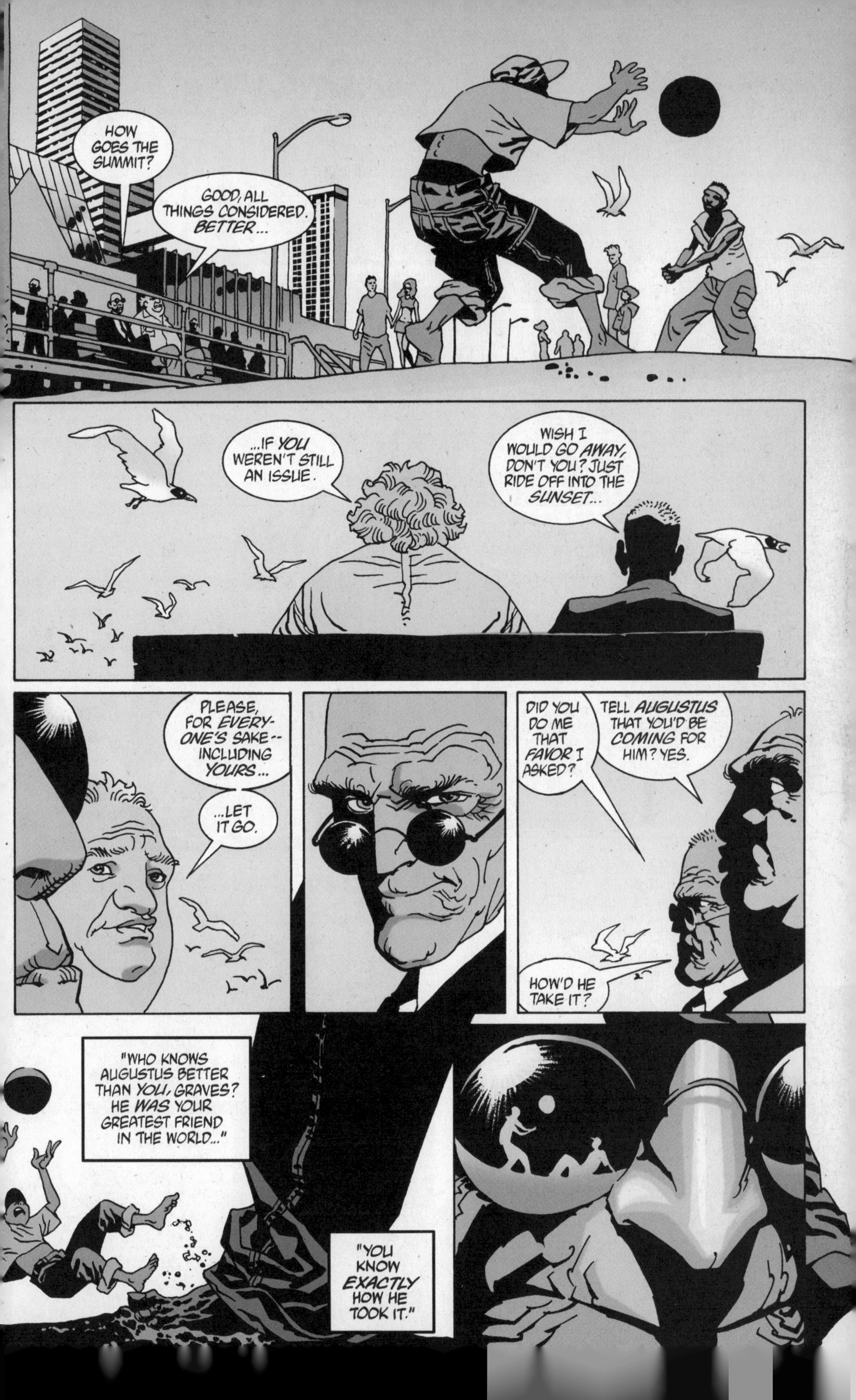
HOW GOES THE SUMMIT?
GOOD, ALL THINGS CONSIDERED. BETTER...
...IF YOU WEREN'T STILL AN ISSUE.
WISH I WOULD GO AWAY, DON'T YOU? JUST RIDE OFF INTO THE SUNSET...
PLEASE, FOR EVERY-ONE'S SAKE-- INCLUDING YOURS...
...LET IT GO.
DID YOU DO ME THAT FAVOR I ASKED?
TELL AUGUSTUS THAT YOU'D BE COMING FOR HIM? YES.
HOW'D HE TAKE IT?
"WHO KNOWS AUGUSTUS BETTER THAN YOU, GRAVES? HE WAS YOUR GREATEST FRIEND IN THE WORLD..."
"YOU KNOW EXACTLY HOW HE TOOK IT."

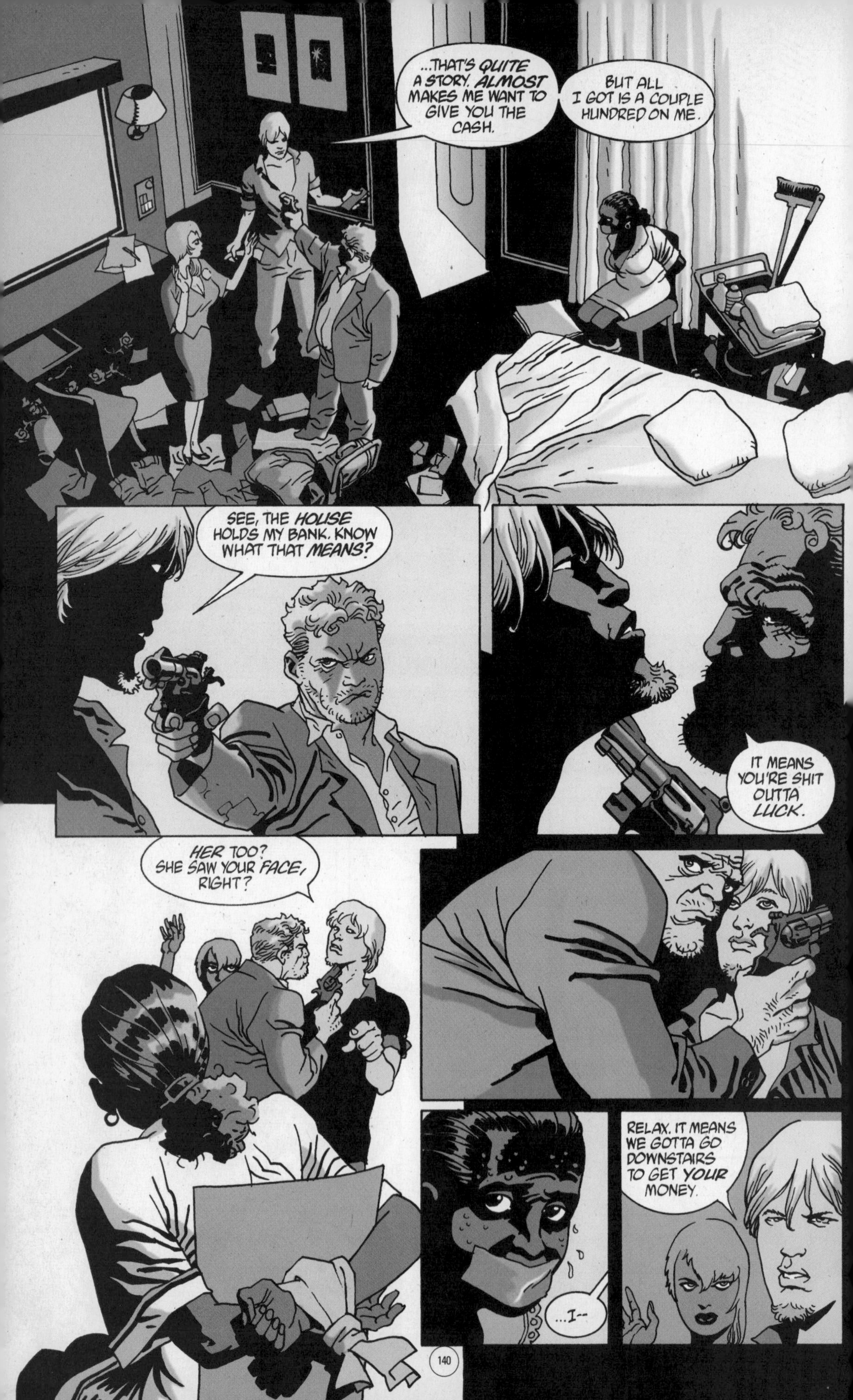
...THAT'S QUITE A STORY. ALMOST MAKES ME WANT TO GIVE YOU THE CASH.
BUT ALL I GOT IS A COUPLE HUNDRED ON ME.
SEE, THE HOUSE HOLDS MY BANK. KNOW WHAT THAT MEANS?
IT MEANS YOU'RE SHIT OUTTA LUCK.
HER TOO? SHE SAW YOUR FACE, RIGHT?
...I--
RELAX. IT MEANS WE GOTTA GO DOWNSTAIRS TO GET YOUR MONEY.

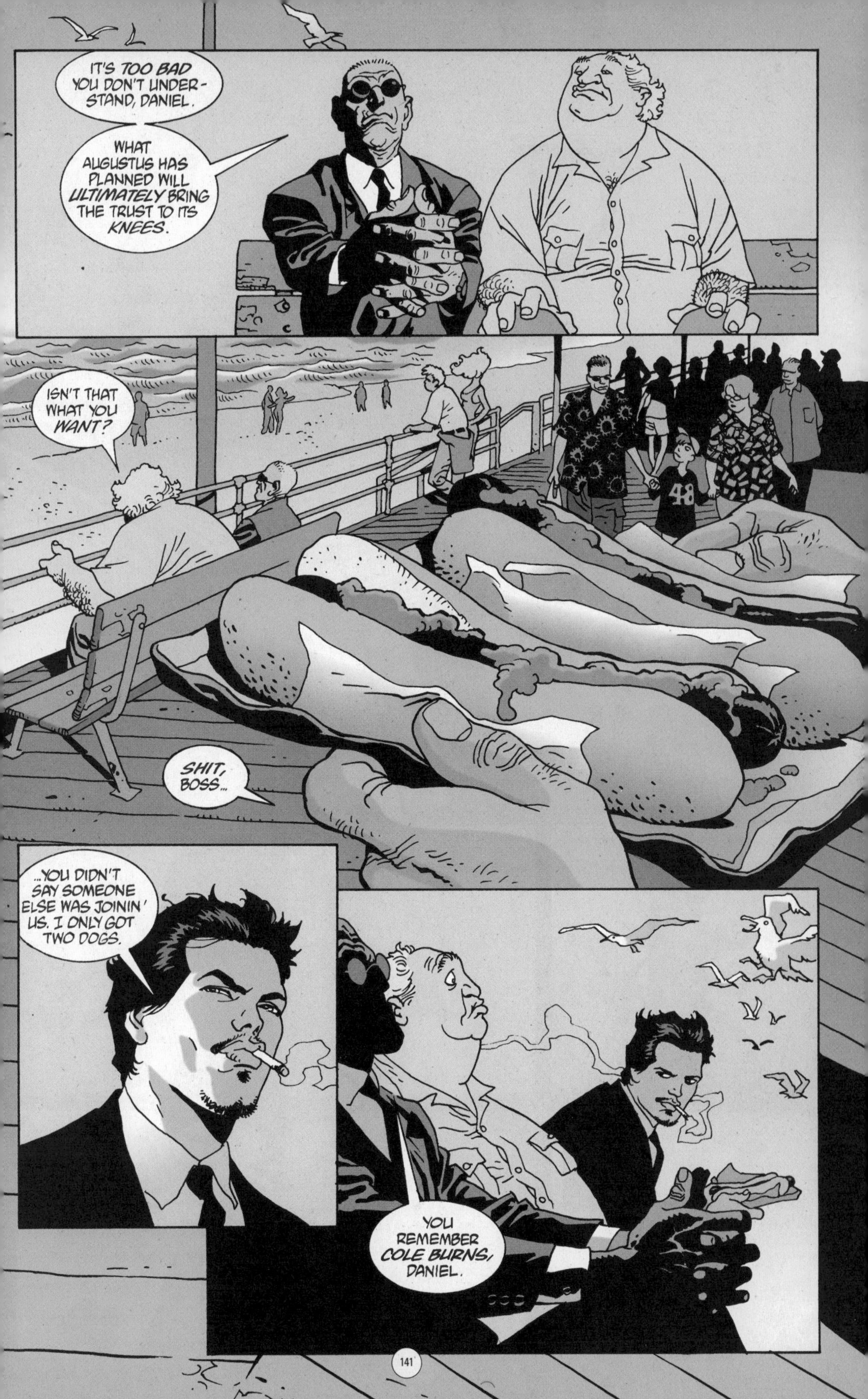

IT'S TOO BAD YOU DON'T UNDER-STAND, DANIEL.
WHAT AUGUSTUS HAS PLANNED WILL ULTIMATELY BRING THE TRUST TO ITS KNEES.
ISN'T THAT WHAT YOU WANT?
SHIT, BOSS...
...YOU DIDN'T SAY SOMEONE ELSE WAS JOININ' US. I ONLY GOT TWO DOGS.
YOU REMEMBER COLE BURNS, DANIEL.

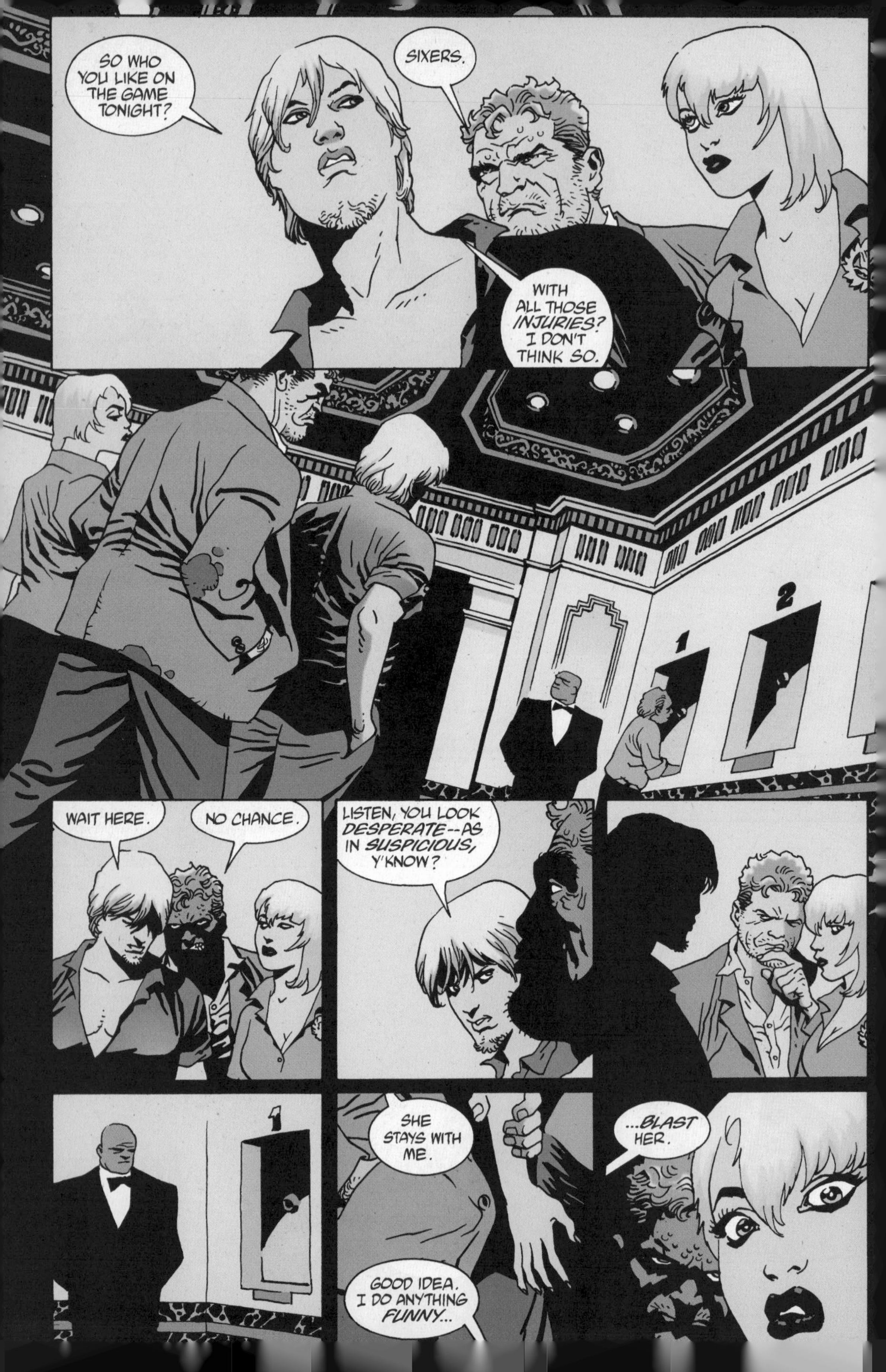
SO WHO YOU LIKE ON THE GAME TONIGHT?
SIXERS.
WITH ALL THOSE INJURIES? I DON'T THINK SO.
WAIT HERE.
NO CHANCE.
LISTEN, YOU LOOK DESPERATE--AS IN SUSPICIOUS, Y'KNOW?
1
SHE STAYS WITH ME.
GOOD IDEA. I DO ANYTHING FUNNY...
...BLAST HER.

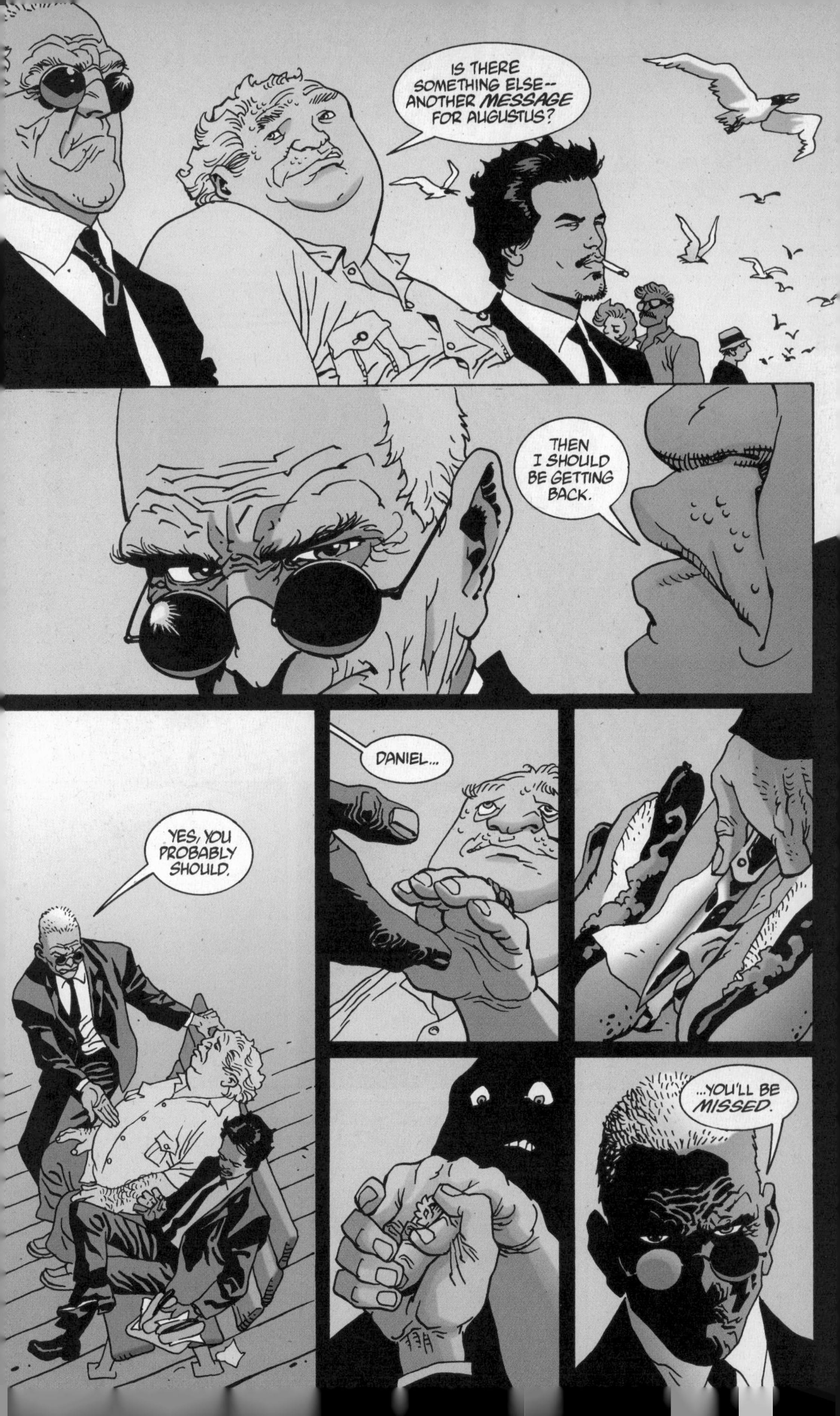
IS THERE SOMETHING ELSE-- ANOTHER MESSAGE FOR AUGUSTUS?
THEN I SHOULD BE GETTING BACK.
YES, YOU PROBABLY SHOULD.
DANIEL...
...YOU'LL BE MISSED.

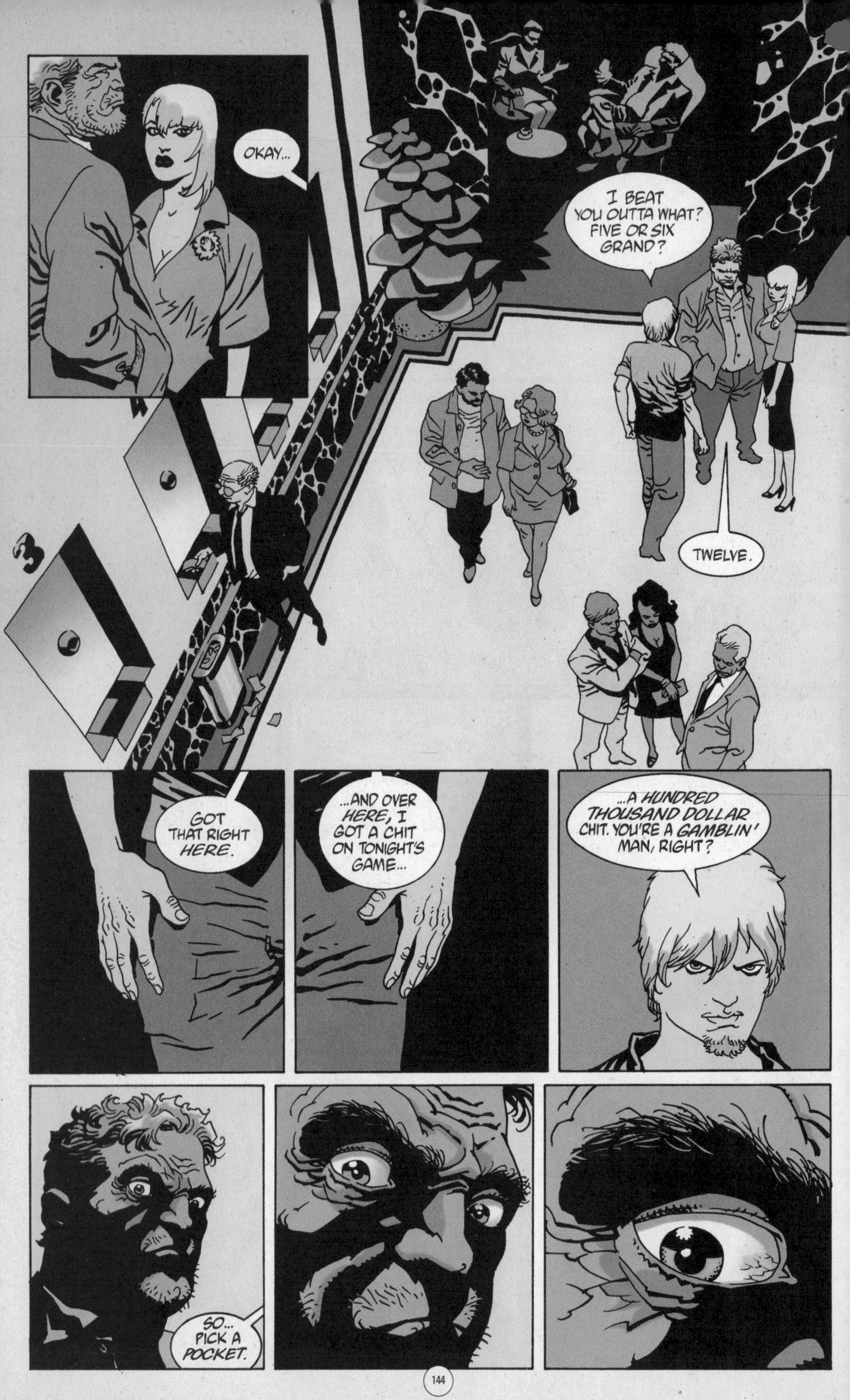
OKAY...
I BEAT YOU OUTTA WHAT? FIVE OR SIX GRAND?
TWELVE.
GOT THAT RIGHT HERE.
...AND OVER HERE, I GOT A CHIT ON TONIGHT'S GAME...
...A HUNDRED THOUSAND DOLLAR CHIT. YOU'RE A GAMBLIN' MAN, RIGHT?
SO... PICK A POCKET.

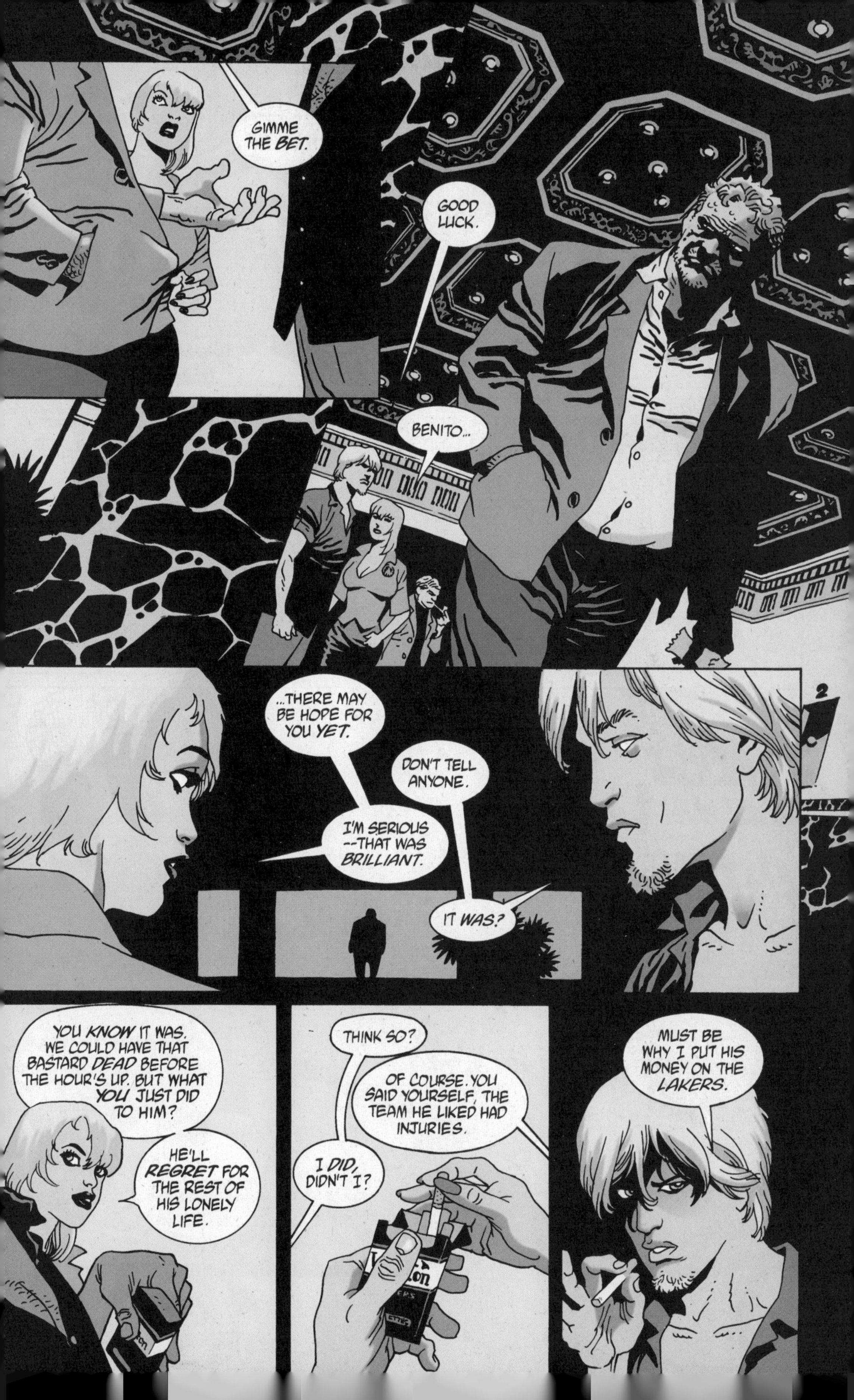
GIMME THE BET.
GOOD LUCK.
BENITO...
...THERE MAY BE HOPE FOR YOU YET.
DON'T TELL ANYONE.
I'M SERIOUS --THAT WAS BRILLIANT.
IT WAS?
YOU KNOW IT WAS. WE COULD HAVE THAT BASTARD DEAD BEFORE THE HOUR'S UP. BUT WHAT YOU JUST DID TO HIM?
HE'LL REGRET FOR THE REST OF HIS LONELY LIFE.
THINK SO?
OF COURSE. YOU SAID YOURSELF, THE TEAM HE LIKED HAD INJURIES.
I DID, DIDN'T I?
MUST BE WHY I PUT HIS MONEY ON THE LAKERS.

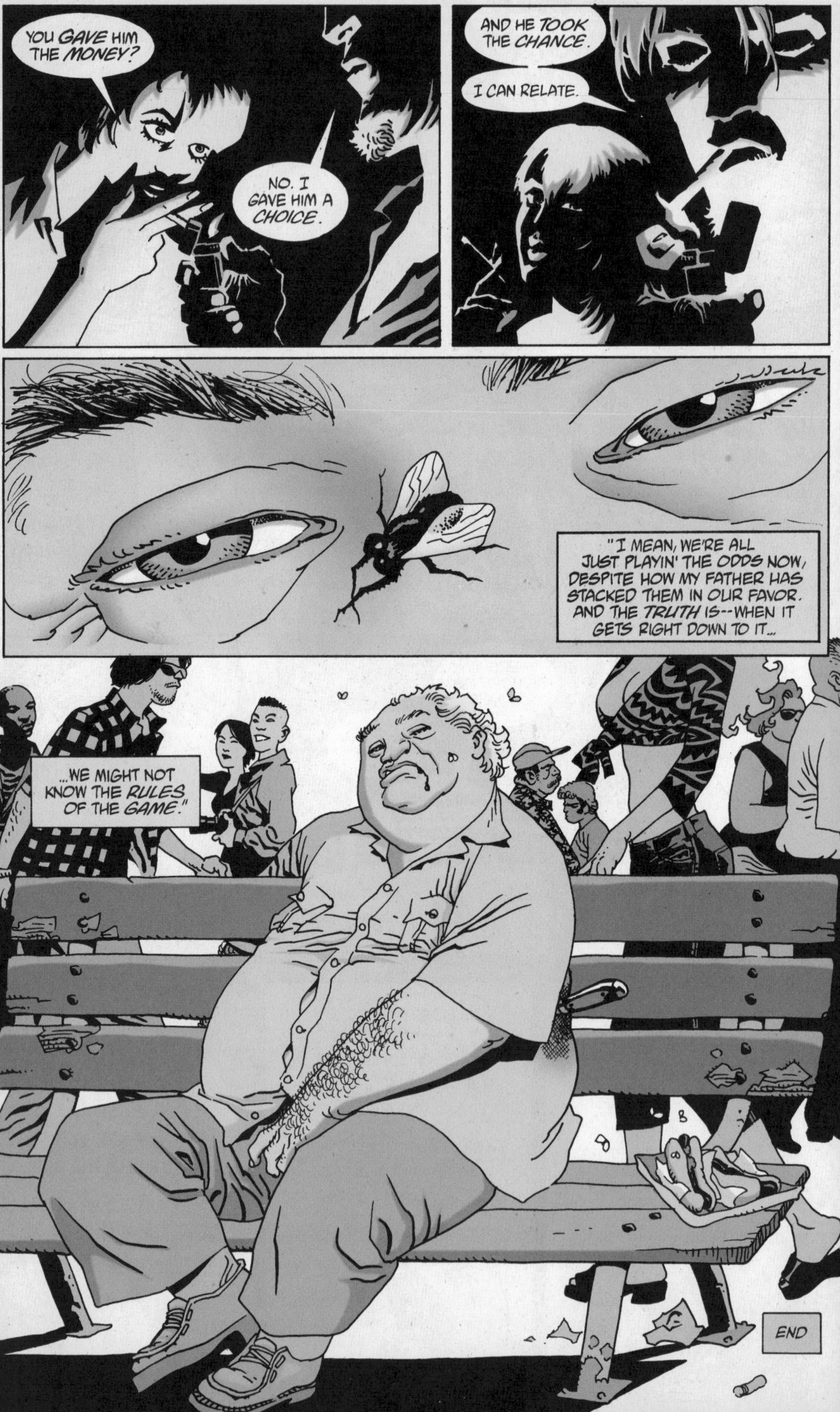
YOU GAVE HIM THE MONEY?
NO. I GAVE HIM A CHOICE.
AND HE TOOK THE CHANCE.
I CAN RELATE.
"I MEAN, WE'RE ALL JUST PLAYIN' THE ODDS NOW, DESPITE HOW MY FATHER HAS STACKED THEM IN OUR FAVOR. AND THE TRUTH IS--WHEN IT GETS RIGHT DOWN TO IT...
...WE MIGHT NOT KNOW THE RULES OF THE GAME."
END

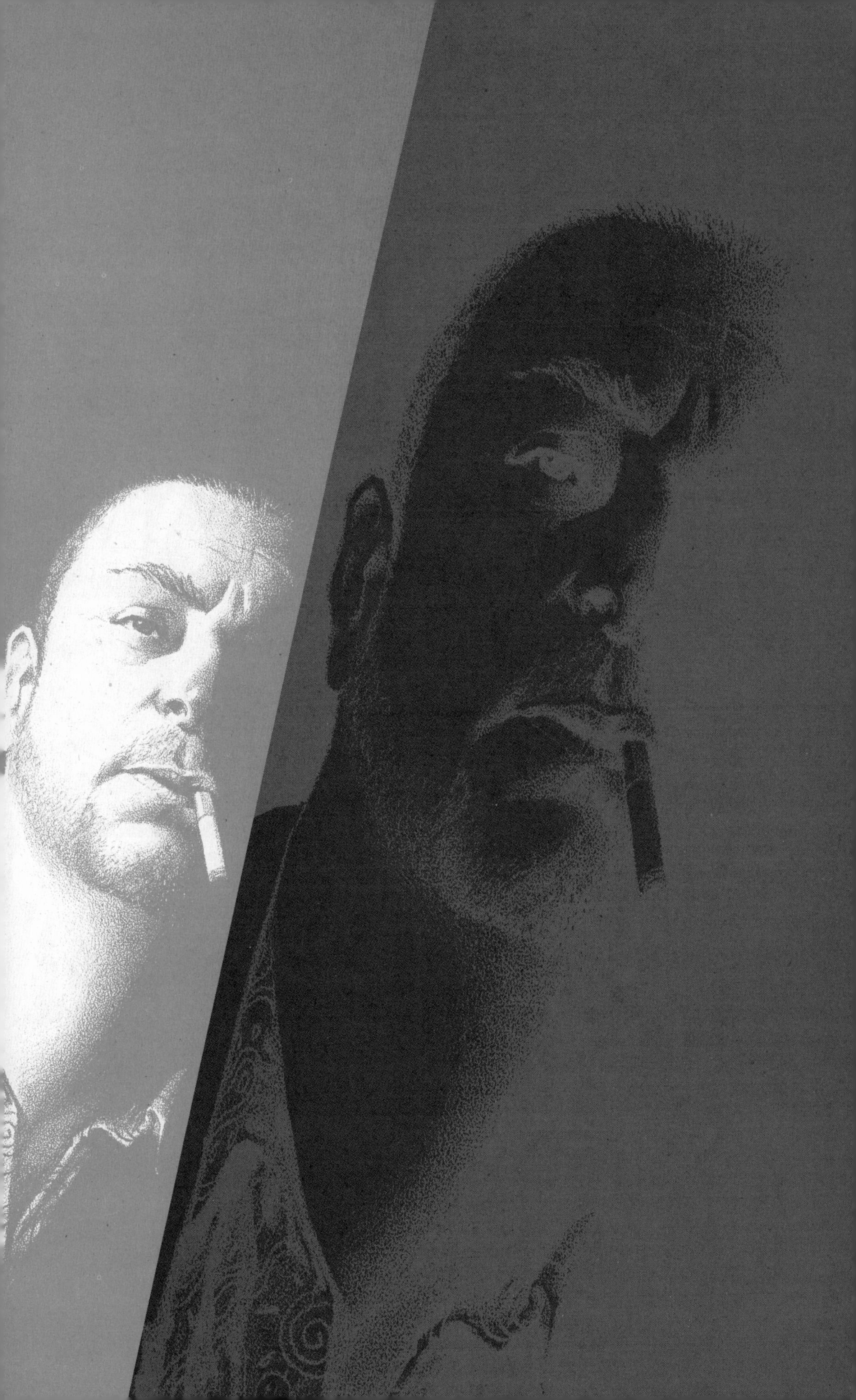

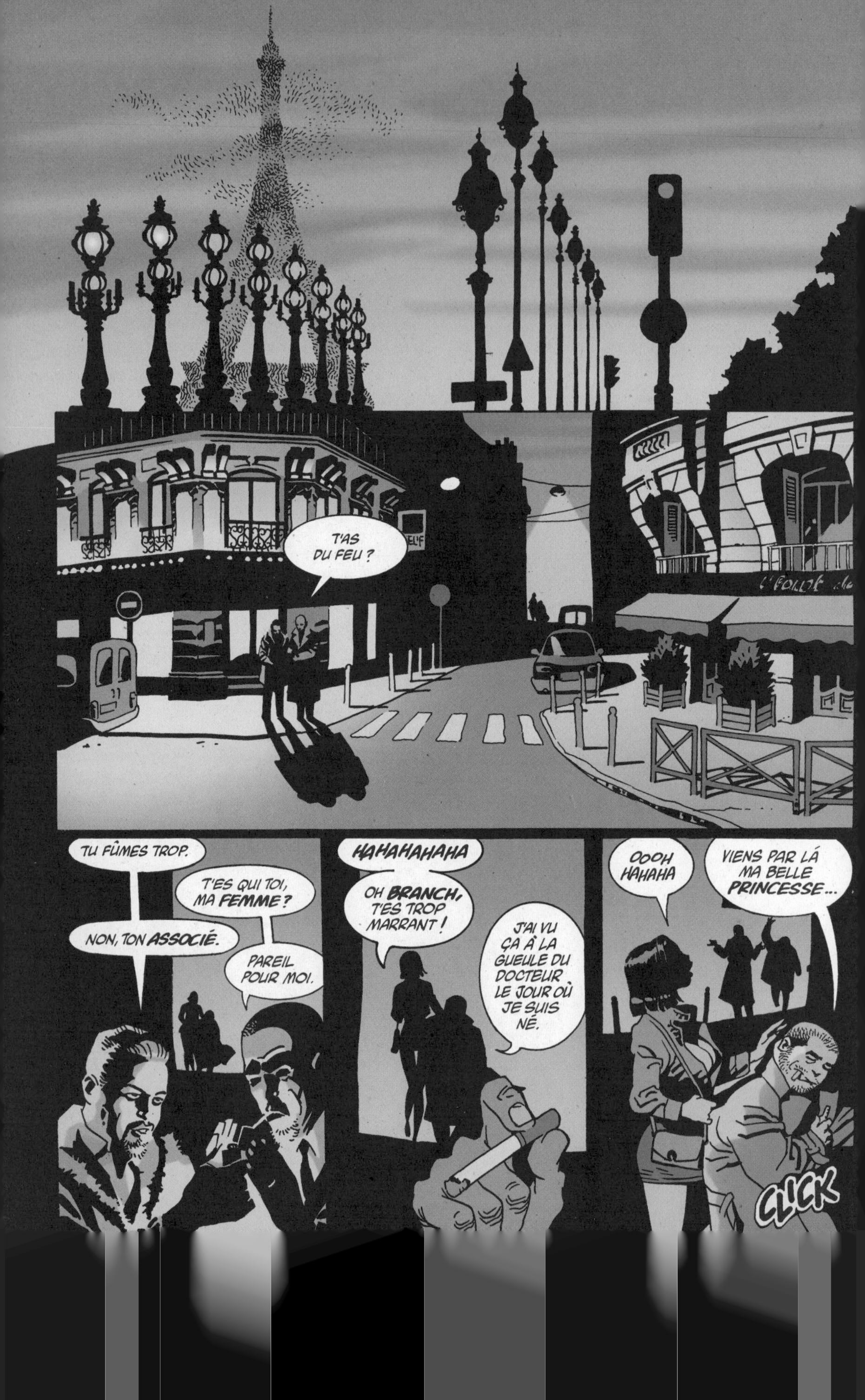
T'AS DU FEU ?
TU FÛMES TROP.
T'ES QUI TOI, MA FEMME ?
NON, TON ASSOCIÉ.
PAREIL POUR MOI.
HAHAHAHAHA
OH BRANCH, T'ES TROP MARRANT !
J'AI VU ÇA À LA GUEULE DU DOCTEUR LE JOUR OÙ JE SUIS NÉ.
OOOH HAHAHA
VIENS PAR LÁ MA BELLE PRINCESSE...
CLICK

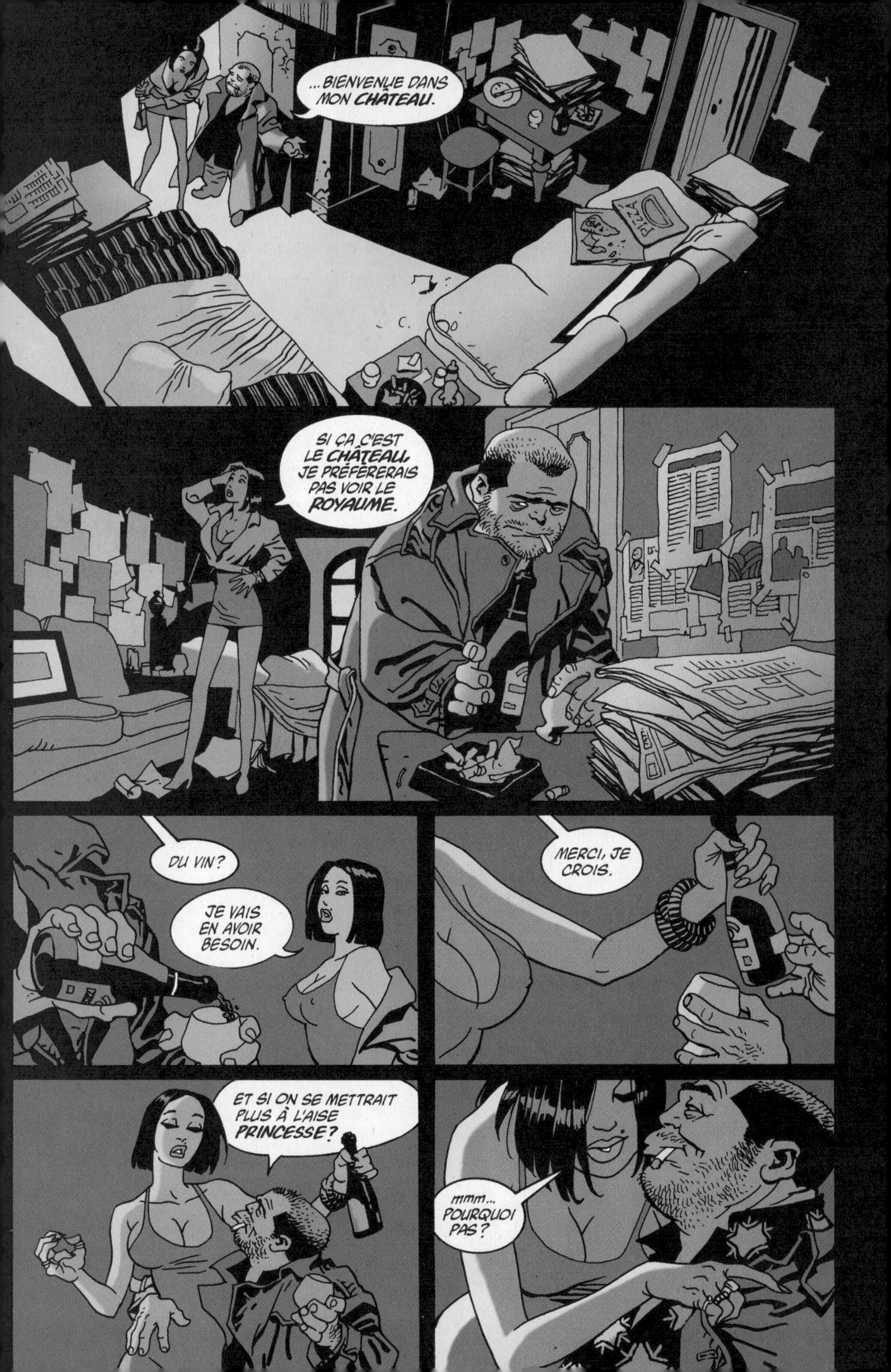
...BIENVENUE DANS MON CHÂTEAU.
SI ÇA C'EST LE CHÂTEAU, JE PRÉFÉRERAIS PAS VOIR LE ROYAUME.
DU VIN?
JE VAIS EN AVOIR BESOIN.
MERCI, JE CROIS.
ET SI ON SE METTRAIT PLUS À L'AISE PRINCESSE?
mmm... POURQUOI PAS?

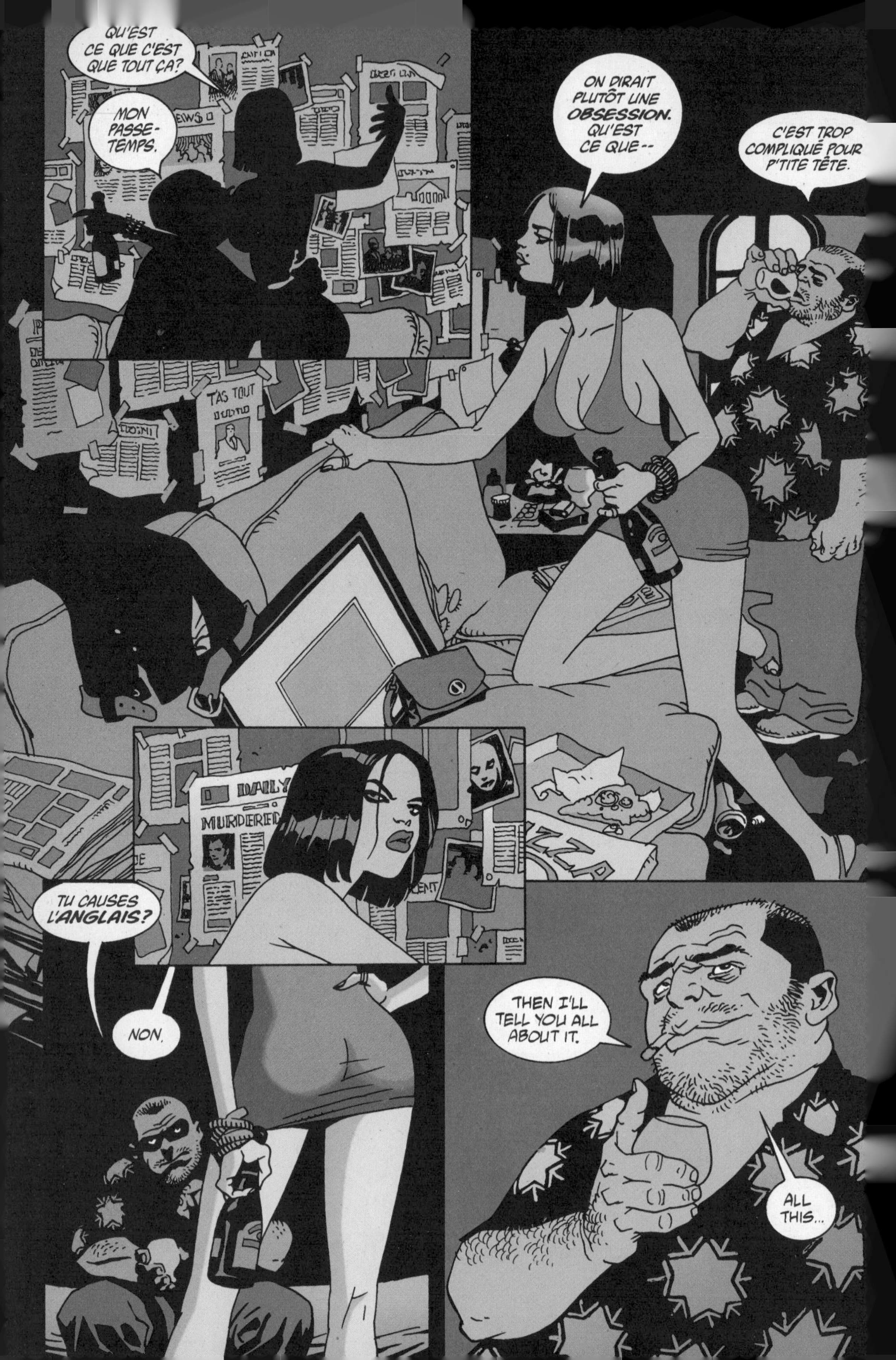
QU'EST CE QUE C'EST QUE TOUT ÇA?
MON PASSE-TEMPS.
ON DIRAIT PLUTÔT UNE OBSESSION. QU'EST CE QUE--
C'EST TROP COMPLIQUÉ POUR P'TITE TÊTE.
TU CAUSES L'ANGLAIS?
NON.
THEN I'LL TELL YOU ALL ABOUT IT.
ALL THIS...

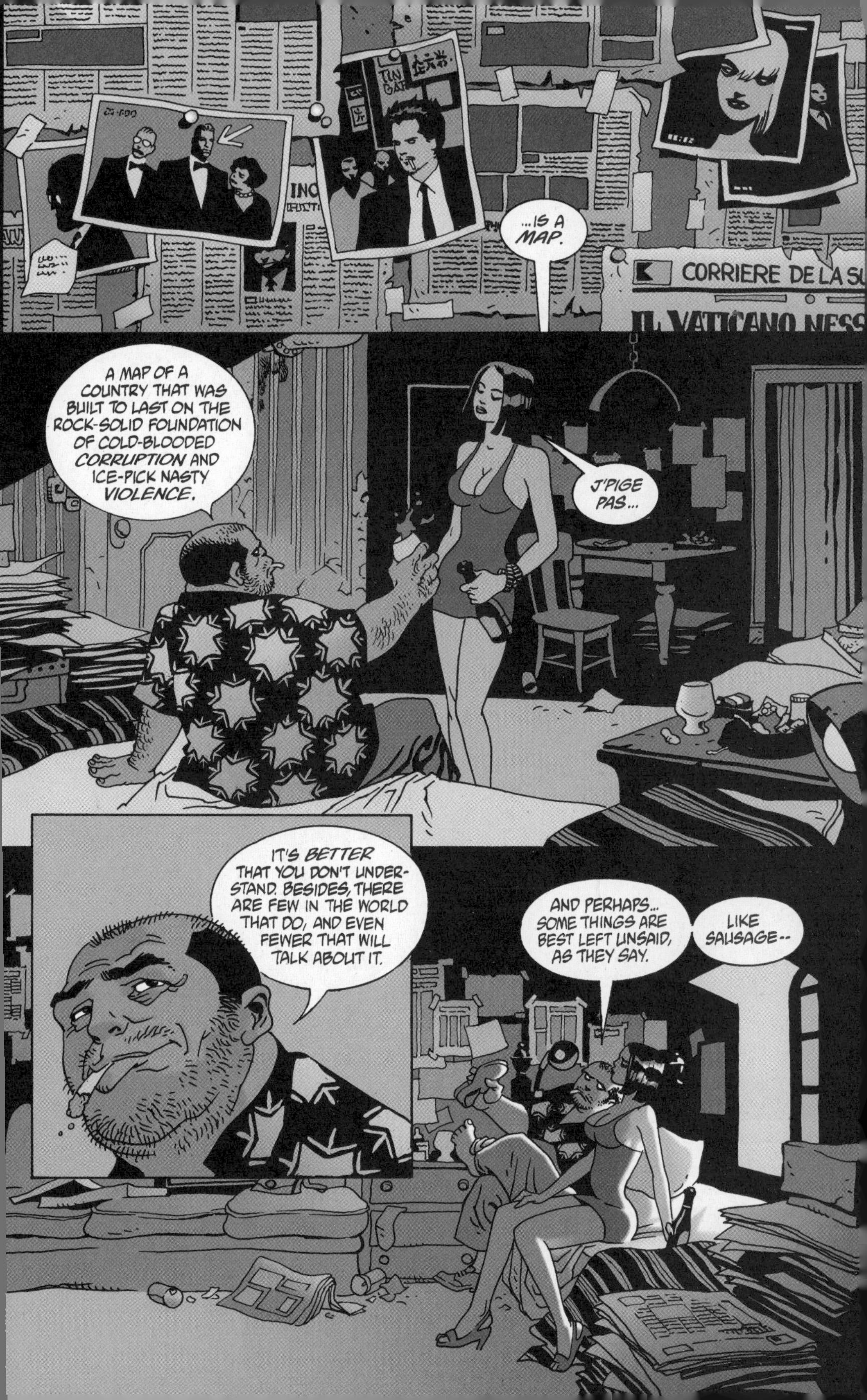
...IS A MAP.
CORRIERE DE LA SU
IL VATICANO NESS
A MAP OF A COUNTRY THAT WAS BUILT TO LAST ON THE ROCK-SOLID FOUNDATION OF COLD-BLOODED CORRUPTION AND ICE-PICK NASTY VIOLENCE.
J'PIGE PAS...
IT'S BETTER THAT YOU DON'T UNDERSTAND. BESIDES, THERE ARE FEW IN THE WORLD THAT DO, AND EVEN FEWER THAT WILL TALK ABOUT IT.
AND PERHAPS... SOME THINGS ARE BEST LEFT UNSAID, AS THEY SAY.
LIKE SAUSAGE--

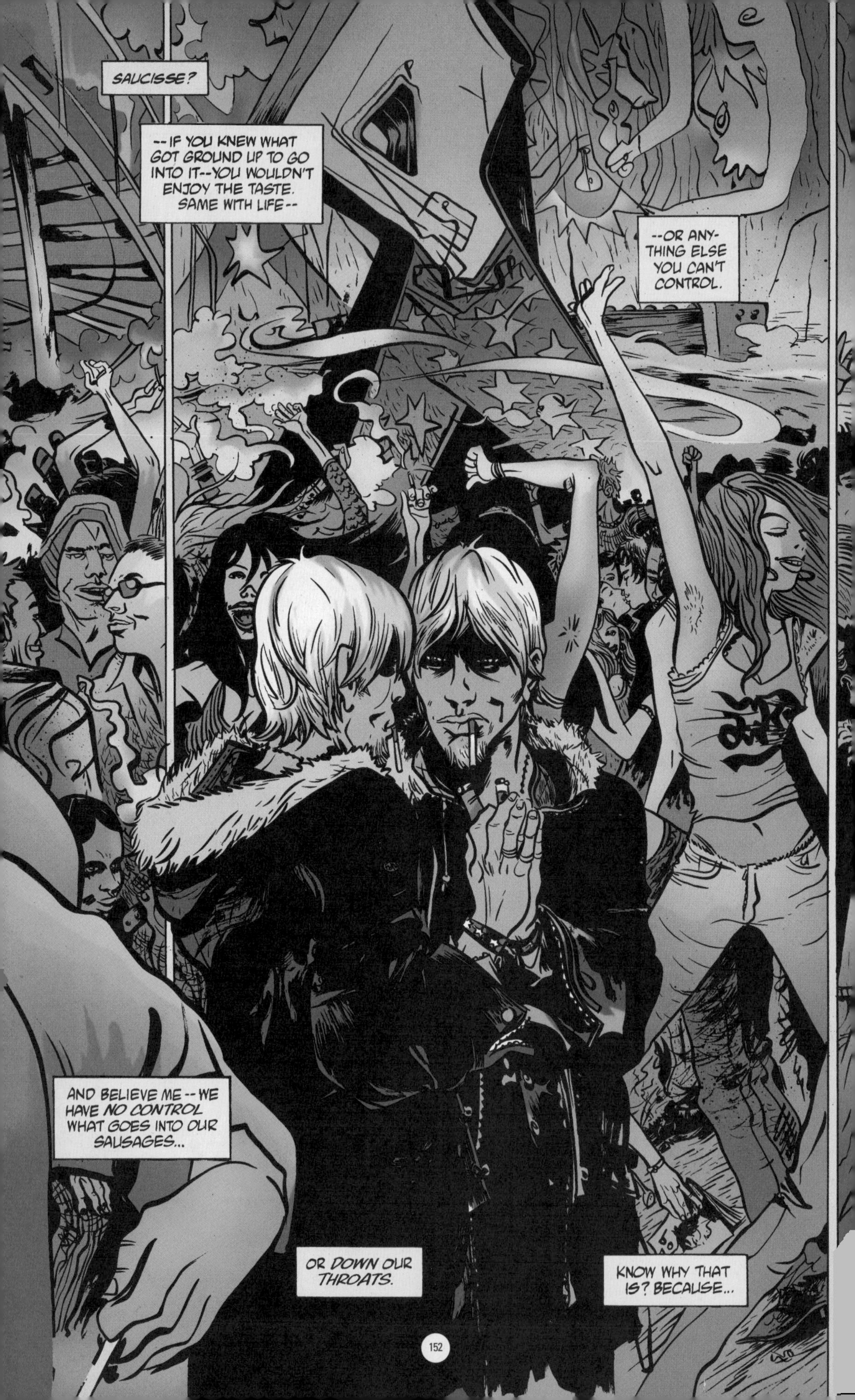
SAUCISSE?
--IF YOU KNEW WHAT GOT GROUND UP TO GO INTO IT--YOU WOULDN'T ENJOY THE TASTE. SAME WITH LIFE--
--OR ANY-THING ELSE YOU CAN'T CONTROL.
AND BELIEVE ME--WE HAVE *NO CONTROL* WHAT GOES INTO OUR SAUSAGES...
OR *DOWN* OUR *THROATS*.
KNOW WHY THAT IS? BECAUSE...

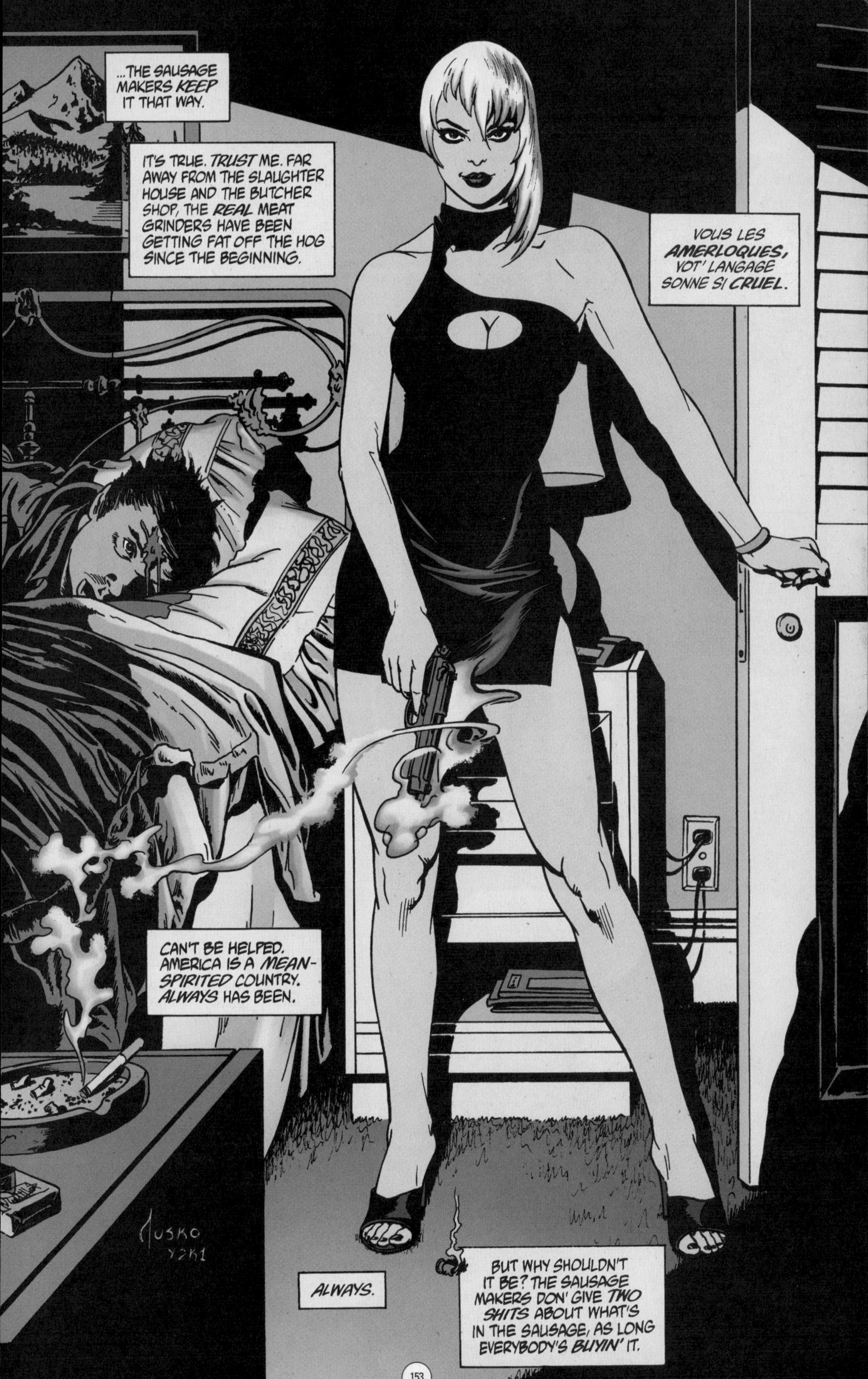
...THE SAUSAGE MAKERS KEEP IT THAT WAY.
IT'S TRUE. TRUST ME. FAR AWAY FROM THE SLAUGHTER HOUSE AND THE BUTCHER SHOP, THE REAL MEAT GRINDERS HAVE BEEN GETTING FAT OFF THE HOG SINCE THE BEGINNING.
VOUS LES AMERLOQUES, VOT' LANGAGE SONNE SI CRUEL.
CAN'T BE HELPED. AMERICA IS A MEAN-SPIRITED COUNTRY. ALWAYS HAS BEEN.
ALWAYS.
BUT WHY SHOULDN'T IT BE? THE SAUSAGE MAKERS DON' GIVE TWO SHITS ABOUT WHAT'S IN THE SAUSAGE, AS LONG EVERYBODY'S BUYIN' IT.

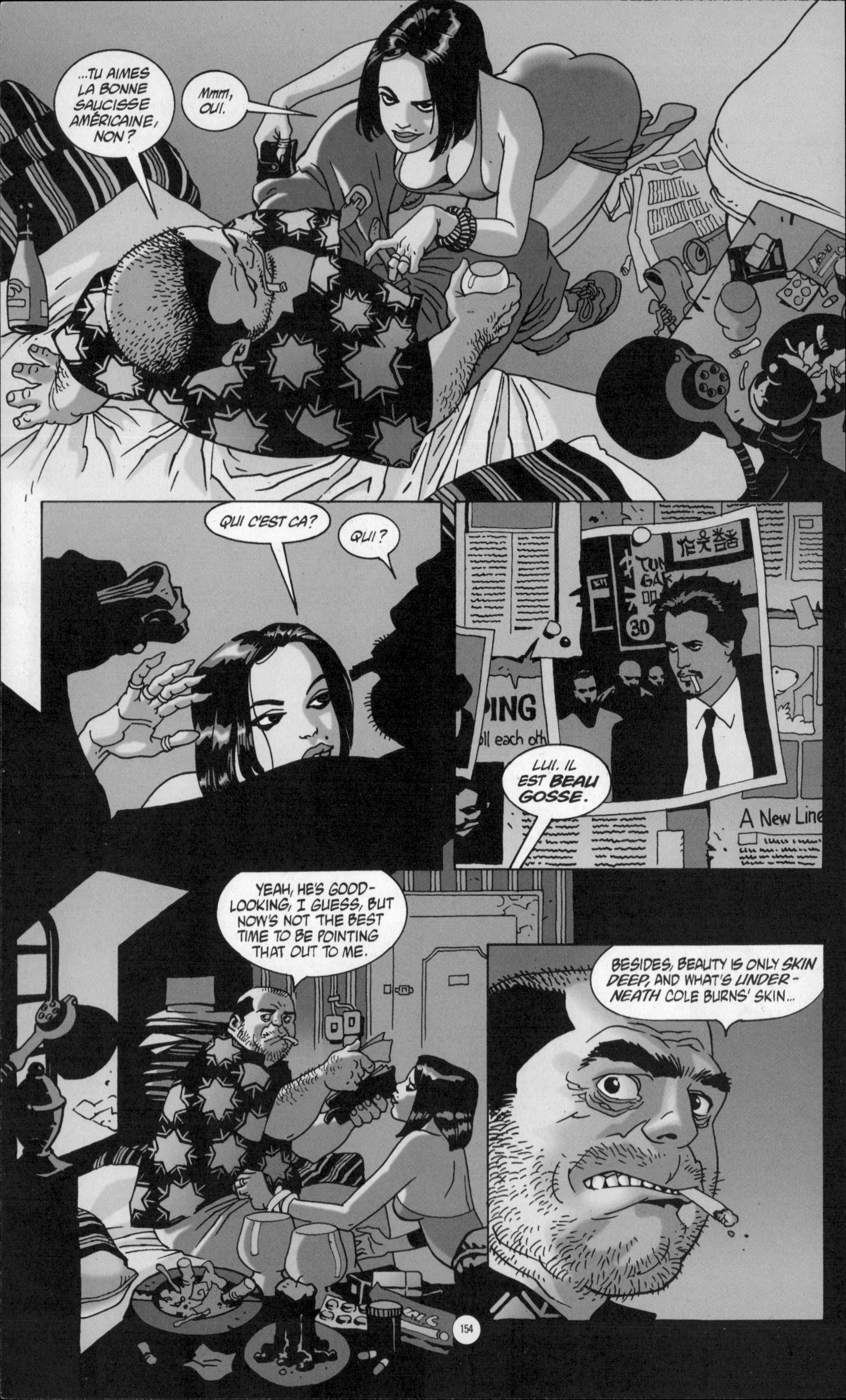
...TU AIMES LA BONNE SAUCISSE AMÉRICAINE, NON?
Mmm, OUI.
QUI C'EST CA?
QUI?
LUI. IL EST BEAU GOSSE.
A New Line
YEAH, HE'S GOOD-LOOKING, I GUESS, BUT NOW'S NOT THE BEST TIME TO BE POINTING THAT OUT TO ME.
BESIDES, BEAUTY IS ONLY SKIN DEEP, AND WHAT'S UNDERNEATH COLE BURNS' SKIN...

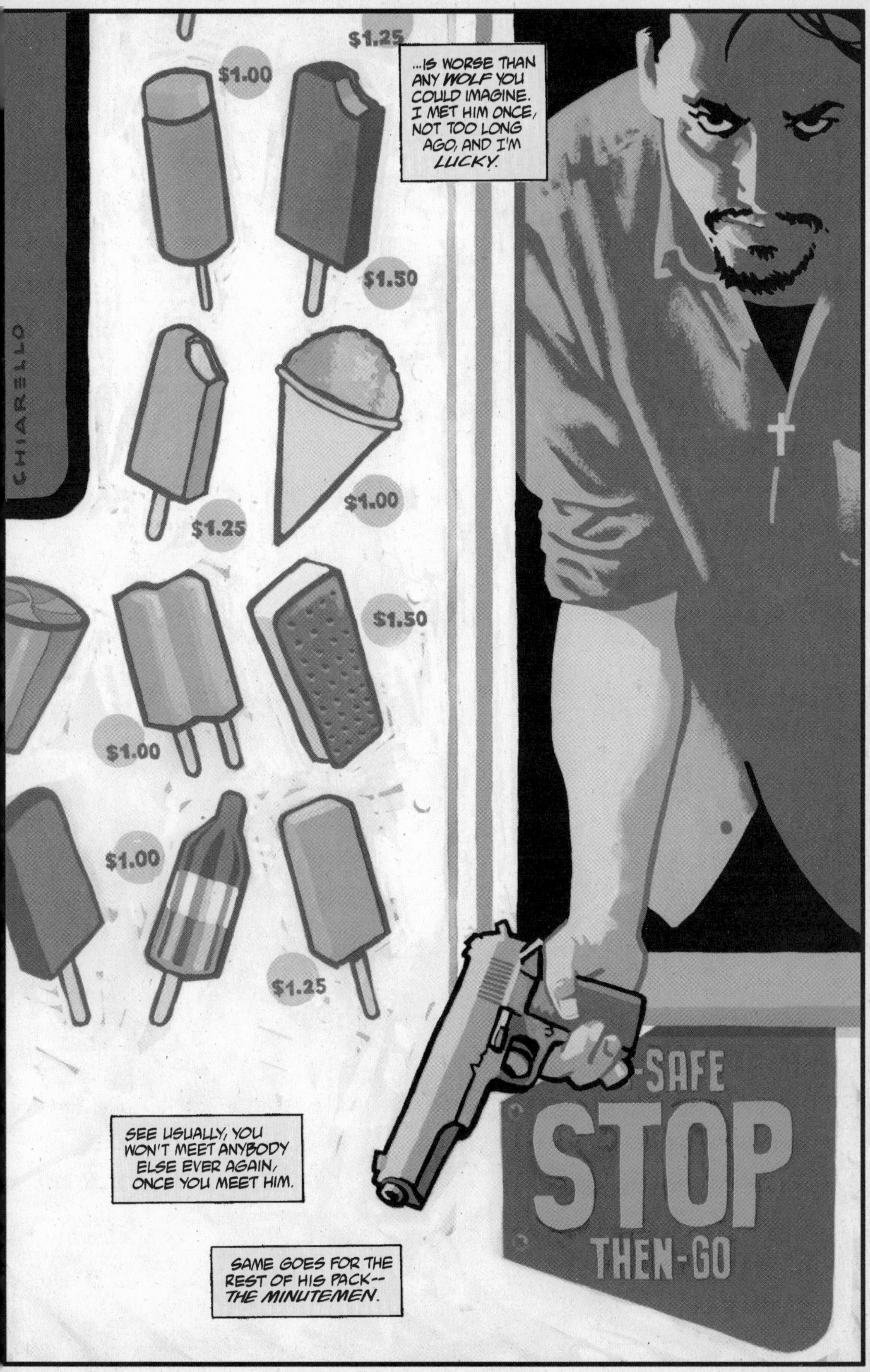

CHIARELLO
$1.25
$1.00
$1.50
$1.25
$1.00
$1.50
$1.00
$1.00
$1.25
...IS WORSE THAN ANY WOLF YOU COULD IMAGINE. I MET HIM ONCE, NOT TOO LONG AGO, AND I'M LUCKY.
SAFE
STOP
THEN-GO
SEE USUALLY, YOU WON'T MEET ANYBODY ELSE EVER AGAIN, ONCE YOU MEET HIM.
SAME GOES FOR THE REST OF HIS PACK-- THE MINUTEMEN.

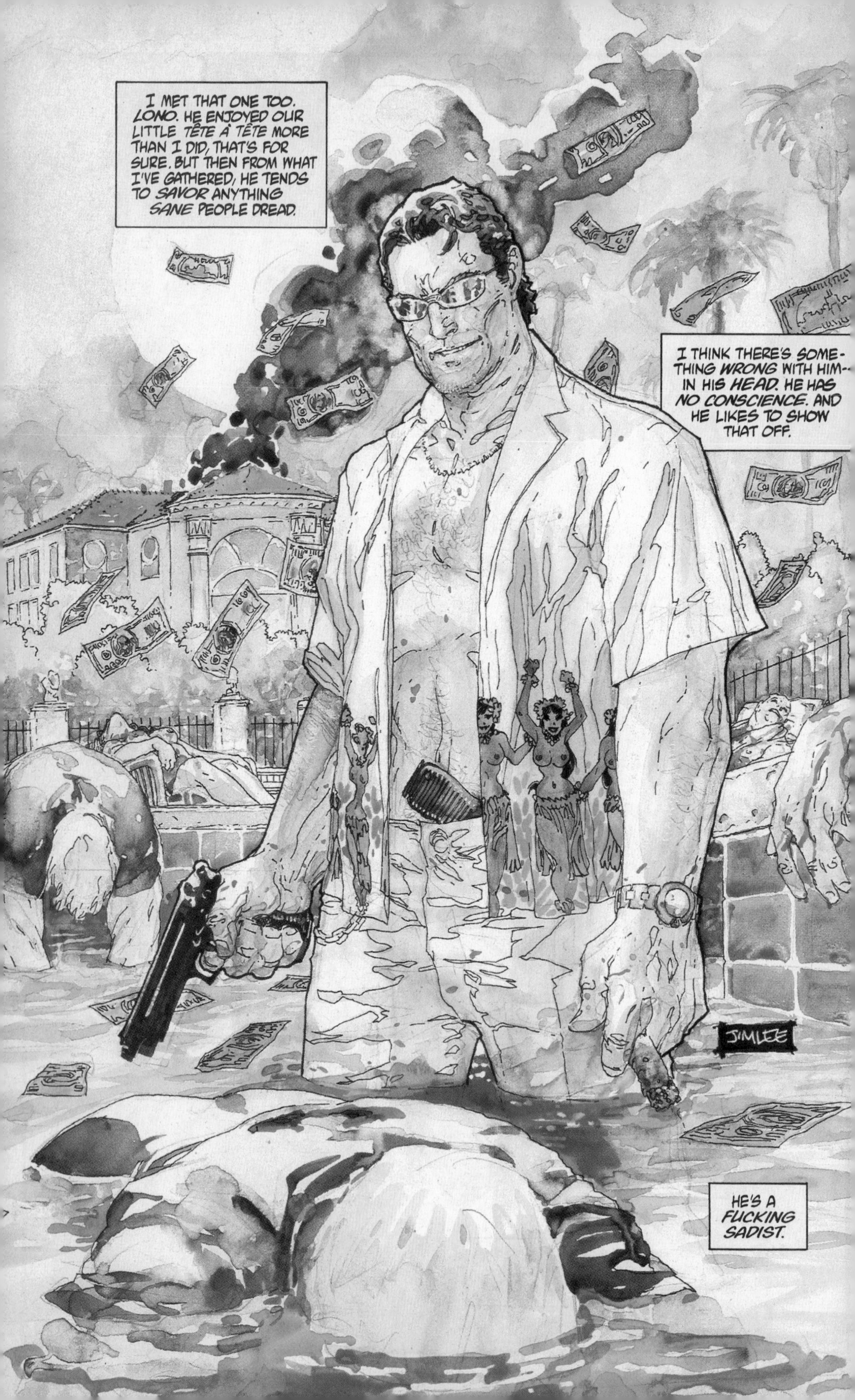
I MET THAT ONE TOO. *LONO*. HE ENJOYED OUR LITTLE *TÊTE À TÊTE* MORE THAN I DID, THAT'S FOR SURE. BUT THEN FROM WHAT I'VE GATHERED, HE TENDS TO *SAVOR* ANYTHING *SANE* PEOPLE DREAD.
I THINK THERE'S SOMETHING *WRONG* WITH HIM-- IN HIS *HEAD*. HE HAS *NO CONSCIENCE*. AND HE LIKES TO SHOW THAT OFF.
JIM LEE
HE'S A *FUCKING* SADIST.

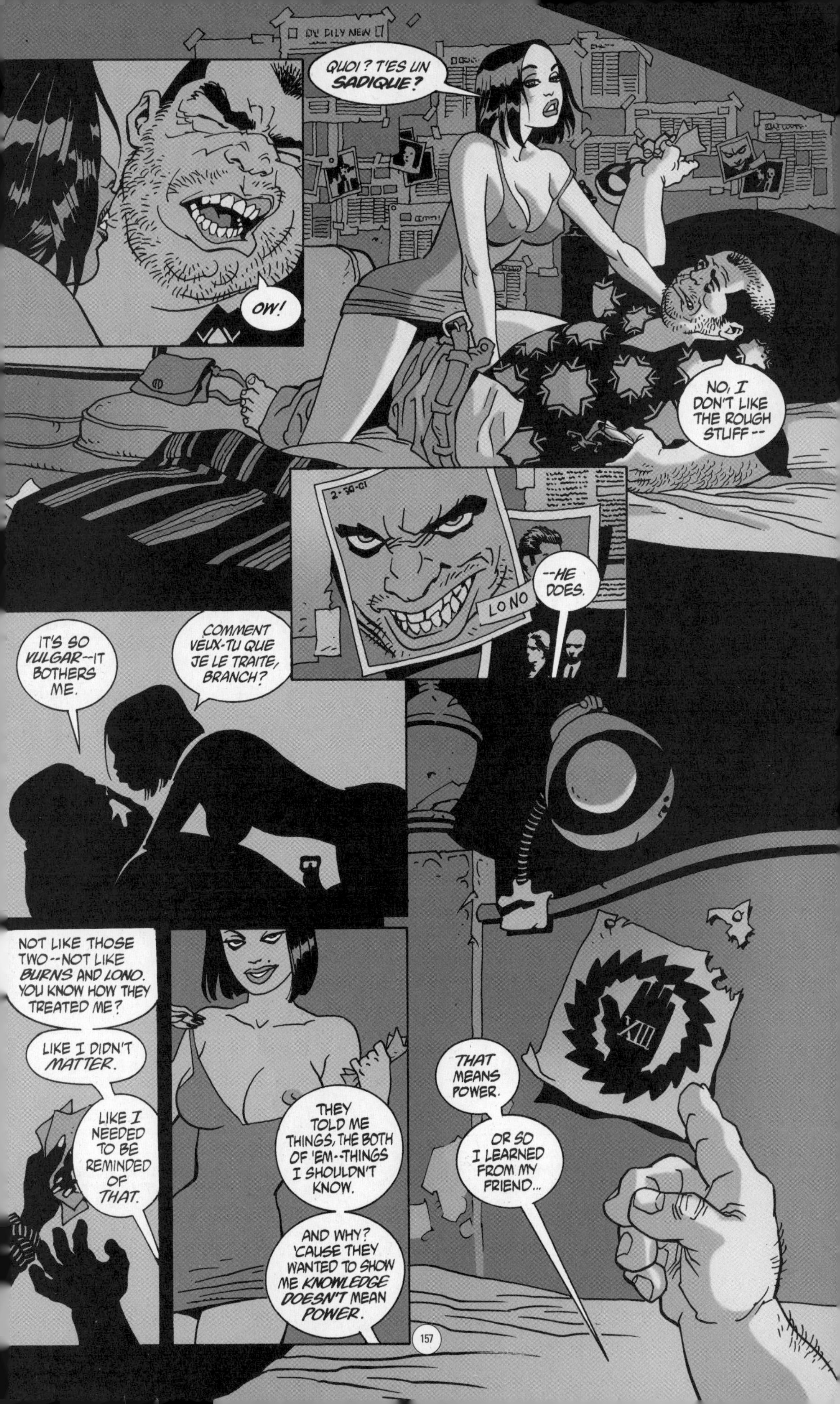

QUOI? T'ES UN SADIQUE?
OW!
NO, I DON'T LIKE THE ROUGH STUFF --
--HE DOES.
LONO
IT'S SO VULGAR--IT BOTHERS ME.
COMMENT VEUX-TU QUE JE LE TRAITE, BRANCH?
NOT LIKE THOSE TWO--NOT LIKE BURNS AND LONO. YOU KNOW HOW THEY TREATED ME?
LIKE I DIDN'T MATTER.
LIKE I NEEDED TO BE REMINDED OF THAT.
THEY TOLD ME THINGS, THE BOTH OF 'EM--THINGS I SHOULDN'T KNOW.
AND WHY? 'CAUSE THEY WANTED TO SHOW ME KNOWLEDGE DOESN'T MEAN POWER.
THAT MEANS POWER.
OR SO I LEARNED FROM MY FRIEND...

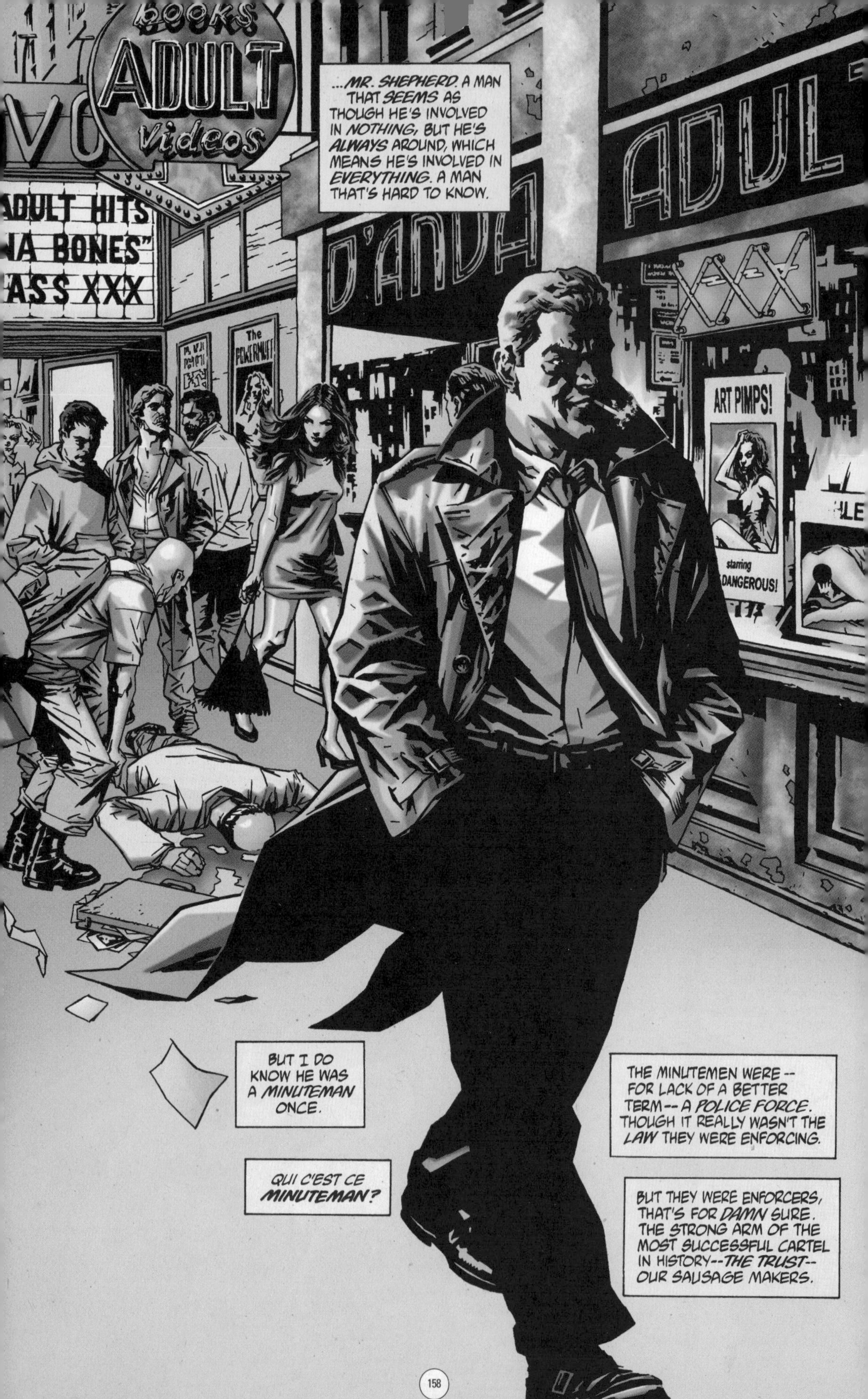
BOOKS
ADULT
videos
ADULT HITS
...MR. SHEPHERD. A MAN THAT SEEMS AS THOUGH HE'S INVOLVED IN NOTHING, BUT HE'S ALWAYS AROUND, WHICH MEANS HE'S INVOLVED IN EVERYTHING. A MAN THAT'S HARD TO KNOW.
D'ANDA
ART PIMPS!
starring
DANGEROUS!
BUT I DO KNOW HE WAS A MINUTEMAN ONCE.
QUI C'EST CE MINUTEMAN?
THE MINUTEMEN WERE -- FOR LACK OF A BETTER TERM -- A POLICE FORCE. THOUGH IT REALLY WASN'T THE LAW THEY WERE ENFORCING.
BUT THEY WERE ENFORCERS, THAT'S FOR DAMN SURE. THE STRONG ARM OF THE MOST SUCCESSFUL CARTEL IN HISTORY--THE TRUST-- OUR SAUSAGE MAKERS.

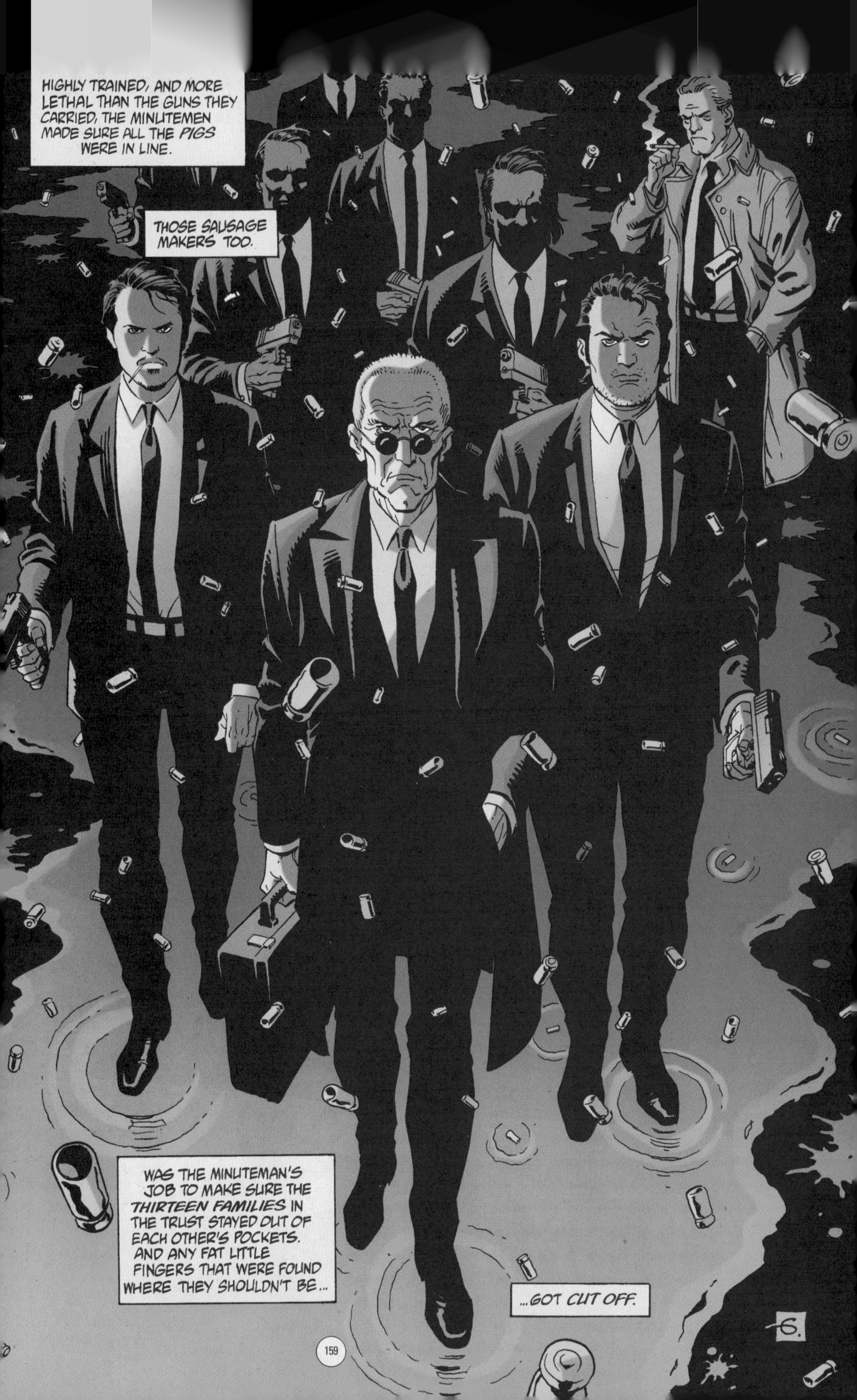
HIGHLY TRAINED, AND MORE LETHAL THAN THE GUNS THEY CARRIED, THE MINUTEMEN MADE SURE ALL THE *PIGS* WERE IN LINE.
THOSE SAUSAGE MAKERS TOO.
WAS THE MINUTEMAN'S JOB TO MAKE SURE THE ***THIRTEEN FAMILIES*** IN THE TRUST STAYED OUT OF EACH OTHER'S POCKETS. AND ANY FAT LITTLE FINGERS THAT WERE FOUND WHERE THEY SHOULDN'T BE...
...GOT CUT OFF.

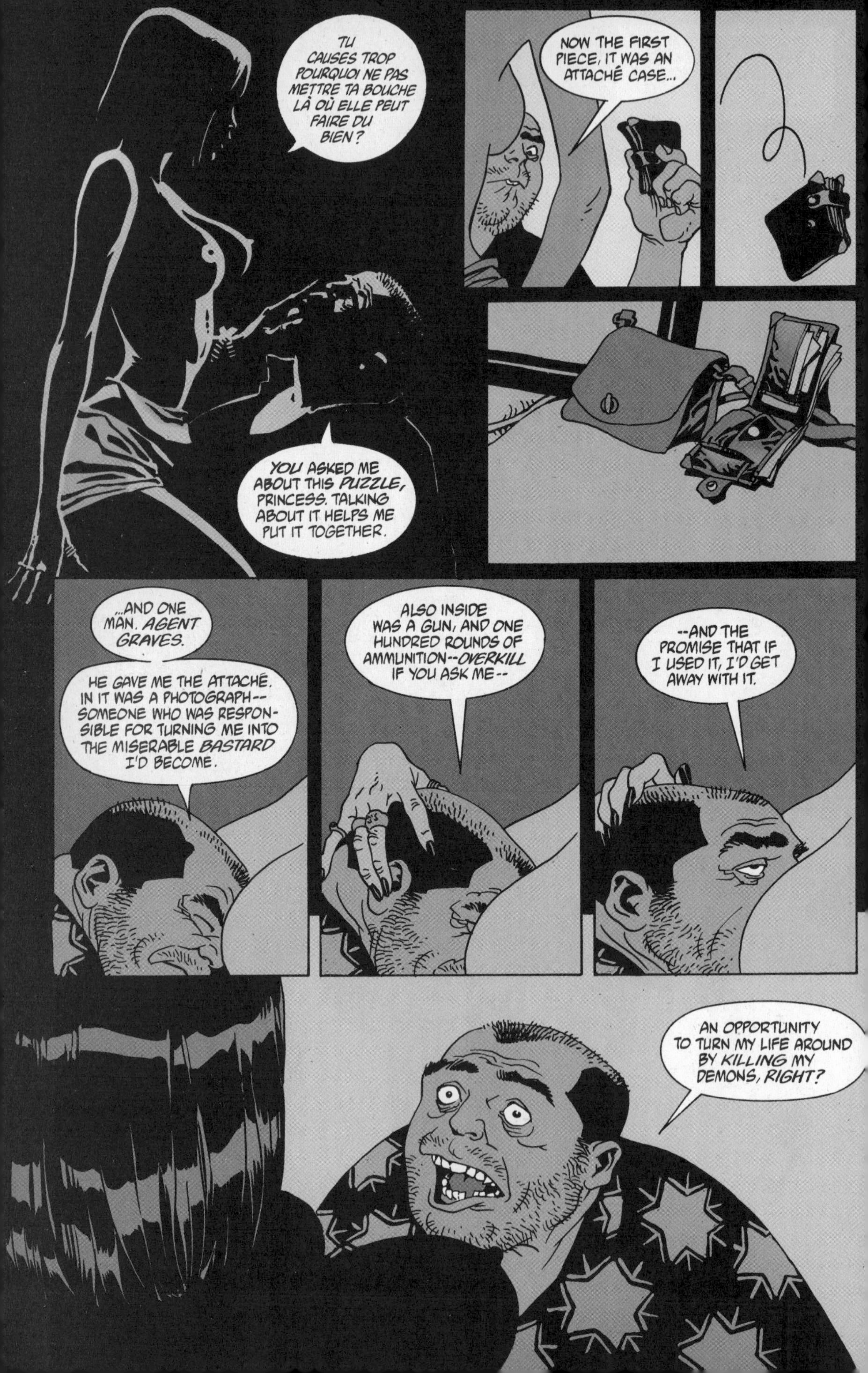
TU CAUSES TROP POURQUOI NE PAS METTRE TA BOUCHE LÀ OÙ ELLE PEUT FAIRE DU BIEN?
YOU ASKED ME ABOUT THIS PUZZLE, PRINCESS. TALKING ABOUT IT HELPS ME PUT IT TOGETHER.
NOW THE FIRST PIECE, IT WAS AN ATTACHÉ CASE...
...AND ONE MAN. AGENT GRAVES.
HE GAVE ME THE ATTACHÉ. IN IT WAS A PHOTOGRAPH--SOMEONE WHO WAS RESPONSIBLE FOR TURNING ME INTO THE MISERABLE BASTARD I'D BECOME.
ALSO INSIDE WAS A GUN, AND ONE HUNDRED ROUNDS OF AMMUNITION--OVERKILL IF YOU ASK ME--
--AND THE PROMISE THAT IF I USED IT, I'D GET AWAY WITH IT.
AN OPPORTUNITY TO TURN MY LIFE AROUND BY KILLING MY DEMONS, RIGHT?

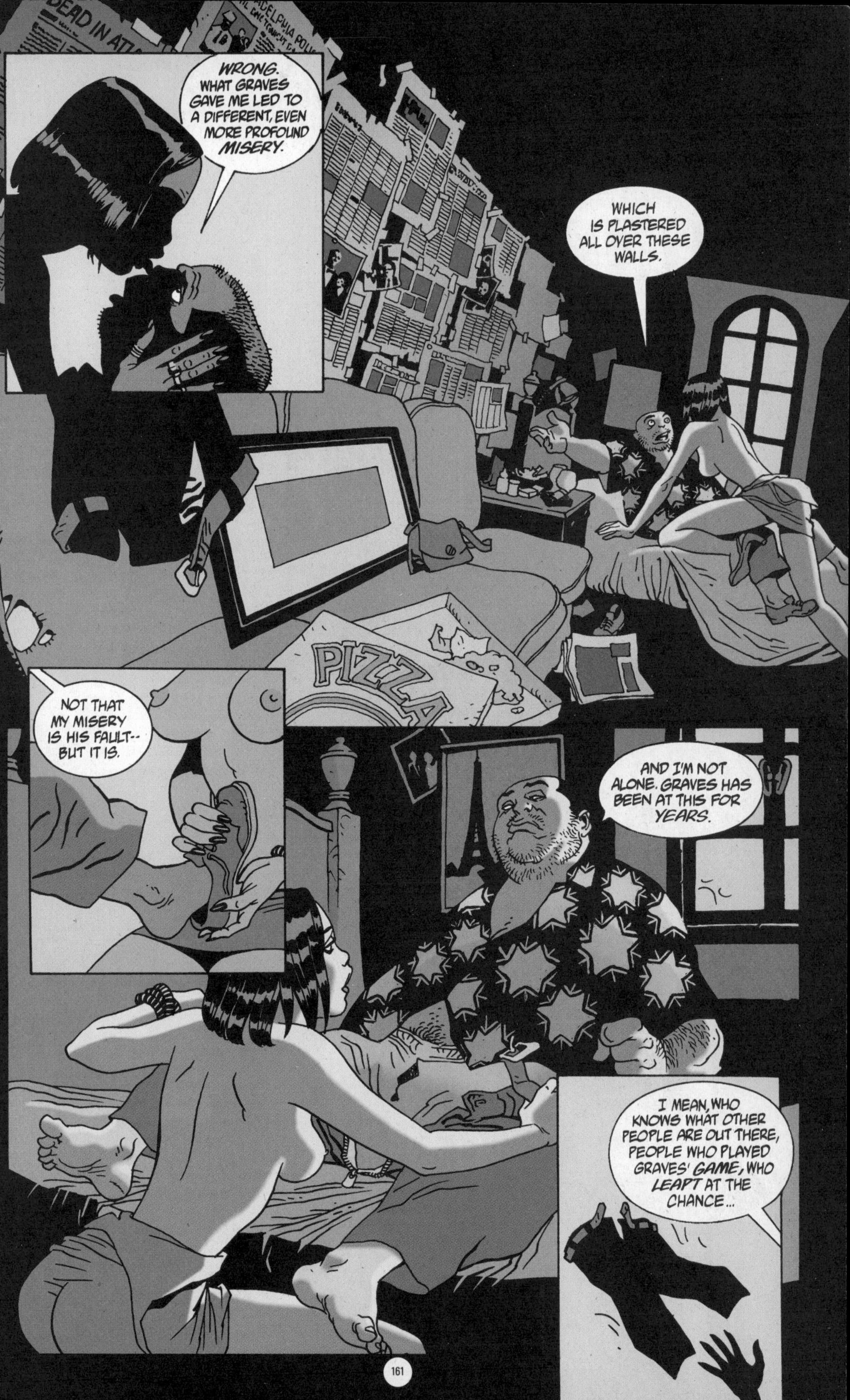
WRONG. WHAT GRAVES GAVE ME LED TO A DIFFERENT, EVEN MORE PROFOUND MISERY.
WHICH IS PLASTERED ALL OVER THESE WALLS.
PIZZA
NOT THAT MY MISERY IS HIS FAULT-- BUT IT IS.
AND I'M NOT ALONE. GRAVES HAS BEEN AT THIS FOR YEARS.
I MEAN, WHO KNOWS WHAT OTHER PEOPLE ARE OUT THERE, PEOPLE WHO PLAYED GRAVES' GAME, WHO LEAPT AT THE CHANCE...

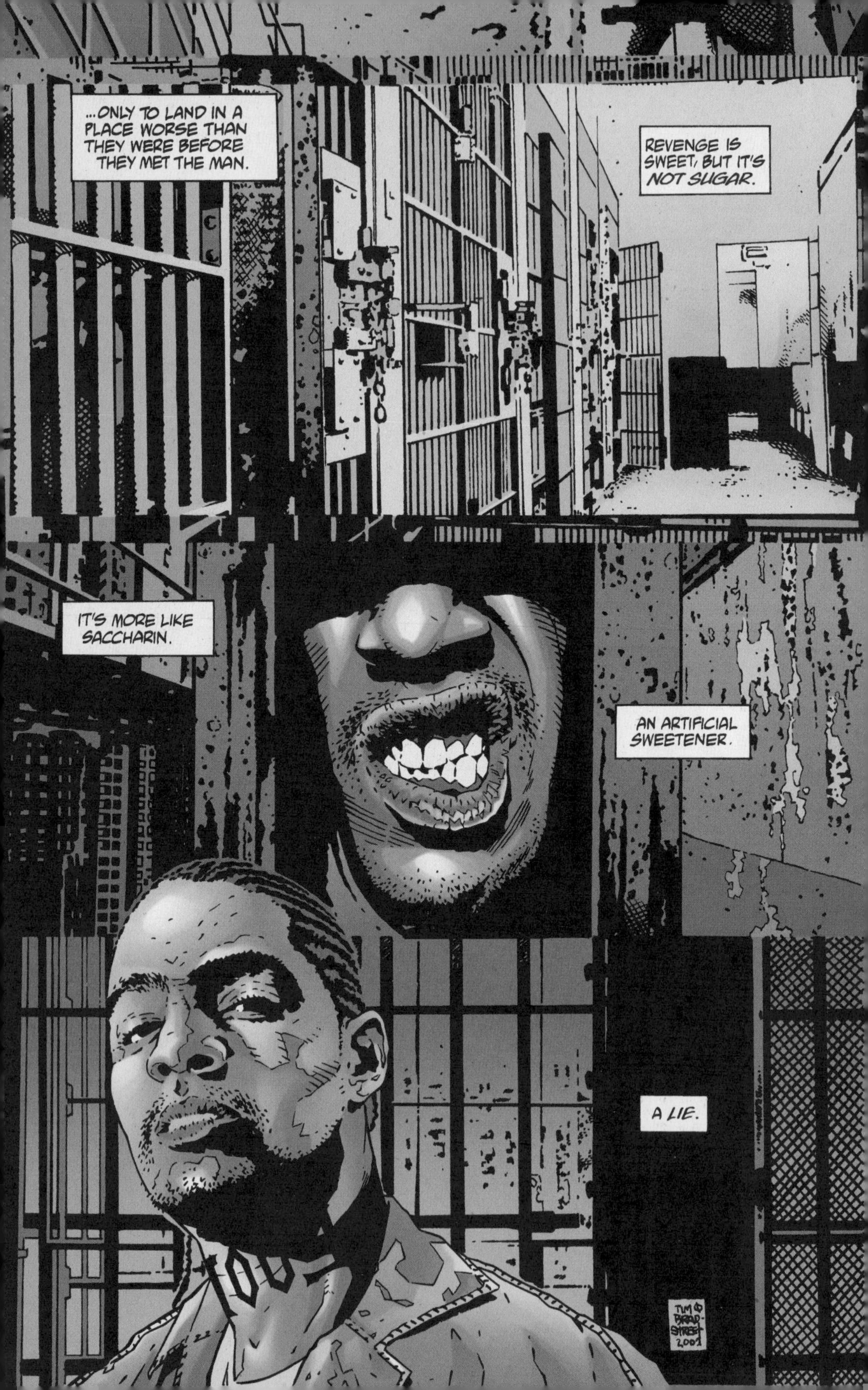
...ONLY TO LAND IN A PLACE WORSE THAN THEY WERE BEFORE THEY MET THE MAN.
REVENGE IS SWEET, BUT IT'S *NOT SUGAR*.
IT'S MORE LIKE SACCHARIN.
AN ARTIFICIAL SWEETENER.
A *LIE*.
TIM BRADSTREET 2001

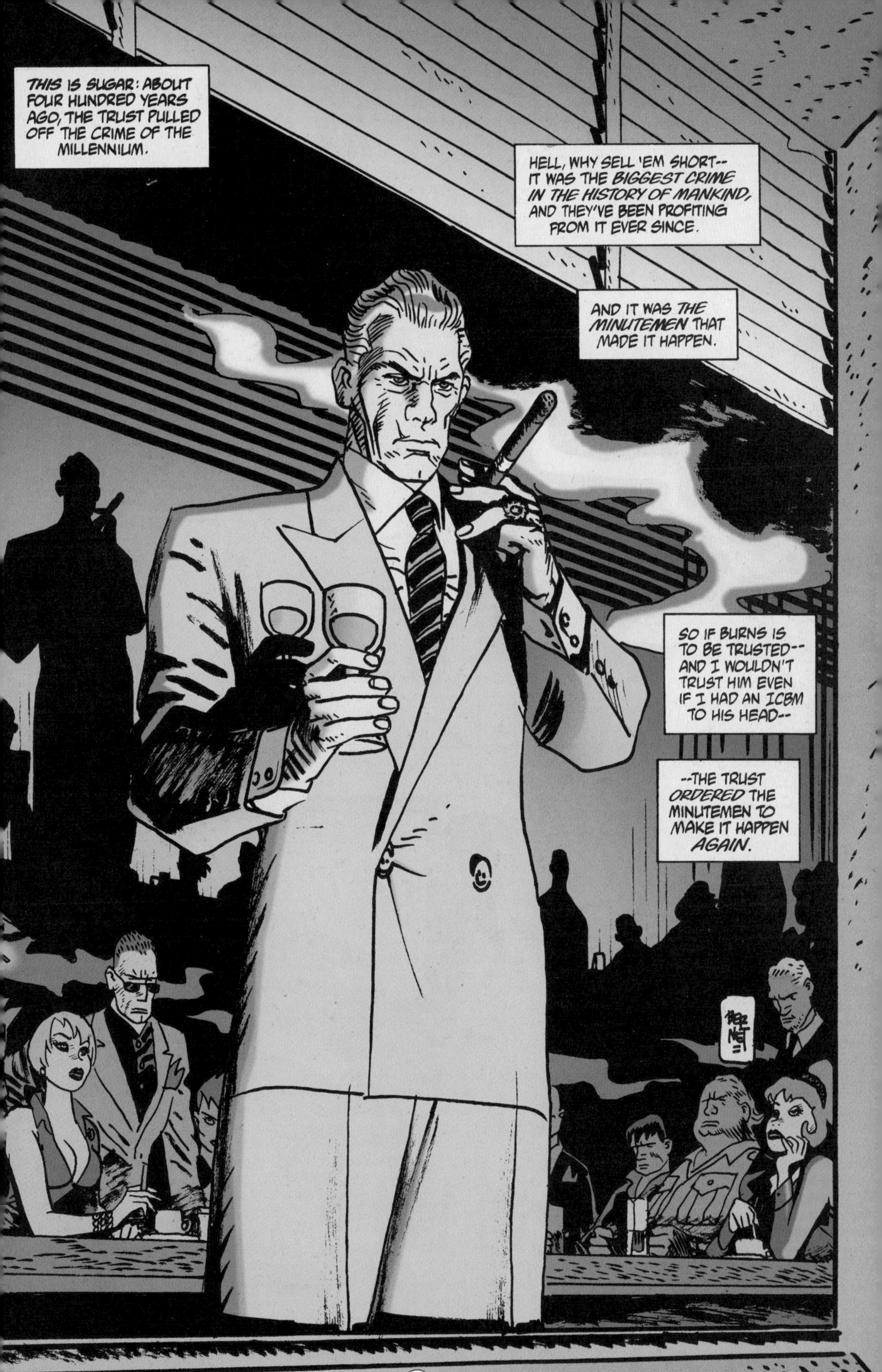
THIS IS SUGAR: ABOUT FOUR HUNDRED YEARS AGO, THE TRUST PULLED OFF THE CRIME OF THE MILLENNIUM.
HELL, WHY SELL 'EM SHORT-- IT WAS THE BIGGEST CRIME IN THE HISTORY OF MANKIND, AND THEY'VE BEEN PROFITING FROM IT EVER SINCE.
AND IT WAS THE MINUTEMEN THAT MADE IT HAPPEN.
SO IF BURNS IS TO BE TRUSTED-- AND I WOULDN'T TRUST HIM EVEN IF I HAD AN ICBM TO HIS HEAD--
--THE TRUST ORDERED THE MINUTEMEN TO MAKE IT HAPPEN AGAIN.

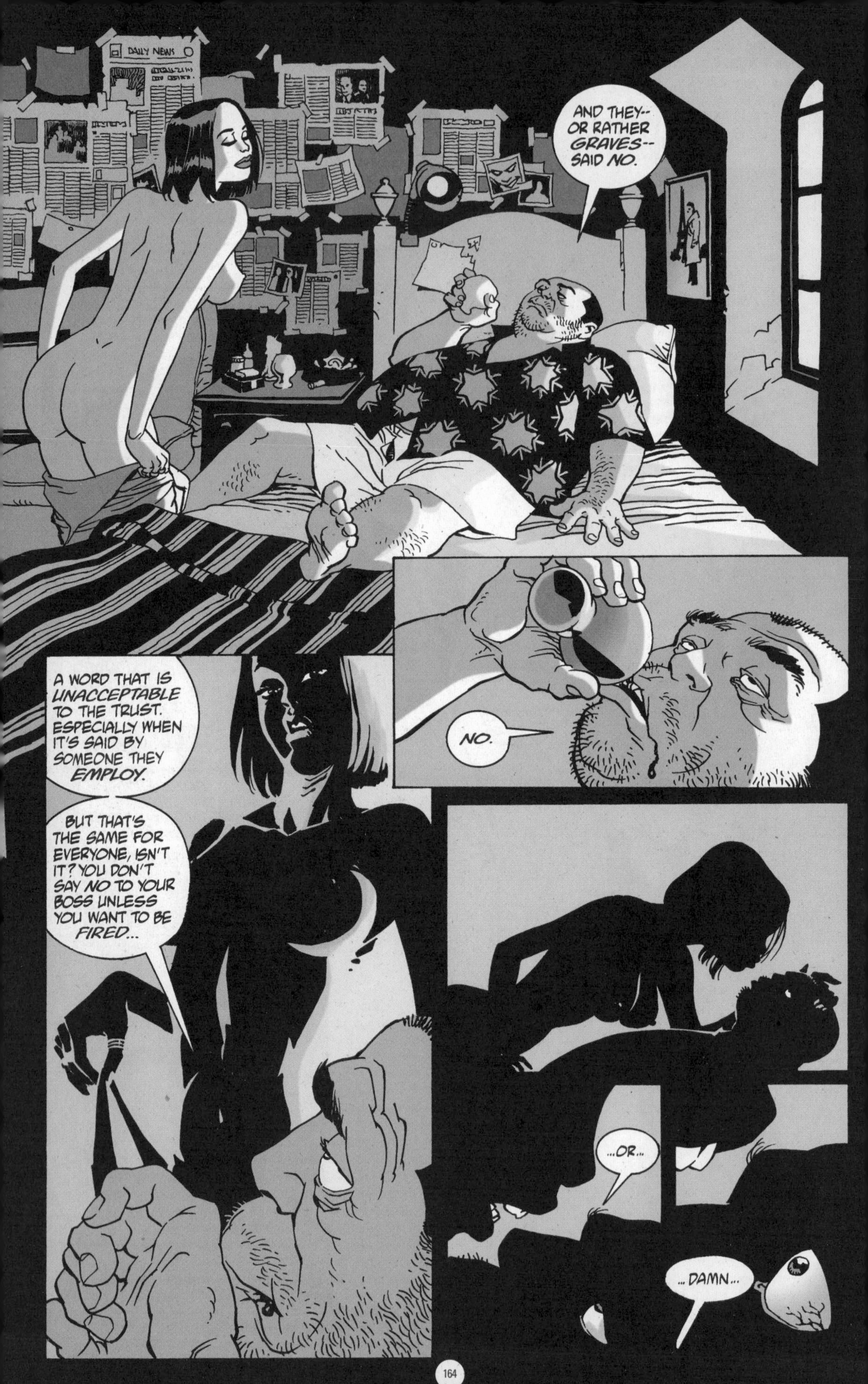
DAILY NEWS
AND THEY-- OR RATHER GRAVES-- SAID NO.
NO.
A WORD THAT IS UNACCEPTABLE TO THE TRUST. ESPECIALLY WHEN IT'S SAID BY SOMEONE THEY EMPLOY.
BUT THAT'S THE SAME FOR EVERYONE, ISN'T IT? YOU DON'T SAY NO TO YOUR BOSS UNLESS YOU WANT TO BE FIRED...
...OR...
...DAMN...

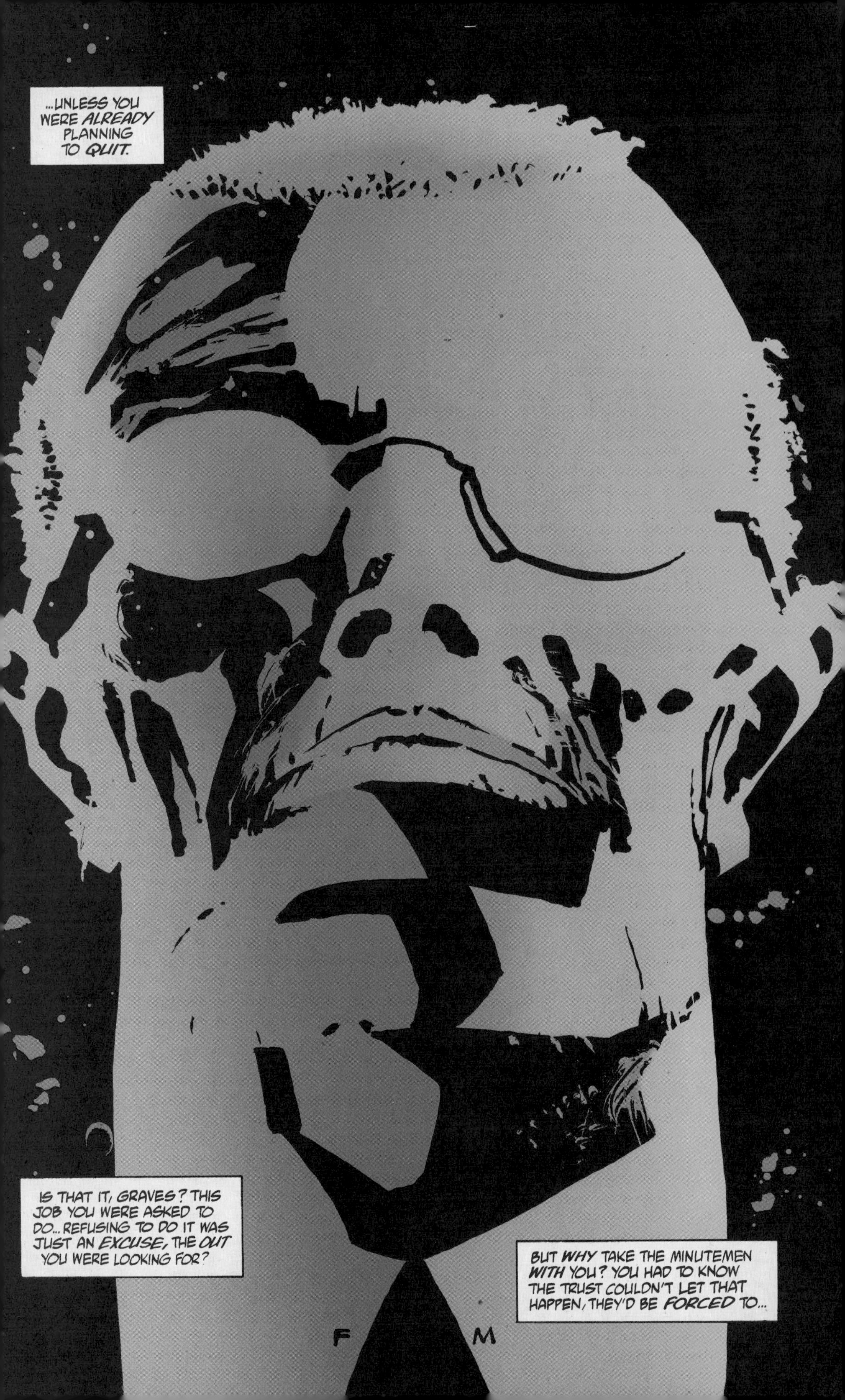
...UNLESS YOU WERE ALREADY PLANNING TO QUIT.
IS THAT IT, GRAVES? THIS JOB YOU WERE ASKED TO DO... REFUSING TO DO IT WAS JUST AN EXCUSE, THE OUT YOU WERE LOOKING FOR?
BUT WHY TAKE THE MINUTEMEN WITH YOU? YOU HAD TO KNOW THE TRUST COULDN'T LET THAT HAPPEN, THEY'D BE FORCED TO...
F M

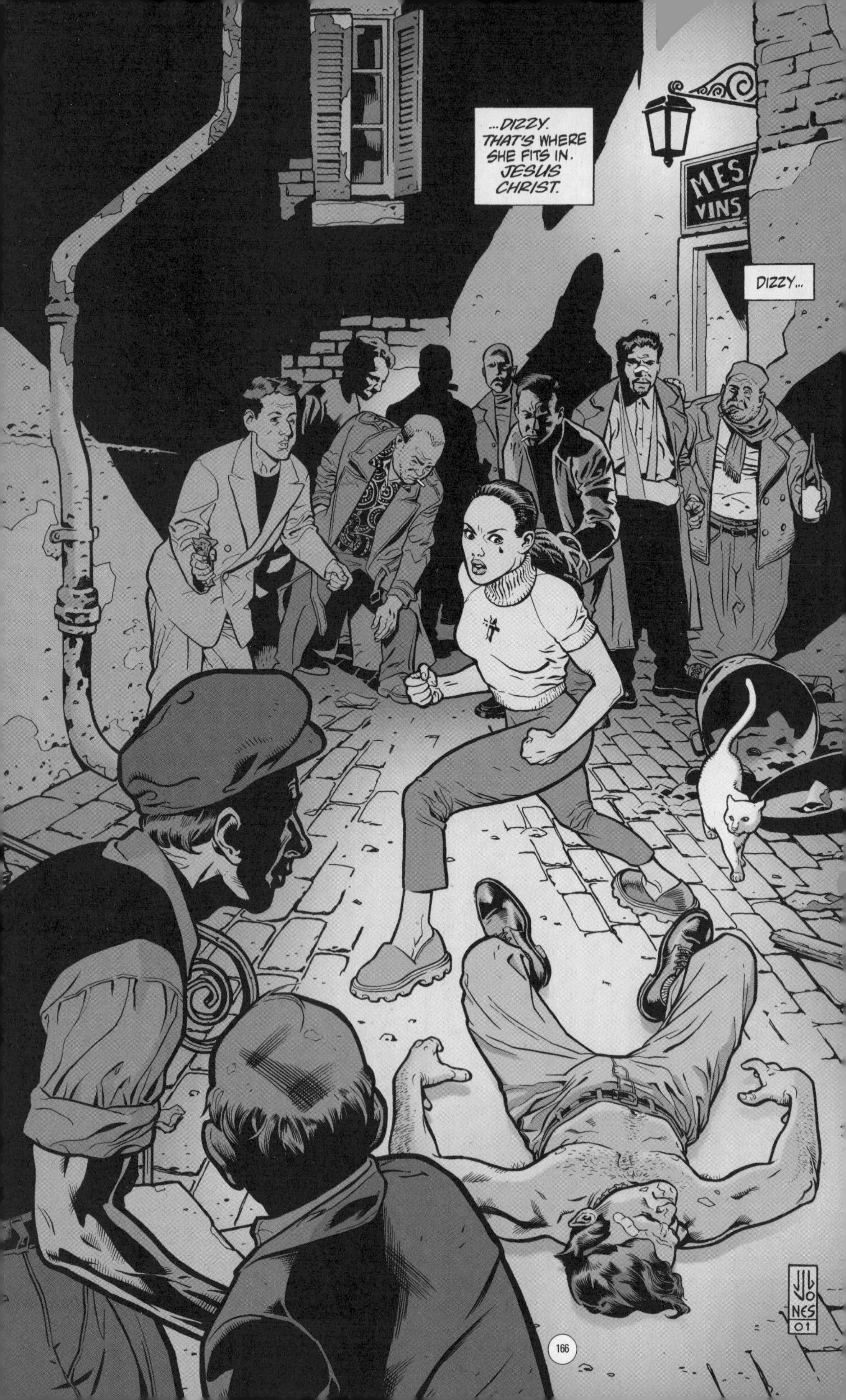
...DIZZY.
THAT'S WHERE
SHE FITS IN.
JESUS
CHRIST.
DIZZY...
MES
VINS

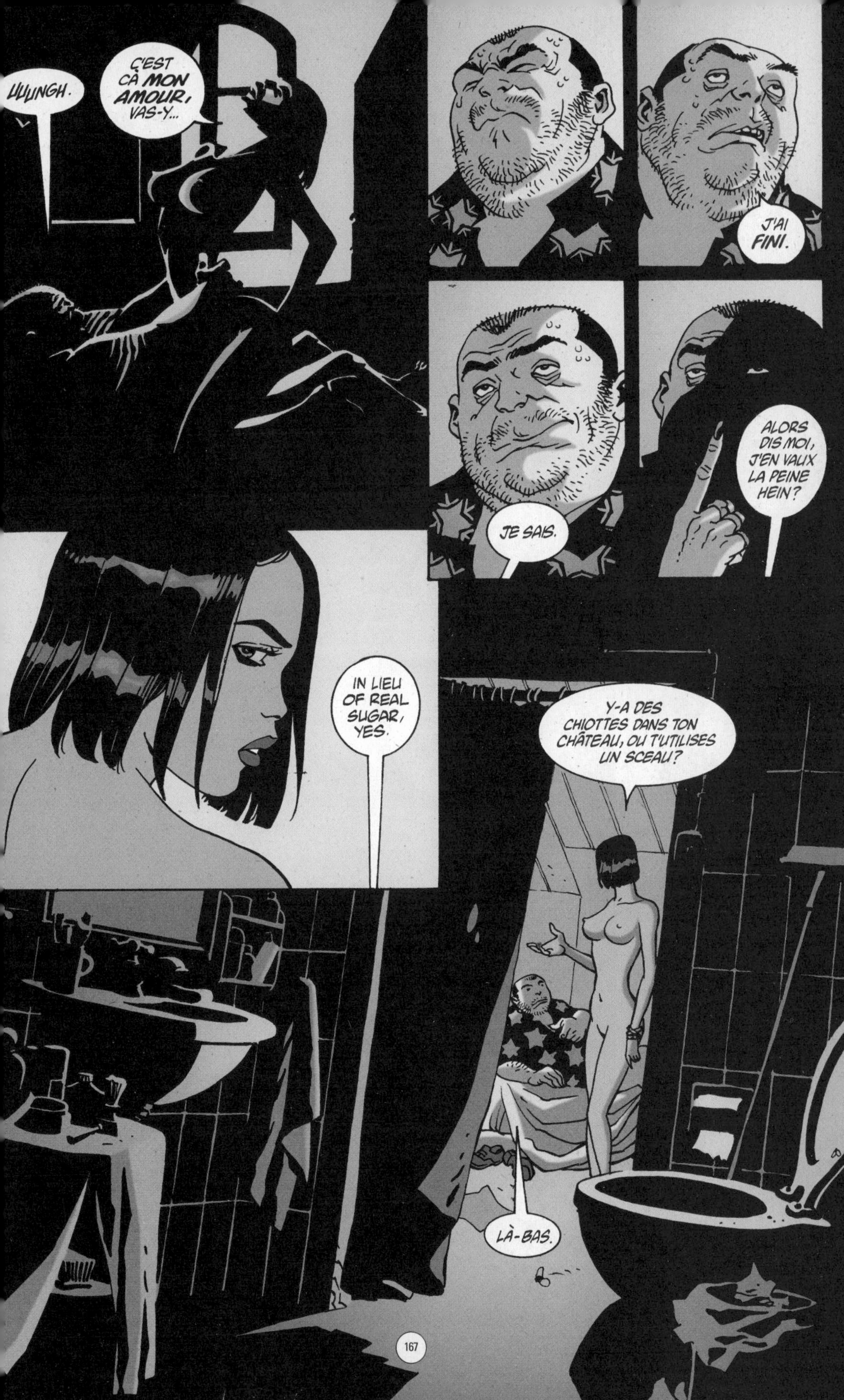
UUUNGH.
ÇEST ÇA MON AMOUR, VAS-Y...
J'AI FINI.
JE SAIS.
ALORS DIS MOI, J'EN VAUX LA PEINE HEIN?
IN LIEU OF REAL SUGAR, YES.
Y-A DES CHIOTTES DANS TON CHÂTEAU, OU T'UTILISES UN SCEAU?
LÀ-BAS.

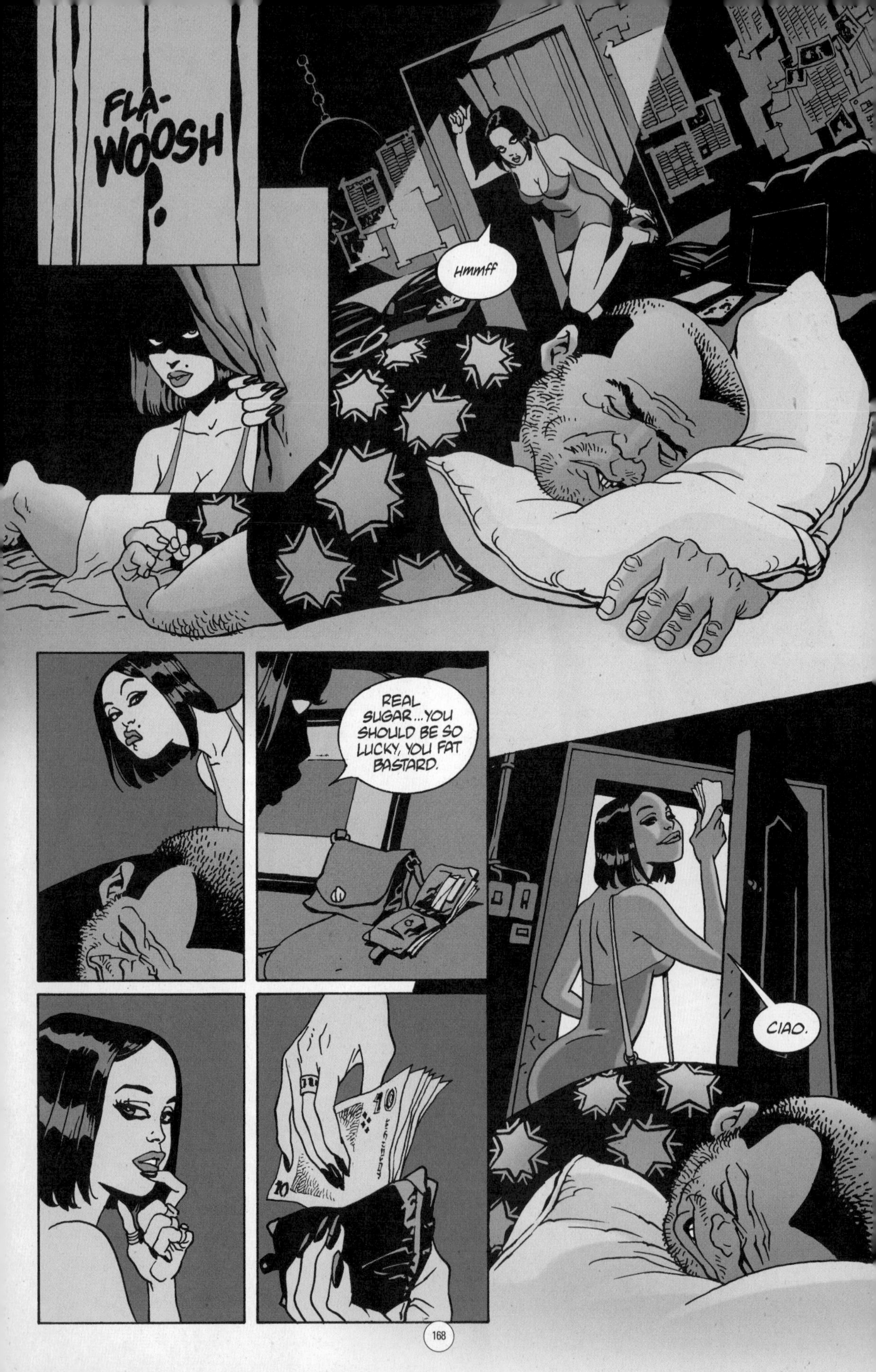
FLA-WOOSH
Hmmff
REAL SUGAR...YOU SHOULD BE SO LUCKY, YOU FAT BASTARD.
CIAO.

Mr. Branch & the Family Tree

Written by
Brian Azzarello

Colorist
Patricia Mulvihill

Letterer
Clem Robins

Separations **Digital Chameleon**

Cover Artist
Dave Johnson

Editor
Will Dennis

Artists
Eduardo Risso
Pgs. 148-151, 154, 157, 160-161, 164, 167-169

Paul **Pope**	Joe **Jusko**	Mark **Chiarello**	Jim **Lee**	Lee **Bermejo**
Pg. 152: Benito Medici	Pg.153: Megan Dietrich	Pg.155: Cole Burns	Pg.156: Lono	Pg.158: Mr. Shepherd

Dave **Gibbons**	Tim **Bradstreet**	Jordi **Bernet**	Frank **Miller**	J.G. **Jones**
Pg.159: The Minutemen	Pg.162: Loop Hughes	Pg.163: Augustus Medici	Pg.165: Agent Graves	Pg.166: Dizzy Cordova

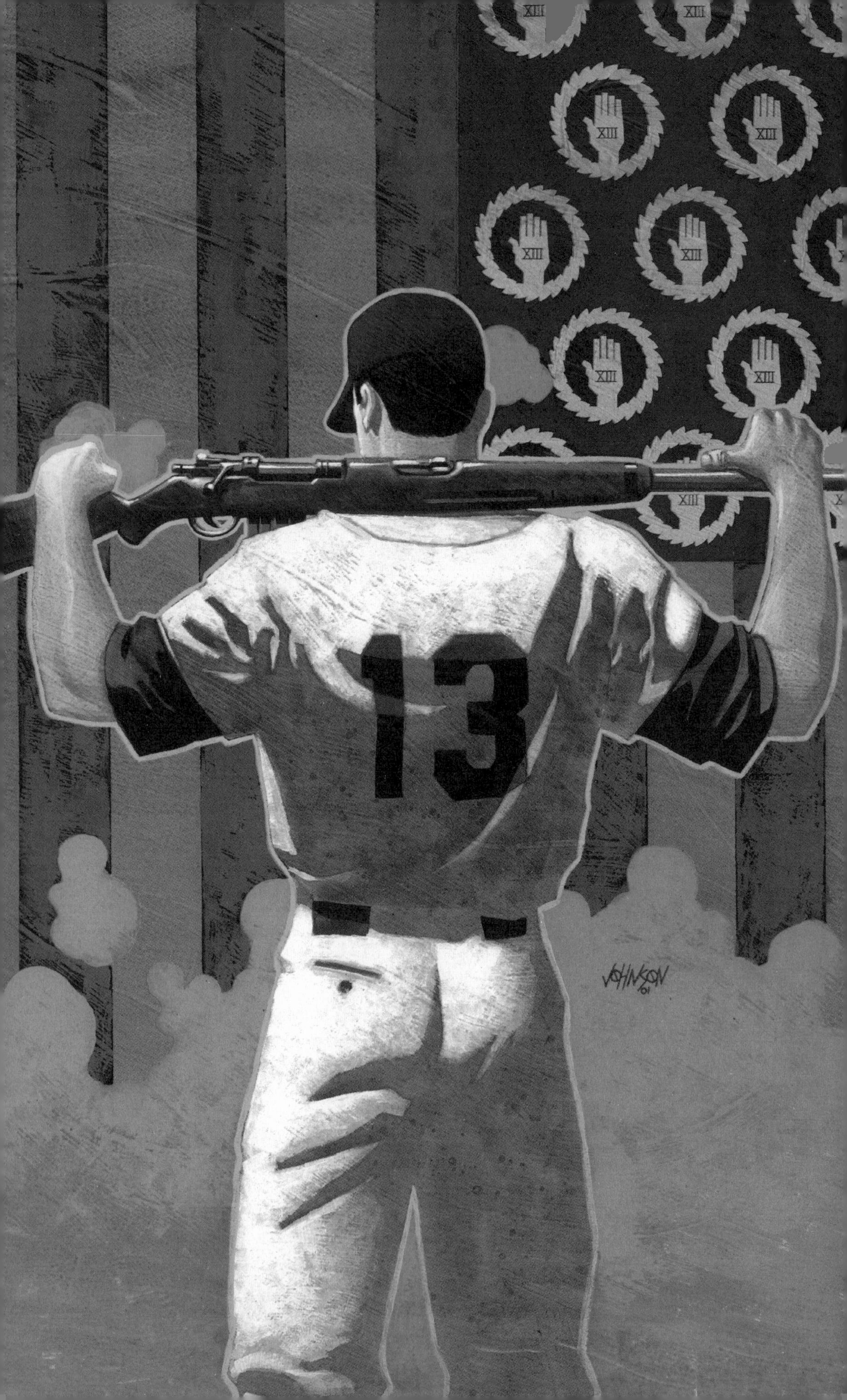
XIII
13
JOHNSON '01

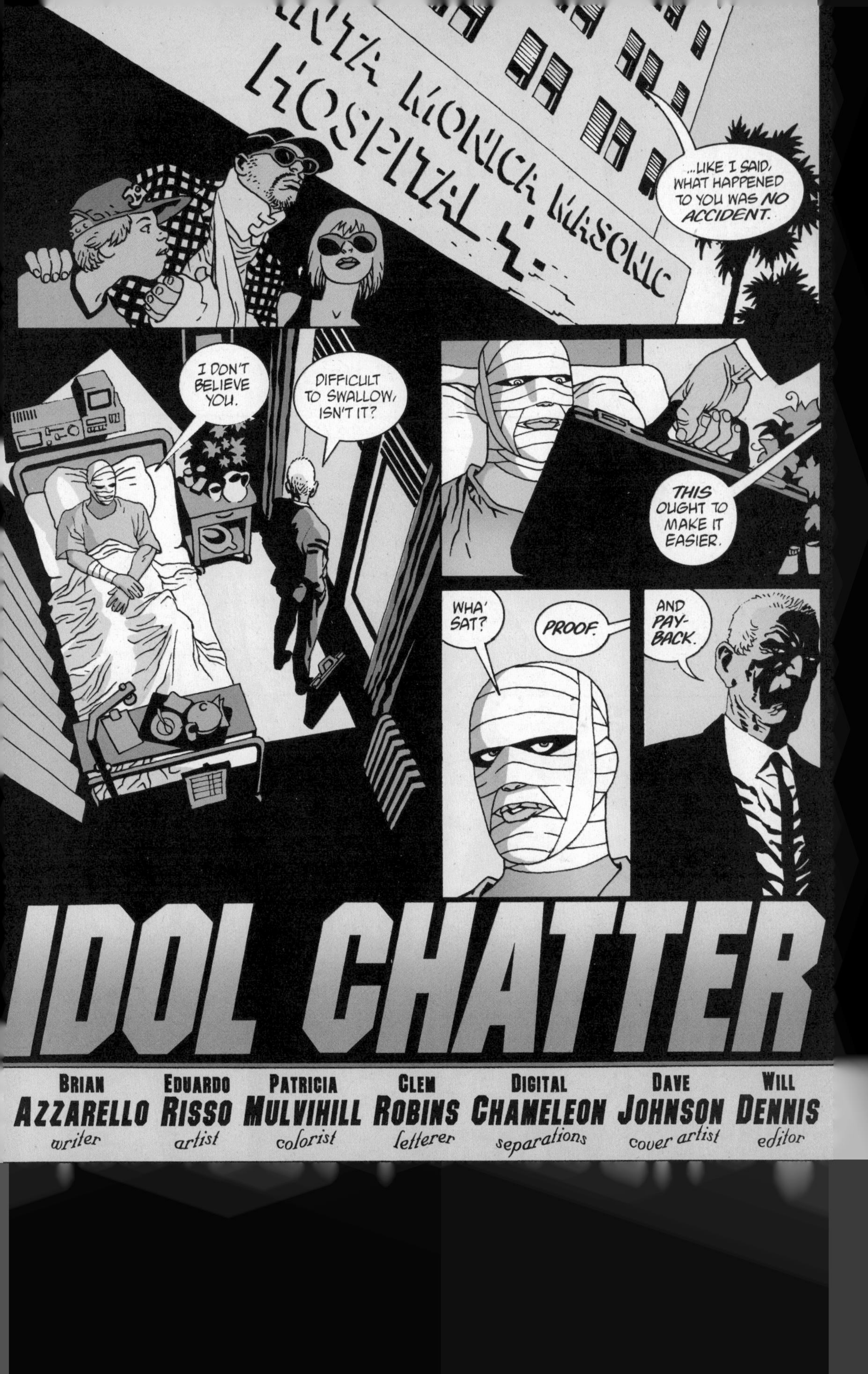
MONICA MASONIC
HOSPITAL
...LIKE I SAID, WHAT HAPPENED TO YOU WAS NO ACCIDENT.
I DON'T BELIEVE YOU.
DIFFICULT TO SWALLOW, ISN'T IT?
THIS OUGHT TO MAKE IT EASIER.
WHA' SAT?
PROOF.
AND PAY-BACK.

IDOL CHATTER

BRIAN AZZARELLO *writer* · EDUARDO RISSO *artist* · PATRICIA MULVIHILL *colorist* · CLEM ROBINS *letterer* · DIGITAL CHAMELEON *separations* · DAVE JOHNSON *cover artist* · WILL DENNIS *editor*

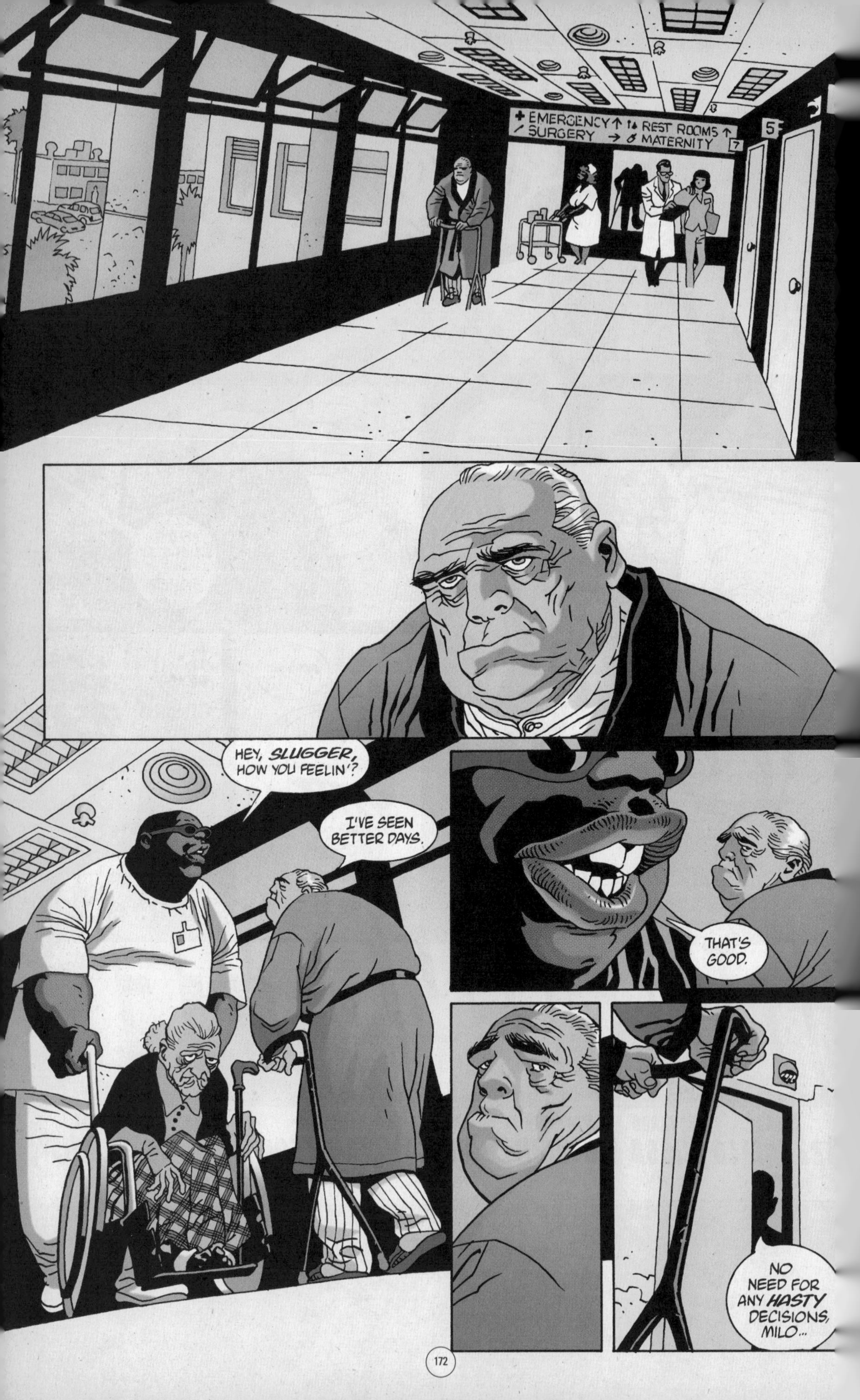
EMERGENCY ↑ ↑↓ REST ROOMS ↑
SURGERY → ♂ MATERNITY
5
HEY, SLUGGER, HOW YOU FEELIN'?
I'VE SEEN BETTER DAYS.
THAT'S GOOD.
NO NEED FOR ANY HASTY DECISIONS, MILO...

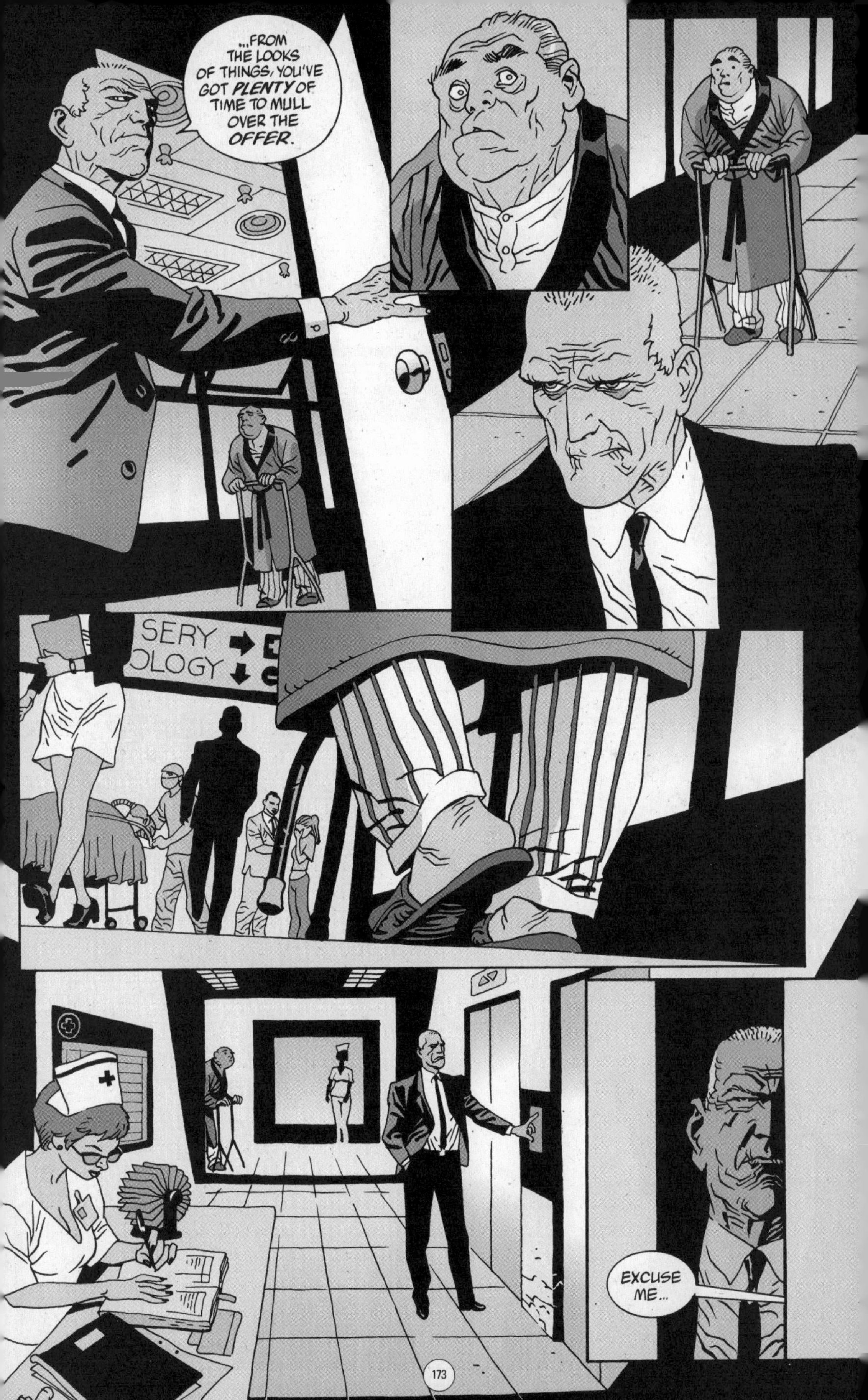
...FROM THE LOOKS OF THINGS, YOU'VE GOT PLENTY OF TIME TO MULL OVER THE OFFER.
SERY
OLOGY
EXCUSE ME...

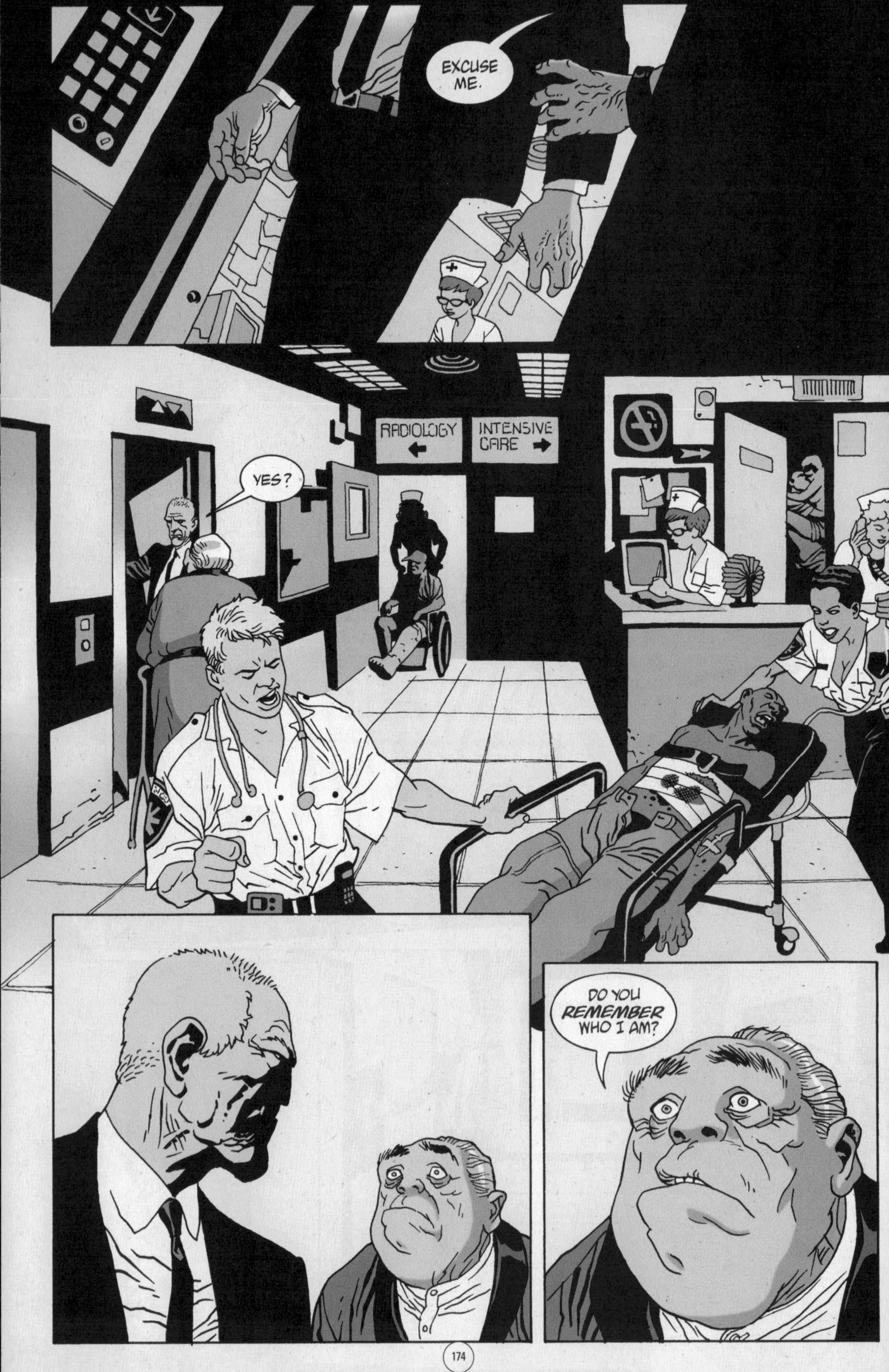
EXCUSE ME.
RADIOLOGY
INTENSIVE CARE
YES?
DO YOU *REMEMBER* WHO I AM?

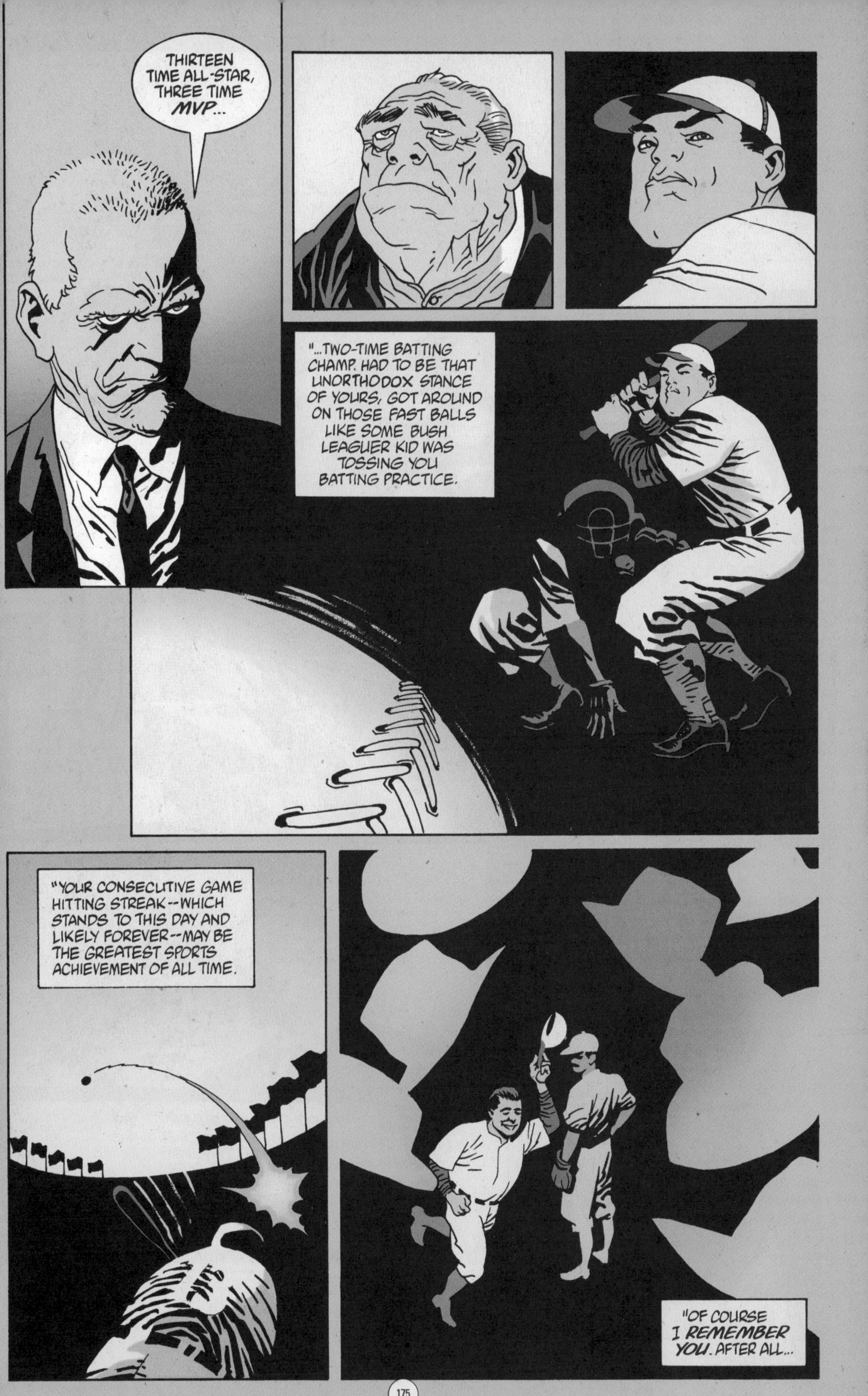
THIRTEEN TIME ALL-STAR, THREE TIME MVP...
"...TWO-TIME BATTING CHAMP. HAD TO BE THAT UNORTHODOX STANCE OF YOURS, GOT AROUND ON THOSE FAST BALLS LIKE SOME BUSH LEAGUER KID WAS TOSSING YOU BATTING PRACTICE.
"YOUR CONSECUTIVE GAME HITTING STREAK--WHICH STANDS TO THIS DAY AND LIKELY FOREVER--MAY BE THE GREATEST SPORTS ACHIEVEMENT OF ALL TIME.
"OF COURSE I REMEMBER YOU. AFTER ALL...

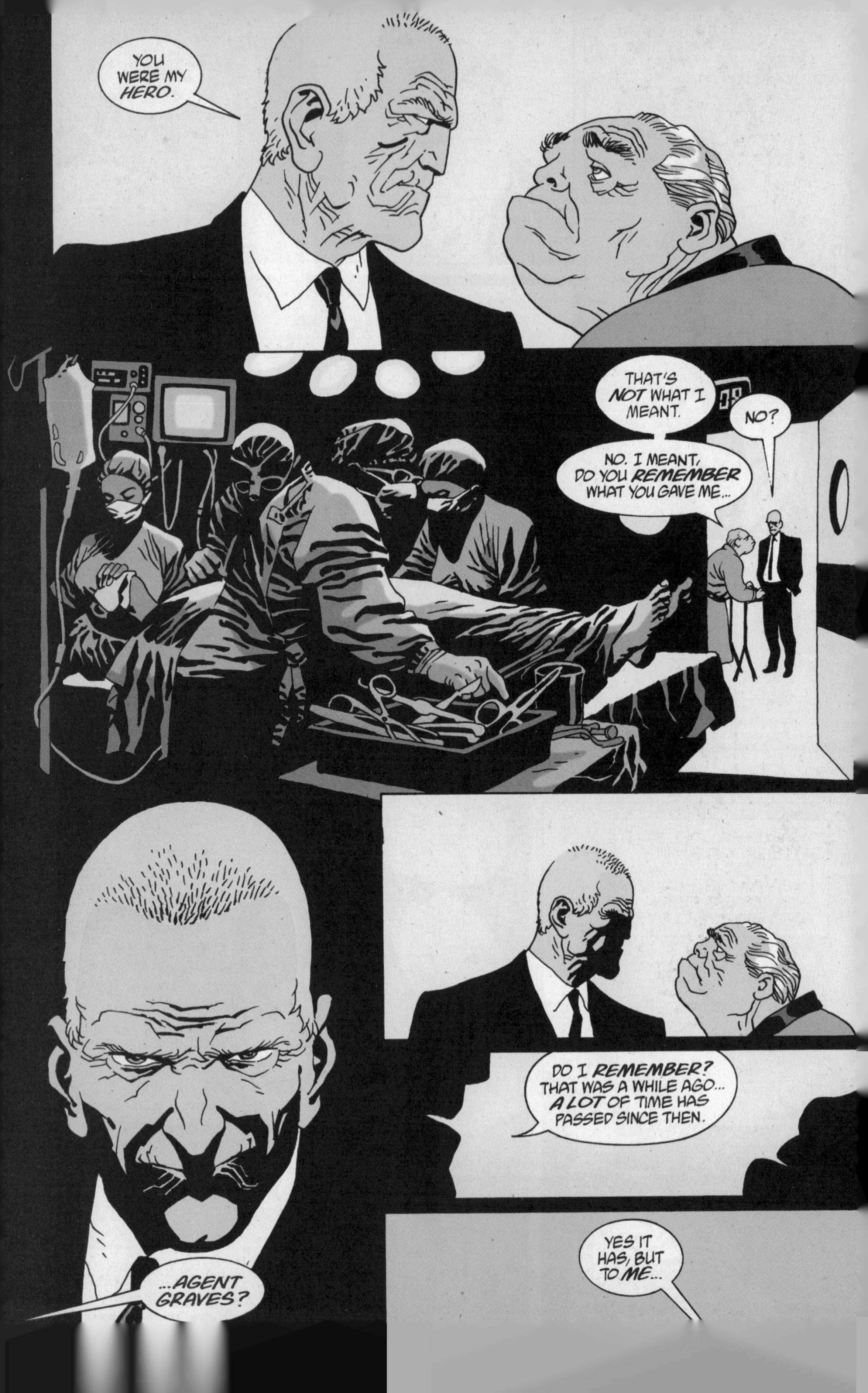
YOU WERE MY HERO.
THAT'S NOT WHAT I MEANT.
NO?
NO. I MEANT, DO YOU REMEMBER WHAT YOU GAVE ME...
...AGENT GRAVES?
DO I REMEMBER? THAT WAS A WHILE AGO... A LOT OF TIME HAS PASSED SINCE THEN.
YES IT HAS, BUT TO ME...

...IT STILL SEEMS LIKE ONLY *YESTERDAY* WHEN WE WERE *TOGETHER*, BABY. THAT GORGEOUS *SMILE* OF YOURS...

...THOSE *LEGS*. *GOD* THOSE *LEGS*.

GOD.

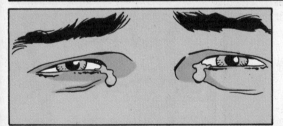

GODDAMN, I MISS YOU.

SHE WAS THE *MOST BEAUTIFUL* WOMAN ON THE *PLANET*.

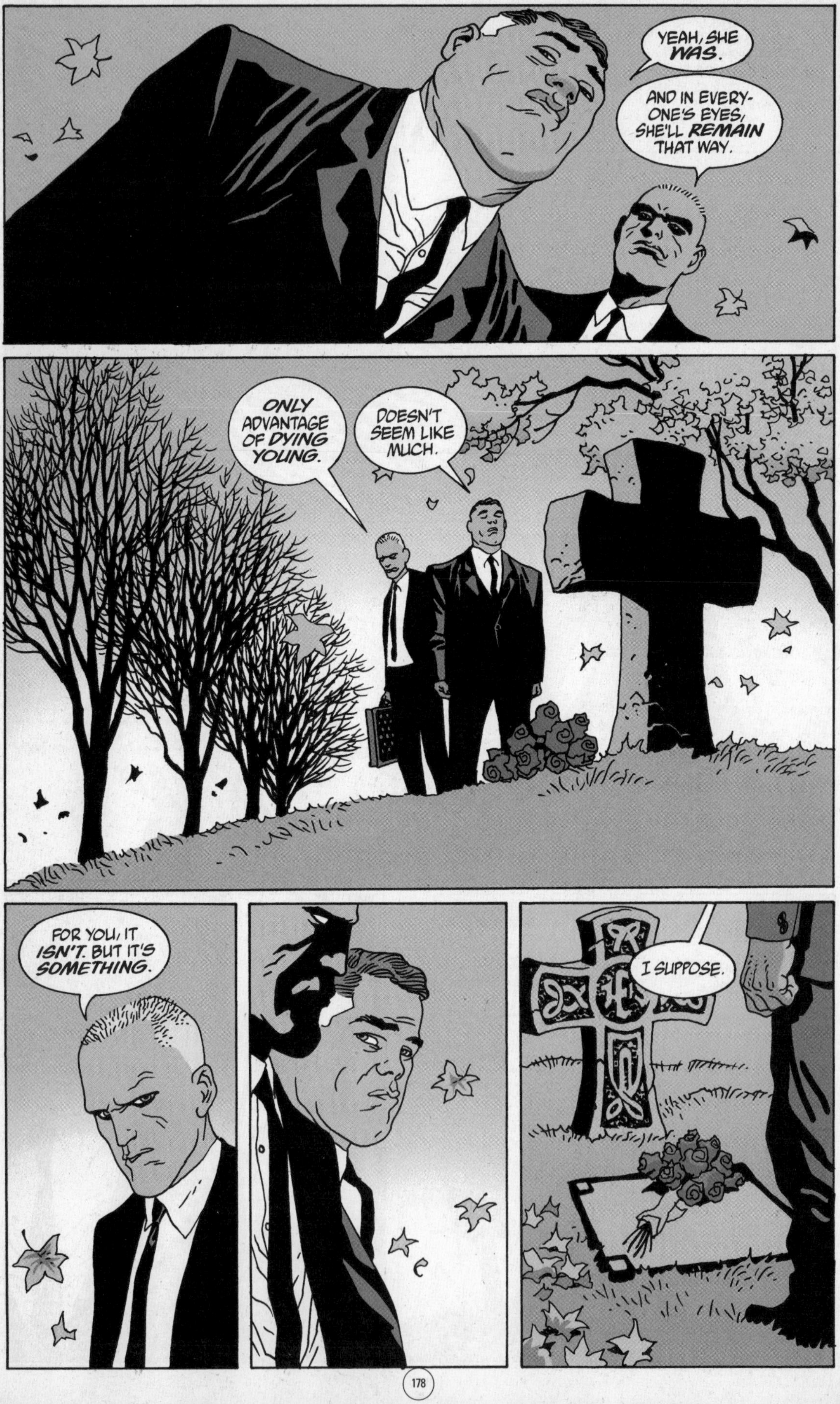
YEAH, SHE WAS.
AND IN EVERY-ONE'S EYES, SHE'LL REMAIN THAT WAY.
ONLY ADVANTAGE OF DYING YOUNG.
DOESN'T SEEM LIKE MUCH.
FOR YOU, IT ISN'T. BUT IT'S SOMETHING.
I SUPPOSE.

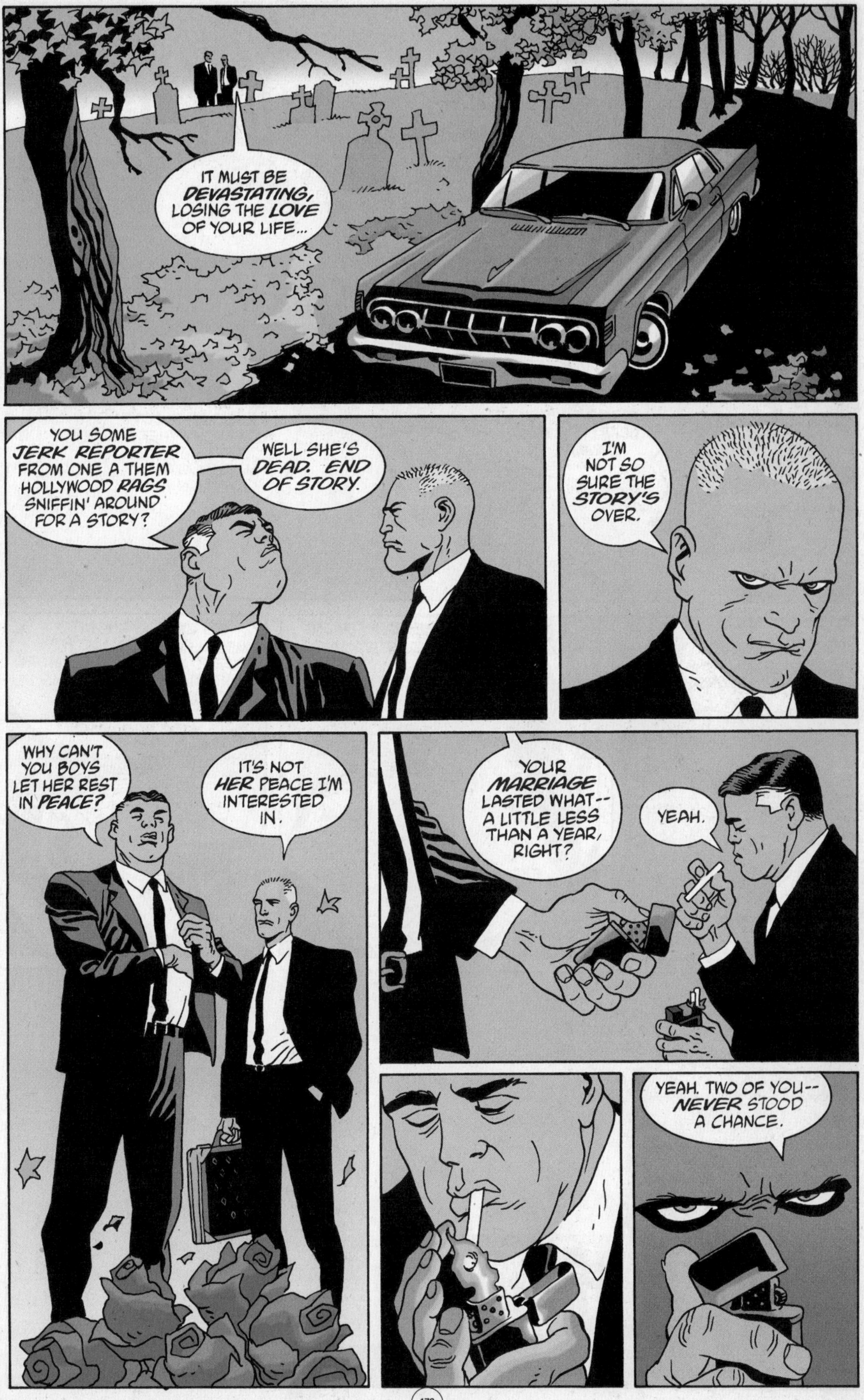
IT MUST BE DEVASTATING, LOSING THE LOVE OF YOUR LIFE...
YOU SOME JERK REPORTER FROM ONE A THEM HOLLYWOOD RAGS SNIFFIN' AROUND FOR A STORY?
WELL SHE'S DEAD. END OF STORY.
I'M NOT SO SURE THE STORY'S OVER.
WHY CAN'T YOU BOYS LET HER REST IN PEACE?
IT'S NOT HER PEACE I'M INTERESTED IN.
YOUR MARRIAGE LASTED WHAT-- A LITTLE LESS THAN A YEAR, RIGHT?
YEAH.
YEAH. TWO OF YOU-- NEVER STOOD A CHANCE.

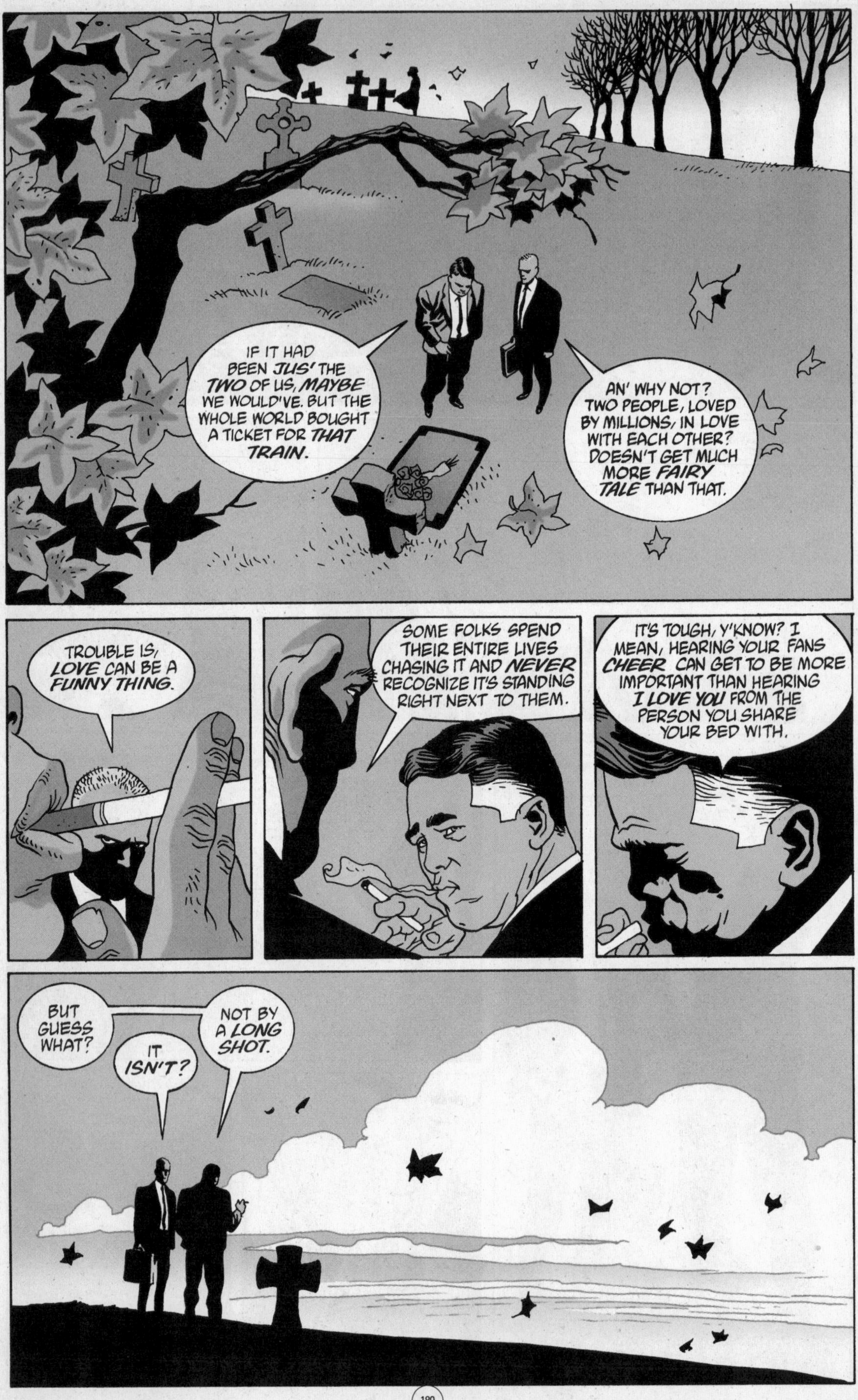
IF IT HAD BEEN JUS' THE TWO OF US, MAYBE WE WOULD'VE. BUT THE WHOLE WORLD BOUGHT A TICKET FOR THAT TRAIN.
AN' WHY NOT? TWO PEOPLE, LOVED BY MILLIONS, IN LOVE WITH EACH OTHER? DOESN'T GET MUCH MORE FAIRY TALE THAN THAT.
TROUBLE IS, LOVE CAN BE A FUNNY THING.
SOME FOLKS SPEND THEIR ENTIRE LIVES CHASING IT AND NEVER RECOGNIZE IT'S STANDING RIGHT NEXT TO THEM.
IT'S TOUGH, Y'KNOW? I MEAN, HEARING YOUR FANS CHEER CAN GET TO BE MORE IMPORTANT THAN HEARING I LOVE YOU FROM THE PERSON YOU SHARE YOUR BED WITH.
BUT GUESS WHAT?
IT ISN'T?
NOT BY A LONG SHOT.

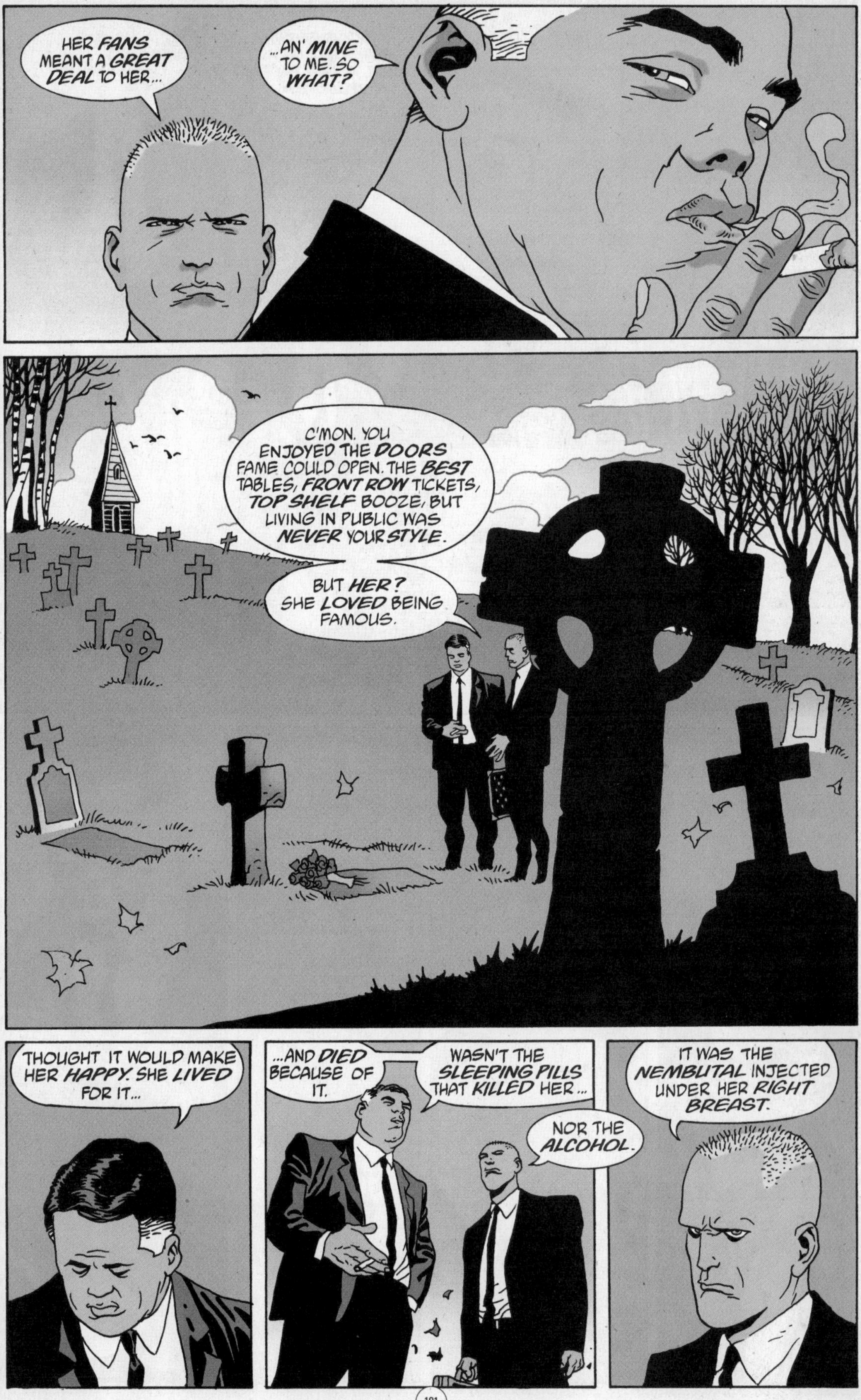
HER FANS MEANT A GREAT DEAL TO HER...
...AN' MINE TO ME. SO WHAT?
C'MON. YOU ENJOYED THE DOORS FAME COULD OPEN. THE BEST TABLES, FRONT ROW TICKETS, TOP SHELF BOOZE, BUT LIVING IN PUBLIC WAS NEVER YOUR STYLE.
BUT HER? SHE LOVED BEING FAMOUS.
THOUGHT IT WOULD MAKE HER HAPPY. SHE LIVED FOR IT...
...AND DIED BECAUSE OF IT.
WASN'T THE SLEEPING PILLS THAT KILLED HER...
NOR THE ALCOHOL.
IT WAS THE NEMBUTAL INJECTED UNDER HER RIGHT BREAST.

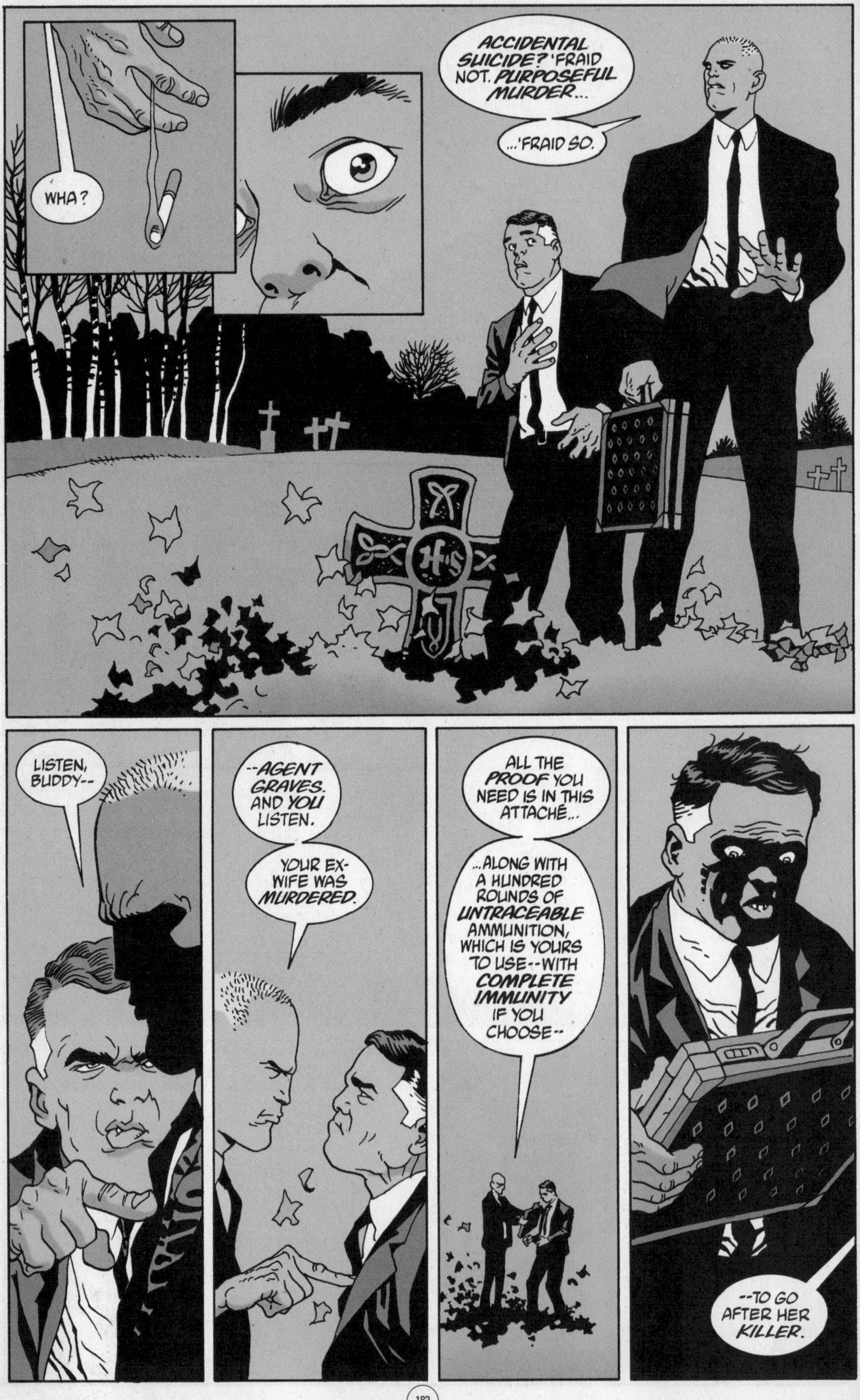
WHA?
ACCIDENTAL SUICIDE? 'FRAID NOT. PURPOSEFUL MURDER...
...'FRAID SO.
LISTEN, BUDDY--
--AGENT GRAVES. AND YOU LISTEN.
YOUR EX-WIFE WAS MURDERED.
ALL THE PROOF YOU NEED IS IN THIS ATTACHÉ...
...ALONG WITH A HUNDRED ROUNDS OF UNTRACEABLE AMMUNITION, WHICH IS YOURS TO USE--WITH COMPLETE IMMUNITY IF YOU CHOOSE--
--TO GO AFTER HER KILLER.

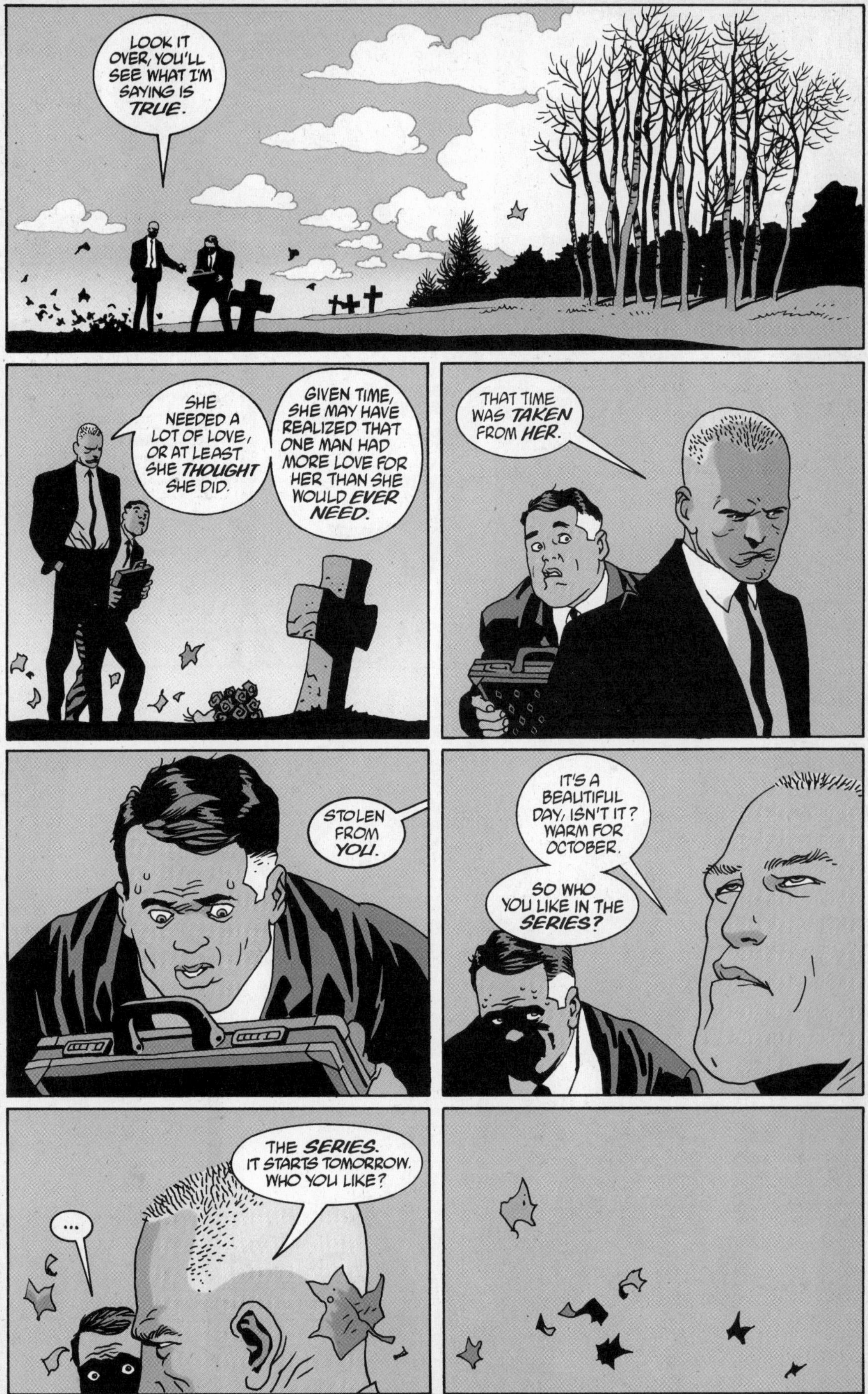
LOOK IT OVER, YOU'LL SEE WHAT I'M SAYING IS TRUE.
SHE NEEDED A LOT OF LOVE, OR AT LEAST SHE THOUGHT SHE DID.
GIVEN TIME, SHE MAY HAVE REALIZED THAT ONE MAN HAD MORE LOVE FOR HER THAN SHE WOULD EVER NEED.
THAT TIME WAS TAKEN FROM HER.
STOLEN FROM YOU.
IT'S A BEAUTIFUL DAY, ISN'T IT? WARM FOR OCTOBER.
SO WHO YOU LIKE IN THE SERIES?
THE SERIES. IT STARTS TOMORROW. WHO YOU LIKE?
...

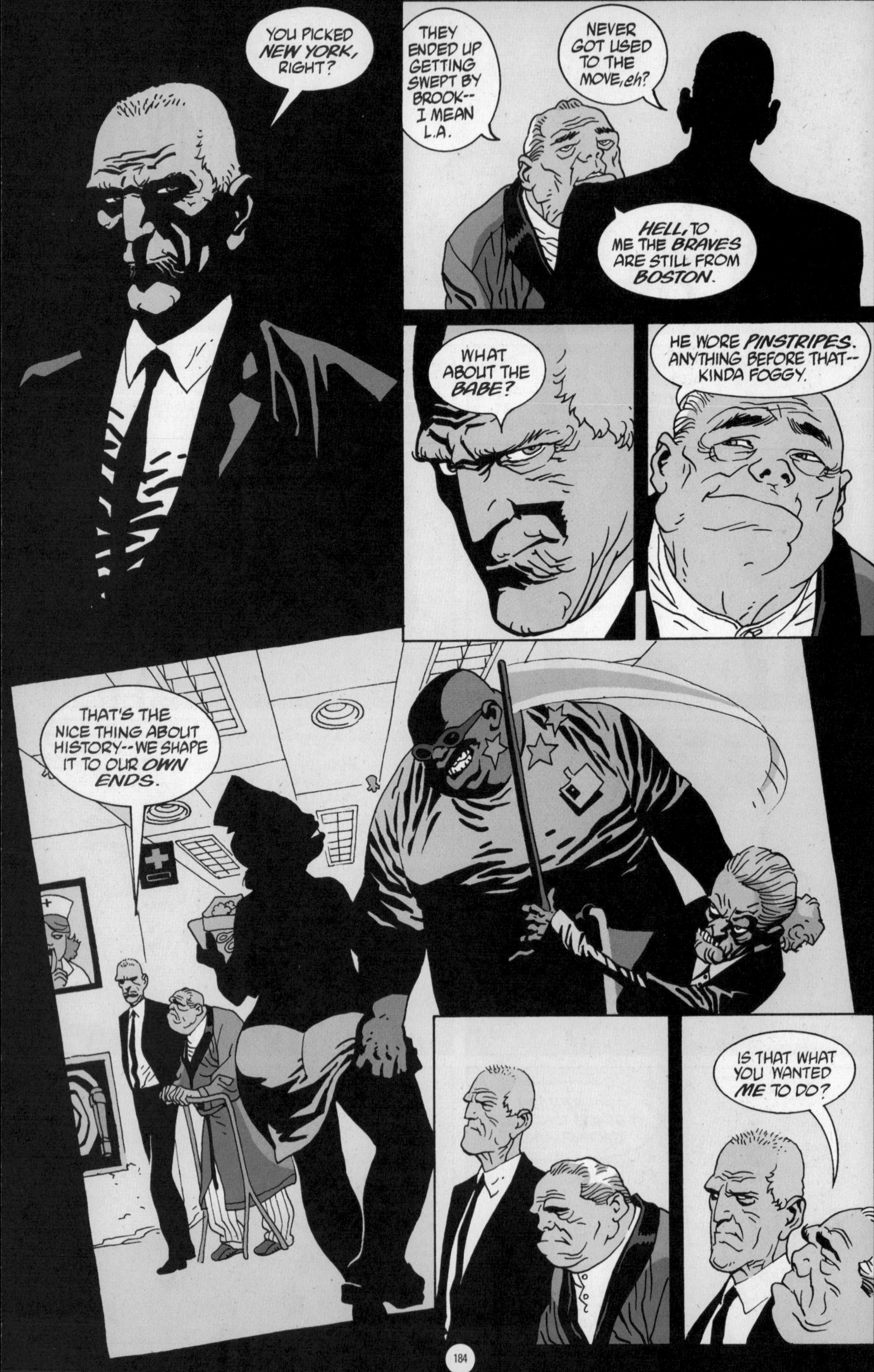
YOU PICKED NEW YORK, RIGHT?
THEY ENDED UP GETTING SWEPT BY BROOK-- I MEAN L.A.
NEVER GOT USED TO THE MOVE, eh?
HELL, TO ME THE BRAVES ARE STILL FROM BOSTON.
WHAT ABOUT THE BABE?
HE WORE PINSTRIPES. ANYTHING BEFORE THAT-- KINDA FOGGY.
THAT'S THE NICE THING ABOUT HISTORY--WE SHAPE IT TO OUR OWN ENDS.
IS THAT WHAT YOU WANTED ME TO DO?

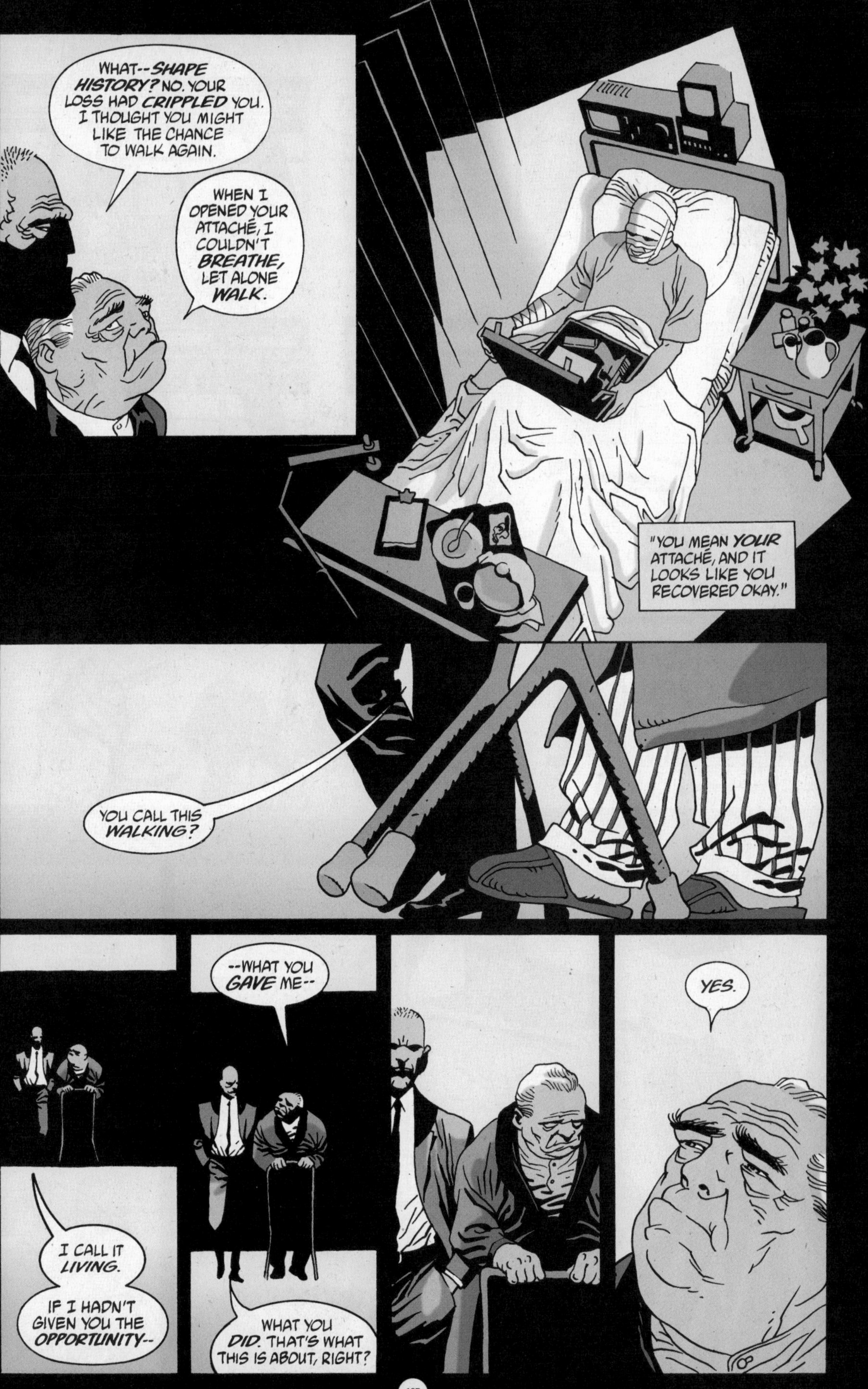
WHAT--SHAPE HISTORY? NO. YOUR LOSS HAD CRIPPLED YOU. I THOUGHT YOU MIGHT LIKE THE CHANCE TO WALK AGAIN.
WHEN I OPENED YOUR ATTACHÉ, I COULDN'T BREATHE, LET ALONE WALK.
"YOU MEAN YOUR ATTACHÉ, AND IT LOOKS LIKE YOU RECOVERED OKAY."
YOU CALL THIS WALKING?
I CALL IT LIVING.
IF I HADN'T GIVEN YOU THE OPPORTUNITY--
--WHAT YOU GAVE ME--
WHAT YOU DID. THAT'S WHAT THIS IS ABOUT, RIGHT?
YES.

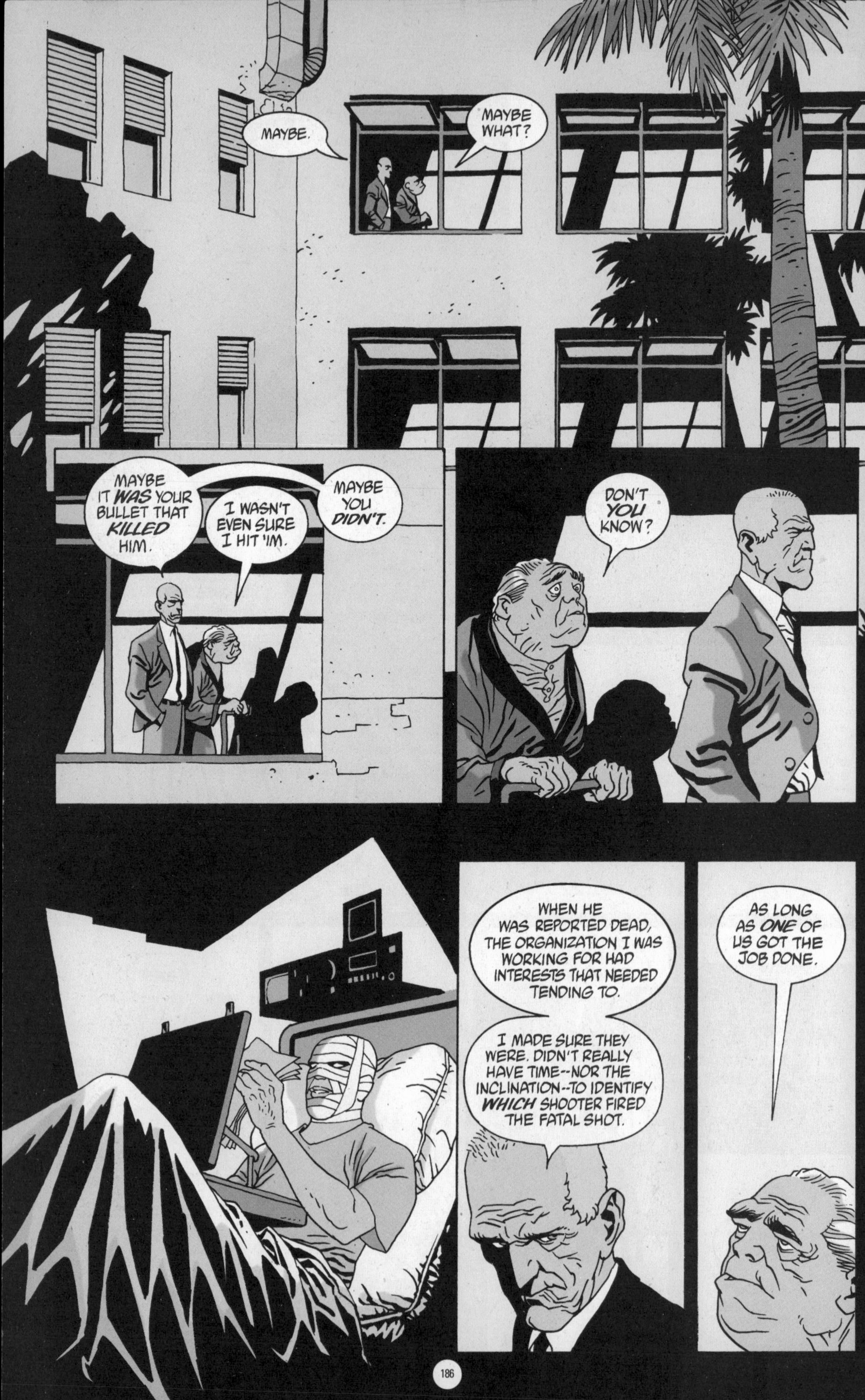
MAYBE.
MAYBE WHAT?
MAYBE IT WAS YOUR BULLET THAT KILLED HIM.
I WASN'T EVEN SURE I HIT 'IM.
MAYBE YOU DIDN'T.
DON'T YOU KNOW?
WHEN HE WAS REPORTED DEAD, THE ORGANIZATION I WAS WORKING FOR HAD INTERESTS THAT NEEDED TENDING TO.
I MADE SURE THEY WERE. DIDN'T REALLY HAVE TIME--NOR THE INCLINATION--TO IDENTIFY WHICH SHOOTER FIRED THE FATAL SHOT.
AS LONG AS ONE OF US GOT THE JOB DONE.

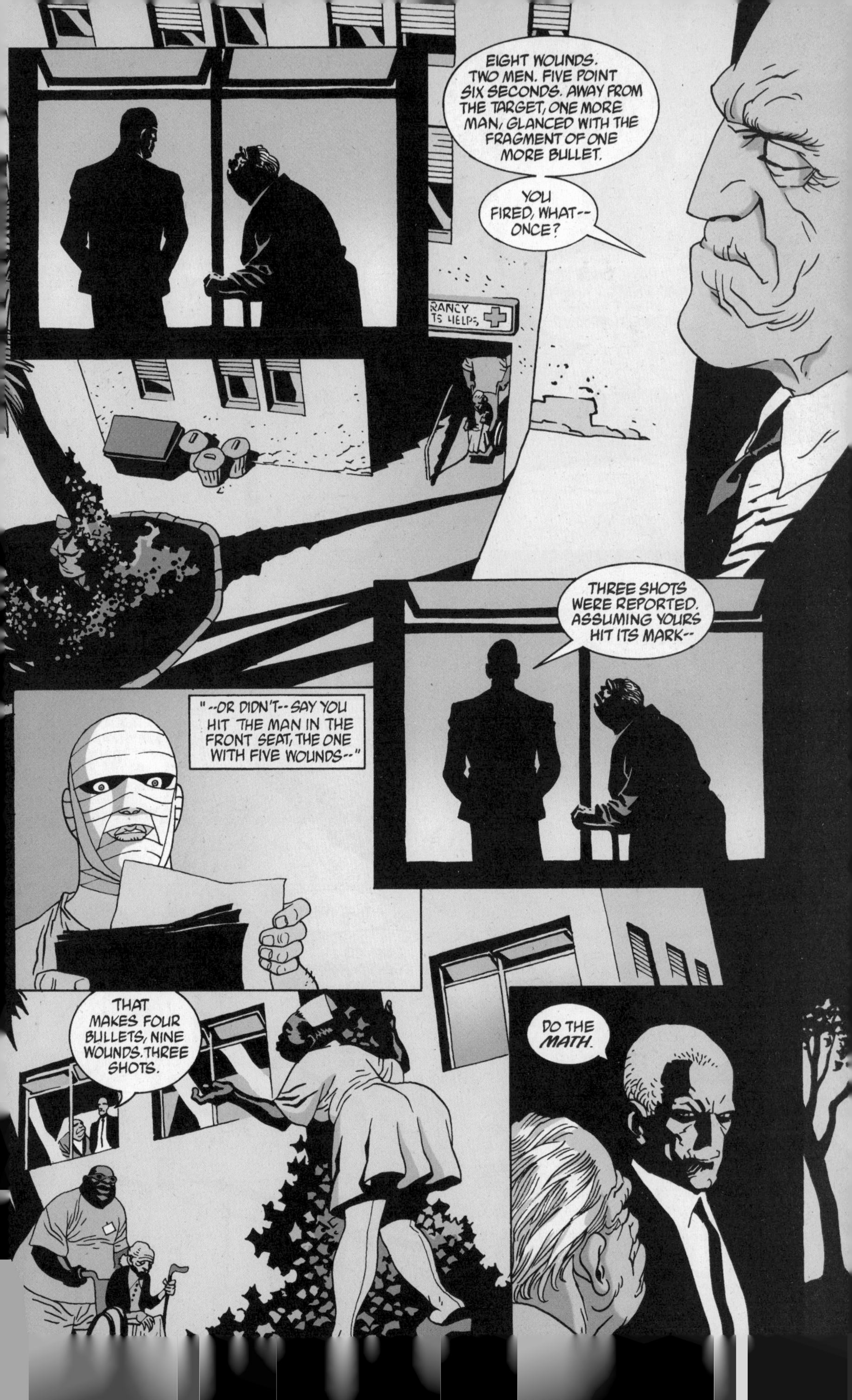
EIGHT WOUNDS. TWO MEN. FIVE POINT SIX SECONDS. AWAY FROM THE TARGET, ONE MORE MAN, GLANCED WITH THE FRAGMENT OF ONE MORE BULLET.
YOU FIRED, WHAT-- ONCE?
THREE SHOTS WERE REPORTED. ASSUMING YOURS HIT ITS MARK--
"--OR DIDN'T--SAY YOU HIT THE MAN IN THE FRONT SEAT, THE ONE WITH FIVE WOUNDS--"
THAT MAKES FOUR BULLETS, NINE WOUNDS. THREE SHOTS.
DO THE *MATH*.

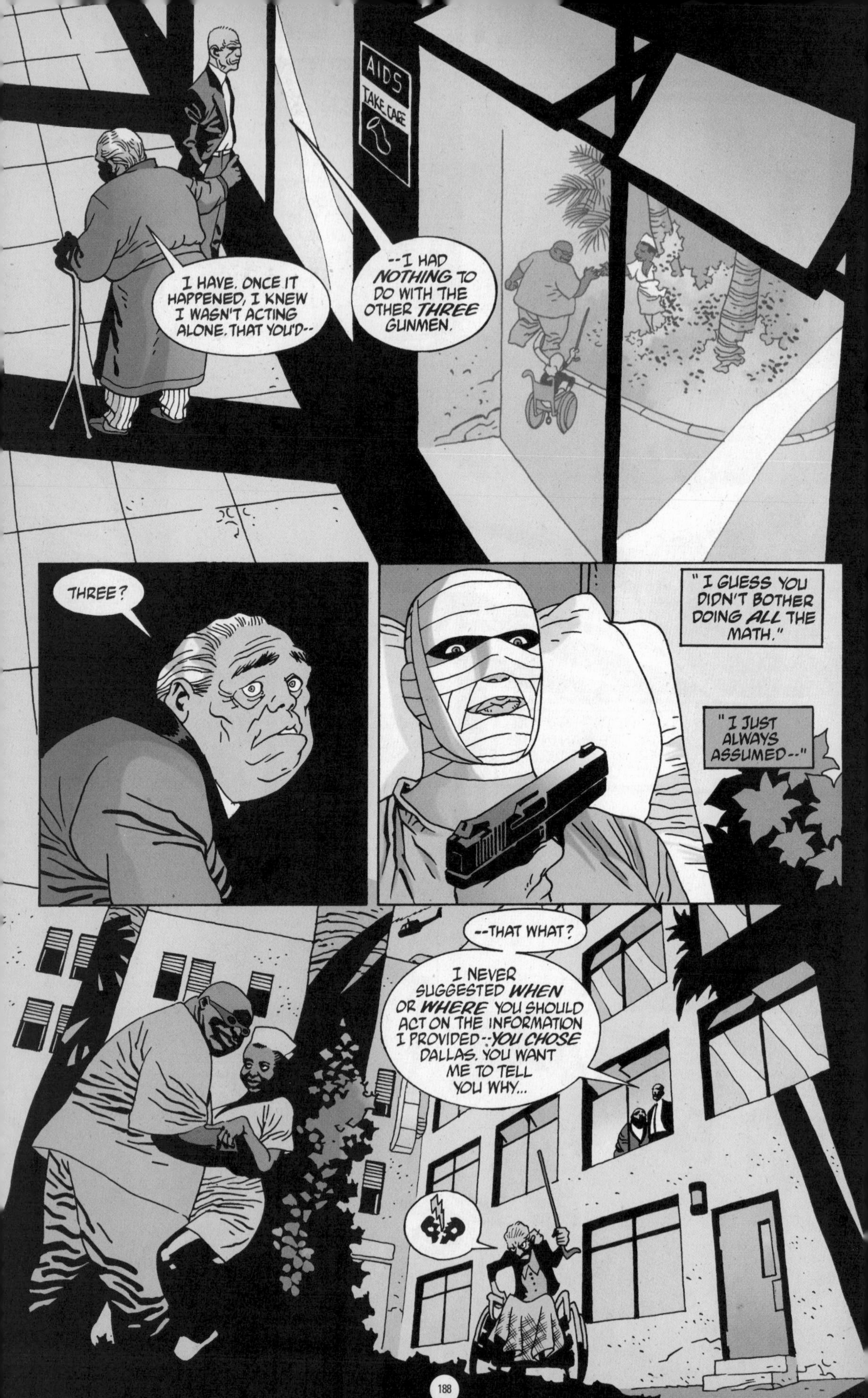
AIDS
TAKE CARE
I HAVE. ONCE IT HAPPENED, I KNEW I WASN'T ACTING ALONE. THAT YOU'D--
--I HAD NOTHING TO DO WITH THE OTHER THREE GUNMEN.
THREE?
"I GUESS YOU DIDN'T BOTHER DOING ALL THE MATH."
"I JUST ALWAYS ASSUMED--"
--THAT WHAT?
I NEVER SUGGESTED WHEN OR WHERE YOU SHOULD ACT ON THE INFORMATION I PROVIDED--YOU CHOSE DALLAS. YOU WANT ME TO TELL YOU WHY...

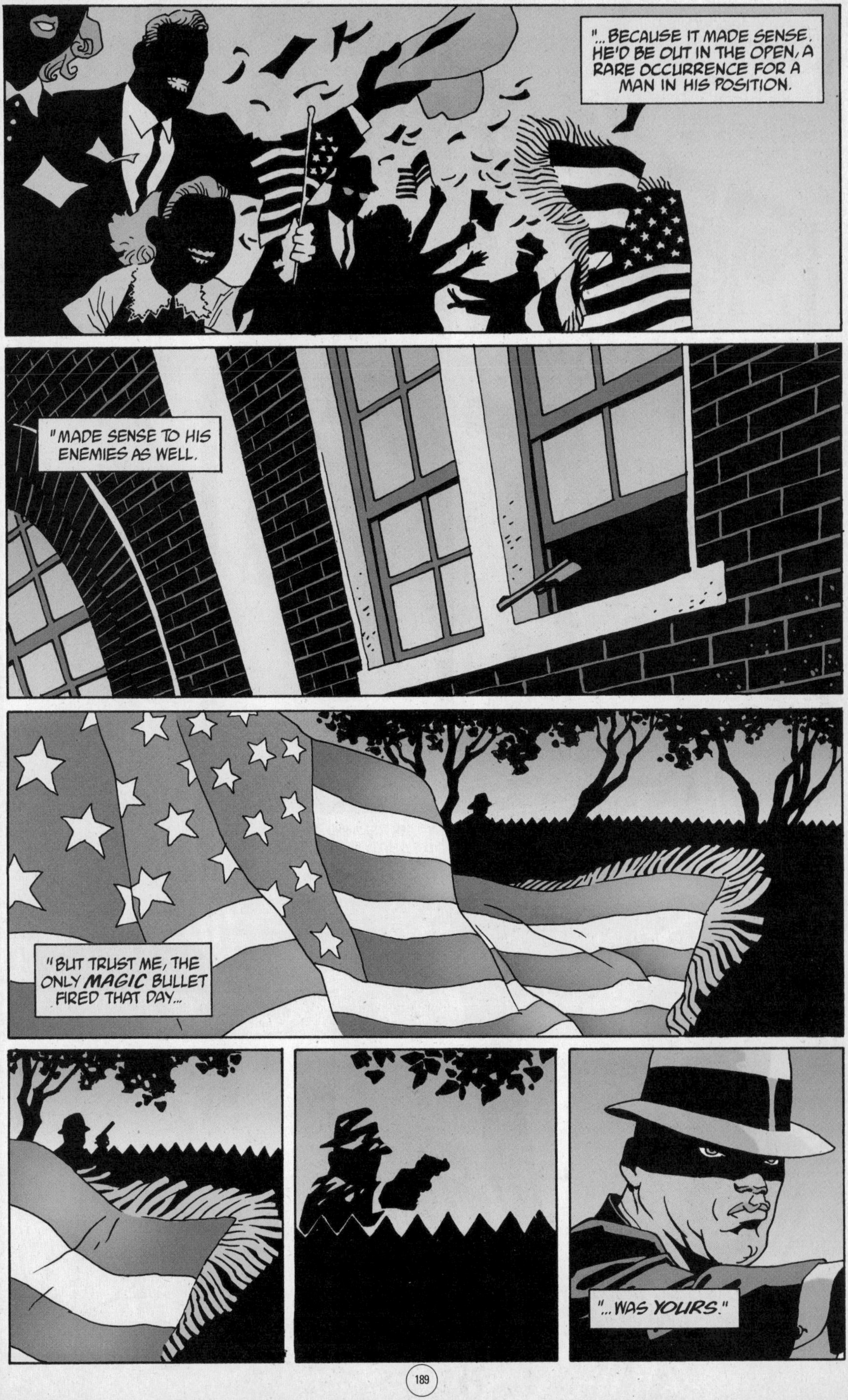
"...BECAUSE IT MADE SENSE. HE'D BE OUT IN THE OPEN, A RARE OCCURRENCE FOR A MAN IN HIS POSITION.
"MADE SENSE TO HIS ENEMIES AS WELL.
"BUT TRUST ME, THE ONLY MAGIC BULLET FIRED THAT DAY...
"...WAS YOURS."

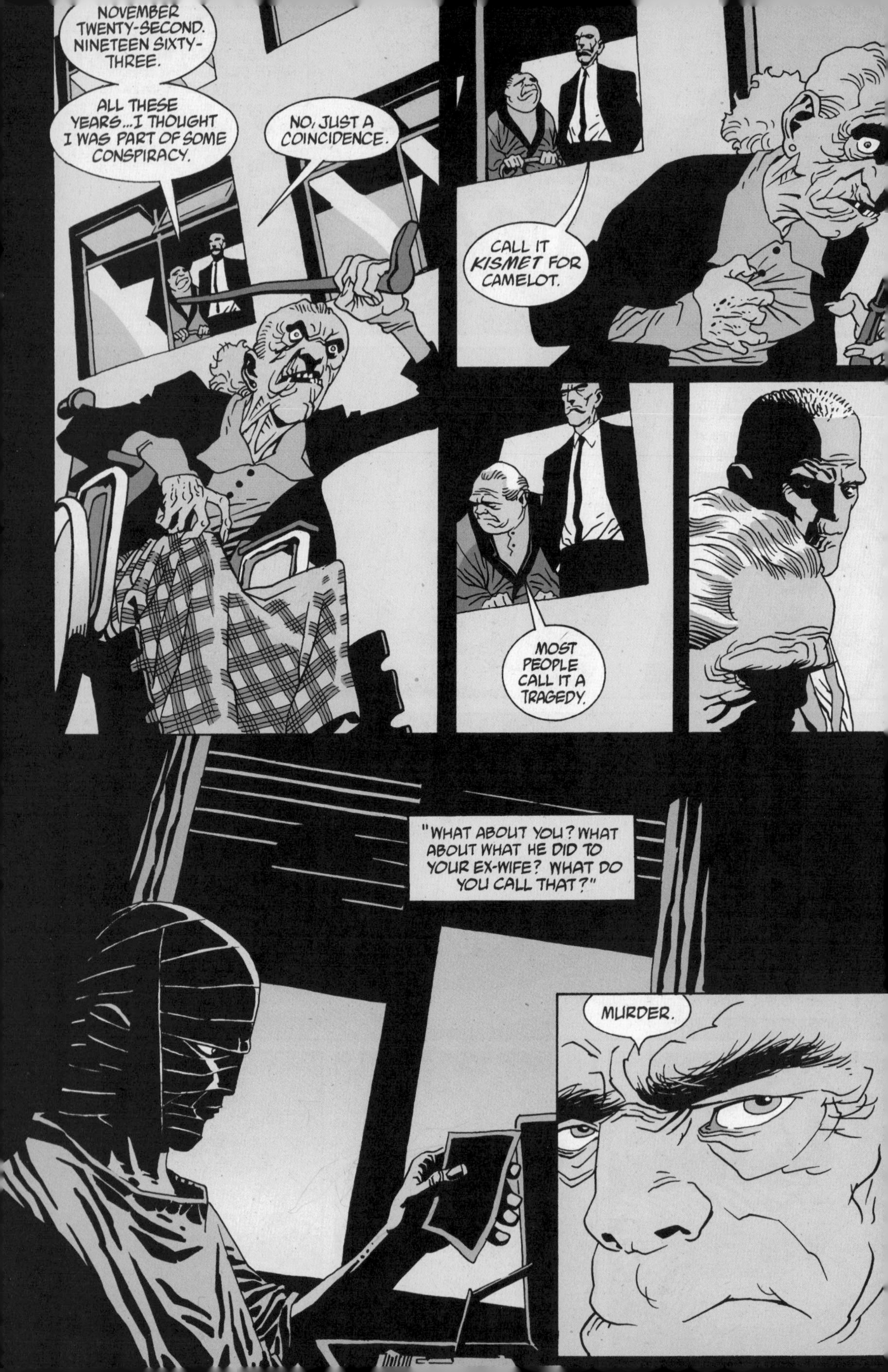
NOVEMBER TWENTY-SECOND. NINETEEN SIXTY-THREE.
ALL THESE YEARS...I THOUGHT I WAS PART OF SOME CONSPIRACY.
NO, JUST A COINCIDENCE.
CALL IT KISMET FOR CAMELOT.
MOST PEOPLE CALL IT A TRAGEDY.
"WHAT ABOUT YOU? WHAT ABOUT WHAT HE DID TO YOUR EX-WIFE? WHAT DO YOU CALL THAT?"
MURDER.

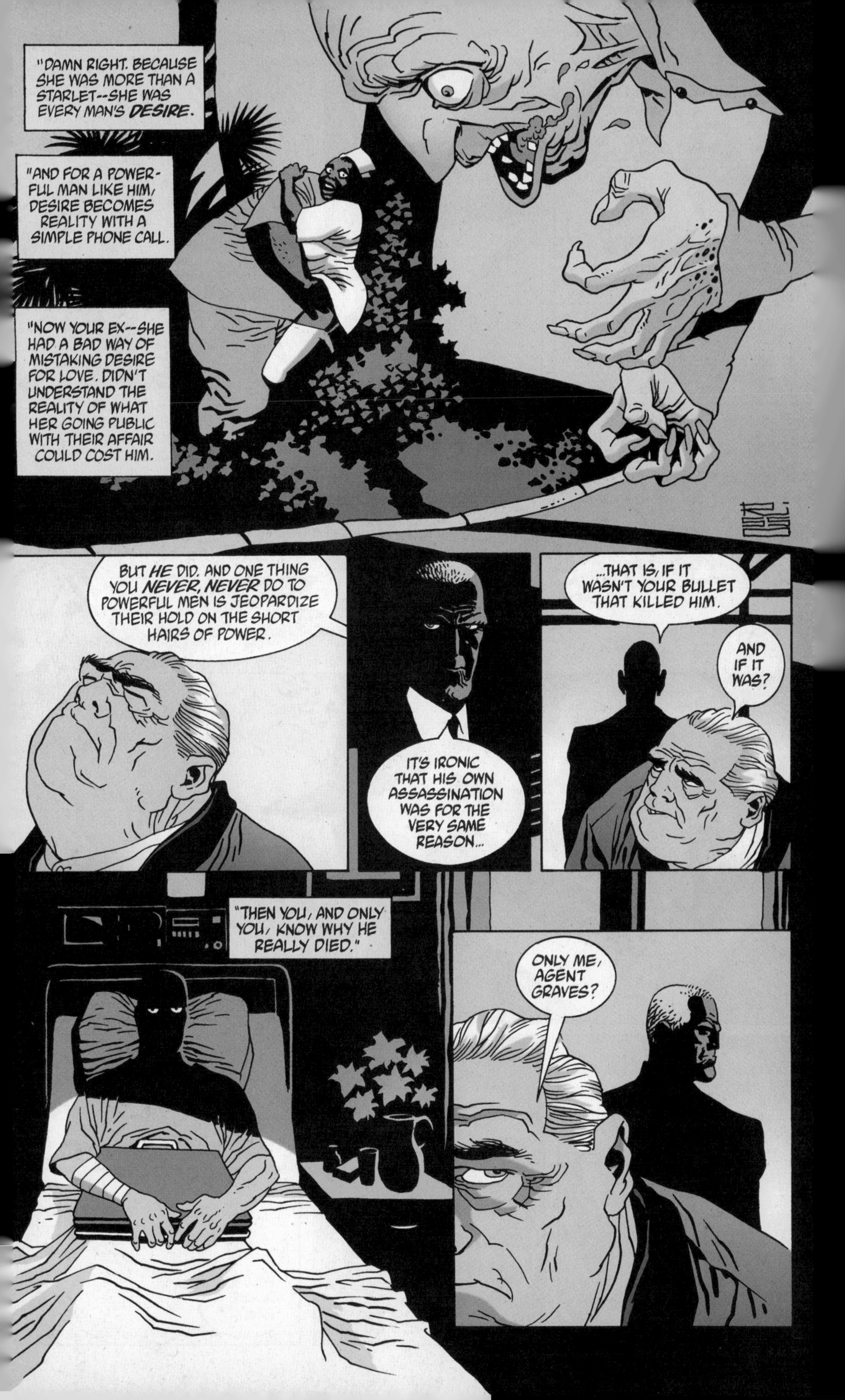
"DAMN RIGHT. BECAUSE SHE WAS MORE THAN A STARLET--SHE WAS EVERY MAN'S **DESIRE**.
"AND FOR A POWERFUL MAN LIKE HIM, DESIRE BECOMES REALITY WITH A SIMPLE PHONE CALL.
"NOW YOUR EX--SHE HAD A BAD WAY OF MISTAKING DESIRE FOR LOVE. DIDN'T UNDERSTAND THE REALITY OF WHAT HER GOING PUBLIC WITH THEIR AFFAIR COULD COST HIM.
BUT **HE** DID. AND ONE THING YOU **NEVER, NEVER** DO TO POWERFUL MEN IS JEOPARDIZE THEIR HOLD ON THE SHORT HAIRS OF POWER.
IT'S IRONIC THAT HIS OWN ASSASSINATION WAS FOR THE VERY SAME REASON...
...THAT IS, IF IT WASN'T YOUR BULLET THAT KILLED HIM.
AND IF IT WAS?
"THEN YOU, AND ONLY YOU, KNOW WHY HE REALLY DIED."
ONLY ME, AGENT GRAVES?

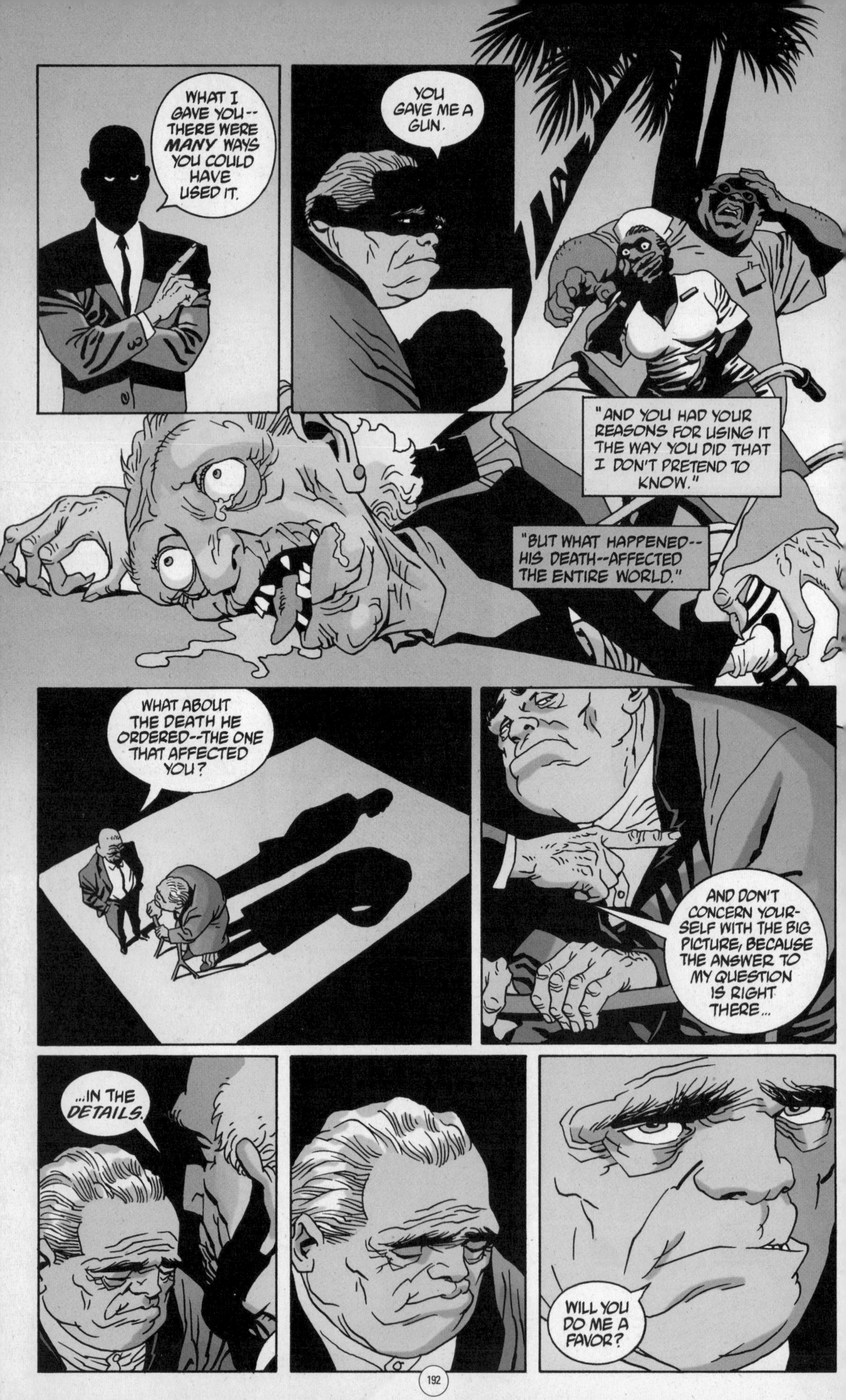
WHAT I GAVE YOU-- THERE WERE MANY WAYS YOU COULD HAVE USED IT.
YOU GAVE ME A GUN.
"AND YOU HAD YOUR REASONS FOR USING IT THE WAY YOU DID THAT I DON'T PRETEND TO KNOW."
"BUT WHAT HAPPENED-- HIS DEATH--AFFECTED THE ENTIRE WORLD."
WHAT ABOUT THE DEATH HE ORDERED--THE ONE THAT AFFECTED YOU?
AND DON'T CONCERN YOURSELF WITH THE BIG PICTURE, BECAUSE THE ANSWER TO MY QUESTION IS RIGHT THERE...
...IN THE DETAILS.
WILL YOU DO ME A FAVOR?

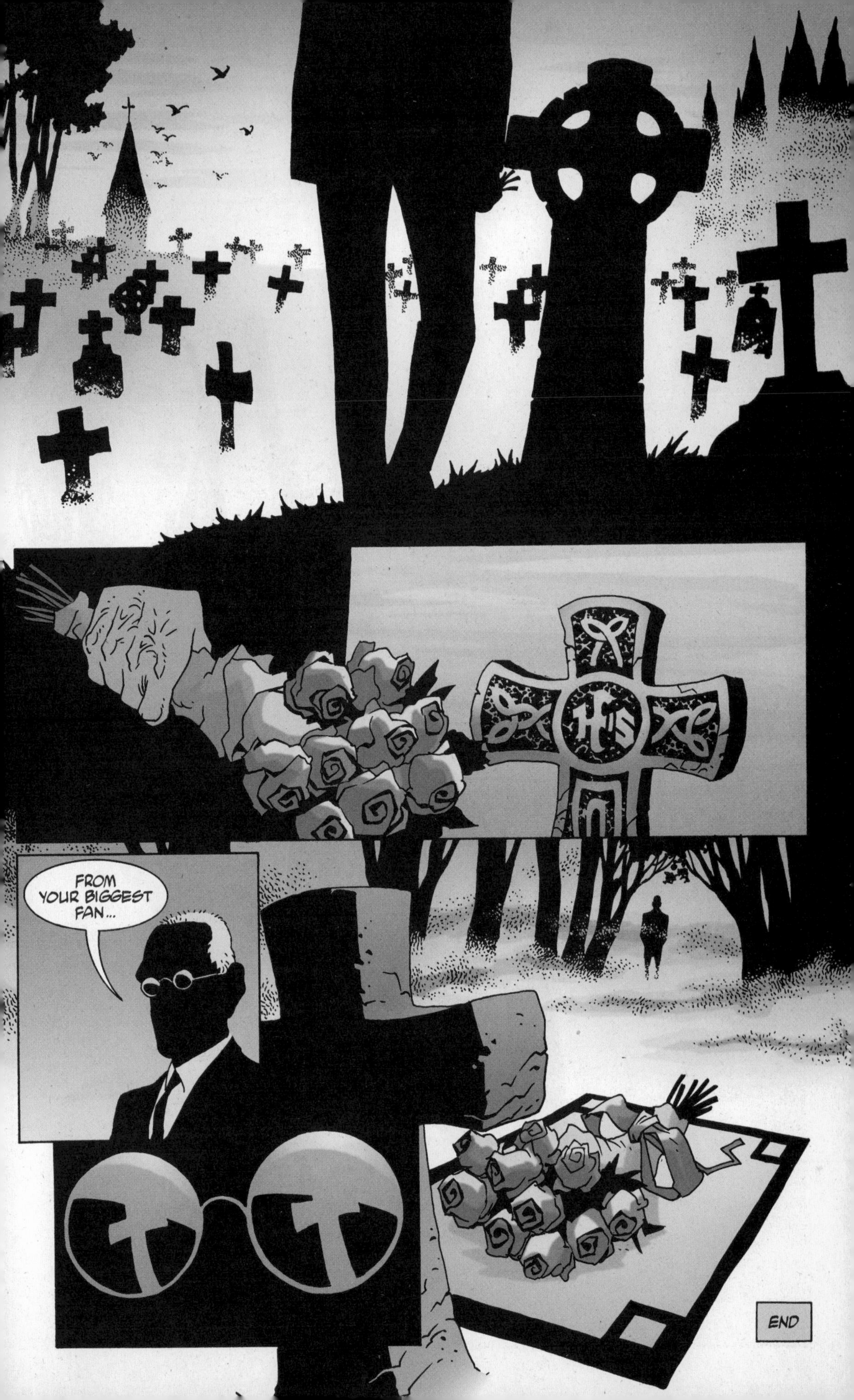
FROM YOUR BIGGEST FAN...
IHS
END

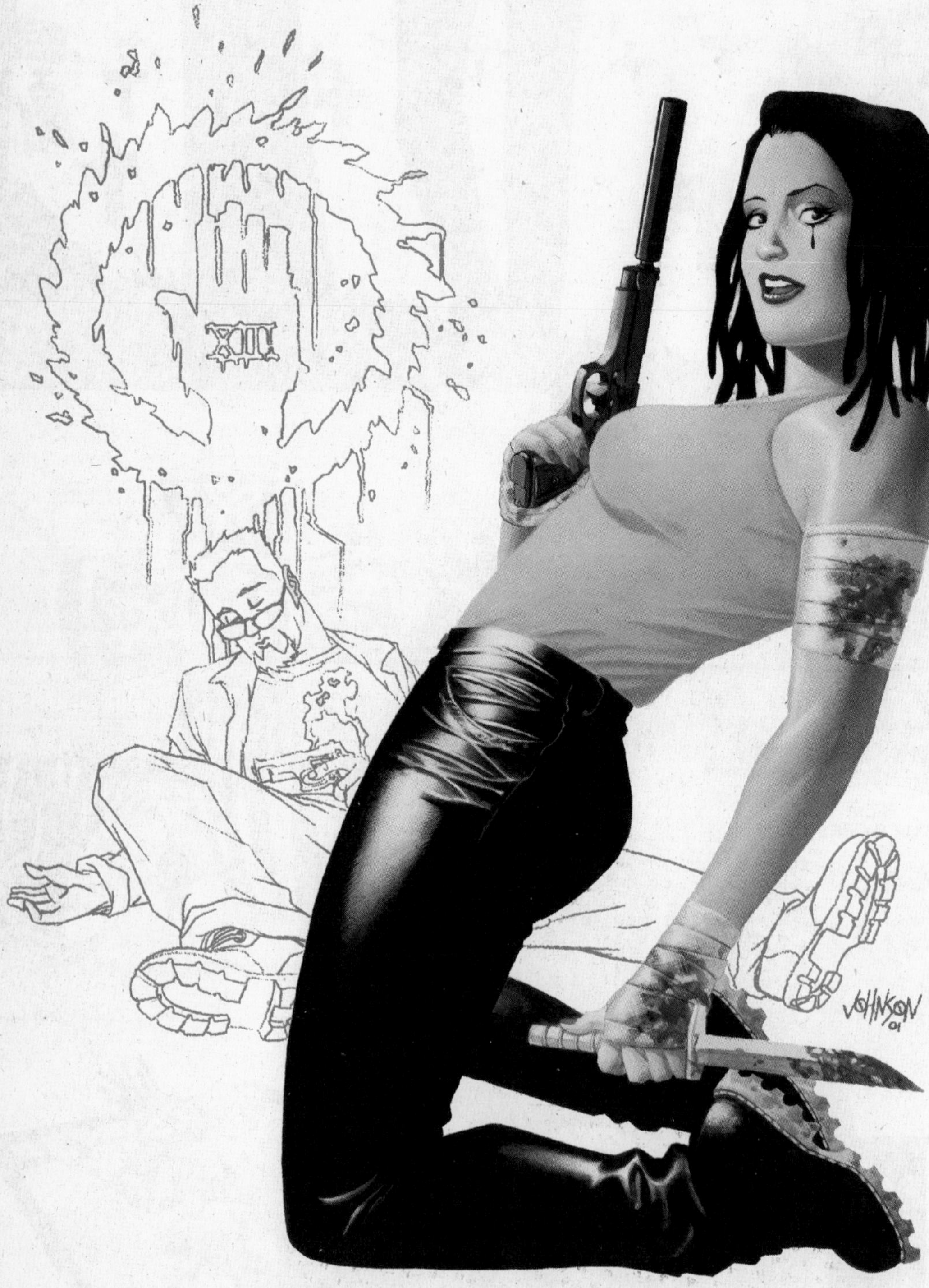
XIII
JOHNSON
'01

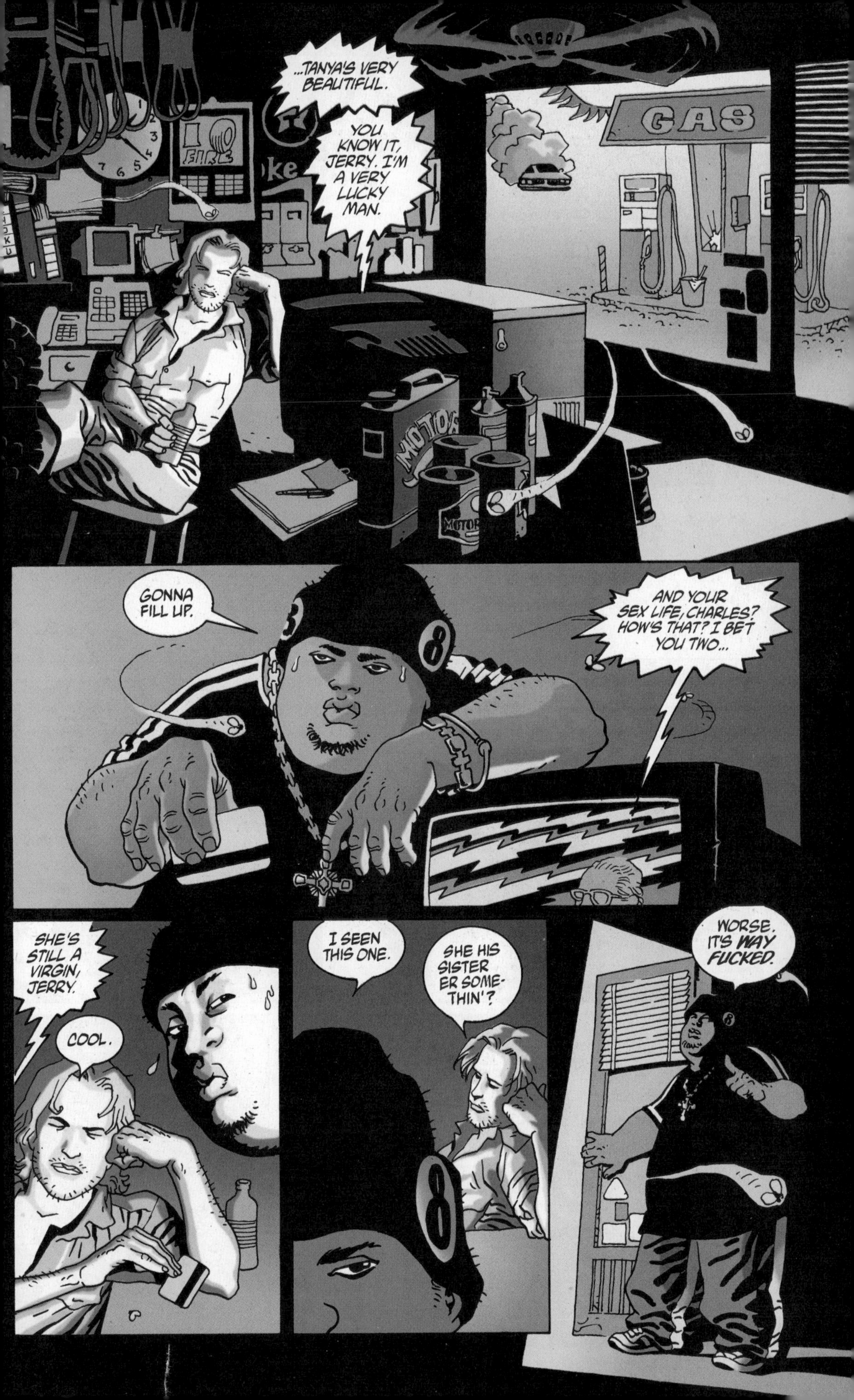

...TANYA'S VERY BEAUTIFUL.
YOU KNOW IT, JERRY. I'M A VERY LUCKY MAN.
GAS
GONNA FILL UP.
AND YOUR SEX LIFE, CHARLES? HOW'S THAT? I BET YOU TWO...
SHE'S STILL A VIRGIN, JERRY.
COOL.
I SEEN THIS ONE.
SHE HIS SISTER ER SOME-THIN'?
WORSE. IT'S WAY FUCKED.

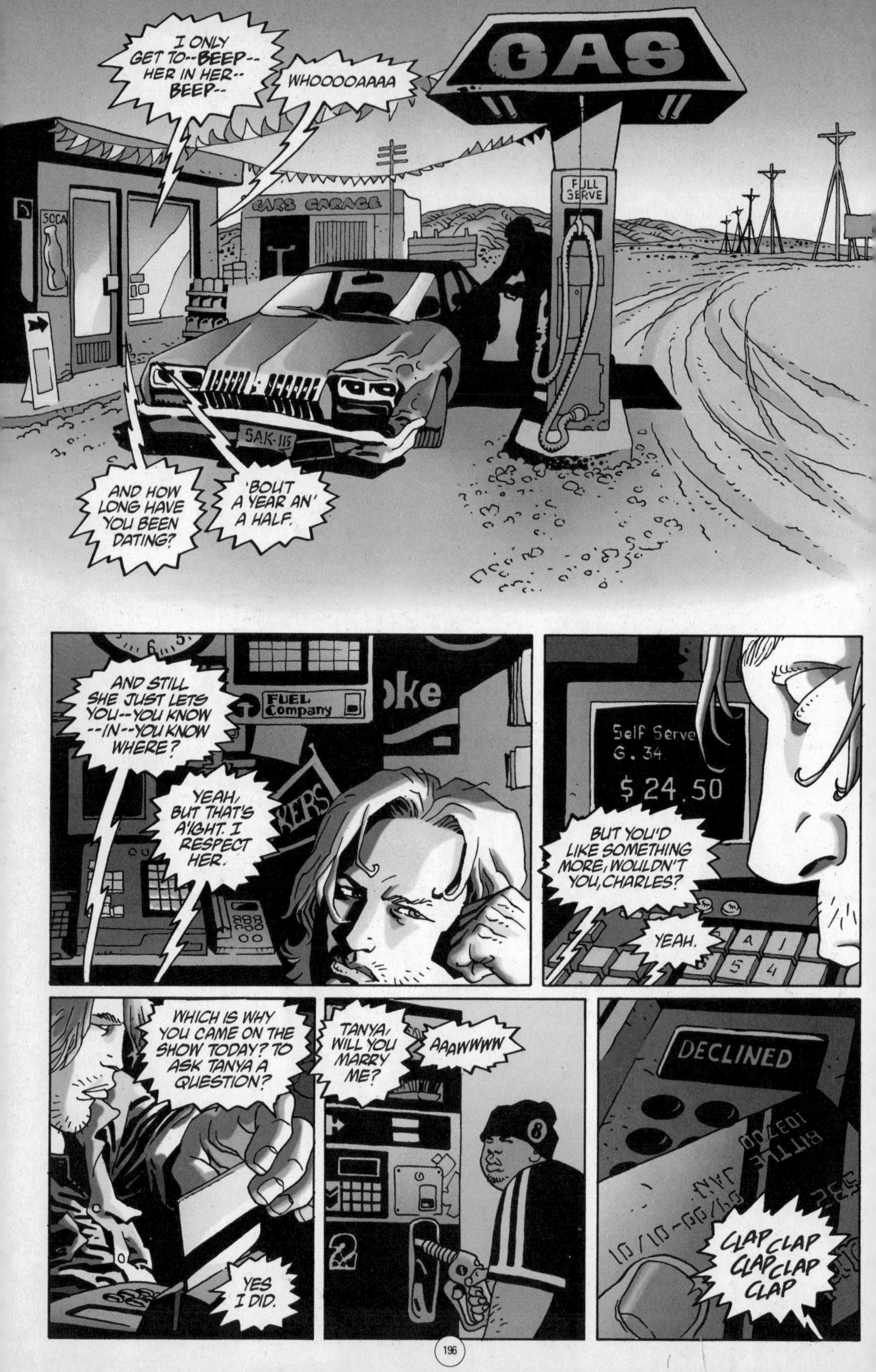
I ONLY GET TO--BEEP-- HER IN HER--BEEP--
WHOOOOAAAA
GAS
FULL SERVE
CARS GARAGE
SODA
SAK-115
AND HOW LONG HAVE YOU BEEN DATING?
'BOUT A YEAR AN' A HALF.
AND STILL SHE JUST LETS YOU--YOU KNOW --IN--YOU KNOW WHERE?
FUEL Company
YEAH, BUT THAT'S A'IGHT. I RESPECT HER.
Self Serve
G.34
$ 24.50
BUT YOU'D LIKE SOMETHING MORE, WOULDN'T YOU, CHARLES?
YEAH.
WHICH IS WHY YOU CAME ON THE SHOW TODAY? TO ASK TANYA A QUESTION?
YES I DID.
TANYA, WILL YOU MARRY ME?
AAAWWWW
DECLINED
CLAP CLAP CLAP CLAP CLAP

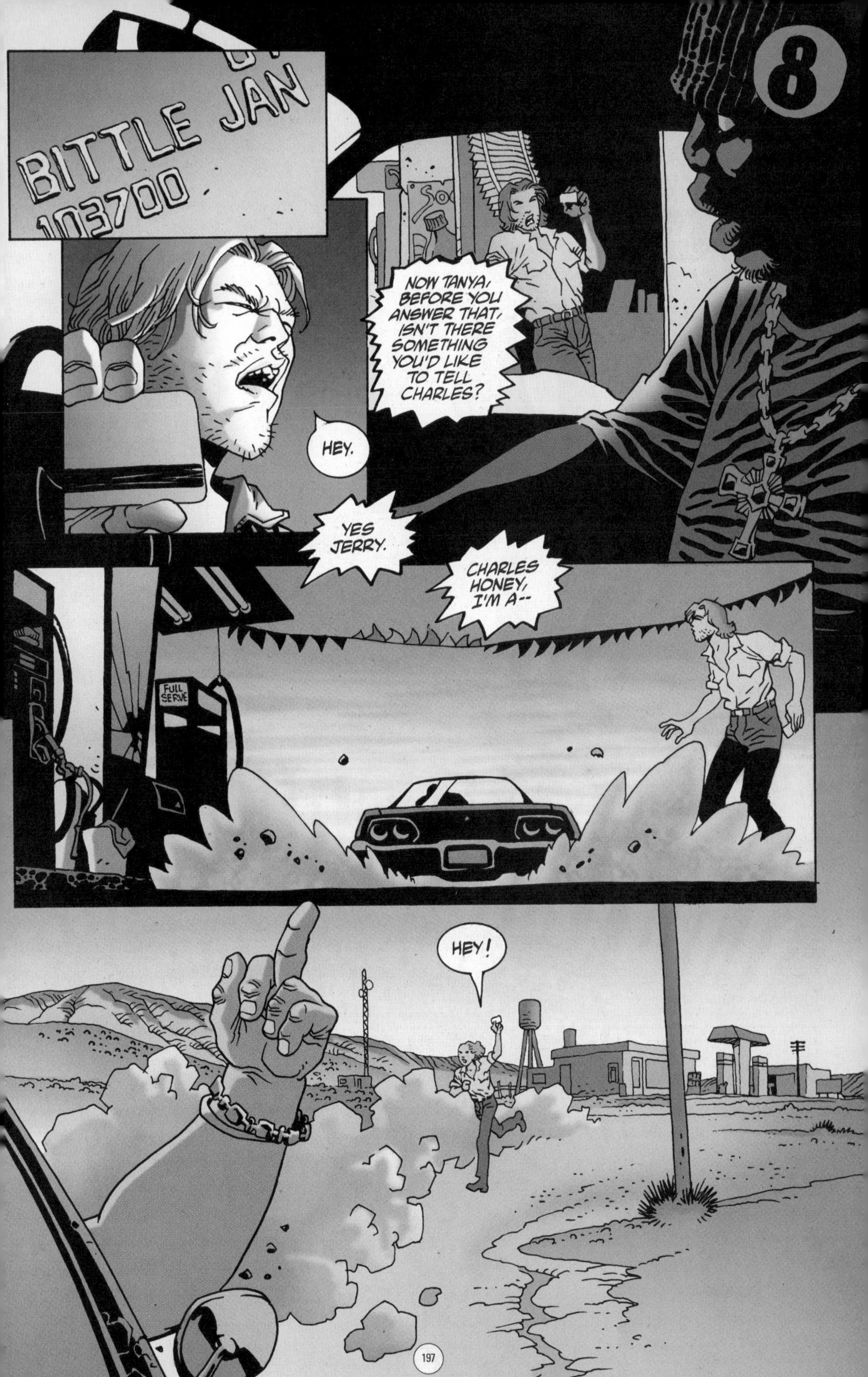

BITTLE JAN
103700
8
NOW TANYA, BEFORE YOU ANSWER THAT, ISN'T THERE SOMETHING YOU'D LIKE TO TELL CHARLES?
HEY.
YES JERRY.
CHARLES HONEY, I'M A--
FULL SERVE
HEY!

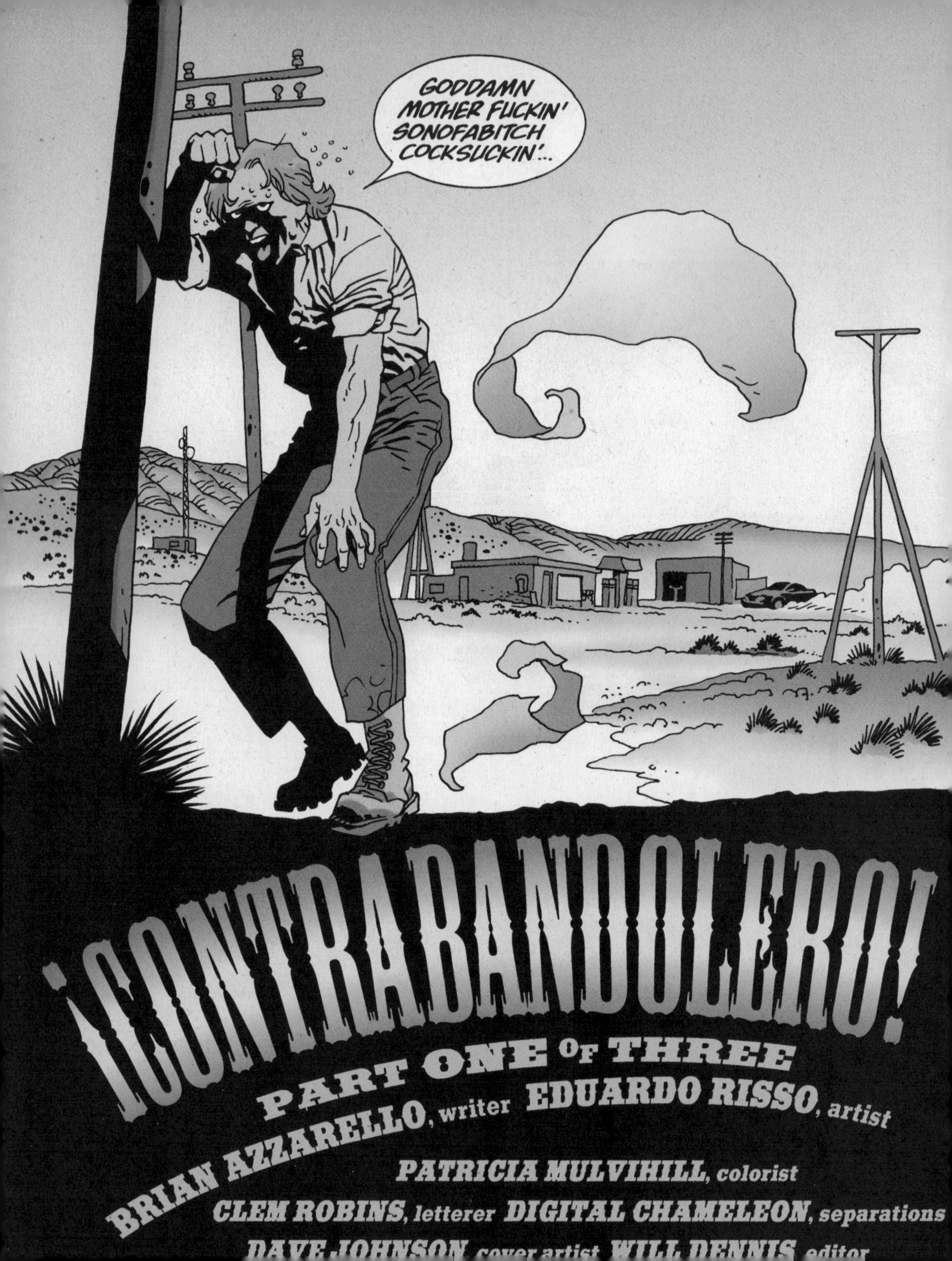
GODDAMN MOTHER FUCKIN' SONOFABITCH COCKSUCKIN'...
¡CONTRABANDOLERO!
PART ONE OF THREE
BRIAN AZZARELLO, writer EDUARDO RISSO, artist
PATRICIA MULVIHILL, colorist
CLEM ROBINS, letterer DIGITAL CHAMELEON, separations
DAVE JOHNSON, cover artist WILL DENNIS, editor

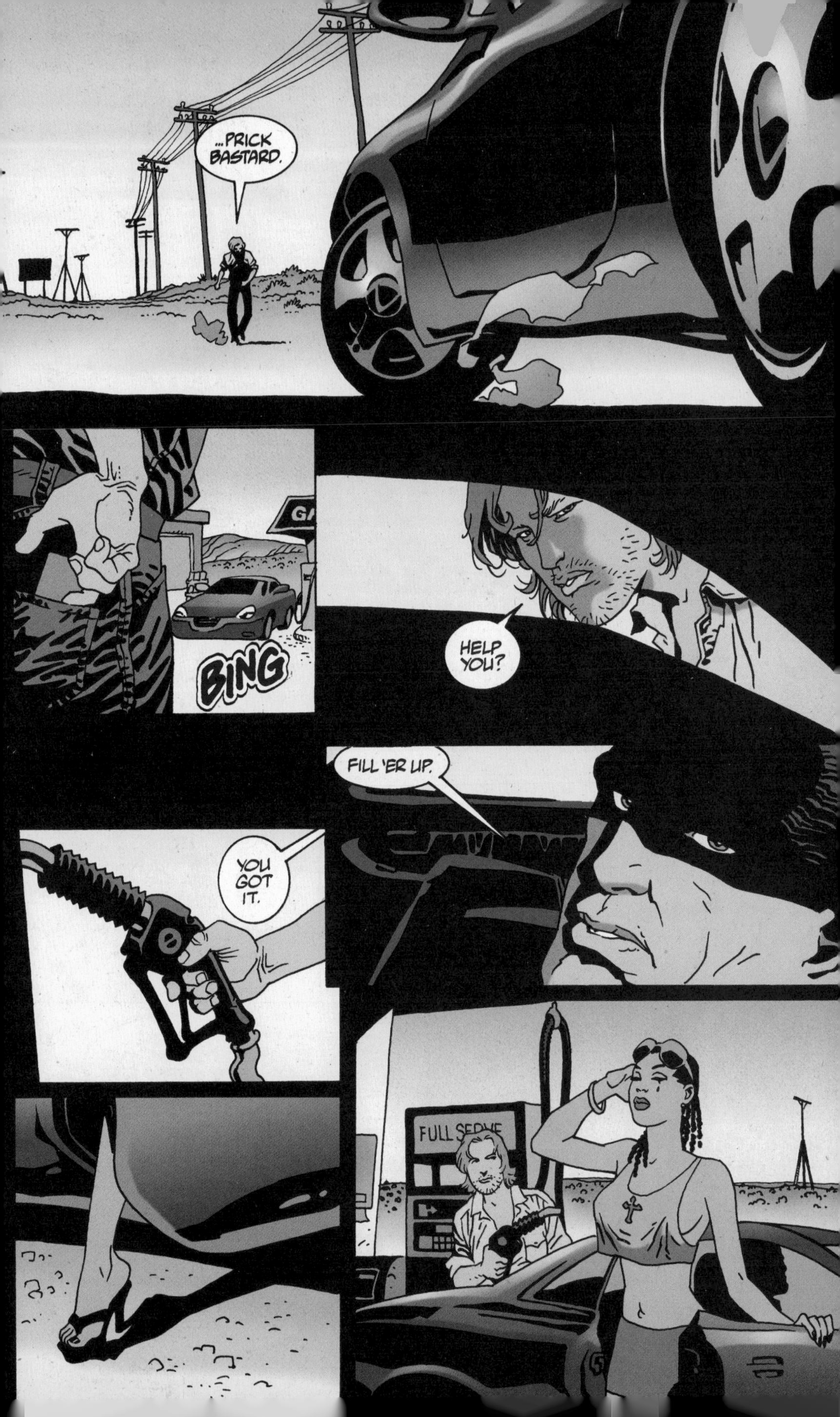
...PRICK BASTARD.
BING
HELP YOU?
FILL 'ER UP.
YOU GOT IT.
FULL SERVE

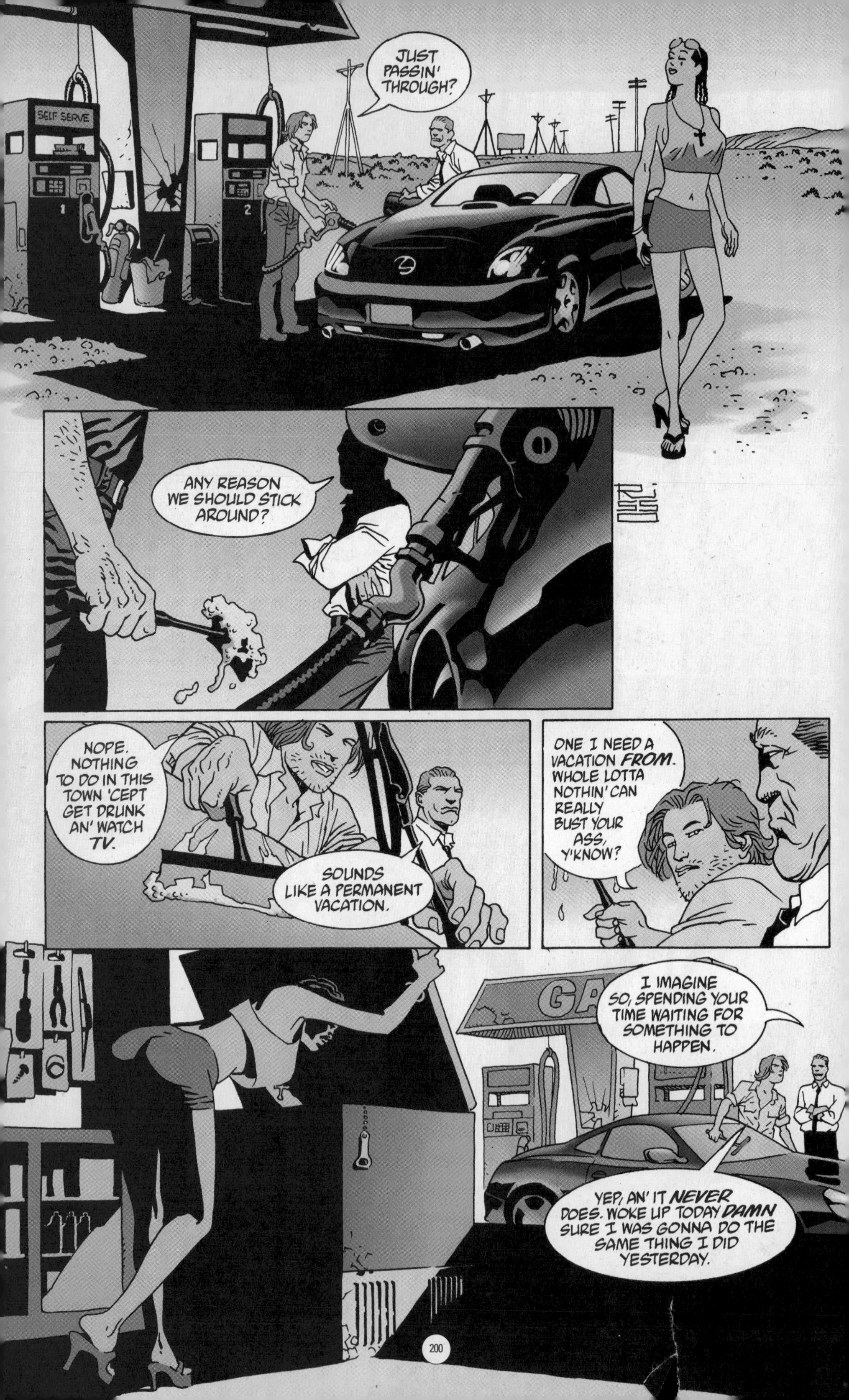
SELF SERVE
JUST PASSIN' THROUGH?
ANY REASON WE SHOULD STICK AROUND?
NOPE. NOTHING TO DO IN THIS TOWN 'CEPT GET DRUNK AN' WATCH TV.
SOUNDS LIKE A PERMANENT VACATION.
ONE I NEED A VACATION FROM. WHOLE LOTTA NOTHIN' CAN REALLY BUST YOUR ASS, Y'KNOW?
I IMAGINE SO, SPENDING YOUR TIME WAITING FOR SOMETHING TO HAPPEN.
YEP, AN' IT NEVER DOES. WOKE UP TODAY DAMN SURE I WAS GONNA DO THE SAME THING I DID YESTERDAY.

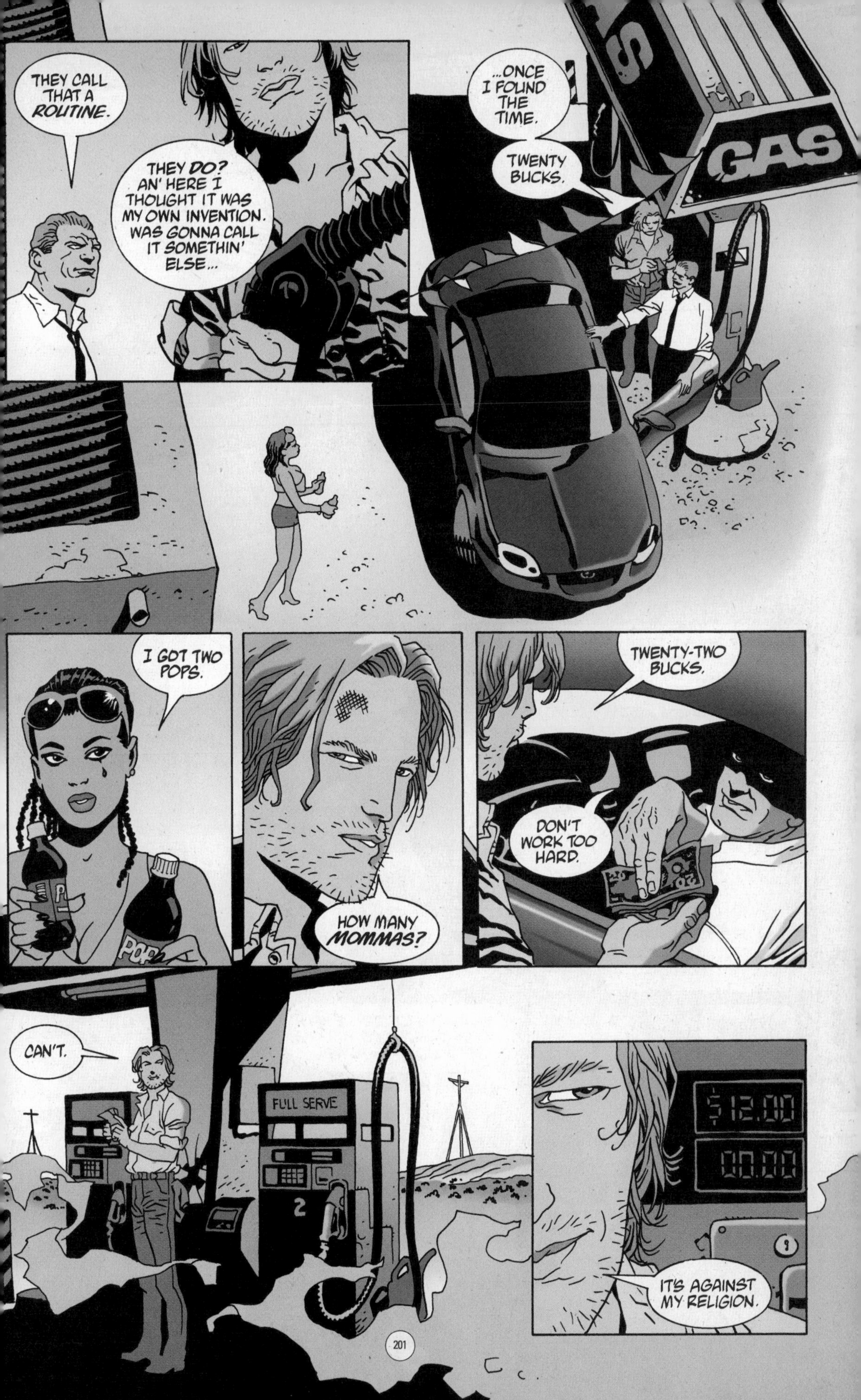
THEY CALL THAT A ROUTINE.
THEY DO? AN' HERE I THOUGHT IT WAS MY OWN INVENTION. WAS GONNA CALL IT SOMETHIN' ELSE...
...ONCE I FOUND THE TIME.
TWENTY BUCKS.
GAS
I GOT TWO POPS.
POP
HOW MANY MOMMAS?
TWENTY-TWO BUCKS.
DON'T WORK TOO HARD.
CAN'T.
FULL SERVE
2
$12.00
00.00
IT'S AGAINST MY RELIGION.

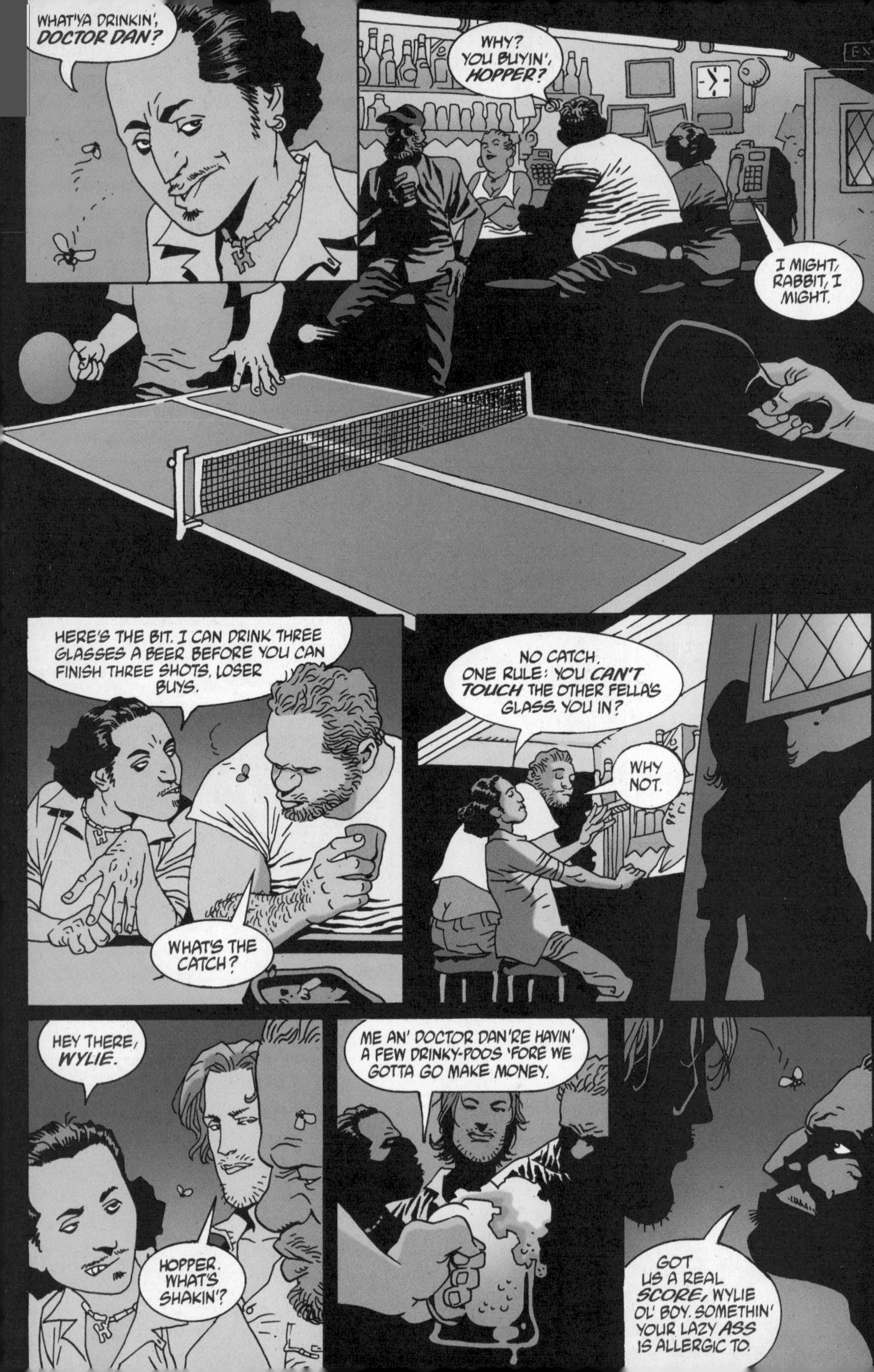
WHAT'YA DRINKIN', DOCTOR DAN?
WHY? YOU BUYIN', HOPPER?
I MIGHT, RABBIT, I MIGHT.
HERE'S THE BIT. I CAN DRINK THREE GLASSES A BEER BEFORE YOU CAN FINISH THREE SHOTS. LOSER BUYS.
WHAT'S THE CATCH?
NO CATCH. ONE RULE: YOU CAN'T TOUCH THE OTHER FELLA'S GLASS. YOU IN?
WHY NOT.
HEY THERE, WYLIE.
HOPPER. WHAT'S SHAKIN'?
ME AN' DOCTOR DAN'RE HAVIN' A FEW DRINKY-POOS 'FORE WE GOTTA GO MAKE MONEY.
GOT US A REAL SCORE, WYLIE OL' BOY. SOMETHIN' YOUR LAZY ASS IS ALLERGIC TO.

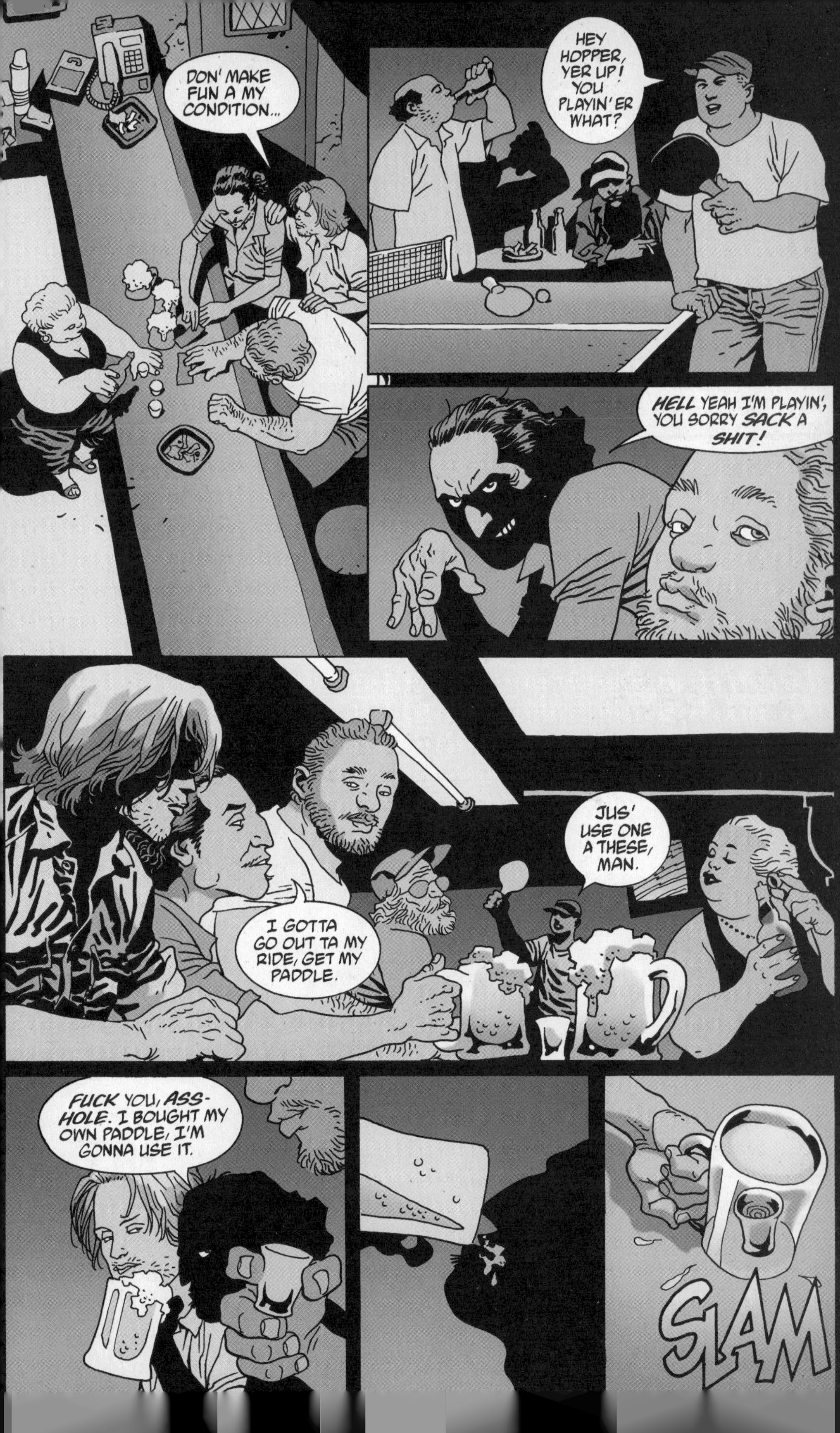
DON' MAKE FUN A MY CONDITION...
HEY HOPPER, YER UP! YOU PLAYIN' ER WHAT?
HELL YEAH I'M PLAYIN', YOU SORRY SACK A SHIT!
I GOTTA GO OUT TA MY RIDE, GET MY PADDLE.
JUS' USE ONE A THESE, MAN.
FUCK YOU, ASS-HOLE. I BOUGHT MY OWN PADDLE, I'M GONNA USE IT.
SLAM

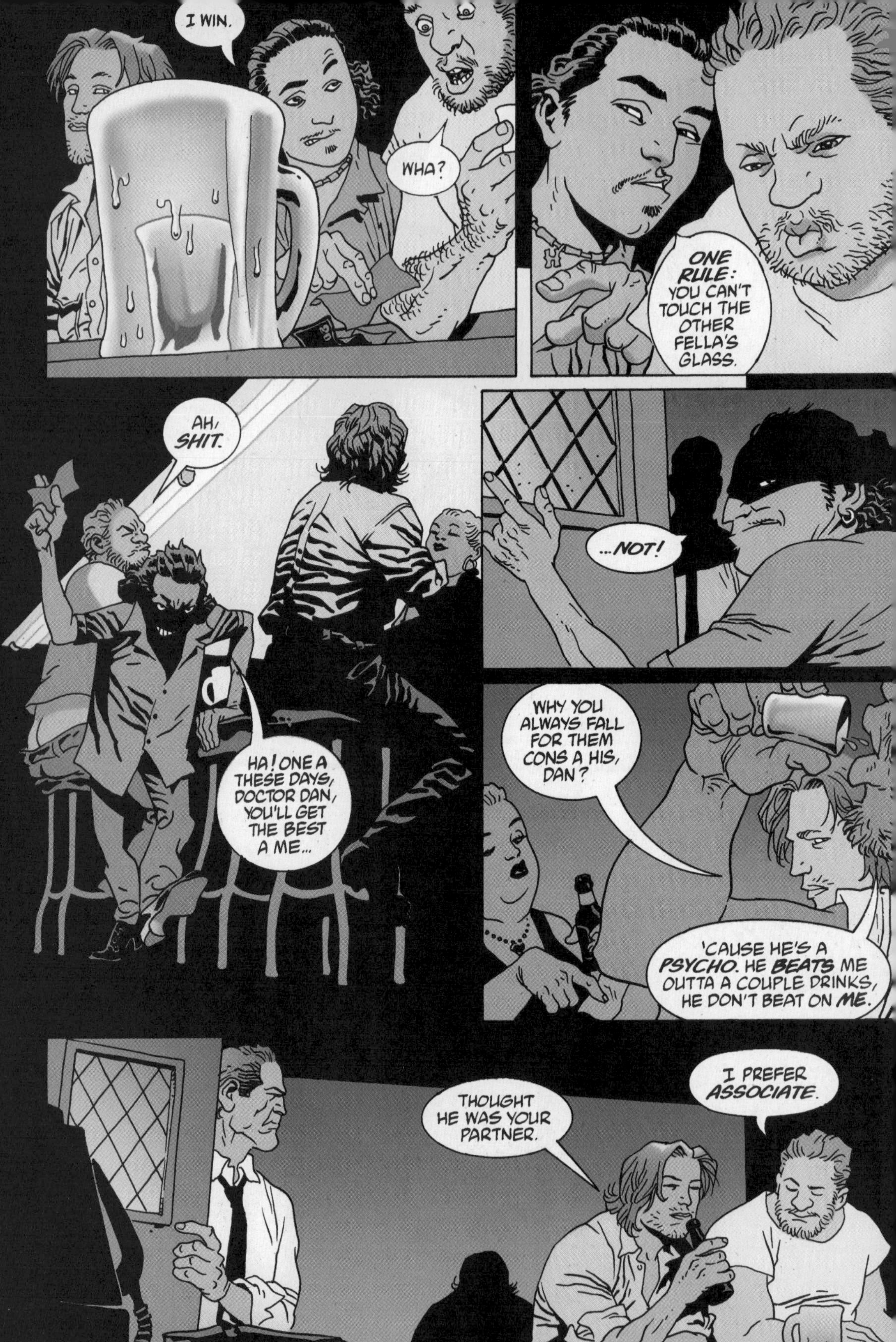
I WIN.
WHA?
ONE RULE: YOU CAN'T TOUCH THE OTHER FELLA'S GLASS.
AH, SHIT.
HA! ONE A THESE DAYS, DOCTOR DAN, YOU'LL GET THE BEST A ME...
...NOT!
WHY YOU ALWAYS FALL FOR THEM CONS A HIS, DAN?
'CAUSE HE'S A PSYCHO. HE BEATS ME OUTTA A COUPLE DRINKS, HE DON'T BEAT ON ME.
THOUGHT HE WAS YOUR PARTNER.
I PREFER ASSOCIATE.

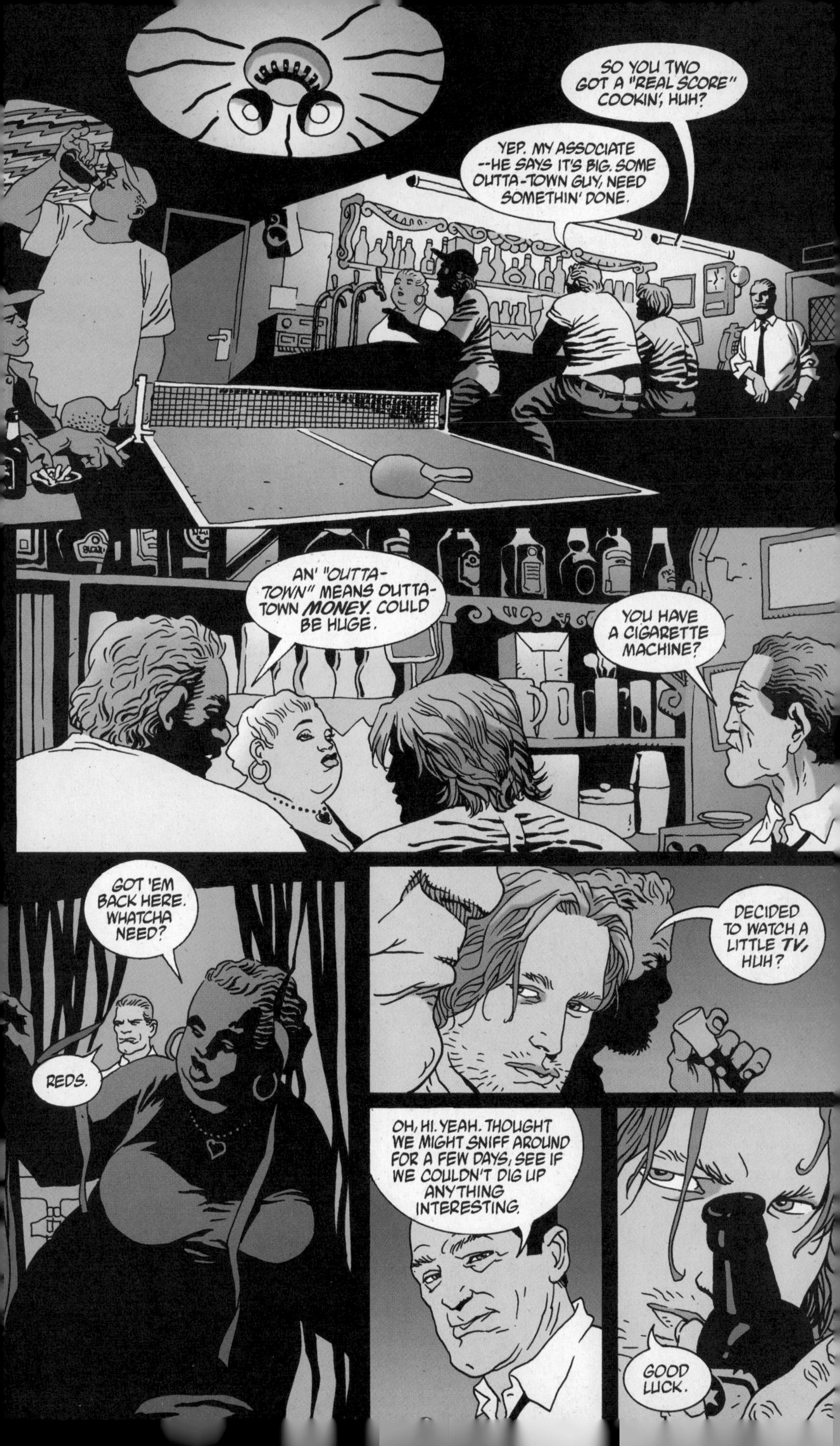
SO YOU TWO GOT A "REAL SCORE" COOKIN', HUH?
YEP. MY ASSOCIATE --HE SAYS IT'S BIG. SOME OUTTA-TOWN GUY, NEED SOMETHIN' DONE.
AN' "OUTTA-TOWN" MEANS OUTTA-TOWN MONEY. COULD BE HUGE.
YOU HAVE A CIGARETTE MACHINE?
GOT 'EM BACK HERE. WHATCHA NEED?
REDS.
DECIDED TO WATCH A LITTLE TV, HUH?
OH, HI. YEAH. THOUGHT WE MIGHT SNIFF AROUND FOR A FEW DAYS, SEE IF WE COULDN'T DIG UP ANYTHING INTERESTING.
GOOD LUCK.

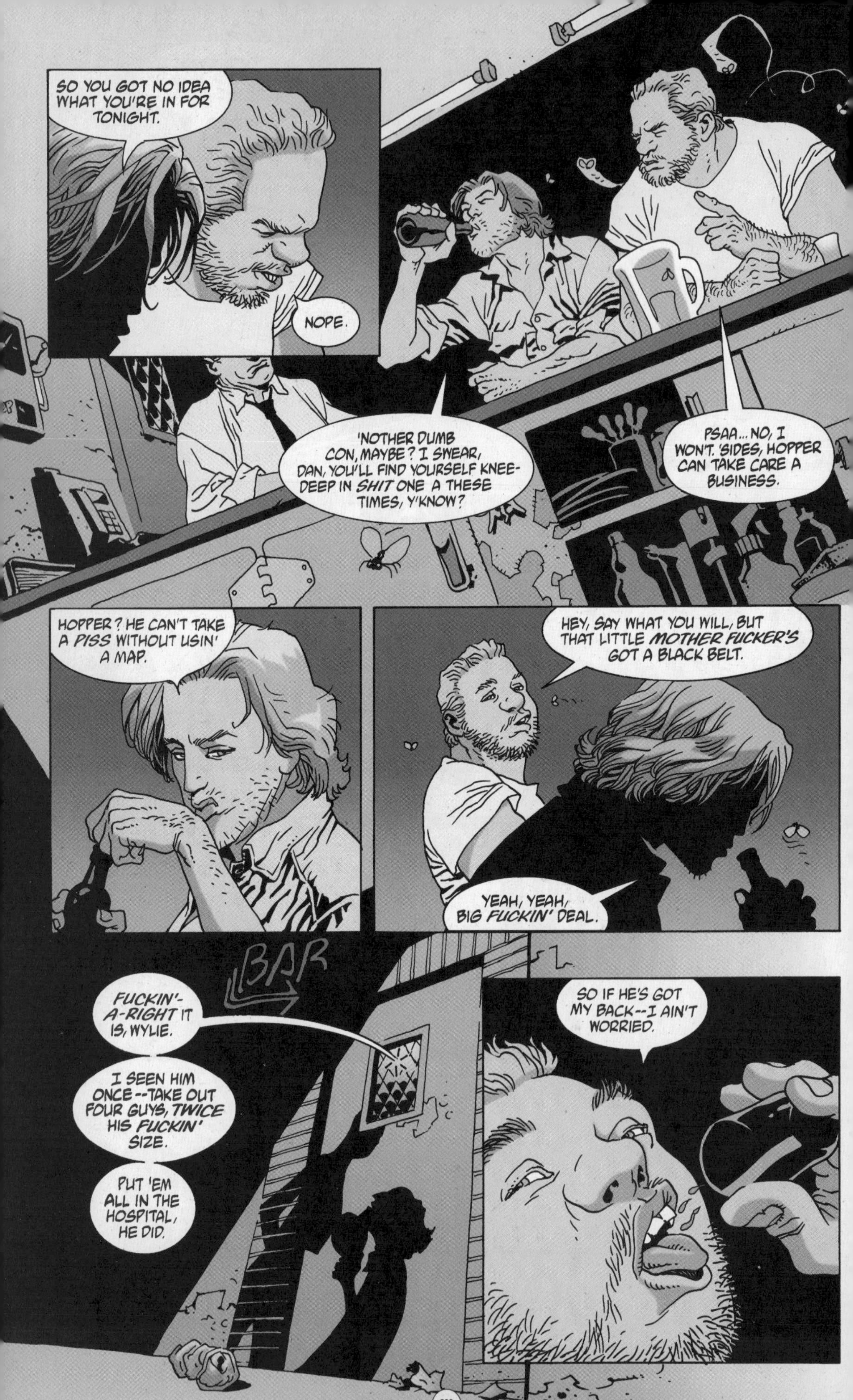
SO YOU GOT NO IDEA WHAT YOU'RE IN FOR TONIGHT.
NOPE.
'NOTHER DUMB CON, MAYBE? I SWEAR, DAN, YOU'LL FIND YOURSELF KNEE-DEEP IN SHIT ONE A THESE TIMES, Y'KNOW?
PSAA... NO, I WON'T. 'SIDES, HOPPER CAN TAKE CARE A BUSINESS.
HOPPER? HE CAN'T TAKE A PISS WITHOUT USIN' A MAP.
HEY, SAY WHAT YOU WILL, BUT THAT LITTLE MOTHER FUCKER'S GOT A BLACK BELT.
YEAH, YEAH, BIG FUCKIN' DEAL.
BAR
FUCKIN'-A-RIGHT IT IS, WYLIE.
I SEEN HIM ONCE--TAKE OUT FOUR GUYS, TWICE HIS FUCKIN' SIZE.
PUT 'EM ALL IN THE HOSPITAL, HE DID.
SO IF HE'S GOT MY BACK--I AIN'T WORRIED.

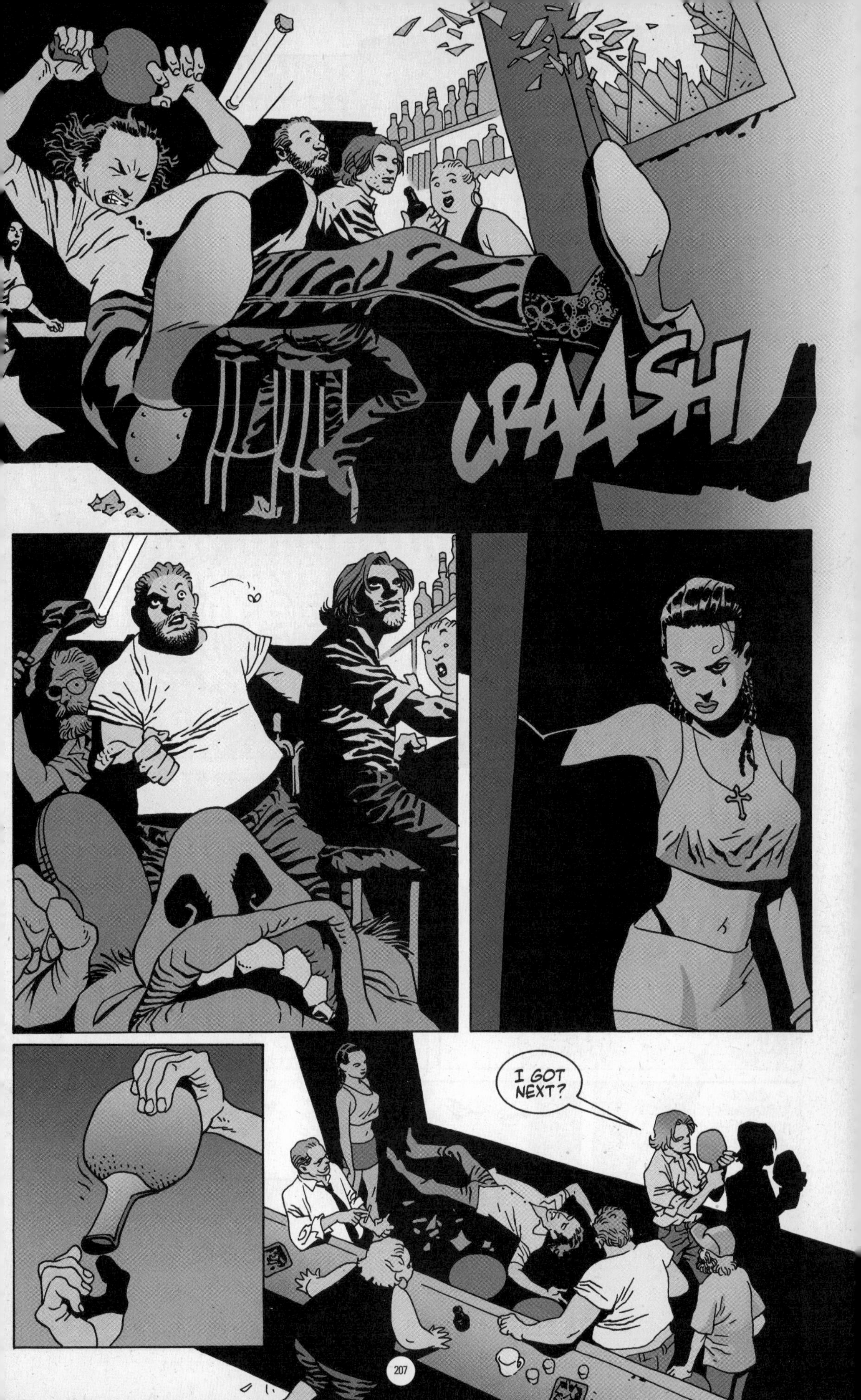
CRAASH
I GOT NEXT?

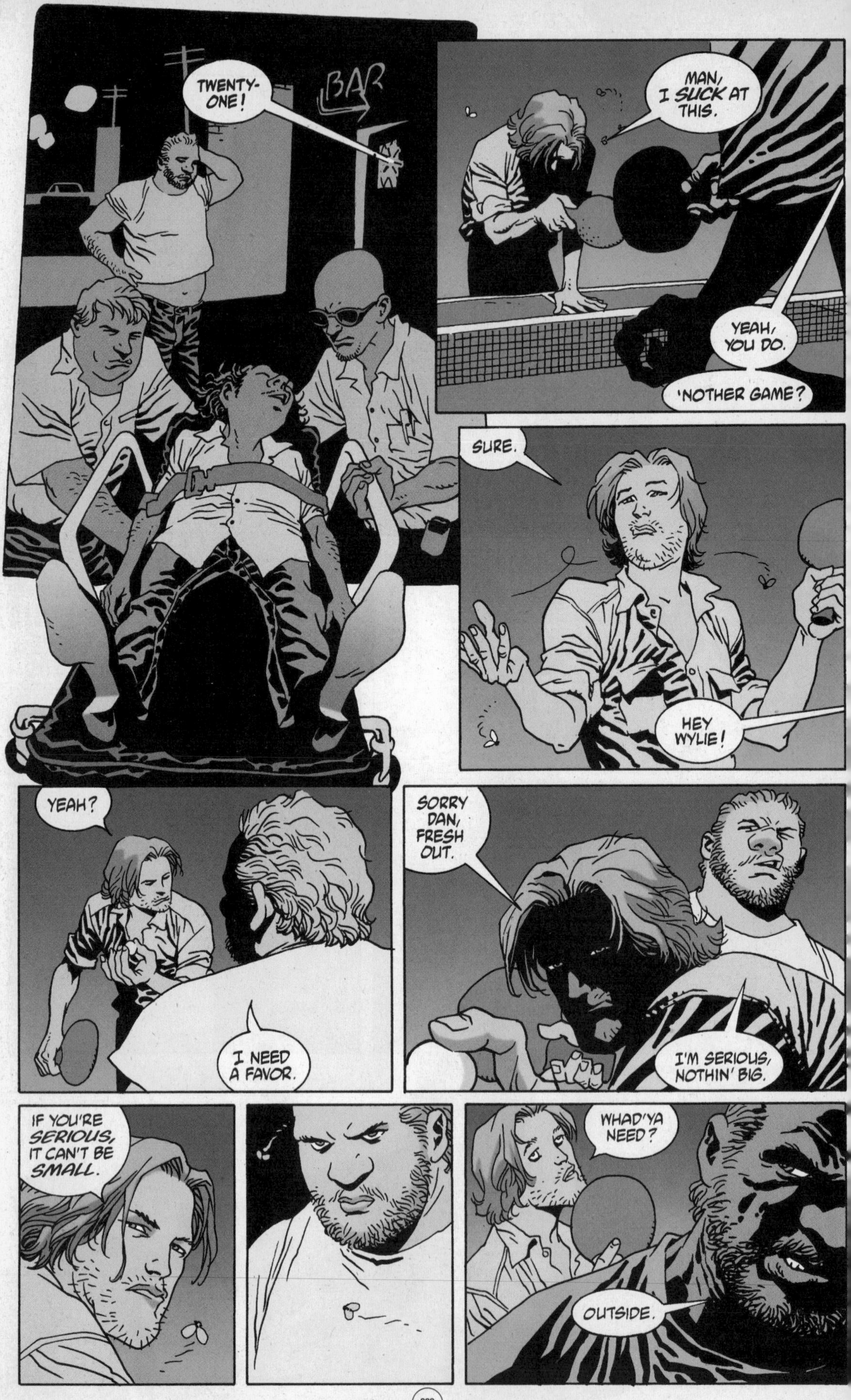
BAR
TWENTY-ONE!
MAN, I SUCK AT THIS.
YEAH, YOU DO.
'NOTHER GAME?
SURE.
HEY WYLIE!
YEAH?
I NEED A FAVOR.
SORRY DAN, FRESH OUT.
I'M SERIOUS, NOTHIN' BIG.
IF YOU'RE SERIOUS, IT CAN'T BE SMALL.
WHAD'YA NEED?
OUTSIDE.

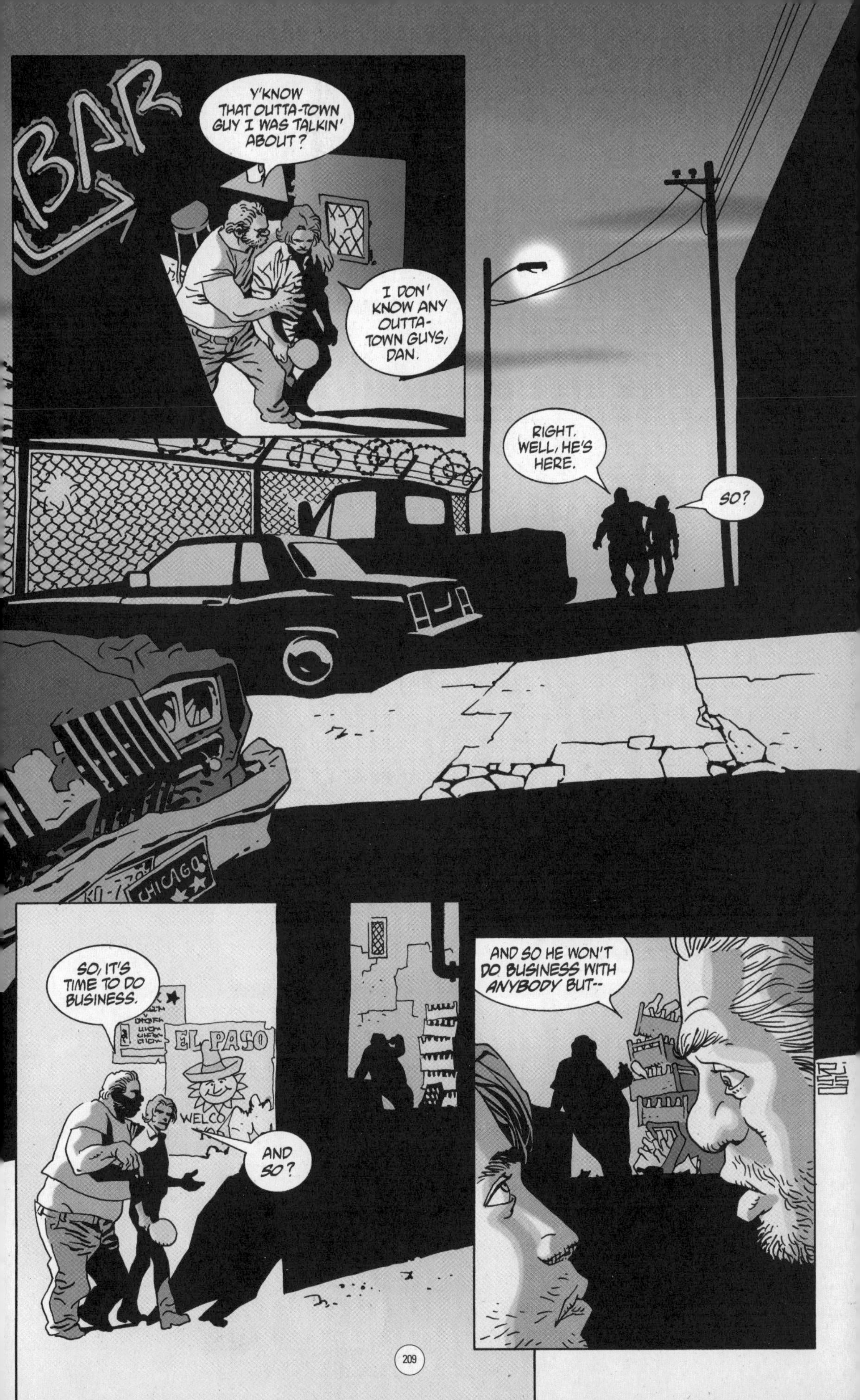
BAR
Y'KNOW THAT OUTTA-TOWN GUY I WAS TALKIN' ABOUT?
I DON' KNOW ANY OUTTA-TOWN GUYS, DAN.
RIGHT. WELL, HE'S HERE.
SO?
CHICAGO
SO, IT'S TIME TO DO BUSINESS.
EL PASO
WELCO
AND SO?
AND SO HE WON'T DO BUSINESS WITH *ANYBODY* BUT--

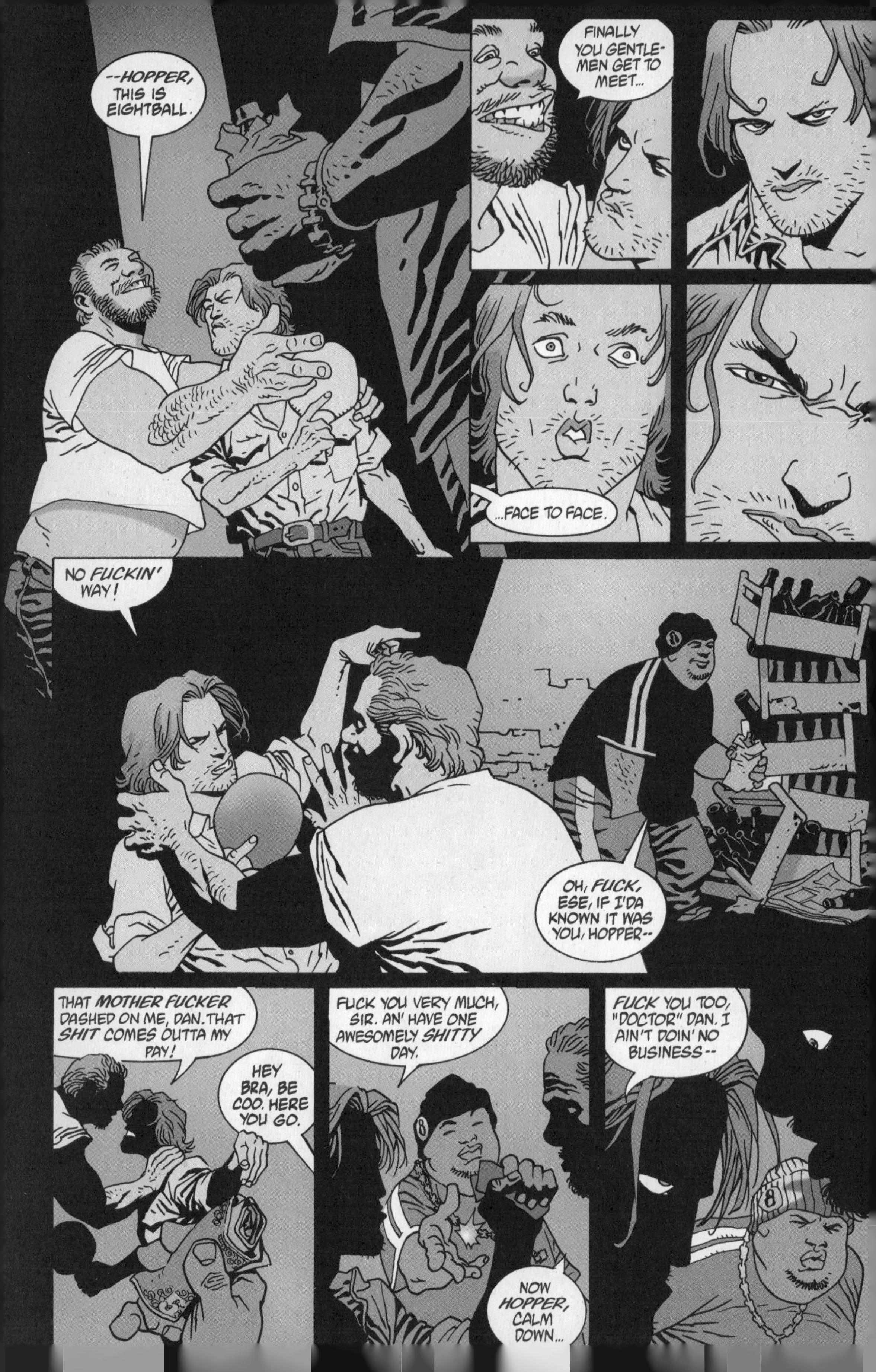
--HOPPER, THIS IS EIGHTBALL.
FINALLY YOU GENTLE-MEN GET TO MEET...
...FACE TO FACE.
NO FUCKIN' WAY!
OH, FUCK, ESE, IF I'DA KNOWN IT WAS YOU, HOPPER--
THAT MOTHER FUCKER DASHED ON ME, DAN. THAT SHIT COMES OUTTA MY PAY!
HEY BRA, BE COO. HERE YOU GO.
FUCK YOU VERY MUCH, SIR. AN' HAVE ONE AWESOMELY SHITTY DAY.
NOW HOPPER, CALM DOWN...
FUCK YOU TOO, "DOCTOR" DAN. I AIN'T DOIN' NO BUSINESS--

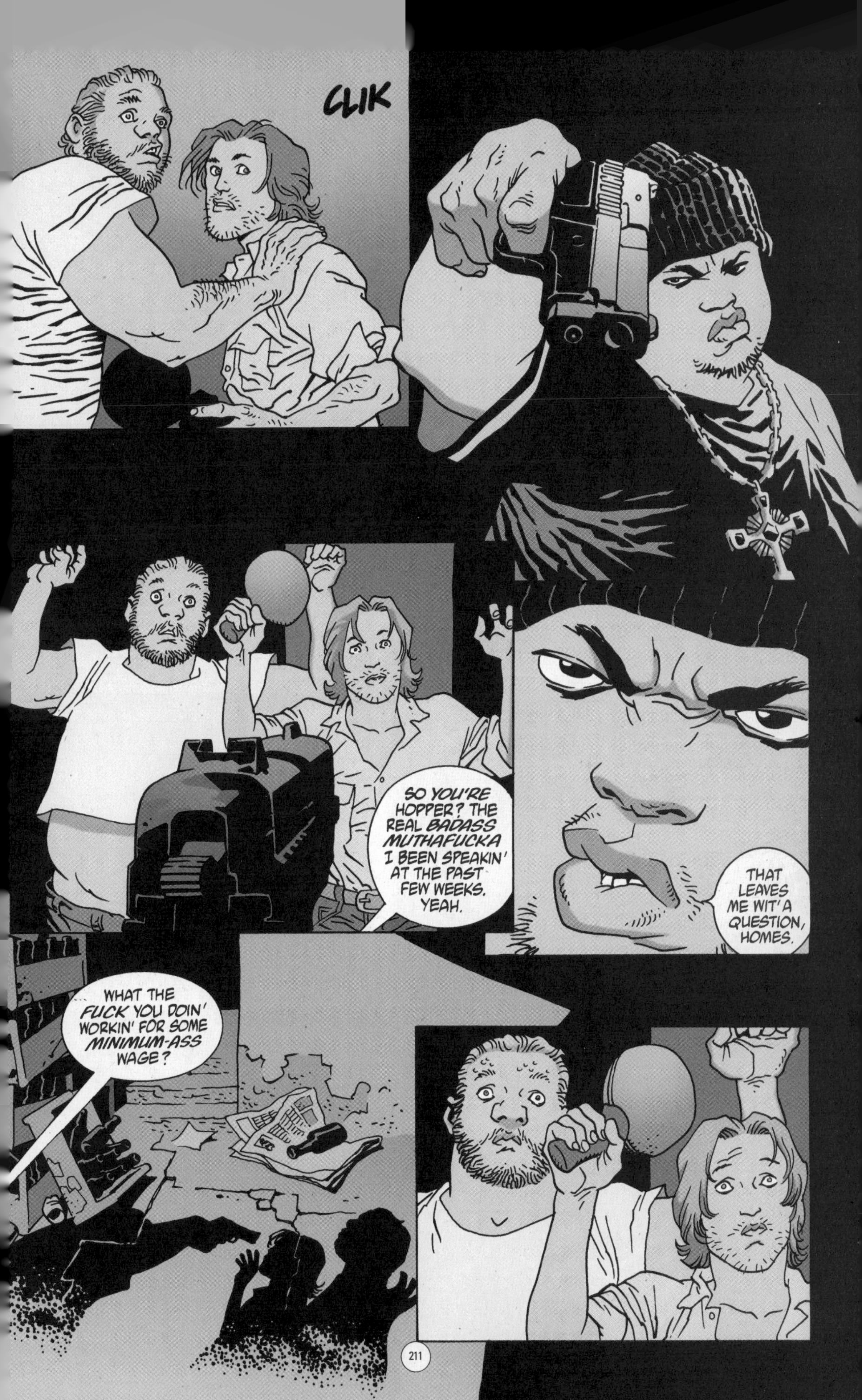
CLIK
SO YOU'RE HOPPER? THE REAL BADASS MUTHAFUCKA I BEEN SPEAKIN' AT THE PAST FEW WEEKS. YEAH.
THAT LEAVES ME WIT' A QUESTION, HOMES.
...WHAT THE FUCK YOU DOIN' WORKIN' FOR SOME MINIMUM-ASS WAGE?

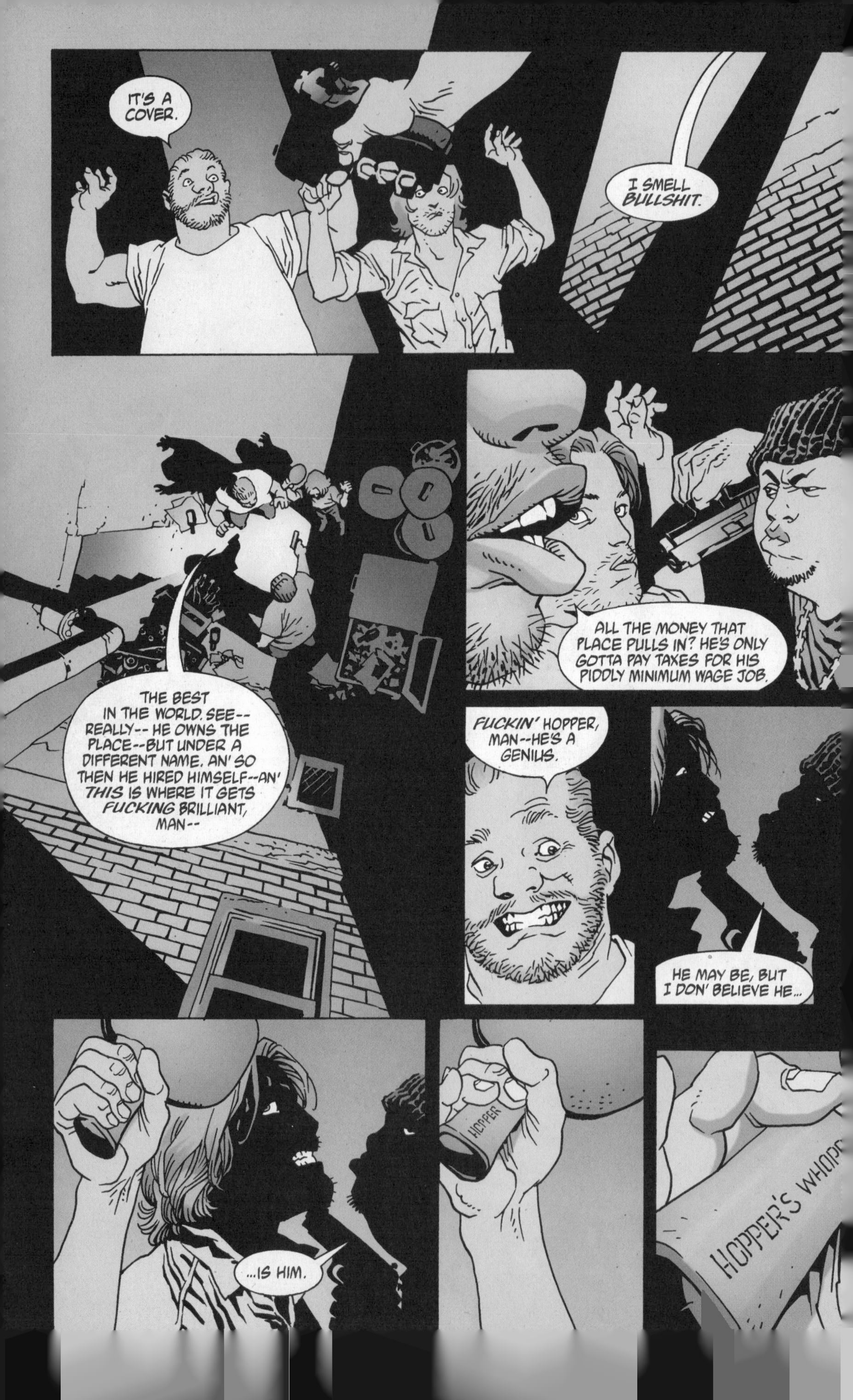
IT'S A COVER.
I SMELL BULLSHIT.
THE BEST IN THE WORLD. SEE-- REALLY-- HE OWNS THE PLACE--BUT UNDER A DIFFERENT NAME. AN' SO THEN HE HIRED HIMSELF--AN' THIS IS WHERE IT GETS FUCKING BRILLIANT, MAN--
ALL THE MONEY THAT PLACE PULLS IN? HE'S ONLY GOTTA PAY TAXES FOR HIS PIDDLY MINIMUM WAGE JOB.
FUCKIN' HOPPER, MAN--HE'S A GENIUS.
HE MAY BE, BUT I DON' BELIEVE HE...
...IS HIM.
HOPPER
HOPPER'S WHOP

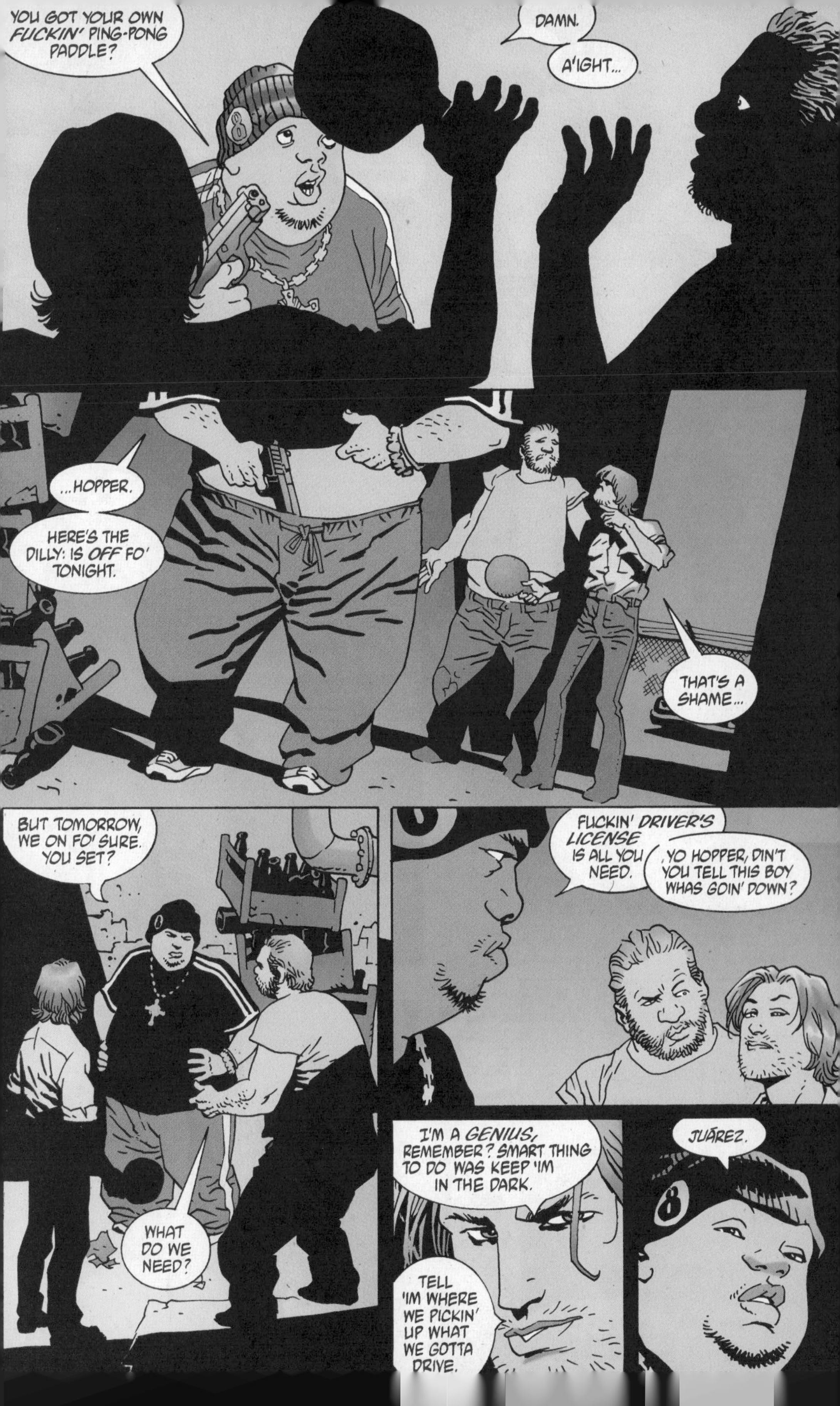
YOU GOT YOUR OWN FUCKIN' PING-PONG PADDLE?
DAMN.
A'IGHT...
...HOPPER.
HERE'S THE DILLY: IS OFF FO' TONIGHT.
THAT'S A SHAME...
BUT TOMORROW, WE ON FO' SURE. YOU SET?
WHAT DO WE NEED?
FUCKIN' DRIVER'S LICENSE IS ALL YOU NEED.
YO HOPPER, DIN'T YOU TELL THIS BOY WHAS GOIN' DOWN?
I'M A GENIUS, REMEMBER? SMART THING TO DO WAS KEEP 'IM IN THE DARK.
TELL 'IM WHERE WE PICKIN' UP WHAT WE GOTTA DRIVE.
JUÁREZ.

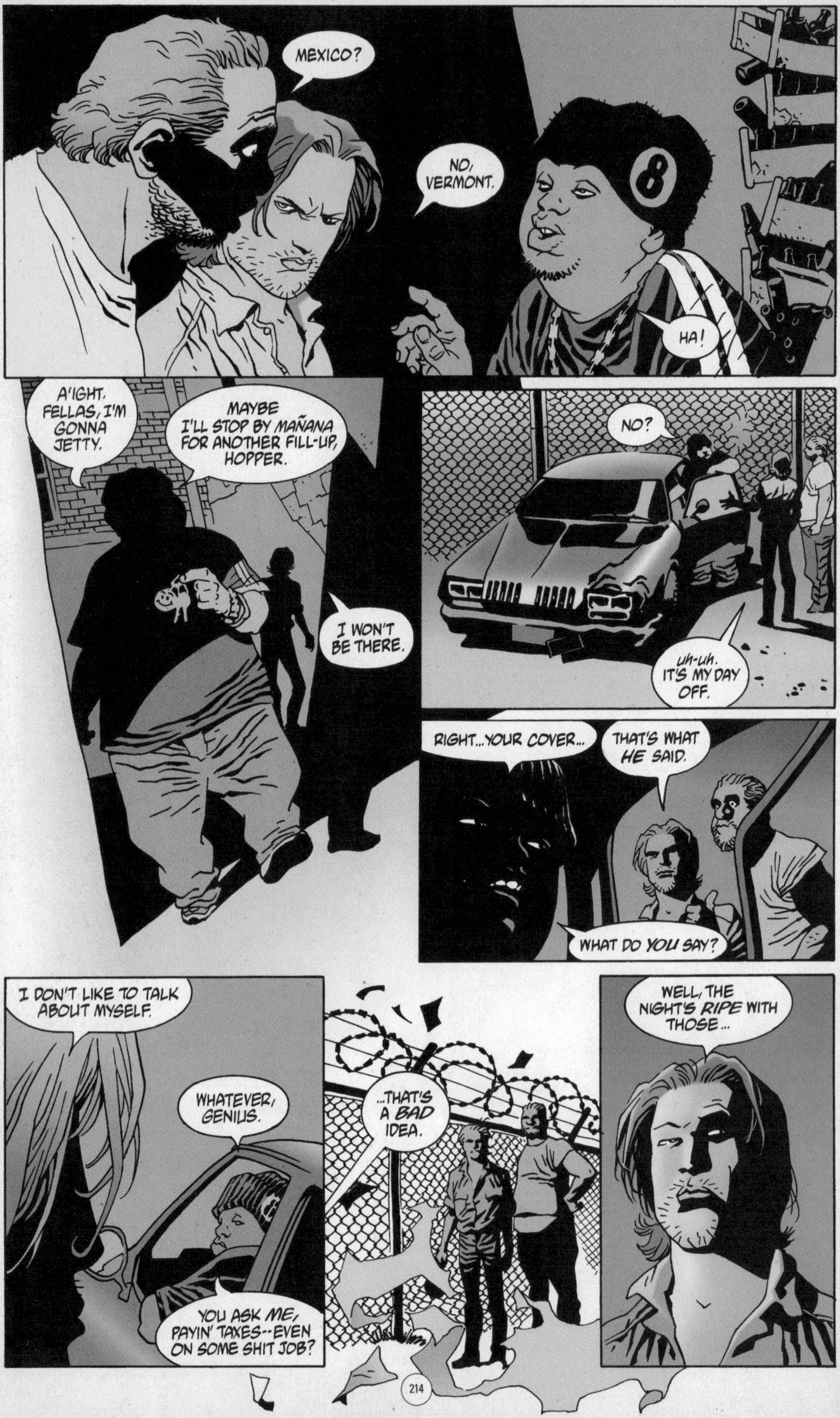
MEXICO?
NO, VERMONT.
HA!
A'IGHT. FELLAS, I'M GONNA JETTY.
MAYBE I'LL STOP BY MAÑANA FOR ANOTHER FILL-UP, HOPPER.
I WON'T BE THERE.
NO?
uh-uh. IT'S MY DAY OFF.
RIGHT... YOUR COVER...
THAT'S WHAT HE SAID.
WHAT DO YOU SAY?
I DON'T LIKE TO TALK ABOUT MYSELF.
WHATEVER, GENIUS.
YOU ASK ME, PAYIN' TAXES--EVEN ON SOME SHIT JOB?
...THAT'S A BAD IDEA.
WELL, THE NIGHT'S RIPE WITH THOSE...

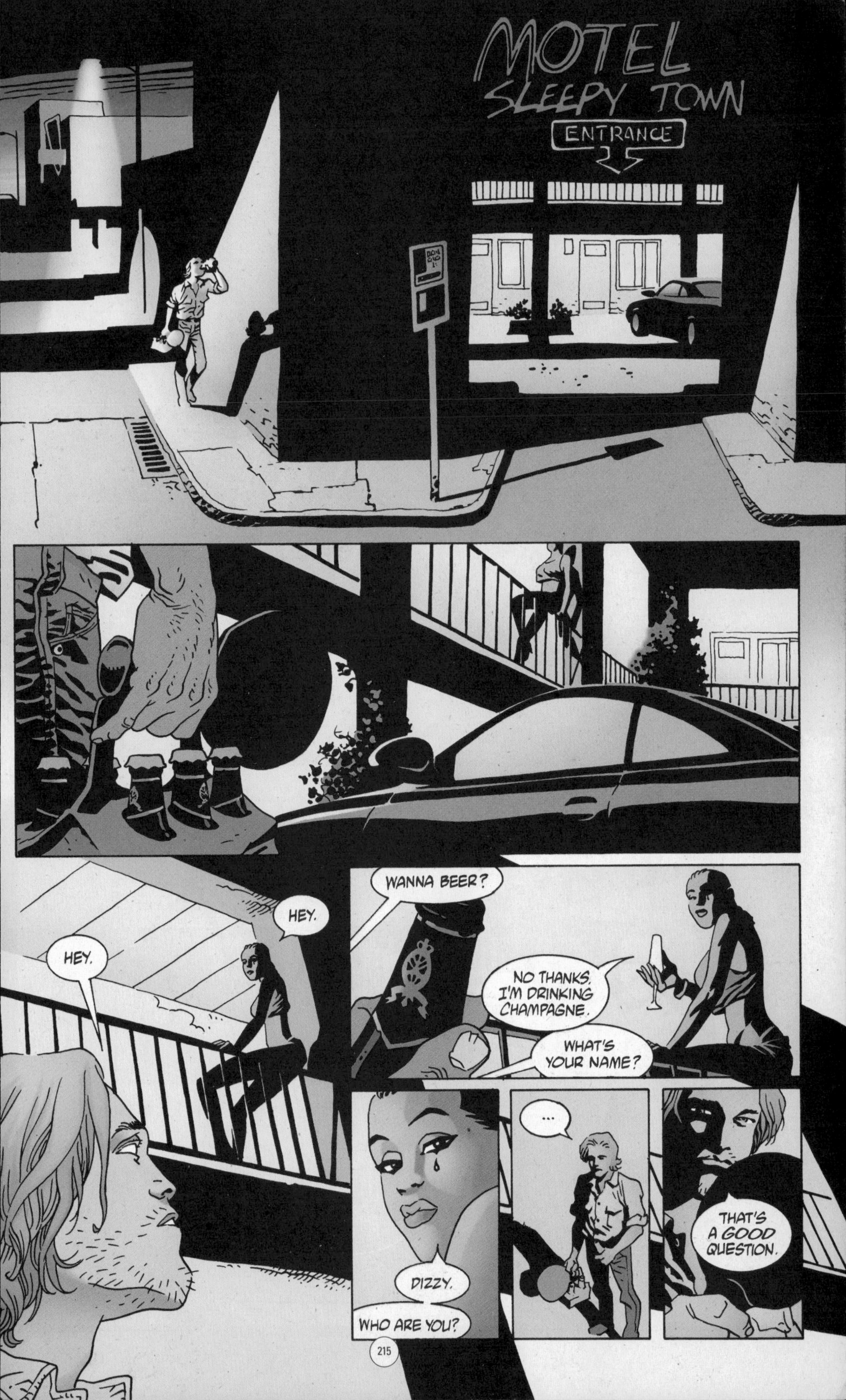
MOTEL
SLEEPY TOWN
ENTRANCE
HEY.
HEY.
WANNA BEER?
NO THANKS. I'M DRINKING CHAMPAGNE.
WHAT'S YOUR NAME?
DIZZY.
WHO ARE YOU?
...
THAT'S A GOOD QUESTION.

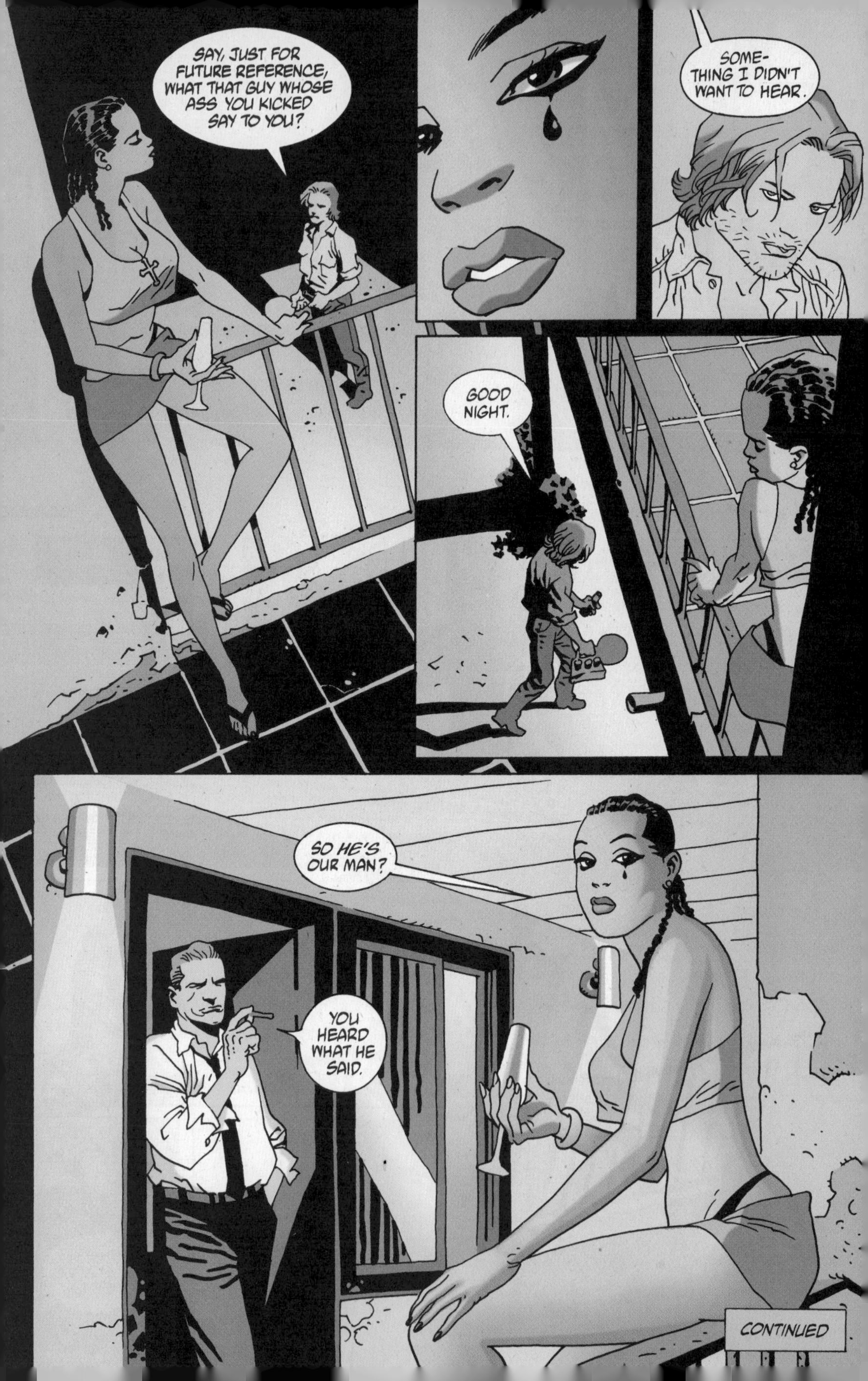
SAY, JUST FOR FUTURE REFERENCE, WHAT THAT GUY WHOSE ASS YOU KICKED SAY TO YOU?
SOME-THING I DIDN'T WANT TO HEAR.
GOOD NIGHT.
SO HE'S OUR MAN?
YOU HEARD WHAT HE SAID.
CONTINUED

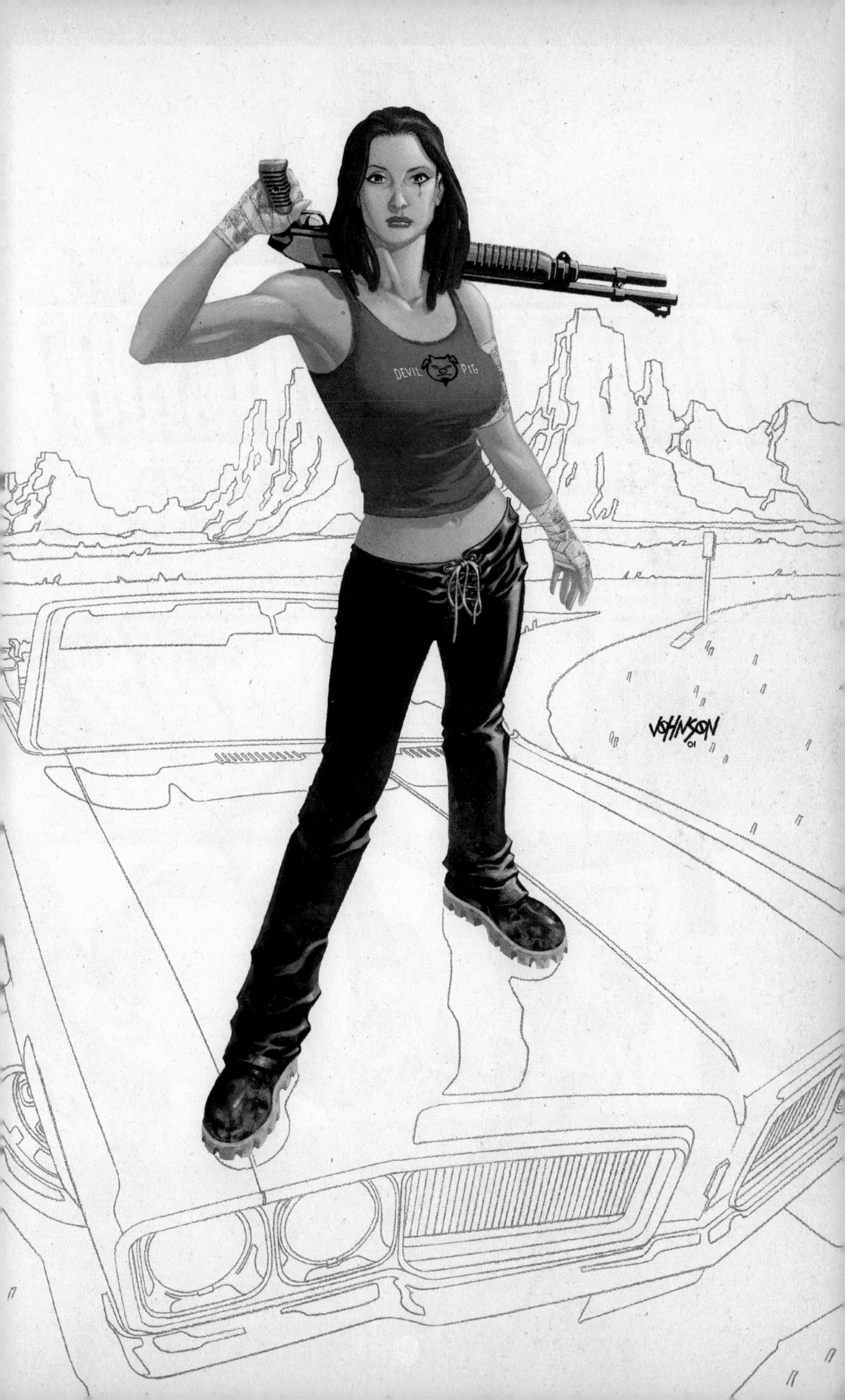
DEVIL PIG
JOHNSON
01

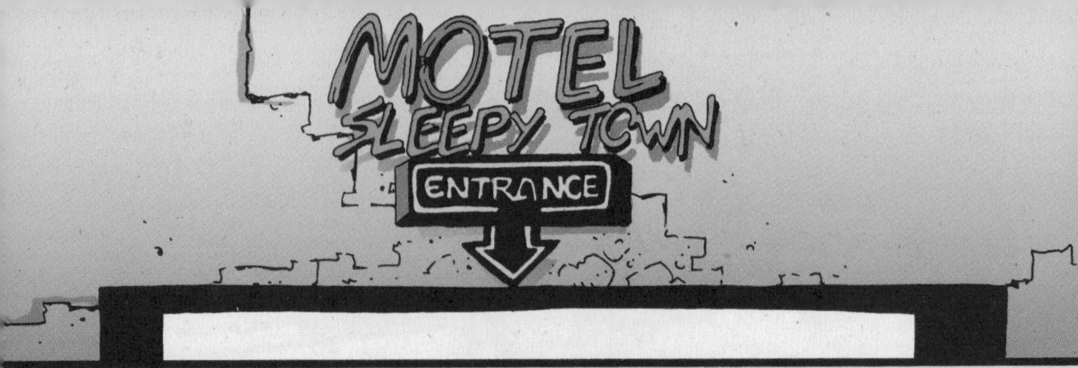
MOTEL
SLEEPY TOWN
ENTRANCE

¡CONTRABANDOLERO!

Part TWO of THREE

Brian Azzarello, writer **Eduardo Risso**, artist

Digital Chameleon, Colors & Seps
Clem Robins, Letterer
Dave Johnson, Cover Artist
Will Dennis, Editor

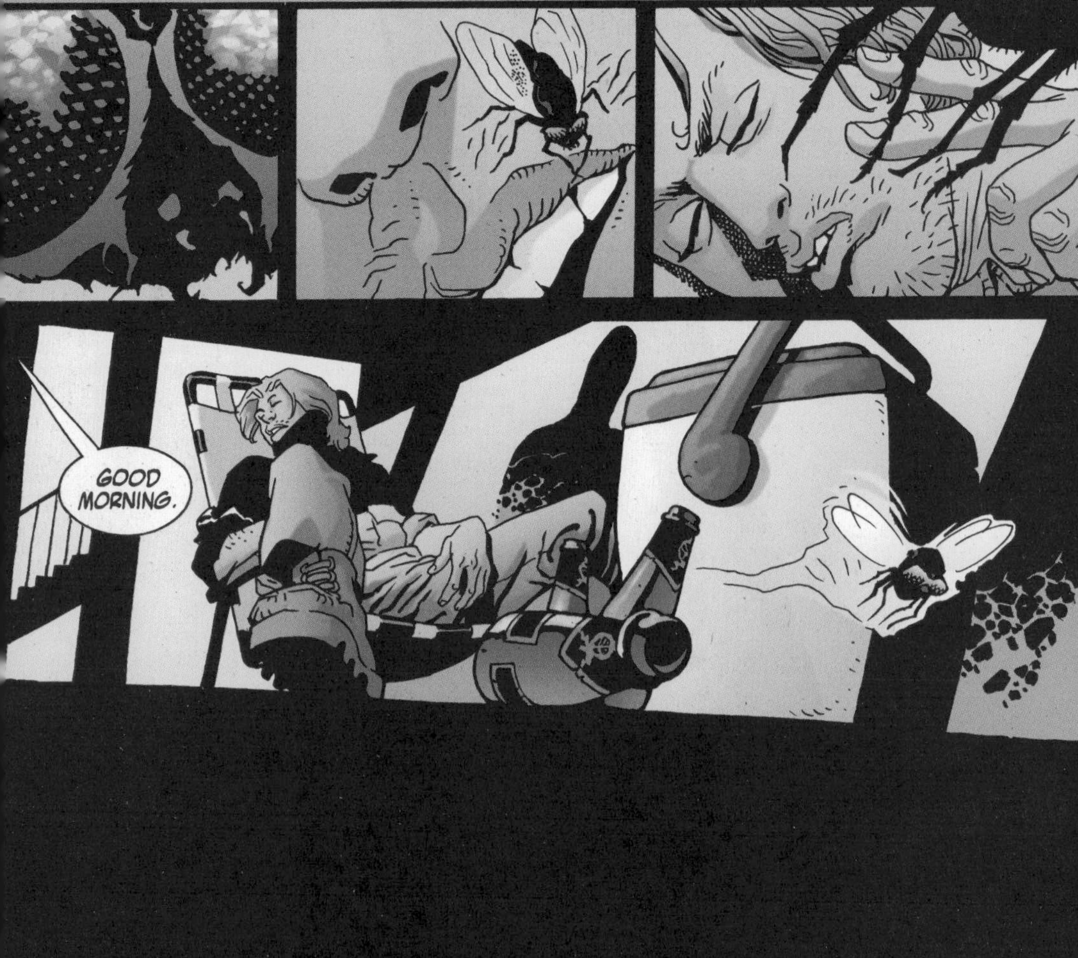
GOOD MORNING.

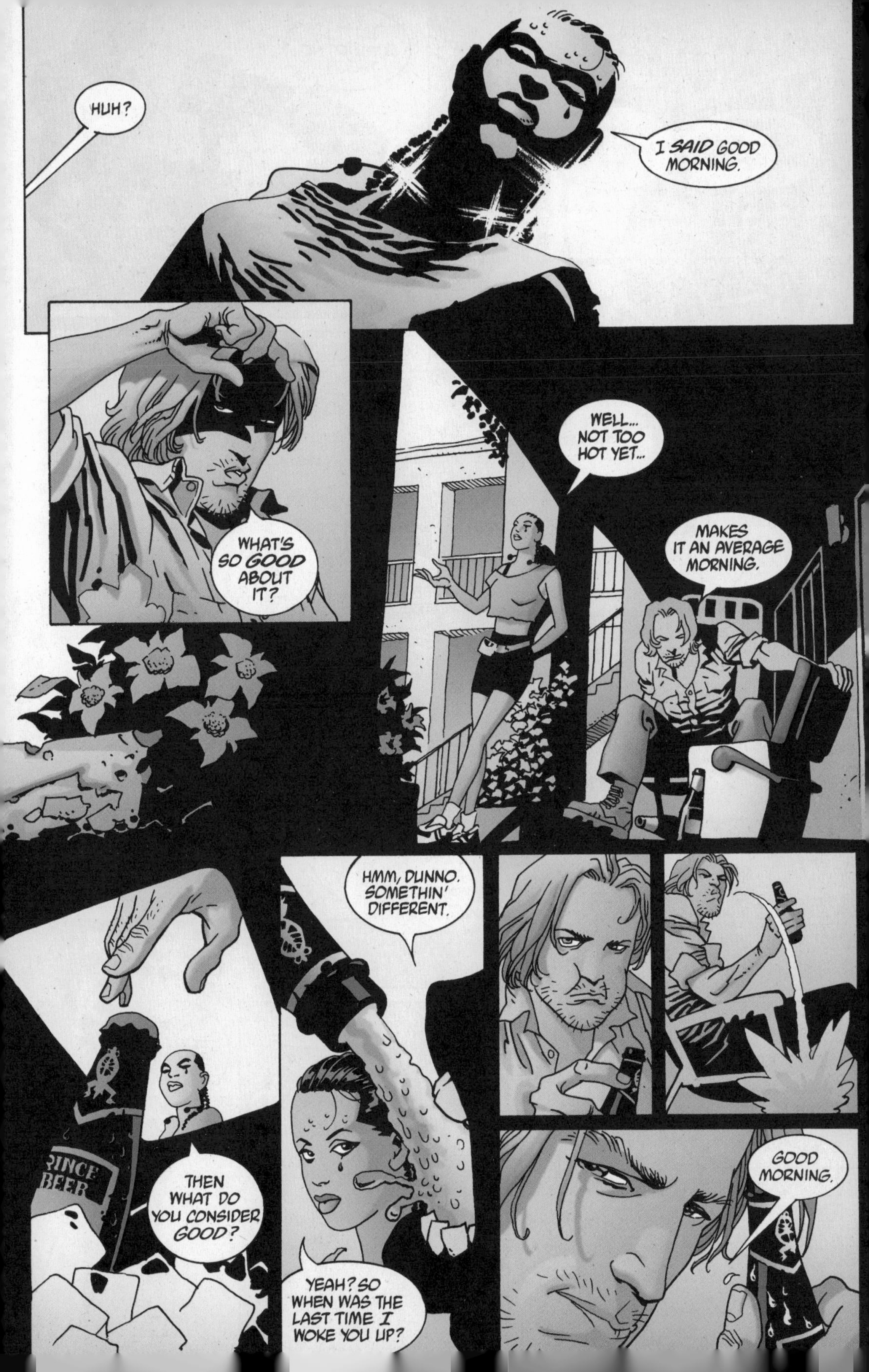
HUH?
I SAID GOOD MORNING.
WHAT'S SO GOOD ABOUT IT?
WELL... NOT TOO HOT YET...
MAKES IT AN AVERAGE MORNING.
THEN WHAT DO YOU CONSIDER GOOD?
PRINCE BEER
HMM, DUNNO. SOMETHIN' DIFFERENT.
YEAH? SO WHEN WAS THE LAST TIME I WOKE YOU UP?
GOOD MORNING.

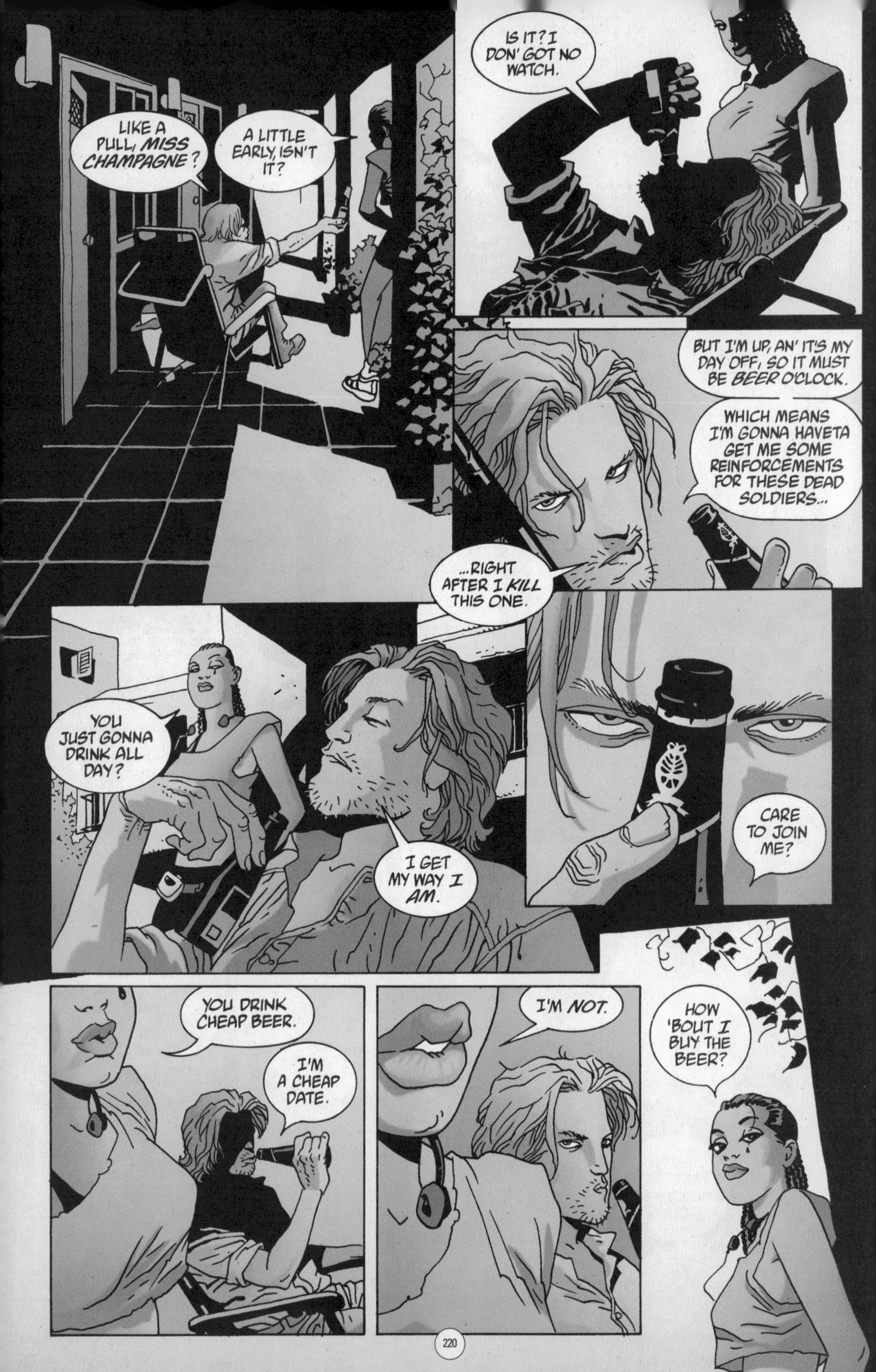
LIKE A PULL, MISS CHAMPAGNE?
A LITTLE EARLY, ISN'T IT?
IS IT? I DON' GOT NO WATCH.
BUT I'M UP, AN' IT'S MY DAY OFF, SO IT MUST BE BEER O'CLOCK.
WHICH MEANS I'M GONNA HAVETA GET ME SOME REINFORCEMENTS FOR THESE DEAD SOLDIERS...
...RIGHT AFTER I KILL THIS ONE.
YOU JUST GONNA DRINK ALL DAY?
I GET MY WAY I AM.
CARE TO JOIN ME?
YOU DRINK CHEAP BEER.
I'M A CHEAP DATE.
I'M NOT.
HOW 'BOUT I BUY THE BEER?

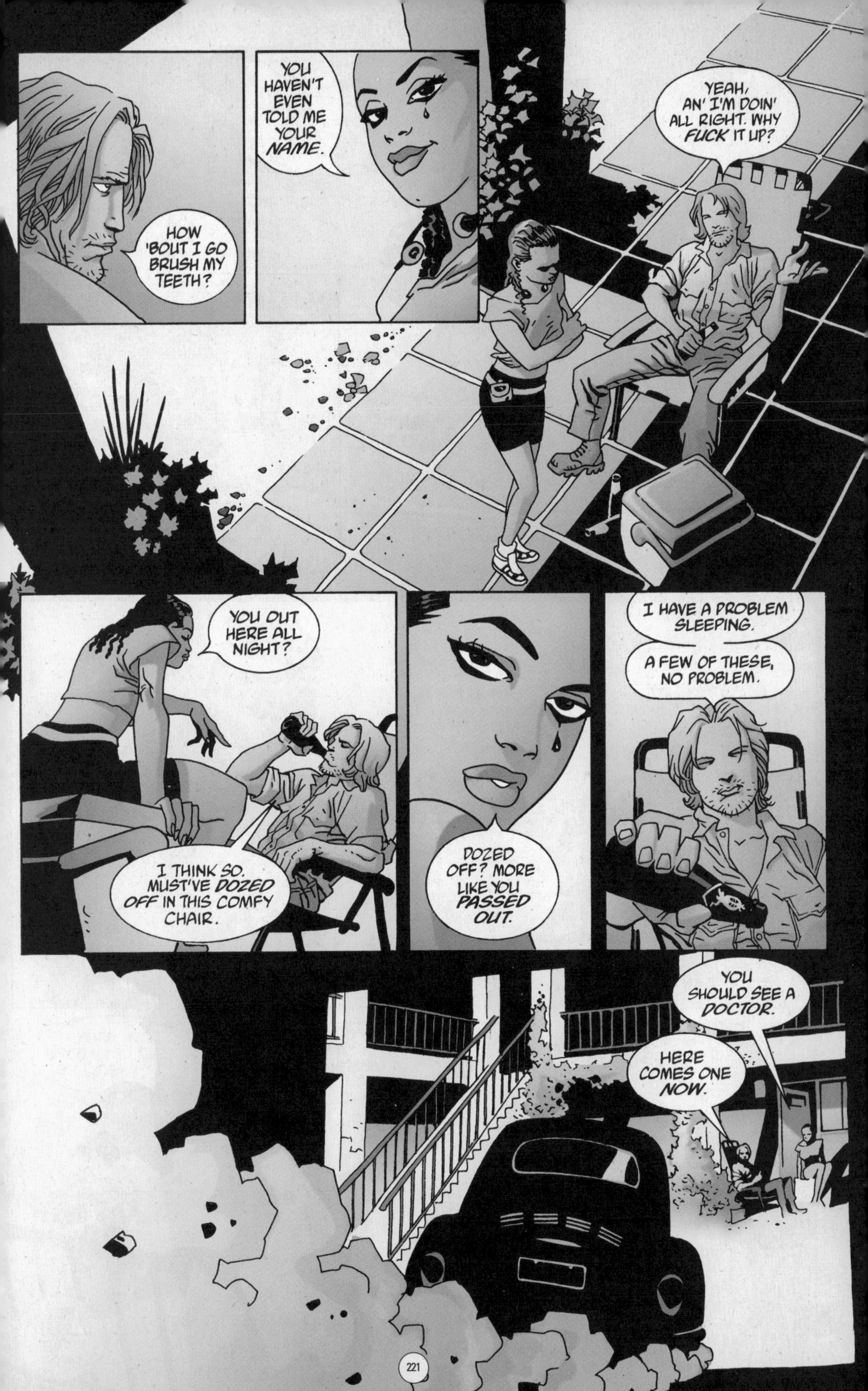
HOW 'BOUT I GO BRUSH MY TEETH?
YOU HAVEN'T EVEN TOLD ME YOUR NAME.
YEAH, AN' I'M DOIN' ALL RIGHT. WHY FUCK IT UP?
YOU OUT HERE ALL NIGHT?
I THINK SO. MUST'VE DOZED OFF IN THIS COMFY CHAIR.
DOZED OFF? MORE LIKE YOU PASSED OUT.
I HAVE A PROBLEM SLEEPING.
A FEW OF THESE, NO PROBLEM.
YOU SHOULD SEE A DOCTOR.
HERE COMES ONE NOW.

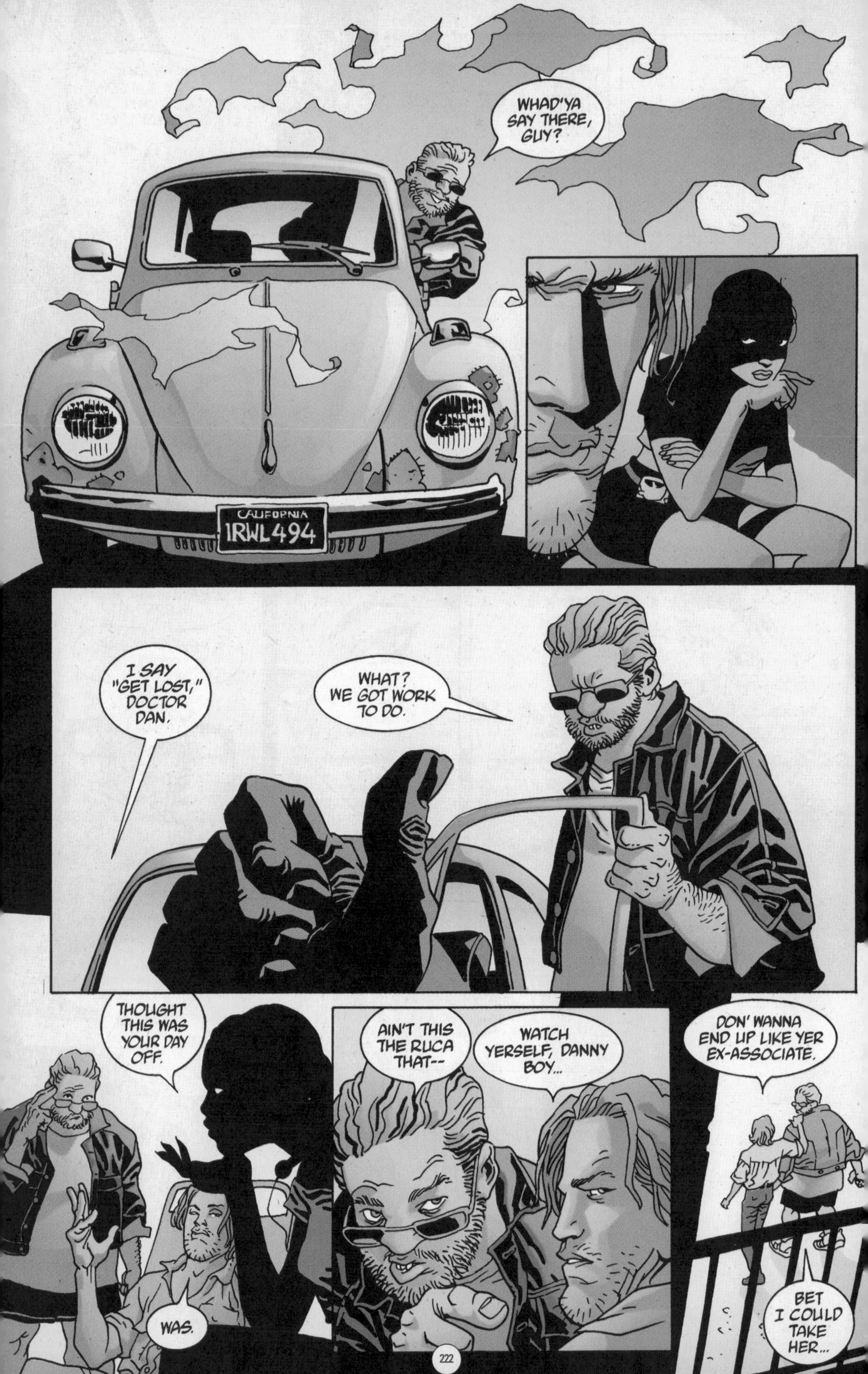
WHAD'YA SAY THERE, GUY?
CALIFORNIA
1RWL494
I SAY "GET LOST," DOCTOR DAN.
WHAT? WE GOT WORK TO DO.
THOUGHT THIS WAS YOUR DAY OFF.
WAS.
AIN'T THIS THE RUCA THAT--
WATCH YERSELF, DANNY BOY...
DON' WANNA END UP LIKE YER EX-ASSOCIATE.
BET I COULD TAKE HER...

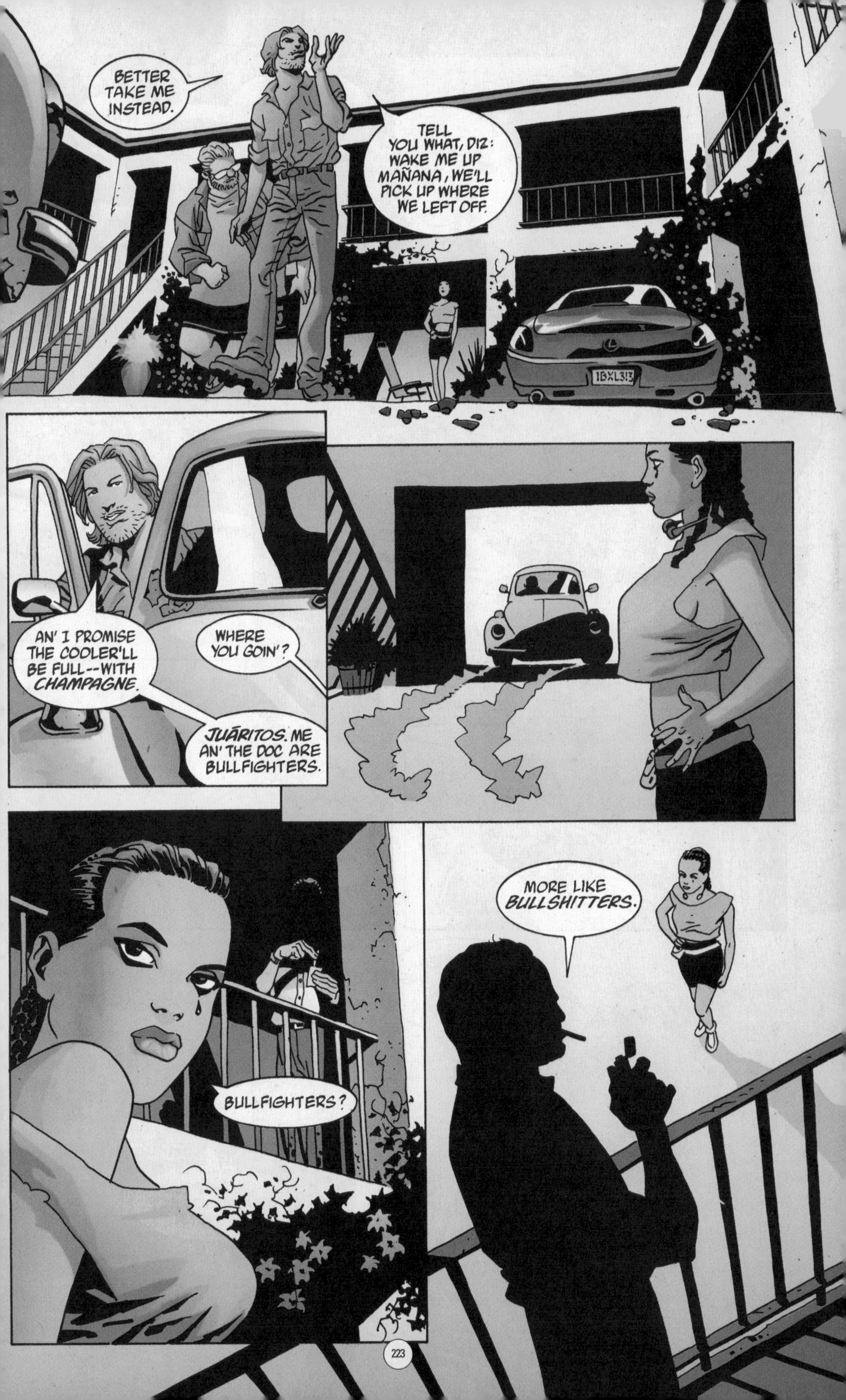
BETTER TAKE ME INSTEAD.
TELL YOU WHAT, DIZ: WAKE ME UP MAÑANA, WE'LL PICK UP WHERE WE LEFT OFF.
1BXL313
AN' I PROMISE THE COOLER'LL BE FULL--WITH *CHAMPAGNE*.
WHERE YOU GOIN'?
JUÁRITOS. ME AN' THE DOC ARE BULLFIGHTERS.
BULLFIGHTERS?
MORE LIKE *BULLSHITTERS*.

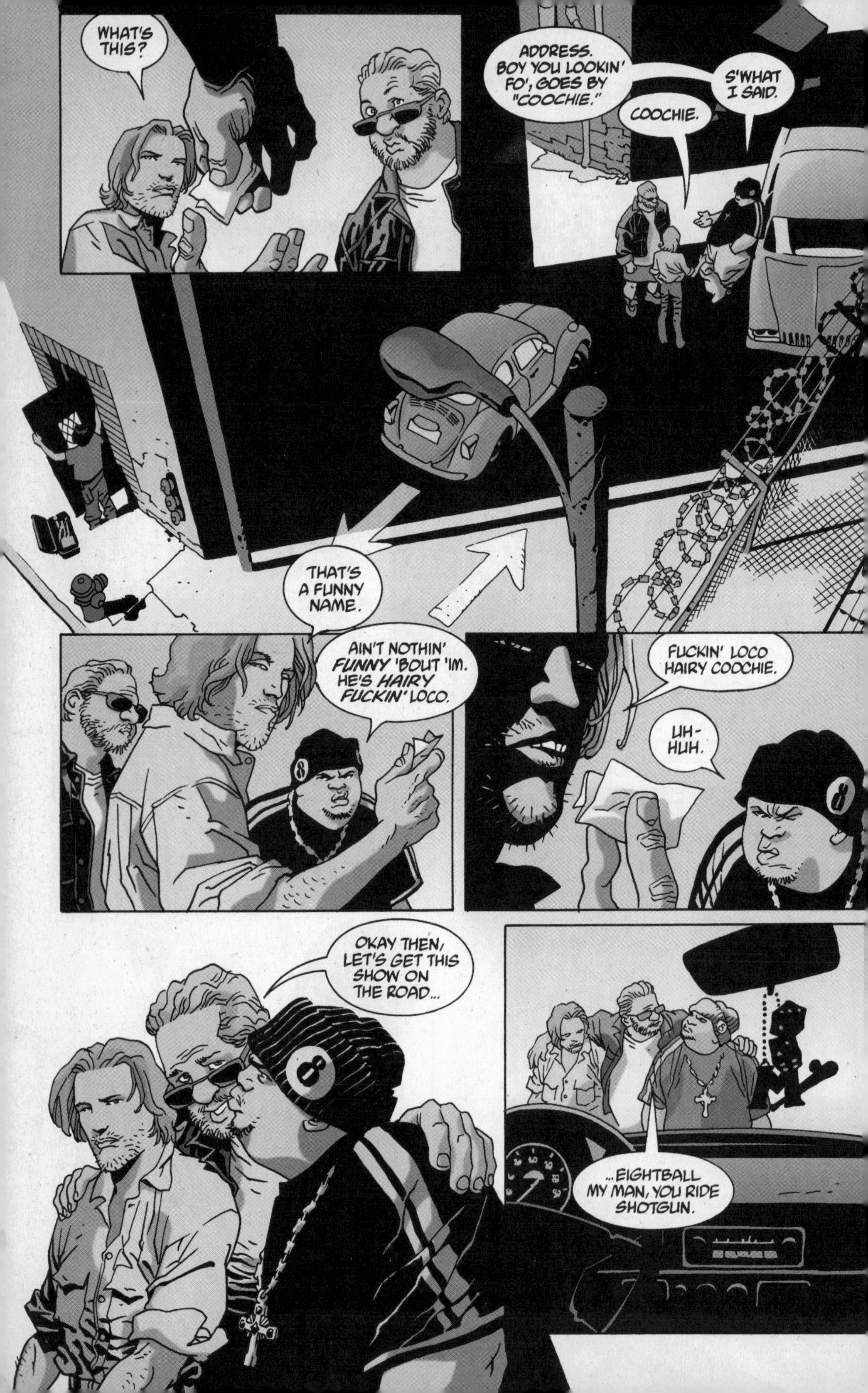

WHAT'S THIS?
ADDRESS. BOY YOU LOOKIN' FO', GOES BY "COOCHIE."
COOCHIE.
S'WHAT I SAID.
THAT'S A FUNNY NAME.
AIN'T NOTHIN' FUNNY 'BOUT 'IM. HE'S HAIRY FUCKIN' LOCO.
FUCKIN' LOCO HAIRY COOCHIE.
UH-HUH.
OKAY THEN, LET'S GET THIS SHOW ON THE ROAD...
...EIGHTBALL MY MAN, YOU RIDE SHOTGUN.

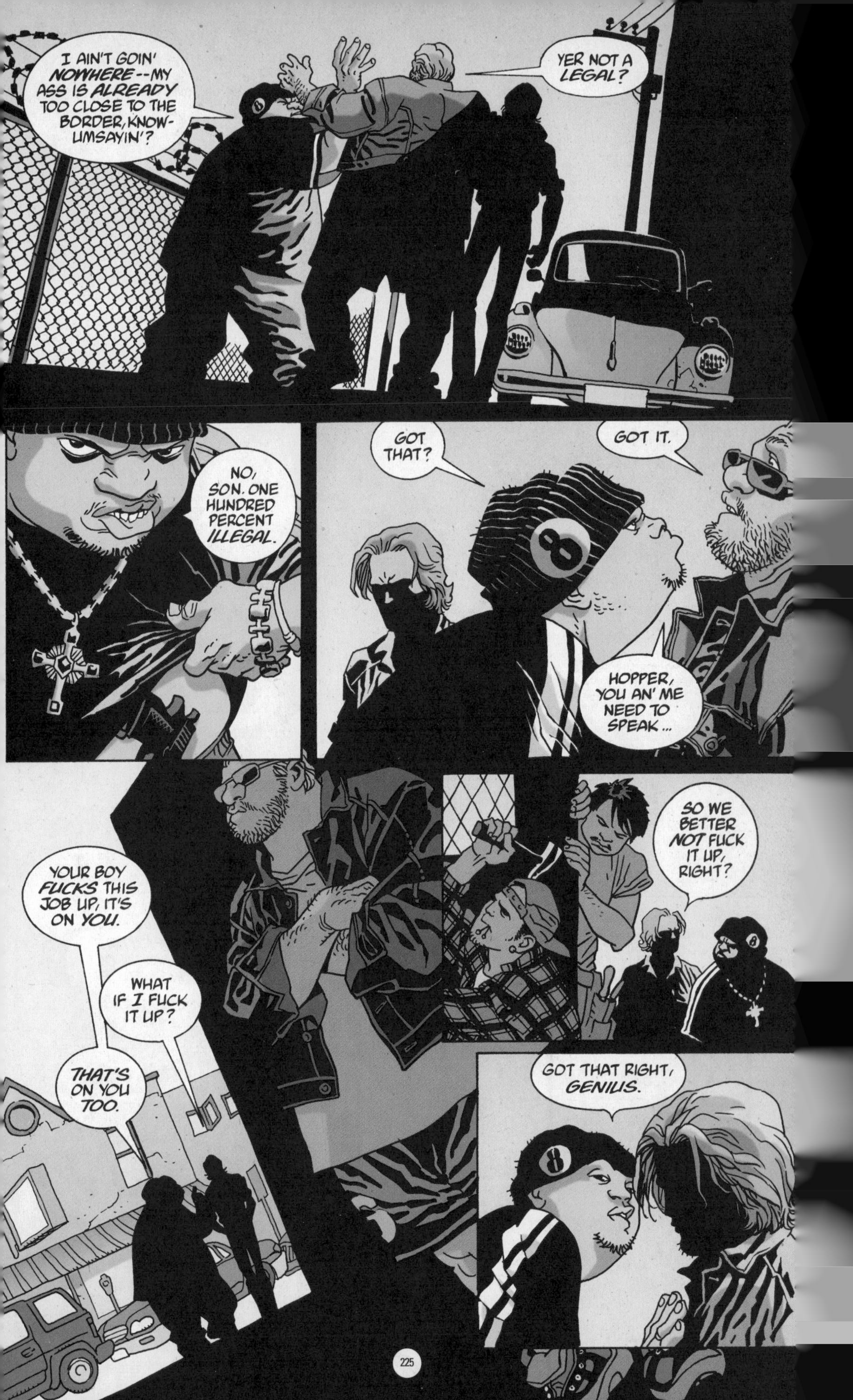
I AIN'T GOIN' NOWHERE--MY ASS IS ALREADY TOO CLOSE TO THE BORDER, KNOW-UMSAYIN'?
YER NOT A LEGAL?
NO, SON. ONE HUNDRED PERCENT ILLEGAL.
GOT THAT?
GOT IT.
HOPPER, YOU AN' ME NEED TO SPEAK...
YOUR BOY FUCKS THIS JOB UP, IT'S ON YOU.
WHAT IF I FUCK IT UP?
THAT'S ON YOU TOO.
SO WE BETTER NOT FUCK IT UP, RIGHT?
GOT THAT RIGHT, GENIUS.

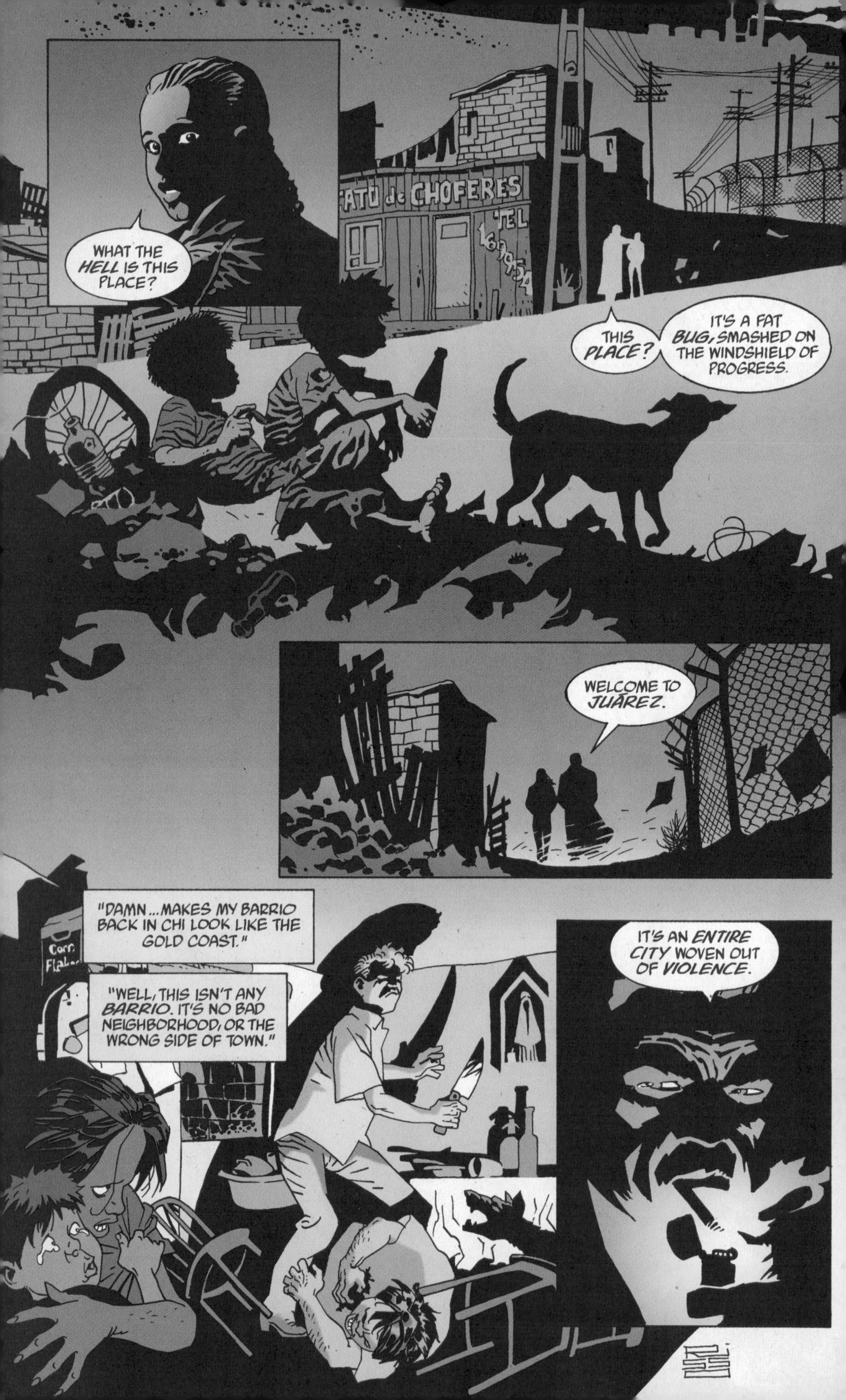
FATU de CHOFERES
TEL
WHAT THE HELL IS THIS PLACE?
THIS PLACE?
IT'S A FAT BUG, SMASHED ON THE WINDSHIELD OF PROGRESS.
WELCOME TO JUÁREZ.
"DAMN... MAKES MY BARRIO BACK IN CHI LOOK LIKE THE GOLD COAST."
"WELL, THIS ISN'T ANY BARRIO. IT'S NO BAD NEIGHBORHOOD, OR THE WRONG SIDE OF TOWN."
IT'S AN ENTIRE CITY WOVEN OUT OF VIOLENCE.

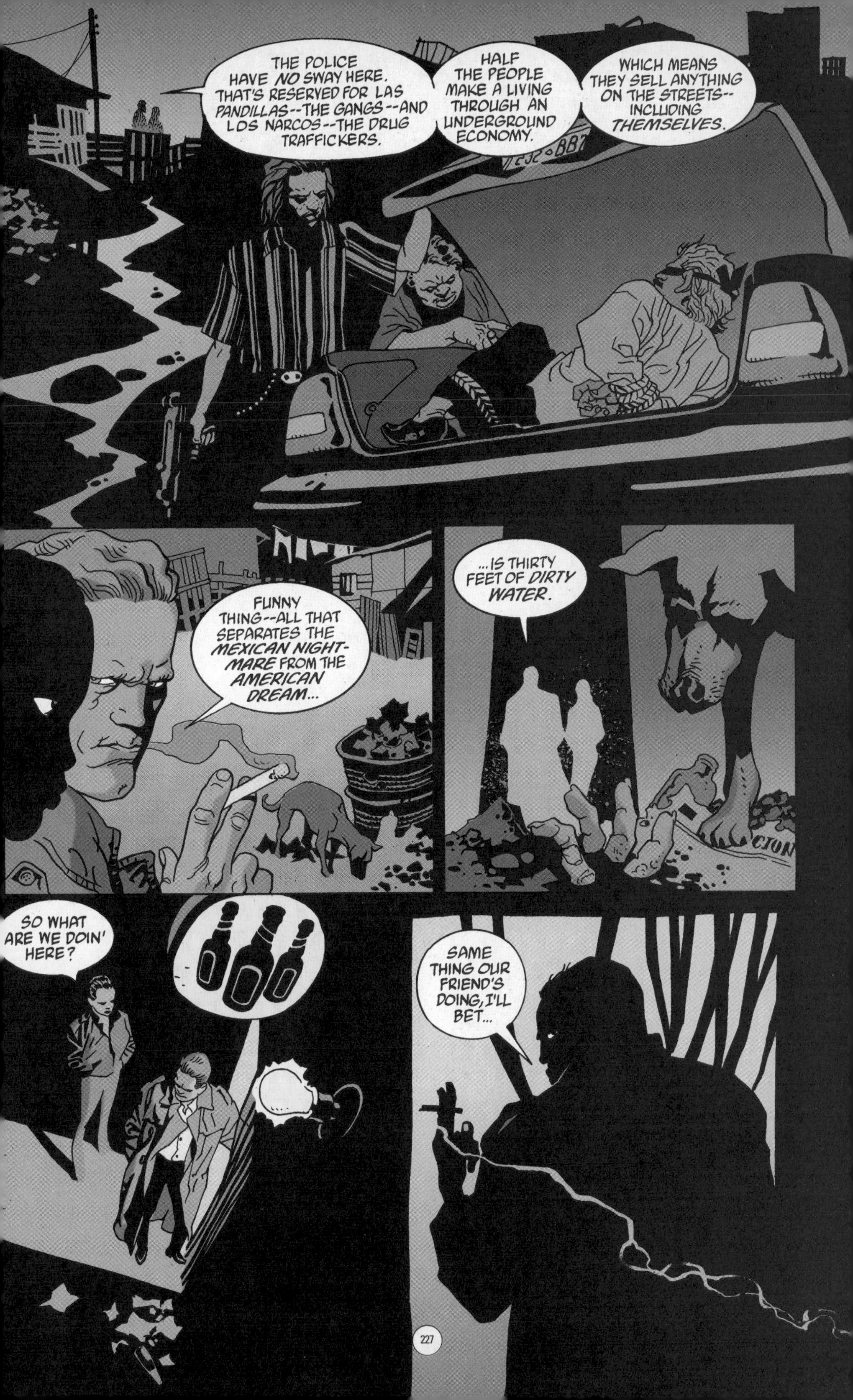

THE POLICE HAVE NO SWAY HERE. THAT'S RESERVED FOR LAS PANDILLAS--THE GANGS--AND LOS NARCOS--THE DRUG TRAFFICKERS.
HALF THE PEOPLE MAKE A LIVING THROUGH AN UNDERGROUND ECONOMY.
WHICH MEANS THEY SELL ANYTHING ON THE STREETS--INCLUDING THEMSELVES.
FUNNY THING--ALL THAT SEPARATES THE MEXICAN NIGHTMARE FROM THE AMERICAN DREAM...
...IS THIRTY FEET OF DIRTY WATER.
SO WHAT ARE WE DOIN' HERE?
SAME THING OUR FRIEND'S DOING, I'LL BET...

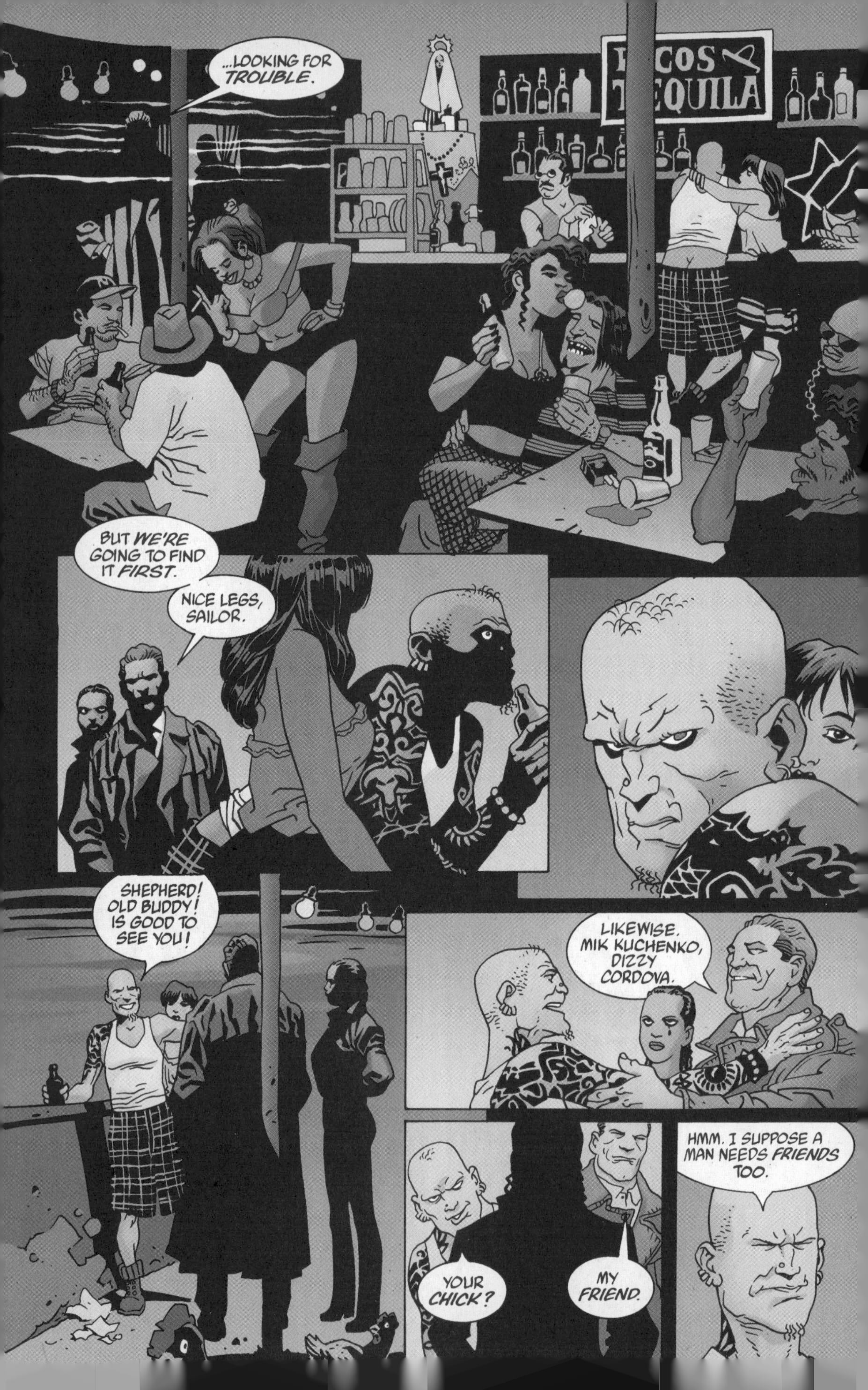

...LOOKING FOR TROUBLE.
PECOS TEQUILA
BUT WE'RE GOING TO FIND IT FIRST.
NICE LEGS, SAILOR.
SHEPHERD! OLD BUDDY! IS GOOD TO SEE YOU!
LIKEWISE. MIK KUCHENKO, DIZZY CORDOVA.
YOUR CHICK?
MY FRIEND.
HMM. I SUPPOSE A MAN NEEDS FRIENDS TOO.

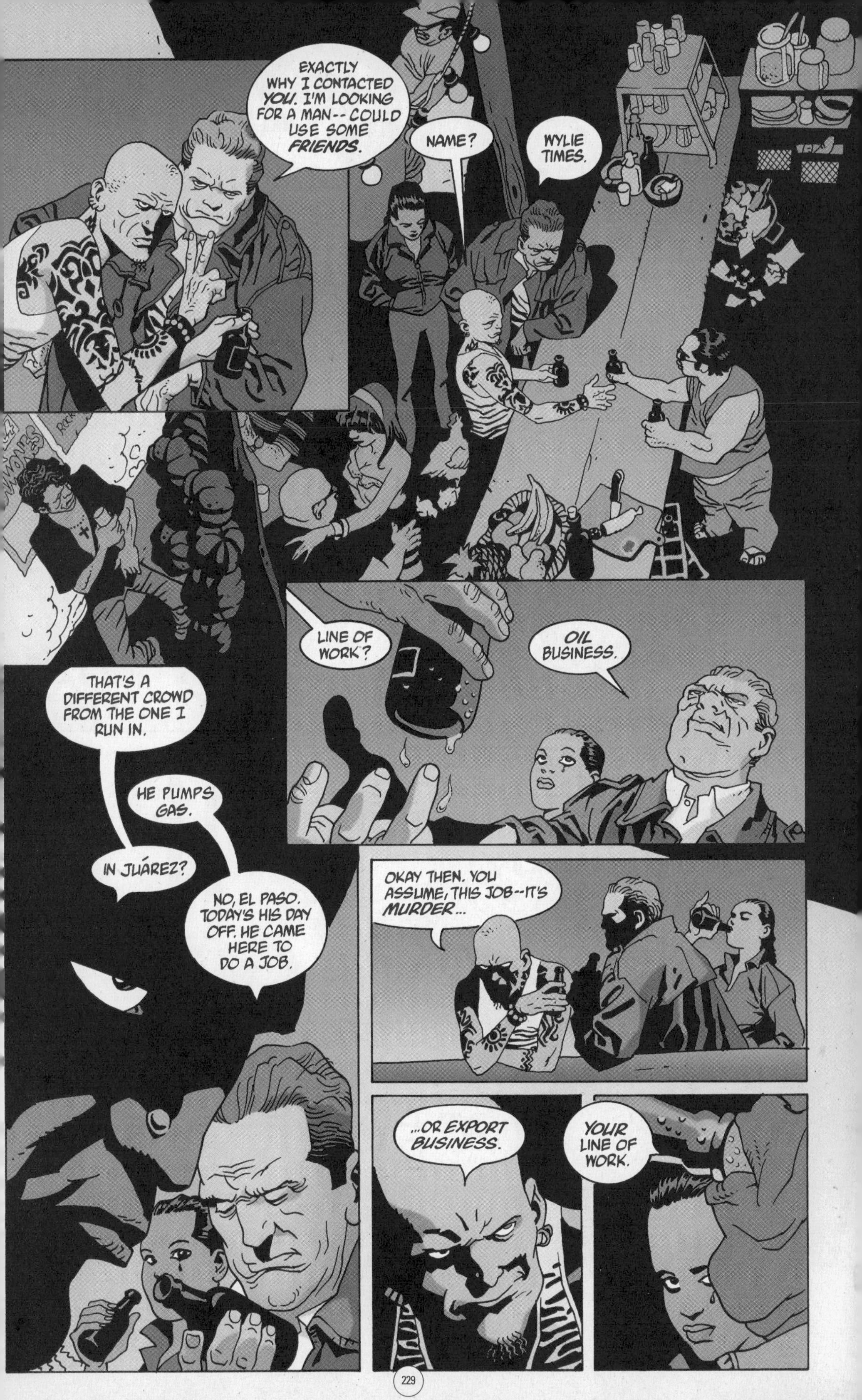
EXACTLY WHY I CONTACTED YOU. I'M LOOKING FOR A MAN-- COULD USE SOME FRIENDS.
NAME?
WYLIE TIMES.
LINE OF WORK?
OIL BUSINESS.
THAT'S A DIFFERENT CROWD FROM THE ONE I RUN IN.
HE PUMPS GAS.
IN JUÁREZ?
NO, EL PASO. TODAY'S HIS DAY OFF. HE CAME HERE TO DO A JOB.
OKAY THEN. YOU ASSUME, THIS JOB--IT'S MURDER...
...OR EXPORT BUSINESS.
YOUR LINE OF WORK.

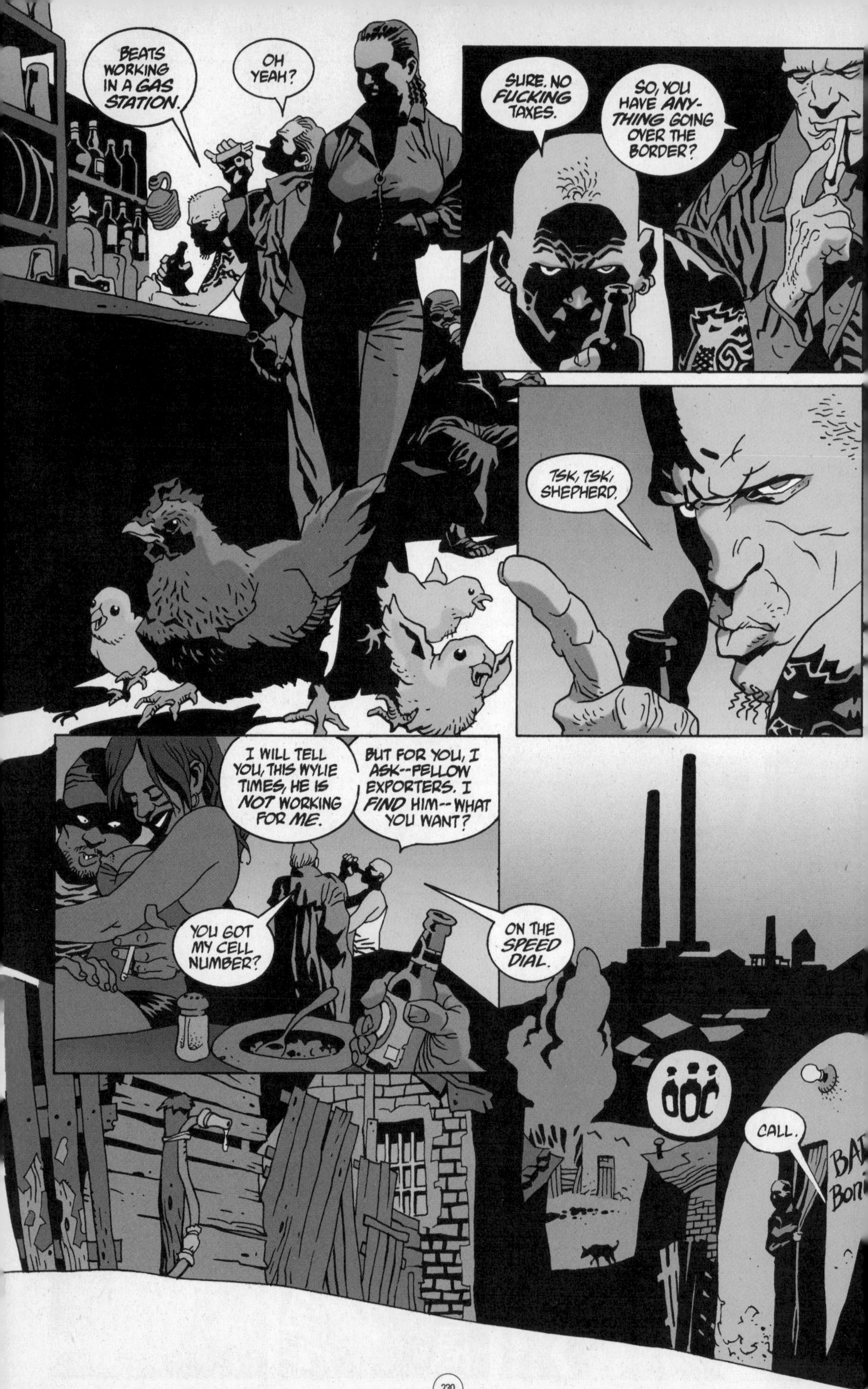
BEATS WORKING IN A GAS STATION.
OH YEAH?
SURE. NO FUCKING TAXES.
SO, YOU HAVE ANY-THING GOING OVER THE BORDER?
TSK, TSK, SHEPHERD.
I WILL TELL YOU, THIS WYLIE TIMES, HE IS NOT WORKING FOR ME.
BUT FOR YOU, I ASK--FELLOW EXPORTERS. I FIND HIM--WHAT YOU WANT?
YOU GOT MY CELL NUMBER?
ON THE SPEED DIAL.
CALL.

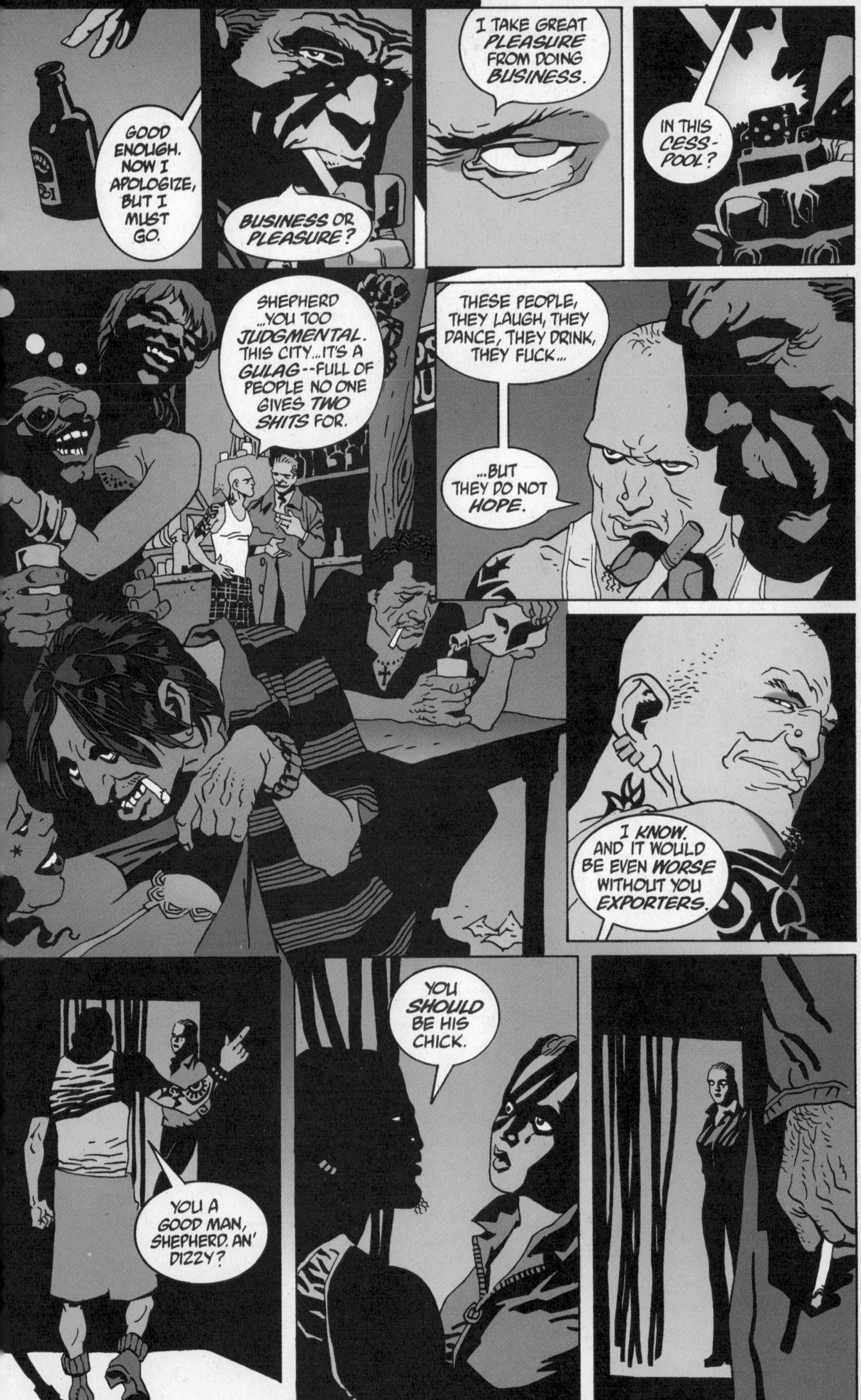
GOOD ENOUGH. NOW I APOLOGIZE, BUT I MUST GO.
BUSINESS OR PLEASURE?
I TAKE GREAT PLEASURE FROM DOING BUSINESS.
IN THIS CESS-POOL?
SHEPHERD ...YOU TOO JUDGMENTAL. THIS CITY...IT'S A GULAG--FULL OF PEOPLE NO ONE GIVES TWO SHITS FOR.
THESE PEOPLE, THEY LAUGH, THEY DANCE, THEY DRINK, THEY FUCK...
...BUT THEY DO NOT HOPE.
I KNOW. AND IT WOULD BE EVEN WORSE WITHOUT YOU EXPORTERS.
YOU A GOOD MAN, SHEPHERD. AN' DIZZY?
YOU SHOULD BE HIS CHICK.

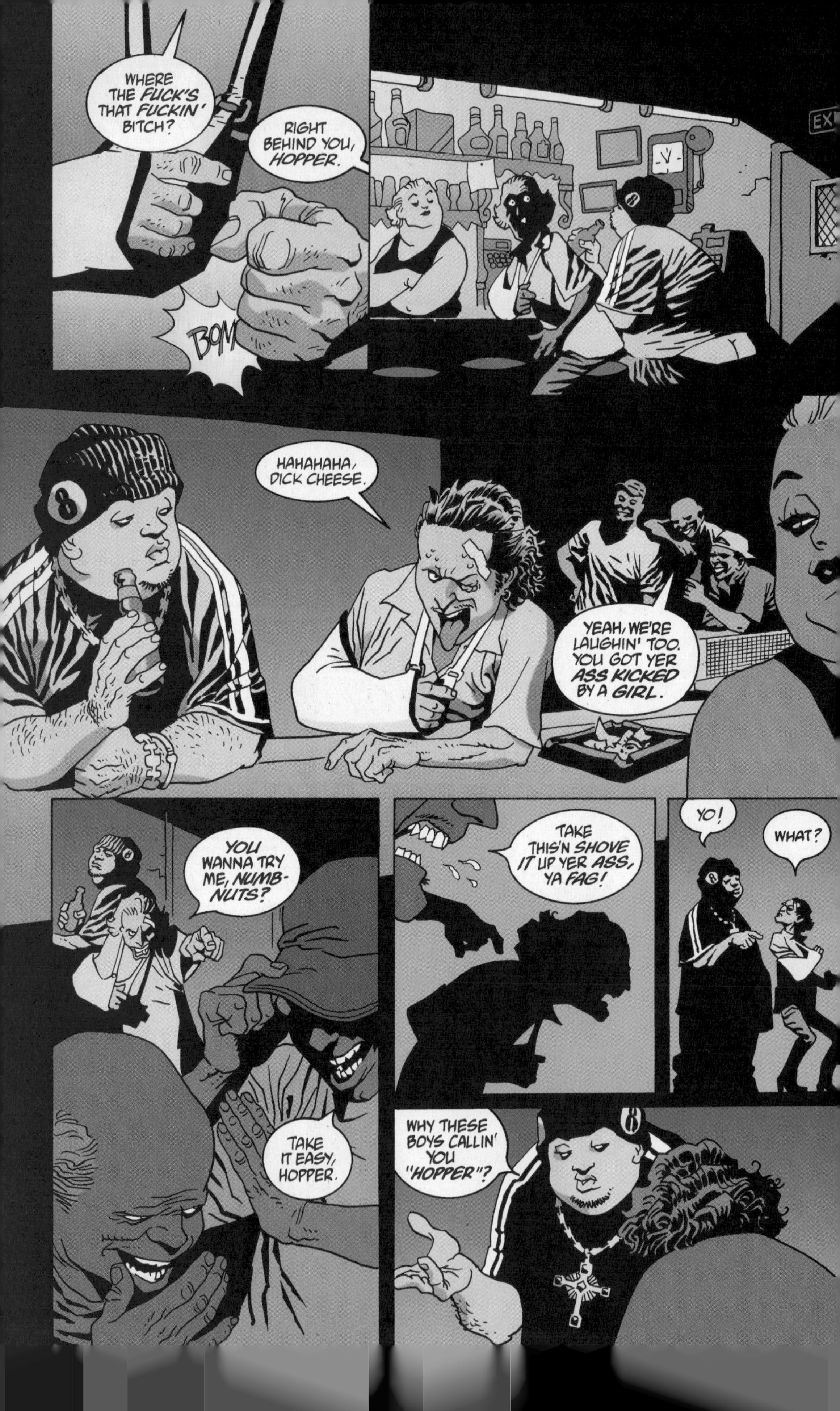
WHERE THE FUCK'S THAT FUCKIN' BITCH?
RIGHT BEHIND YOU, HOPPER.
BOM
EXI
HAHAHAHA, DICK CHEESE.
YEAH, WE'RE LAUGHIN' TOO. YOU GOT YER ASS KICKED BY A GIRL.
YOU WANNA TRY ME, NUMB-NUTS?
TAKE IT EASY, HOPPER.
TAKE THIS'N SHOVE IT UP YER ASS, YA FAG!
YO!
WHAT?
WHY THESE BOYS CALLIN' YOU "HOPPER"?

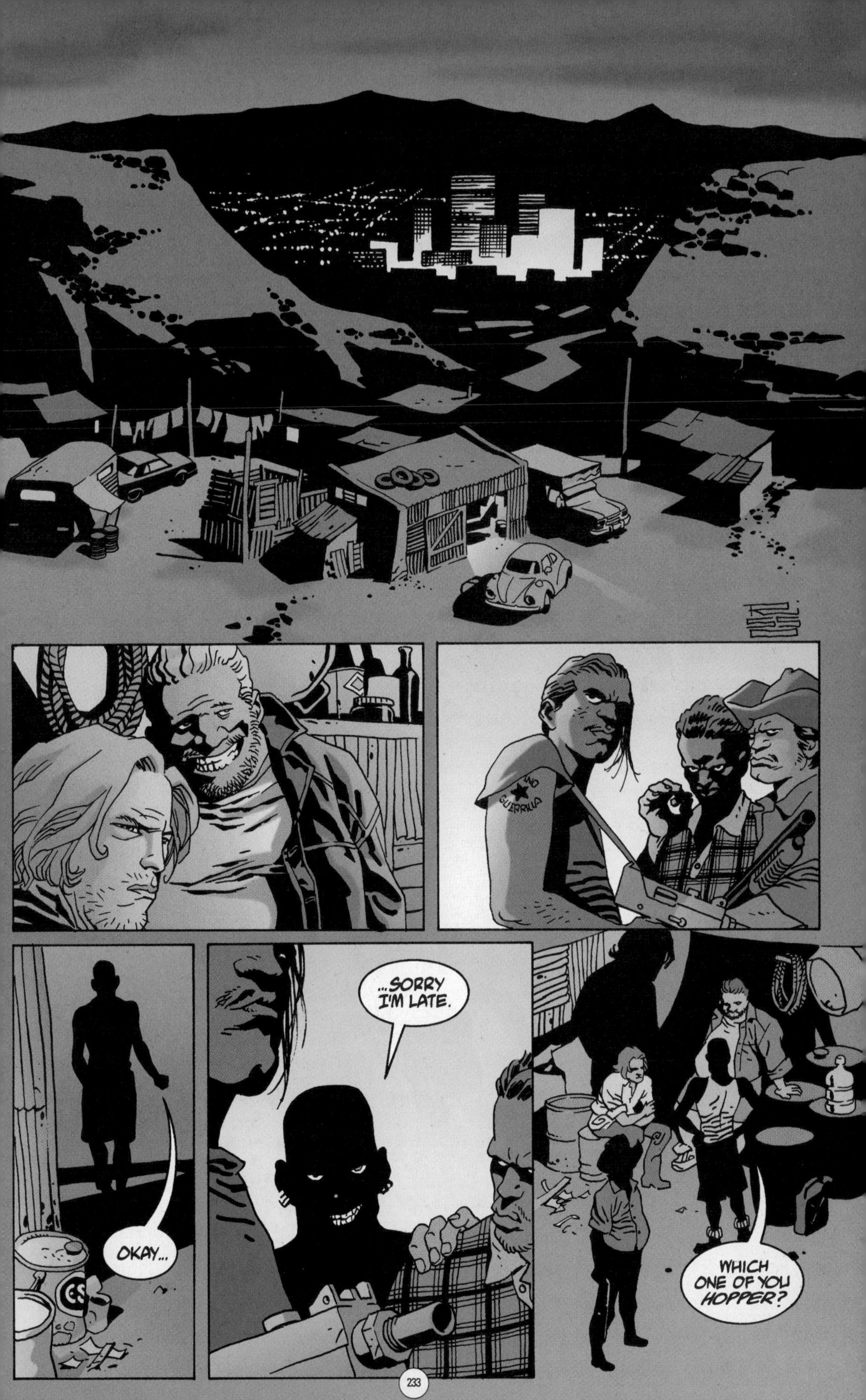
GUERRILLA
OKAY...
...SORRY I'M LATE.
WHICH ONE OF YOU HOPPER?

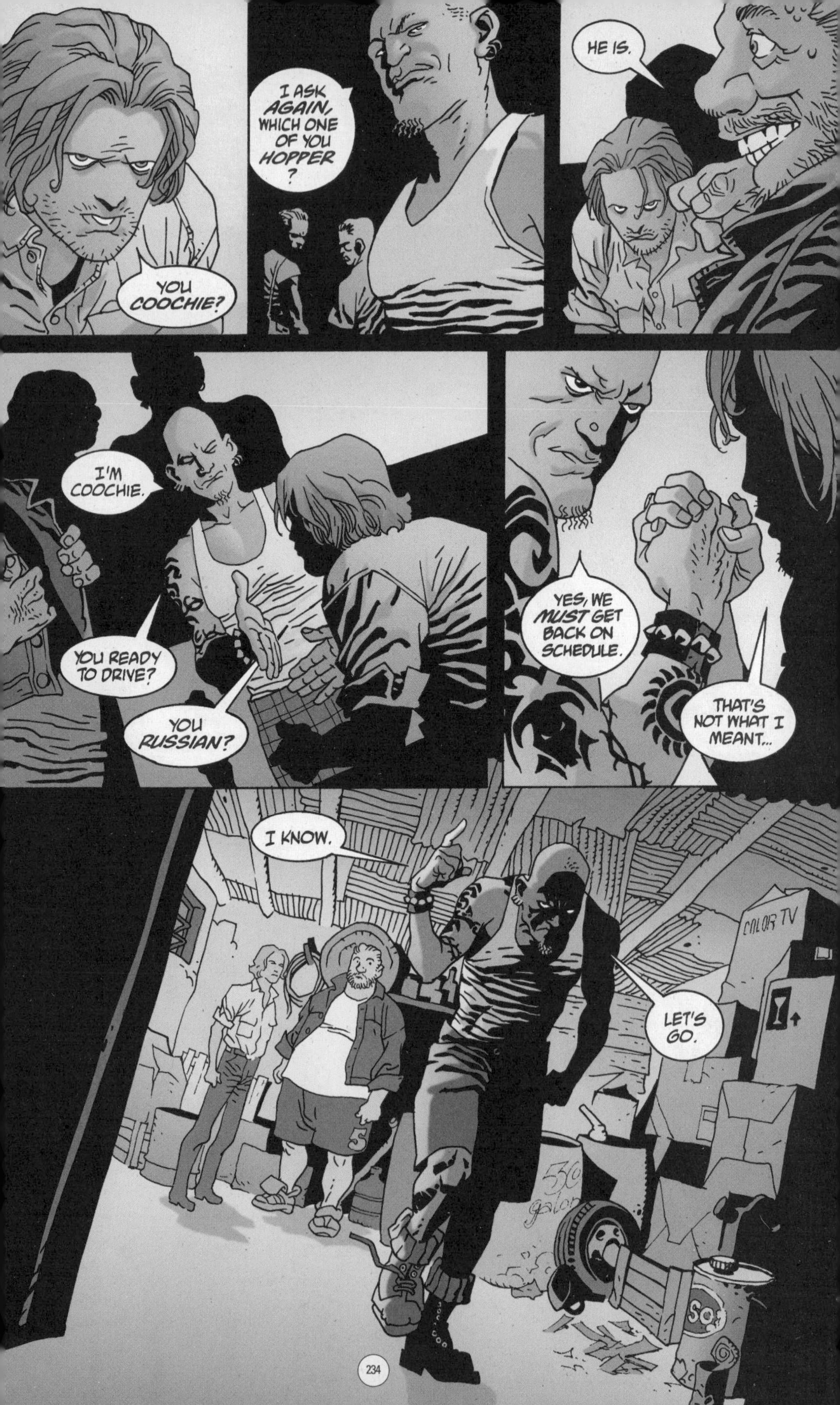
YOU COOCHIE?
I ASK AGAIN, WHICH ONE OF YOU HOPPER ?
HE IS.
I'M COOCHIE.
YOU READY TO DRIVE?
YOU RUSSIAN?
YES, WE MUST GET BACK ON SCHEDULE.
THAT'S NOT WHAT I MEANT...
I KNOW.
LET'S GO.
COLOR TV

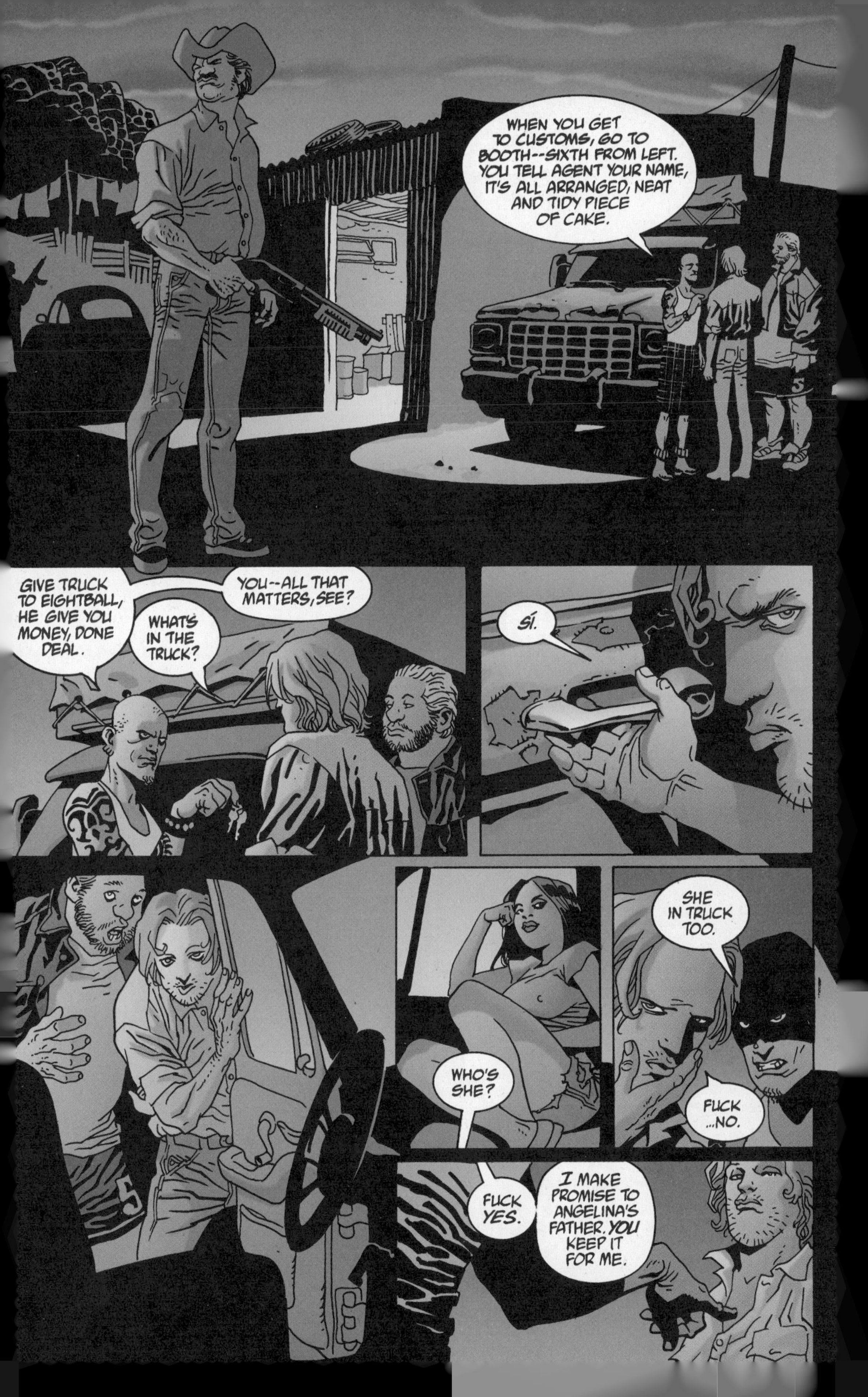
WHEN YOU GET TO CUSTOMS, GO TO BOOTH--SIXTH FROM LEFT. YOU TELL AGENT YOUR NAME, IT'S ALL ARRANGED, NEAT AND TIDY PIECE OF CAKE.
GIVE TRUCK TO EIGHTBALL, HE GIVE YOU MONEY, DONE DEAL.
YOU--ALL THAT MATTERS, SEE?
WHAT'S IN THE TRUCK?
SÍ.
SHE IN TRUCK TOO.
WHO'S SHE?
FUCK ...NO.
FUCK YES.
I MAKE PROMISE TO ANGELINA'S FATHER. YOU KEEP IT FOR ME.

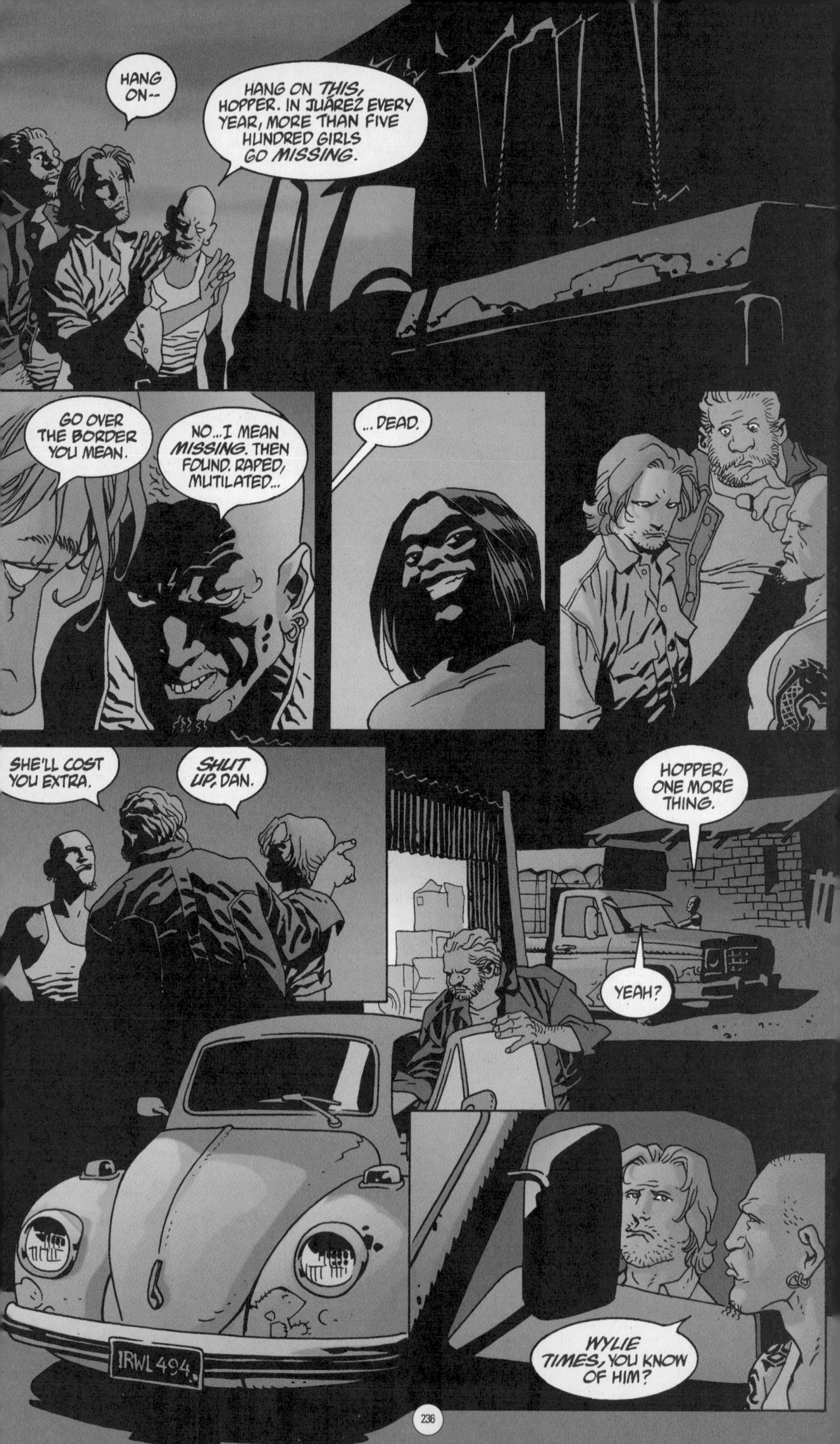
HANG ON--
HANG ON THIS, HOPPER. IN JUÁREZ EVERY YEAR, MORE THAN FIVE HUNDRED GIRLS GO MISSING.
GO OVER THE BORDER YOU MEAN.
NO...I MEAN MISSING. THEN FOUND. RAPED, MUTILATED...
...DEAD.
SHE'LL COST YOU EXTRA.
SHUT UP, DAN.
HOPPER, ONE MORE THING.
YEAH?
IRWL 494
WYLIE TIMES, YOU KNOW OF HIM?

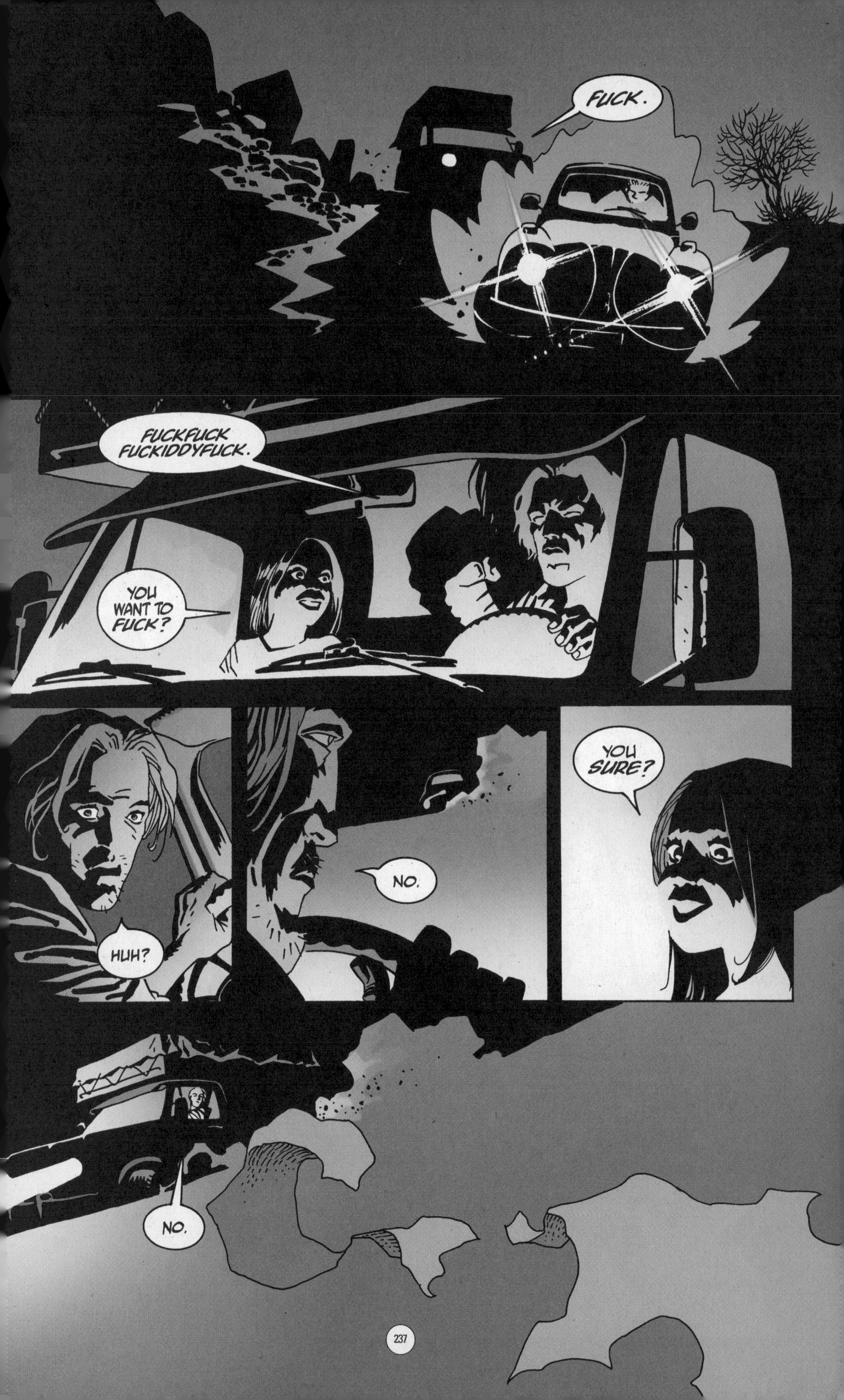
FUCK.
FUCKFUCK FUCKIDDYFUCK.
YOU WANT TO FUCK?
HUH?
NO.
YOU SURE?
NO.

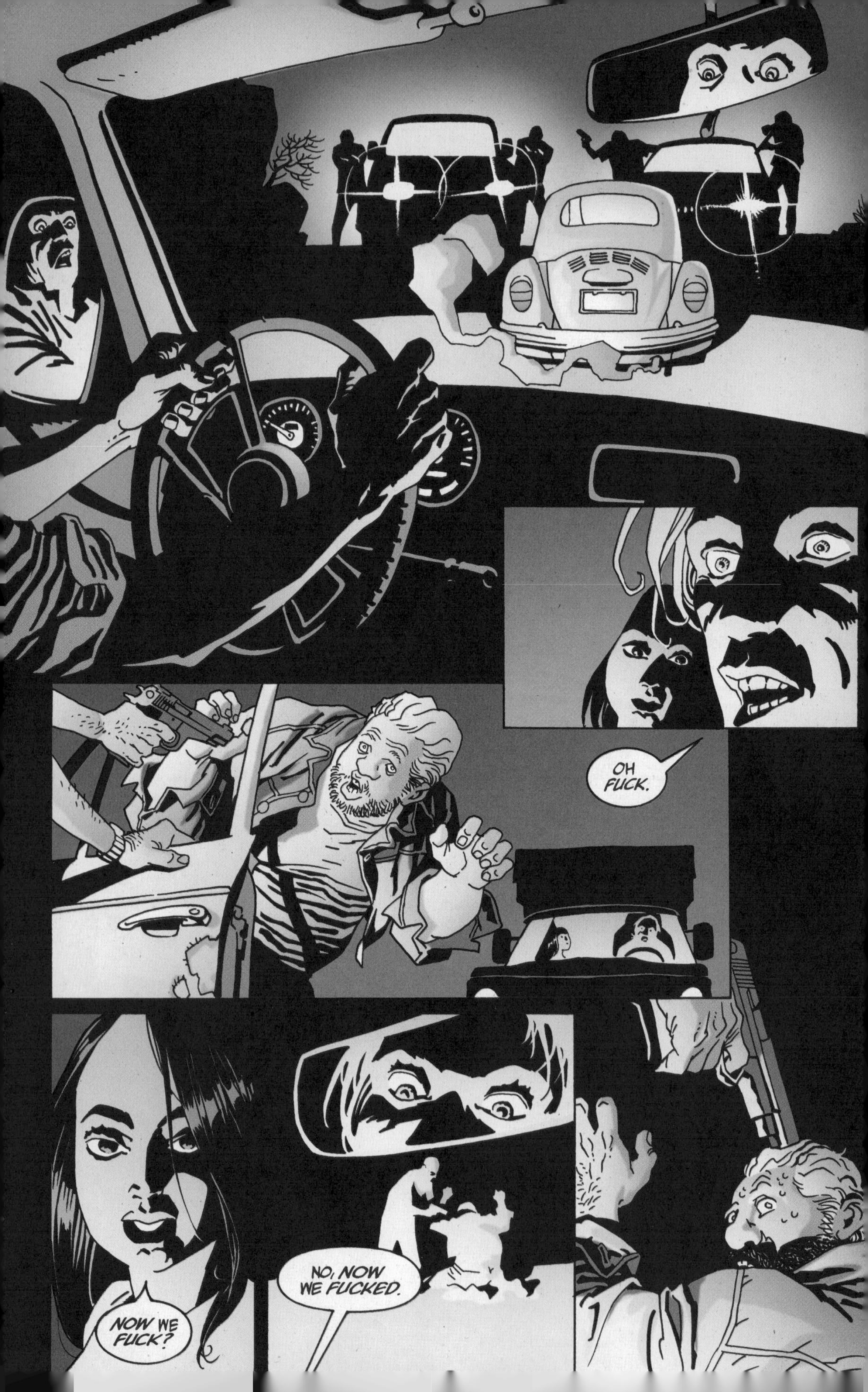
OH FUCK.
NOW WE FUCK?
NO, NOW WE FUCKED.

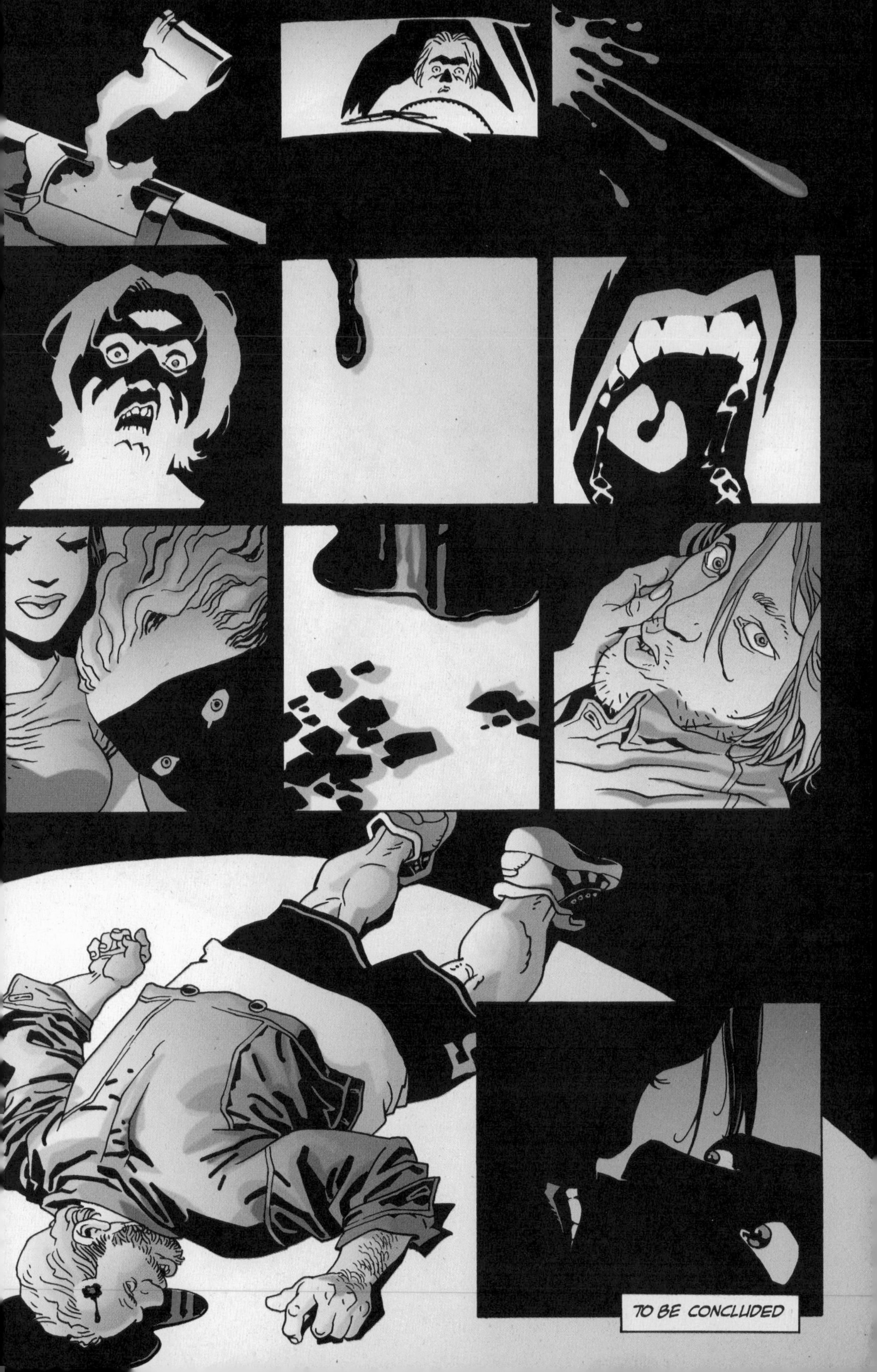
TO BE CONCLUDED

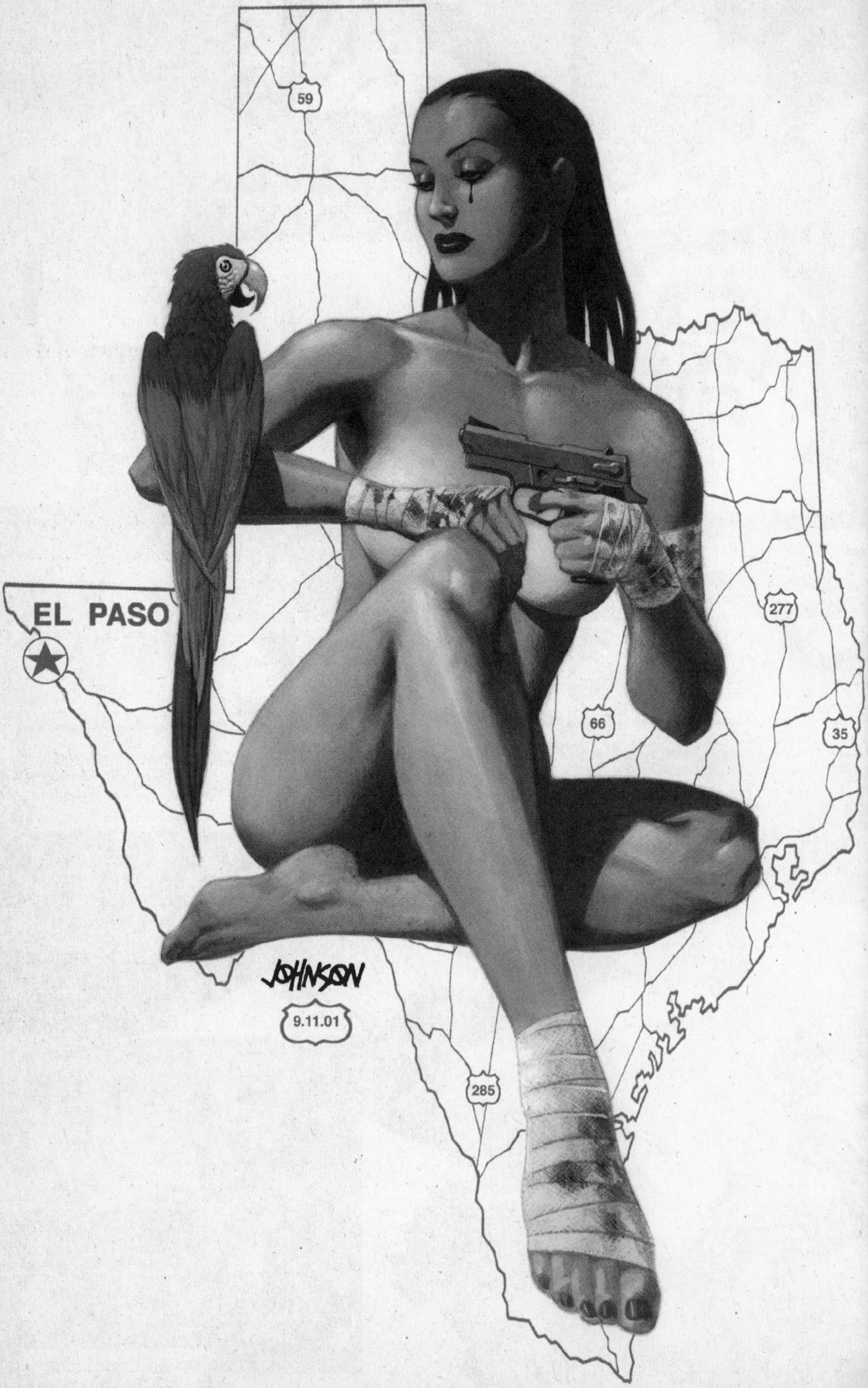

59
EL PASO
277
66
35
JOHNSON
9.11.01
285

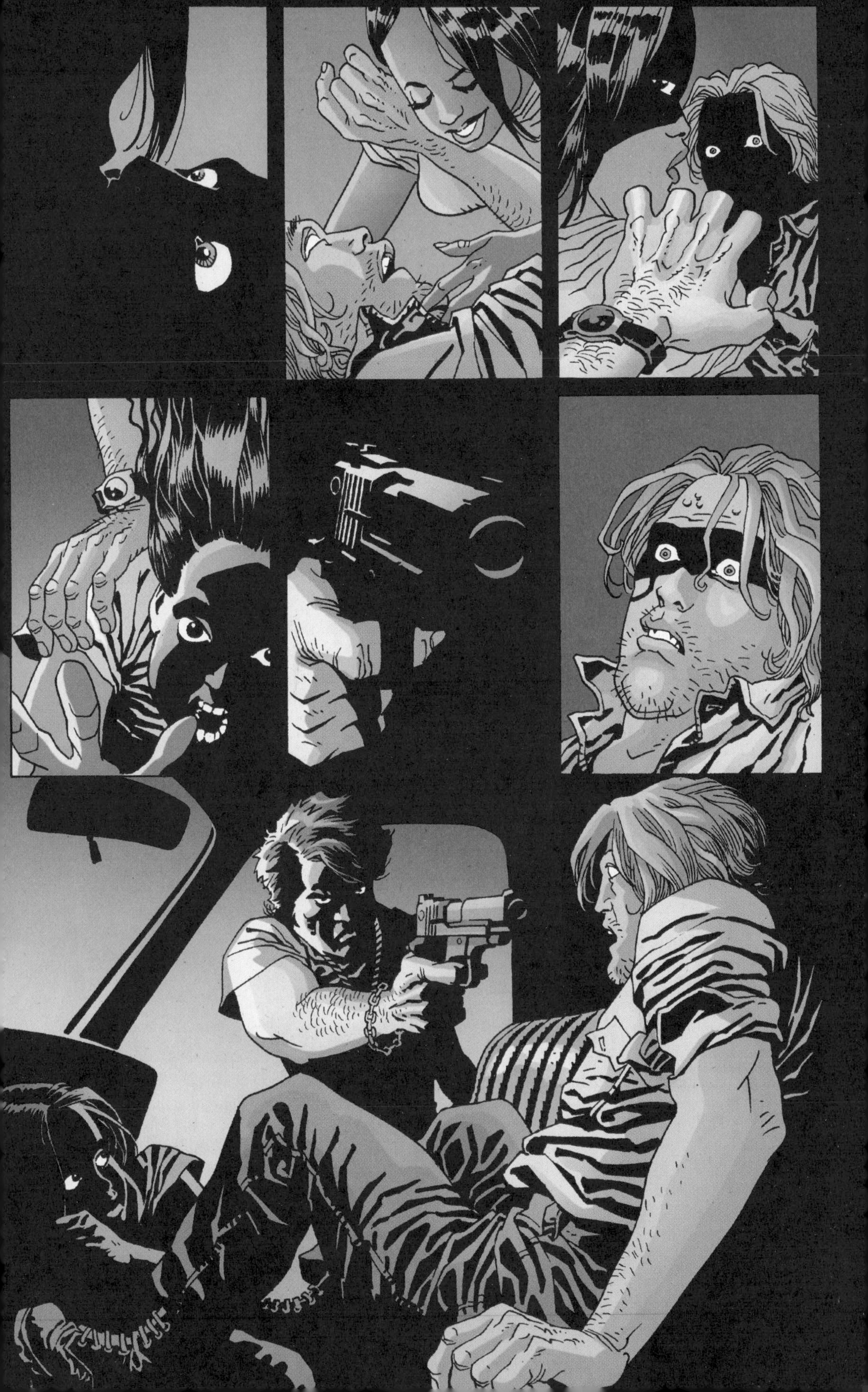

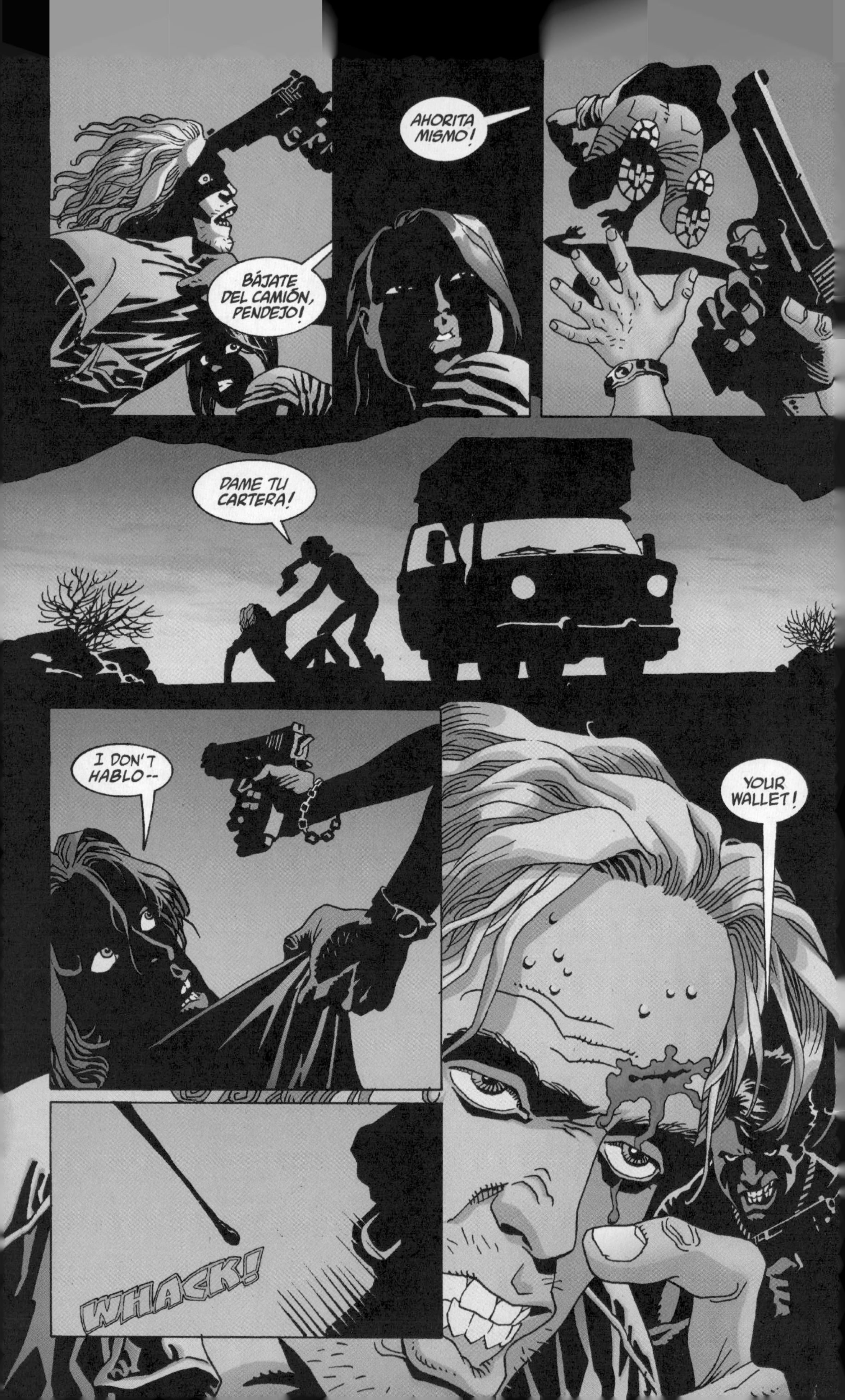
BÁJATE DEL CAMIÓN, PENDEJO!
AHORITA MISMO!
DAME TU CARTERA!
I DON'T HABLO--
YOUR WALLET!
WHACK!

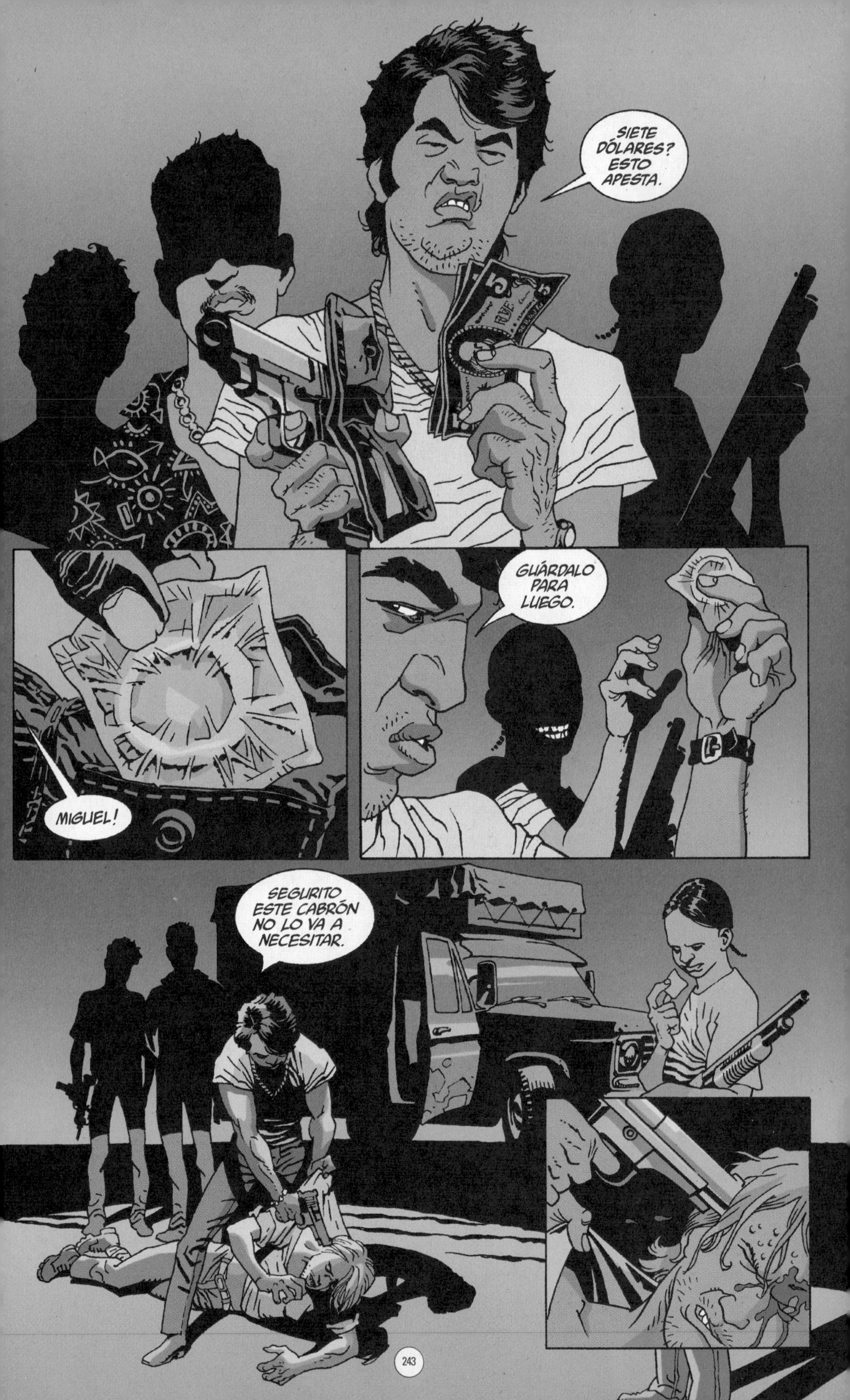
SIETE DÓLARES? ESTO APESTA.
MIGUEL!
GUÁRDALO PARA LUEGO.
SEGURITO ESTE CABRÓN NO LO VA A NECESITAR.

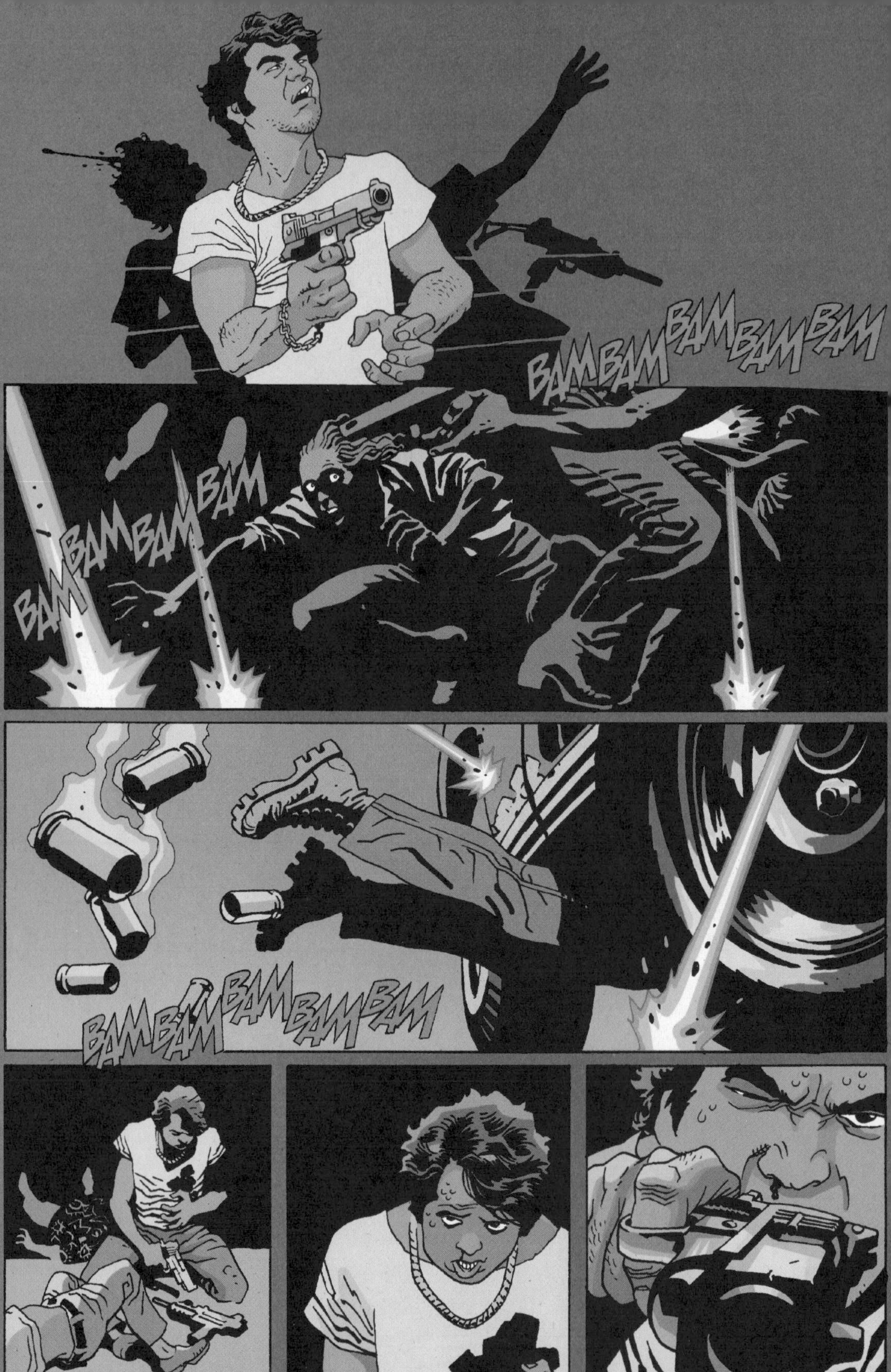
BAM BAM BAM BAM BAM BAM
BAM BAM BAM BAM
BAM BAM BAM BAM BAM

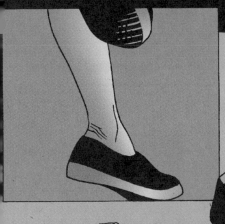

YOU OKAY NOW, BOY-FRIEND?

¡CONTRABANDOLERO!

CONCLUSION

BRIAN AZZARELLO
writer

EDUARDO RISSO
artist

PATRICIA MULVIHILL
colorist

CLEM ROBINS
letterer

DIGITAL CHAMELEON
separator

DAVE JOHNSON
cover artist

WILL DENNIS
editor

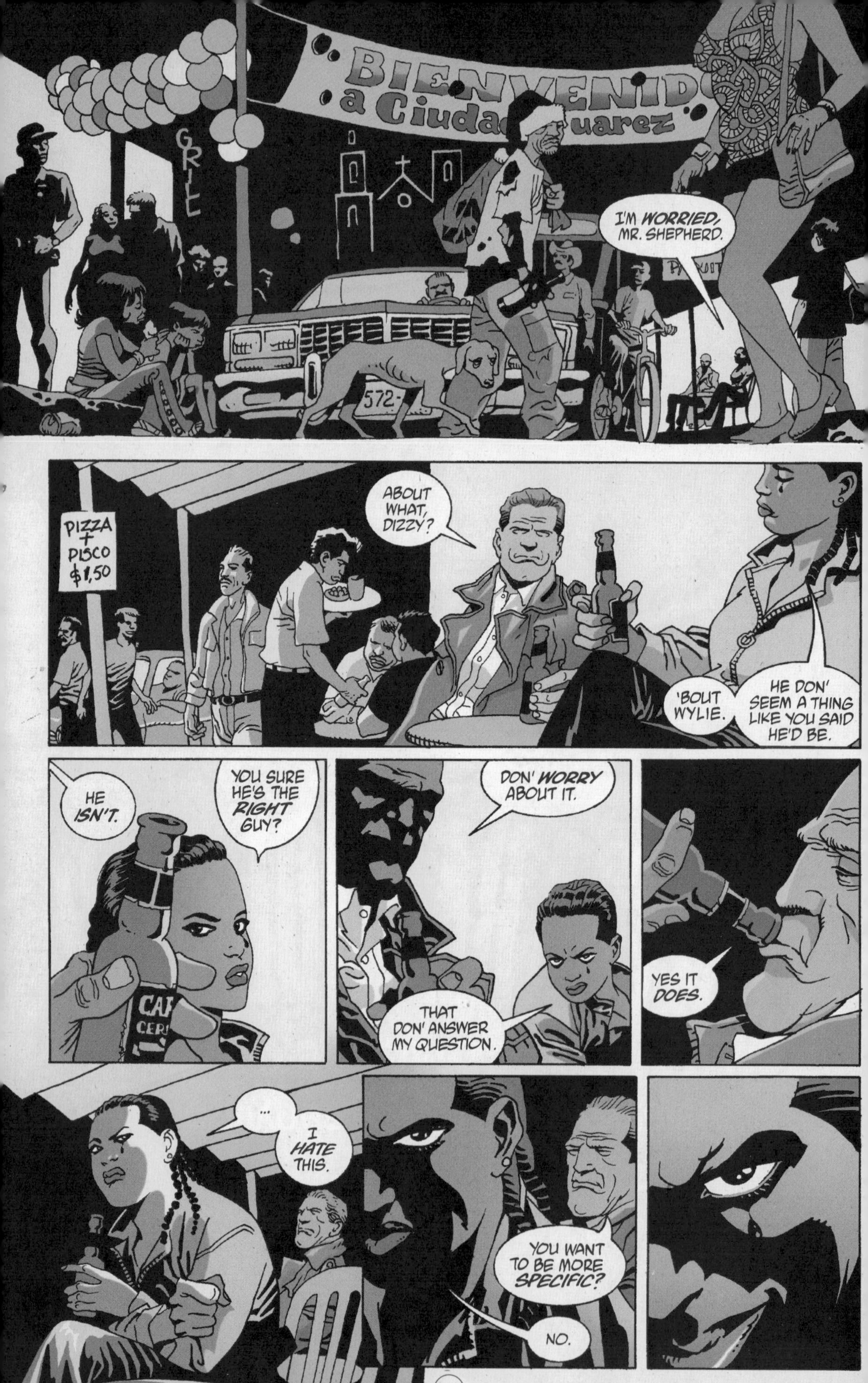
BIENVENIDO a Ciudad Juarez
GRILL
PIZZA + DISCO $1,50
I'M WORRIED, MR. SHEPHERD.
ABOUT WHAT, DIZZY?
HE DON' SEEM A THING LIKE YOU SAID HE'D BE.
'BOUT WYLIE.
YOU SURE HE'S THE RIGHT GUY?
HE ISN'T.
DON' WORRY ABOUT IT.
THAT DON' ANSWER MY QUESTION.
YES IT DOES.
...
I HATE THIS.
YOU WANT TO BE MORE SPECIFIC?
NO.

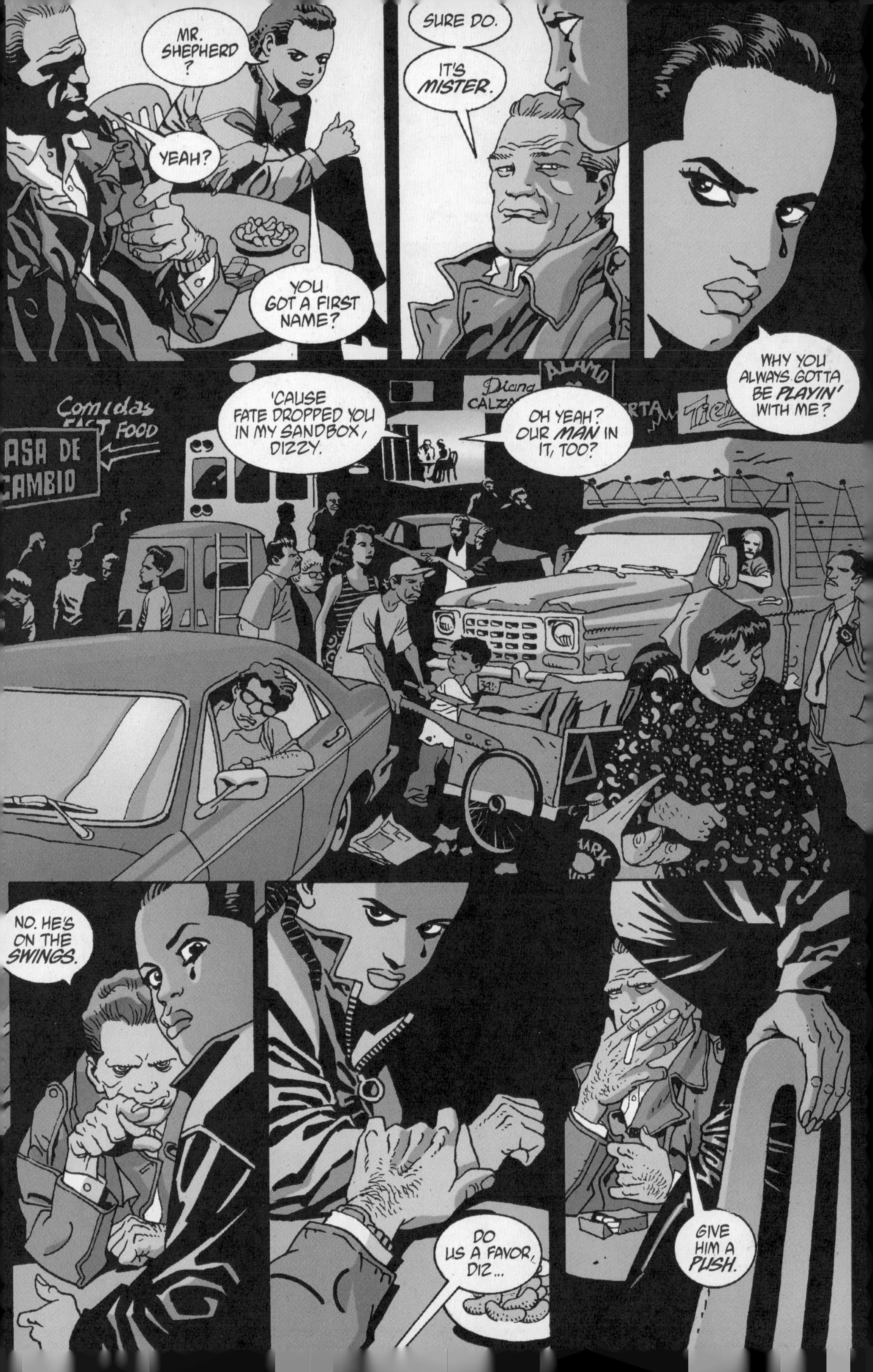
MR. SHEPHERD ?
YEAH?
YOU GOT A FIRST NAME?
SURE DO.
IT'S *MISTER*.
WHY YOU ALWAYS GOTTA BE *PLAYIN'* WITH ME?
Comidas
'CAUSE FATE DROPPED YOU IN MY SANDBOX, DIZZY.
ALAMO
OH YEAH? OUR *MAN* IN IT, TOO?
NO. HE'S ON THE *SWINGS*.
DO US A FAVOR, DIZ...
GIVE HIM A *PUSH*.

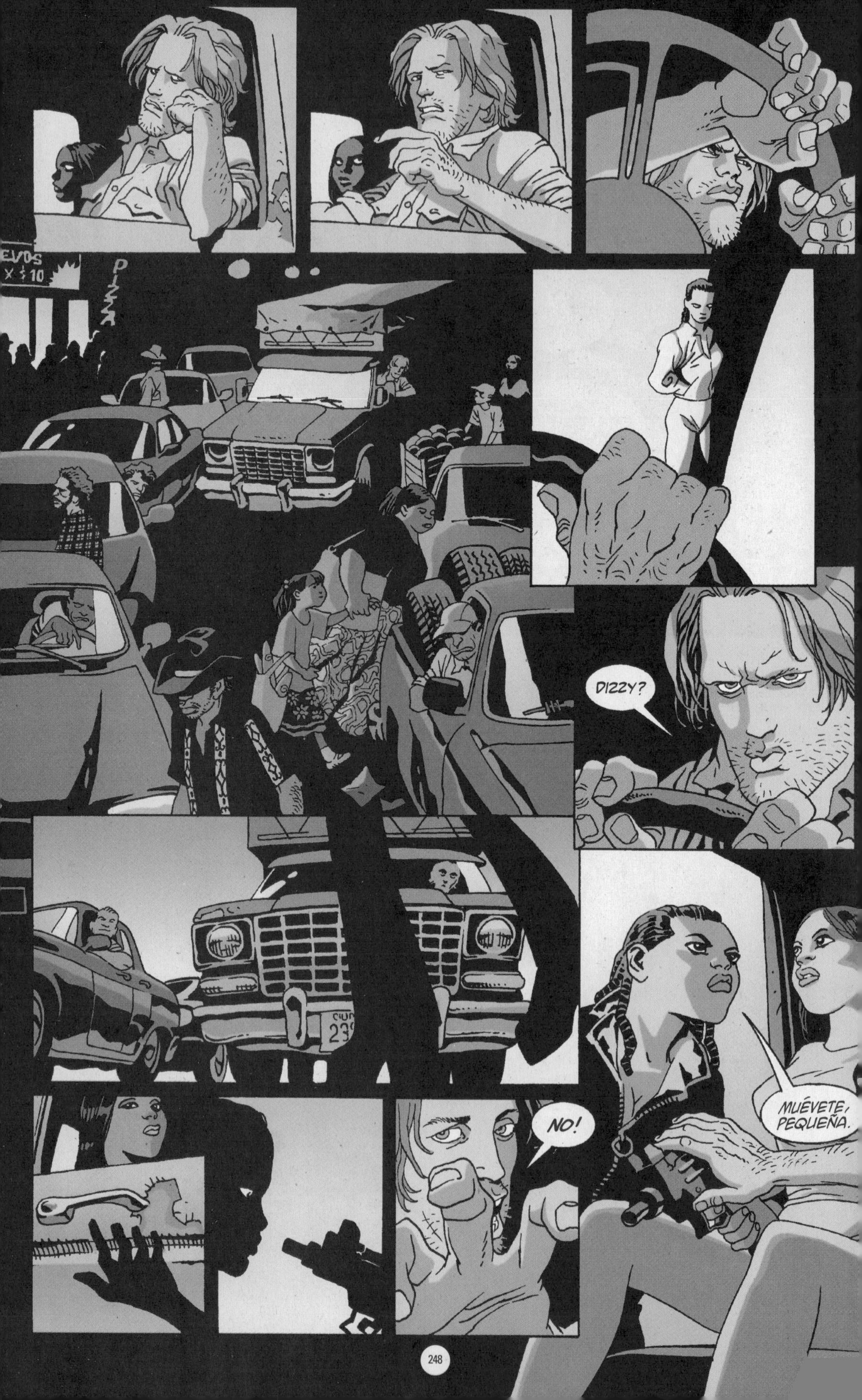
EVOS
X $10
PIZZA
DIZZY?
MUÉVETE, PEQUEÑA.
NO!

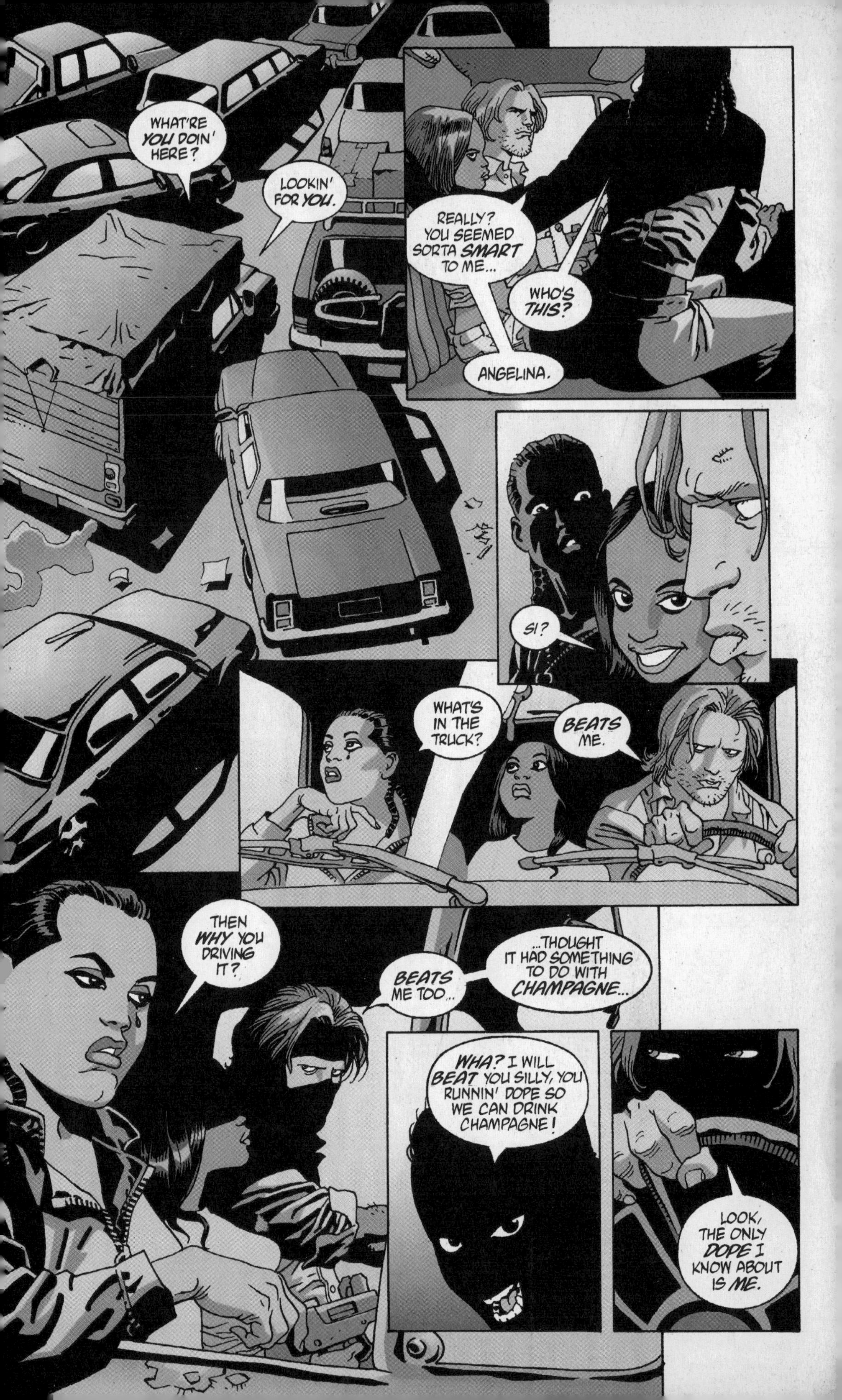
WHAT'RE YOU DOIN' HERE?
LOOKIN' FOR YOU.
REALLY? YOU SEEMED SORTA SMART TO ME...
WHO'S THIS?
ANGELINA.
SI?
WHAT'S IN THE TRUCK?
BEATS ME.
THEN WHY YOU DRIVING IT?
BEATS ME TOO...
...THOUGHT IT HAD SOMETHING TO DO WITH CHAMPAGNE...
WHA? I WILL BEAT YOU SILLY, YOU RUNNIN' DOPE SO WE CAN DRINK CHAMPAGNE!
LOOK, THE ONLY DOPE I KNOW ABOUT IS ME.

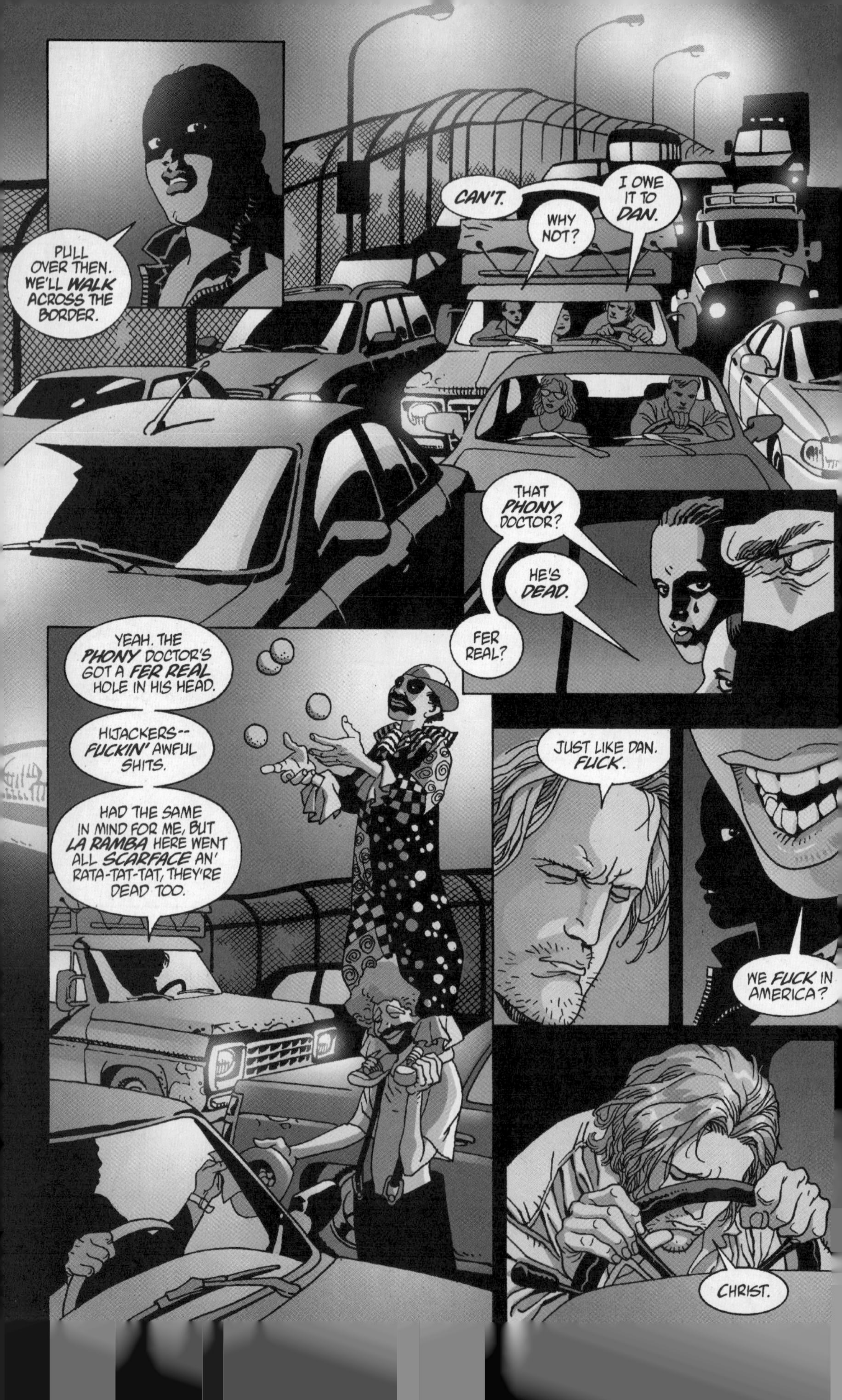
PULL OVER THEN. WE'LL WALK ACROSS THE BORDER.
CAN'T.
WHY NOT?
I OWE IT TO DAN.
THAT PHONY DOCTOR?
HE'S DEAD.
FER REAL?
YEAH. THE PHONY DOCTOR'S GOT A FER REAL HOLE IN HIS HEAD.
HIJACKERS-- FUCKIN' AWFUL SHITS.
HAD THE SAME IN MIND FOR ME, BUT LA RAMBA HERE WENT ALL SCARFACE AN' RATA-TAT-TAT, THEY'RE DEAD TOO.
JUST LIKE DAN. FUCK.
WE FUCK IN AMERICA?
CHRIST.

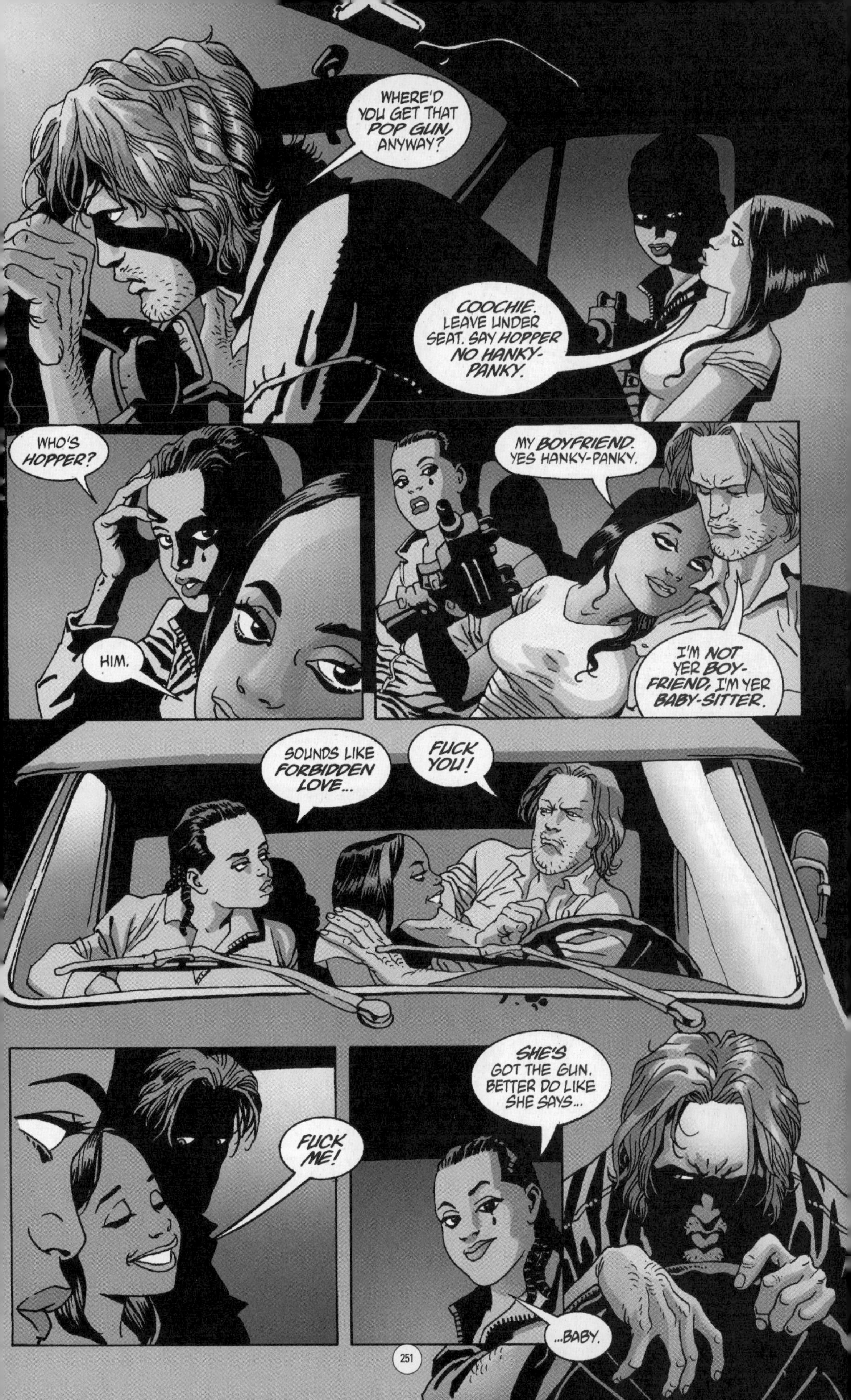
WHERE'D YOU GET THAT POP GUN, ANYWAY?
COOCHIE. LEAVE UNDER SEAT. SAY HOPPER NO HANKY-PANKY.
WHO'S HOPPER?
HIM.
MY BOYFRIEND. YES HANKY-PANKY.
I'M NOT YER BOY-FRIEND, I'M YER BABY-SITTER.
SOUNDS LIKE FORBIDDEN LOVE...
FUCK YOU!
FUCK ME!
SHE'S GOT THE GUN. BETTER DO LIKE SHE SAYS...
...BABY.

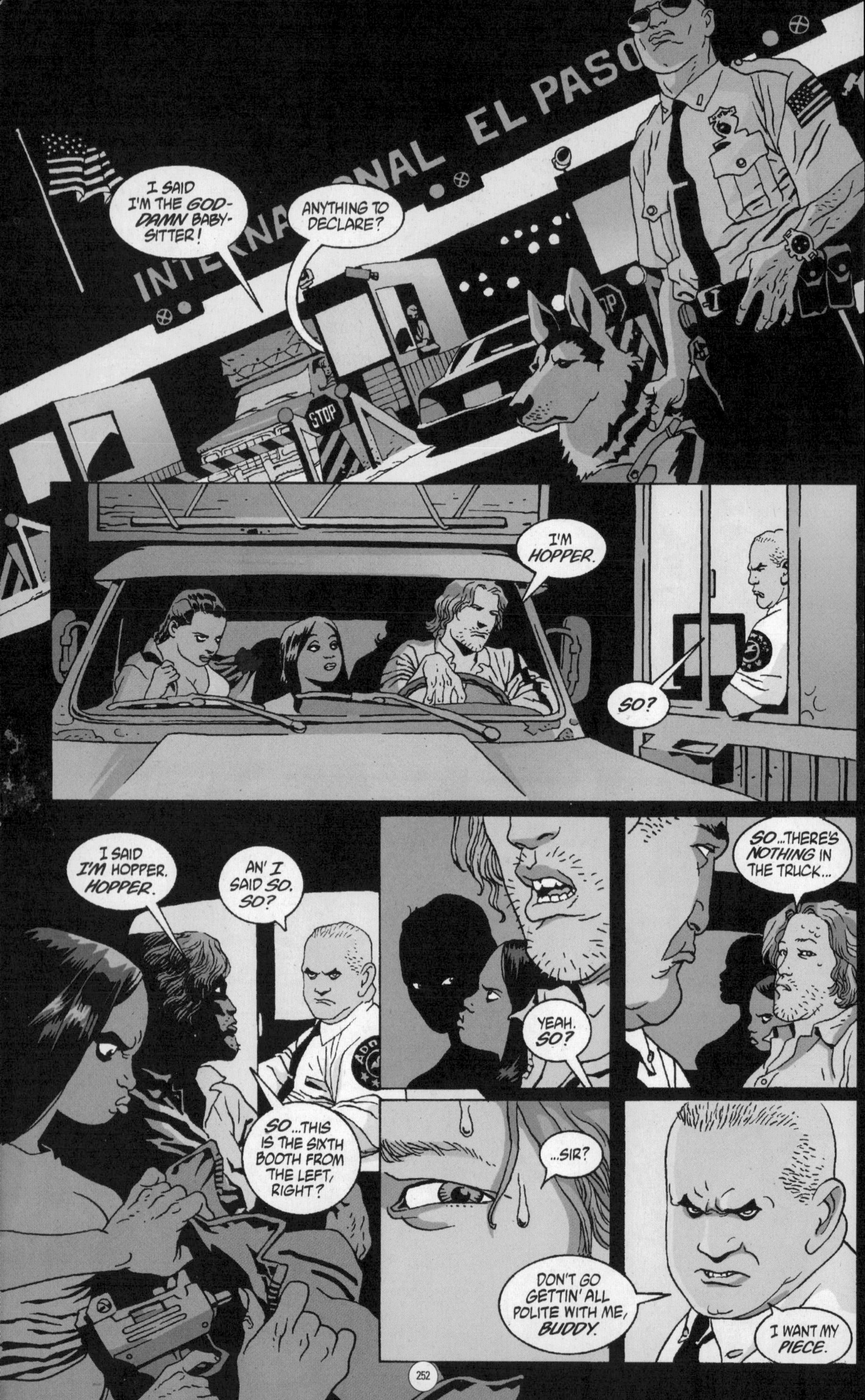
INTERNATIONAL EL PASO
ANYTHING TO DECLARE?
I SAID I'M THE GOD-DAMN BABY-SITTER!
STOP
I'M HOPPER.
SO?
I SAID I'M HOPPER. HOPPER.
AN' I SAID SO. SO?
YEAH. SO?
SO...THERE'S NOTHING IN THE TRUCK...
SO...THIS IS THE SIXTH BOOTH FROM THE LEFT, RIGHT?
...SIR?
DON'T GO GETTIN' ALL POLITE WITH ME, BUDDY.
I WANT MY PIECE.

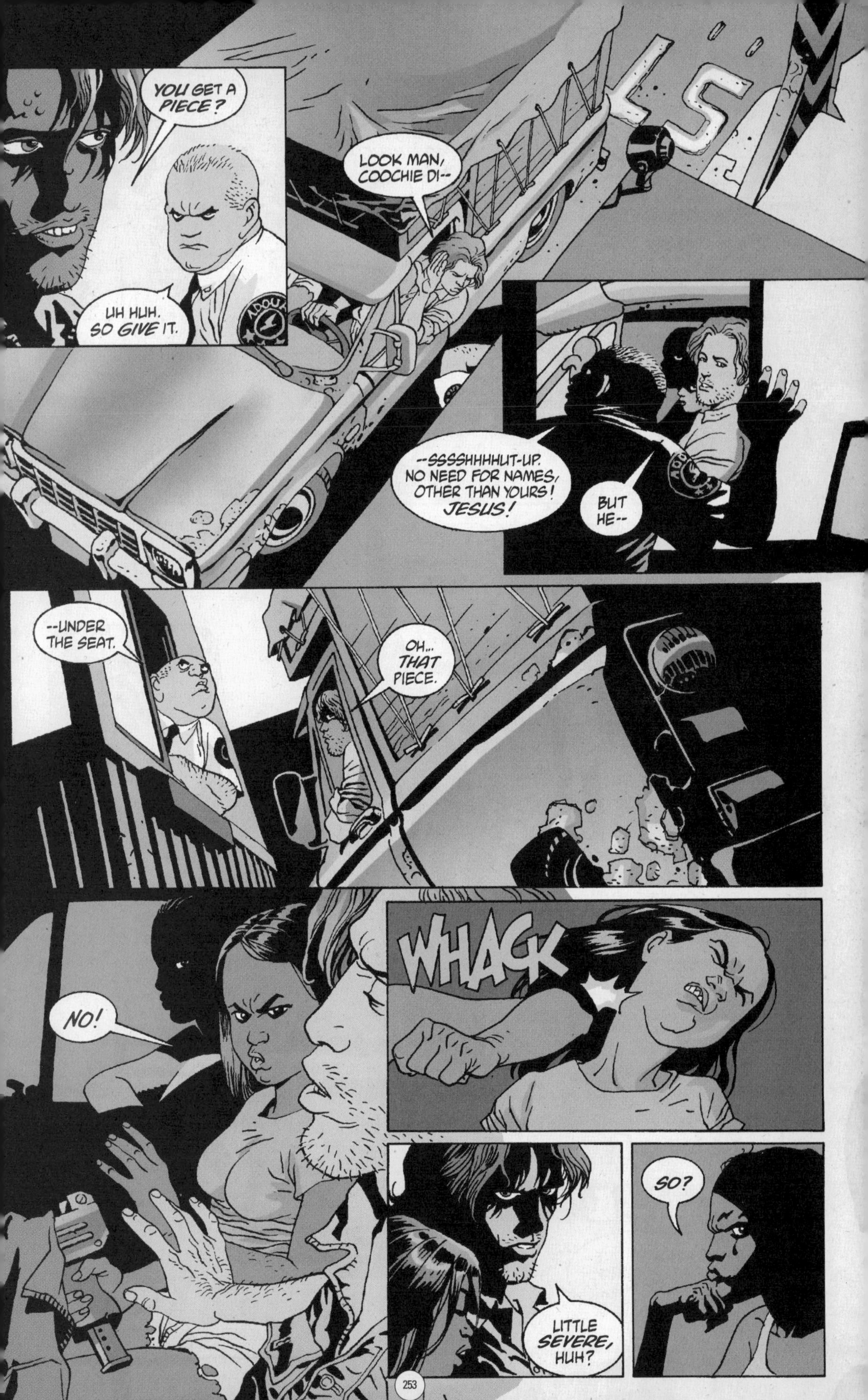
YOU GET A PIECE?
UH HUH. SO GIVE IT.
LOOK MAN, COOCHIE DI--
--SSSSHHHHUT-UP. NO NEED FOR NAMES, OTHER THAN YOURS! JESUS!
BUT HE--
--UNDER THE SEAT.
OH... THAT PIECE.
NO!
WHACK
SO?
LITTLE SEVERE, HUH?

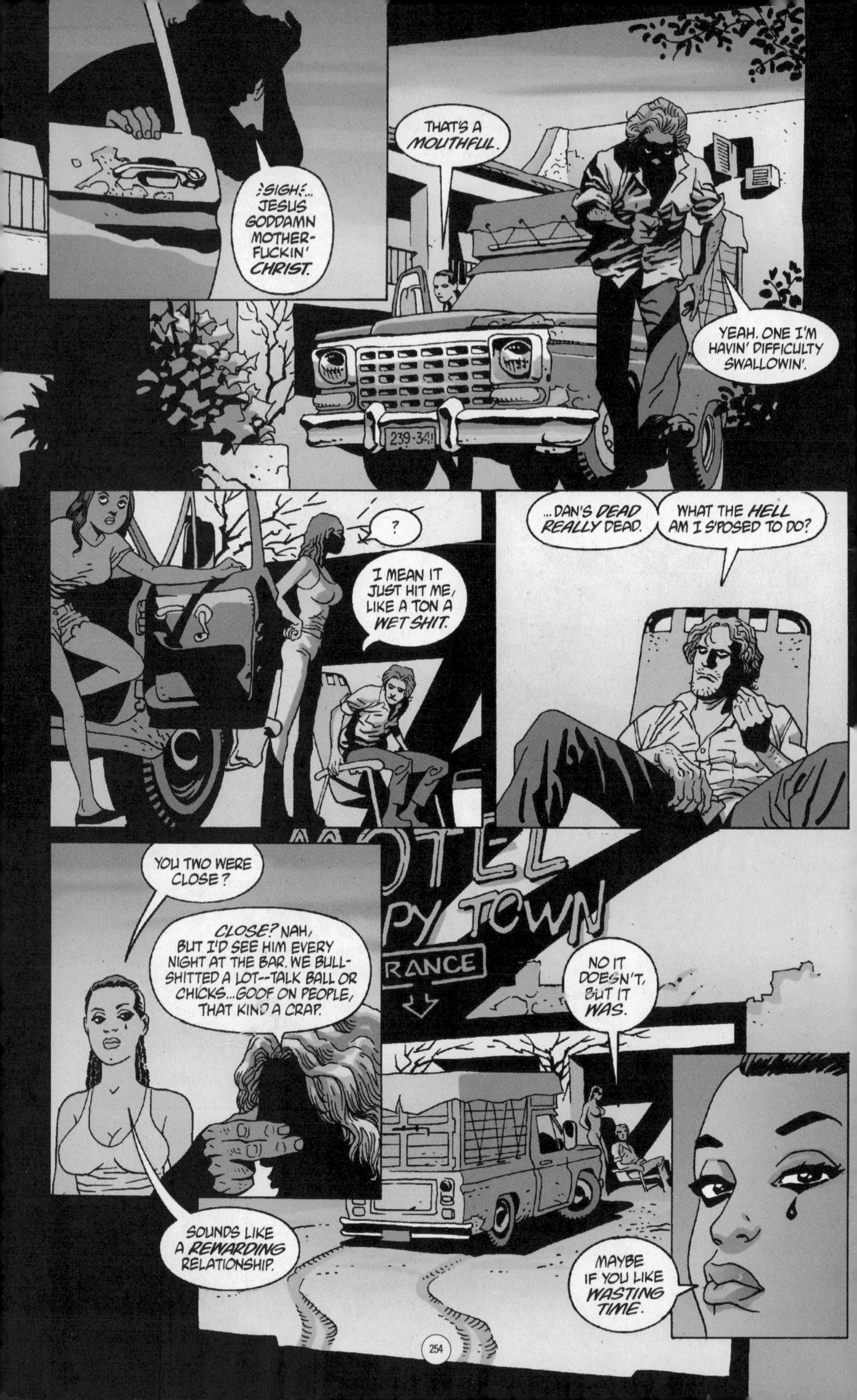

⁝SIGH⁝... JESUS GODDAMN MOTHER-FUCKIN' *CHRIST*.
THAT'S A *MOUTHFUL*.
YEAH. ONE I'M HAVIN' DIFFICULTY SWALLOWIN'.
239-341
?
I MEAN IT JUST HIT ME, LIKE A TON A *WET SHIT*.
...DAN'S *DEAD*. *REALLY* DEAD.
WHAT THE *HELL* AM I S'POSED TO DO?
YOU TWO WERE CLOSE?
CLOSE? NAH, BUT I'D SEE HIM EVERY NIGHT AT THE BAR. WE BULL-SHITTED A LOT--TALK BALL OR CHICKS...GOOF ON PEOPLE, THAT KIND A CRAP.
SOUNDS LIKE A *REWARDING* RELATIONSHIP.
NO IT DOESN'T, BUT IT *WAS*.
MAYBE IF YOU LIKE *WASTING TIME*.

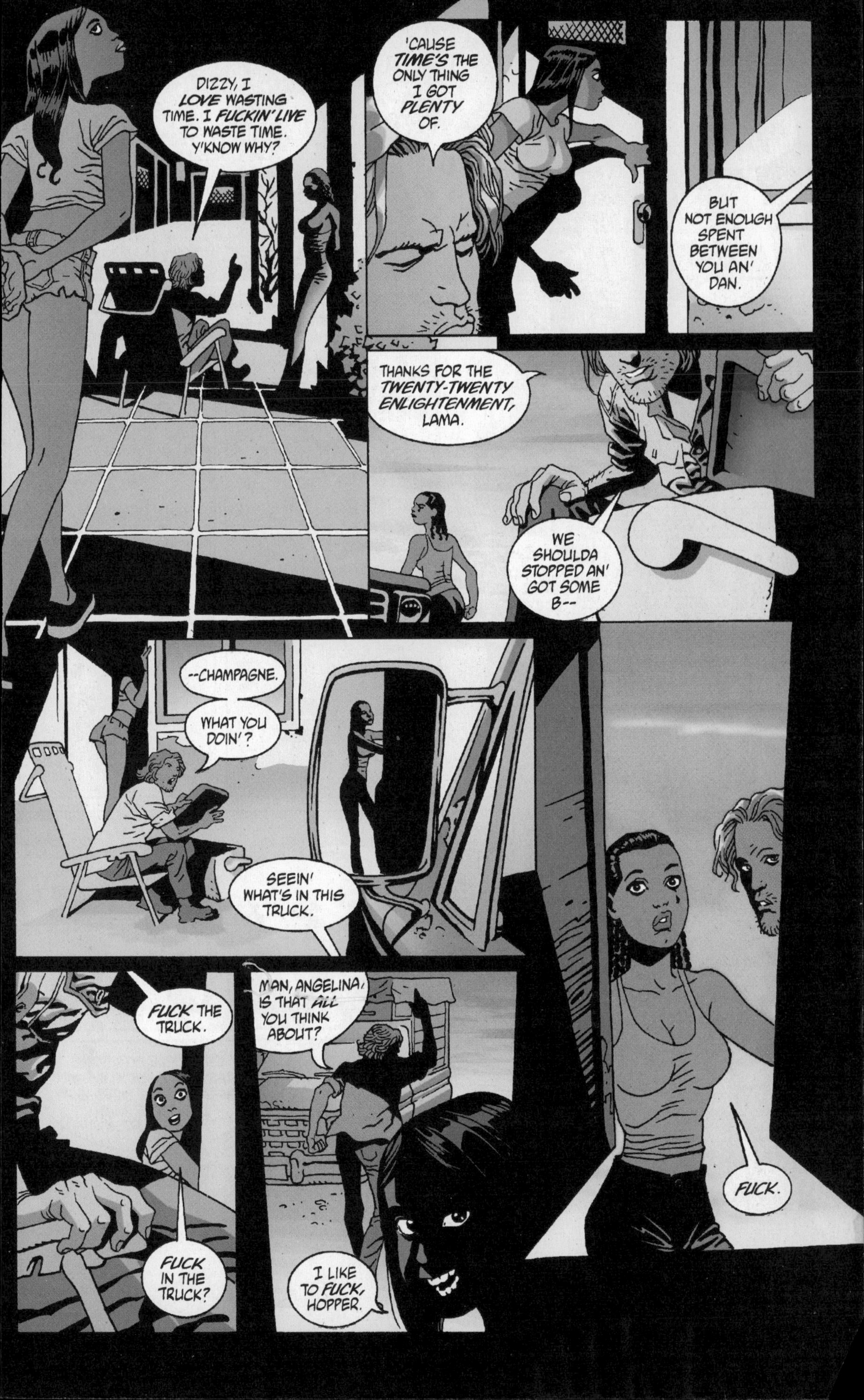
DIZZY, I LOVE WASTING TIME. I FUCKIN' LIVE TO WASTE TIME. Y'KNOW WHY?
'CAUSE TIME'S THE ONLY THING I GOT PLENTY OF.
BUT NOT ENOUGH SPENT BETWEEN YOU AN' DAN.
THANKS FOR THE TWENTY-TWENTY ENLIGHTENMENT, LAMA.
WE SHOULDA STOPPED AN' GOT SOME B--
--CHAMPAGNE.
WHAT YOU DOIN'?
SEEIN' WHAT'S IN THIS TRUCK.
FUCK THE TRUCK.
FUCK IN THE TRUCK?
MAN, ANGELINA, IS THAT ALL YOU THINK ABOUT?
I LIKE TO FUCK, HOPPER.
FUCK.

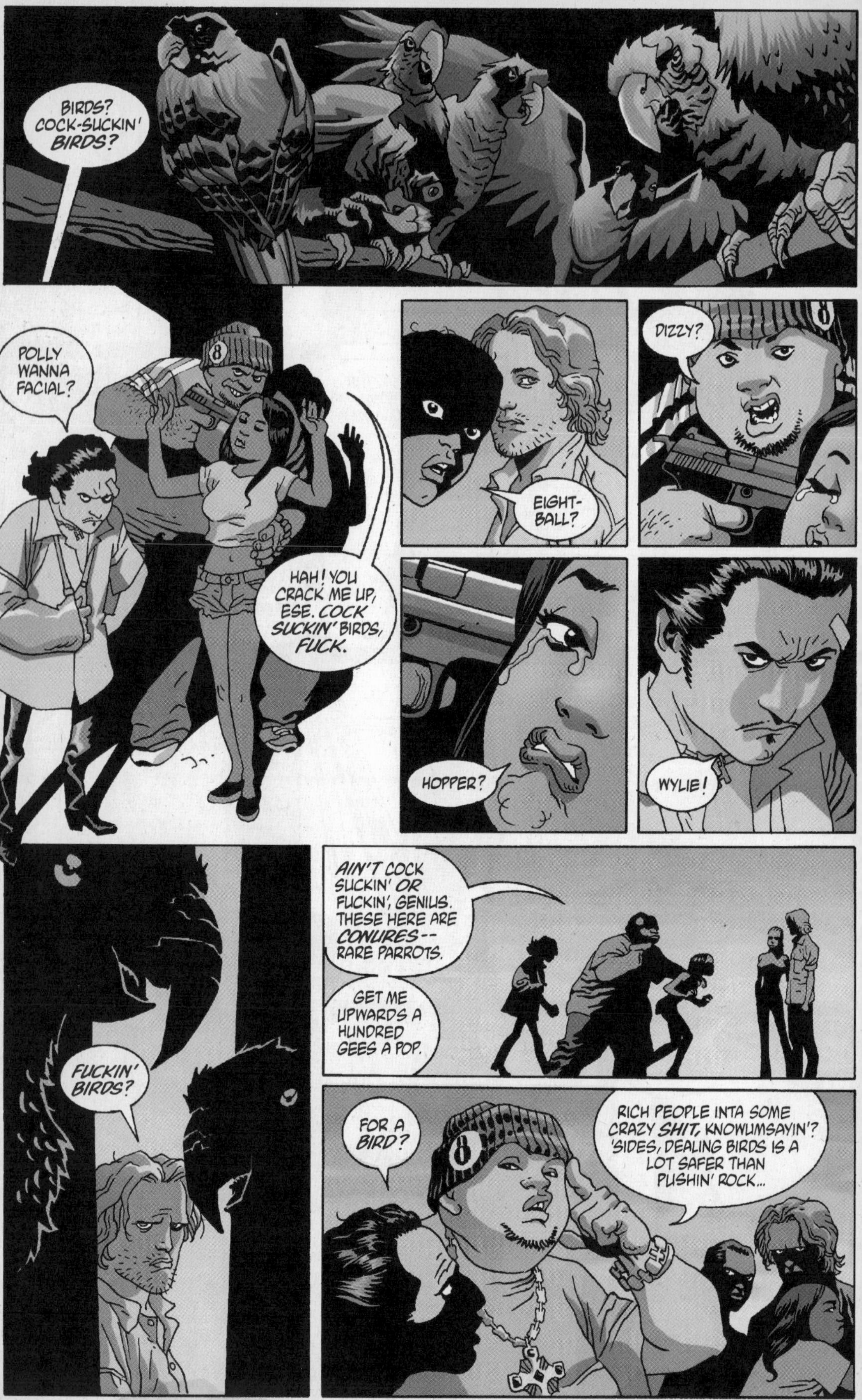

BIRDS? COCK-SUCKIN' BIRDS?
POLLY WANNA FACIAL?
HAH! YOU CRACK ME UP, ESE. COCK SUCKIN' BIRDS, FUCK.
EIGHT-BALL?
DIZZY?
HOPPER?
WYLIE!
FUCKIN' BIRDS?
AIN'T COCK SUCKIN' OR FUCKIN', GENIUS. THESE HERE ARE CONURES-- RARE PARROTS.
GET ME UPWARDS A HUNDRED GEES A POP.
FOR A BIRD?
RICH PEOPLE INTA SOME CRAZY SHIT, KNOWUMSAYIN'? 'SIDES, DEALING BIRDS IS A LOT SAFER THAN PUSHIN' ROCK...

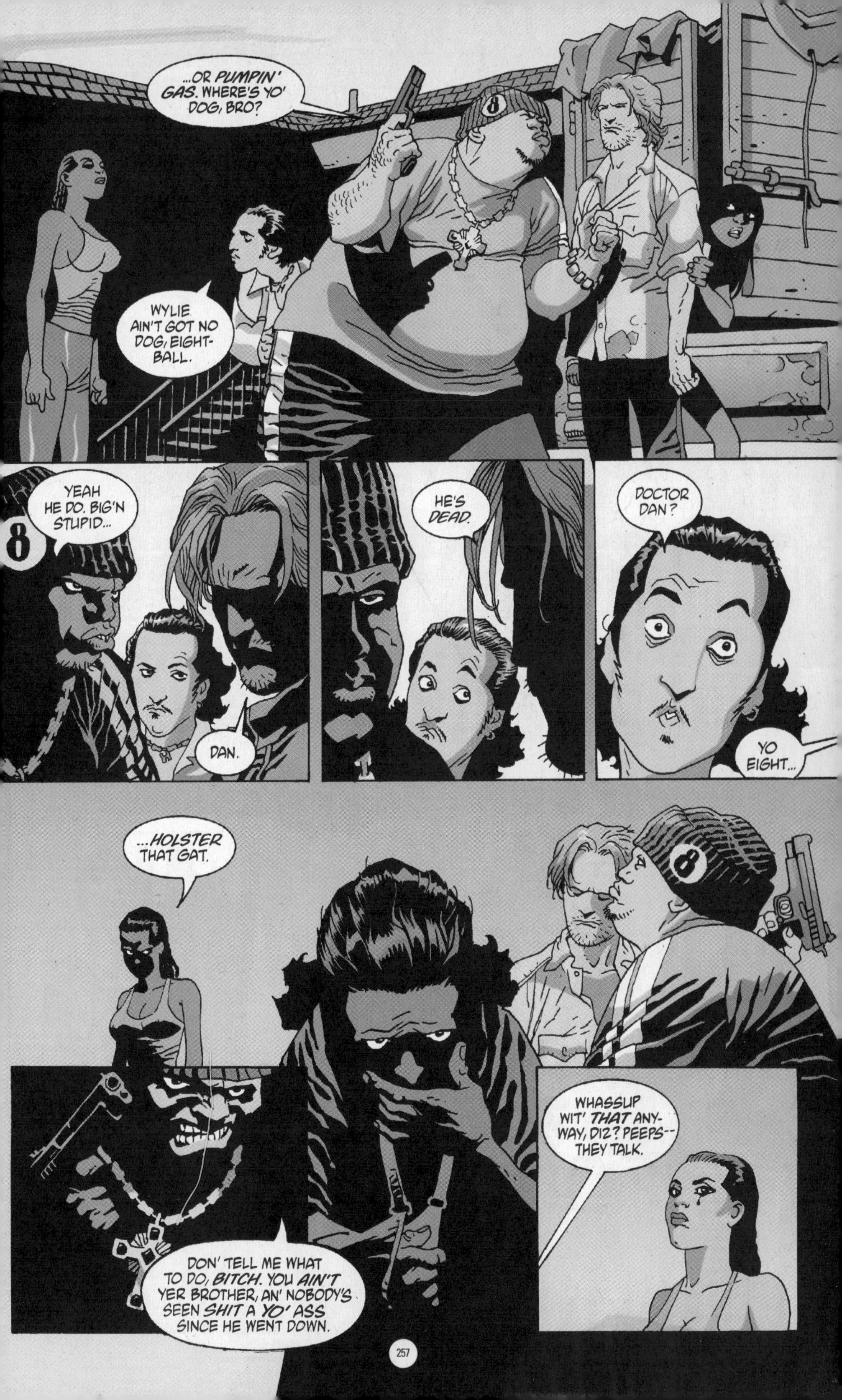

...OR PUMPIN' GAS. WHERE'S YO' DOG, BRO?
WYLIE AIN'T GOT NO DOG, EIGHT-BALL.
YEAH HE DO. BIG'N STUPID...
DAN.
HE'S DEAD.
DOCTOR DAN?
YO EIGHT...
...HOLSTER THAT GAT.
WHASSUP WIT' THAT ANYWAY, DIZ? PEEPS--THEY TALK.
DON' TELL ME WHAT TO DO, BITCH. YOU AIN'T YER BROTHER, AN' NOBODY'S SEEN SHIT A YO' ASS SINCE HE WENT DOWN.

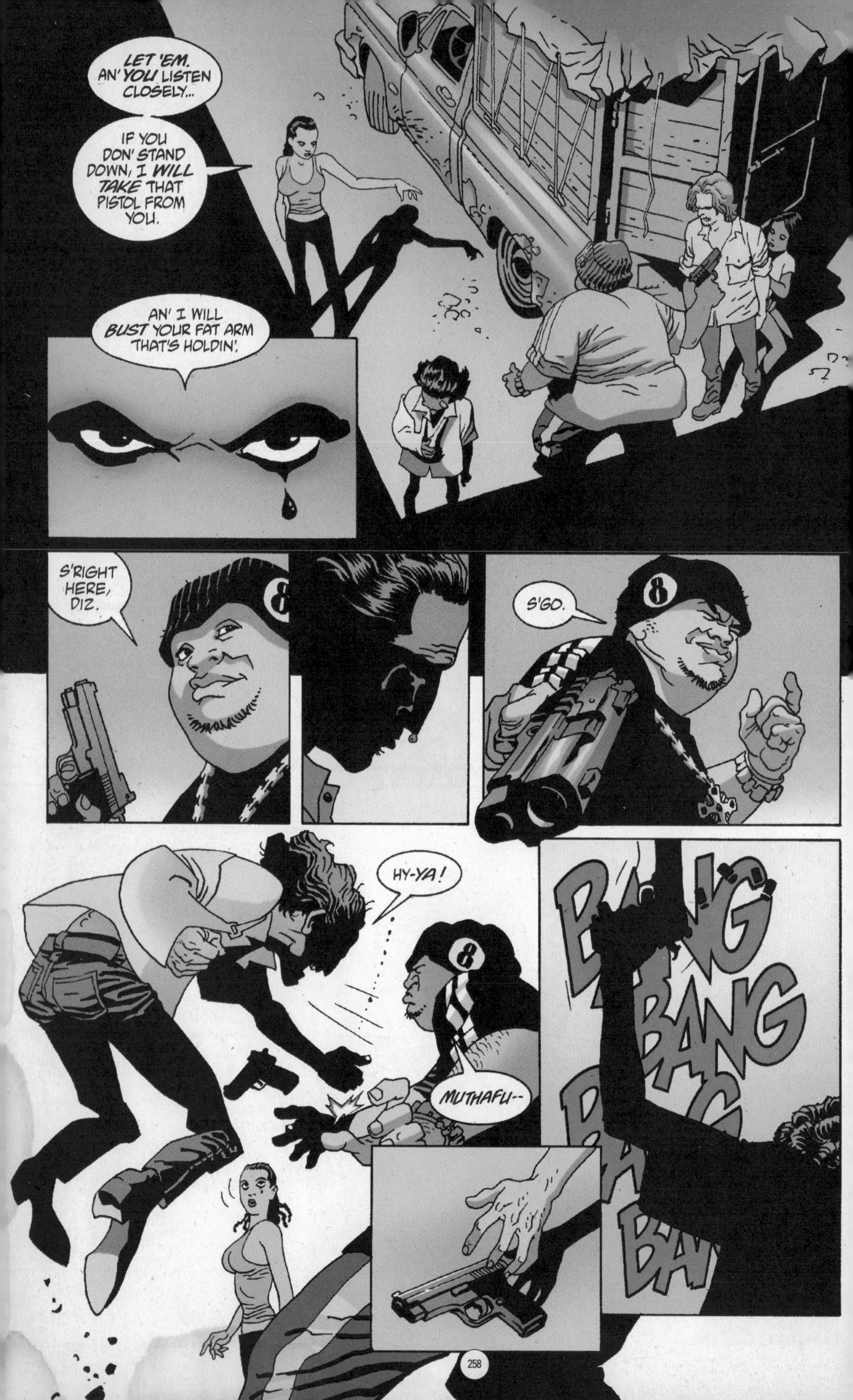
LET 'EM. AN' YOU LISTEN CLOSELY...
IF YOU DON' STAND DOWN, I WILL TAKE THAT PISTOL FROM YOU.
AN' I WILL BUST YOUR FAT ARM THAT'S HOLDIN'.
S'RIGHT HERE, DIZ.
S'GO.
HY-YA!
MUTHAFU--
BANG
BANG
BANG
BANG

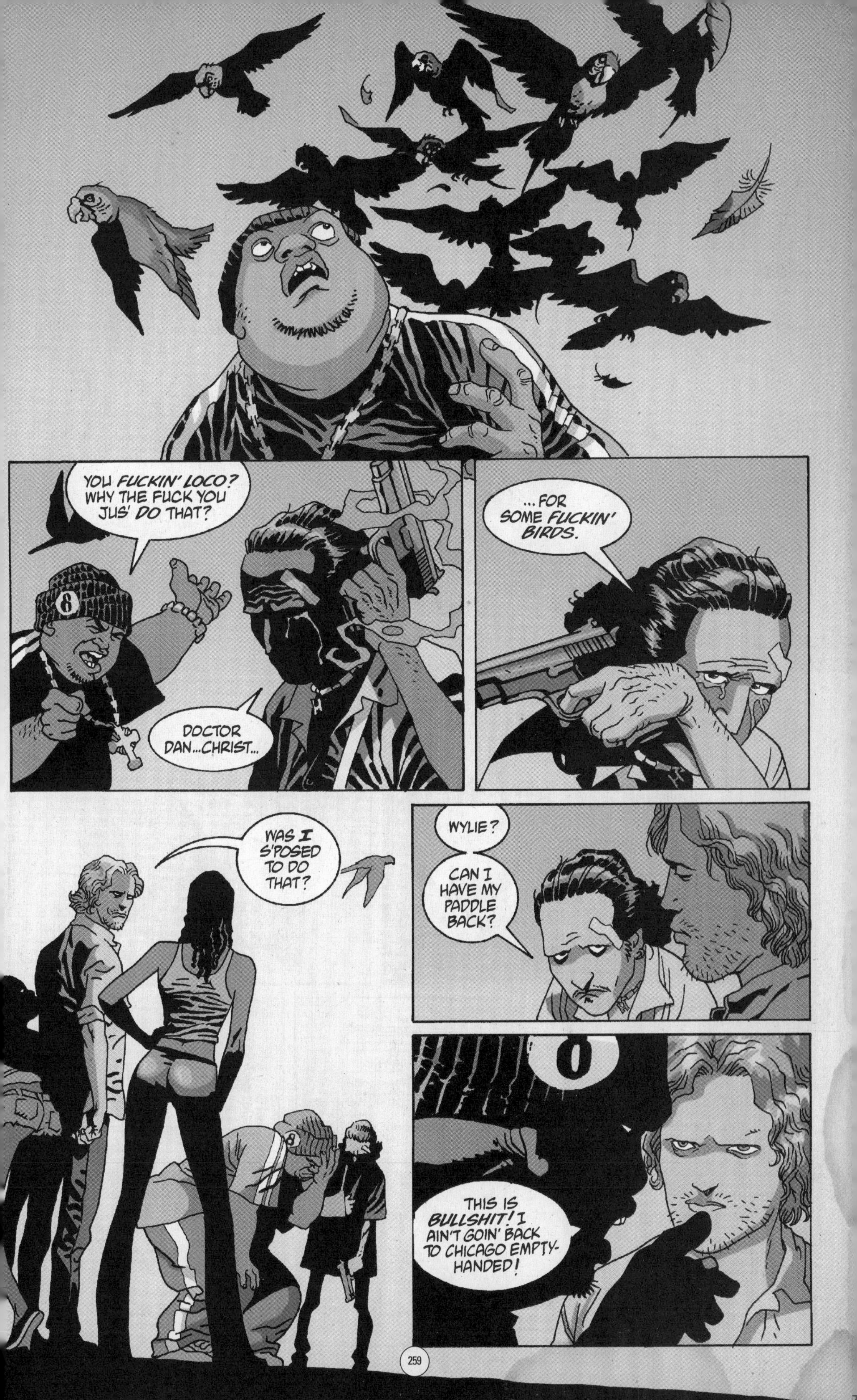

YOU *FUCKIN' LOCO?* WHY THE FUCK YOU JUS' *DO* THAT?
DOCTOR DAN...CHRIST...
...FOR SOME *FUCKIN'* *BIRDS*.
WAS *I* S'POSED TO DO THAT?
WYLIE?
CAN I HAVE MY PADDLE BACK?
THIS IS *BULLSHIT!* I AIN'T GOIN' BACK TO CHICAGO EMPTY-HANDED!

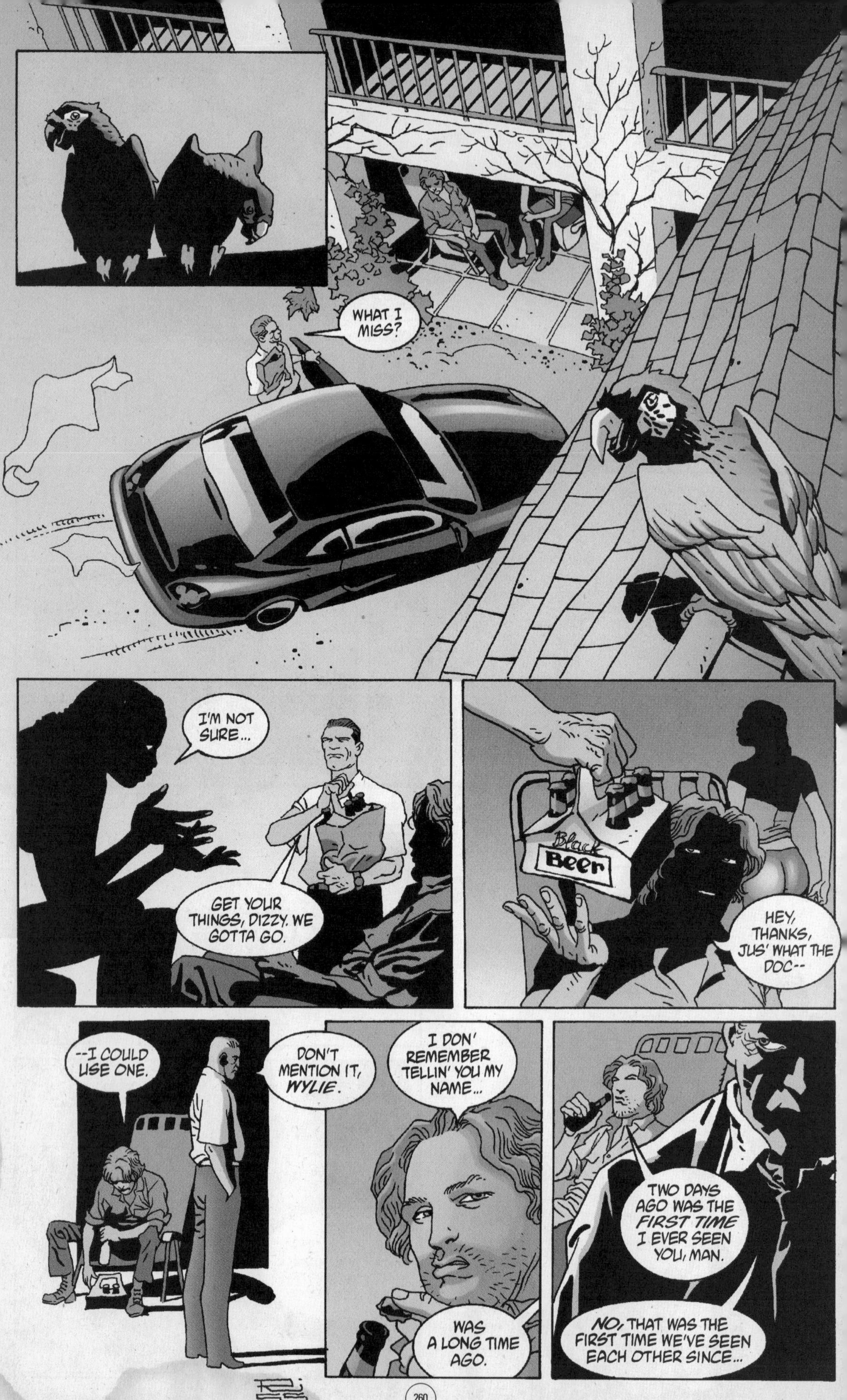
WHAT I MISS?
I'M NOT SURE...
GET YOUR THINGS, DIZZY. WE GOTTA GO.
Black Beer
HEY, THANKS, JUS' WHAT THE DOC--
--I COULD USE ONE.
DON'T MENTION IT, *WYLIE*.
I DON' REMEMBER TELLIN' YOU MY NAME...
WAS A LONG TIME AGO.
TWO DAYS AGO WAS THE *FIRST TIME* I EVER SEEN YOU, MAN.
NO, THAT WAS THE FIRST TIME WE'VE SEEN EACH OTHER SINCE...

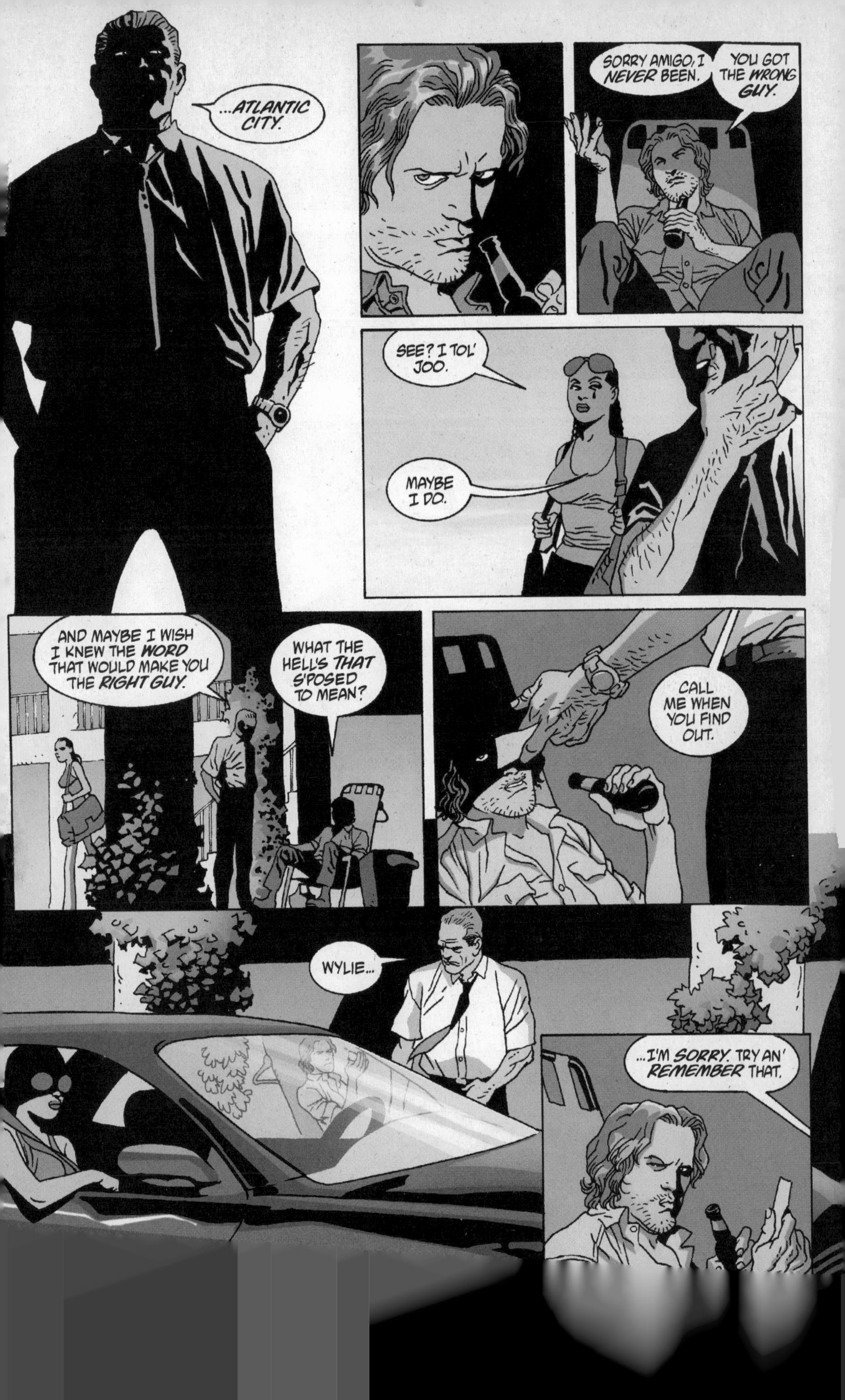
...ATLANTIC CITY.
SORRY AMIGO, I NEVER BEEN.
YOU GOT THE WRONG GUY.
SEE? I TOL' JOO.
MAYBE I DO.
AND MAYBE I WISH I KNEW THE WORD THAT WOULD MAKE YOU THE RIGHT GUY.
WHAT THE HELL'S THAT S'POSED TO MEAN?
CALL ME WHEN YOU FIND OUT.
WYLIE...
...I'M SORRY. TRY AN' REMEMBER THAT.

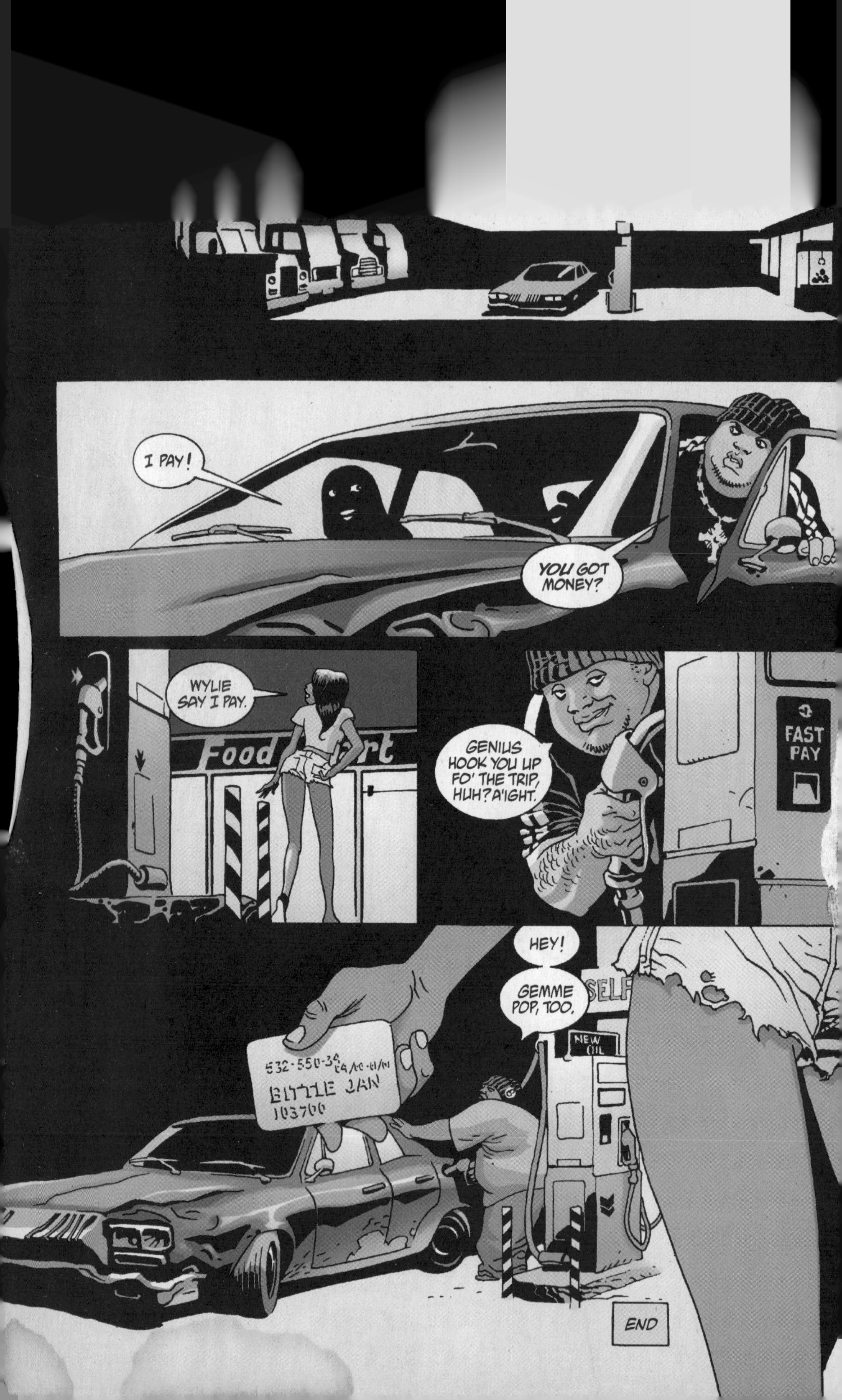
I PAY!
YOU GOT MONEY?
WYLIE SAY I PAY.
Food Mart
GENIUS HOOK YOU UP FO' THE TRIP, HUH? A'IGHT.
FAST PAY
HEY!
GEMME POP, TOO.
SELF
NEW OIL
532-550-34
BITTLE JAN
103700
END